Barr-Cole

EDUCATIONAL SERVICE DISTRICT 112
DIRECT SERVICES
2500 N.E. 65 AVENUE
VANCOUVER, WA 98661-6812

Direct Instruction Reading

Second Edition

Douglas Carnine
University of Oregon

Jerry Silbert
Eugene School District

Edward J. Kameenui
University of Oregon

Merrill, an imprint of
Macmillan Publishing Company
New York

Maxwell Macmillan Canada
Toronto

Maxwell Macmillan International Publishing Group
New York   Oxford   Singapore   Sydney

Cover Art: Marko Spalatin

This book was set in Aster and Univers.

Executive Editor: Jeff Johnston
Production Coordinator: JoEllen Gohr
Cover Designer: Brian Deep

Library of Congress Catalog Card Number: 89-61510
International Standard Book Number: 0-675-21014-3
Printed in the United States of America
    2   3   4   5   6   7   8   9—93   92   91

To those teachers who are always looking for a better way to teach

PREFACE

Direct Instruction Reading attempts to create a learning environment for teaching students in a humane and efficient manner. A learning environment is humane when the environment enhances the student's self-concept. A learning environment is efficient when the maximum amount of learning occurs in the shortest possible time with the least amount of resources.

In the first edition of *Direct Instruction Reading*, we presented in-depth procedures for teaching important reading skills. Since the writing of the first edition, we have learned a great deal through our experiences in working with students and in training prospective teachers. Thus in the second edition, we have made numerous changes throughout the book. Procedures were altered as we found new ways to teach skills. Chapters were reorganized to communicate ideas in a clearer fashion. The emphasis was increased on all aspects of passage reading, including both decoding and comprehending narrative and expository material. Research compiled during the last decade since the writing of the first edition was incorporated. The result is an almost completely rewritten second edition.

The organization of *Direct Instruction Reading* has also changed. The four major parts of this edition are perspective, beginning reading, decoding, and comprehension. We still devote a disproportional amount of the book to beginning reading. The first months of reading instruction are a critical time. The more carefully planned the instruction during this time, the higher the probability of *all* students succeeding. Each part covers (1) specific skills and how to teach them with precise direct instruction methods, (2) related research findings, and (3) application exercises for the classroom. (Answers to these exercises are given in the instructor's manual.)

This edition is not intended to be a definitive handbook. As we work with students, we continue to learn, and this learning enables us to improve our procedures. Procedures can always be improved. The main purpose of the text is to empower teachers by providing them with specific suggestions for problems they will encounter in the classroom. Since many commercial materials are relatively unsystematic, even using direct instruction techniques with them is far from ideal. It is our hope, however, that the systematic procedures recommended here will stimulate the development of even better techniques. Furthermore, we encourage teachers to view learning as an outcome of instruction, rather than a function of the learner. We also encourage commercial publishers to design better programs for students. Overall, we hope that this book contributes to better teaching methods for all students, particularly the hard to teach and lower performing students.

Acknowledgments

We are grateful to many people. Foremost we are grateful to Zig Engelmann, whose empirical approach to instructional design has resulted in the development of many highly effective instructional programs. Many of the procedures in this book were derived from *The Reading Mastery Series* and *The Corrective Reading Series*, authored by Engelmann and his colleagues.

In addition to ideas gained from these programs, many ideas were contributed by colleagues and students, including Gary Davis, Frank Falco, Billie Overholser, Conley Overholser, Abby Adams, Anita Archer, Elain C. Bruner, Linda Carnine, Vonnie Dicecco, Robert Dixon, Phil Dommes, Jane Dougall, Ruth Falco, Mickey Garrison, Alex Granzin, Cheri Hansen, Lisa Howard, Sheri Irwin, Joleen Johnson, Jean Osborn, Mary Rosenbaum, Barak Rosenshine, Sandra Schofield, Marcy Stein, Marilyn Stepnoski, Candy Stevens, and Joan Thormann. Other colleagues provided important support and encouragement, namely, Barbara Bateman, Wes Becker, Meredith Gall, Joe Jenkins, and Ruth Waugh.

We sincerely appreciate the assistance of the following people who reviewed the manuscript and provided constructive feedback for changes: Sara Tarver, University of Wisconsin at Madison; Susan Peterson, University of Florida; Nancy Cooke, University of North Carolina; and Tracy Hall, University of Oregon.

Finally, a sincere thanks to Kay O'Connor and Debbie Evans, who translated almost indecipherable scribbles into an accurately typed manuscript.

D. C.
J. S.
E. K.

CONTENTS

Perspective

Part

Reading is a complex process—complex to learn and complex to teach. Psycholinguists, information systems analysts, reading researchers, and cognitive psychologists each describe the reading process differently. While these descriptions are important to theoretical questions about the reading process, many of them do not address the needs of classroom teachers. Our purpose is not to survey the various theoretical positions, but to explain procedures that teachers can use to improve the reading performance of their students. Our position is that many students will not become successful readers unless teachers identify the essential reading skills, find out what skills students lack, and teach those skills directly.

Success in reading is very important to students, both for academic and vocational advancement and for the students' psychological well-being. Although some students will learn to read in almost any program, other students will not become successful readers unless they receive careful teaching. Our definition of teaching is similar to that of Bateman's (1971, p. 8): "Teaching is the teacher's intentional arranging or manipulating of the environment so that the child will learn more efficiently than if he were to learn incidentally from the world at large."

If teachers are effectively and efficiently to teach reading, they must be knowledgeable in several areas. Teachers must know

1. The essential skills or objectives that make up the reading process and the procedures for teaching those skills.
2. The procedures for evaluating, selecting, and modifying reading programs to meet the needs of all students in their classrooms.
3. The techniques for effectively presenting lessons, including

Chapter

Classroom Reading Instruction

techniques for pacing tasks, motivating students, and diagnosing and correcting their errors.

4. How to individualize instruction by properly placing students in a program, then moving them at an optimal rate through the program.

5. How to organize classrooms to maximize the amount of time students spend engaged in reading instruction.

Perspectives on Improving Student Reading Performance

Effective efficient instruction benefits all students but is essential for instructionally naive students who typically have trouble learning to read. *Instructionally naive students* are those students who do not readily retain newly presented information, are easily confused, and have difficulty attending to an instructional presentation.

There are three basic perspectives toward improving student reading performance. The first, the pessimist's viewpoint, states that the schools can do little unless the student's physical make-up or home and social environment are altered. The second, the generalist's viewpoint, states that the schools can improve reading performance by developing a wide range of abilities which supposedly underlie reading. The third, a direct instruction viewpoint, involves an analysis of how to teach specific reading skills. Each orientation toward reading instruction is discussed below.

Pessimist's Viewpoint

This orientation is typified by an article from a popular news weekly. Mortimer Adler, chairman of the board of editors of the *Encyclopaedia Britannica*, was quoted as saying that there may be good reason for the rising disbelief in the ultimate educability of everyone. He said, "Undifferentiated schooling may be doomed to defeat by differences in the children's economic, social, and ethnic backgrounds and especially differences in the homes from which they come" (New starts for America's third century, 1976, p. 29).

Almost two decades ago, Becker (1973) pointed out the problem with the pessimists' orientation, an orientation tacitly minimizing the importance of teaching:

> As long as the educational climate was such that teaching failures could be blamed on the children, there was no pressure on the teacher to learn more effective means of dealing with children. Over the years, psychologists, mental health workers, and some educators have trained teachers to ship their failures to someone else or at least to blame the child's home background, his low IQ, his poor motivation, his emotional disturbance, his lack of readiness, or his physical disability for the teaching failure. With the recent advent of the label learning disability (for children with normal IQ who fail to learn) there is no teaching failure which cannot be blamed on the child. (p. 78)

An orientation that blames students for their failure is unwarranted and harmful. *Teachers can bring about substantial improvements in students' reading performance.* Problems, such as poverty, a disruptive home life, and physiological impairments, often make teaching more difficult. However, we reject the assumption that improvement in reading achievement is not possible unless there are changes in the children's economic and social environments. Educators cannot use social and home environments as excuses for the poor performance of some students.

There is substantial research indicating that if students are directly taught fundamental reading skills, they will learn to read (Baumann, 1983; Johnson & Baumann, 1985; Becker & Carnine, 1980; Chall, 1988; Englert, 1984; Guthrie, 1977; Kameenui, 1985; Pearson, 1985; Williams, 1985).

Generalist's Viewpoint

Typical of the second orientation toward improving reading performance is the idea that reading performance can be improved by focusing on the *processes* or *abilities* that underlie learning. Focusing on reading skills is felt by this viewpoint's advocates to be an inappropriate emphasis. Once students "learn to learn," "become motivated," or "overcome auditory deficits," reading will be relatively easy for them. The attitudes reflected in this orientation are more constructive than those of the pessimists because the assumption is that students can succeed and what the teacher does will influence the learning of the students. However, the problems with the generalist's viewpoint are these:

1. It draws attention away from the quality of reading instruction. Instead of looking at the way reading is taught, general skills such as visual perception are stressed.

2. Proposed solutions often inadvertently result in students receiving less actual reading instruction than in a normal situation.

3. Data from research reviews do not support a generalist viewpoint (Arter & Jenkins, 1978; Hammill & Larsen, 1974; Kavale & Forness, 1987; Lloyd, 1984).

Two important assumptions of the generalist orientation lack empirical support:

"(a) that the assumed deficiencies in psychological processes can be reliably and validly assessed, and (b) that remediation of these processes will result in improved academic performance" (Haring & Bateman, 1977, p. 138). Chall (1978a) came to a similar conclusion in a separate review: "The research of the past ten years suggests, instead, that good teaching is probably the best way to help the child . . . in most instances, [good teaching] is more effective than perceptual and auditory training" (p. 40).

Direct Instruction

The third orientation and, in our opinion, the best answer to the question of how educators can improve student reading performance is direct instruction. Direct instruction involves teaching essential reading skills in the most effective and efficient manner possible. The effectiveness of this approach has been indicated by large-scale experimental studies with instructionally naive students and by studies which investigated the characteristics of effective teachers.

A federally funded 16-year study called *Follow Through* evaluated several major approaches to educating low-income, primary grade students. Direct approaches were compared with approaches based on language-experience, Piaget's stages of learning, child-development theory, discovery learning, and open education. Only students in a direct instruction approach consistently outperformed control students on basic, cognitive, and affective measures. Guthrie (1977) summarized the *Follow Through* results in this way:

Final answers about teaching are not available from this study (Follow Through)—nor will they ever be—no more than final answers about medicine, engineering, or poetry. A fully complete explanation of education is not likely, since values of the public and research methods are constantly shifting. However, the results of the Follow Through experiment endow us with evidence about the effects of teaching programs at an unprecedented level of certainty. The edge that the more successful programs have over the less successful programs is wide enough to serve as a foothold in the climb to improved, intended education. (p. 244)

A similar conclusion was reached by Rosenshine (1978) after conducting an extensive review of the research literature on teacher effectiveness. In fact, Rosenshine summarized the variables that were associated with student academic success as "direct instruction":

> To give an overview of the results, direct instruction refers to high levels of student engagement within academically focused, teacher-directed classrooms using sequenced, structured materials. As developed below, direct instruction refers to teaching activities focused on academic matters where goals are clear to students; time allocated for instruction is sufficient and continuous; content coverage is extensive; student performance is monitored; questions are at a low cognitive level and produce many correct responses; and feedback to students is immediate and academically oriented. In direct instruction, the teacher *controls* instructional goals, *chooses* material appropriate for the student's ability level, and *paces* the instructional episode. Interaction is characterized as structured, but not authoritarian; rather, learning takes place in a convivial academic atmosphere. (p. 17)

Although the research Rosenshine reviewed focuses on the achievement of low-income,

primary grade students, other researchers (Brophy & Good, 1986; McDonald, 1976; Stanford *Program on Teaching Effectiveness*, 1975; Rosenshine & Stevens, 1986) report similar results with other types of students.

Illustrations of the Three Orientations

Three answers to the question of how to improve reading instruction have been discussed: pessimists look outside the school, generalists look toward abilities that underlie reading, and direct instruction advocates look to improvements in teaching methodology. The following teachers, Ms. Excuse, Mr. Indirect, and Mrs. Direct, illustrate the attitudes and practices implied by these three different orientations. To clarify these orientations, assume these three are sitting in a teacher's lounge discussing students having reading difficulties. Although the discussion is oversimplified, it does portray common teacher attitudes.

The first student they discuss is Arthur, who upon entering fourth grade is placed in a fourth grade reading group. Each day an assignment is written on the chalkboard consisting of a story to read and several written exercises to complete. Unfortunately, Arthur understands only about 60% of the words that appear in the reader and, thus, cannot figure out many of the answers to the written exercises. At the end of the reading period, he hands in his papers. They are returned at the end of the day, full of Xs and sometimes a comment such as "Be more careful." After several days Arthur begins spending more time rough-housing and talking with his neighbors. He seldom completes his assignments. Ms. Excuse complains that Arthur is educationally handicapped, comes from a broken home, and is unmotivated. Mr. Indirect suggests that Arthur be moved to another class where the teacher emphasizes "feeling good" and would work to develop Arthur's self-concept first, and his reading skills second. "After all," Mr. Indirect argues, "You can't read when you don't feel good about who you are." Mrs. Direct suggests *changes in the instructional program to enable Arthur to succeed.* First, she suggests placing Arthur more appropriately in the reading program since he obviously cannot succeed in assignments that assume skills he does not have. Second, she suggests examining the tasks to determine critical component skills and devising strategies to teach these skills. If he is expected to draw inferences and know the meanings of various words for an assignment, inference skills and vocabulary words must be taught before he works the assignment. Finally, Mrs. Direct suggests instituting a system to motivate Arthur since the high degree of failure he has encountered has seemingly made reading distasteful to him.

The next student the three teachers discuss is Janice, a first grader. Janice has been making many errors in reading group. In the past day's lesson, Janice said "at" for *it* and "hum" for *him.* Ms. Excuse explains that Janice is not yet ready to read because she is too immature. Mr. Indirect says it's probably dyslexia and suggests a series of tasks to improve visual discrimination.[1] Mrs. Direct suggests changing the instructional program. First, she suggests testing to see if Janice knows the sound of the letter *i* and has a strategy for reading words. For deficiencies in either skill, Mrs. Direct suggests specific teaching procedures.

The last student is Dale, a sixth grader who forgets how to look up information on different topics in a textbook. The teacher explains that she has taught Dale and the rest of the class how to use a subject index in a textbook several weeks ago. Yesterday, however, when Dale was given a worksheet assignment that required him to list the page numbers in his history book dealing with Egyptian history, he did not remember the subject index or how to use it and began looking at every page in his book to find the pages that discussed Egypt. He ran out of time and was unable to finish the assignment. Ms. Excuse says that Dale did not finish his assignment because he has too many worries about his home life. Mr. Indirect suggests memory training. Mrs. Direct explains that the problem resulted initially because Dale needed *more practice* in using an index. She notes that the sixth grade text doesn't provide enough practice. She says that if Dale had received several exercises in using the subject index immediately following the teacher's initial explanation, he would be more likely to remember when and how to use it. Mrs. Direct suggests reteaching the skill and providing more practice immediately after the reteaching.

After finishing the discussion about the students, the teachers turn to the topic of reading readiness (how to prepare students for reading instruction) discussed in the previous day's staff meeting. Ms. Excuse suggests delaying reading instruction until the students have had enough experiences. She says, "When the child shows a desire to read, we should start teaching." She cannot, however, answer the question of what to do when students do not show an interest in reading.

Mr. Indirect suggests a wide variety of activities seemingly related to reading. He refers to Spache and Spache, who classify these activities under three categories: perceptual motor, form perception, and language and thinking. Perceptual motor training includes exercises to develop

---

1. *Dyslexia* is a term that implies a student has an undetectable constitutional deficit keeping the student from reading successfully. See Harris & Sipay (1975, pp. 136–138) for further discussion.

hand-eye coordination, laterality, directionality, and body image. Form perception training includes some activities closely related to reading, such as matching and reproducing letters and sounds, and other activities, such as working puzzles, drawing pictures, and identifying objects not directly related to reading. Language and thinking training include receptive language exercises (understanding what is said) and expressive language exercises (communicating one's thoughts to another).

He points out that Spaches' book says that students who receive a wide range of readiness training often perform better in reading instruction than students who do not receive any readiness training. Mrs. Direct points out a problem with this approach. She says that if teachers construct and implement a program to teach all the skills, the program might take a full school year. She says the question is which of the skills are the most important and points out that this question is especially critical with instructionally naive students. Efficient instruction is essential for these stu-

dents if they are to learn at a rate that will enable them to participate later in reading activities with their peers.

She explains that teachers have limited instructional time and an enormous amount of information to teach within that time. As a consequence, instruction must be designed and delivered carefully and efficiently, with little or no wasted time.

Note that in each situation Mrs. Direct looked for ways to improve her teaching so that her students would be more likely to succeed in learning to read. In contrast, neither Ms. Excuse nor Mr. Indirect looked at the instructional program as a factor which might be causing the problems. The discussion of these three teachers illustrates the importance of a direct-instruction teacher's attitude. As teachers, we need to seek out ways to improve teaching *in the classroom*. Of course, some students are more difficult to teach than others, but highly skilled professionals *can* teach these students to read. Hopefully this book will contribute to improved reading instruction by providing detailed explanations of effective teaching procedures.

In the following chapter, three critical components of direct instruction are discussed:

1. Organization of Instruction
2. Program Design
3. Teacher Presentation Techniques

Adequate instructional time, well-designed materials, and effective presentation techniques are all essential ingredients of a successful reading program. An excellent reading series in the hands of a knowledgeable teacher will not produce significant gains if instructional time is too limited. Likewise, naive students will not do well in an excellent series with ample instructional time if the teacher cannot present and explain the content clearly. Finally, the potential advantages of adequate time and a teacher who presents well will not be realized if the reading series is too difficult or poorly designed.

Organization of Instruction

Engaged Time

In the last three decades, our knowledge about effective teaching has increased significantly (Brophy & Good, 1985; Murphy, Weil, & McGreal, 1986; Rosenshine & Berliner, 1978; Rosenshine & Stevens, 1985). We now know for certain what we have suspected for a long time, that is, that adequate academic-engaged time is essential if students are to succeed in school.

Reading-engaged time refers to the time students actually spend on reading exercises and activities. Researchers point out that time spent in reading yielded higher correlations with achievement than any other teacher or student behavior studied. Note that engaged time does not refer to scheduled time, but only to the time stu-

Chapter

Direct Instruction

dents actually spend engaged in reading activities. Rosenshine (1978) reviewed studies that found only about 80% of the 85 minutes allocated to reading in second grade were academic-engaged minutes, while in fifth grade about 75% of the 113 minutes were engaged minutes. In class-rooms with little student improvement in reading over a year, students spent only 1 or 2 minutes engaged in fundamental read-ing activities.

Engaged time must be put to good use. First, if students are expected to learn to read, they must be engaged in reading-related activities. On the one hand, re-searchers found positive and usually signif-icant correlations between achievement and engagement in reading activities. On the other hand, time spent on stories, arts and crafts, active play, or child selection of activities *always* produced a negative cor-relation. Second, students should be placed in a reading series at a place appro-priate to their skill level. They should not be placed in material that is too easy, where they just review previously learned material. Nor should their placement be at too advanced a lesson, where they lack essential preskills and make frequent mis-takes (Stallings, 1975).

Similarly, independent reading exer-cises must be instructionally appropriate. They should provide practice for new skills and for previously introduced skills that require continued practice. The exercises should neither be too easy nor too hard. The match between the content of reading exercises (both teacher-directed and inde-pendent exercises) and student skill is the essence of individualizing instruction. Bro-phy and Good (1986) point out the impor-tance of appropriate independent work:

> Student success rates, and the
> effectiveness of seatwork assignments
> generally, are enhanced when teachers

explain the work and go over practice examples with the students before releasing them to work independently. Furthermore, once the students are released to work independently, the work goes more smoothly if the teacher (or an aide) circulates to monitor progress and provide help when needed. If the work has been well chosen and well explored, most of these "helping" interactions will be brief, and at any given time, most students will be progressing smoothly through the assignment rather than waiting for help. (p. 364)

A major research question yet to be answered relates to the optimal amount of engaged time. Approximately how many minutes of reading instruction is required for an instructionally naive student of a given skill level to score at grade level on an achievement test by the end of third or fifth grade? This question encompasses numer-ous other questions relating to various entry-level skills, materials used, degree of teacher proficiency, etc. However, the basic issue is how much time should we devote to reading each day? Among other research issues that affect engaged time are types of schedules, organization of materials, train-ing students in independent work habits, and transition from activity to activity.

Scheduling

Since the amount of engaged time seems to be an important determinant of student success, classroom organization is critical. Teachers need to schedule ample time and implement the schedule effectively, ensur-ing that students do not waste substantial amounts of time during group instruction, independent work, or transitions from one activity to another.

As Brophy and Good (1986) state, "Achievement is maximized when teachers emphasize academic instruction as a major part of their own role, expect their students to master the curriculum, and allocate most of the available time to curriculum-related activities" (p. 360).

Teachers cannot spend 15 minutes getting the students settled in the morning, 5 minutes for transitions between activities, 5 minutes re-explaining assignments and rules that students should understand, and 5 minutes figuring out what to do next while students sit waiting. Teachers working with instructionally naive students must carefully schedule activities so that instructional time is well used and enough time is devoted to priority areas. In some classrooms, less important activities may need to be sacrificed so that enough time is available for reading instruction.

Arranging Materials

In addition to adequate instructional time, organized instruction involves arranging the physical setting and the instructional materials (Englert, 1984). A teacher might save several minutes daily by indicating the page different groups are at with clips in the teacher's guide (a different colored clip for each group) so that the appropriate lesson can be easily and quickly located. Likewise, arranging student materials so the teacher can quickly hand them out when they are needed will save time. More than a decade ago Brophy and Evertson (1976) in studying classrooms in which students made significant academic gains found "(a) each student knew what his assignment was; (b) if he needed help, he could get it from the teacher or from some designated person; (c) he was accountable for completing the assignment appropriately because he knew that his work would be checked" (p. 55). Exercises to be worked independently were placed in folders and placed in the students' desks. Additional independent work was available for students who finished the work in their folders early.

Program Design

Teachers must also be able to evaluate reading programs so they can select programs to meet their students' needs. In addition, they must be able to design lessons for teaching specific skills, which often requires modifying or supplementing certain aspects of a commercial program. Six aspects of direct instruction program design are relevant when selecting a reading program, writing lesson plans, modifying reading programs, and writing IEPs (Individual Education Programs):

1. Specifying objectives
2. Devising strategies
3. Developing teaching procedures
4. Selecting examples
5. Sequencing skills
6. Providing practice and review

Specifying Objectives

Objectives must be stated as specific observable behaviors. Saying that students will be decoding at first grade level by the end of first grade is not specific. The types of words the students will be expected to read must be specified, along with accuracy and rate criteria. The way in which the words will be presented must also be described (e.g., in lists or in passages). For passage reading, the complexity of sentence structure should also be specified.

Objectives of a program should be carefully evaluated according to their usefulness. Since teaching time is limited, skills should be listed in order of importance, with essential skills being taught first. If time allows, less essential skills can also be taught. A skill is essential if it is a prerequisite for a more sophisticated skill or is important in its own right.

An example of a nonessential skill is knowing where to place an accent mark in a word. Since students must be able to decode a word before they can place the accent mark, the skill is not a prerequisite for decoding. Knowledge of accent marks is necessary when students look up a word in a dictionary to figure out its pronunciation. However, that skill does not require the student to place the accent mark; its position is already indicated.

Devising Strategies

Whenever possible, programs should teach students to rely on strategies rather than require them to memorize information. A strategy is taught using a limited set of examples, but can be applied to new examples. For instance in teaching students who know the letters *m, t, r, s, f, d, a, i,* and *o* a sounding-out strategy to decode regular words, the teacher might use the words *mat, Sid, fat,* and *mom* as the initial teaching examples. Once the students master the sounding-out strategy with these words, they can use the same strategy to read words like *sit, mad, ram, it, am, Sam, rod,* and *rid.* Many students learn strategies without being explicitly taught. For instructionally naive students, however, explicit instruction is usually necessary.

The importance of teaching strategies has been extensively analyzed and researched by Ann Brown and her colleagues (Brown, 1976, 1978, 1987; Palincsar & Brown, 1984). As Brown (1976) noted sometime ago:

> Too often educators and psychologists
> draw conclusions about research on an

educationally relevant problem without adequate analysis of the nature of the problem itself. We suspect that there are general *teachable* strategies that young children normally learn by trial and error which greatly facilitate his performance on these tasks. We therefore propose a study of these strategies with an eye toward making them an *explicit* part of reading education. . . . The main problem is one of *externalizing an internal mental event.* (pp. 1, 5)

Some researchers now suggest that strategy deficits account for many, if not most, of the educational problems of handicapped students (Armbruster, Echols, & Brown, 1983; Brown, 1984; Paris & Jacobs, 1984; Simons, Kameenui, & Darch, 1988). Research has shown that training handicapped students to apply various strategies is definitely possible. In fact, the strategy used when reading a passage may be the primary determinant of what is remembered (Zimmer, 1978).

Teachers must take the responsibility for fostering generalization; many students do not spontaneously apply a learned strategy in new situations. Because of the importance of generalization, the amount of practice and range of examples provided must be carefully controlled.

Developing Teaching Procedures

After objectives are specified and a strategy has been devised, the strategy must be translated into a *format* that specifies exactly how the teacher is to present the strategy. The format must include what to say, what words to emphasize, what to ask, how to signal, how to correct appropriately, etc. Providing detailed formats is very helpful because teaching involves very specific behaviors. Teachers do not teach students to decode words in some abstract fashion. They point to particular words, give information, ask questions, etc. Vague teaching procedures do not provide concrete suggestions for teaching a strategy in the clearest possible manner. Most design questions should be worked out *before* the teacher begins the lesson, which is the reason for having formats. Detailed formats free teachers from design questions and enable them to focus their full attention on the students' performance.

Formats often contain two stages: introduction and guided practice. In the *introduction* stage of a format, the teacher demonstrates the steps in a strategy and then provides structured practice in using the strategy. In the guided-practice stage, the student operates with little or no teacher help and is given examples which do and do not call for use of the newly taught strategy. This stage is also called the discrimination stage. These two stages are very important. In the introductory stage, the teacher makes the steps in the strategy overt so that the students can see how to approach similar examples. The importance of making behavior overt has been stressed by various educators. "Interesting behaviors, like sequencing and translation, involve complex chains of covert activities that should be made explicit" (Frase, 1977, p. 189). In the guided-practice stage, the students internalize a strategy, learning to apply it without guidance from the teacher. This stage is an essential step in developing transfer and independent work habits.

Formats must be carefully constructed so that (1) they are easy for the students to understand and (2) they contain only one new skill. For a format to be easily understood, the instructional language must be clear. Words and sentence structures students do not understand should be avoided. This point is simple but often ignored. Formats in the teachers's guides of commercial reading programs often contain words that average and above-average students may understand, but these same words often confuse instructionally naive students. Much student failure in day-to-day lessons is caused by teachers' failing to preteach critical vocabulary.

Furthermore, an acceptable format should teach only one new skill. Formats that attempt to teach more than one new skill cause two problems. First, when students have to learn two new skills at the same time, they are more likely to fail because the learning load is twice as great as when one new skill is introduced. Second, when students fail, the teacher cannot readily tell which skill caused the failure; this makes diagnosis and remediation difficult. For example, in teaching students to decode consonant-vowel-consonant-final *e* (CVCe) words, such as *like* or *fate*, a teacher presents this rule: When a word ends in *e*, say the name for the vowel. Students who were not taught vowel names before encountering this rule would have to learn two new skills at once: vowel names and the rule. Students who say "lik" for *like* may not know the vowel name for *i* or may not know how to apply the rule. Consequently, a teacher would not know whether to help the students with vowel names or with applying the rule.

Selecting Examples

Selecting appropriate examples is a critical part of format construction. Examples at the introduction stage are appropriate only if the student can use the new strategy to come up with the correct answer. For example, when teaching students to decode regular words, the examples would be limited to words that contain only the letters for which students have been taught the letter-sound correspondences. If the students know the letter-sound correspondences for only the letters *m, s, a, d, f, r, t,* and *i*, the teacher should not present the word *met* since it contains an unknown letter (e).

Selecting appropriate examples for the guided-practice stage is more complex. In addition to examples of the new strategy, other examples must also be included. These other examples review previously taught strategies and are in some cases similar to the new examples. A range of examples is necessary so that students are required to differentiate when to use the new strategy and when to use previously taught strategies. If examples of the new CVCe word type are *cane* and *robe*, the teacher might include the words *can* and *rob* in the format. Including these similar words provides important discrimination practice.

Sequencing Skills

Sequencing involves determining an optimal order for introducing new information and strategies. Sequencing significantly affects the difficulty students have in learning some skills. Five sequencing guidelines tend to reduce student error rates:

1. Preskills of a strategy are taught before the strategy itself is presented.

2. Instances that are consistent with strategy are introduced before exceptions.

3. High utility skills are introduced before less useful ones.

4. Easy skills are taught before more difficult ones.

5. Strategies and information likely to be confused are not introduced at the same time.

The most critical sequencing principle is *teaching components of a strategy before the entire strategy is introduced*. Since the components must be taught before the

strategy itself, the components can be referred to as preskills. In the strategy for decoding CVCe words, knowing the names of the vowels is a preskill, which is introduced before the strategy is presented. Another illustration of preskills involves dictionary skills. To prepare older students to locate words in a dictionary, teachers should provide preskills instruction, including saying the alphabet; comparing target words to guide words by looking at the first, second, or third letter; and knowing whether to turn toward the front or back of a dictionary after opening it to a particular page. A final example is sounding out. The preskills of the strategy involve identifying the sound for each letter, blending the sounds, and then saying the blended sounds as a word.

Introducing examples consistent with a strategy before introducing exceptions can be illustrated with the CVCe strategy. Students are first taught a strategy to decode CVCe words in which the initial vowel represents the long vowel sounds. The words *like*, *cone*, and *take*, which are consistent with the strategy, are introduced first. After students become proficient with the strategy, exceptions where the vowel is not represented by its long sound (e.g., *love*, *done*, *live*) are systematically introduced.

The procedure of sequencing *high utility skills* before *less useful ones* can be illustrated with irregular words. Very common irregular words, which students encounter many times in primary readers (e.g., *was*, *said*, *have*), are introduced before less common and, therefore, less useful words (e.g., *tomb*, *heir*, *neon*). Another example involves letters: the letters *a*, *m*, *s*, and *i* are introduced earlier than the letters *v*, *x*, and *j* because they appear more often in words in primary readers. If students learn the more common letters, they will be able to decode more words.

The procedure of *sequencing easy skills before more difficult skills* can be illustrated with letter-sound correspondences and word types. Easier to say sounds (e.g., *a* and *m*) should appear before more difficult to pronounce letters (e.g., *l* and *e*). Similarily, shorter regular words easier that are to soundout than longer regular words should be introduced first.

The procedure of *separating information and strategies likely to be confused* can be illustrated with the letters *b* and *d*, which are similar in shape and sound. If *b* and *d* are introduced within a close span students are more likely to develop confusion between them than if they were separated by a longer time span. If *b* is introduced during the third week of a program, *d* might be introduced in the eighth week, after eight or nine other less similar letters have been introduced. Another illustration involves the similar irregular words *were* and *where*. Since they are similar in sound and shape, they would be introduced several weeks apart.

It is important to note that the sequencing guidelines sometimes conflict with each other. Exceptions to a strategy often need to be introduced early because they are useful. For example, because students cannot decode *was* by saying the most common sound for each letter, *was* is an exception to the sounding-out strategy. However, *was* needs to be introduced early because it occurs frequently in stories for beginning readers. Similar conflicts arise when a skill is difficult, which suggests a late introduction, yet is very useful, which suggests an earlier introduction. Obviously, compromises are necessary to resolve these conflicts. The way a compromise is made usually depends on the relative importance of the guidelines in conflict.

Providing Practice

Learning to read requires lots of practice. Hundreds of repetitions of the same skills may be necessary if an instructionally naive student is to become a mature reader. Therefore, sufficient practice must be provided within each lesson and across lessons. When a new strategy is introduced, within-lesson practice includes a concentrated or massed presentation of examples. The practice is necessary if the student is to master the strategy. Review, which is sufficient practice across several lessons, is needed to ensure that students retain the strategies and information taught in a reading program. A pattern of massed practice in the first several lessons and systematic review later is critical for retention. Teachers must supplement reading programs that do not supply sufficient practice.

Presentation Techniques

Different presentation techniques are appropriate for different stages of reading instruction. For example, during beginning reading, direct instruction involves small group teaching with little independent work. Later the amount of small group instruction decreases, and the amount of independent work increases. An example of how a specific technique is used differently at different times involves diagnosis. Diagnosis of student skill deficits during early decoding instruction is done by listening to students' oral reading responses. In later grades, diagnosis is often based on analysis of students' written answers to worksheet exercises. Another example involves teacher feedback (indicating whether responses are correct or not). For young children, feedback should be immediate; for older children, it can be delayed. (Note that immediate feedback is preferred when any student is learning new, complex material.) In general, a primary-grade teacher must be proficient in the variety of presentation techniques needed to maintain student participation in question-answer exchanges between teacher and students. On the other hand, intermediate grade teachers must be more skilled in managing students who are working independently. In both cases, however, teachers must convey warmth and active demandingness, two aspects of effective teaching identified by Kleinfeld (1975):

> The first and most important characteristic is the effective teacher's ability to create a climate of emotional warmth that dissipates students' fears in the classroom and fulfills their expectations of highly personalized relationships. The second characteristic is the teacher's ability to resolve his own ambivalent feelings about the legitimacy of his educational goals and express his concern for the . . . students, not by passive sympathy, but by demanding a high quality of academic work. (p. 318)

The remainder of this section explains some of the teaching techniques that characterize direct instruction: small group instruction, unison oral responding, signals, pacing, monitoring, diagnosis and corrections, and developing student motivation. Although most of the examples used involve situations in which younger students are being taught, teachers of older students, especially remedial students, should find much of the discussion relevant.

Small Group Instruction

Small groups are recommended for beginning reading instruction because of their efficiency. Beginning reading instruction requires frequent oral responding, which, in turn, calls for teacher feedback. This feedback can be most economically provided through small group instruction. Although students will benefit from ex-

tended periods of individual attention from a teacher every day, most schools cannot afford one-to-one teaching. While some special classrooms may have enough adults to provide intensive one-to-one reading instruction, most classrooms do not have the resources. Therefore, teachers must arrange their schedules to provide for small group instruction. By working with groups of 5 to 10 students at a time for a half hour, the teacher provides students with much more teacher instruction on reading every day than would be available if the teacher worked with individuals.

A critical aspect of small group instruction is forming homogeneous groups of students with similar skills. Such groups allow for more individualization because students with advanced skills can progress quickly through a program while less advanced students receive the extra practice they need. To form homogeneous groups, the teacher divides the students into groups according to pretest performance. Although pretests indicate the skill level of a student at the beginning of a program, they cannot predict how quickly the student will learn new skills. Consequently, teachers should expect to do some regrouping throughout the year.

When forming homogeneous groups, the teacher should make the group with higher performing students the largest and the group with lower performing students the smallest. For example, in a class of 24 students, the advanced group might include 10 students; the next, 8; and the third, 6. This is done to enable the teacher to provide more individual attention to each student in the group.

During small group beginning reading instruction, students are more likely to be attentive if seated close to the teacher. We recommend seating the students in chairs, without desks, in a semicircle or in two rows. The teacher sits facing the group, looking out over the classroom so that he can monitor the entire class. Since the students in the group are facing the board and the teacher, they will not be distracted. Students should be seated about 2 feet from the teacher to make it easier for him to monitor their performance and give encouraging pats or handshakes. It is interesting to note that just the opposite pattern often occurs with less proficient students seated farthest from the teacher (Rist, 1970). Teacher monitoring of distractable and instructionally naive students is easier when they are seated in the middle of the group rather than on the sides (see Figure 2.1).

Unison Oral Responding

A critical feature of efficient small group teaching in the early primary grades is active student involvement. Unison responding, in which all the students respond at the same time, facilitates a high degree of active student involvement. The advantage of frequent unison responses is that all students actively practice each skill throughout an instructional period. Unison responses also provide the teacher with frequent feedback about each student's progress. With younger students, the ratio of teacher talk to student response should be low. That is, teachers should not talk for long without calling for a response to ensure students understand what has been said. In nondirect instructional settings, younger students often do not attend to instruction except when they are expected to answer. When a teacher calls only individuals, some students may answer only once or twice during a period. Such infrequent responding often results in limited practice on the student's part and restricted information about student performance on the teacher's part.

Wait Time

One of the potential disadvantages of unison responses is that the brighter students will crowd out the other students. Allowing wait time or think time followed by a signal can prevent this problem. A signal is a cue given by the teacher that tells students when to make a response. The effective use of signals enables all students to participate, not just higher performing students who, if allowed, will dominate lower performing students. For example, if a teacher points to a letter and asks the students to

Figure 2.1   Suggested Seating Arrangement. An open circle (○) indicates naive or distracted students. Note that these students are not placed next to each other.

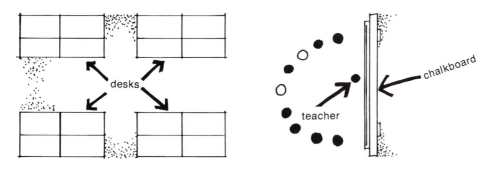

identify it, higher performing students will almost always answer first, discouraging lower performing students from responding and possibly depriving them of needed practice. A signaling procedure can avoid this problem by calling for all students to respond in unison.

The steps in a unison response signaling procedure are the directions, thinking pause or wait time, and response signal (Rowe, 1987). In the directions, the teacher asks the question and tells the students the type of response they are to make. For example, in giving directions for a vocabulary task, the teacher might say, "I'll say two words. If they are synonyms, say synonym. If they are opposites, say opposite. Listen. Big, large. Are they opposites or synonyms?" The question can also be phrased so that students do not respond orally (e.g., "Raise your hand if they are synonyms").

After the directions comes the thinking pause, which lasts for as many seconds as the teacher judges necessary for all students to figure out the answer. The final step is the actual signal to respond. This signal can be a hand drop, clap, or simply a change in voice inflection.

Pacing

Appropriate pacing contributes to student attentiveness and reduces errors. Younger students are usually more attentive to varied, fast-paced representations (as in "Sesame Street") than to slow ones. However, providing a fast-paced presentation does not mean that a teacher rushes students, requiring them to answer before they have had time to determine the answer. The key to providing a fast-paced presentation is to begin the directions for the next question (or for the correction to the current task) immediately *after* the students make a response. A teacher working with younger students might work intensively for a period of 5 minutes and then take a 15-second break, during which time she would acknowledge their efforts with verbal praise and physical contact in the form of handshakes, tickles, pats, etc. A 30-minute instructional session would in fact include about five smaller sessions. As students become more mature, the time they work without a break should increase.

Monitoring

Monitoring student performance in the late primary and intermediate grades is relatively simple (although time-consuming) because assignments are written. In contrast, monitoring the performance of early primary grade students orally responding in unison is not easy. When several students respond at the same time, it can be very difficult for the teacher to hear mistakes made by only one or two of the students, especially when an error sounds similar to the correct response. For example, if a student says the word *sit* instead of *sick* or says the sound /m/ instead of /n/, the error will be difficult to detect. So besides listening to student responses, teachers must monitor student performance by watching their students' eyes and mouths. By watching the students' lips and tongues, the teacher can determine if they are positioned the way necessary to produce the correct response. For example, a teacher points to the letter *m*, and a student responds with her mouth open. Since producing the *m* sound requires closed lips, the student's pronunciation is probably incorrect. In addition, students' eyes should be directed to the letter or word pointed to by the teacher. If a student is not looking at the letter, he may be mimicking other students' responses rather than initiating his own answer.

Simultaneously monitoring every student on every unison response during small group instruction is impossible. Consequently, a teacher must systematically switch from student to student, yet focus primarily on lower performing students. For example, in a group of eight students, five seldom have difficulty while the other three often do. The teacher arranges the students' seats so that the three who have difficulty are seated in or near the center of the group. She watches them for two or three responses and then shifts her attention to the students on the left side of the group for a response or two. Then she shifts her attention back to the students in the middle for several responses before watching the students on the right side. By always returning to the students in the middle and watching them respond, the teacher monitors their responses about twice as often as responses of the higher performing students seated on either side.

Individual tests are a very important monitoring tool because they provide a more accurate indication of mastery than a unison response. If the student makes a mistake when responding individually, the teacher provides more group practice and presents individual tests again later.

During group instruction, teachers usually should give individual tests only after all the students in the group appear to have mastered the examples presented to the group. By providing adequate group practice *before* calling on individuals, the teacher avoids needlessly embarrassing a student. Because individual tests are time consuming, they should not be given to every child after every task. The first priority is to test instructionally naive students most often. The teacher tests them on new skills and the more critical, previously introduced skills. Higher performing students might be tested individually just on tasks on which new skills are introduced.

In addition to individual tests during a group instructional session, a teacher might set up a system to make periodic comprehensive checks on skills introduced to date. By regularly taking data on students' errors, reading rate, and exercises completed, teachers can keep close track of students' progress or lack of progress. Teachers need to know which students are performing well and which are performing poorly. Such information is critical in providing effective remediation and feedback to students. Often, graphs of student performance that show improvement motivate students to do better on their assignments.

The importance of careful monitoring cannot be overemphasized. The sooner a teacher detects a problem, the easier it will be to remedy that problem. Each day a student's confusion goes undetected the student is, in essence, receiving practice doing something the wrong way. For each day a student remains confused, a teacher may have to spend several days reteaching that skill to ameliorate the confusion. Thus, careful monitoring is a prerequisite for efficient instruction.

Diagnosis and Correction

In diagnosing the cause of a student's error during small group instruction, the teacher must first decide whether the error resulted from a lack of knowledge or from inattentiveness, because the cause of an error determines which correction procedure is appropriate. The cues a teacher uses in judging whether inattentiveness is the cause are (a) where the student was looking and (b) what the student was doing during instruction. A student who is looking at the teacher is usually attending, whereas a student who is looking away may not be. The teacher corrects errors caused by inattentiveness by working on increasing the students' motivation to attend.

When errors are judged to result from a lack of knowledge, the teacher must try to determine the specific skill deficit that caused the error. This process, called diagnosis, involves identifying deficits based on recurrent error patterns, not on random errors. The diagnosis procedure is basically the same whether the response is oral or written. If, for example, a student says "sit" for the word *set* and "mat" for *met*, the teacher would diagnose the student deficit as a confusion of the letter-sound correspondence for *e*, since the student said the wrong sound for the letter *e* in both words. In a review of the corrective-feedback research literature, McCoy and Pany (1986) caution teachers to collect specific information on the kinds of oral reading errors children make in order to determine the specific correction procedure.

The correction procedure used in small-group instruction consists of as many as six steps: praise, model, lead, test, firm up, and delayed test. For example, the teacher points to *o* and asks, "What sound?" A student responds, "/ŭ/." First, the teacher praises another student who responded correctly.[1] Second, he *models* the correct answer, saying, "ŏŏŏŏŏ." Third, the teacher may *lead* (respond with them). A lead provides a model as the students respond, ensuring they hear a correct response. Leading is needed only when students have difficulty making the response (saying the sound). Fourth, the teacher tests, asking the students to answer on their own.

The next step is the *firm up*. The teacher repeats the series of tasks that just preceded the missed item and the missed item itself. For example, during second grade, a

word reading exercise might include four lists, each list containing about five words. If a student misses a word, the teacher returns to the beginning of a list and repeats the list. The purpose of the firm up step is to provide students with adequate practice on the missed item.

The last step is a *delayed test* in which the teacher tests the student individually on the missed example at a later time in the lesson. With instructionally naive students, several delayed tests may be given during a lesson so that they will receive repeated practice within a lesson if they need it. If the student makes errors on the delayed test, the teacher corrects the mistake again. A teacher should keep track of student errors so that missed skills can be emphasized on the next day's lesson.

The correction procedure is somewhat different for more advanced items. The teacher models a strategy for answering an item and tests. For example, let's say the students have read a science passage containing the rule, "When objects are heated, they expand." They then work on written exercises of this form: "A metal ball was left outside. It was 40° in the morning. In the afternoon it was 95°. What do you know about the size of the metal ball in the afternoon?" A student responds, "It gets smaller." The teacher would first test to determine the specific cause of the error. Does the student understand critical vocabulary terms (*expand*, in this case), and does she know how to apply the rule? If the student does not know how to apply the rule, the teacher *models* by asking a series of questions. What's the rule that tells about temperature and size? What was the temperature of the ball in the morning? What was the temperature of the ball in the afternoon? So did the ball get hotter? So what happened to its size? Next the teacher tests the student without leading her through the step. The teacher continues

---

1. The purpose of this praise comment is to prevent students from making errors in order to gain teacher attention and also to maintain a positive atmosphere during instruction.

testing until the student makes three or four correct responses in a row to ensure that she is not just guessing. Later in the lesson the teacher presents a delayed test.

Not working on an exercise long enough to bring a student to an acceptable criterion of performance often leads to student failure on later tasks. For example, students who do not practice a set of sounds until they identify them all correctly will have difficulty applying the sounding-out strategy later. In contrast, when teachers correct all mistakes and repeat an exercise until the students can respond to the entire set of questions correctly (called teaching to criterion), students will have relatively little difficulty applying those skills in other situations. Teaching to criterion is a very efficient procedure in the long run. Although 40 to 50 practice examples may be required to bring a group of instructionally naive students to criterion on a new skill the first day it is introduced, only 5 or 6 practice examples may be sufficient the second day, and only 1 or 2 examples on the third day. On the other hand, when teachers do not teach to criterion, students often do not show marked improvement in learning later material.

Motivation

Some students come to school eager to learn and eager to please the teacher. They respond well to simple praise. They work hard and have pride in their work. With such students, motivation is not a concern. Other students have little interest in learning and are not as eager to please. The teacher must accept these students regardless of their attitudes and use techniques to develop an interest in learning. A first step in motivating these students is demonstrating to them that they can succeed in reading. This is done by carefully designing and effectively presenting lesson plans. Second,

the teacher shows students there is a reward in learning to read. At first, with younger students she may use extrinsic rewards such as physical contact, tickles, pats, and handshakes. Eventually, she works toward developing intrinsic motivation.

Higher Performers

Direct instruction procedures are intended to make learning to read easier by breaking complex tasks into their component skills, teaching these components, and demonstrating to students how these are combined. This simplification of complex tasks is particularly important for instructionally naive students, but can also accelerate the learning of instructionally sophisticated students if used appropriately. A potential misuse of direct instruction with instructionally sophisticated students is unnecessarily slowing their speed of learning. When students are required to work exercises they already know or are given unnecessary structured teaching, valuable time is wasted. This situation can be avoided by pretesting all students. Students who do well on pretest exercises without teacher direction do not require structured teaching of the skills contained in those exercises. The teacher should proceed to exercises students cannot do and provide instruction for those exercises. In short, instructionally sophisticated students can benefit from direct instruction if they are moved through a reading program at an optimal rate and are provided no more structure than necessary.

Many educators would disagree, arguing that direct instruction may be appropriate for instructionally naive students but not for instructionally sophisticated students. The evidence in support of this position is sparse, particularly in the area of reading instruction (Cronbach & Snow, 1977). Engelmann and Carnine (1976) found that more sophisticated students perform very well as a result of direct instruction, scoring significantly above grade level on achievement tests and demonstrating an enthusiastic attitude toward learning. Similarly, Guthrie (1977) reported that direct instruction was the only approach in the *Follow Through* study that produced benefits with both low- and middle-income students. Moreover, the incidence of middle-class reading disorders such as minimal brain dysfunction, dyslexia, and learning disabilities suggests that a substantial number of advantaged students would significantly benefit from direct instruction. Since predicting which middle-class students will succeed without careful instruction is difficult, the safest procedure is to teach essential reading skills directly to most students in the early grades, thereby reducing reading failures in later grades. Avoiding direct instruction in the first grade because the students are "too smart" can result in remedial readers in the third and particularly fourth grades. In the fourth grade, reading in the content areas begins, and vocabulary is no longer controlled. These changes result in an explosion of new and difficult words. Students who survived the first three grades through memorization but were not taught basic reading skills encounter serious difficulty in fourth grade. There are too many new words to memorize for students who have not learned generalized word attack skills. If direct instruction is used carefully, it can prevent many of these reading problems. Future research in reading instruction may well point out that many of the procedures involved in direct instruction will be of benefit to all students, not just instructionally naive ones.

Summary

Much of the failure in schools can be attributed to deficits in the instructional system. There are numerous reasons why some students frequently fail. First, many reading programs do not carefully control the introduction of vocabulary, either in decoding or comprehension exercises. Second, preskills of complex strategies often are not taught. Students are expected to learn the component skills that make up a strategy and the strategy itself all at the same time. Third, programs often reflect "a little of a lot" philosophy. Many different skills are presented, but review and practice are minimal and are usually insufficient for many students to master new information and skills. Fourth, teachers are required to cover so many topics every day that finding the time to provide adequate reading practice time is difficult. The result is insufficient reading-engaged time. Fifth, teachers are often not trained to place students carefully in a reading series according to skill level. Sixth, many teachers believe that students should be intrinsically motivated to learn to read and, consequently, are not prepared to manage instruction for students who are not so motivated.

Reading failure can be prevented, however, by efficiently organizing instruction, carefully selecting and modifying reading material, and effectively presenting the material. Students will not only learn the reading competencies needed for success later in life, but they will also feel positive about their ability to function in society.

Research on the Direct Instruction Model: Short- and Long-Term Effects

The best known and largest piece of research on the Direct Instruction Model was the independent evaluation of *Project Follow Through*, conducted by Stanford Research Institute and Abt Associates (Stebbins, St. Pierre, Proper, Anderson, & Cerva, 1977) for the U.S. Office of Education. This longitudinal evaluation examined the impact of eight different instructional models on economically disadvantaged students in the primary grades. This evaluation, although discussed extensively elsewhere (House, Glass, McLean & Walker, 1978; Becker, 1977; 1977), is summarized below.

In general, the national evaluation of *Project Follow Through* found that the Direct Instruction Model had a beneficial effect on the achievement of those low-income students who participated for a full four years (kindergarten through third grade). All students were tested at the end of third grade as part of this evaluation. The results indicated that students taught in the Direct Instruction programs performed at, near, or above the national median in math, language, and spelling. In reading, performance corresponded to the 41st percentile, which is only 9 percentile points below the median. Thus, in most instances the model succeeded in bridging the gap between these low-income students and their middle-income peers.

In a secondary analysis of the achievement data from the study of *Project Follow Through*, Gersten, Becker, Heiry, and White (1984) examined the yearly achieve-

This chapter was written by Craig B. Darch, Associate Professor and Coordinator of the learning disabilities program at Auburn University.

Chapter

3

Research on Direct Instruction

ment test profiles of those students who entered with IQs on the Slosson Intelligence Test of 70 or below. The results of this study found no significant interactions between entry-level IQ and growth on the Wide Range Achievement Test (WRAT) or Total Math on the Metropolitan Achievement Test (MAT). The WRAT is a measure of word identification, while the Total Math score on the MAT is a measure of math problem solving, concepts, and computation.

The low-IQ students who began at the 5th percentile on the WRAT were virtually at norm levels (the 47th percentile) by the end of kindergarten and continued to make slow but steady growth. By the end of the third grade, performance corresponded to the 70th percentile, or a 4.3 grade level. A similar pattern was found for the larger 71-to-90 IQ group. For MAT math, the growth rate for both the below 71 and the 71-to-90 IQ blocks corresponded to 1.0 grade-equivalent unit for each year in school. In general, these results indicate the effectiveness of the Direct Instruction Model with mainstreamed "at risk" and "mildly handicapped" students in elementary grades.

Darch, Gersten, and Taylor evaluated the long-term effects of the Direct Instruction Model in Williamsburg, South Carolina. This study carefully examined the long-term impact of this structured model on the high school performance of the children. The measures used for this study were (a) graduation from high school (versus dropout rate), (b) retention rate, and (c) college acceptance. Two groups of Direct Instruction Follow Through students were included in this study, those who began first grade in 1969 and those who began in 1970. The high school performance of these students was compared to that of demographically similar students who received the traditional elementary curriculum offered by the county. Only students who remained in the county school system from first grade through high school were included. The results revealed that significantly more Follow Through students (93.1%) graduated from high school than comparison students (81.7%). For those students who entered first grade in 1970, the effect was not statistically significant.

Retention rates for grades 4–12, excluding dropouts, were also analyzed. In both groups, significantly fewer Direct Instruction Follow Through students were retained 1 or more years. Similarly, significantly more Follow Through students graduated in 12 years. For the 1969 group, 27% of the Follow Through students were accepted into college compared to only 13% of comparison students. Fewer students who participated in the Direct Instruction program were retained during the 9 years following exit from the program. In general, the results of this longitudinal study indicate benefits to the students in terms of persistence in school and college acceptance. In another study Gersten and Keating (1987) also found that Direct Instruction improved the high school performance of at-risk students.

Meyer (1984) also looked at the long-term academic effects of the Direct Instruction Model in a low-income section in Brooklyn, New York. Meyer's interest was to "trace the performance of Follow Through graduates [children who had either 3 or 4 years in the Direct Instruction program] to see if there appears to be lasting effects in high school from their early childhood participation in the Follow Through program" (p. 382). The results of this study also support the long-term benefits of the Direct Instruction Model. When the Direct Instruction students are compared with local controls, more Direct Instruction students completed high school, fewer Direct Instruction students dropped out of school, and more Direct Instruction students applied and were accepted for college. Comparisons on ninth grade reading and math measures also favored the Direct

Instruction students (see Meyer, 1984 for a discussion of the implication of these results).

Other Direct Instruction Models

The *Follow Through Model of Direct Instruction* is not the only conception of Direct Instruction. There are several definitions and approaches that are labeled as Direct Instruction. The term *direct instruction* was first introduced into the mainstream of educational research by Rosenshine (1976), who used it to capture and refer to patterns of teacher behavior correlated with high levels of student academic achievement. Rosenshine's initial definition of direct instruction focused on teacher behavior and classroom organization, with a particular emphasis on the use of instructional time in the classroom. This conception of direct instruction was based on the naturalistic research of classroom processes conducted in regular education classrooms, often with low-income students. Recently, other researchers have noted that these basic conceptions are equally valid for classrooms with mildly handicapped students (Englert, 1984; Leinhardt, Zigmond, & Cooley, 1981; Reith & Frick, 1982).

Rosenshine and Stevens (1984) concluded that low-performing students repeatedly show higher academic achievement when their teachers follow a consistent practice of demonstration, guided practice, and feedback. In a demonstration, the teacher provides a clear, controlled presentation of a wide range of activities, from decoding words to performing complex cognitive operations involving critical reading skills and general problem-solving strategies. Guided practice, which follows demonstration, allows the teacher to ask questions of students, check for understanding, and give feedback. Finally, during independent practice, the teacher monitors students' work on activities directly related to the new material.

In a recent article, Rosenshine (1986) summarized much of the research in generic direct instruction by specifying how teachers can best affect positive student achievement. He concluded that

> in general, researchers have found that when effective teachers teach concepts and skills explicitly, they: begin a lesson with a short statement of goals; begin a lesson with a short review of previous, prerequisite learning; present new material in small steps, with student practice after each step; give clear and detailed instructions and explanations; provide active practice for all students; ask many questions, check for student understanding, and obtain responses from all students; guide students during initial practice; provide systematic feedback and corrections; provide explicit instruction and practice for seatwork exercises and, where necessary, monitor students during seatwork; and continue practice until students are independent and confident. (p. 61)

Research on Curriculum Design Features	In contrast to the *Direct Instruction Follow Through* studies that looked at the entire model of direct instruction, there is also a large group of studies that have documented the effectiveness of the design of instruction principles of the Direct Instruction Model. These studies are concerned with the analysis of how curriculum should be constructed in order to achieve the greatest learning gains. The studies that evaluate the specific instructional design principles are smaller scale studies with a singular focus. For instance, in a Direct Instruction

program, initial teaching of any problem-solving strategy typically involves explicit instruction on each step in the sequence. Specifically, overt, step-by-step strategies have been developed and empirically field tested to teach students to (a) draw inferences from basal passages (Carnine, Kameenui, & Woolfson, 1982); (b) solve math-word problems (Darch, Carnine, & Gersten, 1984); and (c) learn basic legal concepts (Fielding, Kameenui, & Gersten, 1983).

In other selected studies, Carnine (1977) compared students who learned a sounding-out strategy to identify a set of training words with students who memorized the training words without learning how to sound out words. Both groups required a comparable amount of time to learn to identify the training words; but, on a test of new words, the strategy group identified significantly more regular and irregular words. A second study (Torgesen, 1977) found that while good readers approached memorization in a more organized and active manner and performed relatively well on a recall test, poor readers exhibited different study behavior and did less well on the recall test. However, after poor readers received strategy training on how to study, their performance on the recall test approximated that of the better readers.

The importance of selecting examples is illustrated in a study by Carnine and Kameenui (1978). In learning to identify CVCe words such as *hike* and *came,* one group of students received only introductory examples (all CVCe words: *cape* and *site*) while a second group received both introductory and discrimination examples (CVCe and CVC words: *cap, cape, site, sit*). On a posttest, students who received both introductory and discrimination examples identified significantly more new CVCe words. More than 20 years ago, Ausubel (1967) noted the benefits of sufficient practice as a means of inducing overlearning, or mastery learning:

> Abundant experimental research (for example, Duncan, 1959; Morrisett and Hovland, 1959) has confirmed the proposition that prior learnings are not transferable to new learning tasks until they are first overlearned. Overlearning, in turn, requires an adequate number of adequately spaced repetitions and reviews, sufficient intratask repetitiveness prior to intra- and intertask diversification, and opportunity for differential practice of the more difficult components of a task. Frequent testing and provision of feedback, especially with test items demanding fine discrimination among alternatives varying in degree of correctness, also enhance consolidation by confirming, clarifying, and correcting previous learnings. (p. 239)

Brophy and Evertson (1976) reported that mastery learning levels of 80% to 85% seemed to produce significant learning gains without producing negative student attitudes toward instruction.

The importance of practice is suggested by comparing student performance on two studies in which students learned letter-sound correspondences (Carnine, 1976). In one study, children received as much practice as necessary to master a correspondence before a new letter was introduced.This was the mastery learning study. In the other study, children received a total of 50 practice trials on each letter-sound correspondence. The students in the mastery learning study made 79% correct posttest identifications as compared to a mean of 28% for the students who received 50 trials on each letter.

Research on Direct Instruction Teaching Techniques

Other studies have focused upon the importance of the specific teaching techniques in the Direct Instruction Model. This focus, although different from the studies that evaluated the instructional design principles of the model, is closely tied to the success of this approach. Several studies have validated the importance of pacing of instruction (Carnine, 1976; Darch & Gersten, 1985), use of corrections (Carnine, 1980c; Gersten, Carnine, & Williams, 1982), use of signals (Carnine, 1981b), and use of formats. Gersten, Carnine, and Williams (1982) have comprehensively investigated these instructional variables. Specifically, they identified ten first grade teachers who were all using the same curriculum, *DISTAR* Reading I and II, for an academic year. All were teaching low-income Black and Hispanic children, and their time allocations during the day were virtually identical. Yet, at the end of the year, some classes were above grade level and some at the 22nd percentile. The performances of the two highest achieving and two lowest achieving teachers were analyzed using a contrasted groups design. Results showed that there were distinct differences in observed teacher performance. The higher achieving teachers tended to (a) correct student errors immediately, (b) maintain a student success rate of at least 85% in all reading groups (even the lowest reading group), and (c) pace their lessons at a brisk tempo. These findings were replicated (Gersten, Carnine, Zoref, & Cronin, 1986) with a larger sample. Englert (1984) has replicated these basic findings with student teachers working in classes for handicapped students and using a range of curricula materials. Stallings (1980) and Leinhardt et al. (1981) have also documented the importance of some of these teaching variables.

Small Group Instruction. The research on small group instruction generally shows positive benefits. First, adult supervision apparently contributes to student engagement. Filby and Marliave (cited in Rosenshine, in press) and Fisher, Filby, and Marliave (cited in Rosenshine, in press) found that when students were working with a teacher or another adult, they were engaged from 79% to 88% of the time. In contrast, when students were working alone they were engaged only 68% to 73% of the time. Second, small group instruction seems to be a reasonable alternative to one-to-one instruction. Venezky and Shiloah (1972) reported that performance on language tasks was superior for students working in a small group setting than for students receiving one-to-one instruction. Working with retarded children on language skills, Biberdorf and Pear (1977) reported that group instruction was more efficient in terms of material learned per unit time than individual instruction. Fink and Carnine (1975) and Fink and Sandall (1977) reported similar results. In contrast, a single study (Jenkins, Mayhall, Peschka, & Jenkins, 1974) reported that tutorials in remedial reading were more effective than instruction in small groups. The effectiveness of small group instruction is based on the notion of students with comparable instructional needs. The student grouping in the Jenkins et al. study may not have been comparable in needs. Additional research is needed on the effectiveness of small groups for other aspects of reading instruction and for use in the intermediate grades.

Frequent Oral Responding.   Several studies point to the importance of overt responding. Brophy & Everston (1976) reported that low-performing students are reluctant to respond and are more likely to participate when a group of students is responding. Durling and Schick (1976) and Blank and Frank (1971) reported that overt responding (vocalizing a concept) improved performance when compared to a nonvocalizing treatment. Abramson and Kagan (1975) found that subjects who overtly responded to questions while learning unfamiliar material out-performed students who merely read the material. Frase and Schwartz (1975) reported similar results.

In terms of feedback to overt responses, Tobias and Ingber (1976) reported that feedback yielded superior achievement primarily for students with low pretest scores. Hanna (1976) found that intermediate grade students who received partial or immediate feedback during training answered significantly more posttest items than students who did not receive feedback. When and how to make a transition from overt responding and practice to covert responding are questions that await further research. Brown (1977) and other researchers have emphasized the importance of research on such transitions.

Signals.   During small group instruction, teachers use signals to call for unison responses. Cowart, Carnine, and Becker (1976) conducted a study in which the teachers used signals for several lessons and then did not use signals for several lessons. They found that signaling resulted in more student attending and responding. When the teacher used signals, the children attended about 55% of the time and responded about 80% of the time. When the teacher did *not* use signals, the children attended about 35% of the time and responded 60% of the time. Slight improvement in test scores also accompanied the use of signals. The same study reported comparable signaling effects on attending and responding in an entire class teaching situation. For example, in one classroom of time attending averaged 53% and 54% during the two phases in which the teacher used signals and 41% and 20% during the two phases without signals. The responding percentages were 75% and 79% with signals and 67% and 47% without signals. Other research on the importance of signals has produced few effects. Consequently, we encourage the use of signals primarily as a management tool to secure student participation and to prevent higher performing students from dominating instruction.

Pacing.   The speed with which a teacher presents the tasks in a lesson determines how often students respond and also may affect attending behavior. Rates of presenting beginning reading tasks were compared by alternating rapid and slow pacing of lessons with the two lowest performing first graders from three classrooms serving as subjects (Carnine, 1976b). Attending and correct answers were substantially higher during the fast-rate condition (5 seconds per task) than during the slow-rate condition (14 seconds per task). When the teacher asked approximately 12 questions per minute in the fast-rate condition, the students answered correctly about 80% of the time and were off task only about 10% of the time. When the teacher asked about 5 questions per minute in the slow-rate condition, the students answered correctly about 30% of the time and were off task about 70% of the time. Massad and Etzel (1972) found that preschoolers learned sound-symbol relationships more rapidly and with fewer errors with frequent rather than infrequent responding. They also reported that response frequency influenced performance more than various reinforcement schedules. Although we feel rapid presentations are justified because teachers present more material, research on the effects of rapid presentations beyond the first year of instruction would be useful. Also a more accurate specification of optimal rates for different tasks would provide helpful guidelines for teachers.

Monitoring.   Monitoring is essential both for correcting and reinforcing students' reading behavior. Brophy and Evertson point out the importance of monitoring:

> To find out unambiguously whether or not students really understand, teachers must ask questions or observe student attempts to carry out a learning task. Teachers who do this habitually will find that many students who appeared to have been attentive and to have understood a presentation are unable to apply the new material successfully by answering questions or doing exercises correctly. Thus, when we speak of "monitoring" student learning progress, we mean getting responses, not merely watching facial expressions for signs of inattention or confusion. (1976, p. 68)

Not only is monitoring an indispensable ingredient for knowing when to correct and reinforce, but it also affects how students attend during reading instruction. Carnine and Fink (1974) systematically varied the amount of eye contact directed to two students who were frequently not attending during instruction. They reported that when the teacher maintained eye contact with the first student, the student attended 91% of the time, fell to 62% when eye contact was removed, and increased to 86% when eye contact was reinstated. The second student, who started without teacher eye contact, attended 63% of the time. When eye contact increased, attending increased to 85% and then fell to 60% when eye contact was removed. Brophy and Evertson (1976) found that "More effective teachers moved around the room regularly and visually scanned the classroom regularly to keep continual track of what was going on" (p. 56).

Monitoring occurs in many forms besides teacher contact: checking worksheets, walking around the room as students work at their seats, reading graphs of student performance, etc. The effectiveness of these and other monitoring techniques deserves further research.

Corrections.   Although correcting student errors is usually considered an important part of the instructional process, research on error correction is limited. The importance of correcting mistakes (as opposed to ignoring them) was investigated in a study conducted by Carnine (1976a). Preschool children were taught several sets of facts: first without corrections, then with corrections, again without corrections, and finally with corrections. Accuracy on training questions averaged 55% higher during correction phases than during no-correction phases. In addition to being provided with corrective feedback, students must also attend to the feedback if it is to be effective. Fink and Carnine (1975) reported that student worksheet errors declined significantly when the students graphed their errors as compared with just being told the number of errors. Some educators (Pehrsson, 1974) suggest that errors should not be corrected, which may be reasonable when students have learned a skill and are practicing so that it will become automatic. The question of when and how to correct will be addressed several times later in the book. As with the other presentation techniques, more research questions are unanswered than answered.

Research related to the modeling aspect of a correction indicated that telling adult subjects the answer after an error resulted in quicker learning than just telling the subject whether the answer was right or wrong (Bourne & Pendleton, 1958). Furthermore, requiring the subject to say the answer following an error was more effective than just telling the subject the answer (Suppes & Ginsberg, 1962). Stromer (1975) reported that when corrections (modeling the correct answer following an error) and differential praise were introduced in tutorial situations, errors diminished. Modeling the correct answer, however, is often not sufficient to remedy many error patterns. For example, a study by Jenkins and Larson (1978) has shown that merely modeling the correct answer following a decoding error is not very effective. Only when the teacher provides a model and *extensive practice* did decoding performance improve. In providing practice, the importance of the alternating pattern, in which familiar examples are included along with difficult examples, was suggested in a study by Neef, Iwata, and Page (1977).

Although modeling and providing practice are usually appropriate for correcting mistakes on discrimination tasks (for example, a student identifies *a* as *e*), the procedure can be ineffective with errors that require the application of a multistep strategy. In these situations, the correction should prompt the student to apply the strategy (Siegel, 1977; Siegler and Liebert, 1973). A study by Carnine (1978c) investigated the importance of correcting word-reading errors by prompting students to use an originally taught sounding-out strategy. Three groups of preschoolers were taught eight letter-sound correspondences and then were given practice on the sounding-out strategy until they reached a 100% correct response criterion to a set of six words. After reaching criterion on the training words, the preschoolers received daily word recognition practice, in which four new words were repeated three times. The teacher used a whole word correction procedure in which the teacher identified the word and then asked the students to identify it. The intervention, a sounding-out correction procedure, was introduced with one group at a time. The students were required to sound out and then identify the word that was missed. Consistent improvement was noted in all three groups after the sounding-out correction was introduced, both in correct training responses and correct responses to transfer words. The approximate changes in training performance on word identification were from 30% to 70% correct in group one, 20% to 35% in group two, and 15% to 25% in group three. The smaller changes with each successive intervention suggest that the longer students receive a whole-word correction, the less effective is the introduction of the sounding-out correction. These results are consistent with those of Brophy and Evertson (1976), who found that phonic corrections "were particularly useful for children in general and for low SES children in particular" (p. 85).

Oftentimes errors can be anticipated and prevented. Fink (1976) investigated one such precorrection procedure with two low-performing first graders (mean IQs were 68 and 72) who consistently misidentified vowels when sounding out CVC (consonant-vowel-consonant) and CVCC words. The students received daily practice in identifying letter sounds and in sounding out words. In addition, they were precorrected in this way: each student was instructed to identify the vowel *before* sounding out the word. Initially no precorrection was used. Then a precorrection was used for several days, and then again no precorrection was used. The mean number of correct responses (out of six possible) changed from .71 to 3.75 and back to 1.20 for the first student and from .60 to 2.56 and back to .86 for the second student. Correction is an area that requires numerous studies; whether to correct, when to correct, how often to correct, and the form of the correction are but a few of the variables to be studied. Also, the differential application of correction procedures to students of different skill levels must be investigated. For example, for a fluent fifth-grade reader, a decoding error might be ignored; however, for a second grader, the teacher might model and test the word at the end of a sentence in which the error occurred. For a beginning reader, the teacher might require the student to sound out the word immediately after the error occurred.

Praise. A number of studies have demonstrated that teacher attention is an effective tool in reducing children's inappropriate behavior within large-group instructional settings. Thomas, Becker, & Armstrong (1968) and Madsen, Becker, & Thomas (1968) showed that frequent teacher attention to appropriate behavior in the form of praise was more effective than rules or teacher reprimands in increasing appropriate behavior. Similarly, Hall, Lund, and Jackson (1968) and Cossairt, Hall, and Hopkins (1973) demonstrated that teacher attention through verbal praise and physical contact increased children's study behaviors in a large-group instructional setting. In addition, Cossairt et al. reported that higher rates of teacher praise coincided with higher rates of studying behavior.

Although the effects of positive teacher attention on appropriate classroom behaviors have been well established within large-group instructional settings, its effectiveness within a small group instructional setting has not received much attention. In a study by Kryzanowski (1976), four subjects displayed clear increases in on-task behavior in a small-group instructional setting as a function of increased verbal praise, with the average increase being 47%.

The question remains whether a higher rate of on-task behavior is a necessary prerequisite to a child's learning. On-task behavior may increase a child's opportunity to respond appropriately to every task; however, it does not insure that learning will be more efficient or complete. Siegel and Rosenshine (1973) reported that praise during *DISTAR Language I* small-group instruction was not a significant predictor of child achievement. Thus, high rates of praise may only produce better behaved children and not necessarily smarter ones. Given the contradictory data concerning this question, further research is needed to investigate the effects of praise on learning in a small group instructional setting. Research is also needed on how best to encourage older students in their academic work.

Combined Effects. A final study investigated the combined effects of a set of direct instruction techniques. In a *high-implementation* condition, the teacher used praise, corrections, and rapid pacing, while in a *low-implementation* condition, the teacher seldom corrected, used little praise, and presented tasks in a relatively slow manner (Carnine, 1978d). The subjects were preschoolers who were taught reading in a small-group setting. For assessing the strength of the combined variables, a multielement design with almost daily switches in level of implementation was used.

Both on-task behavior and correct responding remained sensitive to the condition shifts throughout the experiment, with much larger changes occurring for on-task behavior than for academic behavior. The results suggest that this cluster of teacher presentation variables (praise, rapid pacing, and correcting) can strongly affect student behavior and, to a lesser extent, student performance across different educational programs. Children in this study were using the McGraw-Hill *Sullivan Reading* program, while the children in earlier cited research on isolated teacher presentation variables were using *DISTAR* materials or experimenter-designed materials.

Other Outcomes. A final research area of great importance is the effect of a direct approach on other outcomes such as creativity or self-esteem. The studies reviewed by Rosenshine (1979) are uniformly positive. He found that the two *Follow Through* programs that produced the highest proportion of significant positive results on the Coopersmith Self-Esteem Inventory were both highly structured, direct teaching programs. In a study of middle-class students, Solomon (cited in Rosenshine, 1979) found that "control and orderliness" related not only to achievement gain but also to total gain in inquiry skill, creativity, and self-esteem. Solomon elaborates:

> The effective formal classrooms are not cold and critical—McDonald found criticism was relatively rare in California classrooms, being concentrated mainly in the less effective classrooms. Teachers in formal classrooms were warm, concerned, flexible, and allow much more freedom of movement. But they are also task oriented and determined that children shall learn. (p. 40)

Tikunoff, Berliner, and Rist (cited in Rosenshine, 1979) also reported higher achieving classrooms were observed as being "convivial, cooperative, democratic, and warm; whereas in the lower achieving classrooms there was more belittling, shaming of students, and use of sarcasm. Furthermore, competitiveness did *not* distinguish between higher achievement and lower achievement'' (p. 41).

Conclusion.   As stated earlier, these research findings suggest the effectiveness of several direct-instruction presentation techniques. However, the results are not conclusive. Procedures effective with students at a certain age and skill level may not work with students who are more skilled or less skilled. Also, students who have serious behavior problems or who have major academic deficits may not respond to these techniques without concommitant changes in the instructional material and the amount of instruction they receive. The techniques are part of a larger instructional system and alone will not necessarily produce sizable effects.

Although the use of single techniques can have noticable effects in certain situations, usually teachers should think about implementing a set of techniques to teach important reading skills better. Another important point to remember is that as students become more skilled, different instructional procedures will be appropriate. This process is well described by Brophy:

> In particular, it should be noted that what is optimal will change to the extent that the teacher has been successful. That is, a teacher who has brought along a class (or an individual student) nicely through careful structuring eventually will get them to the point where they are ready for some independent responsibility. It is important for teachers to remain aware of this developmental trend, because what is optimal for a child who is having difficulty with initial assignments concerning tool skill mastery and who needs careful structuring and considerable encouragement is very different from what is optimal for this same child when he reaches the stage where he is mastering tool skills and has acquired the independent behavior and learning habits that make it possible for him to profit from independent and self-chosen activities. (1975, p. 16)

A Model of Reading Instruction

This section overviews a scope and sequence for teaching reading. A scope of reading instruction is defined by the major reading skills to be taught. *Sequence* involves an order for introducing the skills. Scope and sequence are directly under a teacher's control. Cognitive structures, maturational levels, and so forth are of less interest because we do not yet understand how teachers bring about changes in these areas through instruction.

Reading skills usually involve decoding and comprehension. *Decoding* is translating printed words into a representation similar to oral language (e.g., reading, either silently or aloud, "I am hot" for the words *I am hot)*. Understanding the representation is *comprehension* (e.g., knowing who *I* in the sentence refers to and how "being hot" feels). Although our major objective is comprehension instruction, a successful reader must be proficient in decoding to comprehend. For example, a 14-year-old student reads a passage about the Civil War and later answers this question about the passage. "By March 15, General Grant had deployed his troops. Should General Lee have attacked General Grant before or after March 15? Explain your answer." The question requires the student to draw an inference, which is a comprehension skill. The inference goes something like this: Grant will have had his forces deployed by March 15. Military attacks should be staged before the opponent has his troops deployed. Therefore, Lee should have attacked Grant before March 15. The student's ability to comprehend the question would be impaired if he decoded *deployed* as *depleted*. Similarly, if he decoded each word in the sentence correctly but did not know the meaning of the word *deployed*, his comprehension also would be impaired. Successful reading requires competency in both decoding and comprehension.

Gough and Tunmer (1986) offer the equation

Reading = Decoding × Comprehension

to point out the importance of both decoding and comprehension to the process of constructing and deriving meaning from words in a text.

Although most reading educators agree about the importance of decoding and comprehension, they disagree about the nature of the reading process, whether it is a holistic, unitary process or a process built upon clusters of subskills. As will become evident throughout this book, we view learning to read as a two-step process. The acquisition of a set of subskills is the first step; the assimilation of those subskills into the holistic act of reading and bringing meaning to the text is the second step. The importance of decoding as a first step in the process of reading is noted by Perfetti (1986) who states, "Final progress in learning to read does depend on learning the principles on which decoding depends . . . . Although many other higher mental processes come into effect in comprehension, decoding and word identification remain as the central recurring parts of reading" (p. 20). In this chapter, a model of decoding will be discussed first, followed by a model of comprehension. It is important to remember that the focus of the models is on *instructional variables* under a teacher's control. The models are not intended as comprehensive representations of what takes place in a reader's mind when a person decodes and comprehends a text. Rather, the models are intended to identify and delineate the instructional features important to the teaching of reading.

Decoding

Our model of teaching decoding is based on the features of several models that have been developed in the past (Calfee & Piont-kowski, 1981; Chall, 1983, 1988; Cunningham, 1975, 1976; Gibson, 1965; Perfetti & Curtis, 1986; Spear & Sternberg, 1986; Stanovich, 1986; Venezky & Calfee, 1970; Williams, 1979). This model acknowledges that reading involves the orchestration of many different skills and types of knowledge. For example, an important skill is that of phonic and structural analysis allowing a reader to break words down into manageable units and to compare those units with the reader's prior knowledge of familiar word parts. For example, when encountering the word *stairs,* the reader recognizes the word part *air,* as in *fair,* and decodes the word. The reader then checks whether this decoding of the word makes sense in the full context of the sentence, as well as in the reader's knowledge of the word; that is, "The man fell down the stars" would not make sense because *stairs* was read as *stars.* If the sentence doesn't make any sense, the reader rechecks his decoding of individual words. By applying phonic skills (reading word parts), general knowledge (knowing word meanings, logical reasoning), and knowing when to make adjustments in the process of reading, the reader is in a position to derive and give meaning to the text.

The decoding of a word then depends on many different kinds of skills and knowledge. A direct instruction analysis of decoding instruction focuses on the (1) decoding units to be taught, (2) the skills necessary to process these units, (3) the knowledge base necessary to understand the meaning of words, and (4) the strategic knowledge necessary to organize information and make adjustments during reading.

Four Aspects of the Decoding Model

The following are descriptions and examples of the four aspects of the decoding model: decoding units, processing skills, knowledge base, and strategic knowledge.

Decoding Units

Decoding instruction begins with the teaching of sounds represented by individual letters, because these are the smallest decoding units. Reading lessons are designed so that only words comprised of previously taught letters and words in the students' speaking vocabulary are presented. When necessary, students orally are taught the meaning of a word before the word is encountered in decoding exercises. For most students, the words introduced in early decoding instruction will be words in their speaking vocabulary and, thus, extensive oral instruction will not be necessary.

As soon as students know sufficient letters, larger units such as words are introduced. When students are able to decode enough words, the teacher introduces phrases, sentences, and passages, as well as the sound correspondences to letter combinations such as *ea, ate, ou, al*, and *ing*. In general, a sequence of increasingly complex decoding units that include letters, letter combinations, syllables, word phrases, sentences, and passages are taught.

Processing Skills

Students must be taught the skills for processing the decoding units. Phonic analysis skills consist of saying the sounds for individual letters (e.g., vowels and consonants) and letter combinations (e.g., *ee, oa, ar*), rhyming words and word parts, breaking larger words into parts, and sight reading. Students must also be taught other skills in addition to phonic analysis if they are to become mature readers. These include structural analysis and contextual analysis skills. Structural analysis involves teaching students to decode multisyllabic words through recognition of root words, prefixes (*re, un, con*), and suffixes (*ness, full, ion*). Contextual analysis involves teaching stu-

dents to rely on the structure of sentences (syntax) and the meaning of words (semantics) as aids in decoding unknown words or in checking the correctness of decoding.

Knowledge Base

A student's knowledge base refers to the different kinds of knowledge a student brings to the reading situation, as well as any knowledge acquired during reading instruction. This knowledge base involves reasoning skills, background knowledge, and the knowledge involved in making sense of words and the logical connections between the text and the reader's experience.

This knowledge base is dynamic and expanding and includes knowledge acquired during previous instruction. Therefore, as the reader acquires the skills for processing the decoding units, these skills become part of the reader's knowledge base. In the beginning stages of reading, this base may be limited primarily to a reader's background knowledge. However, in the advanced stages of reading, this knowledge base will be extensive, including phonic knowledge, semantic knowledge, syntactic knowledge, background knowledge, and knowledge of reading strategies.

Strategic Knowledge

In order to be successful readers, students must be able to make adjustments during the reading process. These adjustments vary depending on the purpose of reading, the reader's skill level, the social context of the reading situation (e.g., individual, small group, whole class), and the reading task requirements (e.g., orally retelling what was read or answering general and specific comprehension questions). This strategic knowledge also includes the reader's ability to monitor the ongoing reading and comprehension process by determining if the words make sense and square with the reader's own experiences. During this monitoring process, the reader orchestrates the various decoding skills and activates the background knowledge necessary for making sense of the text. If the words decoded do not make sense, then the reader makes adjustments in both decoding and comprehension. In general, students must be taught to identify, activate, monitor, and coordinate different kinds of knowledge and information. The process of appraising, managing, and regulating one's performance during reading is often referred to as *metacognition* (Armbruster, Echols, & Brown, 1982; Paris, Wasik, & Van der Westhuizen, 1987). Young and poor readers are known to have problems monitoring and managing reading tasks (Armbruster et al., 1987; Simmons, Kameenui, & Darch, 1988).

Implications for Beginning Reading Instruction

The decoding model can be used to resolve many reading controversies, especially in the area of beginning reading instruction. Although extensive research has been conducted on teaching decoding, educators still disagree on many issues. For teachers of beginning readers, the disagreements result in a bewildering list of choices about what to do. Which of the following should teachers stress:

1. Letter sounds or letter names? That is, pronouncing the sound for *a* as in *cat* or the name for *a* as in *make*. Should students learn sounds before they learn the alphabet?
2. Sounding-out or whole-word reading? That is, identifying a sound for each letter in a word, blending the sounds and identifying the word, or identifying the word as a unit.
3. New words in isolation or in context? That is, presenting new words in lists or in sentences.
4. Accuracy or fluency? That is, correctly identifying words or reading sentences rapidly with expression.
5. Oral or silent reading? That is, students reading aloud or to themselves.

Relying on the decoding model of instruction, these conflicts can be resolved by deciding *when* an objective is appropriate, not whether it is appropriate.

Letter Sounds and Letter Names

We recommend teaching letter sounds before letter names. Although young children are often taught the alphabet as an initial reading skill, knowledge of letter names is not as useful in beginning reading as a knowledge of letter sounds. Letter names bear little resemblance to the sounds said when a word is pronounced. For example, knowing the names of the letters, *r, u,* and *n* will not enable a beginning reader to decode the word *run*. In contrast, knowing the sounds for the letters (/r/ as in *rat*, /ŭ/ as in *up*, and /n/ as in *can*) will help a beginning reader decode the word. An important consideration with letter-sound correspondences is pronunciation variations that result from dialects or regional differences. Instruction should accommodate these variations, unless they are so extreme that students will be unable to decode words correctly. In those situations, teachers should provide practice for troublesome sounds so that word-reading performance is not impeded.

Sounding-out and Whole-word Reading

We recommend that students learn sounding out before they read whole words as units because sounding out provides beginning readers with a relatively easy-to-learn strategy for attacking new words. It also prevents students from becoming confused about the relationship between letters in words and how words are said. Teaching sounding out is best done with a code-emphasis reading program in which words are selected that demonstrate consistent letter-sound correspondences. When sounding out words, students identify sounds, blend them, and identify the word. After students become proficient in sounding out, they must make a transition to whole-word reading which itself involves two stages. In the first stage, students sound out a word subvocally before pronouncing it. In the second stage, students see a word and, without first sounding it out, pronounce it vocally or subvocally. We do not know what goes on in the brain that enables students to recognize words at a glance. All we can say is that recognizing words at a glance is a skill that is acquired with adequate practice. Students vary a great deal in the amount of practice they will require to advance from sounding out words to recognizing words at a glance.

Introducing New Words in Isolation and in Context

During the beginning reading stage, we recommend introducing new words in isolation (in lists) and then in context (in stories). The rationale for this sequence is that when students are acquiring decoding skills, they should be required to focus on the letters and letter combinations that make up the words and to read words using only those cues. Students are less likely to do this when the words are introduced in stories because they can use the context of the story (by saying a word that makes sense in the sentence) or pictures (by looking at objects in the picture to help them guess a word). Students who rely heavily on picture and context cues may attend only to some letters in a word and thus develop ineffective decoding strategies. In word lists, contexts and picture clues are unavailable, thereby increasing the likelihood that the student will attend to all the letters in the words.

Accuracy and Fluency

Accuracy is defined as correctly identifying letters or words. *Fluency* is reading smoothly, quickly, and with expression. The relationship between accuracy and fluency might be better understood in the context of acquisition and proficiency. During the acquisition stage, a new skill is being learned. During the proficiency stage, the skill is practiced so that students can apply it quickly and remember it. Although the two stages overlap to some extent, the intent of each stage differs. During the acquisition stage when a skill is new, mastery of the skill (in this case, accurate decoding) is most important. After the skill has been introduced and practiced to some extent, proficiency (in this case, learning to read fluently) becomes more important. Samuels (1976a) speaks of proficiency as automaticity or "automatic habits" in decoding: "While it is true that accuracy in decoding is necessary in reading, it is not a sufficient condition. In order to have both fluent reading and good comprehension, the student must be brought beyond accuracy to automaticity in decoding" (p. 323).

The progression from accurate to fluent reading makes sense when viewed from a beginning reader's perspective. At first, the student carefully inspects and sounds out each word. The student must remember the sound for each letter, be able to blend sounds, and then transform the blended sounds into a word (e.g., the written word

Sam is sounded out "Ssssaaammm" and then becomes "Sam"). This is the acquisition stage. If a student is encouraged to read rapidly and with expression while still in this stage, she will not have time to process the letters that make up each word. Rather, she may begin guessing, saying any word that makes sense in the sentence; perhaps she will use picture cues that accompany the words or just look at the first letter and guess. However, if the student is given time during the acquisition stage to master sounding out, she will be more likely not to develop guessing habits. It is much easier to increase reading rate with students who have appropriate decoding strategies since the teacher can concentrate solely on rate. As the rate increases, the accuracy stays high. With students who develop strong guessing behavior in early training, rate training is difficult since guessing tends to increase.

Just as stressing fluency too soon causes problems, so can stressing fluency too late. If students are required to sound out every word for months and months, they may become word-by-word readers, which, in turn, may cause serious comprehension problems or result in students not being able to complete assignments since they read too slowly.

Oral and Silent Reading

The long-term objective of reading instruction is for students to read silently, accurately, and with comprehension. However, long-term objectives do not necessarily determine *how to begin* instruction. During early reading instruction, oral reading enables the teacher to keep students actively practicing reading and, in addition, provides information about problems the students may be having. This feedback allows the teacher to correct inappropriate strategies, thereby helping students develop the

skills necessary to become successful readers. In mid- and late-primary grades, students should read silently most of the time; oral reading is used just when teaching specific skills such as reading with expression or in making periodic checks of students' decoding ability. While oral reading does not interfere with improvements in reading rate and comprehension during early instruction, it could interfere at a later stage if ample silent reading practice is not provided.

In summary, with this decoding model the controversy over the scope of decoding instruction (what skills to teach) is transformed into a question of sequencing (when to teach the skills). The alternatives described earlier as either-or questions can now be presented as compatible skills, arranged in sequence:

1. Teach letter sounds, then letter names.
2. Teach sounding out, then sight reading.
3. Teach new words in isolation during the beginning reading stage; later, introduce regular words and high-frequency irregular words in context. (In fact, many words must be introduced in context because of dual pronunciations, e.g., *lead* as in *lead pipe* and *lead the way).*
4. Teach reading for accuracy, then reading for fluency.
5. Teach oral reading, then silent reading.

Each set of objectives contains a short-term objective and a long-term objective. The initial objectives in each set are short-term goals relating to sounds, sounding out, isolated words, oral reading, and accurate reading. These short-term objectives prepare students for the long-term objectives: silently and accurately reading by words and phrases. Just because the short-term objectives are superseded by the long-term objectives does not lessen their importance.

Comprehension

As we noted earlier, beginning reading instruction should stress decoding but not ignore comprehension. As Carroll (1977) notes, "An emphasis on phonics does not mean the attention to meaning must inevitably decrease. Of course, you can teach meaning while teaching phonics, and doing otherwise is counterproductive and absurd" (p. 157). Carroll further points out that reading comprehension also requires language comprehension and cognitive ability (complex reasoning skills) and that there are many more language and reasoning skills that make up reading comprehension than there are decoding skills.

Since almost any set of thoughts or ideas can be written and given to someone to decode and comprehend, comprehension involves almost every type of "understanding" or "thinking." Following Carroll's lead, Jenkins and his colleagues (Jenkins & Pany, 1979; Jenkins, Stein, & Osborn, 1981; Jenkins & Dixon, 1984) emphasize the close relationship between language skills and reading comprehension. These researchers note that students who do well on comprehension questions for passages presented orally also tend to do well on comprehension questions for printed passages. It appears that the same reasoning processes are used to understand what we read as well as what we hear.

However, as Durkin (1981) points out, reading-comprehension instruction involves primarily making sense of written texts. Durkin defines reading-comprehension instruction as "Something a teacher does that ought to help children acquire the ability to understand or work out the meaning of connected text" (p. 518). Our model for comprehension instruction is concerned primarily with "something a teacher does" that provides students with the skills for making sense of texts. Such a model for the classroom teacher is particularly important for comprehension instruction because it is more complex than decoding instruction. As in decoding, we believe this orientation involves the identification of critical skills. In one of the first critical analyses of reading comprehension, Davis (1972) suggested that comprehension skills are hierarchical; that is, skills are built on each other, progressing from simple to complex. In reviewing the research at the time, he rejected an isolated-skills theory in which comprehension is viewed as comprised of many unrelated skills that can be taught in any order. He also rejected a global-skills theory that conceived of comprehension as a single skill. Instead, Davis argued that a hierarchical-skills theory best fit the comprehension research data at the time. We agree that many comprehension skills are hierarchically related. For example, vocabulary knowledge is often a preskill for drawing inferences. Students cannot infer what two antagonists who have frequent altercations will do when they meet at a party, unless they know the meaning of *antagonist* and *altercation*. Yet while comprehension can be viewed as a hierarchical relationship requiring some skills be taught before others, it is also a complex process in which a reader applies various skills and knowledge almost simultaneously. For example, readers asked to draw an inference about the two antagonists in a very brief interval, will have to remember relevant information from the passage, apply inference skills in determining what might happen next, and have appropriate background knowledge. In short, while skills and information can often be taught in a sequential, logical manner, they are applied in an almost instantaneous fashion, and not necessarily in the order they were originally taught.

Research on reading comprehension also points to the importance of background knowledge that a reader brings to the reading task. It is argued that the more a reader knows about a topic and can apply this background knowledge when reading the text, the more he will comprehend. This background knowledge, referred to as *schemata*, is derived from schema theory. Research supports its importance to reading comprehension instruction (Anderson, Spiro, & Anderson, 1978; Anderson, Reynold, Schallert, & Goetz, 1976; Perfetti & Curtis, 1986).

Despite the importance assigned to the role of background knowledge in reading comprehension, Perfetti and Curtis (1986) raise questions about its role in comprehension instruction. They state,

> It is not always clear specifically what people are doing when they are teaching reading 'according to schema theory' . . . the everyday conceptual knowledge that a reader must have to understand ordinary texts is acquired through everyday experience. However, the specific knowledge needed to understand science texts is the result of both everyday experience and specific schooling. (p. 47)

It appears that although a reader's background knowledge is important to successful reading comprehension, specific skill knowledge is also important and must be taught.

Our model of reading comprehension instruction is similar to the one for decoding and consists of the following common elements:

1. *Comprehension units:* The units of instruction in reading comprehension increase in complexity ranging from words, phrases, sentences, and paragraphs to passages and pages of texts.

2. *Processing skills:* The skills for processing the increasingly complex comprehension units consist of rapid decoding, summarizing the main idea or gist of texts, drawing inferences, transforming complex syntactical structures into a simpler form, translating difficult vocabulary into more familiar words, simplifying critical reading and reasoning skills, and so forth.

3. *Knowledge base:* The background knowledge and specific skills knowledge important to understanding and evaluating the message in a text.

4. *Strategic knowledge:* The metacognitive strategies for evoking skills and knowledge designed to monitor and check ongoing comprehension (e.g., Does what we read make sense?).

In each aspect of the comprehension model—comprehension units, processing skills, knowledge base, strategic knowledge—instruction begins with the least complex form and moves to the most complex in an hierarchical fashion:

1. Comprehension units form a hierarchy beginning with single words and continuing to entire passages.

2. Processing skills begin with literal comprehension (such as finding the word *man* and circling it when an illustration of a man is given) and increase in complexity to include complex inferences and evaluations.

3. The hierarchy for knowledge base begins with simple vocabulary (such as knowing the names of common objects) and increases to include more sophisticated vocabulary such as *homo sapiens.*

4. Strategic-knowledge instruction focuses on the monitoring of simple tasks before more complex tasks, and smaller comprehension units before more complex units.

The following examples illustrate how reading comprehension can be viewed as a complex set of different skills and types of knowledge activated in a nearly simultaneous process. In a simple matching item with a picture of a man and the words *cat, man,* and *sad,* a young student would have to know the name of the object illustrated, identify each word listed, then locate and circle the correct word. The comprehension units are words; the processing skills are decoding and following instruction; the background knowledge is the name of the illustrated object and the meanings represented by the printed words; the strategic knowledge is the self-appraisal involved in executing the matching task correctly.

A reader is required to deal with each of these four aspects of the comprehension model at about the same time. A more complex example would be a reaction to this sentence: "Environmentalists claim that conservation measures will not hamper the current economy and in the long run will contribute to employment and capital formation." Critically reading this sentence involves all four aspects of the comprehension model. The comprehension "unit" is not only *that* sentence, but also the *context* from which the sentence was drawn. The processing skills include reading critically and drawing inferences. The knowledge base includes an understanding of many uncommon words. The strategic knowledge includes the regula-

tion and orchestration of the processing skills and knowledge base, and the adjustment required in coordinating these different sources of information. In summary, comprehension can be viewed as a hierarchically ordered sets of skills that develop over time and as a complex process that involves all four aspects whenever a reader is deriving meaning from print.

Four Aspects of the Comprehension Model

The following are examples of the four aspects of the comprehension model: comprehension units, processing skill, knowledge base, and strategic knowledge.

Comprehension Units

The first aspect of the comprehension model is the increasingly larger units that a reader processes. Young readers who attend to one word at a time, forgetting what they read earlier, will have difficulty comprehending a single sentence. Initial exercises for these students should be limited to simple picture-word matching exercises. Similarly, older readers who read at a sentence level can answer questions about individual sentences but may have difficulty with comprehension items requiring them to integrate several paragraphs. As readers become more proficient decoders, comprehension units should expand to phrases, sentences, short passages, and longer passages.

Processing Skills

The second aspect of the Direct Instruction Comprehension Model includes the various skills students apply to what they read. These skills include identifying specific information, rapid decoding, summarizing, simplifying syntactic and semantic information, critical reading, and various study skills including dictionary skills, outlining, and skimming.

Early instruction involves teaching students to answer literal questions (questions to which answers are directly stated in a passage). One literal skill is identifying specific information by answering who, what, when, where, and how questions based on information explicitly stated in a passage. Literal items become more difficult in later grades as the sentence structure becomes more complex. To prepare students for these exercises, the skill of simplifying syntactically complex sentences can be taught. Consider this example of transforming clauses into two simpler sentences. A student reads the sentence, "The tall man, who was seen leaving the cafe with a very old woman, lives near the cafe," and the question, "Who lives near the cafe?" The student may incorrectly respond, "The old woman," because the last part of the sentence reads "a very old woman, lives near the cafe." This type of error can be prevented by teaching students to transform longer, complex sentences into two simpler sentences: "The tall man was seen leaving the cafe with a very old woman" and "The tall man lived near the cafe." The answer to the question, "Who lives near the cafe?" is now obvious. (Note that while most students will not need to be taught explicitly to transform syntactically complex sentences into simpler ones, teachers should be ready to provide the instruction to students who need it.)

One of the skills introduced in later grades is inference, which involves drawing conclusions beyond what is directly stated. Inferences are necessary for students to assimilate new information into their knowledge base. For example, when a twelfth grader reads about the problems of a soybean crop failure in Brazil, she infers that hardships resulting from income loss occur there just as they do in the United States.

She may also use her knowledge of agricultural economics and infer that a drop in soybean production in Brazil will lead to a price increase in anchovies from Chile, since anchovies and soybeans are two major world-wide sources of protein. She infers that when supplies of one protein source become scarce, the price of the other increases.

Knowledge Base

The knowledge base consists of several components such as: (1) acceptable word orderings (syntax), (2) word meanings (semantics), (3) factual information, (4) logic, and (5) frameworks for incorporating new experiences (schema). An example of each component follows.

First is syntax. A student reads, "John ran up the stepped." *Stepped* is a verb and cannot follow *ran up the*. Since the sentence violates known word order rules (syntax), the student rejects her interpretation and checks the sentence again. She notices that the word is *steps*, not *stepped*. Since "John ran up the steps" is consistent with the student's knowledge of syntax, the sentence is acceptable.

Second is an example of semantics (word meaning). A student reads, "Alice tripped and fill against the wall." The syntax is acceptable because *fill* is a verb; however, semantics is violated since *fill* does not make sense in the sentence. Again the student rechecks the sentence and comes up with an acceptable sentence, "Alice tripped and *fell* against the wall."

The third component is factual information. Larry reads, "Jackie works until 5 p.m. every morning." This rendition is rejected because 5 p.m. is in the afternoon, not in the morning. Upon rereading, Larry sees that the sentence refers to 5 a.m., not 5 p.m.

The fourth component, logic, is closely related to the factual-information component. Jason reads, "It was hot and humid on a lazy April afternoon in Minnesota." April in Minnesota is usually cool, not hot and humid. When rereading the sentence, the student finds it is not April but August.

These examples of the importance of a student's knowledge base have all involved decoding errors. Decoding errors were selected to simplify the examples; however, the same process would be involved if a student misconstrued a message even if decoding were not the cause of the error, as illustrated with the next component, schema.

Schema, the fifth component of knowledge base, is a complex relationship involving background knowledge and inferences that allow students to assimilate new information. The following example illustrates how schema operates. Lisa got a letter from an old high school friend. The friend wanted to start a company to make telephones and sell them at a lower price than the telephone company did. He knew he could make them more cheaply because he would simply copy their phones. Lisa was knowledgeable about manufacturing; she had a schema including patents, royalties, and laws protecting copyrights. More specifically, she knew the telephone company had a patent on the design of their phones. Her friend could not copy them without paying a royalty or without being sued. Consequently, her friend would not be able to manufacture the phones as cheaply as he thought. Without a schema involving patents, royalties, etc., Lisa would not have realized that her friend's idea represented infringement of patent laws and would lead to unexpected expense.

It is important to note that what serves as a knowledge base for evaluating and assimilating comprehension units was at one time acquired as a skill, although not necessarily directly taught as a skill. For example, transforming complex syntactic structures into simpler ones is directly taught to some students as a skill. However,

once these students comprehend a syntactic form automatically, the syntactic structure becomes part of the knowledge base for evaluating subsequent comprehension units. In short, the instructional model is portraying a dynamic system in which students learn new skills, then after mastering those skills, use them as a basis for learning more sophisticated new skills and for comprehending more complex material.

Strategic Knowledge

Like the decoding model, the fourth aspect of the Direct Instruction Comprehension Model is concerned with the reader's ability to monitor his or her performance continually during reading and to make adjustments in comprehension when the text doesn't make sense or square with the reader's experience. Baker and Brown's (1982) review of the research on strategic knowledge revealed that less skilled readers experience deficits in a number of areas: for example, these readers were unable to (1) identify the purpose of the reading task, (2) adjust their reading rate according to the material being read, (3) monitor their comprehension of the material being read, (4) employ "fix-up" strategies to correct comprehension failure, (5) relate new information to familiar information, (6) recognize the logical structure of a passage, (7) evaluate a text for clarity, completeness, and consistency, (8) attend to syntactic and semantic constraints, and (9) decide how well the material has been understood. Simmons, Kameenui, and Darch (1988) also found that learning disabled, elementary age children were unable to locate and align story-grammar components such as the problem, attempts, and solution explicitly identified in narrative passages.

Early instruction in strategic knowledge should focus on the development of self-appraisal monitoring strategies and "fix-up" strategies. For example, during the reading of a story, the teacher stops periodically (e.g., after reading the first 3–4 sentences of a paragraph) and asks evaluation questions designed to alert the reader to potential comprehension problems.

Specifically, after reading several sentences students would ask themselves, "Did I understand what I just read?" Students are then told to stop and reread the sentences if they didn't understand what was read or to continue reading if they did. While this self-appraisal strategy doesn't inform the reader of what "understanding" the text means, with adequate prompting and feedback from the teacher the student is alerted to the requirements of successful text comprehension. Students are also taught specific "fix-up" strategies tailored to text features such as difficult vocabulary, story-grammar components, summarization, and so forth. These strategies allow the reader immediately to fix a problem during text comprehension.

In Table 4.1 below, the four aspects of the Direct Instruction Model for Decoding and Reading Comprehension are summarized.

Purposeful Reading

The comprehension model lacks one important ingredient: reader purpose. A reader does not read sentences and aimlessly apply various comprehension skills such as summarizing, simplifying, drawing inferences, etc. A reader's purpose determines the way in which she treats a passage and which comprehension skills she uses. Teachers must be certain to teach students the skills needed for reading with different purposes as well as how to read for different purposes.

Some different purposes for reading include these:

1. To be able to identify and remember specific facts or a main idea.

Table 4.1	A Direct Instruction Model for Decoding and Reading Comprehension	
	Decoding	**Comprehension**
Units	letters, letter combinations, syllables, words	words, phrases, sentences, paragraphs, passages, pages of text
Processing Skills	auditory listening skills, sounding out, sight reading, breaking larger words into parts, identifying letter combinations, and structural units	literal, inference, sequencing summarization, simplifying syntactic and semantic complexities, critical reading study skills, story grammar
Knowledge Base	letter-sound correspondences, familiarity with words, syntax, semantic constraints, knowledge of letter combinations and structural units	vocabulary knowledge, facts, reasoning skills, logic, schemata, syntax, specific-topic knowledge
Strategic Knowledge	monitoring, adjusting, evaluating units, processing skills, knowledge base related to reading text	monitoring, adjusting, evaluating units, processing skills, knowledge base related to understanding text

2. To be able to follow instructions to reach a goal, e.g., assemble a bicycle.
3. To enjoy.
4. To be able to explain the content of a passage to someone else.
5. To be able to accommodate the content into the reader's schema.
6. To critique the logic or data presented in a passage.
7. To edit a passage according to stylistic and organizational criteria.
8. To study according to an assignment or test requirements.

Several comprehension skills may be involved in fulfilling a specific purpose. For example, in pleasure reading, students must develop a story line based on main ideas derived from specific facts in a story. Reading would not be as pleasurable if we did not remember who had done what and when. So even in pleasure reading, we focus on specific details, form main ideas, sequence them, and remember them.

Going a step further, if the purpose in reading a passage is to comprehend it well enough to explain it to someone else, we will approach the material quite differently. In addition to forming main ideas and sequencing them, we will attempt to remember supporting details that justify or make sense out of our main ideas. We will also develop a rationale for selecting specific main ideas and use details from the passage to support our choice. Obviously, our self-imposed criteria for understanding or comprehending a passage are more rigorous if we intend to explain it to someone, rather than just read the passage for pleasure.

The importance of purpose in determining the way we approach a passage suggests that purpose must be considered in any discussion of teaching comprehension. Consider reading with the intent of remembering information or main ideas from a passage for more than just a day or two. Reading for this purpose is seldom taught during the primary stage. Problems occur, however, at the beginning of the intermediate stage, when students are assumed to have had experience in reading and remembering. More specifically, third graders read narrative stories, the content of which they are not usually expected to remember over a period of days. In contrast, fourth graders read expository material with content from areas like social studies and science and are expected to remember the content. Instructionally naive students, who are not trained to "read to remember" in third grade, may have serious problems with content area materials. The implication is that instructionally naive students must be systematically taught to read to remember before fourth grade or at least during fourth grade.

Causes of Comprehension Failure

A deficiency in any of the four aspects of the Direct Instruction Model could interfere with comprehension. The following material will discuss some possible deficiencies.

Inappropriate Units

Students may fail because they do not read in units appropriate to their purpose. Students who cannot process units best suited to their purpose may experience difficulties in comprehension. For example, word-by-word readers may not be able to comprehend the relationship between different parts of a sentence; whereas, students who group words into phrases will. Oakan, Wiener, and Cromer (1967) found that poor readers, who did not organize material into phrases, did better on comprehension measures when the reading material was organized into phrases for them. The phrases were emphasized by leaving extra space between each one. Since methodological concerns about the Oakan et al. study have been raised, their conclusions should be viewed as suggestive rather than definitive.

Skill Deficits

Students may have comprehension problems because they lack various skills needed to comprehend a passage: inference, summarization, simplification, etc. Students who lack these skills entirely, or possess them as oral language skills but do not apply them when reading, will have comprehension problems. A common problem among poor readers is the inability to summarize or extract main ideas from passages (Baker & Brown, 1982). For example, let's say students are presented with this passage:

> the owner of the Yankees made a trade for a new pitcher who was said to be the best pitcher in the league. The next day, the owner said he was looking for a new first baseman and right fielder. The paper quoted the owner as saying, "This year we will be the champs."

The poor reader summarized by saying "The Yankees got a new player." She did not summarize but just picked one of the events in the story. In contrast, another student summarized by identifying the main idea as the owner tries to build a championship team. Obviously the inability to summarize and extract main ideas has a serious effect on comprehension.

Numerous studies point to the importance of well-designed, explicit instructional strategies for teaching students to identify main ideas in narrative-prose comprehension (Baumann, 1984, 1986; Williams, 1986). Jenkins, Heliotis, Stein, and Haynes (1987) succesfully taught low-performing students to compose a summary statement after reading a paragraph of text.

Inadequate Knowledge Base

Students may have difficulties in comprehension because they lack an adequate knowledge base. If the syntactic or semantic load of a passage is too great, students are likely to have difficulty (Kameenui & Carnine, 1982). Consider this sentence: *Naturally, this principle is frequently violated as bureaucratic anonymity is ongoingly disrupted by eruptions of concrete humanity.* This sentence would be difficult for intermediate grade students to comprehend, even if told that the principle referred to was that bureaucracy is an autonomous world of regulations. There simply are too many unfamiliar words, and the sentence structure is too complex.

Strategic-Knowledge Deficits

Research in strategic knowledge or metacognitive deficits has identified two distinct, yet integrally related, components: (a) knowledge or awareness of factors that impede or facilitate learning and (b) the procedures students should employ to regulate cognition (Brown, 1980; Flavell, 1976). The awareness function of strategic knowledge typically centers around four variables (Brown, Campione, & Day, 1981; Flavell & Wellman, 1977): (1) text, (2) task, (3) strategies, and (4) learner (Armbruster, Echols, & Brown, 1983). Specifically, younger and poorer readers are less likely to detect textual inadequacies, confusions, and inconsistencies (Baker & Brown, 1984). Wong and Wong (1986) found that above-average readers were substantially more aware that difficult vocabulary and disorganized passages contributed to passage difficulty than learning disabled students. If students are not alerted to their own difficulties in reading and comprehending a text, comprehension will clearly suffer.

Decoding Deficits

Students with serious decoding problems will be precluded from comprehending a passage. They will misidentify too many words or read so slowly they forget what they have just read.

In summary, comprehension failure can occur when students cannot process printed material in units appropriate for their purpose, when they lack necessary skills for interpreting printed messages, when they do not have an adequate knowledge base for evaluating their interpretation of a printed message, or when they decode so poorly they cannot identify the words correctly or rapidly enough.

Approaches to Improve Comprehension

Two general approaches to improving student comprehension performance are recommended. One approach is to design carefully the comprehension materials from which students work. The other is to teach students strategies they would apply to a wide range of comprehension materials (Kameenui & Simmons, Levin, 1971, 1972). Although combining the two approaches probably has the greatest impact on students' comprehension performance, teachers are more likely to teach essential vocabulary and strategies for working comprehension items than to write a comprehension program. Teachers do not have the time or expertise to write their own comprehension program. Even so, findings that relate to designing comprehension materials will be discussed here as well as findings related to student strategies for comprehending texts.

Designing Comprehension Material

The following illustrative findings relate to constructing comprehension materials:

1. Passages should be previewed and students' background knowledge related to the text's topic should be identified, tapped, and discussed (Anderson, 1977; Mason & Au, 1987; McNeil, 1984).

2. Unknown and potentially difficult vocabulary word meanings should be identified and placed in a separate list for preteaching (Kameenui, Dixon, & Carnine, 1987; Nagy, 1988).

3. Difficult narrative text should be preceded by advance organizers that summarize the upcoming content and relate it to what has come earlier in the program (Richards, 1975–76).

4. Specific questions about the passage should appear frequently throughout a text (Kameenui, Carnine, & Freschi, 1982; Frase, 1968; Frase, Patrick, & Schumer, 1970).

5. Feedback concerning performance on the specific questions should be provided frequently and immediately (Frase, 1967; McNeil, 1984).

The five suggestions do not represent an exhaustive list. They are applicable to all grade levels, but especially to the intermediate grades and beyond. Even if teachers do not write comprehension programs, they can use these findings by designing adjunct materials (e.g., study guides, advance organizers) to support the text materials.

Teaching Strategies

The importance of students having comprehension strategies was illustrated more than twenty years ago in a study by Smith (1967). High-IQ students were better at reading for detail than low-IQ students, but neither group did well at reading for general impressions. When asked about the procedures used in reading for detail, the high-IQ readers specified their strategy; whereas, low-IQ readers could not explain theirs. However, neither group could explain the procedures they followed for a general impression. The results suggest that superior performance of the high-IQ students in finding details resulted from their having a strategy. In reading for general impressions, neither group had a strategy, and neither group did well on those items. Since students who have a strategy perform relatively well, a major goal of comprehension instruction is to teach strategies for various types of comprehension skills.

Summary

This section has included most of the topics discussed later in the book. We have attempted here to make explicit some of the interrelationships among the topics. The topics were discussed in the context of a direct instruction model for decoding and comprehension. In both decoding and comprehension, students need to learn to process increasingly complex units, acquire skills for processing the units, develop a knowledge base for making sense out of what they read and orchestrate the execution of the process. The units in decoding are letters, letter clusters, words, and phrases. The skills for processing the units include phonic, structural, and contextual analysis. The knowledge base is primarily familiarity with words and syntactic structures. For comprehension, the units are words, phrases, sentences, paragraphs, pages, and chapters. The skills are numerous, including summarization, drawing inferences, critical reading, and study skills. The knowledge base is extensive: logic, vocabulary, schema, etc. In addition, the comprehension model must take into account a reader's purpose since purpose determines how a passage is handled. Causes of comprehension failure and avenues for improving comprehension performance can also be accounted for by the model.

Research **Increasingly Larger Units.** Initial units are single, letter-sound correspondences (Wolf & Robinson, 1976; Santa, 1976, 1977); later units extend beyond single letters. These larger units have been referred to as the sound-spelling units, spelling patterns, or letter clusters. Ruddell (1976a) states, "Linguists such as Venezky, Wardhaughn, and Reed have strongly recommended that it is necessary to consider letter patterns beyond the simple sound-letter correspondence level if a more consistent relationship between oral and written language forms is to be realized" (Ruddell, 1976a, p. 24). The importance of students learning to decode increasingly larger units is not a new finding. It was noted by Huey in 1908: "We are brought back to the conclusion of Goldscheider and Muller that we read by phrases, words, or letters as may serve our purpose best. But we see, too, that the reader's acquirement of ease and power in reading comes through increasing ability to read in larger units" (p. 116). More recently, Gibson (1965) identified three phases involved in learning to process larger units: differentiating graphic symbols, learning letter-sound correspondences, and using increasingly larger units of structure.

Various researchers have confirmed that mature readers process larger units than beginning readers. Calfee, Venezky, and Chapman (1969) reported that good readers showed an increasing mastery of multiple-letter groupings through high school. Other research has indicated that mature readers identify

---

clusters of letters rather than individual letters (Spoeky & Smith, 1973; Foss & Swinney, 1973; Savin & Bever, 1970; Glass & Burton, 1973). However, research suggests that when mature readers encounter unfamiliar words, they are able to process them by letters or letter clusters rather than as entire words (Terry, Samuels, & La-Berge, 1976; Baron & Strawson, 1976; Rozin & Gleitman, in press).

Strategies for Processing Units.   Extensive research has been conducted on the importance of teaching strategies for manipulating units of various size: segmenting orally presented words (a teacher says "man" and the students say "mmmaaannn"), combining sounds to form a word (a teacher says "aaaat" and a student says "at"), and blending sounds represented by printed letters (a student says "iiif" for "if"). The studies discussed in Chapter 7, "Auditory Skills," indicate that strategies for manipulating various sized units are correlated with later success in reading and prepare students to decode correctly new words.

Word Familiarity.   The importance of word familiarity in facilitating decoding was suggested in several studies reviewed by Mason, Osborn, and Rosenshine (1977). Similarly, Jorm (1977) reported that familiar words were easier to decode than pseudowords (nonsense words), and pseudowords made up of familiar syllables were easier to decode than pseudowords comprised of unfamiliar syllables. Mason (1977a) found that familiar words were processed as a unit while unfamiliar words were processed at a syllable or letter level. These studies indicate that word familiarity is indeed a significant variable in how readily students can decode words. The implication is that unfamiliar vocabulary should be introduced in oral language exercises before students are expected to decode those words. Teachers will have to devote much more time to vocabulary instruction with lower performing students. Perfettiti and Hogalboam (1975) reported that skilled readers benefited greatly from a small amount of oral exposure, while less-skilled readers required more exposure before their decoding rate improved.

Letter Sounds and Letter Names.   Research findings suggest that knowing letter sounds is more helpful to the beginning reader than knowing letter names. Jenkins, Bausell, and Jenkins (1972) found that while letter-sound training is more difficult than letter-name training, letter-name training did not facilitate word reading. Letter-sound training did. Ohnmacht (1969) also reported that teaching letter names did not facilitate reading performance; however, teaching letter sounds did. Samuels (1971), R. J. Johnson (1970), and Elkonin (1973) reported that teaching letter names did not help students learn to read. Samuels (1972) explained that the frequent emphasis on teaching letter names may have resulted from a confusion between correlation and causation. Knowing letter names is correlated with reading achievement, but does not seem to cause it. The correlation between knowing letter names and doing well in reading probably occurs because children who are taught letter names at home come from a verbally enriched background and do well in reading because of that background, not because they know letter names.

In summary, we are not recommending that students learn only letter sounds, but that they learn letter sounds first and letter names later. Although knowledge of letter names is necessary for later spelling and dictionary tasks, it is not needed for sounding out simple words, a strategy we feel that students need to acquire as early as possible when learning to read.

Sounding-out and Whole-Word Reading. The limited research comparing sounding-out and whole-word reading with naive subjects supports a sounding-out approach. Bishop (1964), in a simulated learning-to-read situation with college students, and Jeffrey and Samuels (1967) and Farmer, Nixon, & White (1976), in teaching 4-to-6 year olds to read vowel-consonant words, reported that a group that was taught a sounding-out strategy read significantly more new words than a group that was taught whole words.

A study by Carnine (1977) replicated and extended Jeffrey and Samuels' findings by requiring students to learn more sounds, read more words, read longer words, and continue in training until they had reached a performance criterion. Both groups in Carnine's study received training on a set of 18 words. The students in both groups were taught to criterion (until they made 18 consecutive correct responses) and then were tested on a set of 6 new words that contained the same letters used in the training words. The sounding-out group in the Carnine study read 91.7% of the new regular words; whereas, the whole-word group correctly identified only 28.3% of the new words. Moreover, the sounding-out group was able to read significantly more irregular words than did the whole-word group. Although students in the sounding-out group correctly read more new words, the time required for them to reach criterion in the training program was actually less, though not significantly so, than for the whole-word group.

It is important to remember that both sounding-out and whole-word strategies are appropriate, but at different times. Sounding out appears to be more effective in initial instruction, but whole-word reading is essential for more rapid, fluent reading. When and how to make the transition are questions that must be answered in future research. In addition, the role of sounding out in decoding irregular words should be investigated.

Introducing New Words in Isolation and in Context. Singer, Samuels, and Spiroff (1973) compared three procedures for introducing new words: words in isolation, words in sentences (context), and words with pictures. Both context and picture clues slowed acquisition. During the beginning reading stage, students often are not proficient enough in decoding to benefit from context clues (Groff, 1976; Hochberg, 1970), and, in fact, the context clues may draw their attention away from the letters that make up the word. In a review of the research on using pictures to facilitate student learning of a sight vocabulary, Samuels (1970) found that pictures hamper performance. The experiments usually compared two groups—one in which a picture appeared with each word and one without pictures. When pictures accompanied the words, students required longer to reach criterion and made more errors than when pictures were not present. More recent research tends to confirm these findings (Harzem, Lee & Miles, 1976). Contrary findings do not test the students on word identification without the pictures (Denberg, 1976). Since the pictures were always present in Denberg's study, the students may have learned nothing more than picture reading. The reason for having illustrations is that they increase student enjoyment (Samuels, Biesbock, & Terry, 1974). We do not recommend that pictures be done away with completely, but rather reserved until after the students complete decoding a portion of a story.

Additional research on context cues is more difficult to interpret since it was not conducted with beginning readers. Although Goodman (1965) found that students correctly identified more words when they were presented in context (rather than in isolation), other researchers did not replicate this effect (Williams & Carnine, 1978). Gibson and Levin (1975) also state that the sooner a child learns what he says is determined by the letters that make up words, the better: "Many children start school with the notion that reading is speaking with books open in front of them. The speech is not nonsensical. Still, the earlier the realization by the child that what he says must be determined by what is printed, the better is the prognosis for early reading achievement" (p. 282).

The issue then becomes how to maximize the probability that students will learn to attend to the letters that make up words. Our suggestion is to teach words in isolation before presenting them in stories. Students cannot read words from context when they appear in isolation. Since they can decode only by attending to the letters in the words, they will more quickly learn that decoding is based on sound-symbol relationships and not on pictures of context. Questions about when to shift the instructional emphasis from reading words in lists to reading words in passages can only be answered through further research.

Accuracy and Fluency.   The importance of some minimal level of accuracy is not disputed (Golinkoff, 1975, 1976), and numerous studies have investigated the relationship between rate and reading achievement. Pace and Golinkoff (1976) found that proficiency in decoding words was related to comprehending word meanings. A similar relationship between decoding speed on isolated words and comprehension test performance was reported by Perfetti and Hogalboam (1975). Speer and Lamb (1976) reported a significant correlation between fluency in identifying letters and letter clusters and first-grade reading achievement. In addition to these correlational studies, two experimental studies have found that students trained to increase their reading rate also demonstrated comprehension gains (Dahl, in press; Waechter, 1972). Perfetti (1977) suggests one possible explanation for this relationship is that slow decoding interferes with recall of previously read material. He found that skilled readers recall 16% more of what they've read (six words back in a sentence) than less-skilled readers. Gough (1976) has a similar explanation: slow decoding results in pauses which disrupt memory processing of what is read.

Little research has been conducted to determine optimal accuracy and rate criteria for developing successful reading behaviors at various skill levels. Research is needed to answer several questions: How accurate should decoding be before rate is stressed? What are optimal decoding and accuracy rates for various reading stages? What are minimal rates that should be reached before new skills are introduced? What kinds of decoding errors should be corrected and when (immediately or at the end of the sentence or paragraph)? How important is oral expressive reading to comprehension? What are efficient procedures for developing reading rate?

Oral and Silent Reading. Neville (1968) reported that reading orally before reading silently resulted in significant differences in reading fluency and number of vocalizations, but not in word recognition and comprehension. Keislar and McNeil (1968) reported significantly higher word recognition and comprehension scores for kindergartners who read orally than for students who read silently. Important questions concerning how much oral reading is appropriate for different stages of acquisition and when it should occur in a lesson with respect to silent reading deserve research attention.

Research in other areas also suggests that practice is more effective with young students if they respond overtly (Durling & Schick, 1976). Similar results were reported with kindergartners in learning tasks involving pictures (Keeney, Canizzo, & Flavel, 1967) and with slow learners in learning tasks involving sentences (Taylor & Whitely, 1972), and with elementary students in recall tasks involving classification (Scribner & Cole, 1972). In all these experiments, students who responded orally during training either remembered more information or were better able to apply the information to new material than were control groups. Although these experiments did not directly relate to decoding instruction, their results suggest that overt responding is beneficial at least during certain stages of skilled acquisition.

A teacher's role in reading instruction consists of two major phases: beginning-of-the-year planning activities and day-to-day implementation. Beginning-of-the-year activities include selecting reading material, setting up a reading program, and testing and placing students in the materials. The on-going daily activities consist of planning lessons, presenting lessons, and conducting follow-up exercises.

Chapter

Classroom Reading Instruction

Beginning-of-the-Year Activities

Selecting Materials

A major objective of this book will be to give teachers specific criteria they can use in evaluating and selecting materials. The following criteria should be considered when selecting a reading program:

1. The major reading-related skills should be taught in a program. The program should adequately present the fundamental core reading and comprehension skills.

2. Opportunities for practice and review of skills should be adequate. Many commercial programs do not provide adequate practice and review of important skills. Programs should provide massed practice on a skill when it is first introduced and then intermittent review of that skill.

3. The sequence and rate at which new skills are introduced should be adequate. A program should introduce skills at a rate and sequence which fosters success for all students.

4. The reading strategies taught in a program should be straightforward and generalizable. Reading programs should teach simple and applicable strategies, not complicated and

restricted ones. Children should be able to use these strategies in many reading situations and without constant teacher assistance.

Obtaining well-constructed materials is critical for teachers working with instructionally naive students, because the quality of the materials can make the difference between success and failure. Teachers working with average students should also select well-constructed programs, because poorly constructed programs can keep the students from learning at an optimal rate. High-ability students will do well in almost any program, if they spend enough time in reading-related activities.

Basal Reader Programs

At the core of reading instruction in most classrooms is the developmental basal reading program, which includes student and teacher materials for grades K–6. In Figure 5.1, Durkin (1987) provides a visual depiction of the core materials in a basal reader program.

Harris and Sipay (1975, 1980) give an excellent description of the contents of basal reading programs:

> Basal reader programs are not simply series of books and accompanying materials. They are preplanned, sequentially organized, detailed materials and methods used to teach and to learn the skills of developmental reading.
>
> The pattern of a graded series starting in first grade, with a controlled vocabulary, gradually increasing difficulty, and a variety of content has not changed greatly since the McGuffey Readers first appeared in the 1830s. For the past fifty or so years, most basal reader systems have been eclectic, trying to achieve a balanced reading program with a broad and varied set of objectives. Until the mid-1960s most of them used a look-and-say procedure for

Figure 5.1

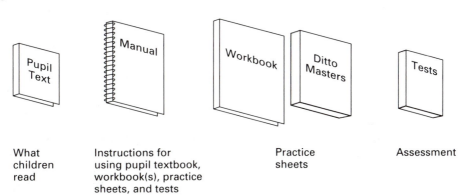

A basal program is composed of a series of readers said to be written at successively more difficult levels. Accompanying each reader is a manual for the teacher, one or two workbooks, ditto-sheet exercises, and end-of-unit, end-of-level tests. Supplementary materials, too numerous to list, include picture, letter, and word cards, and ditto sheet masters and charts for much of what a manual directs a teacher to write on the board.

developing initial reading vocabulary, with phonics and other word-identification skills taught gradually, mainly with the second- and third-grade readers. Since then, however, there has been a decided trend toward more and earlier stress on teaching decoding skills. The following discussion deals with the eclectic basal readers that have been popular since the 1930s and the recent changes in them.

Materials. A representative series starts with one or more readiness books, usually in workbook form. The first actual reading materials are usually three thin paperbacks called pre-primers. However, to dispel the mistaken idea that a given book should only be used in a particular year in school, series are increasingly numbering their books by levels. For example, a first pre-primer following two readiness books would be labeled Level 3. The pre-primers (Levels 3, 4, and 5) are followed by the first hard-covered book (Primer 1 or Level 6), and a first reader (1 or Level 7) which completes the program covered by most first graders. There are usually two second reader books (2 and 2 or Levels 8 and 9), two third reader books, (3 and 3 or Levels 10 and 11) and one thick reader in each of grades 4, 5, and 6. Since the mid-1960s, there have been some departures from this traditional format, such as a choice between a conventional hard-covered reader and the same content bound in two or more paperback units. Also, a few programs now utilize a systems approach, *i.e.,* they provide a large number of components that, through skillful management, can be used to allow for individual differences. The efficacy of such systems has yet to be tested adequately.

Each book in the series is accompanied by a consumable workbook, some of which provide self-help cues at the top of the pages, or have taped directions and answers for self-correction. Other

accessory materials may include exercises printed on duplicating stencils; large cards for group practice with phonic elements, words, and phrases; introductory story cards or charts; correlated filmstrips and recordings; and supplementary paperback storybooks. The recent trend in enrichment is to provide the kinds of materials just mentioned in convenient packages as optional supplements.

Each reader is accompanied by a guide or manual which details the teaching method. Most manuals present a general plan and then give a detailed lesson plan for each selection. The manual, which is really a handbook on how to teach with the pupil book, is either a separate book or is bound together with a copy of the reader. Manuals usually provide more suggestions for skills development and enrichment than are needed for most children. The teacher must therefore judiciously select activities based on the children's needs, as well as determine the appropriate rate of presentation for different groups. (pp. 58–59)[1]

Basal reading programs are developmental because they are designed for students learning to read for the first time. The first books in a developmental series are designed according to the interests of younger students. Later stories and assignments are geared to older students.

Developmental programs can also be used for remedial purposes in some situations. The same program that functions, on the one hand, to teach beginning reading to a first grader can also be used as a remedial program for a second grader, be-

---

1. From *How to Increase Reading Ability: A Guide to Developmental and Remedial Methods,* 6th ed. by Albert J. Harris and Edward Sipay. Copyright © 1975 by Longman, Inc. Reprinted by permission of Longman.

cause the interest levels of first and second graders are fairly close. On the other hand, programs designed for first graders usually cannot be used for older students who have not mastered skills normally taught in first grade. These students need programs designed for their interest level and greater sophistication.

Supplementary Materials

In addition to the basal programs there are a great number and variety of other commercial materials. First, there are materials designed to teach or provide extra practice in decoding skills. Foremost among these materials are series of workbooks designed to provide supplementary practice on phonics. Most supplementary decoding material is designed for use in the early grades (first grade through third grade) since it is during these grades that most basic decoding skills are taught. Second are materials designed to teach or provide extra practice on comprehension and study skills. These materials are usually designed for use in the intermediate grades (fourth grade through sixth grade) since the emphasis switches from decoding to comprehension and study skills in these grades.

A third type of material is designed for the remedial reader, the student who is unable to decode and comprehend materials written for his grade level. Considering the significant number of students reading below grade level, it is surprising that there are few comprehensive programs that provide carefully integrated decoding and comprehension instruction for the remedial reader. The majority of commercially available materials for remedial readers deal only with some decoding or comprehension skills. High-interest/low-vocabulary books (books focusing on themes that interest older students but which use words usually taught in

the primary grades) make up the bulk of material designed for remedial readers. In addition to these materials are programs with activities for reteaching important decoding and/or comprehension skills. However, these programs usually are not very comprehensive. For example, a decoding program may include reading words in lists but not reading passages, an activity critical in developing fluency in using phonic, structural, and contextual cues.

Modifying Basal Reading Programs

Durkin (1987) points out that there are approximately 17 basal reader programs on the market. Since the reading materials market is very competitive, publishers constantly revise and update their materials (Durkin notes that "At any given time, three or four will be best sellers." p. 417).

During the 1980s, basal reading programs have come under increasing examination by parents, teachers, school administrators, and educational researchers. This close scrutiny of basal reading programs is in part a result of the important role the basal program play in teaching reading. In fact, basal reader programs are such a prominent part of American classrooms that Osborn, Jones, and Stein (1985) have called for "educators to raise some questions about these programs" (p. 9). Questions about commercial reading programs have been raised for sometime now (Beck, McKeown, McCaslin, & Burkes, 1979; Durkin, 1981; Jenkins & Pany, 1978) and continue to be raised. For example, a special issue of *The Elementary School Journal* (Hoffman & Roser, 1987) was devoted to "The Basal Reader in American Instruction." The articles in this issue range from improving the quality of instruction provided in basal readers (Beck & McKeown, 1987; Durkin, 1987) to arguing that commercial reading materials should be removed from elementary classrooms

(Shannon, 1987). Several researchers have conducted intensive descriptive analyses of basal-reader programs in an effort to determine the quality of the instructional procedures recommended to teachers (Armbruster & Gudbrandsen, 1986; Durkin, 1981). The attention given to commercial reading programs is also evidenced by the federal government's interest in this issue. For example, a national invitational conference was sponsored by the Office of Special Education Programs of the U.S. Department of Education to discuss the results of a study on the "usability" of textbooks, in which special attention was given to reading programs (Education Development Center, Inc., 1988).

Throughout the text, we will refer to exercises from basal readers and make recommendations for modifying the exercises to facilitate high levels of student success.

Setting Up a Reading Program

After teachers select reading instruction materials, they must decide how to use the materials. More specifically, they must schedule adequate instructional time and specify how the time will be spent. There are two aspects to consider in setting up a total reading program:

1. Ensuring that the program does in fact provide time for teaching all basic reading skills.
2. Deciding on the type of instruction that is suitable: highly structured, teacher-guided instruction or more loosely structured, child-guided instruction.

A total reading program includes adequate provision for decoding, comprehension, study skills, recreational reading, writing, and spelling. The amount of time devoted to these activities should depend on the skill levels of the students. Teachers working with students whose home environments provide a great deal of informal instruction in basic skills need not spend as much time on these skills as teachers working with students from homes in which informal instruction is limited. Students performing below grade level should spend more time on basic skills since they must acquire more than a year's worth of skills if they are to progress at a rate that will enable them to catch up to their peers.

Furthermore, the teacher must take responsibility for providing adequate time. For example, if a teacher feels that students are unlikely to read outside of school and that their fluency indicates they need more reading practice, she must take the responsibility to provide the extra practice. In the upper grades, a teacher might do this by incorporating reading activities into all content area instruction (math, social studies, science, etc.) and by scheduling time into the day for recreational reading. These and other procedures for low-performing and remedial readers are discussed in detail later in the book.

Besides adequate instructional time, teachers must also provide a suitable type of instruction. The type of instruction students receive can vary from highly structured, small group instruction in which the teacher presents simple skills a step at a time and calls for frequent oral responses to unstructured student-centered learning activities in which the students work with minimal teacher guidance. During the early primary grades (K–2), the majority of instruction should be conducted in structured, small group situations, which allow teachers to closely monitor student performance and correct errors as soon as they occur. During the intermediate grades, the type of instruction used will vary according to the students' skill levels. Students performing at or above grade level can benefit from more loosely structured, child-centered activities. Students performing below grade level may still require a more structured type of instructional setting.

In a typical intermediate-level classroom, a teacher might have two programs: one for students performing at or above grade level and one for students performing below grade level. The program for the higher performing students may include a high proportion of independent activities (e.g., research projects, independent use of audio-visual aids, etc.). Teacher-student contact would consist of individual conferences and group discussions. The program for lower performing students would include more small group instructional sessions in which activities were carefully planned to present skills in an efficient manner. Likewise, the teacher would endeavor to present skills in a manner which kept the students performing at a high success rate (90% or above) since lower-performing students are more likely to be discouraged by failure.

In some schools, reading specialists or other trained auxiliary personnel are available to assist teachers with lower-performing students. These students may be taken from a classroom for 30 minutes to 1 hour for special reading instruction. The instruction provided by the classroom teacher and the specialist must be carefully coordinated; that is, both should be teaching the student the same reading strategies. Similarly, the information being presented to the student should be carefully controlled. For example, it would be *inappropriate* for one teacher to present letter-sound correspondences in one sequence while the other teacher presented them using another sequence. Conflicting approaches overload students with too much information and confuse and frustrate them. Furthermore, teachers should not shirk their responsibility to teach reading because a student is receiving outside instruction. Lower performing students generally need more practice than average students to master skills. Therefore, the teacher should provide practice and instruction in addition to that provided by the specialist.

Remedial Reading Instruction

Students unable to read books at their grade level are often pre-empted from success in school since their limited reading ability handicaps their performance in nearly all other subject areas. Below-grade-level reading can result from a decoding deficit, a comprehension deficit, or a combination of the two. Regardless of the cause of the deficit, six guidelines are relevant to teaching remedial readers: provide extra instruction, start the extra instruction as soon as any deficiency appears, use highly trained personnel, select a program that teaches essential skills and teaches them well, move remedial students through the instructional program as rapidly as possible, and motivate the students to achieve.

Extra Instruction

The more deficient a student is in reading, the greater the amount of instruction the student should receive. A student should receive an extra 15 to 30 minutes of direct instruction for each year the student is below grade level. A student 2 years below grade level should receive about 1 hour of extra instruction during the day. A student decoding several years below grade level is in serious trouble. An enormous amount of practice is required to develop decoding fluency. A fifth-grade student reading at a second-grade level, for example, must progress 3 years in 1 year to catch up and to perform at grade level.

Early Remediation

The sooner remediation begins, the more likely the student can be helped. Helping a second grader overcome a 1-year deficit is much easier than helping a fifth grader overcome a 3-year deficit. Younger students not only have less to make up, but they also tend to have better attitudes because they have not failed for as long a time. Another reason for beginning remediation as soon as possible is that students identified as needing special help in early grades can continue to receive it, thus preventing failure in later grades.

Balow (1965) found that remedial instruction was effective in dealing with the problems of the disabled reader, but he also noted that severe reading disability is not corrected by short-term intensive treatment and needs continual attention.

Careful Instruction

The more severe the student's deficit, the more careful the instruction must be. The instruction of remedial students must be monitored quite carefully by highly trained teachers. In the past, students in need of remedial help were often sent to volunteers or other untrained personnel who were asked to help the students. Many remedial readers need the help of the most highly trained professional, because they have developed serious confusions that must be carefully and consistently corrected. Volunteers and other untrained personnel are often unaware of how crucial many student errors are and do not know how to deal with them. Volunteers can perform very useful functions such as listening to

the students read and making simple corrections (telling the student the word and recording the error). However, they should not assume larger responsibilities unless they receive training and are monitored.

Well-designed Program

The greater the students' deficit, the more they will benefit from a well-designed program that teaches essential skills. The guidelines for evaluating commercial programs for remedial readers involve the same variables as any reading program: sequence, rate, teaching procedure, and practice. However, two additional factors must be considered for remedial students. First, the program must focus on the essential skills that will prepare the students to handle decoding and comprehension exercises at their own grade level. Second, the program should be designed to interest older children. Pictures and story themes designed for first or second graders are often rejected by older students.

Rapid Progression

The more deficient a student is in reading skills, the more quickly she must progress through the program. Since a remedial student is already behind, she must progress at a rate of more than 1 year for each year of instruction. If the student only progresses 1 program year for each instructional year, she will never reach grade level. To move students at the maximum rate, the teacher must know both the student's deficiencies and the order in which skills are introduced in a reading program. The teacher should spend time only on those lessons that focus on student deficits. The identification of lessons that focus on student deficits is much easier with programs that focus on essential skills.

Motivation

The more highly motivated a remedial reader is, the greater the student's progress and success. Unmotivated students will not receive the full benefit of increased instructional time, careful teaching, and a well-designed program. Without motivation, covering more than 1 year of program in 1 school year is unlikely; the student will continue making the same errors and will perform poorly on new skills.

Remedial readers are often unmotivated and understandably so. Think what it would be like to be in a failure situation day after day. No matter how hard you try, things don't get better. You can't succeed, and you can't get out of the situation. The failure has to be faced day after day, year after year. Think what that failure would do to your self-image and of how you might react. Then think of the remedial reader who has failed day after day, year after year.

Foremost in establishing motivation is providing a program in which the student can succeed. This occurs when the student is placed appropriately in a program that teaches only essential skills, is given extra practice, and is taught in a very careful manner. After the student is shown that he is succeeding in *reading* (and is not told that success in reading is unimportant), the student's attitude and motivation will begin to change.

Second, the student must have a goal. Sometimes it involves having a point system or contract that states the student will receive a certain grade, privilege, or prize for reaching a certain performance level. The point system or contract must be carefully designed so that earning the grade or privilege is neither too difficult nor too easy. The grade or privilege must be a functional reward, which means the student will work for it, and the student's daily successes must be clearly tied to his progress toward earning the grade or privilege.

Testing

Tests given at the beginning of the school year should be designed to help teachers (1) place students of similar ability and knowledge in homogeneous groups, (2) place the groups at appropriate starting lessons in materials being used in the classrooms, and (3) identify skills and/or information the students lack which might keep them from succeeding in reading. Throughout this book, we will recommend testing procedures that teachers at various grade levels, who are faced with testing 25 to 30 students, might use at the beginning of the year. Our procedures are designed to take relatively little time per student (5 to 10 minutes) and to be administered by a volunteer or teacher aide with minimal supervision.

There are two basic types of tests usually used to place students in reading instruction: norm-referenced tests and criterion-referenced tests. Norm-referenced reading tests measure the students' general knowledge and skills in reading, but not the skills presented in any particular program. The results from a norm-referenced test allow for several types of comparisons. Two of the more common comparisons are percentile and grade level. Percentiles tell how the student stands in regard to other students of that age or grade level; e.g., a 35th percentile score means the student scored above 34% of similar grade or age students taking the test, but below 65% of similar grade or age students taking the test. Grade-level scores indicate the average year and month in school that corresponds to a particular score. The major advantage of norm-referenced tests is that they allow for comparisons of different programs. Students from different programs can be given the same test to determine if some programs seem to result in better student performance than other programs. One problem with using a norm-referenced test to compare various programs is that the test probably covers the content of some programs more than others (even though it is not supposed to), which means that the test is biased toward some programs. An even greater disadvantage of norm-referenced tests is that they provide little information about how to instruct a student. That is, a percentile or grade equivalent score does not really indicate where to place a student in a commercial program or what a student's skill deficits are.

The second type of test, criterion-referenced tests, focuses on specific skills, thereby providing the teacher with information about what skills the student has and has not mastered. Criterion-referenced tests either focus on the skills from a commercial program or on important skills independent of any programs. Throughout this book, we will refer to the following types of criterion-referenced tests, which we recommend using to help place students in a program.

The first type of criterion-referenced test is an informal reading inventory (*IRI*), which is used to place students at their instructional level in a graded series of books.[2] The test is constructed by selecting sample passages from sequential levels of the reading series. Informal reading inventories should be used as the prime tool in placing students in basal reading programs. A more in-depth discussion of the use of informal reading inventories will appear in later sections.

A second type of criterion-referenced test focuses on various word attack skills. The diagnostic test of word attack skills can be used (1) to help the teacher group beginning readers who do not know enough words to read a selection in an informal reading inventory, and (2) to help the teacher identify specific word attack deficits. Sample tests and directions for administering the tests for each reading level appear in the appropriate testing sections for beginning, primary, and intermediate reading stages.

The third type of criterion-referenced test is designed to test comprehension skills. Students should be grouped according to how they can decode and comprehend. For example, a student who can decode at a sixth grade level but is unable to do comprehension exercises appropriate for that grade level may be placed, depending on the severity of the comprehension deficit, in a lower group or, if placed in a higher group, may receive instruction geared toward specific deficits. Since the number of comprehension skills is much greater than the number of decoding skills, a beginning-of-the-year comprehension test can test only a small sample of the total number of skills. More thorough comprehension testing can be done during the school year.

Day-to-Day Implementation

After students are grouped and placed in a commercial or teacher-made program, a teacher presents individual reading les-

---

2. *Instructional level* refers to an appropriate level to begin instruction with a student. The student should not know all the material presented at that level since, if he did, no new instruction would be going on. Similarly, the level should not be too difficult since this will cause frustration for the student. A student's instructional level will vary depending on the student's personality. Some students will tolerate difficult situations better than others. In general, an instructional level in a reading book is one at which a student can decode at about a 95% accuracy level in decoding and can comprehend the major theme of the material.

sons. The three components of an on-going implementation are planning, presentation, and follow-up.

Planning

A teacher must plan daily activities for the instructional session and for independent work. The plan must be realistic. Often, teacher guides from commercial programs suggest a variety of tasks that would take many hours to present. The teacher must decide which of these tasks is necessary. In like fashion, he must plan seatwork assignments appropriate for the amount of time available.

More important than planning the *amount* of material to present is planning for the *quality* of the material. Most commercial reading programs will require modifications to make them effective with instructionally naive students. The teacher must be prepared to simplify teaching explanations and provide for extra practice when appropriate. As an author of a major basal program said, "Our series was not designed for the slow learner, the non-English speaking child. . . ." (Chall, 1967, p. 194). In commenting on materials available for teaching vocabulary, Hunres (1976) noted that they are "haphazard—in organization, sequencing, and presentation" (p. 1).

The extent of program modification is determined primarily by student performance. If students have no difficulty learning the skills as presented in a program, little modification will be needed. However, if students have difficulty, major modifications may be necessary. Nearly all commercial reading programs are characterized by two critical instructional design deficits in their handling of comprehension: insufficient practice and inadequate teaching procedures. First is insufficient practice. In the typical program, a new comprehension skill often appears in one lesson and then disap-

pears for several weeks only to reappear again in a single lesson. Programs seldom provide enough introductory or review examples for instructionally naive students either to master a new skill or to remember it.

The second problem is the lack of procedures for teaching students strategies for working various types of comprehension activities. Programs often provide students with one or two sample items and expect them to formulate their own strategies as they work through the remaining items. While some students can learn a strategy from a few sample items and from working practice items, many need to be directly taught strategies. They either take too much time to come up with a workable strategy, or the strategy they devise is faulty.

In addition to planning and modifying instructional activities, the teacher must ensure that the work students are to do independently is appropriate. During seatwork activity, the teacher should assign tasks containing skills the students have mastered in an instructional setting. Teachers do not want to include practice on skills the students have not mastered since such practice may be counterproductive. If, for example, teachers assign an activity which involves the student in identifying words that begin with the /n/ sound and the student is confused between the /m/ and /n/ sounds, the activity may result in the student's receiving practice in misidentifying *n*, making the confusion more difficult to remedy.

Presenting a Lesson

A lesson consists of two major sections: (1) teacher presentation and (2) independent work.

The teacher presentation exercises usually involve decoding and comprehension activities (and possibly handwriting and spelling). For example, the decoding exercises during a second grade lesson might include sound identification exercises, several introductory words to illustrate a new decoding skill, and a list of discrimination words to provide practice on the new skill and on previously introduced skills recently causing students difficulty. The exercises on identifying sounds and reading words are constructed to prepare students not only for the passage and written items for that lesson, but also for upcoming lessons.

Comprehension activities during teacher presentation usually include instruction on critical words (i.e., words students probably do not know and are inadequately explained in the passage). Comprehension instruction may also be designed to introduce or provide practice on various strategies: how to draw inferences, how to paraphrase sentences with complex structures, how to summarize, etc. Finally, the teacher presentation includes going over any independent seatwork assignments that give directions the students are not likely to understand.

Follow-up

Follow-up exercises are intended to deal with major problems that occur during passage reading or during the written exercises. If students have decoding problems with a particular sound or word type, the teacher presents word lists or a passage that contains several examples of the troublesome skill during follow-up. If students have difficulty with a certain type of comprehension exercise, the teacher might review it with the students and then give them more practice on the same type of exercise, but with different items.

Summary

A reading teacher's role can be seen as occurring in two phases: beginning-of-the-year activities and day-to-day implementation. Beginning-of-the-year activities include selecting materials, setting up a program, planning for use of auxiliary personnel, and testing. In selecting materials, teachers should consider the skills presented, practice and review, sequence and rate of introduction, and the use of strategies. In setting up a program, teachers should plan schedules that allow adequate instructional time and decide on the amount of structure appropriate to the students' skill levels. Teachers and auxiliary personnel, whether aides or reading specialists, must coordinate their services to individual students so that their efforts complement each other and are not in conflict. Finally, testing is important for identifying specific skill deficits, grouping students, and placing them in an instructional program.

Day-to-day implementation includes planning, presentation, and follow-up. Planning is needed to construct appropriate teacher presentations and independent work activities for the students. The planning often requires modifying program lessons for use with low-performing students. Presenting a lesson includes the teacher presentation, passage reading, and the monitoring of independent work. Follow-up is devoted to extra teaching on skill areas difficult for the students.

Part

Beginning Reading:

The First Months of Instruction

2

The beginning reading stage refers to the period when students are learning to decode the first several hundred words presented in the classroom reading program. Some students may come to school able to decode many words. For these students, little instruction is needed before they can complete the beginning stage. Other students will enter school with very little ability to decode words. These students may require anywhere from 3 months to 1 year of instruction before completing the beginning stage.

Code-Emphasis vs. Meaning-Emphasis Programs

Controversy surrounds the beginning reading stage. First, there is the controversy of which reading approach to use. There are two major reading approaches: the code emphasis and the meaning emphasis. They differ in the manner they teach decoding. Beginning reading programs emphasizing letter-sound regularity are code-emphasis programs; code-emphasis programs are usually referred to in lay terms as phonics programs; those stressing the use of common words are called meaning-emphasis programs.

Code-emphasis programs initially select words made up of letters and letter combinations representing the same sound in different words. This consistency between letters and their sound values enables students to read many different words by blending the sounds for each new word. For example, the word *sat* is sounded out as "sssaaat" and pronounced "sat." The word *land* is sounded out as "lllaaannnd" and pronounced "land." The letter *a* represents the same sound in *sat* and *land* as well as in other words initially appearing in a code-emphasis program. In code-emphasis programs, a new word generally is not introduced until students have mas-

Chapter

6

An Overview of Beginning Reading

tered the letter-sound correspondences that make up the word. For example, the word *mat* is not introduced until the students know the sounds for the letters *m*, *a*, and *t*.

In contrast, meaning-emphasis programs initially select words that appear frequently in print regardless of their letter-sound irregularity. The assumption is that frequently appearing words are familiar and, consequently, easier for students to learn. Students are encouraged to use a variety of sources—pictures, context of the story, word configuration, and initial letter—as cues to use in decoding words. Unlike the code-emphasis programs, the meaning-emphasis programs do not control words so that the same letter represents the same sound in most initially appearing words. For example, it would not be uncommon to see the words *done*, *to*, *not*, and *book* among the first 50 words introduced in a meaning-emphasis program. Note that in each word, the letter *o* represents a different sound.

We recommend using a code-emphasis program approach during the beginning stage over a meaning-emphasis approach because a code-emphasis approach more readily allows the teacher to present reading instruction in a more efficient and humane manner. Instruction is efficient when the teacher can present the maximum number of skills in the minimum amount of time. Instruction is humane when students encounter a high degree of success.

Instruction can be presented more efficiently in a code-emphasis approach than in a meaning-emphasis approach because a code-emphasis approach better facilitates generalization. The introduction of each new letter-sound correspondence results in the students reading many new words. For example, let's say that the students already know the sounds for the

letters *m*, *s*, *t*, *f*, *d*, *r*, *n*, *h*, *k*, *l*, *a*, *o*, and *c*. The introduction of the letter *i* results in the student being able to read these words: *sit*, *in*, *hid*, *lid*, *tin*, *Tim*, *hill*, *sin*, *miss*, *kiss*, and *fill*. In a meaning-emphasis approach, each word is introduced as a separate unit.

Instruction can be presented in a more humane manner in a code-emphasis program than in a meaning-emphasis program. The former more readily allows the teacher to provide each student with a higher degree of success in the reading process.

When word reading is introduced in a code-emphasis approach program, students are taught an overt strategy—saying the sounds for each letter in the word in a left-to-right progression, then saying the blended sounds at a normal rate. If a student misreads a word, the cause of the error and an effective remediation procedure are clear. For example, if a student says "mud" when encountering the word *mad*, the teacher checks to see if the student knows the sound for the letter *u*. If the student does not know the correct sound, the teacher presents exercises to teach the missed sound. Words with the letter *u* would be avoided until the reteaching is accomplished.

In summary, the code-emphasis approach facilitates the use of simple teaching procedures and allows for effective corrections. The students learn a strategy that is used again and again.

In contrast, meaning-emphasis programs do not teach the student to rely on a single strategy because there is little consistency between letter-sound relationships, especially regarding vowel sounds. The students are encouraged to use a variety of strategies to decode words. Students are told to use the initial sound, the shape of the word, the context of the sentence in which the word appears, and the pictures on the page in which the word appears as cues to decoding the word. This reliance on a multifaceted approach results in relatively long, complex teacher explanations. For example, a typical meaning-emphasis program might introduce the word *cat* using the following steps:

1. The teacher writes a sentence on the board that has the word *cat,* and reads the sentence.

2. The teacher then displays flash cards containing the words *can* and *cat,* and asks the children how they are alike.

3. The teacher reminds the children that the middle letter represents the short vowel sound in each word.

4. Finally, the children are asked to read the word *cat* and identify the final sound.

This explanation contains words that more naive students may not understand (e.g., middle, final). Also, there is a relatively high degree of teacher talk. The higher the ratio of teacher talk to student response, the less attentive students are likely to be.

If a student misreads a word in a meaning-emphasis approach program, there is no simple correction available to the teacher that corrects the immediate mistake and prevents the error from reoccurring.

Let's say a student is reading the sentence: *The boy saw a little bird.* When coming to the word *saw,* the student says "said." A correction the teacher might use would involve explaining that the word *saw* could not be *said* because it does not end with *d* and does not make sense in the sentence. The correction tells the student why a word couldn't be *said,* but does not provide him with a strategy enabling him to figure out the word. The student might say "sees" the next time he encounters the word in a sentence.

The relatively complex teaching strategy and the relatively long teaching demonstrations inherent in a meaning-emphasis approach places the instructionally naive student at risk. Students who are inattentive to begin with are not likely to attend to teaching demonstrations that do not consistently demand active involvement.

We strongly recommend the use of a code-emphasis approach as the tool for teaching beginning reading. The importance of students receiving the highest quality of instruction available during the beginning reading stage cannot be overemphasized. For the child, initial reading instruction represents his first big challenge in the school setting. Every child should be guaranteed the right to successfully meet this challenge.

Our experience in the schools over the past twenty years has led us to a strong belief that virtually all the reading failure in the early grades could be avoided if teachers: (1) were given well-constructed code-emphasis instructional materials, and (2) received adequate on-the-job training in how to present reading instruction to groups of six-year-old students. Our experience in training teachers has shown that the average person will need 50 to 60 hours of preservice and on-the-job supervision to become skilled in presenting beginning reading instruction in a humane and efficient manner. This book cannot take the place of this type of training. What this book can do, however, is to help the teacher learn the specific details of what a code-emphasis approach reading program should include and to become aware of the specific teaching techniques that foster student attentiveness and success.

Key Terminology

Throughout these beginning chapters, we will use several key terms. The definition of these terms and an explanation of their importance follows.

Most Common Sounds

The most common sound of a letter is the sound that a letter most usually represents when it appears in a short, one-syllable word, such as *man* or *bled*. Table 6.1 lists the most common sound of each of the 26 letters. The word next to each letter illustrates the most common sound of that particular letter.

Stop Sounds vs. Continuous Sounds

A continuous sound is a sound that can be said for several seconds without distorting the sound. A stop sound can be said for only an instant. Words beginning with a stop sound are more difficult for students to sound out than words beginning with a continuous sound. For example, the word *pad* is more difficult to sound out for beginning readers than the word *sad* because *pad* begins with a stop sound. Because of the difference, a slightly different procedure is used when the teacher presents stop sounds than is used to teach continuous sounds. The list in Table 6.1 designates which letters correspond to stop sounds and which letters correspond to continuous sounds.

Regular Words

A regular word is any word in which each letter represents its respective, most common sound. For example, the words *am*, *cat*, *mud*, *best*, and *flag* are regular words because each letter represents its most common sound.

Irregular Words

During the beginning reading stage, any word in which one or more letters does not

Table 6.1		Most Common Sounds of Single Letters	
Continuous Sounds		**Stop Sounds**	
a	(fat)	b	(boy)
e	(bet)	c	(can)
f	(fill)	d	(did)
i	(sit)	g	(got)
l	(let)	h	(his)
m	(mad)	j	(jet)
n	(nut)	k	(kiss)
o	(not)	p	(pet)
r	(rat)	q	(quit)
s	(sell)	t	(top)
u	(cut)	x	(fox)
v	(vet)		
w	(wet)		
y	(yes)		
z	(zoo)		

represent its most common sound will be considered an irregular word. The word *was* is irregular because the letters *a* and *s* do not represent their most common sounds.

Consonant Blends

A consonant blend occurs when 2 or 3 consonants appear consecutively in a word and each consonant represents its most common sound. Consonant blends may appear at the beginning or end of words. Table 6.2 illustrates common-initial and final-consonant blends. Words that begin with consonant blends are more difficult to decode than words that begin with single consonants. An initial-consonant blend that contains a stop sound will make a word more difficult to decode than will a consonant blend with two continuous sounds.

Regular Word Types

Regular word types may be described by the patterns of vowels and consonants they contain. Table 6.3 lists word types in their relative order of difficulty. In the first col-

---

Table 6.2   Consonant Blends

Initial Consonant Blends

Two-letter Blends Continuous Sounds First				Two-letter Blends Stop Sound First				Three Letters	
fl	(flag)	sc	(scat)	bl	(black)	pl	(plug)	scr	(scrap)
fr	(frog)	sk	(skip)	br	(brat)	pr	(press)	spl	(split)
sl	(slip)	sp	(spin)	cl	(clip)	tr	(truck)	spr	(spring)
sm	(smack)	sq	(square)	cr	(crust)	tw	(twin)	str	(strap)
sn	(snip)	st	(stop)	dr	(drip)				
sw	(swell)			gl	(glass)				
				gr	(grass)				

Final Consonant Blends

Two-letter Blends Continuous Sounds First				Two-letter Blends Stop Sound First		Three Letters	
ft	(left)	nd	(bend)	ct	(fact)	words formed	
ld	(held)	nk	(bank)	pt	(kept)	by adding an	
lk	(milk)	nt	(bent)	xt	(text)	s to 2-letter	
lp	(help)	sk	(mask)	bs	(cabs)	blends (e.g.,	
lt	(belt)	st	(west)	ds	(beds)	belts, facts)	
mp	(lamp)	ls	(fills)	gs	(rags)		
ms	(hams)			ps	(hips)		
ns	(cans)			ts	(bets)		

Table 6.3   Simple Regular Words—Listed According to Difficulty

Word Type	Reason for Relative Difficulty/Ease	Examples	Notes
VC and CVC words that begin with continuous sound	Words begin with a continuous sound.	it, fan	VC and CVC are grouped together because there are few VC words.
VCC and CVCC words that begin with a continuous sound	Words are longer and end with a consonant blend.	lamp, ask	VCC and CVCC are grouped together because there are few VCC words.
CVC words that begin with stop sound	Words begin with a stop sound.	cup, tin	
CVCC words that begin with stop sound	Words begin with stop sound and end with a consonant blend.	dust, hand	
CCVC	Words begin with a consonant blend.	crib, bled, snap, flat	Words that begin with two continuous consonants are the easier of words that begin with blends. These words are grouped with the rest of blends since there are relatively few such words.
CCVCC, CCCVC, and CCCVCC	Words are longer.	clamp, spent, scrap, scrimp	

umn, the letters V and C are used to describe the various types. V stands for vowel and C stands for consonant. A CVC word begins with a consonant letter, followed by a vowel, and another consonant. The word *sat* is a CVC word since *s* is a consonant, *a* is a vowel, and *t* is a consonant. The second column indicates the reason for the word type's relative difficulty. The third column illustrates each word type. This table provides general guidelines, not hard and fast rules for the teaching of each word type.

Some students may find words of an earlier type more difficult than words of a later type.

An Overview of Decoding Instruction—Beginning Stage

During the beginning stage, the major part of instruction revolves around teaching students how to decode regular words. We recommend teaching students an overt strategy of sounding out words. In sounding out, the students start at the beginning of the word and say the sound corresponding to the first letter. They then advance in a left-right progression, saying the sound for each successive letter and blending the sounds without pausing. The blending results in a word such as *Sam* being sounded out "Sssssssaaaaaammmmmm." Finally the blended word is said at a normal rate "Sam."

The following are preskills that help students to sound out words:

1. A knowledge of letter-sound correspondences in the word. (Note that word reading can begin as soon as the students know enough sounds of letters to form words. The students need not master all letter-sound correspondences before word reading begins.)

2. The ability to imitate a model of a word in which each sound is held several seconds with no pause (e.g., the teacher says "mmmaaannn" and the student says "mmmaaannn").

3. The ability to translate a series of sounds into a meaningful word (e.g., the teacher says "mmmaaan" and the student says "man").

The imitating and translating skills are called auditory skills because they can be presented verbally without any reference to printed material.

The first week of instruction will consist primarily of letter-sound correspondence and auditory-skill training.

Sounding-out instruction can begin when the students know 4 to 6 letter-sound correspondences. The first sounding-out exercises are word-list exercises in which the teacher points to the letters in a word while the students say and blend the sounds, then say the word at a normal rate.

When the students demonstrate mastery on teacher-prompted sounding out, the teacher introduces sounding out exercises in which the students point to the letters in the word as they blend sounds.

Passage reading, in which the students read stories composed of words taught in word-list exercises, begins with just one or two sentences. The length of stories and the time devoted to passage reading grows gradually until, near the end of the beginning stage, almost two-thirds of decoding instruction focuses on passage reading.

A gradual transition is made over a period of weeks from sounding out to sight-word reading in which the students do not vocally sound out a word before saying it at a normal rate.

Initial word-reading exercises are done with regular VC and CVC words that begin with continuous sounds. More difficult regular word types are introduced only when students demonstrate mastery of easier types.

Irregular words, words in which one or more letters do not represent their most common sound, are not introduced until students have developed fluency in sounding out regular words.

In summary, decoding instruction begins with the teacher presenting component skills that students will need when the students read words. The teacher presents letter-sound correspondences and auditory skills that students will employ when reading words. The initial word-reading instruction involves the teacher instructing the students how to sound out regular words. A gradual transition is made from exercises where students vocally sound out words with a good deal of teacher prompting to later exercises where students read words independently without vocally sounding them out. The key teacher behavior is to provide students with adequate practice to facilitate high accuracy before proceeding to new steps.

Comprehension

During the first year of reading instruction, the words students will be able to read will represent only a small fraction of the words in the students' expressive and receptive vocabulary. Written comprehension exercises are limited to relatively simple, literal and inferential questions. Limiting comprehension activities is unnecessary and inefficient. All students can benefit from ORAL instruction in a wider range of comprehension and vocabulary skills than can be presented in written exercises.

The type and quantity of comprehension instruction during the beginning reading stage depends on the entering skills of the children. Since the words introduced in most commercial reading programs are selected to be within the vocabulary of the *average* child, relatively little work needs to be done on these words with most students. Comprehension training for average and above-average students can consist of oral training in reasoning skills and more sophisticated vocabulary.

Low-performing students, however, may require a great deal of training in basic vocabulary and expressive language. They will not know the meaning of words encountered in primary reading books. Equally important, they may not understand many terms teachers commonly use during instruction. To prepare lower performing students for the tasks they will encounter, a teacher should provide instruction in basic language and vocabulary. Early lessons should include instruction in various attributes of objects such as color, shape, texture, and size; labels for common classroom objects, use of comparatives and superlatives, pronoun usage, and prepositions.

In summary, oral language training during the beginning reading stage will benefit all students, but it is especially critical for instructionally naive students. Without extensive oral training, these students are likely to have serious problems with later comprehension activities.

Application Exercises

1. **a.** Write B if the word begins with a consonant blend.
   b. Write E if the word ends with a consonant blend.
   c. Circle the consonant blend in each word.

clip	step	desk	clamp
must	lamp	milk	splint

2. Classify each of the following words under the appropriate heading below

strip	step	ant	crust
camp	fled	bets	bled
mud	must	snap	top
best	cop	brat	set
strap	ask	grab	bust

    a. VC and CVC words that begin with continuous sound:

    b. CVC words that begin with stop sound:

    c. CVCC and VCC words:

    d. CCVC words:

    e. CCVCC, CCCVC, and CCCVCC words:

3. Put *s* over each letter that represents a stop sound. Put *c* over each letter that represents a continuous sound.

    a b c d e f g h i j k l m n o p q r s t u v w x y z

4. Identifying words students will not be able to decode is an important teaching skill. Assume that students know the most common sound of all individual letters. Circle any single letter the student will not be able to decode, which means the word itself is probably not decodable. For example, the letter *g* in *gin* would be circled since *g* is not representing its most common sound.

cent	tab	put
must	cut	fat
cab	gin	send
pin	rust	son
was	ten	con
gas	some	hat
wish	fast	mind
tent	bent	dent
	walk	cub

Chapter

7

Auditory Skills

This section explains how to teach three auditory skills: (1) segmenting a word into its component sounds, (2) telescoping a series of blended sounds into a word, and (3) rhyming with different initial sounds to form new words. It is important to note that these three skills are primarily auditory, which means that the teacher does not present written letters or words to students. Instead, the exercises are conducted orally with the teacher saying sounds and requiring students either to repeat the sounds or say the sounds another way. The student is not required to look at a word and read it. The student merely listens to sounds and responds.

Teaching these auditory skills early is necessary to lay the groundwork for later reading skills such as sounding out words and blending.

Preskills for Sounding Out Words

Two auditory skills directly relate to sounding out words. The first auditory skill is telescoping sounds to form a word. The teacher says a series of blended sounds, then the student translates the series of sounds into a word said at a normal rate ("aaammm" becomes *am*). This skill prepares the student to identify words after having sounded them out.

The second skill is segmenting a word into sounds. The teacher says a word, slowly breaking it down into its component sounds. Then the student segments the word.

Telescoping and segmenting words does the following:

1. Shows the student that words are composed of discrete sounds.

2. Provides practice in saying sounds before the letter-sound correspondences are introduced. This practice is particularly important for difficult-to-say sounds.

3. Prepares students for later sounding-out exercises which require blending (saying sounds without pausing between them).

Since auditory skills do not require knowledge of letter-sound correspondence, instruction on these skills can begin on the first day of instruction, before any letter-sound correspondences have been introduced. Telescoping sounds to form a word is the easier auditory skill and should be introduced first. Segmenting a word into sounds can be introduced when students are able to telescope a group of words with no errors. This is usually within several days.

These auditory tasks should be continued for the first few months of instruction. Four to six words should be included in each auditory exercise. As a general rule, auditory exercises should include words and sounds that students will be asked to decode in the near future.

Telescoping Sounds

Telescoping sounds requires the student to translate a series of blended sounds into words said at a normal rate. When sounding out a written word, students will hold each continuous sound for 1 to 2 seconds, thus producing a series of sounds, "mmmaaannn." Then they will have to telescope this series of sounds into a word pronounced at a normal rate, "man." A format for teaching telescoping appears in Table 7.1. The teacher says a word slowly, pauses an instant, and then says, "What word?" The students reply by saying the word at a normal rate.

Correcting Mistakes

Students may make three types of mistakes when telescoping sounds to form a word: saying the word slowly (imitating the teacher), leaving out a sound (the teacher says "sssaaat," but the child leaves off the final consonant, saying "saa"), and mispronouncing a sound (the teacher says "ssseeelll," but the student says "sil"). The correction procedure, which is the same for all types of mistakes, consists of the teacher's (a) modeling the correct re-

Table 7.1 Format for Telescoping Sounds

Teacher	Students
1. (Teacher gives instructions.) Listen, we're going to play a say-the-word game. I'll say a word slowly, then you say the word fast.	
2. (Teacher says the word slowly, then students say it fast.) Listen. (Pause.) iiiifffff. What word? (Signal.)	"If."
3. (Teacher repeats step 2 with four more words: sat, Sid, am, fit.)	
4. (Teacher repeats the set of words until students can respond correctly to all the words, making no errors.)	
5. (Teacher gives individual turns to several students.)	

sponse, (b) leading the students by responding with them, (c) testing the students on the missed word, and (d) returning to the first word in the format.

Here is a typical correction sequence: The teacher is presenting these words: *if, sat, Sid, am, fit.*

- Teacher says, "Sssssiiiiid."
  Student says "sad" instead of "Sid."
- Teacher says correct answer, "Sid."
- Teacher models entire task:
  My turn. (Pause.) "Sssssiiiiid." What word? "Sid."
- Teacher leads—teacher and student respond together: "Sssssiiiiid." What word? (Signal.)
  "Sid." (Teacher says, "Sid" with the students.)
- Teacher tests—only students respond.
  Your turn. (Pause.) "Sssssiiiiid." What word? (Signal.) "Sid."
- Teacher returns to first word in format:
  Let's see if we can do all the words without making any errors.

Usually one or two students in a group will make an error while the rest of the students respond correctly. Teachers should occasionally begin the correction procedure by praising a student who responded correctly. (e.g., "Good answer, Tommy.") This praise will demonstrate to students that the teacher places importance on correct responding. Teachers should not be negative with students who make errors. Praise a student who got the answer right. The praise keeps the lesson positive and motivates other students.

The teacher does not generally signal out the students who made the error, but presents the correction to the entire group, having all the students respond. When presenting individual turns, the teacher should test a student on any word the student missed during the exercise.

Segmenting a Word

Segmenting a word format (see Table 7.2) teaches students to say a word slowly by holding each continuous sound for about $1\frac{1}{2}$ seconds and by switching from sound to sound without pausing. The teacher models by saying a word slowly. Then the students imitate the teacher.

Correcting Errors

Students can make three types of mistakes in segmenting a word: not saying the correct sound, pausing between sounds, or not switching sounds when the teacher signals for the students to say the next sound.

The correction procedure for not saying a correct sound includes these steps:

1. Stop the students as soon as you hear the wrong response and say the correct sound.
2. Model the correct response.
3. Lead the students in making the response.
4. Test the students.
5. Return to the beginning of the task.

Here is a typical correction sequence:

- Examples being presented:
  am, not, rug, sad
- Error
  When segmenting "nnnooot," a student says "nnnuuu."
- Teacher stops the student as soon as she hears "uuu."
- Teacher says correct sound, "Ooooo."
- Teacher models (emphasizing the sound the student said incorrectly):
  My turn. Nnn*ooo*t.

Table 7.2   Format for Segmenting

Teacher	Student
1. We're going to say words slowly.	
2. First word: **sad.**	
I'll say it slowly. Listen. (Pause.) Ssssaaaddd.	
You say it slowly. Get ready. (Teacher signals each time	
students are to switch to the next sound.)	*"Ssssaaaddd."*
3. (Teacher repeats procedure in step 2 with 3 more words.)	
Next word: **me.**	
I'll say it slowly. Listen. (Pause.) Mmmmeee.	
You say it slowly. Get ready. (Signal.)	*"Mmmmeee."*
Next word: **mom.**	
I'll say it slowly. Listen. (Pause.) Mmmmooommm.	
You say it slowly. Get ready. (Signal.)	*"Mmmmooommm."*
Next word: **fit.**	
I'll say it slowly. Listen. (Pause.) Ffffiiittt.	
You say it slowly. Get ready. (Signal.)	*"Ffffiiittt."*
4. Teacher repeats the set of words until students can say	
every word slowly, making no errors.	
5. Teacher gives individual turns to several students.	

- Teacher leads:
  Listen. Nnnn*ooo*t. Say it with me.
  Get ready. (Signal.) "Nnnooot."
- Teacher tests:
  Listen. Nnnnooot. You say it slowly.
  Get ready. (Signal.) "Nnnooot."
- Teacher returns to first word in task.

The correction procedure for student pausing between sounds is basically the same as for mispronounced words except that the teacher does not have to say a missed sound. The teacher tells the students not to stop between sounds. Then the teacher models, leads, tests, and returns to the first word of the task.

    The correction procedure for students failing to switch sounds when the teacher signals would begin with the teacher prais-ing students who followed the signal, then modeling, leading and testing as above.

Segmenting and Telescoping

The two auditory skills are combined in a single format in Table 7.3. This format can be introduced when students are able on the first trial to respond correctly to all the words in a segmenting format without making any errors.

Critical Behaviors— Saying the Word Slowly

When saying a word slowly in an auditory-skills format, the teacher: (a) says each continuous sound for about 1½ seconds, (b) does not pause between sounds, and (c) is

Table 7.3

Table 7.3   Segmenting and Telescoping—Combined Format

Teacher	Students
1. First you'll say a word slowly, then you'll say it fast.	
2. Listen. (Pause.) Rrrraaannn. Say it slowly. Get ready. (Teacher signals each time students are to switch to the next sound.)	*"Rrraannn."*
What word? (Signal.)	*"Ran."*
3. Listen. (Pause.) Sssiiiccck. Say it slowly. Get ready. (Signal.)	*"Ssssiiiick."*
What word? (Signal.)	*"Sick."*
4. Listen. (Pause.) Mmmmaaad. Say it slowly. Get ready. (Signal.)	*"Mmmaaaad."*
What word? (Signal.)	*"Mad."*
5. Listen. (Pause.) iiiiffff. Say it slowly. Get ready. (Signal.)	*"Iiiiffff."*
What word? (Signal.)	*"If."*
6. Teacher repeats steps 2 through 5 until students are able to respond correctly to all words.	
7. Teacher gives individual turns to several students.	

careful not to distort any sound. When saying the final consonant of a word, the teacher must be careful not to add an "uh" sound, but to say the word *sad* as "sssaaad," not "sssaaduh." Similarly, teachers must be careful not to add an "uh" sound to words that begin with stop sounds (*b, c, d, g, h, j, k, p, q, t*). The teacher pronounces a word such as *pin* by combining the |p| and |ĭ| sound and then elongating the |ĭ| sound, pronouncing *pin* as "piiiiiiinnnnn" not as "puhiiiiiinnnnn."

Note that in all three formats the teacher is directed to pause before saying a word slowly (segmenting a word). The pause should be just for an instant. The purpose of the pause is to ensure that the students hear the word as a distinct unit.

Signaling

The telescoping and segmenting tasks are among the first tasks presented to students at the beginning of the year. When presenting the exercises to the students, the teacher not only teaches the telescoping and segmenting skills, but also teaches students how to respond as a member of a group. The teacher must present the signal to respond in a manner that makes it clear to the students exactly when they are to respond and when to listen. When speaking to the students the teacher can hold up her hand in front of her (as someone indicating another person to stop).

In the telescoping exercises, the teacher signals the students to respond by moving her hand up an inch or two, then quickly moving it down like a drummer. The up-down motion should be done crisply and without hesitation. The students respond on the down motion, just as the teacher's hand hits an imaginary drum. The up-down motion should be done the same way every time. Any hesitation or inconsistency makes a unison responding difficult because the students don't know when to respond.

The signal for segmenting a word begins the same way with the teacher holding her hand in the stop position. The teacher signals the students to begin responding by using the up-down motion. One-and-a-half seconds later the teacher repeats the up-down motion again, then $1\frac{1}{2}$ seconds later she repeats the motion. The students switch from sound to sound on each movement, not pausing between them. The signaling procedure is summarized in this way:

```
sssssssssssssaaaaaaaaaammmmm
|              |           |
up-down    up-down     up-down
motion     motion      motion
```

A slightly different signaling procedure is necessary when words begin with stop sounds (*b, c, d, g, h, j, k, p, q, t*). When the teacher models these words, the teacher says the first two sounds of the word as one unit. For example, when segmenting the word *hat* the teacher says "haaat." The teacher says the initial consonant sound for an instant and then begins the next sound without any pause or distortion.

To signal to the students that this type of word is different, the teacher makes two rapid up-down motions while saying the first two sounds of the word. The teacher holds the vowel slightly longer than usual (about 2 seconds), then makes another up-down movement, to signal students to say the third sound.

Monitoring Students

When students respond orally in unison, hearing an incorrect response can be difficult; therefore, the teacher should look at the students' mouths as they make the responses. The position of the students' lips and tongues helps to tell the sounds

the students are making. For example, if a student's mouth is open when the student is supposed to be making the |m| sound, the teacher knows the student is not making a correct response.

The teacher should also watch the students' eyes. The students' eyes should be directed toward the teacher's face. Young children unconsciously watch an adult's mouth movements to learn how to say sounds and words. Hence, students should watch the teacher's mouth as she models. Watching the students' eyes also lets the teacher know if the students are attending to the teacher's signals.

Pacing

As a general rule, the teacher should keep the time between when the students respond and when the teacher begins the instructions for the next word to just an instant.

When presenting a format the teacher presents several words in a row, pausing no longer than one second to make a quick one- or two-word praise comment (e.g., good, great) between the student response and the instructions for the next word. After a set of several words, the teacher can spend 5 to 15 seconds praising students.

The concept of presenting a set of tasks with little extraneous language between each task is an important one. Presenting a set of tasks with no interruption is a very powerful method for keeping students attentive.

The number of words in a set and the relative intensity of teacher praise depends on the difficulty the students have with the formats. The less difficulty students have, the more words should be included in a set and the less effusive the praise.

Individual Turns

As a general rule, when a format is presented, the teacher has the students respond in unison. The teacher has the students respond in unison until the teacher is fairly certain all students can respond correctly to all the words. Then individual turns are given. The main purpose of individual turns is to make a final check to see whether students are able to respond correctly. During the first week of instruction, an individual turn on segmenting a word may be given to most students. Later, fewer individual turns are needed. The teacher may give an individual turn to each weaker students, but just to 1 or 2 stronger students. The purpose of giving individual turns to higher performers is not only to monitor their performance, but also to ensure that the teacher does not inadvertently stigmatize some students as lower performers by always calling on just them for individual turns.

Selecting Examples

Selecting words to use in telescoping and segmenting tasks is relatively simple. The basic rule is to use regular words that will appear in early word-reading tasks. On the first day of instruction, the teacher selects 4 words, including some from the first word-reading task in the program.

The initial auditory tasks is done with the easiest type of words, VC and CVC words beginning with continuous sounds. More difficult types of words are presented in auditory tasks a week or so before that type is introduced in word-reading exercises.

The teacher must make certain the list is not too predictable because a predictable list may cause the students to anticipate words and not attend carefully to what the teacher says. For example, if the same vowel appears in all words, the words form a predictable order; the students may then respond according to the pattern rather than to what the teacher says. If the teacher presented the following set: *Sam,*

lap, rat, man, the students might start anticipating that all words have the |ă| sound.

To avoid a predictable list, the teacher constructs a list in which the same letter does not appear in the same position in more than two consecutive words.

Rhyming

Rhyming is another valuable auditory skill because it: 1) prepares students to see the relationship between letter clusters that represent the same sounds in different words, such as *fan, pan, tan,* and *man,* and 2) prepares students for sounding out words that begin with stop sounds. Rhyming can be introduced when the students have mastered the segmenting and telescoping skills.

In the rhyming format (see Table 7.4), the teacher writes several letters on the board (e.g., *m, r, s*) and models by saying a series of rhyming words, beginning with those letters (e.g., *mat, rat, sat*), then tests the students.

On the first lessons that rhyming is presented, the letters written on the board should have continuous sounds. After the students can correctly do the rhyming tasks with continuous sounds, words that begin with stop sounds can be included. For example, a set might include these words: *fill, hill, pill, mill.*

The correction procedure follows these steps:

- Teacher says the correct answer.
- Teacher models:
    My turn. Rhymes with at. (Signal.) Mat.
- Teacher leads:
    Let's do it together.
    Rhymes with at. (Signal.) "Mat."
    (Teacher respond with the students.)
- Teacher tests:
    Your turn. Rhymes with at. (Signal.) "Mat."
- Teacher returns to first word in format.

Table 7.4   Rhyming Format

Teacher	*Students*
(Teacher writes on board:)	

m →

s →

f →

1. Listen. I'm going to rhyme with (Pause.) **at**. What am I going to rhyme with? (Signal.)	*"At."*
2. (Teacher models:) (Teacher puts finger on ball of first arrow and says:) My turn: Rhymes with **at**. (After a 1-second pause, teacher moves finger rapidly across arrow and says:) Mat.	
3. (Teacher repeats step 2 with remaining arrows.)	
4. (Teacher tests:) (Teacher puts finger on ball of first arrow and says:) You're going to rhyme with **at**. What are you going to rhyme with? (Signal.)	*"At."*
Rhymes with **at**. (After a 1-second pause, teacher moves finger quickly across arrow.)	*"Mat."*
5. (Teacher repeats step 4 with remaining arrows.)	
6. (Teacher gives individual turns to several students.)	

Application Exercises

1. The teacher is presenting the format for telescoping a word. Specify all the steps in the correction procedure for the following error. Tell what the teacher says and does.

   Teacher says "mmmuud what word?" Student says "mad."

2. The teacher is presenting the format for segmenting a word. Specify all the steps in the correction procedure for the following errors.

   Teacher says "fffiiit. Say it slowly." Student says "fff (pauses) iiit."

3. Classify each of the following words under the appropriate heading below.

mud	hid	fled	ramp
stamp	ran	sid	frog
cop	slid	hot	fit
best	stink	ten	strap
runt	lid	splint	

a. VC and CVC words that begin with continuous sound:

b. CVC words that begin with stop sound:

c. CVCC and VCC words:

d. CCVC words:

e. CCVCC, CCCVC, and CCCVCC words:

4. Identifying words students will not be able to decode is an important teaching skill. Assume that students know the most common sound of all individual letters. Circle any single letter the student will not be able to decode, which means the word itself is probably not decodable. For example, the letter *g* in *gin* would be circled since *g* is not representing its most common sound.

chest	lamp	rub
bent	ten	find
cent	bath	fit
son	rust	slim
rob	camp	limp
was	mend	pen

5. The teacher is selecting words to use in teaching the segmenting format during the first week of instruction. Examine each list of words and indicate by specifying *acceptable* (A) or *unacceptable* (U) whether or not the teacher followed the example-selection guidelines for segmenting. If the teacher did not follow the guidelines specify the violations.

List A	List B	List C
brat	mud	mad
ham	sad	if
sit	lid	sit
fun	mad	sam
last		

Students should be taught letter-sound correspondences to prepare them for sounding out words. When students sound out words, they must produce the sound represented by each letter in the word, blend the sounds, and then identify the word. In this section, the details pertaining to teaching letter-sound correspondences are explained.

Sequence

Here are four guidelines for determining an order for introducing letters:

1. Introduce initially only the most-common sound for a new letter.
2. Separate letters that are visually or auditorily similar.
3. Introduce more useful letters before less useful letters.
4. Introduce lower-case (small) letters before upper-case (capital) letters.

Introduce the Most Common Sound

The most common sound of a letter is the sound that is usually pronounced for the letter when it appears in a short word, such as *man* or *sit*. The chart presented earlier in Table 6.1 illustrates the most common sound for each of the 26 letters.

The letters are grouped as continuous sounds or stop sounds. Remember, a continuous sound can be said for several seconds without distorting the sound. All vowels and some consonants are continuous sounds. A stop sound can be pronounced for only an instant. Next to each letter in Table 6.1 is a word in which the letter represents its most common sound. (Note: Phonemes and graphemes are the words used by linguists to describe sounds and the letters that represent them. Phoneme

Chapter

Letter-Sound Correspondence

means sound. Grapheme is a letter or a series of letters that represents one sound.)

Separate Visually or Auditorily Similar Letters

The more similar two letters are, the more likely students will confuse them. Separating similar letters from each other in their order of introduction reduces the possibility of student confusion. The greater the similarity between two sounds or letters, the greater the number of letters that should separate them. Two factors determine the probability of confusion: auditory similarity (how alike the most common sounds of two letters are) and visual similarity (how alike in appearance the two letters are). The following sounds are auditorily similar: /f/ and /v/, /t/ and /d/, /b/ and /d/, /b/ and /p/, /k/ and /g/, /m/ and /n/, /ĭ/ and /ĕ/, and /ŏ/ and /ŭ/. The following letters are visually similar: b and d, b and p, q and p, n and m, h and n, v and w, and n and r.

Similar sounds should be separated by the introduction of at least three other dissimilar sounds. For example, if the sound /t/ is introduced on lesson 40, the sounds /r/, /l/, and /m/ might be introduced before /d/, which is auditorily similar. Students have the most difficulty with pairs of letters that are both visually and auditorily similar: (b, d), (m, n), (b, p). These letters (plus e and i) should be separated by at least 6 other letters. Students can also be expected to have some trouble with letters

just visually similar. If possible, the members of these pairs should also be separated.

Introduce More Useful Letters First

More useful letters are those that appear most often in words. Learning such letters early enables students to decode more words than learning less useful letters. For example, knowing the sounds for the letters s, a, t, and i will allow students to decode more words than knowing the sounds for j, q, z, and x. Vowels are the most useful letters. More useful consonants are b, c, d, f, g, h, k, l, m, n, p, r, s, t. Less useful consonant letters are j, q, z, y, x, v, and w.

Introduce Lower-Case Letters First

Lower-case letters should be taught before upper-case letters since the majority of words in reading material is composed of lower-case letters. A student knowing all lower-case letters would be able to decode all the words in the following sentence: "Sam had on his best hat." A student knowing only upper-case letters could read none of the words. An exception to this guideline can be made for lower-case and upper-case letters that look exactly the same, except of course for size (e.g., sS, cC). These lower- and upper-case letters may be introduced at the same time. Upper- and lower-case letters are classified according to their visual similarity in Table 8.1.

Table 8.1				Upper-and Lower-Case Letters Grouped According to Visual Similarity								
Dissimilar				**Same**					**Moderate Similarity**			
aA	eE	qQ	bB	cC	kK	oO	pP	sS	fF	mM	jJ	nN
rR	dD	gG	hH	uU	vV	wW	xX	zZ	tT	yY	lL	il

A Sample Sequence

Table 8.2 contains one possible order for introducing letters. We are not suggesting that this is the only or even the best sequence for introducing letters. It is just one sequence that derives from the guidelines specified here. Note the following about Table 8.2:

1. The letters visually and/or auditorily similar—*e, i; b, d; m, n;* and *b, p*—are separated by 13, 7, 13, and 6 letters, respectively. Other potentially confusing pairs (*d, t; f, v; h, n; k, g; v, w; n, r*) are also separated.

2. Upper-case letters not the same in appearance as their respective lower-case letters are introduced after most lower-case letters have been introduced. Upper- and lower-case letters that are identical are introduced at the same time and, thus, these upper-case letters are not listed on the chart.

3. More useful letters are introduced before less useful letters. The lower-case letters *j, y, x, q,* and *z* are introduced toward the end of the sequence. The first two letters, *a* and *m,* were chosen not only because they are more useful letters, but also because they are easy to pronounce. Starting with easy-to-pronounce letters makes initial sounds tasks easier for instructionally naive students.

Rate and Practice

The rate at which new letters are introduced is always contingent on student per-formance. Teachers working with students who enter school with little knowledge of letter-sound correspondence will find an optimal rate (one which introduces new letters quickly while minimizing errors) for introducing new letters is about one each second or third day. This rate assumes that the teacher presents daily practice on isolated sounds. Without adequate daily practice, an optimal rate is not possible. However, the rate of introduction should always be dependent on the students' performance. When the first 5 letters are being taught, a new letter should not be introduced if the students are unable correctly to produce the sound for each of the previously introduced letters. Rather than presenting a new lesson, the teacher should review previously taught lessons for several days, concentrating on the unknown letters. After the first 5 letters have been introduced, a new letter can be introduced if the students are having difficulty with just one letter-sound correspondence; however, that letter should not be similar to the letter being introduced. For example, a new vowel (*e*) can be introduced even though students are having difficulty with *b* and *d*. However, the vowel *e* should not be introduced if the students are having difficulty with any previously introduced vowel since all vowel sounds are similar.

Procedure for Teaching Letter-sound Correspondences

The basic procedure for teaching letter-sound correspondences involves an introductory format and a discrimination for-

---

Table 8.2   An Acceptable Sequence for Introducing Letters

a m t s i f d r o g l h u c b n k v e w j p y T L M F D I N A R H G B x q z J E Q mat. In the introductory format, the teacher models and tests on the new letter-sound correspondence. In the discrimination format, the teacher tests the new letter-sound correspondence along with previously introduced letters. The introductory format is used the first lesson or two a new letter appears. The discrimination format starts after two letters have been introduced and appears in every subsequent lesson.

Introductory Format

In the introductory format, the teacher first models by saying the sound, then tests by having the group say the sound. The teacher first has the students respond in unison. Then when the teacher thinks that the group can respond correctly, the teacher tests students individually (see Table 8.3).

Discrimination Format

In the sounds-discrimination format, students receive the practice they need to quickly and accurately say the sound for different letters, a skill necessary for sounding out words. A new letter-sound correspondence is taught in the introductory format. If the students have no difficulty saying the sound, the letter can appear in the discrimination format on the next lesson.

Table 8.3	Introductory Format for Letter-Sound Correspondences	
	Teacher	*Students*
1.	(Teacher writes on the board: m.) When I touch under the letter, you say the sound. Keep saying the sound as long as I touch it.	
2.	(Teacher *models* the sound. Teacher holds her finger under the letter and says:) My turn. (Teacher moves finger out and in, touching under the letter for 2 seconds if it is a continuous sound and for an instant if it is a stop sound. Teacher says the sound while touching under the letter, then quickly moves her finger away from the letter and immediately stops saying the sound.)	
3.	(Teacher *tests* by having the group say the sound several times by themselves, and finally gives individual tests to all students. The purpose of the individual test is to enable the teacher to correct mispronounciations early.)	
a.	(Teacher points under the letter and says:) What sound? (Signal.) (Teacher touches under letter for about 2 seconds.)	*"mmmmmmm"*
b.	(Teacher repeats step *a* several times, touching under the sound from 1 to 3 seconds.)	
4.	(Teacher tests the students individually.)	

The teacher writes the new letter several times on the board intermingled with previously introduced letters. The new letter is written several times to prevent the students from cueing on where the letter is written rather than on the shape of the letter. The teacher follows an alternating pattern in which he gradually increases the number of other letters pointed to between each occurrence of the new letter. The format shown in Table 8.4 illustrates the introduction of the letter *f*. During the first month of reading instruction, two isolated sounds-discrimination exercises should be

Table 8.4   Discrimination Format for Letter-Sound Correspondences

Teacher	*Students*
(Teacher writes on board several letters that have been previously taught, along with the new letter. Note that the new letter appears several times in different positions:)	

```
                         i
a          f                       m
    s           n             f
       r            f               o
```

1. (Teacher gives instructions.) When I touch under a letter, you say the sound. Keep saying the sound as long as I touch under it.	
2. (Teacher tests new sound. He points to the first letter, pauses 2 seconds, moves his finger out and in, touching under the letter for about 2 seconds if it is a continuous sound, and for an instant if it is a stop sound.) (Teacher immediately either corrects or points to the next letter.)	*Students say the sound.*
3. (Teacher tests on all letters. He points to a letter, pauses 2 seconds, then moves his finger out and in, touching under the letter.) (The teacher follows an alternating pattern in which he gradually increases the retention interval for the newly introduced letter by pointing to more review letters before returning to the new letter. For example, if the new letter is *f,* the teacher points to the letters in this order:)	*Students say the sound.*

```
  f    a    f    r    m    f    s    i    o    f    n    i    r    o    f
```

4. (Teacher gives individual tests. Every day the teacher should test several students on all vowels introduced up to that time and test individual students on any sounds that have caused difficulty for them in the past week.)

included in each lesson: one early in the lesson and one later in the lesson. The reason is simply to provide extra practice. Later in the program when students begin reading words, the word reading itself will be a form of practice for letter-sound correspondences and only one discrimination letter-sound correspondence task needs to be presented in a lesson.

As with the introductory sound format, the teacher has the group respond in unison until it appears all students are responding correctly to all sounds. Then the teacher gives individual turns.

Note that the discrimination format directs the teacher to pause 2 seconds after pointing to a letter before signaling the students to respond. This pause is to allow the students time to think of their response. After the students know about 12 letter-sound correspondences, the teacher can decrease the pause to about a second on letters introduced prior to the current week.

Critical Behaviors

Signaling

The teacher should concentrate on teaching students to respond to her signal during the first days of instruction. To follow the touching signal, students begin saying a sound as soon as the teacher touches under the letter and continue to respond as long as she touches it. Teaching students to say a sound continuously for several seconds is a very important preskill for sounding out words. When students initially sound out a word, they will say each sound for 1 to 2 seconds. During the time they are saying one sound, they simultaneously look ahead to the next one. For example, while the students say the /m/ sound in *mad*, they look ahead to figure out the

sound for the letter *a*. Students who cannot hold a sound for several seconds are likely to have difficulty sounding out words.

When signaling, the teacher points under the letter (not touching the board), making certain that no student's vision is blocked by any part of the teacher's hand or body. The out-and-in motion is done crisply with the finger moving away from the board (about 3 inches) and then immediately back to the board (see Figure 8.1). When the finger touches the board below the letter, the students are to respond. The out-and-in motion is done the same way every time it is used. Any hesitation or inconsistency makes a unison response difficult because the students cannot tell when they are supposed to answer. The teacher signals the students to stop responding by moving her finger away from the board in a rapid, distinct movement.

A modified signaling procedure is used for the stop sounds (/b/, /c/, /d/, /g/, /h/, /j/, /k/, /p/, /q/, /t/, and /x/). Since these sounds can be pronounced for only an instant, the teacher signals by touching the board below the letter for only an instant.

Modeling

Continuous consonant sounds should be said without any distortion. The letter *m* is said "mmmm," not "uummm" or "mmmmmuuu." Saying a stop sound without adding a slight vowel sound is impossible. However, teachers should try to minimize the vowel sound. The letter *d* should not be pronounced "duh." Vowel sounds must also be pronounced accurately. Some teachers have a tendency to distort vowel sounds. They start out with a distorted sound and then change it into the correct sound (e.g., pronouncing *i* as "uuiii") or start with the correct sound and then distort it (e.g., pronouncing *i* as "iiieee"). Care should be taken to avoid distorting sounds.

Figure 8.1   Point, Out-In, and Touch Signal

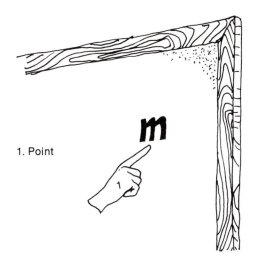

1. Point

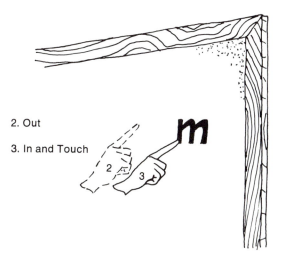

2. Out

3. In and Touch

Pacing

Pacing a task is not only an important method for maintaining student attention, but it also affects academic performance. Pacing should be fast enough to keep the students attending, but not so fast they begin to guess and make errors. A basic pacing rule in presenting the letter-sound correspondence discrimination format is for the teacher to provide a "thinking pause" before giving the signal for the students' response. Then after the students respond, quickly move to the next letter. The thinking pause gives all students enough time to come up with a response. A longer thinking pause may be given for sounds that have caused the students diffi-culty in previous lessons. However, the teacher should provide extra practice on that letter so that by the end of the discrim-ination format, the students can respond with only a 2-second pause.

The thinking pause concept is illus-trated below. Let's say that the teacher is presenting a letter-sound correspondence task with the letters *m*, *s*, and *d*. The students had trouble with the letter *d* on the previous lesson. Note how the teacher gives more thinking time for the letter *d*.

- Teacher points to *m*, pauses 2 seconds, then signals.
- Immediately after students respond, teacher points to *s*.
- Teacher pauses 2 seconds, then signals.
- Immediately after students respond, teacher points to *d*, and says, "Remember this tough sound," then pauses 4 seconds before signaling.

Another critical aspect of pacing is im-mediately moving to the next letter after the students make a correct response. Note above that immediately after the students make the response for the letter *m*, the teacher moves to the next letter *s*, then gives the students time to think. The rapid movement after students respond is a big help in keeping students attentive.

Developing Automaticity

The goal of the letter-sound correspondence formats is not only to enable students to produce the sound associated with the letter, but also to allow them to make the response with relative ease.

In the discrimination format, we recommended that teachers use a 2-second thinking pause before signaling. As the school year progresses, the thinking pause should be gradually reduced; so, by the time 12 letter-sound correspondences have been introduced, the students can respond with no more than a 1-second thinking pause before each letter.

Teachers working with instructionally naive students may find the students need a great deal of practice to increase their rate. To keep the students' frustration level low, the teacher starts the discrimination format with a 2-second thinking pause before each signal. When the students can respond correctly to all the letters with no more than a 2-second pause, the teacher challenges the students by saying, "You did a great job. I'll go faster this time."

Monitoring

Monitoring student performance during group responding is done by listening to the students' responses and watching their mouths and eyes. Since the teacher cannot watch every student on every response, she watches only a few students at a time. She continually scans the group, focusing on one or two students for one response and then shifting attention to other students for the next response. The teacher looks at a student's eyes and mouth. If a student's eyes are not directed toward the letters, the student is probably not paying attention. Looking at the student's mouth indicates whether the student is responding cor-

rectly. To produce a sound, a student's lips and tongue must be in a certain position. For example, when a student makes the /l/ sound, his mouth should be open with the front edge of the tongue touching the upper palate. If the student's mouth or tongue is not in this position, he is probably not pronouncing the sound correctly. For some sounds—(c, g), (d, t), (f, v), (p, b), (s, z), and all short vowel sounds—the teacher cannot rely on looking at the student's mouth because the lips and tongue are placed in similar positions for more than one sound. Consequently, the teacher must listen very closely to these sounds.

Even when the teacher listens and watches carefully to unison student responses, she cannot be certain that all students are responding correctly. Individual turns at the end of a format are given to help the teacher find which letters the student does not know. In the introductory format, teachers give individual turns to every student. The purpose is to ensure that the students are saying the new sound correctly. The faster the teacher spots a mispronunciation error, the easier it will be for the teacher to correct the error. In the discrimination format, teachers test several students each day on all the vowels introduced up to that time, plus any troublesome consonants.

Teachers should test all students weekly or biweekly on all the letters introduced to date in order to determine if students can produce the sounds for all letters with no more than a 2-second pause. During this test, which is not be presented during group instruction, the teacher should let students respond at their own rates. Teachers should record not only the sounds the students are unable to say correctly, but also the sounds the students *can* say correctly, yet take more than 2 seconds to produce.

Correcting Mistakes

There are three types of errors: a confusion error (saying the sound for a different letter), a pronunciation error (saying a sound in a distorted manner), and a signal error (not beginning the response when the signal is given). The basic correction for all the errors includes these five steps:

1. Directing a specific praise comment toward a student who responds correctly.
2. Modeling the correct answer.
3. Leading, if necessary.
4. Testing the group on the missed letter, then alternating between the missed letter and other letters in the format.
5. Retesting, later in the lesson, individual students who made an error.

Confusion Errors

In a confusion error, a student might say *"m"* for *n*. The teacher would do the following:

1. Specifically praise a student who responded correctly.
2. Model the missed letter. "Listen: mmm."
3. Test the students on the missed letter, then alternate between it and other previously identified letters that have been *Correctly* identified. If the student said a sound represented by another letter, the teacher does not include this letter in the firm up. If the student said *n* for the letter *m*, the letter *n* would not appear in the firm up for *m*. The teacher gradually increases the number of review letters that are included. The teacher

continues to alternate between the missed letter and familiar letters until the students identify the missed letter correctly after at least 3 other letters are tested just prior to the missed letter. The examples might look like this: first a test on *m*, then an alternating pattern of *a, m, s, i, m, r, f, g, m*.

4. Retest students later in the lesson who have made errors on *m*. The teacher retests by pointing to *m* and asking, "What sound?" If the student misses the letter, the teacher should follow the procedure in steps 2 and 3.

Keep in mind that the sooner confusion errors are spotted, the easier it will be to correct them. Older students who have been confused on a pair of letters for years will take much more time to remedy than younger students.

If a student is having chronic problems with a pair of letters (e.g., *b* and *d*), the teacher might work on one letter of the pair and exclude the other letter from the practice sets. When the students are able to identify correctly the letter being presented for three consecutive days, the teacher can reintroduce the other letter of the pair.

Pronunciation Errors

Pronunciation errors can be as serious as confusion errors, especially if made on vowel sounds. The more distorted the pronunciation of a sound, the greater the students' difficulty will be in discriminating it from other sounds appearing in later lessons. For example, if a student distorts the /ĭ/ sound so that it is very similar to the /ĕ/ sound, she will have difficulty when the /ĕ/ sound is introduced and may confuse /ĭ/ and /ĕ/ in word reading, saying "led" for *lid*.

The correction for a mispronunciation error is similar to that for a confusion error. When a student mispronounces a sound, the teacher does the following:

1. Praises a student who responded correctly.

2. Models, saying the correct response. "Listen: Mmmmm."

3. Leads, checking to see whether the lips and tongue of the student who made the mistake are positioned properly. If the position is incorrect, the teacher models again saying, "Watch my mouth when I say the sound." The teacher says the sound and watches the student's eyes to make certain the student is attending. Next, the teacher leads by having the students say the sound with him while watching the student's mouth. Leading is used most often when students mispronounce a sound.
   Listen: Mmmm. Say it. "Mmmm." (Teacher responds with students.) Listen again: Mmmm. Say it. "Mmmm." (Teacher responds with students.)

4. Tests, alternating between the missed letter and other letters, using the same pattern as for confusion errors.
   Teacher points to each letter and asks, "What sound?"

5. Retests later in the lesson.

The main difference in the correction procedure for pronunciation errors and the correction procedure for confusion errors is in the lead step. In the lead step, the teacher says the sound, then has the students say the sound with her. The teacher directs the students to watch her mouth as she says the sound. Watching the teacher's lips and tongue as she says the sound will help the students in placing their lips and tongues in the correct position to say the sound. The teacher may have to present 5 to 15 repetitions before the students make an acceptable response. Note above that before each student response, the teacher models saying the sound, then has the students say the sound with her.

The teacher should set a reasonable goal for the lead step. If the student does not have any speech problems, the goal is to have the student say the sound perfectly. If the student has a lisp or other speech problem, the teacher should set a reasonable approximation of the sound as a goal. The teacher should continue the lead step until the student can make two consecutive acceptable responses. Quite often a student who has an initial difficulty saying a sound will make an acceptable response, but on the next trial will make an unacceptable response. Providing extra practice for students to make two consecutive acceptable responses will result in steady improvement over a period of days. A student may need 15 repetitions before he's able to make an acceptable response the first day, then only 10 responses the next day, and fewer each following day. Providing practice to help students say sounds correctly is very challenging for the teacher. She must decide what response from the student will be the goal for each session. She must be careful not to set up unreasonable goals. The outcome of instruction is not only for the student to produce the desired response but also to see himself as a capable person. During instruction she should be very encouraging. After several student responses, the teacher should encourage the students and praise them for their effort: "You guys are working hard. This is a tough sound." When a student finally makes two consecutive acceptable responses, the teacher should act very excited and praise the student profusely: "That's great! You did it. I knew you would be able to do it. You didn't give up and you got it right. Great, great, great!!!"

Teachers working with students who have poor enunciation should provide extra practice in imitating sounds. The teacher should do a daily exercise in which students simply imitate sounds the teacher says. The teacher says a sound for several seconds, then has the student say it for several seconds. The teacher, therefore, can introduce a sound in imitating exercises a week or so before it appears in words presented during the auditory tasks.

Signal Errors

In a signal error, students do not begin and/or end their responses when the teacher signals. Teachers should expect some students to need many signal corrections the first several days of isolated sounds instruction. To make learning to follow signals easier during the first few days of instruction, the teacher can exaggerate each part of the signal. After pointing to the letter, the teacher exaggerates the "out" portion of the signal by moving her hand 6 inches from the board, rather than just 3 inches. She can also emphasize when to begin responding by hitting the board to create a "thud," which tells the students to respond. To exaggerate the end of the signal, the teacher moves her hand 6 inches in a quick motion, away from the board.

A second prompt a teacher can use to train students to follow her signals involves varying the interval for holding a sound. Each time the teacher signals the students to respond, she touches under the letter for a different amount of time. For example, the teacher might touch under the letter for 3 seconds the first time, then 1 second, and finally 2 seconds. The purpose is to show the students that they should hold the sound as long as the teacher points to the letter and not for some fixed interval. If the teacher points to every letter for the same amount of time, the students will soon learn to ignore the signal.

During the first few days of sounds instruction, teachers should be effusive with their praise for students learning to follow the signals. Nearly all students can learn to follow sound signals in one or two days if they are motivated. The teacher can make the exercise into a game. The teacher can challenge the students with a statement such as, "I'm going to try to trick you. It's really hard to watch my finger and say the sound just when I'm touching." This game format is usually very motivating for students.

After the first week of instruction, the teacher should correct a signal error the same way as a confusion error: 1) praising a student who responded correctly 2) modeling 3) testing the missed letter by alternating and 4) retesting later in the lesson.

Selecting Examples

The introductory sounds format includes just the letter being introduced. A new letter appears for 2 or 3 consecutive lessons. The discrimination format includes 6 to 8 letters. For the first week or two, selecting examples is easy; all previously introduced sounds are included in the format. After the students know more than 8 letters, the teacher must select which letters to include. Including all the letters introduced so far makes the format too time consuming. The following guidelines can be used to select letters for the discrimination format:

1. a. As a general rule, include the new letter in the discrimination format on the second day the letter appears in the introductory format.
    b. If the new letter being introduced is visually and auditorily similar to

Table 8.5 Sample 4-Day Example Selection Sequence for Letter-Sound Correspondence Tasks

Day	1	2	3	4
Introductory Format	b	b	b	
Discrimination Format	c u h	h o i	b u i	u c b
	l o g	b u l	h a t	o d i
	i a	c r	c l	t f

a previously introduced letter, do not include the similar previously introduced letter in the discrimination format on the lessons in which the new letter appears in the introductory format. Thereafter include the similar letter every day for the next two weeks.

2. Once a new letter is introduced in the discrimination format, it should appear daily for about two weeks.

3. Put extra emphasis on vowels. Include all vowels introduced to date in almost every lesson.

The chart in Table 8.5 demonstrates the integration of example-selection criterion into daily lesson construction. The chart shows the examples that might be included in the introductory and discrimination formats during the time in which the letter *b* is introduced. Note that on days 1, 2, and 3, the letter *d* does not appear in the discrimination format since *b* is appearing in the introductory format. On day 4, the letter *d* appears along with the letter *b*. The teacher concentrates on providing discrimination practice on *b* and *d*, as well as reviewing other earlier introduced letters. Note also the extra review on vowel letters, as well as the consonant *c, l,* and *h* which were recently introduced.

Application Exercises

1. Below are lists of letters in the order they are introduced in several hypothetical reading programs. Next to each letter is the sound value taught for the letter. Write *acceptable* (A) next to the *one* program in which the sequence is acceptable. Write *unacceptable* (U) next to the *one* program that has such severe violations it should not be used with low-performing students. Tell why the sequence is unacceptable. For the other programs, specify the sequencing guideline which is violated in each one and tell what step might be taken to modify it to increase the probability of student success.

Program A

1. a /ă/   2. i /ĭ/   3. e /ĕ/   4. u /ŭ/   5. o /ŏ/   6. b /b/   7. f /f/   8. d /d/

Program B

1. m /m/   2. a /ă/   3. f /f/   4. d /d/   5. s /s/   6. o /ŏ/   7. g /g/   8. h /h/

Program C

1. m /m/   2. M /m/   3. a /ă/   4. A /ă/   5. s /s/   6. S /s/   7. d /d/   8. D /d/

Program D

1. m /m/   2. a /ă/   3. d /d/   4. s /s/   5. i /ĭ/   6. b /b/   7. r /r/   8. n /n/

2. The sequences below indicate the letters *(s, a, m, r,* and *f)* a teacher presented in a sound-discrimination task. Next to each letter is a plus (+) if the student responded correctly or a minus (−) if the student responded incorrectly. For each series of responses, indicate by checking *acceptable* or *unacceptable,* whether the teacher followed the recommended correction procedure. If not, explain the violation.

   Sequence 1—acceptable unacceptable why?
   s+   r+   m+   a−   (teacher corrects) a+   m+   a−   (teacher corrects) a−
   Sequence 2—acceptable unacceptable why?
   s+   a+   m−   (teacher corrects) m+   s+   m+   a+   s+   m+   f+   r+   a+   m+
   Sequence 3—acceptable unacceptable why?
   s+   a−   (teacher corrects) a+   m+   r+   f+   m+   s+   r+   m+

3. The teacher is presenting the sound-discrimination format. The task includes these letters: *m, a, s, d, i, f, c,* and *e.* The student has identified *m, a, s,* and *d* correctly, but then says /ĕ/ for the letter *i.* Specify the steps (including the examples) the teacher should take to correct the error.

4. **a.** Circle the lower-case letters not highly similar to the upper-case letters.
   b. Place an S over each letter that represents a stop sound.

   a   b   c   d   e   f   g   h   i   j   k   l   m   n   o   p   q   r   s   t   u   v   w   x   y   z

5. The letters:

   a   m   t   s   i   f   d   r   o   g   l   h   u   c   b   n   v

   have been presented to a reading group.
   a. A student does not know the letter b. The letter e is the next letter to be introduced. What should the teacher do?
   b. A student does not know the letter i. The letter e is the next letter to be introduced. What should the teacher do?
   c. A student does not know the letters b and t. The letter e is the next letter to be introduced. What should the teacher do?

Chapter

Sounding Out Regular Words

Regular words are words in which each letter represents its most common sound. For example, the word *sat* is regular because the letters *s*, *a*, and *t* each represents its most common sound.

Regular word-reading instruction can begin when students have mastered four to six letter-sound correspondences and the auditory skills of segmenting and telescoping the easiest word types to decode (i.e., CVC words beginning with continuous sounds).

Regular word-reading instruction begins with word list exercises in which students are taught to sound out regular VC and CVC words that begin with continuous sounds. The teacher prompts the students by pointing to the letters in a word as the students blend the sounds together to form a meaningful word. Word-list sounding out is continued for several months. Passage-reading exercises, in which the students read a story, are introduced when they can sound out simple words in lists with relative ease. Passage reading is a more difficult task for students, since they can no longer rely on the teacher to prompt them by pointing to the letters.

Scope and Sequence

The chart in Figure 9.1 summarizes the decoding related content of daily lessons during the early weeks of instruction. Sounding out, auditory preskills, and letter-sound correspondence exercises, as well as letter copying and writing, are included in lessons.

Keep in mind that this scope and sequence chart is based on the assumption that the students begin instruction with no knowledge of these reading-related skills. Students who enter school with some knowledge of these skills will be able to progress at a more accelerated rate.

Note on the chart that the first lessons include only letter-sound correspondences, auditory skills, and letter writing. During the first lessons, students learn not only these skills, but also how to respond to the teacher's signals. Sounding out is not introduced until the students know four to six letter-sound correspondences. All initial sounding out is done with VC- and CVC-regular words that begin with continuous sounds, the easiest type of word. Also note that only a couple of words are presented in the early word-list sounding-out exercises. Students can be expected to need quite a few practice trials before they are able to sound out a new word without distorting the sounds. Few words are included in the initial exercises so that a teacher can bring the students to a high level of performance on sounding out the words. A high level is reached when the students can correctly sound out each word in the task without error.

Passage reading is introduced after students have sufficient practice reading words in lists. Students will differ in the amount of practice they need on sounding out words in lists. Passage reading can be introduced when students can do a 4-word, word-list exercise without making an error. On the chart we recommend that passage reading be introduced 10 days after sounding out is introduced. Remember, it is the students' performance that dictates when new skills are introduced. When a student can perform without error on a format, the teacher can introduce new skills. The chart in Figure 9.1 only shows "average" amounts of time a teacher can expect to present a skill.

Teaching Procedures

Sounding out is initially presented in *word-list* exercises where the teacher writes the words in lists, then prompts the students by pointing in a left-to-right progression to the letters in the words. The students say the sounds as the teacher points to the letters.

Passage reading, in which the students point to and concurrently say the sound in

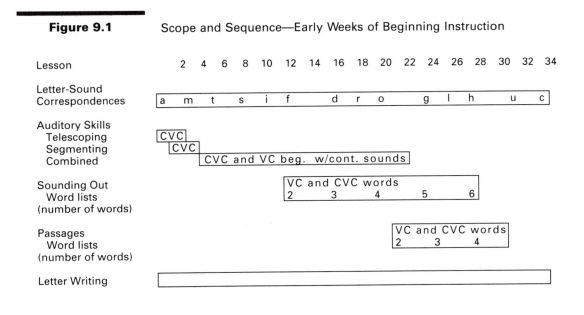

Figure 9.1   Scope and Sequence—Early Weeks of Beginning Instruction

words, is introduced after students master the word-list exercises.

Word Lists

Word lists are the vehicles the teacher uses to introduce and provide initial practice for new word types. Word-list exercises are also used to introduce words that will appear in stories. Words can be written on a chalkboard, overhead, or on a $8\frac{1}{2} \times 11$ sheet of paper. If the teacher writes the words on a sheet of paper, we recommend constructing a display made on one side with a piece of 10×12 cardboard and on the other with a piece of clear acetate. The acetate is fastened to the cardboard on one side and on the bottom. The teacher slips the paper on which the word list is written into the acetate container. The advantage of the container over the chalkboard is that the teacher can hold the acetate container in front of her and point to the words without turning her back to the students.

Guidelines for Constructing Word Lists

- The initial word-list exercise should include only two words since in this initial exercise the students will be learning the mechanics of sounding out and are likely to need a good deal of repetition before they can sound out words correctly.

- The number of words in word lists should increase gradually. The number can be determined by the students' performance. A general rule is to include the number of words the student can be brought to mastery on within a 5-to-7-minute period. Mastery is reached when the students are able to respond consecutively to all the words in a list without making an error.

- Words should include only letters students have mastered in letter-sound correspondence tasks. Mastery is demonstrated when a student does not make an error on a particular sound for two consecutive lessons.

- When a new letter first appears in word-list exercises, that letter should appear in about a third to half of the words in the list.

- Word lists should be construed in an unpredictable manner. Generally the same letter should not appear in the same position for more than two words in a row. For example, a list such as *sat, mit, rut, fat* would be inappropriate since the same letter, *t*, appears in the same final position in all the words. The problem with lists such as this is that such predictability may inadvertently encourage student nonattentiveness as they anticipate rather than examine letters.

The chart in Figure 9.2 illustrates the integration of these example-selection guidelines into daily lessons. The chart shows instances presented in the letter-sound format and the word-list sounding-out format over a 4-lesson period during the sixth week of instruction. The students already know about 15 letter-sound correspondences and have been sounding out words for about 3 weeks. The letter *u* is introduced in the introductory format for letter-sound correspondences in lesson 31. Previously introduced letters are reviewed in the letter-sound discrimination format. The words in the word-list exercise in lesson 31 include only letters previously mastered. Note that the letter *l* appears in three words. The letter *l* was recently introduced and receives more practice. Note also that the letter *u* does not appear in word-list

Lesson	31	32	33	34
Letter-sound Intro	u	u		c
Letter-sound Disc	h l g a i r d f	u a i g h l t	u i r d h l a o	c r o u l h t d
Word-list sounding out	fill	ran	lot	rug
	if	fill	mad	in
	lot	it	lid	lad
	lad	lit	if	mud
	am	mom	Sam	mat

exercises until lesson 34. There is a 3-day period for the students to practice the letter-sound correspondence for *u* before reading words with these letters. Remember that student performance dictates when new skills are introduced. If the students are having difficulty with *u* in the letter-sound correspondence format, words with *u* should not be presented. A final note concerns the word *fill*. Even though *fill* is technically a CVCC word, it is included as an easier word type since it includes only 3 sounds.

Teaching Procedure for Sounding Out Words in Lists

Introductory Format

The format for introducing sounding out appears in Table 9.1. The teacher introduces sounding out by demonstrating (modeling) how to sound out a word. The teacher points to each letter for about $1\frac{1}{2}$ seconds and says the sounds for the respective letters, not pausing between the sounds. Note the similarity between this task and the auditory segmenting skills tasks. The students have learned in the auditory skills task to pronounce a series of sounds without pausing between each sound, and to follow a teacher's signal of when to switch from sound to sound. In the sounding-out task, the students say the sounds when teachers point to the letters. After the teacher models sounding out a word, she has the students respond with her (lead). The purpose of responding with the students is to ensure that they hear the correct response. People who have not worked with young students usually do not realize how difficult sounding out is for them. To read a word, the student says the first sound, then, while saying the first sound, he must examine the next letter to determine its sound. The student then says the next sound without distorting either sound. This is a difficult coordination task for young students. The teacher responds with the students since it is predictable that they will make errors at first. The teacher repeats responding with the students until they appear able to respond correctly without prompting. Then the students respond without any leading (test).

The introductory format is presented daily until the students are able to sound out the words correctly in the format with no more than two practice trials for each word.

Table 9.1   Introductory Format for Sounding Out Words in Lists (Illustrated with the CVC Word Type)

Teacher	Students
(Teacher writes on board: am, fit.)	
1. Teacher states instructions. "Watch. When I touch a letter, I'll say its sound. I'll keep saying the sound until I touch the next letter. I won't stop between sounds."	
2. Teacher *models* sounding out the first word. "My turn to sound out this word." Teacher touches under each letter that represents a continuous sound 1 to $1\frac{1}{2}$ seconds and under letters that represent stop sounds for only an instant. "Aaaammm."	
3. Teacher *leads* students in sounding out the word. Teacher points to left of word. "Sound out this word with me. Get ready." (Signal.) Teacher touches under letters. The teacher sounds out the word with students until they respond correctly.	*"Aaaammm."*
4. Teacher *tests* the students on the first word. Teacher points to left of word. "Your turn. Sound out this word by yourselves. Get ready." (Signal.) Teacher touches under letters.	*"Aaaammm."*
5. Teacher has several students sound out the word individually. "Billy, sound it out. Get ready." (Signal.)	*"Aaaammm."*
6. Teacher repeats steps 2 through 5 with the word *fit*.	

Critical Behaviors

Signaling

An illustrated explanation of the signaling procedure for sounding out appears in Figure 9.3.

Monitoring

The teacher monitors by watching the students' eyes and mouths and by listening to their responses. To coordinate pointing to the letters with watching students is difficult. The teacher should quickly glance at the letters to determine where to point next, and then, look at the students before pointing to the next letter. All these movements are done in an instant. The key is to watch the students' mouths when they say a new sound, since the position of their mouths provides feedback about the correctness of their responses and also informs the teacher whether students are responding.

Pacing

The teacher should point to each letter long enough for the students to say its

Figure 9.3   Signaling Procedure

1. Instructions: Teacher points to the page about an inch to the left of the first letter in the word. "Get ready."

2. The signal for the first sound: Teacher looks at the students to see if they are attending, then quickly touches under the *m*. Teacher holds finger under *m* for about 1 to $1\frac{1}{2}$ seconds.

3. The signal for the second sound: Teacher *quickly* makes a loop, moving his finger from the first letter to the second letter, *a*, and holds his finger under *a* for about 1 to $1\frac{1}{2}$ seconds.

4. The signal for the third sound: Teacher loops *quickly* from *a* to *d* and instantly removes his finger from the page. When signaling for the students to say a stop sound, the teacher touches under the letter for an instant and then moves his hand quickly away from the letter.

sound and look ahead to the next letter. This will be between 1 and $1\frac{1}{2}$ seconds for each continuous sound. Not pointing to a sound for a long enough time is probably the most common mistake teachers make. The importance of allowing adequate time cannot be overstated.

Students may have to sound out a word several times before they can blend the sounds without error. The pacing of these repetitions is important. For each repetition, the teacher says, "Again," points to the left of the word, and then pauses about 2 seconds before beginning the signal.

Shorter pauses before beginning signaling may not give the students time to focus on the beginning of the word.

The teacher can expect more instructionally naive students to need 10 to 15 repetitions on the lead step during the first lessons when sounding out is taught. A great deal of skill is needed to give the children adequate practice and still to make the reading lesson enjoyable for the students. One way to keep lessons enjoyable is to provide little 15 to 20-second breaks after each 5 or so practice trials. During the break, the teacher encourages the students: "You kids are working so hard. These are really hard words and you've almost got them." When the students finally sound out all the words correctly, the teacher should act very excited and proud of the students. "You did it! I'm so proud of you. Let's clap our hands loud so everybody knows what hard workers we are."

Providing the practice students need to respond correctly to all words consecutively in the early days will result in steadily improving student performance. Not providing adequate practice will result only in minimal daily improvement.

Discrimination Format

In the discrimination format (see Table 9.2) for sounding out words in lists, the teacher tests the students on sounding out a set of words. The discrimination format replaces the introductory format when students' performance in the introductory for-

mat indicates they no longer require the teacher to lead. Specifically, after the teacher models sounding out a word in the introductory format, the students can (with generally only 1 or 2 practice trials) sound it out correctly.

Critical Behaviors

Pacing

The students should not be asked to say it "fast" (at the normal rate) until they have sounded out the word acceptably (i.e., saying each sound correctly and not pausing between sounds). The teacher should say, "Say it fast" immediately after the students correctly sound out the word. Any pause makes translating the blended sounds into a word said at a normal rate more difficult. Likewise, in the discrimination format, the teacher should not praise after the students sound out the word, but should hold the praise until after the students say the word at a normal rate.

Table 9.2	Discrimination Format—Sounding Out Words in Lists	
	Teacher	*Students*
1.	Teacher states instructions. "You're going to sound out each word. After you sound out the word correctly, you'll say it fast."	
2.	Teacher points to left of first word. "Sound it out. Get ready." Teacher touches under each letter (except stop sounds) for 1 to $1\frac{1}{2}$ seconds. After the student sounds out the word correctly, the teacher immediately says, "What word?"	
3.	Teacher repeats step 2 with remaining words written on the board.	
4.	Teacher gives individual tests. Teacher calls on several students to sound out a word.	

Individual Turns

Remember, individual turns are given only when the students responding in unison appear to have mastered all the words. Keeping all the students in a group attentive while one student is given an individual turn is very important. The more students are attentive and actively practicing word reading, the faster they will progress.

During individual turns the teacher should tell the other students to read the words to themselves. The teacher can encourage students to read to themselves by initially using effusive praise: "Randy and Ginger are reading to themselves. They are going to be good readers because they are practicing. Let's clap for them."

Correcting Mistakes

Two common errors made during sounding out are pausing between sounds and saying a sound incorrectly. Pausing errors involve the student's stopping between sounds, which can result in the student leaving out a sound when saying the word the fast way. For example, in sounding out the CVC word *sat*, a student pauses between the first and second sounds, "sss (pause) aaat." When translating these blended sounds into a word, the student may leave off the sound preceding the pause, translating "sss (pause) aaat" into "at."

Below is the correction procedure for pausing errors. The teacher:

1. Models. As soon as the teacher hears the error, she says: "Don't stop between sounds. Listen to me sound out the word without stopping." (Teacher points to letters and sounds out the word.)

2. Leads by responding with the students. "Sound it out. Get ready." (Teacher responds with students.)

3. Tests by having the students sound out the word themselves. "Sound it out. Get ready."

4. Returns to the first word in the list and repeats all the words in the list until the students can sound out all the words consecutively without an error. (Note: If there are more than 4 words in a list, the teacher simply returns to a word 4 words earlier in the list rather than to the beginning of the list.)

5. Individual turns. At the completion of list, individual turns are given to students who missed the word.

The teacher should sometimes begin the correction procedure by praising one of the students who responded correctly. "Nice job, Randy. You didn't stop between the sounds."

Teachers sometimes cause pausing errors and sound errors by not pointing long enough to each letter. If the teacher moves too quickly from one letter to the next, some students will not have time to look ahead to the next letter and, consequently, will guess or pause. If students make many of these errors, the teacher should consider whether he is causing the error and try pointing longer. Teachers also sometimes cause student errors by not signaling clearly. Teachers should make certain their signals are not causing student errors.

Sound errors involve the student's saying a sound that is not the most common sound of a letter. In sounding out the word *fat*, a student says the sound /ī/ when the teacher points to the letter *a*.

The correction for sound errors is somewhat different. In correcting a sound error, the teacher uses a limited model, which involves first modeling and testing only the sound missed rather than the entire word. For example, if the teacher points to the letters in *sip* and the student responds "sssaaa," the teacher immediately says "iiii." Next, the teacher points to *i* and asks, "What sound?" The teacher then tests students on the entire word. Below is a sample sounds-correction for a student who said /ă/ for *i* in sounding out the word *sit*.

1. *Limited model.* As soon as the teacher hears the sound error, the teacher says the correct sound, "/iiiii/."
2. *Tests.* The teacher tests the whole group on the missed sound, carefully monitoring individuals who originally made the error. Teacher points to *i*. "What sound?" Teacher signals by touching *i*.
3. *Tests.* The teacher tests the whole group on sounding out the word. "Sound it out. Get ready." (Signal.)
4. The teacher returns to the first word in the list and repeats all the words until the students can correctly sound out each word in the task. (Note: If there are more than 4 words in the list, the teacher just goes back 4 words.)
5. *Individual turns.* At the completion of the list, individual turns are given to students who made errors.

A third type of error that occurs when the teacher is presenting the discriminations involves the student saying the word incorrectly after sounding it out, usually leaving out the initial sound. For example, the student sounds out "sssaat" and when the teacher asks "What word?" the student says "at."

This type of error is usually a result of the student pausing between the first two sounds when sounding out the word (e.g., *sat* is sounded out "ssss [pause] aaaat").

The steps in the correction procedure for this type of error are:

1. The teacher says the word. "That word is *sat*."
2. The teacher models sounding out and saying the word. "My turn. Sssăăăt. What word?" "Sat."
3. The teacher tests and leads if necessary. "Sound it out. Get ready. (Signal.) What word?" (Signal.)
4. The teacher returns to earlier word in list.
5. Individual turns.

Teachers should record the errors students made. Table 9.3 shows a simple recording form that can be used over a week's time. The names of the students in a group are written in the spaces in the left column. Across from each student's name are boxes for each day of the week. The teacher records errors the student made in the appropriate box. If a student makes an error in a letter-sound-correspondence task, the teacher writes the letter and over the letter writes the sound that the student said. In a sounding-out task, the teacher can write the word the student was reading, then write the response the student said over it.

Precorrecting

Precorrecting is a valuable technique for minimizing errors students make in a lesson. In a sounding-out precorrection, the teacher prompts the students on a letter that has caused them difficulty in earlier lessons before having them sound out a word with that letter. For example, if the students were having difficulty with *e*, the teacher would point to *e* in the word *met* before having the students sound out the

Table 9.3   Weekly Record-Keeping Form

Weekly Record Keeping Form

Student	Monday	Tuesday		Wednesday	Thursday	Friday
Bill	(n) m					
Francine	(sad) sid	(t) d	(mit) mid			
José						
Elwin	(i) e	(i) e	(lid) led			
Marcy						

word and ask, "What sound?" The teacher would then have the students sound out the word.

A possible danger with using precorrections is in using them too much, making some students dependent on them. If precorrections are overused, the students will not try to remember difficult sounds because they expect the teacher to identify them. Teachers can avoid developing dependency by precorrecting a sound only for a few lessons. Precorrections are particularly appropriate when new, difficult letters appear in words or when a letter that has caused students difficulty appears in a word.

Introducing New Word Types

Regular words can be classified by type according to their relative difficulty to decode. The types are listed below, according to their relative difficulty—easy to difficult:

- VC and CVC that begin with continuous sounds (e.g., *at, sam*)
- CVCC that begin with continuous sounds (e.g., *runs, lamp, fist*)
- CVC that begin with stop sounds (e.g., *hot, cap*)
- CVCC that begin with stop sounds (e.g., *cast, hand*)
- CCVC in which both of the initial consonants are continuous sounds (e.g., *slap, frog*)
- CCVC in which one of the initial sounds is a stop sound (e.g., *crib, stop*)
- CCVCC words (e.g., *brand, clump*)
- CCCVC and CCCVCC words (e.g., *split, sprint*)

Sounding-out instruction begins with VC and CVC words that start with continuous sounds. Instructionally naive students may require 20–30 lessons of practice with this type of word before they are able to sound out a set of these words with relative ease. Teachers often underestimate the amount of practice needed by lower performing students to become proficient in sounding out words. During these first months of instruction the students will be learning many new letter-sound correspondences. Integrating all the new correspondences when sounding out words requires a great deal of practice. The amount of practice needed will vary from student to student.

The students' performance tells the teacher when the student is ready to learn a new skill. When a student can sound out a set of 4 CVC words beginning with continuous sounds without error on the first trial for two consecutive days, CVCC words beginning with continuous sounds can be introduced. No special teaching procedure is required for introducing CVCC words. The teacher writes 3 CVCC words on the board and uses the introductory sounding-out format. This format is repeated daily until the students can sound out the 3 words with no more than 1 error during the format. Then the introductory format is dropped and CVCC words are included in the discrimination format. Half the words in the discrimination format should be CVC words while the other half should be CVCC words.

Words Beginning with Stop Sounds

CVC words beginning with stop sounds can be introduced when students master CVCC words. Remember, student performance is always the key factor that determines when something new can be introduced.

Several modifications in the teaching procedure are necessary for words that begin with a stop sound. First, the sounding-out signaling procedure has to be modified slightly. The letter for the stop sound is touched for just an instant, followed by a quick movement to the next letter, which is pointed to for slightly longer than usual, about $1\frac{1}{2}$–2 seconds. When modeling how to sound out the word, the teacher does not pause at all between the initial stop sound and vowel. The word *can* would be modeled "caaaannnn" with no pauses. (Note: Words

beginning with the stop sound /h/ often cause students particular difficulty. When words beginning with *h* are introduced, include at least 3 such words in a format, such as *hit*, *hug*, and *him*, to provide massed practice.)

During the first week when stop-sound-first words appear, the teacher can use a precorrection in which she has the students say the sound of the letter following the stop sound before they sound out the word. For example, before the students sound out the word *cut*, the teacher points to *u* and asks, "What sound?" If this precorrection is used, the teacher should have the students sound out the entire word list again later without using the precorrection so that the student does not become overly dependent on the precorrection. Furthermore, the precorrection should not be used for more than one week.

CVCC words beginning with stop sounds (e.g., camp, hunt, test) can be introduced when students are able to sound out CVCC words beginning with continuous sounds and CVC words beginning with stop sounds.

Words Beginning with Blends

Words that begin with initial blends (two consecutive consonants) are introduced next. This type can be divided into words that begin with two continuous sounds (e.g., *snap*, *frog*, *sled*), and words in which one of the initial consonants is a stop sound (e.g., *stop*, *club*, *grab*, *spin*). There are not many regular words that begin with two continuous consonants; moreover, these words will usually not present difficulty for students. Words where one of the two initial consonants is a stop sound, such as *step* and *skin*, will require careful teaching and a great deal of practice.

In addition to providing sounding-out practice, the teacher can also present several supplementary exercises. First is the auditory-skills task in which students telescope a series of blended sounds into a word said at a normal rate. (See pages 77–78.) This auditory exercise should be started a week or so before students begin reading words containing initial blends, then can be continued daily for about two weeks. When presenting the auditory format, the teacher includes words the students will be asked to decode within the next few days.

Precorrections can also be used when words containing blends are first introduced. The precorrection involves the teacher pointing to the letter with which students are likely to have problems. If the word contains a stop sound, the teacher points to the letter following that stop-sound letter (e.g., in *step*, the teacher would point to *e* and in *cram*, *r*). If the word does not contain a stop sound, the teacher would point to the second consonant in the blend (e.g., the teacher would point to *l* in *flap* and *r* in *frog*).

Example selection criteria are very important. Word lists, in the discrimination format, should contain a mix of words from the various types introduced to the current day. About half the words should be of the most recently introduced type and half a mix of words from earlier types. The purpose of the mix is to buttress against students not attending carefully to the letters in a word. For example, if students read lists of words all having the letter *l* as the second letter, some students might become careless and often include the /l/ sound when sounding out a word.

Passage Reading

Passage reading refers to an activity where each student is given a story and expected to read the words orally. Sounding-out passage reading is significantly more difficult than word-list sounding out. In word-list exercises, the teacher points to the letters and the students say the sound in passage. In passage-reading exercises, the student must learn to coordinate independently moving from letter-to-letter and concurrently saying the sounds.

When to Introduce

Sounding-out passage reading can be introduced when students are able to sound out the words in a word-list task with relative ease. This level of mastery would be indicated by the students not making more than 1 error on a 5-word sounding-out word-list task for two consecutive days.

As students progress through the beginning stage, the proportion of the lesson devoted to passage reading gradually increases until late in the beginning stage nearly two-thirds of decoding instruction revolves around passage reading.

Constructing Passages

During the first weeks of passage reading, the passages students read should contain only words that have previously appeared in word-list exercises. Including previously taught words will help make the transition from word-list reading to sounding-out passage reading easier.

Initially the passages should be very short, containing only two to four words. The teacher should expect to correct some students many times when passage reading is introduced. If the initial passages are too long, students may find passage reading too frustrating. The passage length should increase gradually. Passage-reading exercises, during the beginning stage, should be structured so that students are likely to attend to the letters in the words and nothing else. Consequently, picture cues should be avoided because some students will try to use them as an aid in decoding words. A student might look at the first letter in a word, then look at the picture to find an object whose name starts with that letter. For example, when reading the sentence "Tom had a rock," a student might look at a picture, then begin reading "Tim had a . . .," and then, not knowing the /o/ sound in the next word, *rock*, refer to the picture for help in figuring out the word. If the picture shows a child holding a rock, the student is likely to use the picture as a cue for decoding the word. An effective way to avoid problems with pictures is to construct pages so that pictures appear only at the end of the passage. The students see the picture only after they read the passage.

Teaching Procedures

We recommend that students respond in unison, saying each sound as they move their fingers from letter to letter. Words to be read in early passage-reading exercises should be written large enough to allow the student to place his finger under each letter. Passages to be read during the first three weeks should be written with an arrow under each word. The arrows would resemble these:

(A big ball appears at the beginning of each arrow; small dots appear under each letter.) Requiring students to respond in unison and to touch each letter encourages students to apply the sounding-out strategy, fosters attentiveness and maximizes the amount of active practice students receive. Such a procedure is especially important with instructionally naive students, who tend to be very distractible. The touching procedure and unison responding also make monitoring easier, since they

enable the teacher more easily to see and hear students respond. The format for sounding-out passage reading appears in Table 9.4. Note that the signaling procedure for unison responding is difficult to learn. In a teacher-training program at the University of Oregon, numerous hours are spent in preservice, training prospective teachers to use the signaling procedure for conducting unison-response passage reading. If these procedures are not implemented correctly, they will not be productive. It would be more productive simply to call on students to read individually while other students follow along.

Critical Behaviors

Signaling

Because the students are looking at their stories and not at the teacher, the signal for unison responding must be audible. Students cannot look at the passage while simultaneously watching for the teacher's signal. The audible signal we recommend has two parts—a "get ready" and a clap (or finger snap). The "get ready" tells the students to prepare; the clap indicates that they are to begin the response. The critical teacher behavior in making the signal effective is a consistent 1–second pause between the "get ready" and the clap. Consistency is necessary so that students will be able to use the "get ready" as an effective cue by expecting the clap 1 second after they hear "get ready."

During the first days of passage reading, the students may need to sound out each word several times. To ensure that repetitions are done quickly and with little confusion, the teacher must use a clear signal for instructing the students to return to the first letter of a word. The teacher can do this by saying, "Again, back to the big ball of the arrow." After giving this instruction several times, it can be abbreviated to

Table 9.4   Format for Sounding-Out Passage Reading

Teacher	Students
1. "Everybody, touch the big ball for the first word."	*Students touch ball of first arrow.*
2. "We are going to sound out the words. When I clap, touch the first little dot and say the sound above it. Keep on saying it until I clap again, then move your finger and say the next sound. Don't stop between sounds."	
3. "Get ready." Teacher pauses 1 second then claps. After 1 to $1\frac{1}{2}$ seconds, teacher claps for next sound. Then 1 to $1\frac{1}{2}$ seconds later she claps for last sound.	*Students say sounds, pointing to the dots under the letters as they say sounds.*
Step 3 is repeated until the students sound out the word without an error. Then the teacher asks, "What word?"	*Students say the word at a normal rate.*
4. a. "Touch the big ball of the next arrow."	*Students put finger on ball of next arrow.*
b. "Get ready." Teacher pauses 1 second then claps. After 1 to $1\frac{1}{2}$ seconds teacher claps for next sound. Then 1 to $1\frac{1}{2}$ seconds later, she claps for last sound.	*Students say sounds, pointing to dots under the letters as they say sounds.*
c. After students sound out the word without any errors, the teacher asks, "What word?"	*Students say the word at a normal rate.*
5. Teacher repeats step 4 with the remaining words in the sentence.	
6. Teacher repeats steps 4 and 5 with the next sentence.	
7. Teacher gives individual turns. Several students sound out a word or two.	

"Again." The teacher should make certain all the students are touching the ball of the arrow before signaling the group to sound out the word another time.

Monitoring

The monitoring techniques used in sounding-out passages in unison are similar to those a teacher uses in word-list exercises. As in word-list reading, the teacher watches the student's mouth and notes if the student's lip movement is appropriate for each sound. For example, if a student's lips do not come together at the end of the word *ham*, the teacher knows that the student made an error. To say the word *ham*, the lips must be pressed together for the final "mmmmm" sound. The teacher also watches the student's fingers, noting if the student is pointing to the appropriate letter.

Individual turns are also used to monitor a student's performance. As a general rule, individual turns should not be given until the group has read the passage in unison with no errors. Individual turns serve as a check to see if students are actual participants in the group reading (students often become quite good at mimicking other students rather than actually reading), and to see if the teacher has provided enough practice. During individual turns, the students who are not reading should follow along, touching the letters as the reader says the sounds. Since the teacher can hear the responses of the student who is reading, she watches the eyes and fingers of the other students who are following along. The students who are not reading are more likely to be inattentive. To increase the probability of students being attentive, the teacher should instruct the nonreaders to whisper the sounds as they point to them.

Correcting Mistakes

Initially some students will have difficulty following the signal for shifting from letter to letter. The teacher corrects by modeling and, if necessary, by leading (physically moving the student's finger from one letter to the next. Some students may initially require 10 to 20 repetitions before they respond to the signal by touching and saying the next letter. The teacher should use the same techniques discussed in the pacing section (see page 104) to motivate students and to keep them from getting discouraged.

Students may misidentify a sound. The correction is similar to that specified in the word-list reading section. The instant the teacher hears an error, she models the correct sound, and tests by having the students sound out the word again. As the final part of the correction, the teacher has the students return to the beginning of the sentence and reread the sentence. When the students reach the missed word again (after having returned to the beginning of the sentence), they are receiving a delayed test on that word. The purpose of rereading the sentence is to demonstrate to the students that the teacher places a great importance on reading a passage accurately.

If the students miss a sound in a word near the end of a sentence, the teacher can let the students continue reading the sentence, then say, "Let's go back to the beginning of the sentence and read it again with no mistakes." Again, a good deal of teacher skill is required to help students reach a high level of performance and, at the same time, keep the lesson positive and motivating for the students.

Application Exercises

1. (For an aid in doing this exercise, see the word lists in Appendix A.)

  a. Students have been taught to read CVC words that begin with continuous sounds and know the most common sounds for these letters: *f, t, l, m, d, s, r, a, i, o*. List four words that could be included in a word-reading task.

  b. Students have been taught to read CVC words that begin with continuous and stop sounds and know the most common sounds for these letters: *f, l, m, d, t, s, r, h, i, o, a*. Assume the letter *h* has been introduced 3 days earlier. Make a list of 10 words for a word-reading task. Four of the words should include the letter *h*. Three of the words should begin with continuous sounds.

2. The teacher is presenting a word-list sounding-out format. In the following situations, specify what the teacher would do and the wording the teacher would use to correct the student's error when it occurs.

    a. When sounding out the word *mud,* student pauses after saying *m.*

    b. When sounding the word *mud* a student says /i/ when the teacher points to *u.*

3. Assume that you have taught a group of students the following skills:
The most common sound of these individual letters
    a i o u b c d f g h k l m n p r s t v w
How to decode these word types: VC and CVC that begin with continuous sounds; CVC that begin with stop sounds; CVCC that end with consonant blends.

    Circle each of the following words students will not be able to decode. Next to each circled word write the abbreviation for the explanation below that tells why students can not decode the word. These are the possible explanations:

Letter (L)—The word is regular, but a letter the students do not know appears in the word.
Word Type (WT)—The word is a type that has not been taught.
Not Regular (NR)—The word is not regular. Some letter(s) do not represent its most common sound.

jet	_____	rag	_____	said	_____
slim	_____	hot	_____	stand	_____
big	_____	clap	_____	tag	_____
red	_____	put	_____	of	_____
last	_____	best	_____	ramp	_____
trap	_____	list	_____	stop	_____
was	_____	talk	_____	sink	_____
if	_____	Sam	_____	fit	_____

4. The words in a word-reading task are *sam, rid, mad, it, at.* Below are four sequences of examples a teacher presented to different groups. A plus (+) indicates a correct response; a minus (−) indicates an error. (1) Tell whether each sequence represents an acceptable firm up, and (2) explain what is wrong with the unacceptable sequences. Assume all errors were word-identification errors.

    a. Sam (−) (teacher corrects) rid (−) (teacher corrects) mad (−) (teacher corrects if (+) at (+)

    b. Sam + rid + mad + if + at +

    c. Sam + rid + mad − (teacher corrects) Sam + mad − (teacher corrects) Sam + rid + mad + it +

    d. Sam + rid − (teacher corrects) Sam + rid − (teacher corrects) mad + if + at + Sam + if + at +

5. Assume the students know the common sound of the following letters: *a, m, t, s, i, f, d, r, o,* *g, l, h, u, c, b, n.* The teacher has created two word lists that are unacceptable. Examine the word lists below. For each word list, indicate whether the list is *acceptable* or *unacceptable* and explain your answer.

List A	List B	List C
dug	dad	rug
run	rim	bat
hut	den	fin
fun	got	hot
hug	hug	dig

6. List these words according to their relative difficulty to sound out. Provide a brief explanation for your sequence.

lamp, stop, bet, clamp, slam, run, best

7. The students are sounding out the sentence: "Sam sat in mud." When sounding out mud, a student says "a" for *u.* Tell all the steps in the correction procedure. Tell what the teacher says and does.

In sight-reading exercises, the students do not sound out words vocally, but say them at a normal rate. Sight-word reading is introduced in the word-list exercises. Students initially sight read several words they sounded out earlier in the lesson. The number of words in sight-reading exercises increases gradually until the students sight-read all of the words in a list.

Sight-reading words in passages follows the same pattern as sight-reading words in lists. Initially, students might sound out a 10-sentence story, then sight-read 1 of the sentences. The number of sentences a student sight-reads increases gradually until he or she can read the entire story by sight-reading.

Sight-Reading in Word Lists

Sight-reading in word lists may be introduced when students can consistently sound out a set of four CVC words that begin with continuous sounds without an error.

Introducing Sight-Reading in Lists

Two formats—an introductory format and a practice format—can be used to teach sight-reading. The introductory format (see Table 10.1) is designed to teach students to sound out a word to themselves (subvocally), then say it out loud at a normal rate. This format begins with the teacher modeling how to sound out words subvocally, then say the words out loud at a normal rate. The model is followed by a step in which the teacher instructs the students to sound out words to themselves (as she points to the sounds), then say the words out loud at a normal rate. This step is very important, especially for instructionally naive students. It overtly shows them what to do in sight-reading exercises.

Chapter

Sight-Word Reading

Table 10.1	Format for Introducing Sight-Reading Words	
	Teacher	*Students*

Teacher writes on board: sat, mud, fit, sad.

1. Teacher models.
   a. "You are going to read these words without saying the sounds out loud."
   b. "My turn. Watch my mouth. I'll say the sounds to myself, then I'll say the word." Teacher points to the first word, moving lips and whispering each sound as she points to each letter. After saying the sounds subvocally, she says "What word?", signals, and says the word "sat."
   c. Teacher models with one more word.

2. Teacher tests group on all the words.   *Students sound out words, whispering sounds. "Sssaaat."*
   a. "Your turn." Teacher points to left of first letter. "As I point to the letters, sound out this word to yourselves." Teacher loops from letter to letter touching under each continuous sound letter for about one second. "What word? (Signal.)"   *Students say word at normal rate. "Sat."*

   b. Teacher repeats step 2(a) with remaining words in list. Teacher presents the list until students correctly identify all words.

Without this step, some more passive students might not sound out words but rely on guessing. The format is presented daily until the students are able to respond correctly to all words on the first trial for two consecutive days. Then a sight-reading practice exercise where the students practice sight-reading without any teacher prompting replaces the introductory format.

Practicing Sight-Reading in Lists

Table 10.2 contains the format for practicing sight-reading in word lists. In this format, the teacher tells the students to sound out the words to themselves, then say the word the fast way out loud when the signal is given. The students read the list of words at least two times. The goal of the first reading is to have students identify each word within 3 seconds. The goal of the second reading is to have students identify each word with only a 2-second pause.

Critical Behaviors

A critical teaching behavior is deciding how long a pause should be given to enable the students to figure out a word. The goal of the first reading of a list is to enable the students to respond to each word with no

Table 10.2   Practice Format for Sight-Reading Words in Lists

	Teacher	Students
Teacher writes on board: sad, not, fit, am, sun, fin.		

1. "You're going to read these words the fast way. When I point to a word, sound it out to yourself. When I signal, say the word the fast way."

2. Students read words with a 3-second pause.
   a. Teacher points to left of the first word, pauses 3 seconds, then says, "What word?", and signals.   *"Sad."*
   b. The teacher continues the same procedure, as in step 2(a), with the remaining words.

3. Students read entire word list again with a 2 second pause.
   a. Teacher has the students read words again with only a 2-second-pause.

4. Teacher gives individual turns.
   a. Teacher points to word, pauses 2 seconds, then calls on a student.
   b. Teacher repeats step 4(a) with remaining words.

---

more than a 3-second pause before the signal. Some students may need longer than 3 seconds to sound out a word. During the first several weeks, up to 5 seconds can be allowed to let the students figure out a word. After 5 seconds, the teacher should give the signal for the students to respond, even if it appears that not all students have figured out the word. Allowing the students too much time may inadvertently reinforce student indecisiveness. Some students take a long time to figure out a word because they start to sound it out, say 1 or 2 sounds to themselves, then stop and start over again. Allowing too long a period may inadvertently show students that this behavior is acceptable. Remember, the teacher can usually determine what a student is doing by watching the student's mouth.

If any student in the group needs more than 3 seconds to figure out a word in a list,

the teacher should provide extra practice. This is done by either returning to the beginning of the list or returning 4 words earlier in the list, whichever is less, and representing the words. When the words are re-presented, the students receive extra practice. The extra practice is critical to enabling the students to develop adequate fluency.

A problem with repeating a set of words several times is that the students may memorize the words on the page according to their position. If the teacher covered all the words with her hand, the students could say the words. To minimize the possibility of students memorizing the position of words, the teacher can present the words in a different order each time the list is repeated.

The teacher should be certain to keep the student's motivational level high by using praise. Remember, praising students when they respond correctly is a very powerful motivator for young students. When returning to an earlier word in a list, the teacher can make a comment such as, "You certainly are working hard. Let's go back and see if we can read a little faster." Be certain to praise effusively when a student who has had difficulty finally succeeds.

Signals

The teacher points just to the left of a word, pauses to let the students figure out the word, then says, "What word?", and moves her finger using the same out-in motion described earlier for the isolated letter-sound correspondence format (see Figure 8.1).

The teacher should be watching the students when she gives the signal for the students to respond. Watching the students is critical. It enables the teacher to see if the students are attentive and helps to determine if the students made a correct response.

Individual Turns

Keeping students attentive during individual turns is a challenge for the teacher. The teacher should not call on students in a predictable order. Pacing is very important. The teacher points to a word, pauses long enough for all the students to figure out the word, then calls on an individual student to respond. The critical behavior involves allowing enough time for *all* the students to figure out the response, *before* calling on an individual student.

The teacher can make up an activity game such as "I'm going to see if I can trick you. I'll point to a word and give you time to figure it out, then I'll call on someone. You won't know who until I call on you. Don't get tricked." The teacher should strongly praise students who answer correctly immediately when their name is

called. "That was great. You are a hard working reader."

Sometimes teachers call a student's name before pointing to a word. The problem with doing this is that once a student knows that he won't be called on, the student is much less likely to be attentive.

Correcting Mistakes

The correction procedure for misidentification errors involves: giving a limited model identifying the missed sound (e.g., if student says "fat" for *fit*, teacher points to *i* and says, "This says *i*"), having the students sound out the word vocally and say it fast, then returning to an earlier word in the list. The teacher goes back 3 or 4 words and re-presents the words. At the end of the lesson, the teacher retests students individually on any words they have missed.

Below is an example of a limited model-correction procedure. A student said "fat" for *fit*.

1. Teacher gives limited model: (Teacher points to *i*.) "This says *i*. What sound?" (Signal.) "i."
2. Teacher has students sound out word: "Let's sound out the word. Get ready." (Teacher points to left of first letter, pauses, then loops under each letter.) "What word?" (Signal.) "Fit."
3. Teacher goes back several words in the list and repeats the list. "Let's read these words perfectly."

Example Selection

The critieria for constructing word lists to be sight-read is basically the same as for selecting words for sounding-out exercises.

● Words should include only letters that students have demonstrated mastery on in letter-sound correspondence tasks.

- Words should be listed in an unpredictable order. The same letter should not appear in the same position in more than 2 consecutive words.
- Words of a new type should make up one third to one half of the list.

The word-list exercises during the beginning stage will include both sounding-out and sight-reading activities. When sight-word reading is first introduced, the introductory sight-reading format should be presented with just 3 or 4 words the students sounded out earlier in the lesson. The number of words to be sounded out increases gradually over a period of weeks until the students sight-read all the words sounded out earlier in the lesson. In future lessons, the teacher can change the pattern by gradually reducing the number of words that are sounded out. Word-list reading exercises, near the end of the beginning stage, might include 15 words. The students sounds out 5 words of the newest type introduced, then sight-reads all the words. Keeping sounding out alive throughout the beginning stage is important to buttress against the possibility of students adopting guessing strategies.

Table 10.3 includes a summary of the number of words that might be included in word-list exercises throughout the begin-

ning stage. Note that the word-list exercises do *not* grow above 15 words. The reason is that during the beginning stage, most of the practice will be in the form of passage reading.

Passage Reading

Passage reading refers to activities in which students read stories. Sight-word passage reading involves the students reading a story, and saying the words at a normal rate rather than sounding them out vocally.

Introducing Sight-Word Reading

Sight-word passage reading can be introduced when students have had adequate practice with the sight-word list reading to enable them to read the words with no more than a 3-second thinking pause for each word on the first reading.

In sight-reading stories, students simply say the word after the teacher signals. They do not sound out the word vocally. To facilitate the transition from sounding-out to sight-reading passages, the teacher has the students first sound out a passage, then sight-read one or two sentences in the same passage.

A format for introducing sight-reading passages appears in Table 10.4. This format is presented for one week. In this introduc-

Table 10.3	Relationship of Sounding Out and Sight-Reading During Beginning Reading Stage					
Lesson		30	50	70	90	110
Words to be sounded out only		6	8			
Words to be sounded out, then sight read			4	10	6	5
Words to be sight read only					8	10

Table 10.4   Introductory Format for Passage Sight-Reading

Teacher	Students
1. Teacher says, "You're going to read the words in this story the fast way. When I signal, you'll say a word the fast way."	
2. Students read the first sentence, teacher says:	
a. "Touch the first word."	*Students touch under first letter of first word.*
b. "Figure out the word. Move your finger under the sounds and say the sounds to yourself." (Pause up to 3 seconds.)	*Students touch letters and sound out word subvocally.*
"Get ready." (Signal.)	*Students say the first word.*
c. "Next word. Say the sounds to yourself." (Pause up to 3 seconds.)	*Students sound out word subvocally.*
"Get ready." (Signal.)	*Students say the next word.*
d. Teacher repeats step 2(c) with remaining words in the sentence.	
e. Students are to reread the sentence if they needed more than 3 seconds to figure out any word in the sentence.	
3. Teacher repeats step 2 with remaining sentences.	
4. Teacher has individual students read a sentence.	

tory format, the teacher prompts the students to sound out each word to themselves before saying the word. We recommend unison responding to increase student attentiveness. A sentence is reread until the students are able to identify each word in the sentence with no longer than a 3-second pause.

Critical Behaviors

Signaling

When reading a passage, the students are looking at their stories, not at the teacher. The signal for students to respond in sight-word passage reading must be an auditory signal. We recommend the signal begin with the teacher saying, "Get ready," paus-

ing for a second, then making a noise such as a clap or finger snap. The length of time between the "Get ready" and the clap should be consistent. Think of it as hitting a drum. The drummer says, "Get ready," then lifts his drum stick and hits the drum.

Monitoring

The procedures for monitoring unison responding during sight-reading are the same as those used during sounding out: Listen carefully to the students' response, check whether the students are pointing to each word, and watch their lips and eyes.

The teacher should tell students always to keep their eyes on their story. Sometimes students may look up after each word. This looking up slows down the task.

The teacher should praise students for keeping their eyes on the book during the entire story.

Pacing

Immediately after the students say a word correctly, the teacher should say, "Next word." The students are immediately to begin sounding out the next word to themselves. The teacher allows them time to figure out the word, then says, "Get ready," and signals. If the students respond correctly, the teacher immediately says, "Next word," then pauses several seconds to let the students figure out the word. (Teachers should allow for longer pauses for words that occur at the beginning of a new line of print, since students must move their fingers down to the next line and back to the left side of the page to locate the next word.)

Practicing Sight-Word Passage Reading

We recommend that students continue sounding out the words in stories for several weeks after sight-word passage reading is introduced. The purpose is to buttress against the possibility of students adopting a guessing strategy. Students can read half of the story sounding out words, then read the entire story by sight-reading. Table 10.5 contains a format for presenting sight-word passage reading after the first week.

The format has 3 parts. In part 1, the students sight-read the story a sentence at a time in unison. (The teacher no longer prompts the students to sound out the words themselves.) In part 2, the teacher writes on the board any words the students missed during the passage reading and conducts a sight-word-list reading exercise. In part 3, the teacher calls on individual students to read a sentence at a time.

Critical Behaviors

Comprehension

The teacher asks comprehension questions periodically. The comprehension questions should include literal questions such as who, where, what, and when questions, and some simple inferential questions such as, "Why were they sad?"

Adequate Practice

The teacher should provide students with adequate practice to gradually increase their reading rate. The teacher works toward increasing fluency by gradually decreasing the number of seconds allowed to figure out words when conducting sight-word-unison passage reading. During the first weeks of passage sight-reading, students repeat sentences until they are able to read all the words with no longer than a 3-second pause. This translates to an appropriate rate of 20 words per minute. Higher performing students may require few, if any, rereadings to read at this rate. Lower performing students, however, may require numerous repetitions. When the students are able to read at the rate of 20 words per minute without the need of rereading, the teacher can decrease the pause time to about 2 to 2½ seconds (a rate of about 25–30 words per minute). This rate in turn can be increased later by decreasing the pause time to 1½ seconds between words.

Teachers working with lower performing students may note that students need repetitions on virtually every sentence before they are able to read at the specified rate. We strongly recommend scheduling another 15–20 minute reading period later

Table 10.5   Format for Practicing Sight-Reading a Passage

Teacher	Students

Part 1: *Students sight-read story in unison.*

1. Teacher says, "We're going to read the words in the story the fast way. Each time I signal, say a word the fast way."

2. "Touch the beginning of the story." (Pause.)   *Students touch.*

3. "Figure out the first word." (Pause.) "Get ready." (Signal.)   *Students say first word.*

4. **a.** "Next word." (Teacher pauses while students figure out the next word.) "Get ready." (Signal.)
   b. Teacher repeats step 4(a) with remaining words in sentence.
   c. (If students need more than specified pause time for any word or make an error, the teacher has students reread the sentence.)

5. "Touch the first word in the next sentence." (The teacher has the students read the sentences using the same procedure as in steps 3 and 4.)

Part 2: *Teacher firms up missed words.*

1. Teacher writes missed words on the board. The students sound out, then identify each word.

2. Students sight-read the list.

Part 3: *Individual turns*

1. Teacher calls on individual students to read a sentence at a time, asking comprehension questions.

in the day for such students. This practice is necessary to enable the students to develop adequate fluency. Without the extra practice, the students will fall behind their peers. The importance of providing extra practice for students during first grade cannot be emphasized too much. Beginning in second grade, an increasing proportion of school activities (e.g., social studies, science, etc.) are conducted with the whole class. Students who read too slowly may not be able to keep up. Not only may they be subjected to frustration, but they will not be able to benefit from the practice other students receive during these activities.

Motivation

The teaching procedures call for students to reread a sentence if a word is missed or if the students have taken too long to figure out a word. Providing such practice is necessary for students to read a passage fluently and accurately. However, teachers must be prepared to use a combination of techniques to keep students from viewing reading as a dull, repetitive task.

One important technique teachers can use is making the rereading a challenge. If students need to reread a sentence, the teacher challenges them to read better. For example, the teacher might say, "Let's read this sentence again. You did pretty well. I bet you'll do it perfectly this time." The teacher rewards the students when they meet the challenge. Phrasing the challenge positively is important, since it contributes to a positive attitude toward reading. For students who require several rereadings before reading a sentence acceptably, physical rewards, such as handshakes, should be given as well as verbal praise. When rewarding students, the teacher comments on their persistence, saying, for example, "Good reading. You worked hard and didn't give up. You worked till you got it right. I'm proud of you." In addition to using challenges and rewards, teachers can keep rereading from being boring by inserting short breaks after each 5 to 10 minutes of reading. During the break, the teacher can conduct an enjoyable game such as "Simon Says" for about 30 seconds. Remember, that the teacher's most powerful motivation tool is praising students who perform in a desired manner. Praise should always be stated specifically so it's clear to the other students what behaviors the teacher considers important.

Signaling and Pacing in Individual Reading

No signals are necessary during individual reading since the students are not responding in unison. However, to encourage attentiveness, students who are not reading aloud should point to each word as it is read.

The teacher calls on students in an unpredictable order. If students can predict when they will be called on to read, some are likely not to attend until it is almost their turn. Others may look ahead to find "their" sentence and practice it. Sometimes inattentive students should be called on to read again after only one other student has read. This indicates to students that, even though they may have just finished a sentence, they cannot become inattentive because they might be called upon again soon. Students should read only 1 or 2 sentences in a row, since the longer one student reads, the greater the probability some other students will become inattentive. The more inattentive the students in a group, the fewer the number of consecutive sentences any one student should read.

Students should be instructed to stop at periods in order to read in more meaningful units. The pause also enables the teacher to call on a new student to read. The teacher calls on the new student immediately after one student says the last word of a sentence. This quick pace enhances student attentiveness and maintains story continuity.

During individual turns, some students will read in a very quiet voice, making it difficult for other students to follow along. Imploring or nagging a student to read louder will not usually change the student's behavior. Providing strong reinforcement for students who do speak in an acceptably loud voice will often be effective in eliciting louder responses from a student who is reading too quietly. The reinforcement can be in the form of praise after a student reads, such as "Great job, Erika. You read with a big voice," or the teacher can reward the student with a tangible reinforcer (e.g., stickers) at the end of the group session for reading in a "big" voice

Correcting Errors

During unison reading the teacher should make a correction if any student says the wrong word. The correction procedure for misread words during sight-passage reading in the beginning stage is to (1) stop the students; (2) instruct the group or individual to sound out the word, then say it at a normal rate; and (3) direct the students to return to the beginning of the sentence and reread the sentence. For example, if during unison reading the students are reading "A cat went in it," and the teacher hears a student say "was" for *went*. The teacher should say "Everybody, let's sound out the word. Put your finger on the first sound. Get ready." (Signal.) After the students sound out the word correctly, the teacher tells the students to return to the beginning of the sentence and has the student reread the sentence.

The words missed during passage reading should be included in the part 2 firm up and in the next lesson's word-list exercise.

A second type of error that might occur during unison sight-passage reading is the signal error. A student does not respond when the signal is given, either responding an instant after the rest of the group or not at all. The correction procedure for this type of error is the same as for the wrong-word error. The teacher has the students sound out the word, then return to the beginning of the sentence. A teacher must be very careful in handling signal errors. If several students in a group make signal errors, there is the high probability that the teacher is not allowing students adequate time to figure out the word. In such cases, the teacher should increase the amount of time she gives students to figure out words before signaling.

During the first week of unison sight-passage reading, the teacher should make it clear through praise that she wants the students to respond on her signal. She can do this by having the students read the first sentence of a story, continuing to the end of the sentence even if some students make signal errors then effusively praising the students who read on signal: "Mary read great. She said every word when I signaled. Let's clap for Mary." The teacher then challenges the students and repeats the sentence. "I wonder if you can all answer as well as Mary did. This is difficult stuff." The teacher repeats the sentence until all students are responding on signal. Thereafter, the teacher challenges the students: "Let's see if I can trick you on the rest of the story. Let's see if you can answer correctly on signal every time." As a general rule, any signal errors thereafter should be handled by having the group sound out the word, then returning to the beginning of the sentence. To keep the instructional setting positive, the teacher should be very encouraging: "That was a tough word. Let's sound it out . . . Now let's go back to the beginning of the sentence. I bet that word won't trick us again."

Finding the Beginning of a Sentence

A critical part of the story-reading correction procedure is to have the students immediately reread a sentence in which they made an error. After telling the students to sound out the missed word, the teacher instructs the students to go back to the first word in the sentence.

A great deal of time can be saved if the students are able to find the first word of the sentence quickly. A format for teaching this skill appears in Table 10.6. This format should be presented early in the school year. The format has four parts. In part 1, the teacher holds up a story and models how to find the end of a sentence. In part 2, the teacher has the student go through the

Table 10.6   Format for Finding First Word of Sentence

Teacher	*Students*

Part 1:   *Teacher models finding end of sentences.*

1. Teacher holds up a story that is at least 4 sentences long.
2. "You can tell where a sentence ends by looking for a little dot, called a period."
3. (Teacher points to first word in the story.) "This is where the first sentence begins. I'll move my finger and stop at the period."
4. (Teacher moves finger from word to word and stops at the period.) "This period tells us that this is the end of the first sentence."
5. "I'll move my finger from word to word; say 'period' when I get to the next period." (Teacher moves finger from word to word, pointing at the space between each word for an instant.)
6. (Teacher repeats step 5 with remaining sentences.)

Part 2:   *Teacher tests finding end of sentences.*

1. "Put your finger on the first word of the story."
2. "Move your finger from word to word. Stop when you get to the period at the end of the sentence."
3. (Teacher repeats step 2 with remaining sentences.)
4. (Teacher repeats steps 1 through 3 if students had any difficulty.)

Part 3:   *Teacher models finding beginning of sentences.*

1. "I'll show you how to find the beginning of a sentence."
2. (Teacher holds up a story and points to the period at end of the last sentence in the story.) "Here's the end of the last sentence in the story."
3. "Watch me find the beginning of that sentence." (Teacher moves finger from word to word until she reaches the preceding period.) "Here's the period." (Teacher points to word after period.) "This is the first word of that sentence."

Table 10.6   Continued

Teacher	Students

4. "Now I'll find the first word of this sentence." (Teacher points to preceding sentence, moves from word to word, and stops just before period.)

Part 4:   *Students practice finding the beginning of sentences.*

1. "Look at your stories."

2. "Touch the period at the end of the story."

3. "Move your finger back until you come to the first word of that sentence."

4. (Teacher points to last word of sentence.) "Move your finger back until you come to the first word of this sentence."

5. Repeat step 4 with remaining sentences.

story, finding the end of each sentence. During this part, the teacher must monitor the students carefully to make certain they move their fingers word-by-word until they get to the period. Part 2 is presented daily until the students are able to find the end of sentences in a story without making any errors.

Parts 3 and 4 teach the students how to go back and find the first word in a sentence. In Part 3, the teacher models. She holds up a copy of the story and models how to return to the beginning of sentences. In Part 4, the students practice finding the beginning of sentences.

Individual Checkouts for Rate and Accuracy

We recommend that students be tested weekly on reading an entire passage. The individual checkouts begin when the students are sight-reading passages about 40 words in length. The teacher would put in some type of motivator to ensure that students really try (e.g., "If you can read this whole passage in less than 2 minutes with 3 or fewer errors, you'll get two stars on the chart next to your name. If you have trouble, I'll let you practice by yourself and you can try again, for one star.") The individual checkouts will provide valuable information to the teacher. The checkouts will show if the student is receiving adequate practice in developing rate and accuracy. The students should read a story that is of equal length to the stories currently being read. The teacher times the student and records any errors the student made.

Table 10.7 shows a chart that can be used to record student performance over a period of several weeks. The teacher records the time it took each student to read the passage and the words the student missed. This data, along with the data on student performance during daily lessons, will help teachers diagnose and remediate errors.

Table 10.7 Record Form—Individual Checkouts

Student Name	Lesson		Lesson		Lesson	
	Time	Errors	Time	Errors	Time	Errors

Diagnosis and Remediation

A student's performance on individual checkouts will often indicate the need for remediation procedures, either in regard to specific skills or fluency. Teachers should record daily errors on a form like that shown in Table 9.3. Teachers should also use the student's performance on individual checkouts, story reading, and word-list exercises to look for error patterns. Error patterns may indicate that a student needs extra practice on a previously taught component skill or that a teacher is making an error in the way he is presenting a format. A teacher error is indicated if several students in a group are making the same type of mistakes. For example, if several students are responding late during unison reading, the teacher may not be providing adequate time to figure out a word before signaling; thus, he should alter his presentation to provide students with a longer thinking pause.

The type of error patterns teachers should look for in word-reading tasks are specific letter-sound correspondence errors, word-type errors, random-guessing errors, and fluency errors.

Letter-Sound Correspondence Errors

A specific letter-sound correspondence error is indicated when students mispronounce the same letter in several words.

For example, a student says "mat" for *mit*, "hum" for *him*, and "ten" for *tin*. The student's performance seems to indicate that the student does not know the most common sound for the letter *i*. The teacher should test the student individually by asking her to say the sound for *i*. If the student does not know the sound, the letter-sound correspondence should be reintroduced in the next lesson. The teacher presents the letter in an introductory format, then stresses it in a letter-sound-discrimination format for several days. During the days the letter is being reintroduced, the teacher precorrects words containing that letter. In the precorrection, the teacher tells the students the letter's sound before asking them to read words that contain the letter.

After several days, the teacher presents an introductory word list of 3 to 5 words, all containing that particular letter. This list is followed by a discrimination list of 8 to 10 words in which about half of them include the letter students had missed.

Word-Type Errors

A word-type error is indicated when a student misses several words of a particular type. For example, a student says "lam" for *lamp* and "ben" for *bent*. On both words, the student left off the second consonant of a final consonant blend in a CVCC word. To remediate a word-type error, a teacher presents daily word-list reading exercises focusing on that particular word type. She first presents an introductory list of four words, all of which are of that particular type. (For example, if students had difficulty with CVCC words, the teacher might include the words *lamp, sink, bust, bent*, all of which are CVCC.) Next the teacher presents a discrimination list of about eight words. Half the words should be of that particular type. The other half should be from easier types and to provide discrimination practice. A list focusing on CVCC words might include

these words: *sand, tan, bust, bus, bent, can, lamp, men.*

Fluency Errors

If a student reads much more slowly than the rest of the group, he should either be provided with extra practice or be placed in a lower group. The extra practice can be done on isolated letter-sound correspondences, word-list reading and passage reading. Sometimes late responding is caused by a student's lack of ability to say the sounds for letters at a rapid enough rate to sound out words quickly. As a check, the teacher can ask the student to produce the sounds of all letters introduced to date. The teacher then notes the letters the student was unable to recognize instantly and provides practice on them. In addition to extra practice, the teacher can also use a slightly longer thinking pause on word-reading tasks so that the student does not develop a habit of copying the responses of higher-performing students.

Random-Guessing Errors

A random-error pattern is indicated when a student is making errors on more than 10% of the words in exercises, and the errors do not involve a specific letter or word-type pattern. Random-error patterns often simply result from the student's not examining a word carefully. The student might just look at several letters and say any word which contains those letters. Sometimes this guessing is caused by a student not being able to respond at the rate the teacher is signaling. If so, practice should be provided and a longer thinking pause used during group reading. If the student is able to read at the rate the group is reading, the remedy lies in increasing the student's motivation to read accurately. (See Chapter 19 for a discussion on motivational techniques.)

Application Exercises

1. A teacher is having a group of students sight-read the following sentence in unison: "Sam had a big cast." Several students say "cat" when the teacher signals for "cast." Specify all the steps the teacher takes to correct this error. Tell what the teacher says and does,

2. Assume that you have taught a group of students the following skills: Letter-sound relationships:

   a, i, o, u, b, c, d, f, g, h, l, n, m, p, r, s, t, w

   How to decode these word types: VC, CVC, and CVCC words that begin with either continuous or stop sounds:

   a. Circle each of the following words the students will not be able to decode. Next to each of those words write the letters for the explanation below that tells why the student can not decode the word:
   Letter (L)—A letter the students do not know appears in the word.
   Word Type (WT)—The word type has not been taught.
   Not regular (NR)—The word is not regular; a letter(s) does not represent its most common sound.

cop	_____	tin	_____	spot	_____	drug	_____
said	_____	test	_____	mad	_____	kept	_____
last	_____	bust	_____	sip	_____	sand	_____
gram	_____	was	_____	can't	_____	Stan	_____
must	_____	gin	_____	don't	_____	big	_____
had	_____						

   b. The errors for each of the two students below are listed. For each student (1) diagnose the problem, (2) specify whether an isolated letter-sounds task is called for, and (3) construct an introductory word list and a discrimination word list to remediate the problem. Be certain to include only letters the students have been taught.

   Student A
   errors: The word was *tin,* student said "tun."
          The word was *sit,* student said "sat."
   diagnosis:_____
   sound tasks: yes_____no_____
   examples for introductory list_____
   examples for discrimination list_____

   Student B
   errors: The word was *land,* student said "lad."
          The word was *fist,* student said "fit."
   diagnosis:_____
   sound tasks: yes_____no_____
   examples for introductory list_____
   examples for discrimination list_____

c. Below are three word lists a teacher constructed for a practice exercise. Two are unacceptable. Tell why.

List A	List B	List C
bunt	hunt	bent
mint	win	win
hunt	sand	rust
pant	past	sand
lint	wig	will
	till	top

3. A teacher is presenting a practice sight-reading word list exercise with these words: rag, must, sink, fun, fin. The goal of the exercise is for students to identify each word with no longer than a 2-second think pause. When the students come to the word "sink," several students need 4 seconds to figure out the word. Tell what the teacher is to do.

4. In a practice sight-word-list reading exercise, a student says "ham" when the teacher signals for the students to respond to "him." Tell what the teacher says and does to correct this error.

A code-emphasis approach program is carefully controlled to ensure that nearly all words students encounter during the beginning stage contain letter-sound correspondences the students know. When the students encounter a word containing a letter-sound correspondence they do not know, that word is considered an irregular word. There are two types of irregular words:

1. Some words are considered irregular in an early part of a program, but not in a later part because the words contain phonic elements that will be taught in the future. The word *park* is an example of such a word. During the beginning stage, *park* is irregular because the *a* does not represent the /ă/ sound. During the later stages of reading, students will be taught the sound for the letter combination *ar* and will be able to decode the word *park*.

2. Some words will always be considered irregular because they contain letter-sound correspondences unique to that word or a few words. Examples of this type of irregular word include *was, they, none,* and *done.*

When to Introduce

Learning to decode irregular words is an important step for beginning readers because a new strategy is involved. The reader cannot simply sound out a word, then translate the blended sounds into a word. For example, *was* is sounded out as "wwwăăăsss" but is pronounced "wuz."

We recommend delaying the introduction of irregular words until students can sight-read regular CVC words in a list at a rate of about a word every 3 seconds. This

Chapter

11

Irregular Words

rate, though quite slow in terms of the advanced reader, is adequate at the beginning stage to indicate student mastery of the sounding-out skill. The reason for delay in the introduction of irregular words is to make initial reading instruction easier for the students by simply letting them concentrate on the mechanics of sounding out regular words.

Because of the complexity of decoding irregular words, students need a great deal of practice to master each individual word. Therefore, the introduction of the first several irregular words should be carefully spaced out—1 every four to six lessons.

The next 10 or so irregular words can be introduced at a somewhat faster rate of about 1 new word every 3 lessons. The students' performance, of course, is the key determinant of how quickly new irregular words can be introduced. During the introduction of the first 10 irregular words, a new irregular word should not be presented if students miss any previously introduced irregular words in word-list reading or in passage reading.

After several weeks, a teacher can introduce a new irregular word even if a student is having difficulty with a previously introduced irregular word. However, the new word should not be similar to the word the student is having difficulty with. For example, a teacher would not introduce the word *where* if students are having difficulty with *were*, but could introduce *where* if students are having difficulty with *said*. If students are having difficulty with more than one previously introduced word, no new words should be introduced.

Sequence

If a teacher is using a commercial program, the words in upcoming passages will dictate the order that irregular words are introduced. The teacher will introduce irregular words according to the order they appear in the program.

If a teacher is constructing a program, the following factors should be considered when making a sequence: frequency, similarity, type of irregularity, and presence of related words.

Frequency

As a general rule, words that appear more often in children's literature should be introduced before words that appear less often. The sequence of words is not particularly critical as long as the general rule is followed. Appendix B contains a list of 400 high-frequency words.

Similarity

Some irregular words are very similar to other irregular words (e.g., saw-was, of-off, were-where). The introduction of these pairs should be planned so that one of the two words is introduced at least 15 lessons before the other. The separation allows students to master the first word before encountering the second and, thus, decreases the probability of the students confusing them.

Type of Irregularity

After the beginning stage is completed, students begin to learn to decode units of letters. Many letter units are predictable in relation to the sounds they make. Foremost are words that end in a VCE pattern (vowel/consonant/letter e) and have a long vowel sound, as in *hate, like, note*, and words that contain a letter combination usually representing a particular sound (e.g., *ar* in shark, *ea* in seat). A list of common letter combinations appears in Table 16.1.

As a general rule, words that contain a VCE pattern or a letter combination should not be presented as irregular words during the beginning stage, with the exception of very common words such as *name* and *told*. The reason is students will learn generalizable strategies that allow them to decode these words. Spending time in the beginning stage teaching a word as an individual word is not efficient if soon thereafter the students learn a strategy which allows them to decode a wide range of words, one of which is the irregular word.

Related Words

Some irregular words will be related because they have the same letter-sound correspondences. Examples of some common related irregular words appear below:

walk	none	some	other
talk	done	come	mother
chalk			brother
give	to	any	most
live	do	many	post
			ghost

As a general rule, related words should be taught one after another or introduced together.

Teaching Procedure

Two procedures are discussed for introducing irregular words. The first procedure can be used to introduce the first 10 irregular words presented in the program. The second procedure is used to introduce new irregular words after the first 10 words.

The strategy we recommend for introducing the first 10 irregular words involves the student sounding out the word as it is written, then translating that series of sounds into the correct pronunciation. *Was*

is sounded out as "wăăăsss," but is pronounced "wuz." The word *walk* is sounded out as "wwwăăălllk," but is said "wauk." Even though this procedure is somewhat cumbersome, it has several advantages. First, it increases the probability that students will carefully continue to attend to the letters making up a word. It shows students that the same basic strategy (i.e., to start with the first letter, say the sound, then blend the sounds for the remaining letters in left to right sequence, one sound for one letter) can be used to decode all words, even though some are pronounced differently than the blended sounds indicate. Without this demonstration, some students may develop the misrule that since sounding out does not work on some words, it will no longer work on any words. Second, it prepares students for later spelling exercises by demonstrating that students cannot rely solely on how a word sounds to spell out words.

Table 11.1 contains the format for introducing irregular words during the beginning stage. The format starts with a model: The teacher says the irregular word, then sounds it out saying the most common sound for each letter, then says it again as a meaningful word. The teacher then tests the students, asking them to say the word, sound it out, then say the word again as it is pronounced.

Critical Behaviors

Demonstrating

The teacher must clearly demonstrate that the irregular word is pronounced differently than it is sounded out. When sounding out the word, the teacher must say the most common sounds. To keep students from making errors when sounding out a word, the teacher can point to a letter in the word that is pronounced differently

Table 11.1   Introductory Format for Irregular Words

Teacher	Students
1. Teacher tells students a new word, then sounds it out. Teacher points to *was*. "Everybody, this is a funny word. The word is 'was.' What word?" (Signal.)	"Was."
"Listen to me sound out the word." Teacher touches each letter. "Wwwwăăăsss. That's how we sound out the word. But here's how we say it: *was*. How do we say it?" (Teacher touches word.) "Yes, *was*."	"Was."
2. Teacher has students sound out the word and then say it. Teacher points to the left of was. "Now you are going to sound out *was*. Get ready." Teacher touches under each letter for about a second.	"Wwwwăăăsss."
"But how do we say the word?" (Signal.)	"Was."
"Remember, how do we say the word?" (Signal.)	"Was."
3. Teacher gives individual turns on step 2.	

than its most common sound, and ask the students "What sound?" before having the students sound out the word.

Correcting Mistakes in Introductory Format

Students make two types of errors in step 2 of the introductory format: (1) when sounding out the word, they may say the sounds for how the word is pronounced, rather than the most common sound for each letter (e.g., when sounding out the word *was*, the student says /ū/ instead of /ă/ for a); and (2) after sounding out the word, they may say the word as it is sounded out, rather than as it is said (e.g., after sounding out the letters in *was* as "wwwăăăsss," the student says "wăs" instead of "wuz").

The correction procedure for both errors is (1) to model by repeating the task and saying the correct answer; (2) to test; by returning to the beginning of step 2 and (3) to retest by repeating the format later in the lesson. For example:

- Error
  Student says /ū/ when sounding out the word *was*.
  Teacher models.
  My turn to sound out *was*. Listen: Wwwăăăsss.
  Teacher tests.
  Sound out *was*. Get ready. (Signal.) "Wwwăăăsss."
  How do we say the word? (Signal.) "Was."
  Later in the lesson the teacher repeats the format.

- Error
  After sounding out *of*, student responds "ŏf" when the teacher asks,

What word?
Teacher models.
We say of.
What word? (Signal.) "Of."
Teacher tests sounding out and saying word.
Sound out of. Get ready. (Signal.) "Ŏŏŏfff."
How do we say the word? (Signal.) "Of."
Later in the lesson, the teacher repeats the format.

Modified Introductory Format

The procedure for introducing irregular words after the first 10 words have been presented involves the teacher telling the students the word, then having the students repeat the word, spell it by letter names, and say the word again:

1. This word is *giant*. What word? (Signal.)
   "Giant."

2. Spell *giant*. (Signal.)
   "G-i-a-n-t."

3. What word did you spell? (Signal.)
   "Giant."

4. Yes, *giant*.

The purpose of having students spell words is to ensure they attend to the letters in the word. Spelling replaces sounding out because spelling the word allows for a faster-paced presentation. Obviously, this format would not be introduced until the students know the names of all letters. Letter names can be taught after students know the most common sound of all letters.

Facilitating Retention

Students will require considerable exposure to a word before they can be expected to learn it and retain the word. New words should be systematically introduced and practiced.

A new irregular word should be presented daily for 3–4 days using one of the introductory formats. On the third day, the new irregular word is incorporated into a practice sight word-list exercise along with regular words and previously introduced irregular words. The new irregular word appears daily in the word-list exercise until the students are able to identify it correctly for two consecutive days. Then the new irregular word is incorporated into stories to be read in passage-reading exercises; the new word appears at least every second day for several more weeks in either a word-list or passage-reading exercise.

Correcting Mistakes in Sight-Reading

When the teacher asks students to identify an irregular word in a sight-practice word list, students may make two types of misidentification mistakes: (1) saying the word as it is sounded out (saying "wăs" instead of "wuz") or, (2) saying a different word (saying "saw" instead of "wuz"). The correction procedure for either errors is the same:

1. The teacher tells students the word and asks them to repeat it. "This word is *was*. What word?"

2. The teacher has students sound out the word or say its letter names, depending on what procedure was used to introduce the word.

3. The teacher asks how the word is pronounced. "How do we say that word?" or "What word?"

4. The teacher backs up 4 words in the list and has the students reread that part of the list.

5. Later in the lesson, the teacher retests by calling on the student who missed the word to identify it.

If a previously introduced irregular word is missed more than once, it should be reintroduced in the next lesson and stressed in the word-list exercise for several days. For example, if students had trouble with the word *put* in Monday's lesson, the teacher should reintroduce *put* in an introductory format on Tuesday and include it in sight-word list exercises daily until the students correctly identify the word for two consecutive days on the first trial.

The teacher can incorporate a more powerful correction technique into a word-list exercise by using an alternating pattern: The teacher presents the missed irregular word, one of the other words, and then returns to the missed word. She returns to the missed word several times during the task, but each time only after having presented more review words. For example, if the irregular word *said* is in a word list with *was, the, walk,* and *lamp,* and the student misread *said,* the teacher could present the words in this order: *said, was, said, walk, the, said, walk, the, lamp, said.* Note that more words appear between each successive presentation of *said.* The teacher keeps alternating between the missed word and review words until the student is able to identify the new irregular word correctly three times.

Application Exercises

1. Assume that you have taught a group of students the following skills:
   The most common sound for all single letters except *e, b, q, w, x, y,* and *z.*
   How to decode these word types: VC, CVC, CVCC, and CCVC words that begin with continuous or stop sounds.

   a. Circle each of the following words the students will not be able to decode. Next to each of those words, write the abbreviation for the explanation below that tells why the student cannot decode the word.
      • Letter (L)—The word is regular, but contains a letter that the students do not know.
      • Word Type (WT)—The word is a type that has not been taught.
      • Irregular (I)—The word is irregular.

fled	_____	list	_____	you	_____	nest	_____	hot	_____
clap	_____	stamp	_____	slam	_____	rump	_____	slug	_____
push	_____	bet	_____	was	_____	son	_____	stink	_____
led	_____	stop	_____	tint	_____	spot	_____	bent	_____
cut	_____	said	_____	snag	_____	free	_____	home	_____

   b. A teacher circled the errors students made when reading stories. The word above the circled word is what the student said. Your assignment is to first diagnose what skill the student needs help with, then to specify what the teacher would include in the remediation exercise. Remember if a student has difficulty with a particular letter, include isolated-sounds practice and a group of introductory and discrimination words.
      If the problem is with a word type, only introductory and discrimination words are called for.
      Be specific. List the examples you would include in the tasks. Be certain to include only letters students have been taught.

Student 1

            fat   sap

Dan had a flat hat with a snap.

Student 2

                    cot   dad

Tim's hand had a cut on it. His mom did act fast. His mom is not a dud.

Student 3

            fat   lip

Tam has a fast cat. It has a limp.

Student 4

This student missed no words; however, he read quite slowly when given an individual turn. What should the teacher do?

2. This exercise introduces letter combinations (two or more letters which usually represent the same sound(s) in a significant number of words). Although letter combinations will not be discussed until later in the book (Chapter 16), we include them now so the reader may receive adequate practice to develop fluency in recognizing and pronouncing them. Assume the students know the most common sound of all single letters and these letter combinations: *th, sh, ch, ck, ar, ee, ea,* and *or.* Circle any letter or letter combination the students will not be able to decode, which means the word itself is probably not decodable. For example, the *ar* in warm would be circled because it does not represent its most common sound (see list of letter combinations in Table 16.1).

charm	east
par	sea
warm	head
shark	porch
need	worm
been	corn
peek	world
dead	short
weak	chef

3. A teacher is presenting the introductory format for irregular words. In step 2, the teacher has the student sound out "wăs," then asks how the word is pronounced. Some students say "was," pronouncing the word phonetically. Specify what the teacher says and does in correcting.

4. Put a check next to each of the six irregular words below that would not warrant frequent review during the first year of decoding instruction.

knob	was	scent
your	scenic	see
said	good	route
any	of	talk
pry	scarce	they

5. The teacher is presenting a discrimination sight-reading format which includes the words *flag, must, said, him, slip, was.* A student says "sad" for *said.* Specify what the teacher would do and the wording the teacher would use to correct the student's error when it occurs, then tell what the teacher would do after making the correction.

Chapter

12

Vocabulary and Language Skills

All students should receive at least 15 minutes daily instruction during the beginning stage in vocabulary, language, and comprehension skills. This is additional time beyond the 30 to 35 minute block devoted to decoding.

We recommend that the vocabulary, language, and comprehension tasks be presented orally. During the beginning stage, students read only a small fraction of the words in their receptive and expressive vocabularies. Oral instruction introduces a much wider range of concepts than if the teacher limits the instruction to the words students are taught to decode.

The scope of skills presented depends on the student's language skills. Many students do not enter school with adequate vocabulary and sufficient language skills. These beginning readers do not understand the meaning of many words commonly used in directions given by teachers (for example, find the letter *under* the *last* car, touch the *narrow stripe* in the first column, find the letter in the *lower right-hand corner*). For these students, instruction in basic vocabulary and oral language is needed to succeed in reading instruction. For students who enter school with basic language skills, instruction can begin with more advanced concepts such as inferences and reasoning skills.

Vocabulary Teaching

The procedures for teaching vocabulary are critical for teachers working with instructionally naive students. Teaching vocabulary to average and above-average students is relatively easy because these students have a good understanding of language and a sizeable vocabulary. Instructionally naive kindergartners, on the other hand, do not know many common words, have difficulty repeating statements of more than four or five words, and are confused by unclear demonstrations.

Vocabulary can be taught orally by the use of modeling, synonyms, and definitions. Modeling is used when verbal explanations of a new word include words students do not understand. For example, when teaching the preposition *over*, the teacher cannot explain why something is *over* without using the term *over* or a synonym for *over* such as above. Modeling is used primarily to teach the word labels for common objects, actions, and attributes.

Synonyms are used when a student knows a word(s) that can explain the meaning of a new, unknown word. For example, a student knows the word *over* but does not know *above*. Instead of introducing *above* through modeling examples, the teacher tells the students that *above* means *over* and then tests the students to make sure that they understand the synonym. Similarly, if a student knows the meaning of *wet*, the teacher can use a *little wet* to explain the meaning of *damp*. (Note: Initial synonyms do not have to be precise. They must, however, be designed to give students an approximate meaning that can be refined as they encounter the word in later reading.)

Definitions are used when students have adequate language to understand a longer explanation and when the concept is too complicated to be explained through a synonym. The teacher constructs a definition by specifying a small class to which a new word belongs and then by telling how the word differs from other members of the class. For example, a simple definition of *service station* might be "a place where gasoline is sold and cars are repaired." Service station is in the class of *places*. It differs from other places because gas is sold and cars are repaired there. After a definition is given, examples are presented to test the students' understanding of the definition.

Example Selection

The most important aspect of teaching vocabulary, regardless of the procedure used, is selecting a set of appropriate examples. A set of examples is appropriate only if it demonstrates the teacher's intended meaning. A set of examples may be inappropriate if the student learns an interpretation other than the intended one. For example, a thick pen and a thick pencil are presented as examples of *thick*. Since both of these objects are writing tools, some students might interpret *thick* as having something to do with writing rather than with size.

Learning a vocabulary word implies applying the word correctly to a set of examples. When a baby first learns the word *dog*, the baby may think that the word *dog* refers solely to the dog in his house. Through further experience, the child learns to expand his definition of *dog* to a whole set of dogs, many with different appearances. For learning to take place in the classroom, a teacher must provide enough positive examples of a new word so the student can respond to a full range of possibilities.

Selecting examples that show the range of *positive examples* is the first step in constructing a set of examples. To teach the class the word *container*, the positive examples might be a garbage can, a cardboard box, a drawer, and a glass vase. Having this wide variety of positive examples rules out the possibility of the student misconstruing the concept of container as being something square or something made of metal. The examples also set a base for fostering generalization to things not presented in the lesson (e.g., a plastic can or metal box). When teaching the preposition *over* (as in "the pencil is over the table"), the pencil should not just be presented above the center of the table, since young children might think that *over* has something to do with "in the middle" or a height of about 1 foot. To illustrate the full range of possibilities, the teacher presents the pencil in many different positions by holding it an inch or two above the table, then several feet above it, and then over the table's left and right side.

In addition to positive examples, an appropriate set of examples should also include *negative examples*. Negative examples rule out incorrect generalizations. For example, in teaching the concept *pet*, if only positive examples of *pet* were presented (dog, cat, goldfish, canary), some students might generalize that all animals are pets. In presenting the term *vehicle*, some positive examples might include an airplane, truck, boat, plane; negative examples might include a kite and a buoy. When possible, negative and positive examples, which are exactly alike except for the presence or absence of the new concept, should be presented. The positive and negative examples form a pair. Each pair of examples can be referred to as a *minimally different pair*. Minimally different pairs focus student attention on the characteristics that determine whether an example is positive. The advantage of using minimally different pairs is illustrated in the following examples for teaching the color *orange*. A teacher might use these minimally different pairs of objects for teaching *orange*:

1. Two identical shirts, except that one is orange and one is red.

2. Two identical pieces of paper, except that one is orange and one is blue.

3. Two identical plastic disks, except that one is orange and one is brown.

4. Two identical crayons, except that one is orange and one is green.

By varying the color in each pair of objects, the teacher demonstrates the critical characteristics. Misinterpretations that orange has something to do with shape, texture, or size are ruled out. Likewise, any confusion between *orange* and *red* is ruled out by including *red* as a negative example.

Teaching Procedure for Modeling

Modeling is used when it is impossible to use language to explain the meaning of a word. Modeling is used primarily to teach concepts like color, size and shape covered in preschool and kindergarten. Modeling's basic procedure involves three steps: (1) modeling positive and negative examples of the new concept, (2) testing the students on their mastery of the examples for the new word, and (3) presenting different examples of the new word, along with examples of other previously taught words. As in decoding, review should be cumulative. Newly introduced words should be reviewed heavily at first by appearing daily for at least two or three lessons, then less frequently by appearing every other day for a week or two, and then intermittently thereafter. Also, as in the case of introducing new decoding skills, the introduction rate of vocabulary words is dependent on the students' mastery of previously introduced words.

Table 12.1 includes object, color, adverb, and adjective formats for teaching basic vocabulary. Each format has three basic steps: model, test, and integrated test. Each format contains positive and negative examples and instructional wording. The examples in each presentation were selected to show the range of positive examples and eliminate possible incorrect generalizations. For example, in teaching *mitten* the positive examples vary in color and material, showing that color and material are irrelevant to whether an object is a mitten. Also, minimally different positive

Table 12.1   Format for Teaching Vocabulary: Modeling Examples

	Object	Adjective (Color)	Adverb	Adjective (Texture)
Step 1: *Teacher models positive and negative examples.*	"This is a mitten" or "This is not a mitten." *Examples:* brown wool mitten brown wool glove red nylon glove red nylon mitten blue sock blue mitten	"This is orange" or "This is not orange." *Examples:* 2" red disk 2" orange disk 4x4" orange paper 4x4" brown paper	"This is writing carefully" or "This is not writing carefully." *Examples:* write on board, first neatly, then sloppily hang up coat, first carefully, then carelessly arrange books, first carelessly, then carefully	"This is rough." *Examples:* red flannel shirt red silk shirt piece of sandpaper piece of paper smooth book cover rough book cover
Step 2: *Teacher tests.* Present positive and negative examples until the students make six consecutive correct responses.	"Is this a mitten or not a mitten?"	"Is this orange or not orange?"	"Is this _____ carefully or not carefully?"	"Is this rough or not rough?"
Step 3: *Teacher tests by asking for names.* Present examples until students make six consecutive correct responses.	"What is this?" glove mitten sock mitten mitten glove	"What color is this?" orange brown orange red	"Show me how you _____ carefully." or "Tell me about how I'm writing" (quickly, slowly, carefully, etc.)	"Find the _____ that is rough." or "Tell me about this shirt" (rough, red, pretty, etc.)

and negative pairs are included (e.g., a mitten and a glove of the same size, material, and shape). Similarly, the positive examples of the color *orange* in Table 12.1 include a range of objects and minimally different positive and negative examples. Also, note the minimum use of language. Teacher talk is minimized to facilitate pacing and student attentiveness.

The students are tested by asking them to respond to the object as an example or not an example of the new concept (e.g., *heavy* vs. *not heavy*). Requiring students to say "heavy" or "not heavy" provides better practice than a "yes/no" response when the question "Is this heavy?" is presented.

Critical Behaviors

Modeling. When modeling, examples must be presented rapidly in order to keep a student's attention. The teacher should present the examples in a lively fashion, stressing the key words: "This is a *mitten.*" "This is *not* a *mitten.*"

Testing the New Word. The teacher presents the task until students can respond correctly in consecutive order to a group of at least 3 positive and 3 negative examples (6 in all). A teacher can conclude only *after* students make correct responses to all the positive and negative examples that the students understand the new word. Examples should not be presented in a predictable order. Never use a yes-no-yes, no-yes-no pattern. Vary the number of consecutive positive and negative instances.

Teaching Procedure for Synonyms

Teaching new vocabulary through synonyms is similar to the procedure of teaching modeling examples, except that the teacher first equates a new word (*huge*)

with a known word(s) (*very big*) rather than modeling examples. The teacher gives the synonym: "Here's a new word, *huge*. Huge means very big." Next, the teacher tests a set of positive and negative examples for the new word saying, "Tell me if it is huge or not huge." Then, the teacher provides practice in applying several recently taught synonyms: "Is this huge? Is this damp? Is this tiny? Find the one that is huge." The purpose of this review is to build retention.

The selection of synonyms must be made very carefully. Students *must* understand the meaning of the familiar word because it is intended to "explain" the new word. It is inappropriate to use the term *textile* to explain *fabric* because most students do not understand the synonym *textile*. On the other hand, using the synonym *strong* to explain *sturdy* is reasonable because most students know the meaning of *strong*.

Teachers can find potential words to use for synonyms by referring to a dictionary or thesaurus. One or more of the words will probably be familiar to students and appropriate to use.

Table 12.2 illustrates a synonym teaching format with the word *sturdy*. The major steps include the teacher presenting the synonym, testing positive and negative examples, and then reviewing the new word and previously introduced words.

Teaching Procedure for Definitions

The third procedure for teaching vocabulary is through definitions. Although definitions can be constructed in several ways, we will focus on a procedure that is applicable to most words and suited to most young students. The procedure includes two steps:

1. Identifying a small class to which a word belongs.
2. Stating how the word differs from other members of that class.

Table 12.2   Format for Teaching Vocabulary Through Synonyms

	Teacher	Students

1. Teacher states the new word and the equivalent, familiar word and then tests.
   a. "Here is a new word. Sturdy. Sturdy means strong."
   b. "What does sturdy mean?" (Signal.)   *"Strong."*

2. Teacher presents positive and negative examples until the students make 6 consecutive correct responses. Examples are not repeated in the same order.
   a. "Tom leaned against a pole. The pole fell over. Was the pole sturdy or not sturdy?" (Signal.)   *"Not sturdy."*
   b. "Tom leaned against another pole. The pole didn't move. Was the pole sturdy or not sturdy?" (Signal.)   *"Sturdy."*
   c. "A house didn't shake at all in a high windstorm. Was the house sturdy or not sturdy?" (Signal.)   *"Sturdy."*
   d. "A different house fell down when the wind started blowing. Was the house sturdy or not sturdy?" (Signal.)   *"Not sturdy."*
   Note: The teacher can also provide practice by asking the students to generate examples. "Tell me about something that is sturdy."

3. Teacher reviews new word and other previously introduced words.
   a. "Is it mild out today? How do you know?"
   b. "Is that bench sturdy? How do you know?"
   c. "Is my desk tidy? How do you know?"

In constructing definitions, teachers must make them understandable to students, rather than make them technically correct. For example, a *liquid* might be defined as something poured. Although scientists might disapprove of this definition, it is adequate to teach the meaning of *liquid* to young children. Definitions are also kept understandable by using words that students understand.

Some sample definitions appear below. Note the effort to keep them as simple as possible.

		Class	Differs from other things in the class
1.	Container:	an object	you can put things in
2.	Vehicle:	an object	that can take you places
3.	Seam:	a place	where 2 pieces of material are sewn together
4.	Glare:	to look	at someone as if you are angry

Table 12.3   Format for Teaching Vocabulary with Definitions

Teacher	Students
1. Teacher states the new word and its definition and has students say definition.	
a. "An exit is a door that leads out of a building."	
b. "What is an exit?" (Signal.)	*"A door that leads out of a building."*
2. Teacher presents positive and negative examples.	
a. Teacher holds up a picture or points to an open closet door. "Is this an exit or not an exit?" (Signal.)	*"Not an exit."*
"How do you know?"	*"It doesn't lead out of the building."*
b. Teacher holds up a picture of a movie theater, points to an open exit door and asks, "Is this an exit or not an exit?" (Signal.)	*"An exit."*
"How do you know?"	*"It leads out of the building."*
c. Teacher continues presenting examples until the students answer six consecutive questions correctly.	
3. Teacher reviews words recently introduced.	
a. Teacher holds up picture of barracks. "What is this?" (Signal.)	*"A barracks."*
"How do you know?"	*"It's a building full of bunk beds."*
b. Teacher holds up a picture of an exit. "What is this? How do you know?" etc.	

The format for teaching vocabulary through definitions appears in Table 12.3. First, the teacher tells the students the definition and has them repeat it. Second, the teacher tests the students on positive and negative examples to ensure that students understand the definition and that they are not just memorizing a series of words that has no meaning. Third, review of previously introduced words is presented.

Written Vocabulary Exercises

During the beginning reading stage, written vocabulary exercises usually involve students selecting a word or phrase that defines a picture. A student may either: (1) look at a picture and select a word, (2) read a word and select a picture, or (3) answer a question based on an attribute of the object illustrated in the picture. Each type of exercise is illustrated in Figure 12.1.

The simplest type of picture-related vocabulary item is multiple choice with one obviously correct alternative. Items increase in difficulty as more alternatives seem reasonable, even though only one answer is correct. For example, a picture shows a young boy. The answers are: boy, kitten, man. A student may think that *man*

Figure 12.1

(1) Picture to label   (2) Label to picture   (3) Attribute of picture

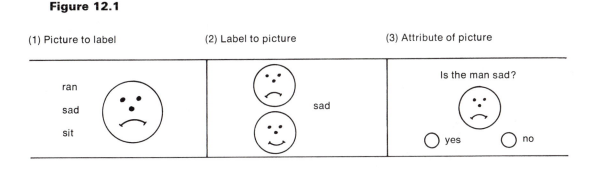

is correct. However, the correct answer is *boy* because the person in the illustration is young. Vocabulary items are also more difficult when they ask about object attributes rather than object names. In Figure 12.2 item a, which involves naming an object, is easier than item b, in which the students must identify an attribute of an object. In item b, the student must make the association between pillow and soft.

Many students can work this simple type of picture-related item without any teacher guidance. Obviously, these students do not need the teaching procedure. However, instructionally naive students need directed teaching. Students should be led through several structured examples daily for 2 or 3 days. The items should include only words that are labels for objects. The teacher (1) asks the students what they see in the picture, (2) tells them to touch and read each word, and (3) asks if the picture shows that word. Students should be taught to examine all the choices in a multiple-choice exercise before selecting the correct answer, preparing them for more difficult items that contain more than one plausible answer.

A significant proportion of students will need directed teaching on items that involve object characteristics. For example, an item shows a picture of a pillow and has the words *set, soft,* and *still* under the picture. The teacher first has the students say the name of the object in the picture and decode each word, asking if that word names the object. Next, the teacher tells the students that since no word names the object, one of the words must tell about the object. The teacher has the students decode each word and asks, "Is a pillow _____?" The students must

Figure 12.2

a)   b)

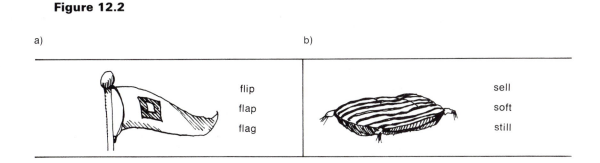

know the vocabulary words used in the task (e.g., the students must know the meaning of *soft*).

Language Skills

Beginning language teaching should include not only vocabulary, but also a multitude of other skills such as plurals, pronouns, classification, polar concepts, information, and reasoning.

In this section, we'll discuss just three language skills to exemplify the activities that should be included in the curriculum for instructionally naive students. The skills are statement repetition, sentence comprehension, and similarity comparisons. We'll conclude with a discussion of how language and vocabulary skills are presented in commercial programs.

Statement Repetition

Statement repetition refers to a student's ability to say verbatim a statement by the teacher. Instructionally naive students typically have difficulty repeating statements verbatim. In kindergarten it would not be unusual to find a significant number of students who could not repeat the sentence "The big tree does not have round leaves."

The inability to repeat statements often handicaps students in the later grades when they attempt comprehension activities. The students have difficulty studying because they cannot say sentences to themselves accurately.

Teachers should test statement repetition ability during the first school week by asking students to repeat several 6 to 10 word sentences (e.g., A little boy walked to the store yesterday; my friend has a big dog and a little cat). If a student does not repeat the sentence correctly, the teacher repeats it again and asks the student to say it again.

Students who are not able to repeat the sentence correctly within two trials will need practice on statement repetition. Such practice should consist of short drills (3 to 5 minutes) in which students practice saying statements. Practice should start on sentences of a length a word or two longer than those a student can say without error.

Teaching Procedure

Providing sufficient practice is the key to improving statement repetition performance. Table 12.4 presents a format. The teacher first models by saying the statement and then tests by asking the students to repeat it. If the students are unable to say the statement, the teacher says it again, stressing deleted or mispronounced words. After two such corrections, the teacher can lead the students by responding with them. The teacher might say the statement several more times. Then the teacher judges how closely the students are repeating the statement correctly. If they need only a few more trials, the teacher continues modeling and leading. On the other hand, if the students appear to need many more trials, the teacher uses a part firming technique in which the teacher first models, leads, and tests on just the first part of the statement and then the entire statement. The final step in the format is modeling the statement in a normal speaking manner and testing the students on saying the statement in a normal fashion. Without this final step, students may develop a stilted, singsong way of saying statements.

Critical Behaviors

Modeling and Pacing.   Each word in the sentence should be said at a normal pace. Teachers have a tendency to speak slowly in statement repetition tasks. A slow model

Table 12.4   Format for Statement Repetition

Teacher	Students
1. **a.** Teacher models and tests entire statement. "Listen. The little cat is under the old table. Say that." (Signal.)	
b. If students cannot say the statement, the teacher repeats step 1(a), stressing words the students left out. "The *little* cat is under *the old* table." Say it.	
c. If students cannot say the statement after several attempts, the teacher goes on to step 2.	
2. **a.** Teacher models, leads, and tests, saying the entire statement. "Listen. The little cat is under *the old* table. Say it with me." (Signal.) "The *little* cat is under *the old* table."	*"The little cat is under the old table."*
b. If the students cannot say the statement after several leads, the teacher goes on to step 3.	
3. **a.** Teacher models, leads, and tests on the first part of the statement and has students repeat it. "Listen. The *little* cat is under." (Signal.) "Say it with me." (Signal.) "The little cat is under." "Say it by yourselves." (Signal.)	*"The little cat is under."* *"The little cat is under."* *"The little cat is under."*
b. Teacher models, leads, and tests, saying the entire statement. "Listen. The little cat is under *the old* table. Say it with me." (Signal.) "The *little* cat is under *the old* table."	*"The little cat is under the old table."*
c. Teacher models and tests, saying the statement at a normal pace. "Listen, the little cat is under the old table. Say it by yourselves." (Signal.)	*"The little cat is under the old table."*

makes repeating the statement more difficult for the students.

Correcting Mistakes. When the teacher models the entire statement, some students may leave out a word. For example, the teacher says, "This ball is not big," but the student says, "This ball not big." The correction procedure is to model the statement again, stressing the word left out, "This ball *is* not big."

A second type of error involves mispronunciation. If the word is 1 or 2 syllables, the teacher corrects by stressing the missed sound. If the student says "ba" instead of "bat," the teacher says "bat," stressing the final /t/ sound. If the student says "mid" instead of "mud," the teacher says "mud," stressing the /u/ sound. If the word is more than 2 syllables, the teacher can use a part firming procedure: model, lead, and test on the first part of the word, and then the entire word. For example, if a student has difficulty saying the word *experiment*, the teacher could model, lead, and test on "experi," then *experiment*.

Sentence Comprehension

Introducing Question Words

Sentence comprehension begins with exercises to teach students how to identify *what* happened in a sentence, *who* was involved, *when* the event happened, *where* the event occurred, and *why* the event occurred. Who, what, when, where, and why are referred to as question words.

Students should be able to repeat five-to-seven-word statements (e.g., The boy ran in the park, The girl hit the ball) before questions about sentences are introduced. If students cannot retain the information in a sentence long enough in order to repeat that sentence, they are unlikely to remember the information from the sentence needed to answer simple *who* or *what* questions.

The rate for introducing new question words is determined by student performance. A new question word is not introduced until the students have mastered questions involving previously introduced question words.

Sequence

Who and *what* questions (see Table 12.5) should be presented first because they are easiest: "John went to the store. Who went to the store?" "John." "What did John do?" "Went to the store." *Where* and *when* can be introduced next. And *how* and *why* are introduced later because they are more difficult.

When students answer *who* and *what* questions without difficulty, *where* questions can be introduced. A phrase telling

---

Table 12.5   Format for Introducing Question Words *Who* and *What*

Teacher	Students
1. Teacher models. "John ran in the park. Who ran in the park? John. What did John do? Ran in the park."	
2. Teacher provides practice and tests.	
a. "Listen. Tom fell off his bed. Say that." (Signal.)	*"Tom fell off his bed."*
b. "Who fell off the bed?" (Signal.)	*"Tom."*
c. "What did Tom do?" (Signal.)	*"Fell off the bed."*
3. Teacher repeats steps 2(a-c) with these sentences and questions:	
a. Ann hit the ball. Say that. (Signal.)	*"Ann hit the ball."*
Who hit the ball? (Signal.)	*"Ann."*
What did Ann do? (Signal.)	*"Hit the ball."*
b. The cat ate the food. Say that. (Signal.)	*"The cat ate the food."*
Who ate the food? (Signal.)	*"The cat."*
What did the cat do? (Signal.)	*"Ate the food."*
c. The dog jumped up and down. Say that. (Signal.)	*"The dog jumped up and down."*
Who jumped up and down? (Signal.)	*"The dog."*
What did the dog do? (Signal.)	*"Jumped up and down."*

---

where would be inserted in each sentence and a *where* question asked in addition to the *who* and *what* questions.

For example:
Sentence: A girl played soccer in the park.
Questions: Who played soccer?
What did a girl do?
Where did the girl play soccer?

When students are able to answer the who, what, and where questions without difficulty, *when* phrases can be introduced. Table 12.6 includes a format for presenting *when* and *where* phrases.

After students can discriminate between *when* and *where* phrases, they can be introduced to *when* and *where* questions. The teacher uses all four question words to do this (see Table 12.7).

The next step is to introduce *how*. The procedure for doing this is to model the answer for one or two *how* questions and then test the students on a series of sentences (see Table 12.8).

The last step is to introduce *why* (see Table 12.9). The procedure for teaching *why* is similar to the procedure for teaching earlier question words because the teacher gives examples with *why* and then provides discrimination practice. A teacher should not always include the word *because* in sentences that call for a response to a *why* questions, since students may acquire a misrule that *because* is the only word that tells why. To prevent students from learning this misrule, teachers include examples containing *to* (He went home to get his coat), *since* (He ran home since it was late), and finally *and* (He fell down and cried).

After several days of practice on *why* questions, they can be introduced into exercises that include other question word items.

Similarity Comparisons

Similarity comparisons involve examining several objects or actions and determining

---

Table 12.6   Format for Introducing Question Words *When* and *Where*

Teacher	Students
1. Teacher models.	
a. "I'll say phrases that tell *when*. Yesterday morning tells when. Last night tells when. Before it got dark tells when. After dinner tells when."	
b. "Now I'll say phrases that tell *where*. In the park tells where. At the beach tells where. On my chair tells where. Under the couch tells where."	
2. Teacher tests. "I'll say a phrase. You say if it tells when or where."	
a. "In the park." (Signal.)	"Where."
b. "After dinner." (Signal.)	"When."
c. "Yesterday morning." (Signal.)	"When."
d. "On my chair." (Signal.)	"Where"
e. "At the beach." (Signal.)	"Where."
f. "Last night." (Signal.)	"When."

Table 12.7   Format for Using Four Question Words

Teacher	Students
1. Teacher says, "John played in the park yesterday morning. Say the sentence." (Signal.)	*"John played in the park yesterday morning."*
a. "Who played in the park?" (Signal.)	*"John."*
b. "What did John do in the park?" (Signal.)	*"Played."*
c. "Where did John play?" (Signal.)	*"In the park."*
d. "When did John play?" (Signal.)	*"Yesterday morning."*

ways they may or may not be similar. Student success on similarity comparison items is particularly dependent on the student's knowledge of the common dimensions between objects and events. Some major dimensions are listed below:

1. *Classification* (A knife and a saw are the same because they are both tools.)
2. *Use* (A knife and a saw are the same because they both cut.)
3. *Materials* (A knife and a brush are the same because their handles are often made of wood.)
4. *Parts* (A knife and a saw are the same because they both have handles.)
5. *Location* (A toothbrush and a hairbrush are the same because they are both found in a bathroom.)
6. *Attributes* (Many objects are the same because of their shape, color, and texture.)

If students are not knowledgeable about the dimensions relevant to the comparison of items, they will not understand the item. For example, if students do not know the class of tools or that a knife and a brush both have handles, they will fail an item that asks how a knife and a brush are the same.

The first step in teaching similarity comparisons involves expanding the stu-

Table 12.8   Format for Introducing *How*

Teacher	Students
1. Teacher models. "She ran like a deer. How did she run? Like a deer."	
2. Teacher tests.	
a. "He worked quickly. How did he work?" (Signal.)	*"Quickly."*
b. "He wrote carefully. How did he write?" (Signal.)	*"Carefully."*
c. "They worked like dogs. How did they work?" (Signal.)	*"Like dogs."*

Table 12.9   Format for Introducing *Why*

Teacher	Students
1. Teacher models. "He cried because he was hungry. Why did he cry? He was hungry."	
2. Teacher provides practice and tests.	
a. "Since she was late to school, she ran. Why did she run?" (Signal.)	"She was late."
b. "He went home to get his coat. Why did he go home?" (Signal.)	"To get his coat."
c. "She tried her best and won the race. Why did she win the race?" (Signal.)	"She tried her best."
d. "They lost because they made mistakes. Why did they lose?" (Signal.)	"They made mistakes."

dents' understanding of *same* by showing them that things are the same when they possess similar attributes. Many students understand the concept *same* in a limited sense (i.e., whether two objects look alike). Table 12.10 includes a format designed to expand the students' understanding of *same*.

Students have more trouble with items when asked how two objects differ than they do with items that ask how objects are the same. This difficulty is sometimes caused by the students not knowing what *different* means and sometimes by a lack of vocabulary. The format in Table 12.11 presents the concept of *different*. Note how similar it is to the format for teaching how objects are the same.

Commercial Programs

Although all basal reading programs include exercises designed to teach vocabulary and language skills, none of these programs provides for the comprehensive and systematic teaching of language skills instructionally naive students need to learn

at an optimal rate. Most programs use inappropriate teaching demonstrations and provide insufficient practice.

Major modifications are necessary to make basal reading programs suitable tools for teaching naive students vocabulary and oral language skills. Modifying the vocabulary and oral language component of a program is much more difficult than modifying the decoding component of a program, since constructing demonstrations to teach the meaning of a new word can require many illustrations or objects. Our suggestion is not to modify the vocabulary and language teaching component of reading programs, but to obtain a program specifically designed to teach vocabulary and language skills to instructionally naive students. When selecting a program, teachers should spend most of their time examining *how* the programs teach skills, rather than determining what skills are taught, since most programs cover basically the same content. Teachers should look at individual lessons, noting the formats and examples used. The wording in the formats should be simple and direct. The examples,

Table 12.10   Format for Teaching the Concept of *Same*

	Teacher	Students
1.	Teacher says, "Let's see some ways a chair and a table are the same."	
a.	"Does a chair have legs?" (Signal.)	*"Yes."*
	"Does a table have legs?" (Signal.)	*"Yes."*
	"So a chair and a table are the same because they both have legs. A chair and a table are the same because they both . . ." (Signal.)	*"Have legs."*
b.	"Can a chair be made of wood?" (Signal.)	*"Yes."*
	"Can a table be made of wood?" (Signal.)	*"Yes."*
	"So a table and a chair are the same becuase they both . . ." (Signal.)	*"Can be made of wood."*
c.	"Is a chair in the class of furniture?" (Signal.)	*"Yes."*
	"Is a table in the class of furniture?" (Signal.)	*"Yes."*
	"So a table and a chair are the same because they are both . . ." (Signal.)	*"In the class of furniture."*
d.	"Name three ways a chair and a table are the same." Teacher calls on individuals and accepts appropriate answers.	

as mentioned earlier, are critical. Example selection is the key to effectively teaching vocabulary. Note if positive and negative examples are provided. If the program does not provide adequate examples, it will not be effective with instructionally naive students.

After looking at the way several tasks are constructed, teachers should look at 5 to 10 consecutive lessons to see how many times each new skill or word is reviewed. The purpose is to determine the adequacy of initial practice and review. If a new skill or word is not reviewed, many students will not learn it. Programs with inadequate review are difficult to modify.

In summary, examine a beginning-language program by looking at *how* it teaches language skills and vocabulary rather than by looking at what it claims to teach. Look at (1) the language used in the formats, (2) the adequacy of example selection, and (3) the provision for review.

An example of an effectively constructed program designed to teach basic vocabulary and language skills is the DISTAR Language Series. This series is designed to be taught independently of decoding; thus, it can be used in conjunction with any commercial reading program. The program begins by teaching simple vocabulary (e.g., words like *big, red, in, on*) and expressive-language tasks (e.g., teaching students to say statements like "The ball is not big"), and it eventually teaches complex reasoning and inference skills. Two levels of the program can be used during the beginning stage. Level 1 is

Table 12.11   Format for Teaching the Concept of *Different*

	Teacher	Students

1. Teacher says, "Let's see how a chair and a table are different."

a. "Does a chair have a back?" (Signal.) → *"Yes."*
"Does a table have a back?" (Signal.) → *"No."*
"So a table and a chair are different because a chair has a back but a table doesn't."

b. "Do you usually sit on a chair?" (Signal.) → *"Yes."*
"Do you usually sit on a table?" (Signal.) → *"No."*
"So a table and a chair are different because . . ." (Signal.) → *"You sit on a chair but you don't sit on a table."*

c. "Does a table have a top?" (Signal.) → *"Yes."*
"Does a chair have a top?" (Signal.) → *"No."*
"So a chair and a table are different because . . ." (Signal.) → *"A table has a top but a chair doesn't."*

d. "Tell me three ways a chair and a table are different." Teacher calls on individuals.

e. "Now tell me some ways a chair and a table are the same." Teacher calls on individuals and accepts appropriate answers.

---

used with instructionally naive students because it stresses basic vocabulary teaching and expressive language. Level 2 is used with average and above-average students during beginning reading. It stresses reasoning skills, rather than basic vocabulary. Level 2 is used with instructionally naive students after they complete Level 1.

DISTAR Language I is unique because it provides for cumulative introduction and practice of skills (as new skills are introduced, previously introduced skills are reviewed) and introduces new material at a realistic rate. For example, prepositions are introduced at the rate of about one each 5-10 lessons; *on* appears in lesson 28, *over* in lesson 31, *in front of* in lesson 36, *in* in lesson 47, *in back of* in lesson 57, *under* in lesson 67, *next to* in lesson 76, and *between* in lesson 86. When a new preposition is introduced, previously taught ones are reviewed.

The DISTAR Language I program also uniquely emphasizes expressive language. Tasks range from early ones designed to identify statements (e.g., "This is a dog," or "This is not a dog") to more complex statements (e.g., "This rabbit will eat the big apple that has leaves."). Simple reasoning skills are also introduced in Level 1. Level 2 reviews the vocabulary from Level 1 and presents more complex reasoning tasks like absurdities, descriptions, definitions, multiple classifications, and analogies.

Application Exercises

1. For each of the following sets of examples, specify at least one misinterpretation a student might learn.

    a. *rough*
negative examples: desk top and mirror
positive examples: wool shirt and burlap bag

    b. *narrow*
positive examples: a picture of a narrow European street and a narrow alley next to the school, with buildings on each side.
negative examples: none

    c. *vehicle*
positive examples: 4-door sedan, 2-door sedan hatchback
negative examples: none

2. Assume you are working with young children (5–6 years old). Tell which method—examples only, synonyms, or definitions—you would use to teach the following words. (A synonym can be a word or a phrase.)

    a. avoid

    b. damp

    c. striped

    d. in

    e. between

    f. delivery truck

    g. cashier

3. On the following picture-comprehension item, the student makes this wrong response: How would you determine what caused the error?

4. Specify the correction procedure for the following error:

    a. The teacher asks students to repeat this statement: The old man is walking the little dog. A student says, "The man walking dog."

5. Assume that a group of students knows the most common sound for all individual letters and the most common sound for the following letter combinations: *ai, ar, ay, ch, ea, ee, ing, oa, or, ou, sh,* and *th.* Underline every letter that the students will not be able to decode:

spout	some	peach	round	chef
boat	broad	gain	pour	mind
walk	tough	chord	starch	hound
again	round	steak	put	been
much	stain	gray	park	road
bread	street	beach	groan	storm
four	strap	steel	torn	none

6. Construct a set of 8 examples to teach the concept "tall." Half the examples should be positive examples and half negative examples. Specify the teacher wording in presenting and testing the examples you constructed to teach "tall."

Chapter

Using
Commercial
Materials: The
Beginning
Reading Stage

asal reading programs are the teacher's main tool in providing reading instruction for her students. Basal reading programs are complete packages of teaching materials, organized by grade level, with most programs beginning at kindergarten and continuing through eighth grade. Currently, there are about fifteen basal reading programs available.

Most basal readers will need varying degrees of modification to make them suitable tools for teaching the instructionally naive student. This section discusses when and how to make these modifications with kindergarten and first-grade level materials.

Kindergarten/Readiness

Nearly all basal reading materials have a set of materials designated as kindergarten or readiness materials. The materials include a teacher presentation book, a student workbook, and various charts and displays.

The kindergarten/readiness levels, as a rule, have serious instructional design deficits which hamper their effectiveness in presenting instruction to the instructionally naive student. One way to critique the kindergarten/readiness materials is to say "They provide too little of too much." So many skills are presented that adequate practice to develop mastery is not provided. The lack of practice also results in skills being introduced too fast.

A second major problem with the basal kindergarten/readiness programs is the relatively sophisticated use of language used to present concepts. Suggested teacher explanations utilize terms and sentence structures which can be difficult for naive students to comprehend. Similarly, suggested activities often assume that students have mastered component skills not taught in the program, which naive students are unlikely to possess.

A more in-depth look at the manner in which kindergarten-level basal materials present letter-sound correspondences, auditory skills, word-attack skills, and language and vocabulary skills follows. The discussion of the kindergarten materials concludes with recommendations for the use of these materials.

Letter-Sound Correspondence

We recommended that students be taught the most common sound of letters prior to the names of letters. We also recommended introducing lower-case letters before upper-case letters.

Both these recommendations are not followed in typical basal programs. Letter names and letter-sound correspondences, as well as upper and lower-case letters, are often simultaneously introduced.

A second recommendation involves carefully sequencing the introduction of letters in an order that decreases the probability of students having difficulty. This guideline is often not adhered to. For examples, in the readiness level of the Ginn Reading Program (© 1987), the first letter-sound correspondences introduced are for the letters *m, t, c, b, n, k, d, s,* and *g.* Note that two pairs of similar letters (*b* and *d, m* and *n*) are introduced relatively near each other.

A third recommendation is to provide systematic practice and review. This guideline is extremely important to fostering student retention. Most programs had serious practice and review problems; in particular, after the initial presentation of a letter-sound correspondence it was not unusual to see that letter not presented again for weeks. For example, in Houghton Mifflin Reading (© 1987), letter-sound correspondences are presented in the readiness

level in sets of 4 letter-sound correspondences. The sound for the letter *j* is taught in Lesson 56 and practiced daily until Lesson 63. However, throughout the next 62 lessons of the 125-lesson program, there are only a couple of activities that review the *j* letter-sound correspondence.

Auditory Skills

In Chapter 7 we described two skills, segmenting and telescoping, that were component skills of sounding out.

Most basal programs do not present tasks similar to the auditory tasks described in Chapter 7. Instead, auditory tasks of relatively complex natures are presented. In a typical task the teacher says two words, then asks the students if the words begin with the same sound. Similar tasks in which the teacher asks about the middle and final sound also are presented. In these tasks, the student is assumed to be able to isolate the sound within the context of the word. The report of the Commission on Reading pointed out the problem with such tasks:

> Children who do not already have some idea of the sounds in the letters in *sit* may not be able to single out the short i sound when they hear the word spoken. Hence when the teacher tells the children that the letter *i* has the sound you hear in the middle of *sit*, they may not be able to make the connection. (p. 40)

The tasks also tend to be wordy and potentially confusing for the instructionally naive student. A typical task taken from Lesson 3 of the Ginn Reading Program directs the teacher to tell the students that the teacher will describe a turkey. The teacher's guide then directs the teacher to tell the students that if the word that describes the turkey begins with the same sound as the word turkey, they should lift the letter *t* and trace the letter in the air. The teacher's guide presents the sentence "Is it a tall turkey?" emphasizing the words *tall and turkey*. Then, using the same sentence form, the teacher substitutes the following words for *tall*: tired, muddy, terrible, tough, little, and tiny. The activity concludes with the teacher writing on the board all the words that begin with *t*. The teacher reads each word, then asks a pupil to circle the *t* at the beginning of the word. Activities such as this can inadvertently teach students the misrule that looking at only the first letter of a word can help you decode the word.

Word Attack Skills

We recommended that word attack skills instruction in the form of sounding out begin when the students know 6 to 8 letter-sound correspondences. The reasons we made this recommendation were: (1) students need a lot of practice to master sounding out; (2) students who learn 6 to 8 letter-sound correspondences and can master the auditory telescoping and segmenting skills have the preskills needed to begin sounding out; and (3) starting sounding-out instruction as early as possible will help the instructionally naive student to progress at a rate that enables him/her to master decoding at an early age and, thus, be able to participate fully in the whole-class instruction in the later grades.

Sounding-out exercises also serve as an important vehicle for reviewing letter-sound correspondences. Each time students sound out a word, they are practicing the letter-sound correspondences. The review helps the students develop automaticity.

The kindergarten/readiness programs do not teach sounding out. Some introduce about 15 irregular, high-frequency words. Houghton Mifflin Reading (© 1986) introduced the words: *go, I, to, a, we, can, not, you, will*, and *help*. Note that in each of the four words where the letter *o* appears, it represents a different sound. The methods for introducing the irregular words used a mixture of phonic and contextual analysis. For example, to introduce the word *we*, the Houghton Mifflin program recommends that the teacher place a word card with the word *we* in a pocket chart, then say, "This word begins with the sound for *w*, the sound you hear at the beginning of *worm*. I'm going to read a sentence and leave out this word. Think of a word that makes sense and begins with the sound for *w*. Listen: He won't see us if _____ hid behind the chair" (p. 365). Tasks such as these have the potential to confuse instructionally naive students because the tasks make extensive use of language.

Language Skills

The kindergarten/readiness programs usually present a wide range of language activities. Lack of careful control of teacher wording, inadequate example selection, and inadequate review characterize the language teaching. For example, the Scribner Reading Series introduces the prepositions *above* and *below* in Lesson 21 of the kindergarten/readiness book. Then, with the exception of a review exercise on Lesson 23, does not present the concept again in the 92-lesson program.

Recommendations

Decoding

Discussing the use of the kindergarten/readiness programs brings to light another important question: When should word reading instruction begin? This question is particularly relevant for students in lower socio-economic areas. We recommend that formal reading instruction begin in kindergarten. Even though kindergarten students may not progress as rapidly through a reading program as first grade students will, they will receive a substantial head start. They will enter first grade with a set of reading skills they would not otherwise possess.

Since younger students are more instructionally naive, the instruction provided to kindergarten students must incorporate sound instructional design principles. The teacher's wording and examples presented should be carefully controlled. SRA Reading Mastery I program (© 1988) provides an example of an instructional program which carefully incorporates instructional design principles.

Kindergarten teachers may find themselves in a situation where the use of a particular kindergarten/readiness program that is not instructionally sound is mandated. In such instances, we recommend incorporating Direct Instruction principles into the use of the materials.

Letter-sound correspondences can be taught, using the principles specified in Chapter 8. Preparing letter-sound correspondence exercises is not very time consuming. The teacher can follow the order letters are introduced in the basal program, unless there are serious violations of sequencing principles (e.g., *b* and *d* are being introduced too near in sequence). Serious sequencing violations should be remedied by altering the sequence. If upper- and lower-case letters are introduced simultaneously, the teacher can delay the introduction of the dissimilar upper-case letters. Letter names can be introduced when the students know the sounds of most of the letters.

Auditory Skills

The teacher should present telescoping and segmenting skills early in the school year

and continue presenting them throughout the year, introducing more difficult word types when the students master easier word types. Rhyming also should be introduced when the students can do telescoping and segmenting without difficulty.

A typical workbook activity in a kindergarten basal program will ask students to indicate if the object represented by a picture begins or ends with a particular sound. For example, a worksheet might have pictures of a frog, a hat, and a rug. The student is asked to circle the words that end with the same sound the word *dog* ends with.

The value of these exercises is questionable. Does learning to do the exercises really prepare students to read? There is no empirical evidence to support their use. If a teacher does present the tasks, she should be prepared to modify the wordings of teacher directions and provide extra vocabulary teaching.

A teacher cannot assume that students understand what is meant by first, middle, and last sound. Nor can she assume students can extract a sound from a word.

A preskill exercise involves teaching the students to segment a word the teacher says at a normal rate (i.e., the teacher says "rug", the students say "rrrruuuug"). The teacher presents this skill through modeling and testing.

> My turn to say the sounds in the word *rug*.
> *Rug*. Listen: *Rrrrruuuug*.
> You're going to say the sounds in the word *rug*. Get ready. (Teacher signals by lifting one finger at a time.)
> *Rrrrruuuuug*.

The teacher models and tests on several words, then simply tests on several words. The exercise is continued daily until the students can respond correctly to 4 words presented without a teacher model. Next a new exercise can be introduced in which the teacher says a word slowly, then identifies the first, middle, and last sound (see example at bottom of page).

These preskill exercises will give the teacher an effective correction procedure to use if a student makes an error on the workbook exercise.

Word-Attack Skills

We recommended teaching students to sound out regular words. When the students know 6 to 8 letter-sound correspondences, the teacher can use the procedures specified in Chapter 9. The teacher would begin sounding-out instruction with VC and CVC words that start with continuous sounds and contain letters that have already been introduced.

Language Skills

Most reading programs contain language and vocabulary activities inappropriate for instructionally naive students. Major modifications are necessary to make most commercial reading programs suitable for teaching these students vocabulary and oral language skills. Modifying the vocabulary and language component of a program is much more difficult than modifying the decoding component of a program since constructing demonstrations to teach the meaning of a new word may require many illustrations or objects. Our suggestion is not to modify the language and vocabulary component of kindergarten programs, but rather to obtain an instructionally sound program such as DISTAR-Language to use as a vehicle for teaching vocabulary and language skills.

First Grade Programs

This part will be divided into discussions of code-emphasis programs and meaning-emphasis programs.

A code-emphasis reading program controls the introduction of words so that new words are composed of letter-sound correspondences that have been taught previously. Words that do not contain previously introduced letter-sound correspondences are treated as irregular words and constitute a small percentage of the words introduced in the early lessons.

A meaning-emphasis program does not control the introduction of words according to the regularity of the letter-sound correspondences in the words. Letter-sound correspondences are not a factor the au-

Teacher	Students
My turn. Listen: *mmmuuud.*	
The first sound is /m/.	
The middle sound is /ŭ/.	
The last sound is /d/.	
Your turn. Say the sounds in mud.	
Get ready. (Signal.)	"Mmmmuuud."
What's the first sound? (Signal.)	"Mmmm."
What's the middle sound? (Signal.)	"Uuuu."
What's the last sound? (Signal.)	"D."

thors use in constructing stories in early lessons.

Code-emphasis Programs

There are two basic types of code-emphasis programs: programs that use *explicit* phonics and programs that use *implicit* phonics.

The approach described in this text exemplifies *explicit* phonics. Sounds associated with letters are identified in isolation, then blended together to form words.

In implicit-phonics instruction, the sound associated with a letter is never supposed to be pronounced in isolation. To introduce a new letter-sound correspondence, the teacher typically writes a list of words on the board that begin with the same sound, then asks the students how the words are similar. For example, the teacher writes the words *map, mud*, and *meal* on the board, then elicits from the students that the letter *m* stands for the sound you hear at the beginning of the words.

A major problem with implicit-phonics programs is that they introduce new word types without enough practice for the students to develop mastery of easy-type words. For example, Table 13.1 shows the words introduced in the first 22 lessons of the Scribner program (a popular implicit-phonics program). Note the high number of words of the more difficult type.

Instructionally naive students entering school with no reading skills typically need at least three to six weeks of instruction to master sounding out VC and CVC words that begin with continuous sounds and to begin making the transition from sounding out to sight-reading.

Explicit-phonics programs typically introduce new word types at a more realistic rate. We recommend that teachers using a code-emphasis program carefully examine the first 20 lessons of the program. If sounding out is not taught and new word types are introduced too quickly, the teacher should delay instruction in that program and

Table 13.1		Words Introduced in First 22 Lessons of Scribner Program			
VC & CVC Continuous		**CVC Stop**	**CVCC**	**CCVC**	**CCVCC**
an	nap	Dan	ramp	drum	stand
Nan	map	Dad	nips	drip	stamp
Ann	in	pan	naps	drop	
ran	rip	pad	pumps	drops	
and	us	pup	pants	trip	
add	miss	dump	dust	stop	
run	pass	pump	must	spot	
am	mop	pin	past		
mad	of	did			
mud	it	dip			
up	sat	mops			
	sit	tip			
	ant	to			
	not	pass			

present a preprogram that teaches students the sounding-out word-attack skills.

The depth and length of the preprogram would depend on the skills the students possess when entering first grade. Students who know most letter-sound correspondences may need only a couple of weeks of practice to master sounding out and make the transition to sight-reading. A 20-lesson preprogram appears in Appendix C. The preprogram in Appendix C outlines the examples that might be used in teaching auditory skills, letter-sound correspondences, and word-attack skills. Teachers working with higher performing students may be able to complete several lessons a day.

Students who enter first grade with knowledge of 10 or fewer letter-sound correspondences will need significantly more instruction. Ideally we recommend the use of a well-constructed, thoroughly tested explicit-phonics program with these students. The SRA Reading Mastery I program incorporates the principles discussed in this book. The program was carefully field tested and is part of a sequential series that progresses through a sixth level. A second alternative is to use a supplementary program designed to teach explicit phonics to the beginning reader. One such program was constructed by three teachers who read the first edition of this text. They spent several years developing a set of teacher and student materials for teaching beginning reading skills. The program is entitled *The BEST Phonics Program*. (Information on this program can be obtained by writing to: Jerry Silbert, P.O. Box 10459, Eugene, Oregon, 97440.) Upon completing the preprogram, students should be placed in a basal program lesson that contains only the letter-sound correspondences and word types the students have learned.

The teacher should be prepared to modify the teacher presentation techniques suggested in the teacher's guide. The teacher presentation suggestions in implicit-phonics programs are often too wordy and discourage a high degree of attentiveness by the students. Letter-sound correspondences are introduced in exercises in which the students listen to sets of words and determine if they begin or end with the same sound; e.g., "Listen as I say two words. If both words end with the same sound as *pig*, raise your left hand. Bug, dog" (Scribner, p. 50). Word-reading exercises introduce words by telling the students the word, then asking them questions about which letter stands for the sound at the beginning of the word, the middle of the word, and the end of the word. Passage reading is sometimes done silently.

Here are some suggestions for presenting lessons from code-emphasis programs. The first step is to examine the words in the upcoming five lessons. The teacher notes (1) any regular-word types more difficult than the types previously introduced; (2) irregular words; and (3) new letter-sound correspondences to be introduced.

The teacher then constructs tasks for the daily lessons. Each lesson should have the following parts:

1. Letter-Sound Correspondence Task.
   Introduce and review letter-sound correspondences using the procedures in Chapter 8.

2. Auditory Skills.
   Present a telescoping and segmenting exercise in which difficult type words to be introduced in the near future in word-list exercises are practiced. (Use procedures in Chapter 7.)

3. Word-List Exercises.
   Construct word lists that contain regular words to be introduced in upcoming stories. Focus on words with newly introduced letters and

words of the more-difficult type. Sound out some words and sight-read some words. (Use procedures in Chapters 9 and 10.)

4. **Irregular Words.**
Introduce irregular words several lessons before they appear in passages. After the first 10 to 15 words have been introduced, the teacher no longer needs to sound out irregular words, but can say the word and have the students spell the words (assuming the students know letter names). See Chapter 11.

5. **Passage Reading.**
Incorporate the procedures in Chapters 9 and 10. The students should read the story twice. In the first reading, the teacher concentrates on decoding. In the second reading, the teacher concentrates on decoding and comprehension.

Meaning-emphasis Programs

Sight-word reading begins in the initial lessons of first-grade meaning-emphasis programs. Between one-half and three-fourths of the words students encounter initially will be irregular words. This high level of irregularity makes it virtually impossible for the teacher to present any clear, overt word reading strategy to the students. It is not unusual to see a high proportion of instructionally naive students and a substantial proportion of average-performing students flounder in meaning-emphasis programs. Students typically overrely on context or picture cues and develop guessing strategies.

We strongly suggest that any student who enters first grade unable to read at least 50 words be placed in an instructionally sound code-emphasis program instead of a meaning-emphasis program.

The more instructionally naive the student, the longer the student should remain in the code-emphasis program. Ideally, students should remain in the code-emphasis program until they can (1) decode all types of regular words; (2) know the most common sound of all single letters, several common letter combinations (th, sh, wh, ch, ar, ea) and several affixes (er, ing, ed, est, y, le); (3) read words with these letter combinations and affixes; and (4) apply the CVCe rule involving the initial vowel representing its name in words (e.g., *ride* and *hope*). (Note: Procedures for teaching these skills are discussed in Chapters 16 and 17.)

When the students know the skills described above, the teacher will be more readily able to provide a successful experience for the students in the meaning-emphasis program. We have found that placing the students at an early lesson in the meaning-emphasis program makes the transition from code-emphasis the smoothest. Even in the early lessons of a meaning-emphasis program, students will encounter CVCe words with letter combinations and words with affixes. The students will practice these word types as they read the early stories.

Using the Basal Reading Program

We recommended that students not be placed in most basal reading first-grade materials until the students have learned varying degrees of word attack skills. In this part, we shall discuss how to incorporate direct instructional principles into teaching lessons from basal reading programs.

Progressing at an Optimal Rate

A critical teaching skill for both code- and meaning-emphasis programs is knowing how to move a group at an optimal rate. A rate is optimal when a teacher spends no more time on a task than necessary for students to master it. The students' performance dictates the rate of progress. On the one hand, if students require a substantial number of corrections before successfully completing a lesson, the teacher will not be able to present more than a lesson a day. On the other hand, if students are able to complete the tasks in a lesson with few corrections or repetitions, the teacher can proceed at a faster rate than a lesson each day.

There are two ways in which a teacher can present more than a lesson a day. One is simply to present the tasks from several lessons in the time set aside for one lesson. The other way is to skip lessons. Teachers can skip lessons if they see that students have little difficulty with the tasks in a current lesson and that no new skills are introduced in the following lesson. The teacher then skips to the next lesson in which a new skill is introduced. She can continue skipping until the students' performance on a skill indicates they need the continued practice on that skill rather than an introduction of a new skill.

Teachers should be careful to take both rate and accuracy into consideration before deciding to skip lessons. Skipping a student who performs accurately, but is slow in responding, would be inappropriate.

Monitoring, Diagnosis, and Remediation

Monitoring is a critical teacher skill to ensure that all students are, in fact, mastering the skills the teacher is presenting.

During group instruction, a teacher monitors by looking at and listening to students and by giving individual turns. In addition to the monitoring done during group instruction, teachers should set up a supplementary individual testing system in which weekly or biweekly in-depth tests of students' performance are given. The tests should include all the letters, sounds, and irregular words introduced to date, as well as five regular words of the most recently introduced word type.

Administering comprehensive individual tests is time consuming. The average classroom teacher does not have time to give more than one or two tests daily and, thus, can only test students about once a month. If possible, teachers should use a volunteer, parent, or an older student to administer the tests.

The teacher makes the test by writing the letters and words on a sheet of paper, then writing the same words and letters on a group-answer form similar to that in Table 13.2.

When administering the tests, the tester writes a plus (+) across from each letter or word said correctly and a minus (−) across from each letter or word said incorrectly. For each error, the tester writes in what the student says. If the student does not answer, the tester writes NR (No Response). If the student responds correctly, but takes longer than a second to produce a sound, the tester marks an L (Late) in the space across from that letter. If a student identifies a word correctly, but takes longer than 3 seconds to figure out the word, the tester marks an L in the space across from the word.

The teacher should use the results of the comprehensive individual tests in evaluating his teaching, in regrouping students, and in planning remediation lessons. A teacher can use the results to evaluate his teaching by noting how well the group as a whole performs. If several students perform below a 85% accuracy criterion, the teacher must improve daily monitoring procedures to ensure tasks are repeated until students have mastered them. Similarly, if several students in the

Table 13.2   Group-answer Form

Letters, Sounds, and Words	Students		
	1/25/89	1/25/89	1/25/89
Letters/Sounds	Jim	Sarah	Tammy
m	+	+	+
a	+	+	+
s	+	+	+ L
d	+	+	+ L
f	+	+	+
l	+	+	+ L
r	+	+	+
t	+	+	+
c	− NR	+	+ L
o	+	+	+
n	+	+	+
g	+	+	+
b	+	+	+
u	+	+	− ŏ
k	+	+	+
Irregulars			
was	+	+	+ L
put	+ L	+	+ L
pull	+	+	+ L
walk	+	+	+ L
said	+ L	+	− sad
Regulars			
last	+	+	+ L
cent	+	+	+ L
ask	+	+	+ L
lift	+	+	+ L
sand	+	+	+ L

group respond late to more than one or two letters or words, the teacher is probably not providing enough practice.

The results of the individual tests may also help to regroup students. If one or two students perform significantly more poorly than the other students in the group, the teacher should consider either placing these students in a lower performing group or providing them with extra practice to improve their performance. Conversely, students who are noticeably more fluent in reading words than other students in their group may be considered for placement in a higher performing group.

The third way teachers can use the tests' results is by planning lessons to remedy specific skill deficits. If several members of a group miss more than 2 or 3 letters or words, the teacher should consider not progressing in the program, but rather, repeating several lessons and concentrating on deficits. If the students' accuracy is high, but they answer slowly, the teacher should concentrate on providing the practice needed to increase fluency.

Tests for Placement and Grouping

The following material discusses tests that can be used initially to group and place students entering kindergarten or first grade. The two tests we recommend are a diagnostic test of word attack skills and a language screening test. Both tests should be given during the first few days of school.

When reading this section, keep in mind that the procedures are designed for use by a classroom teacher with 20 to 30 students in her class. Consequently, the testing procedure is as brief as possible. Also realize that any beginning-of-the-year testing and grouping procedure will not be 100% accurate. A student's performance on one test may not indicate what the student knows. Similarly, a test of what a student knows at a particular point in time will not indicate how quickly he will be able to learn new skills.

Grouping students is a difficult task since it involves balancing what is ideal for each individual student with what is practical for the entire class. Classroom teachers do not have the luxury of making decisions based solely on what is best for each student. Since the time available for instruction is very limited, teachers must balance the needs of each student with the needs of other students. How to group the students initially and how quickly to move a group through a program are complex questions.

Diagnostic Test of Word Attack Skills

The beginning level of the diagnostic test of word attack skills (Table 13.3) tests students' specific letter-sound correspondence knowledge and simple word attack strategy skills. The test is to be administered individually. It should take no longer than 5 minutes per child.

Materials

The teacher needs a copy of the test form (Table 13.3) and a class record form (Table 13.4). When preparing the test form for reproduction, use a primary typewriter or print with large letters.

Table 13.3		Diagnostic Test of Word Attack Skills—Beginning Readers' Section										
a	m	t	s	i	f	d	r	o	g	l	h	
u	c	b	n	k	e	v	p	y	j	x	w	q

		D	A	R	H	G	B	E	Q		

1	2	3	4	5
it	cat	must	flag	stamp
am	him	hats	step	strap
if	hot	hand	drop	split
sam	tag	last	skin	skunk
mad				

Seating Arrangement

The student should be seated at a desk facing away from the rest of the class. The teacher should be seated to the side of the student so that the student cannot see the teacher recording errors.

Administering and Scoring

Step 1—Test Letter-sound Correspondences (Lower-case Letters). Point to each letter and ask the student "What sound does this make?" On the class-record form (Table 13.4), write a plus (+) for each sound correctly produced. If a student tells you the letter name, say to the student, "Yes, that's the letter name, but can you also tell me the *sound* it makes?" If the student cannot tell you the sound but does know the letter, write LN (Letter Name) next to the letter. If a student does not respond in 5 seconds and seems unable

to answer, tell the student the sound, mark the letter with a zero, and move to the next letter. Continue testing letters until the student makes three incorrect responses in a row.

Step 2—Test Letter-sound Correspondences (Upper-case Letters). The procedure is the same as for step 1 above.

Step 3—Test Regular Words. Point to each word and ask "What word is this?" Repeat this question with each word in column 1, then columns 2, 3, 4, and 5. On the class record form, write a plus (+) next to words correctly read. Write a zero (0) next to each word not read correctly. If the student misidentifies a word then immediately corrects himself, count it as correct. If a student does not respond in 5 seconds, give the answer, then move to the next word. Continue testing until the student misses 3 words in a row.

Table 13.4 Record Form for Diagnostic Test of Word Attack Skills—Beginning Level

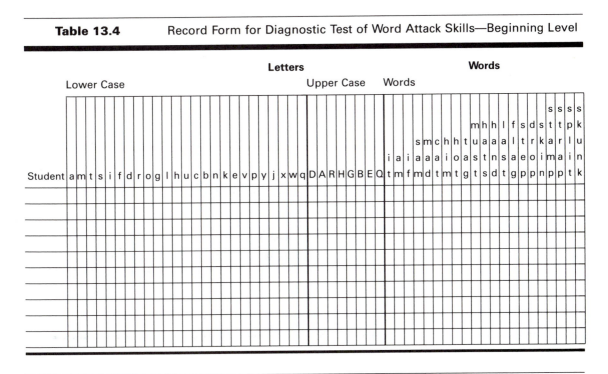

Oral Language Screening Test

The oral language screening test is designed primarily to alert teachers to students who have vocabulary and/or language deficits. It should be administered to all students during the first days of school. The test results can also be used to help in forming groups.

Materials

The teacher needs a test form (Figure 13.1) and a class record form (Table 13.5).

Teacher Directions

Start at item 1 and test all items.

Recording

Use the class-record form (Table 13.5). For a correct answer, write a plus (+) under the appropriate heading. For an incorrect answer, write a zero (0).

Informal Reading Inventory

An informal reading inventory is a test in which students read selected passages

---

Figure 13.1   Oral Language Screening Test

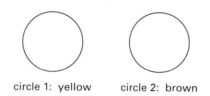

circle 1: yellow   circle 2: brown

Directions—Color circle 1 yellow. Color circle 2 brown.

1. (Point to circle one and ask) "What color is this?"
2. (Point to circle two and ask) "What color is this?"
3. "I'll say sentences. Say them just the way I say them. Listen." (pause) "A big boy sat on a dirty bench." (Repeat the sentence once if the student did not say it verbatim. If the student says it correctly verbatim on the first or second trial, score the item correct.)
4. "Listen." (pause) "Mary was baby-sitting for her little sister last night. Say that." (Repeat the sentence once if the student did not say it verbatim. If the student says it correctly verbatim on the first or second trial, score the item correct.)
5. "I'm going to say a sentence, then ask you some questions. Listen carefully. A little cat slept in the park yesterday. Listen again. A little cat slept in the park yesterday." "Where did the cat sleep?" (In the park)
6. "When did the cat sleep in the park?" (Yesterday)
7. "How are a mouse and a cow different?" (Accept reasonable answers.)
8. "Listen. Monday, Tuesday, Wednesday, Thursday, Friday. Say that." (Repeat the days once if the student did not say them correctly. If the student says them correctly on the first or second trial, score the item correct.)
9. "What is a person who fixes your teeth?"
10. "What is a pencil usually made of?"

Table 13.5   Record Form for Oral Language Screening Test

Student's Name	1 yellow	2 brown	3 statement (1)	4 statement (2)	5 where	6 when	7 different	8 days	9 dentist	10 wood

from a reading textbook. The purpose of the test is to determine at which appropriate lesson the students in the textbook should be placed. Students who read 12 or more words on the beginning level diagnostic test of word attack skills should be given an informal reading inventory. (Directions for constructing and administering an informal reading inventory are included in Chapter 20.)

Summarizing Test Results

The results of the tests should be listed on a class summary form (Table 13.6). The students should be listed according to the total number of letter-sound correspondences correctly identified on the diagnostic test of word attack skills. Students who made the fewest correct responses should be listed first. Across from the student's name, the number of correctly identified letters (total of lower and upper-case) and words should be written along with the number of items the students answered correctly on the language test. The class summary form is the basis for grouping students.

Grouping Beginning Readers

The more homogeneous a reading group, the easier it will be for the teacher to progress at an optimal rate and provide each student with a success-filled learning experience. Most first grade teachers divide their classes into 3 or 4 reading groups. The group with the highest performing students should contain the most students (8 to 12 students). The group with the lowest performing students should contain the fewest students (3 to 6 students).

The number of letter-sound correspondences and words the student knows

Table 13.6   Class Summary Form for Beginning-of-the-year Testing

| | Phonics Test | | Language Test |
	Letters Correct	Words Correct	Items Correct
Song Yan	0	0	6
Samuel	0	0	8
Jason	2	0	4
Cheryl	2	0	5
Elvin	2	0	9
Eric	3	0	6
James	4	0	8
Mary	5	1	8
Roberto	5	0	5
David R.	5	1	8
Lois	9	2	6
Alex	9	0	9
Phillipe	9	2	7
Gerald	10	2	8
Dianne	10	1	8
David P.	10	3	9
Sean	11	2	9
Toni	12	4	10
Dina	14	3	8
Jerome	14	2	10
Sandy	20	12	10
Alfred	21	14	10

should be the main factors the teacher considers when forming groups. The teacher should try to form groups in which the number of letter-sound correspondences the student knows are within 4 or 5 letters of each other.

Let's examine the class summary of a typical first grade classroom in a low to mid-socio-economic area (see Table 13.6). We start with the students who know the most sounds—Alfred and Sandy. Alfred and Sandy both know 20 or more letter-sound correspondences and have identified 12 or more words. These students are performing at a much-higher level than the students just below them. These higher performing students present a problem. Making a group of 2 higher performing students would not be efficient use of teacher time. The optimal solution would be to consult with other first grade teachers to see if they have children performing at a similar level and to create a group with 10 or 12 students. Sometimes the alternative of grouping students from several classrooms is not available, however. If that is the situation, the teacher might consider grouping the higher performing first graders with the second grade group.

Now let's look at the remaining 20 students. Let's say the teacher wants to form three reading groups. The highest reading group should contain the most students. The grouping of students in Table 13.6 who know 9 to 14 sounds would result in a group of 10 students. The lower 10 students in the room know 0 to 5 letter-sound correspondences. The students who know 3, 4, or 5 letter-sound correspondences would be in one group, while the students who know 0 to 2 letter-sound correspondences would be in the other group.

Teachers must keep in mind that the initial groupings are tentative. No matter how much time is devoted to pretesting, some regrouping will always be necessary. Regrouping should be done after the first week or two of instruction. The student's performance should serve as a basis for changing group assignments. A student who makes few errors and is facile (does not hesitate) in responding during instruc-tion might be moved to a higher group, while a student who makes more errors than other members of the group might be moved to a lower group.

Indications that a student might be ready to be moved to a higher group include mastering new skills with much less practice than required by the other students in the group, and being ready to answer before the other students.

Students may possibly belong in a lower group when the opposite occurs: the student always needs many more practice examples to master a new skill than the other members of the group or the student is often not ready to answer when the others are.

Early regrouping is very important. If regrouping is delayed too long, students who could progress at a faster rate might be separated from the higher group by several skills, making regrouping difficult.

Application Exercises

1. Below are the first 20 words in two hypothetical reading programs.

Program A

| sat | ram | fat | mam | am | it | cat | ram | was | sit | fit |
| ham | go | tan | Sid | mad | dad | had | sad | dim | | |

Program B

| Robin | Larry | house | go | into | the | was | happy | new |
| soon | at | if | when | there | what | did | them | you | find |

Which program is probably a code-emphasis program? Which program is probably a meaning-emphasis program? Explain your answers.

2. Below are the words introduced in the first 20 lessons of three hypothetical code-emphasis programs.

Lesson	Program A	Program B		Program C
1	Sam, am	at, tam	a	During the
2	at, sat	Tim, mit	m	first 15
3	mad, tam	rat, rim		lessons, the
4	Tad, mat	sit, sat, Sam	s	program
5	it, sit	mad, rid, did		teaches

Lesson	Program A	Program B		Program C
6	Tim, mit, miss	if, fat	t	auditory
7	rim, ram, rat	gas, dig, tag		skills but
8	rid, mam	ham, him, his		not word
9	fit, fat	hot, hit, rot	r	reading.
10	if, dim	lit, hill, till		
11	rag, tag	tan, man, Don		
12	gas, go	pan, pot, Pam	i	
13	fill, till	hut, mud, hum		
14	lad, lid, to	tub, but, sub	f	
15	had, ham, has	kiss, kit, kid		
16	hig, him	cat, sick, lock	if, sat	
17	cat, sick	net, ten, bet	am, Sam	
18	tack, sack	wet, wing, was	rat, at	
19	hot, sock, lock	tax, Tex, box	sad, sit	
20	mom, lot, Tom	yes, yet	Sid, ram	

a. For each program, fill in the chart below with the letters introduced in each lesson.

	1	2	3	4	5	6	7	8	9	10	11	12	13	14	15	16	17	18	19	20
A																				
B																				
C																				

b. Tell which program would be the easiest to use with low-performing students. Explain why.

c. Tell which program would be the next easiest to use with low-performing children. Explain why.

d. Tell which program would be the most difficult to use with low-performing students. Explain why.

3. Below is a summary table which shows the performance of Mr. Andrews' first graders on the diagnostic phonics test. Make two groups. Tell which students would be in each group.

	m	a	s	d	f	i	c	n	t	o	r	l	h	g	u	b	T	L	M	F	k	th	e	v	p
John	o	o	o																						
Ann	+	+	+	+	+	+	o	+	+	o	+	+	+	+	o	+	+	+	+	+	+	+	o	o	o
Sue	+	+	+	+	+	+	+	+	+	o	+	+	+	o	o	o									
Ramon	+	+	+	+	+	+	+	+	+	+	+	+	o	+	+	+	+	o	+	+	+	+	o	+	+
Dina	+	+	+	o	+	o	+	+	+	+	o	o	o												
Rachel	+	+	+	o	+	o	+	+	+	+	o	+	+	o	o	o									
Sandy	o	o	o																						
Thomas	+	+	+	+	+	o	+	+	o	o	o														
Jill	o	+	o	o	o																				
Jason	o	o	o																						

4. Below is a scope-and-sequence chart of the skills taught in a hypothetical reading program.

Lesson	Letter-sound Correspondences	When the Word Types First Appear	Irregular Words
1	m		
4	s		
6	a		
9	t		
11	r		
14	g		
16	i		
19	f	CVC (continuous)	
22	n		
25	d		
28	o		
31	h		
34	l	CVC (stop sounds)	was
37	b		said
40	u		have
46	c	CVCC	give
50	k		no, go
55	p		the
60	v	CCVC	were
63	e		of
68	j		most

a. Specify the tasks you would include in Lesson 31 on this program. For each task, write the page in this book on which the format appears. Also write the examples you would use in each task. Use the lessons in Appendix C as a guide.

b. Specify the tasks you would include in Lesson 68 of this program. For each task, write the page in this book on which the format appears. Also write the examples you would use in each task. See page 162 for an outline of tasks to include.

Chapter

14

Research on Beginning Reading Instruction

Code-Emphasis vs. Meaning-Emphasis Programs[1]

Numerous researchers have focused on the effectiveness of code-emphasis and meaning-emphasis beginning-reading programs. The most frequently cited of these reviews is Chall's *Learning to Read: The Great Debate* (1967a). This book reviews 25 studies of early reading Chall judged as "acceptable" conducted between 1900 and 1960. In addition to these later research reports, Chall's 1967(b) work focused on findings from clinical settings and her own examination of reading textbooks. The impact of this landmark work has been substantial (Chall, 1983). Chall reported that code-emphasis programs surpassed meaning-emphasis programs for teaching students word recognition, oral reading, and spelling. These findings held for lower performers as well as average and above-average students. Since 1967 basal readers typically have introduced more phonics, and the developers of standardized tests have included subtests to measure decoding skills at the lower elementary level.

Research Since 1967

Numerous studies completed in the two decades since 1967 also have addressed the question of the relative effectiveness of code-emphasis and meaning-emphasis approaches to early reading instruction. For example, a team of researchers from ETS completed an extensive review of research on beginning reading (Corder, 1971). This report concluded that generally no conclusion could be drawn from previous research because of the quality of the earlier

1. This section of the chapter was written by Linda A. Meyer, Assistant Professor in Educational Psychology and Scientist at the Center for the Study of Reading, University of Illinois, Champaign-Urbana.

studies. Dieterich (1973) used the Corder Report as well as research on the Initial Teaching Alphabet (ITA) and the Bleismer-Yarborough work to prepare an ERIC document on *Methods and Materials in Reading*. Dieterich stated that "one of the few conclusions of reading research in which we can have a high degree of confidence is that earlier and more systematic instruction in phonics is essential" (p. 7).

In 1968 Dykstra, one of the coordinators of the 27 United States Office of Education studies, produced a paper entitled "The Effectiveness of Code and Meaning-Emphasis Beginning Reading Programs." In comparing the results from eight code- and meaning-emphasis programs, Dykstra concluded that "Data from the Cooperative Research Program in First Grade Reading Instruction tend to support Chall's conclusion that code-emphasis programs produce better overall primary grade reading and spelling achievement than meaning-emphasis programs" (Dykstra, 1968, p. 22). In his later work, Dykstra (1974) has supported his earlier conclusions even more strongly.

The *Follow Through* program implemented in grades kindergarten through third grade for compensatory education students included a direct teaching method for a systematic-code approach. Other models ranged from those with a cognitive emphasis to those that had an affective emphasis. Each type of model was implemented in a variety of settings.

Stallings (1975) and Abt Associates (1977) found higher beginning reading achievement as measured on word recognition, vocabulary, and comprehension with the Metropolitan Achievement Test (MAT) in the Direct Instruction Model, grades 1 through 3. Kennedy's (1978) reexamination of these data found that the Direct Instruction results were fairly consistent across settings. House, Glass,

McLean, and Walker (1978), however, judged variations from site to site within models to be greater than between model differences and, thus, cautioned against acceptance of the Abt conclusions. Wisler, Burns, and Inwamoto (1978), however, declared the Direct Instruction Model an exception to the other *Follow Through* early childhood models in overcoming disadvantages for poor children. They concluded that, although Direct Instruction had not been uniformly successful everywhere and with all measures, it did show the best general pattern of success.

Although the *Follow Through* studies were conducted for reasons different from the USOE research, the results are quite similar. In addition, research comparing matched control groups in two different communities (Meyer, Gersten & Gutkin, 1983; Meyer, 1983) both show results significantly favoring students in the *Follow Through* sites despite differences in the communities. These studies and a follow-up study reported by Meyer (1984) all attribute reading performance in the lower elementary grades and comparisons in high school reading, as well as more general measures of school success such as high school graduation and application to college, to differences in early-reading curricula. Furthermore, Meyer's follow-up study (1984) revealed a strong correlation ($r = 78$) between children's third grade and ninth grade reading ability.

Analytic and Synthetic Phonics

As general acknowledgement regarding the importance of phonics grew from the late 1960s, research then began to focus on what kind of phonics instruction produced higher student achievement. Phonics in these studies is usually referred to as analytic when children must derive letter-sound relationships from words. Phonics is classified as synthetic when letter sounds are taught directly in isolation, then must be blended to form words. Most studies comparing analytic and synthetic phonics have been conducted in regular classroom settings. In most of this work, students are taught to read nonsense words, then tested on new words constructed from the same letters that they have been practicing. Nine studies fall into this category.

Fox and Routh (1976), Carnine (1977), Haddock (1978), Yawkey (1973), and Haddock (1976) worked with students who were either four or five-years old. In 5 of these studies, the teaching of specific letter-sound correspondences prevailed; whereas, whole-word instruction was more prevalent with the other two groups. The final group was instructed on letter names only. In addition, all of the students in these groups received blending training. Yawkey's results significantly favored letter name and blending training over whole-word instruction. Fox and Roth found no significant differences with blending training for 4-year-old nonsegmenters, i.e., those students who could not break words down into their constituent phonemes. All of the other studies in this group yielded significant results for the letter-sound training groups.

Six more studies of this same type have been conducted with first-grade students. Treatments were generally similar to those described for preschool students. With the exception of one study conducted by Muller (1973a), all of the other results (Jeffrey & Samuels, 1976; Jenkins, Bausell, & Jenkins, 1972) showed significant results on a transfer test for children who received letter-sound training and blending.

Fifteen additional studies have been conducted in classrooms to test the effectiveness of analytic vs. synthetic phonics instruction. Most of these studies compared students' outcomes on word recognition, oral reading of text, silent reading and comprehension, vocabulary, decoding, spelling, or a total reading score. Several of these studies (Hayes & Wuerst, 1967, 1969; Wyatt, 1976; Putnam & Youtz, 1972; Lynn, 1973; Pittsburgh LRDC, undated; Hayes & Wuerst, 1967, 1969; Putnam & Youtz, 1972; Lynn, 1973; Grant, 1973; and Hayes & Wuerst, 1967, 1969) found synthetic phonics to produce either significantly better or at least results equal to those for analytic phonics approaches. Only one study (Putnam & Youtz, 1972) found results that favored analytic phonics, and these researchers commented that by the second grade, the direct phonics group outperformed the indirect phonics group on comprehension.

Research with Special Students

Five studies (Richardson, Winsberg & Binler, 1973; Sabatino & Dorfman, 1974; Enfield, 1976; Biggins & Uhler, 1979; Williams, 1980) with special populations have compared the results of direct and indirect phonics with special students. These populations have ranged in exceptionality from students who were neurologically handicapped to students who were educably mentally retarded, or to children who were residents in special schools. The students ranged in age from 6–17 years. In all but one study (Sabatino & Dorfman, 1974), where the dependent measure was spelling, results favored the analytic-phonics method. With this group, results were equal for synthetic and analytic phonics in terms of word recognition. Thus, synthetic phonics appears to be more successful with exceptional populations than is an analytic phonics approach. Most recently (1985) the Commission on Reading, when reviewing research on these two phonics methods, concluded that results favor a synthetic-phonics approach (Anderson, Hiebert, Scott & Wilkinson, 1985) in *Becoming a Nation of Readers*. Synthetic phonics was also found to be superior to analytic phonics in a meta-analysis conducted by Pflaum et al. in 1980. Similar results are apparent by the end of kindergarten in a longitudinal study of reading-comprehension acquisition (Meyer, Hastings, Wardrop, & Linn, 1988). In this program of research, students taught to read with a synthetic-phonics approach appear to maintain higher achievement in reading compared to students taught with analytic-phonics methods through at least second grade.

In summary, one can conclude from almost four decades of research on beginning reading that phonics programs have produced results superior to meaning-emphasis approaches in the early grades. Furthermore, synthetic phonics appears to yield better results in beginning reading than does an analytic phonics approach.

Vocabulary and Language Skills

Beginning readers bring a variety of vocabulary and language skills to the instructional setting (Stanovich, 1986). These skills have been acquired through everyday experiences with the environment. Our emphasis is on instructional procedures that will utilize students' abilities to learn language. This emphasis seems appropriate because students who do well on oral language tasks tend to do well on written comprehension tasks (Anderson & Freebody, 1983; Jenkins & Pany, 1977; Perfetti, 1977; Berger, 1975).

Vocabulary[2]

Although research suggests that vocabulary can be developed and expanded

through classroom experiences and visual aids such as films or field trips (Hargis et al., 1988; Davis, 1968; McCullough, 1969; Lieberman, 1967) and context clues (Nagy, Anderson, & Herman, 1987; Perfetti, 1986; Jenkins & Dixon, 1983; Gipe, 1978; Wittrock, Marks & Doctorow, 1975), vocabulary can also be taught more directly (Graves, 1987; Chall, 1983; Jenkins & Pany, 1976; Petty, Herold, & Stoll, 1968; Otterman, 1955). Explicit vocabulary instruction is most appropriate for the beginning reader because he or she has limited reading skills and, therefore, cannot totally rely on context to derive word meanings. At this stage, the primary focus in reading instruction is on decoding: students are learning to "process the medium" of written text (Chall, 1987). Even after students have become efficient decoders, explicit vocabulary instruction continues to be "a useful adjunct to the natural learning from context" (Stahl & Fairbanks, 1986, p. 100).

Many of our specific guidelines for teaching basic vocabulary have been validated in experimental research. One of the points made in Chapter 12 is that *a presentation should be consistent with only one interpretation*. If a presentation is consistent with several interpretations, students may learn an interpretation other than that intended by the teacher. An application of this principle is illustrated in Figure 14.1, which contains positive and negative examples of the discrimination *on*. The pair of examples from teaching set *a* illustrates the minimum difference between positive and negative examples of *on*. In set *a* the number of possible interpretations for *on* is minimized because of the small differences between the positive and negative examples. In contrast, the subsequent sets of examples (sets *b* through *e*) differ in terms of several features, which suggest additional interpretations. A student with set *e* examples might learn that *on* means a

2. This section was written by Geneva Blake and David Evans who are doctoral candidates in Special Education at the University of Oregon.

Figure 14.1

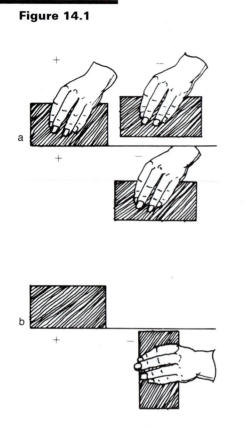

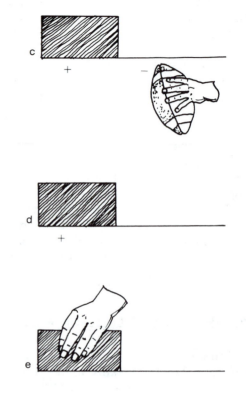

block, something not held in a hand, horizontally positioned objects, etc. None of these interpretations is possible from set *a*. When Williams and Carnine (1981) presented examples similar to those in Figure 14.1 to different groups of preschoolers, they found a significant linear trend between the number of possible interpretations and errors on a transfer test. Preschoolers presented with set *a* examples responded correctly to 10.2 transfer items, whereas, preschoolers presented with set *e* responded correctly to 5.0 transfer items. In other words, the greater the number of possible interpretations consistent with a teaching demonstration, the greater the likelihood some students will learn an interpretation other than the one intended by

the teacher. Designing a presentation as in set *a* that is consistent with only *one* interpretation increases the likelihood of students not becoming confused with what is relevant.

Ensuring a presentation is consistent with only one interpretation requires selecting not only minimally different positive and negative examples (whenever possible), but also *a range of examples*. For example, Flanders (1978) worked with a student who did not understand the difference between singular and plural nouns; e.g., the experimenter would present two sets of examples (one dog and two dogs), touch the one dog and ask, "Am I touching dogs?" The student would be likely to answer, "Yes." Flanders followed a commonly used procedure to teach the student to answer correctly questions involving singular and plural nouns. The problem was that the procedure implied a misinterpretation. All examples were presented in pairs: a single object for singular and two identical objects for plural. Testing revealed that the student had learned the misinterpretation that plural meant two. The teacher presented a set of 4 objects, pointed to the 4 objects, then asked "Am I touching dogs?" The student answered, "No" and pointed to the two dogs, saying, "dogs".

Other research suggests that misinterpretations can result from a limited range of negative examples. In one study, Carnine (1976c) presented students with a narrow sample of negative examples keyed on the features of the negatives but not the positives. The same positive examples (figures with saw-toothed edges) were presented to three groups of students. One group of students was presented with straight-sided negatives (or a narrow range of negative examples), while two other groups were presented negatives with many different characteristics (a full range of negatives). The group with the narrow range of negatives did poorly on a transfer test because they identified figures with straight sides as negatives and everything else as positives, regardless of whether the figure had saw-toothed edges. The preceding two studies suggest that a full range of positive *and* negative examples is need to ensure appropriate "generalization."

Another study by Carnine (1976a) suggests the importance of presenting intended, irrelevant characteristics in both positive and negative examples. An irrelevant feature appearing only in positive examples may be treated as relevant, whether or not the teacher "intends" for a feature to be relevant (Reynolds, 1961). One group of students in the Carnine (1976a) study was

presented with a concept that had both a dotted pattern and three points. The students treated the points as critical. The concept for another group had the dotted pattern in both positive and negative examples with only the three points in positive examples. These students treated dots as critical. The point is that students learn what is easiest (Samuels, 1976b). Consequently, teachers must be certain that what is easiest for students to learn is what the teacher wants them to learn.

Sequencing Examples

Several procedures are relevant for sequencing examples. First, minimally different positive and negative examples of a discrimination should be sequenced adjacent to each other, simultaneously rather than successively. Sequencing minimally different examples in this way increases the awareness of the discriminations' relevant features (Granzin & Carnine, 1977). Students taught conjunctive and disjunctive concepts with simultaneously presented minimally different positive and negative examples reached criterion in about half as many trials as students presented the same examples presented successively, with multiple differences between adjacent examples. Similar results have been reported by Stolurow (1975); Tennyson, Steve, and Boutwell (1975); and Tennyson (1973).

A second sequencing procedure involves, whenever possible, positive and negative examples generated by changing a single stimulus (a dynamic presentation) rather than presenting a set of discrete stimuli, either simultaneously or successively (a static presentation). Carnine (1978f) reported faster acquisition and higher transfer scores for preschoolers who were taught to discriminate between *diagonal* and *convex* with a dynamic rather than static presentation. In the dynamic treatment, examples of diagonal were generated by rotating a single-line segment. In the static treatment, examples consisted of pairs of line segments drawn on cards. The differences in trials to criterion was 46.4 versus 10.6 for diagonal and 5.8 versus .05 for convex.

Carnine (1980a) also compared all three sequencing procedures discussed above. Preschoolers were taught a discrimination defined by an angle using material developed by Trabasso (1963) in his study on various types of prompts. Preschoolers who received the dynamic presentation with minimum differences reached on an average of 7.6 trials; preschoolers who received a static presentation with minimum differences took 12.8 trials; finally, preschoolers who received a static presentation with multiple differences required an average of 26.0 trials. Similar results have been found with severely handicapped individuals (Gersten, White, Falco & Carnine, 1982).

The importance of carefully sequenced examples and nonexamples in the teaching of vocabulary has also been highlighted in research conducted with students in the upper elementary grades by Tennyson and his colleagues (e.g., Tennyson & Cocchiarella, 1986; Tennyson & Park, 1980), Klausmeier and his colleagues (e.g., Klausmeier & Feldman, 1975; Klausmeier & Allen, 1978), and more recently by Petty & Jansson (1987).

Language Skills

The importance of statement repetition has not been documented in experimental research; however, there is correlational evidence to suggest its importance. After comparing the high and low performers on their ability to remember what they just read, Perfetti said, "The point at which it seems adaptive to forget the words recently heard appears to be the end of a sentence (Jarvella, 1971). Up to that point, it is helpful to remember the sequence of words or phrases verbatim so that the unheard portion of the sentence (e.g., the verb) can be related to the first part of the sentence" (1977, p. 33). Perfetti's work underscores the importance of students being able to remember words in a sentence. If a reader cannot say a sentence verbatim, she probably has difficulty remembering sentences that are read.

Beginning Decoding Instruction[3]

The controversy regarding decoding skills has spanned for several decades (Bond & Dykstra, 1967; Chall, 1967; Guthrie, Martuza, & Seifert, 1979). In her chapter, "The Case for Explicit Decoding Instruction," Williams (1985) concluded that the resistance to direct-decoding instruction cannot be due to a lack of empirical data, but is more likely due to the fact that "data do not necessarily determine educational practice" (p. 211). She posited that practitioners perceive direct-decoding instruction as a laborious process that fails to resolve quickly the reading difficulties of low performers. Irrespective of the perceived demands of decoding instruction, there is substantial data indicating that low-achieving readers' deficits originate from underlying bottom-up or code-based deficits and that these deficits are best resolved through direct instruction (Perfetti, 1985; Spear & Sternberg, 1986; Stanovich, 1986).

---

3. This section was written by Deborah C. Simmons and Cynthia C. Griffin. Deborah C. Simmons is a research assistant Professor in Special Education at George Peabody College, Vanderbilt University. Cynthia C. Griffin is an instructor and research assistant in the Department of Special Education at the University of Florida.

There is further evidence indicating the correlational, if not causal relationship linking the difficulties students experience in beginning decoding activities and their subsequent inability to comprehend what they read. (Perfetti, 1985; Spear & Sternberg, 1986; Stanovich, 1986). The effects of decoding deficits have been found to delay the automaticity students need for word recognition. This lack of automaticity is thought to be a primary impediment to higher-level comprehension (LaBarge & Samuels, 1974; Perfetti, 1985). As Stanovich (1986) noted, "Comprehension fails not because of over-reliance on decoding, but because decoding is not developed enough" (p. 373). Based on the documented difficulties of poor readers on decoding tasks and the relationship between decoding deficits and comprehension, Williams (1985) reported that "We have enough data to justify teaching decoding explicitly" (p. 207).

The beginning reading deficits of low-performing readers encompass a host of decoding skills ranging from phonemic awareness to the process of recoding symbols into sounds and then into words. This review examines research regarding the efficacy of direct instruction in the following decoding skill areas: (a) phonemic awareness, (b) letter-sound correspondences, (c) regular word reading, (d) irregular word reading, and (e) passage reading.

Phonemic Awareness

Empirical findings suggest that phonemic awareness, or the ability to perceive a word as a sequence of individual sounds, is positively correlated with early reading success (See Stanovich, 1986; Williams, 1984 for reviews). Extant research indicates that some functional level of phonemic awareness facilitates reading acquisition and, specifically, that children who perform successfully on tasks of phonemic awareness

are more likely to be successful at learning to read than children unable to perform phonemic-awareness tasks (Perfetti, 1986). Several studies where phonemic-awareness skills were taught directly indicated significant advantages for the experimental groups in both word recognition and spelling (Bradley & Bryant, 1985; Fox & Routh, 1976; Williams, 1979, 1980). Despite the apparent advantages of auditory-skills training, there is limited evidence that phonics programs ever teach students to segment words into parts or to blend these parts into words (Williams, 1985). Furthermore, there is preliminary evidence that students do not induce independently the skills of segmenting and sound blending (Haddock, 1978). Such findings suggest the need for explicit instruction in the skill of segmenting and sound blending. Teachers should not assume that students will implicitly learn these skills or that they will be transferred to new-word types.

Phonemic-awareness Skills and Instruction. Various kinds of phonemic-awareness skills have been studied including the ability to divide words into parts, to blend phonemes into recognizable words, and to add or delete phonemes from various parts of words (Ehri, 1984). Lewkowicz (1980) identified ten separate categories of phonemic-awareness tasks and targeted the tasks of segmenting or sound analysis and sound blending or sound synthesis as particularly relevant for beginning reading acquisition. Williams (1979) explicitly taught both phoneme analysis and phoneme blending to learning disabled students and found significant improvements in both decoding acquisition and transfer tasks. Bradley and Bryant (1985) examined the effects of two sound-categorization treatments, one with letter instruction and one with sounds-only to a conceptual categorization treatment and to a no-treatment control group. Marked differences between groups were observed favoring the sound-categorization-plus-letters treatment in both reading and spelling achievement.

Perfetti, Beck, and Hughes (1981) conducted a longitudinal study of beginning readers using tasks analogous to the segmenting and sound blending tasks identified by Lewkowicz. One group of students was directly taught synthesizing or blending procedures for combining word sounds. Instruction for the two comparison groups was based on the basal reading series. Findings from the year-long study indicated that phonemic awareness both precedes and follows progress in reading unfamiliar words. From their results, the researchers concluded that the relationship between phonemic knowledge and learning to read is not unidirectional, but rather reciprocal. Learning to read, on the one hand, depends on phonemic awareness and, on the other hand, is furthered by the experience of reading itself. Ehri (1983) similarly noted the reciprocal relationship between linguistic or phonemic knowledge and reading achievement.

Letter-sound Correspondence Training

In general, the research concerning teaching letter-sound correspondences relates to sequencing and practice considerations.

Separating the Introduction of Similar Letters. Research investigating the separation of letters has studied the effect of letters of similar shape and/or sound (Carnine, 1976d, 1980b, 1981a). These three studies by Carnine demonstrated the superiority of teaching sequences that separate the introduction of visually and/or auditorily similar stimuli over methods that simultaneously introduce similar stimuli. A study that focused on visual similarity was a match-to-sample visual-discrimination task in which preschoolers were shown a target letter and asked to match it to one of four alternatives (Carnine, 1980b). Two groups of preschoolers were trained until they reached criterion on each of three consecutively presented match-to-sample tasks. One group was presented tasks in which similar letters were separated; the other group received alternatives in which similar letters appeared together. In the similar-separated treatment, the first set of alternatives included only one similar alternative to the target letter. In the second set, two of the alternatives were similar. In the third set, all the alternatives were similar. Preschoolers in the similar-separated treatment reached criterion on a match-to-sample posttest in significantly fewer trials than the similar-together treatment. The means were 31.0 and 69.1 trials respectively. Carnine suggested that the more rapid learning of the similar-separated groups does not imply that visual-discrimination training should not include similar alternatives, but rather, that the factor of deciding when to introduce similar letters in the instructional set is of critical importance.

A study investigating the procedure for separating auditorily similar sounds (Carnine, 1976d) used a sound-symbol paired-associate task in which the similar sounds were /e/ and /i/. The order of introduction for the similar-separated group was e, c, m, s, i, while the order for the similar-together group was e, i, u, s, c, m. In Experiment 1, first graders in the similar-separated group made significantly more correct training responses than first graders in the similar-together group (51.7% versus 33.1%). Experiment 2 measured trials to criterion rather than the number of correct responses to a fixed-trial presentation. Preschoolers in the similar-separated treatment reached criterion on /e/ and /i/ in significantly fewer trials, a mean of 178.0 versus 293.2 trials.

A limited amount of research has been conducted examining methods to reduce problems associated with letter-sound correspondences both visually and auditorily similar. Carnine (1981a) used experimental geometric figures and labels that approximated the difficult discriminations encountered by young children in school (e.g., /b/ vs. /d/) to investigate different methods of integrating a new, similar symbol into a set of familiar symbols. Students were assigned to one of four groups where experimental stimuli consisted of (a) Similar Shapes Only, (b) Dissimilar Shapes, (c) Similar Shapes Distributed, and (d) Similar Shapes and Names. Results indicated that the mean number of trials to criterion of the Similar Shapes and Names group was significantly higher than the mean of the other three conditions. Implications of this study suggest the importance of strategically separating similar letter-sound correspondences in initial teaching sequences.

Practice. Research related to the amount and the specifics of practice has been rather limited since the first edition of this text. No new studies pertinent to letter-sound correspondence practice issues were identified in our search. A summary of earlier research follows; readers may refer to the original edition for more detailed descriptions of the referenced studies.

Carnine (1976d) conducted a study investigating the effect of a cumulative introduction procedure where students were trained to criterion on a letter-sound correspondence prior to the introduction to a new member. The cumulative-practice schedule was contrasted with a simultaneous-introduction procedure where six letters were introduced consecutively on a daily basis, regardless of student performance on prior letter-sound correspondences. Results indicated that not only did the cumulative-

introduction group require a fewer number of trials to reach criterion than did the simultaneous-introduction group, but it also identified a significantly greater number of letter-sound correspondences on a post test measure.

Kyraznowski and Carnine (1978) investigated the efficacy of massed vs. distributed practice of letter-sound correspondences using two groups of preschoolers. With a massed practice schedule, the same letter was presented several times in a row; with a distributed schedule, a letter was followed by a different previously introduced letter. Results indicated that students who received the distributed form of practice correctly identified a significantly greater number of posttest responses (72% vs. 38%).

Sounding Out Words. A growing body of data seems to point to the validity of teaching sounding out. Muller (1973), Ramsey (1972), and Richardson and Collier (1971) reported that blending is a necessary component skill for successfully applying a sounding-out strategy to unfamiliar words. Ramsey (1972) found that 40% of the errors made by nonreading second graders were due to blending difficulties. Coleman (1970) noted that blending is a strategy that students can apply to many different words, but direct instruction with many sounds is necessary before students will acquire the generalized skill. Skailand (1971) and Silberman (1964) reported that, if subjects were taught sound-symbol relationships but not blending, they would not be able to use sounding out as a decoding strategy. Bishop (1964), Jeffrey and Samuels (1976), Carnine (1977), and Vandever and Neville (1976) reported that teaching letter-sound correspondences and sounding out resulted in students correctly identifying more unfamiliar words than when students were trained on a whole-word strategy. Haddock (1976) and Chapman and Kamm (1974) found that only when blending is directly taught will students successfully use a sounding-out strategy for attacking words.

A rhyming approach to blending was found to be effective in both the Haddock (1976) and Chapman and Kamm (1974) studies. Through direct instruction in rhyming, children tended to learn to recognize phonetically similar elements (Venezky Shiloah, & Calfee, 1972). Venezky also reported a significant positive correlation between reading achievement and rhyming performances. Recognition of phonetically similar elements through rhyming instruction should assist students quickly to identify letter combinations and syllables.

Because of individual learner differences, a specific number of examples will never be appropriate for teaching a sounding-out strategy to all students. A mastery learning approach, in which examples are presented until the student reaches a specified performance standard, probably results in higher retention scores than presenting the same number of examples to all students. Jeffrey and Samuels (1976) taught students a word-reading strategy with a fixed number of practice trials on a set of training words. Carnine (1977) taught students a similar strategy, but with a mastery learning design. Subjects in the Carnine study identified about 92% of the transfer words correctly, while Jeffrey and Samuels' subjects identified only about 31% of the words correctly. Since different subjects were used in the two studies, the comparison of a mastery learning and fixed practice design is at best suggestive. Research that directly addresses the question is needed.

Introducing word types according to their relative difficulty was also recommended in this section. In a study on word difficulty (Carnine & Carnine, 1980), children in a synthetic phonics program (Engelmann & Bruner, 1974) were tested on three types of untaught words: CVC words with an initial stop sound, CVCC words with an initial continuous sound, and CCVC words. Students were presented with five examples of each word type (for a total of 15 words). The mean percent of correct responses was 71% for CVC words, 40% for CVCC words, and 22% for CCVC words. All differences were significant, suggesting that CVC words are easier to decode using a sounding-out strategy than either CVCC or CCVC words, and that CVCC words are easier than CCVC words.

The question of how initially to teach word recognition is very important. As mentioned earlier, Singer, Samuels, and Spiroff (1973) compared words in isolation, words in context, and words with pictures. Presenting words in isolation was the most effective procedure. Shankweiler and Liberman (1972) reported that the ability to recognize words in lists is highly correlated with accurately reading words in context. Discrimination word lists also reduce confusion errors in later reading activities. Samuels and Jeffrey (1966), McCutcheon and McDowell (1969), and Otto and Pizillo (1970, 71) reported that discrimination lists (made up of similar words) resulted in fewer incorrect responses to similar transfer words than did training on lists where the words were dissimilar. Students who learned the discrimination list usually required longer to reach criterion, but the improved word-recognition skills probably warranted the additional time.

From their research on word reading, Rayner and Posnansky (1978) concluded that "since beginning readers focus so heavily on beginning letters, we suggest that a great deal of discrimination training in which the first letter is held constant will prove beneficial for children" (p. 187). Discrimination training is particularly important since primary students often mistakenly learn to identify words based on the first two letters. Venezky (1975) pointed out that 75% of the common words that appear in primary readers can be discriminated on the basis of the first two letters. Unfortunately, relying on initial letters is inappropriate since it is a useless strategy after third grade.

The ineffectiveness of picture cues has been demonstrated in several studies (Harzem, Lee & Miles, 1976; Samuels, 1970). Similarly, research on configuration as a basis for word recognition has yielded negative results (Edelman, 1963; Smith, 1969; McClelland, 1977). Word configuration supposedly allows students to identify words on the basis of their contours such as ⬜ for little. Marchbanks and Levin (1965) tested beginning readers' preferred cues in word identification by asking them to select one word from a set of alternatives that was most similar to a standard. Children tended to use word configuration as a *least* preferred cue, after initial, final, and medial letters.

Decoding

The remainder of this book will deal with skills taught after the beginning stage. We can expect students progressing at an average rate to have mastered the beginning-stage skills sometime in mid-to-late first grade. Instructionally sophisticated students who enter school with many skills may take a much shorter time to master these skills. Conversely, instructionally naive students may need more than a year to master the beginning-level skills. Earlier in the book we recommended providing an extra daily reading period for lower performing students. If this extra time is provided, and if the teacher has adequate training to develop her presentation skills, we have found that nearly all students will be able to finish the beginning-level skills by the end of the first grade.

Decoding and comprehension teaching continue throughout the primary (grades 2 and 3), intermediate (grades 4–6), and middle- and high-school level. The relationship between decoding and comprehension instruction changes as students progress through the grades. At the beginning of the primary grades, a lot of time is devoted to teaching decoding skills because students need to learn generalizable skills that will enable them to decode many words. By the end of the primary grades, most specific word attack skills have been taught and decoding instruction focuses mostly on introducing difficult irregular words that students will encounter in upcoming passage reading and comprehension exercises. The proportion of the lesson devoted to teaching comprehension skills grows as the time spent on decoding decreases.

Decoding Instruction

A phonetic language is a language where each letter always represents only one

Chapter

Overview of Decoding

sound, regardless where the letter appears in a word. For the aspiring reader, English is not, unfortunately, a highly phonetic language. Although about half the letters in the English language are highly regular in that they nearly always represent the same sound, the other half of the letters are quite irregular. The sound these letters make varies considerably, depending on the context in which they appear. To determine what sound a particular letter represents, the reader must take into account the letters that follow it in a word. For example, if the letter *o* is followed by another *o*, the letter *o* may make the /oo/ sound as in *moon*, or the /oo/ sound as in *blood*. Similarly, when *o* is followed by the letter *u*, the /ou/ sound as in the word *sound*, or the /oo/ sound as in the word *would* is produced. The letter *o* can also represent or combine with other letters to make the /ŏ/ sound as in the word *mom*, the /ō/ sound as in the word *hope*, and the /ŭ/ sound as in the word *done*. Obviously, the sound the letter *o* makes is determined by the letters that follow it.

The consonant *t* is also not consistent. If *t* is followed by the letter *h*, the *t* and *h* join to represent either the voiced /th/ sound as in *that*, or the unvoiced /th/ sound as in *thought*. But if *t* is followed by *ion*, the *t* represents the /sh/ sound as in *action*. Again, the sound the *t* represents is determined by the letters that follow it.

If English were a highly phonetic language, the job of teaching students to decode would be practically finished by the end of the beginning stage. The students would learn the letter-sound correspondences and how to blend in a left-right progression. The only major teaching steps remaining would be to provide practice and introduce longer words.

However, since English is not a highly phonetic language, a lot of teaching needs to be done after the beginning stage to produce literate readers. One should look at the beginning-reading stage as the time when the foundation for future learning is being established.

During the beginning-reading stage, students receive the practice that will enable them to succeed in later instruction. As students practice the skill of sounding out words letter by letter, they develop the ability to see units of letters rather than merely individual letters. As the students progress through the beginning-reading stage, they should receive adequate practice to enable them to read one-syllable words relatively quickly, without subvocally sounding out the word first. The nearly instantaneous decoding of words indicates that the students are processing letters as a unit rather than as a series of individual letters.

Teaching students to decode in the primary and intermediate grades involves three skills: *phonic analysis, structural analysis,* and *contextual analysis. Phonic-analysis* skills help students figure out letter-sound correspondences. *Structural-analysis* skills help students decode multisyllabic words. *Contextual-analysis* skills help students use the context of a sentence to figure out irregular words.

Phonic Analysis

Teaching students the relationship between units of letters and their sounds is referred to as phonic analysis. During the beginning stage, we recommend teaching the most common sound for individual letters. In the primary grades, we recommend students learn sound correspondences for groups of letters we refer to as letter combinations. An example of a letter combination is *ar*, which usually represents the /ar/ sound as in the word *far*. Learning the sound for this letter combination enables students to decode a set of previously "irregular" words (e.g., *bark, barn, farm, cart, hard, start, card, star, dark, harm*).

We also recommend teaching students a rule for decoding words with a VCe pattern such as *like, made,* and *hope.* In VCe words, a single vowel is followed by a consonant and a final *e.*

Structural Analysis

Structural analysis involves teaching students to decode words formed by adding prefixes, suffixes, or another word to a base word. The word *repainting* is formed by adding the prefix *re* and the ending *ing* to the base word *paint* (*re* + *paint* + *ing* = *repainting*). Spelling changes are often made when word parts are combined. For example, note what happens when the ending *ed* is added to *hope* and *hop* (*hope* + *ed* = *hoped, hop* + *ed* = *hopped*). *Hoped* is formed by dropping the *e* in *hope. Hopped* is formed by doubling the final *p* in *hop.* These spelling changes require the students to learn skills to discriminate similar words such as *hoped* and *hopped.* Another example of a spelling change occurs with words that end with the letter *y.* The *y* is often changed to an *i* (e.g., *try* + *ed* = *tried, happy* + *est* = *happiest, marry* + *ed* = *married*). Exercises that show students how word parts are combined will help students decode words with spelling changes.

Contextual Analysis and Irregular Words

Teaching students phonic and structural-analysis skills will allow them to decode a great number of words. However, there will still be words the students are not able to decode because they contain letter-sound correspondences they do not know. We call these words "irregulars."

Contextual analysis is a useful tool to help students in decoding irregular words. It involves teaching students to rely on the syntax (word order) and semantics (word meaning) of the sentence in which a word appears, as well as letter-sound-correspondence knowledge as an aid to decoding the word. The first type of context cue, syntax (word order), limits the number of possible words that can come next in a sentence. Thus, syntax cues allow students to make inferences regarding the possible pronunciation of a word. For example, the next word in the sentence "John ran to the _____" might be any of several nouns (e.g., *store, shore, station*), but could not be a verb (e.g., *stay, shave*), adverb (e.g., *slowly*), or pronoun (e.g., *she,* etc.). The second type of context cue, semantics (word meaning), further limits the number of possible words that can come next in a sentence. For example, although the next word in the sentence "Alice threw away the _____" must be a noun, only certain nouns make sense (e.g., *cup, old clothes, broken TV,* etc.). Other nouns would not make sense and would not come next in the sentence (e.g., *Jerry, woman, railroad,* etc.). Since context cues (semantic and syntactic) restrict the words that can come next in a sentence, students are more likely to be able to figure out the pronunciation of an unknown word in context than when it appears in a list of words.

Students also use context cues to check their decoding of words in passages. If a student reads the sentence "The rabbit went *hopping* down the street" as "The rabbit went *hoping* down the street," he can infer he made a decoding error since the sentence does not make sense. The student needs to reanalyze *hoping* to correct the sentence.

Comprehension

The emphasis of reading instruction gradually shifts as students move through the grades from learning to read (decoding) to reading to learn (comprehension). By the intermediate grades, passage-reading instruction focuses primarily on comprehension. Most of the reading lesson at this point deals with teaching specific comprehension skills and applying these skills to comprehend passages.

During the primary grades, phonics instruction includes teaching students: (1) the most common sound(s) represented by several consecutive letters (referred to as letter combinations), and (2) a strategy to decode words which contain a VCe pattern in which the initial vowel represents its long sound and the final *e* is silent as in *make, hope,* and *use.*

Words with Letter Combinations

A letter combination is a group of consecutive letters that represents a particular sound(s) in the majority of words in which it appears. Knowing the most common sounds of letter combinations greatly expands students' abilities to decode new words. For example, a student who can decode all types of regular words and has just learned the *ee* letter combination will be able to decode these new words: *bee, bleed, beet, breed, peel, see, teen, wee, creek, deer, flee, fleet, green, greet, jeep, keep, weep, canteen, indeed, upkeep,* and *fifteen.*

Table 16.1 lists the letter combinations that we suggest presenting. We recommend presenting the letter-sound relationship for a letter combination if the letter combination represents one sound in over half the words in which it appears and if it appears in 5 or more common words. The letter combinations are listed alphabetically in the left column of the table. The second column contains words that illustrate the most-common sound of each letter combination. The third and fourth columns give data from a computer analysis of the most common 17,300 English words (Hanna et al., 1966). The third column lists the percentage of total words in which the letter combination represents its most common sound. (Note that these percentages vary

Chapter

16

Phonic Analysis

Table 16.1   Letter Combinations

Letter Combination	Sample Word	Percentage	Frequency	Type
ai[a]	maid	90%	254	vowel digraph
al[b]	halt	NA	NA	l-controlled
ar	car	75%	518	r-controlled
au	haul	94%	146	vowel digraph
aw	lawn	100%	75	vowel digraph
ay	stay	97%	131	vowel digraph
ch	chip	63%	313	consonant digraph
ea[a]	beat	60%	294	vowel digraph
ee[a]	need	98%	285	vowel digraph
er	fern	97%	313	r-controlled
igh	high	100%	88	vowel digraph
ir	first	100%	104	r-controlled
kn	know	100%	41	consonant digraph
oa	load	94%	126	vowel digraph
ol[b]	hold	NA	NA	l-controlled
oo	boot	59%	173	vowel digraph
or	short	55%	312	r-controlled
ou	cloud	84%	285	vowel diphthong
ow	own	50%	124	vowel digraph
oy	toy	98%	48	vowel diphthong
ph	phone	100%	242	consonant digraph
qu	quick	100%	191	none
sh	shop	100%	398	consonant digraph
th[c]	thank	74%	411	consonant digraph
ur	burn	100%	203	r-controlled
wh	whale	85%	89	consonant digraph
wr	wrap	100%	48	consonant digraph

[a]When computing percentages from the Hanna et al. study (1966), we combined some combinations that were followed by r (air, eer) with the respective combination without r (ee, ai). We found that even though there is a sound difference when r follows the combinations, students can decode words by pronouncing the most common sound of the letter combination and then saying the /r/ sound.

[b]The percentage and frequency of the l-controlled letter combination was not available.

[c]Although /th/ represents the unvoiced sound in most words (e.g., think), in many high-frequency words (this, that, them, than, then, the, those, these) the th is voiced. We recommend introducing this less-common, or minor sound of th first, because students use it in sounding out many high-frequency words.

from study to study, depending on the sample of words used.) The fourth column gives the number of words in which the particular letter combination represented its most common sound. In the fifth column, the letter combinations are classified as vowel digraph, consonant digraph, r-controlled vowel, or diphthong. A digraph consists of two consecutive letters that represent one sound. An r-controlled vowel is a vowel followed by the letter *r*. A diphthong consists of two consecutive vowels, each which contributes to the sound heard.[1]

Preskills

The first letter combinations can be introduced after students know the most common sounds of about 20 single letters and can decode passages made up of regular words at a speed of about 20 words per minute. This speed indicates that students are no longer laboriously sounding out but beginning to perceive words as units, which makes decoding words that contain letter combinations much easier.

Sequence

Two factors determine the order in which letter combinations are introduced in a reading program. The first is the number of words in which the letter combination appears. When planning a sequence for introducing letter combinations, the number of words containing the letter combination should not only be considered in terms of total occurrence, but also in terms of how many words are common in primary grade literature. For example, although the digraph *ph* appears in a large number of words, many of these words are fairly uncommon words (words which would not appear in primary grade books). Consequently, *ph* would not be introduced as early as indicated by its frequency of oc-

---

1. The distinction between which letter combinations are digraphs, diphthongs, or r-controlled vowels is more important to speech teachers than reading teachers. Nonetheless, reading teachers should be aware of the terms since they often appear in teacher's guides and professional literature.

currence. However, the letter combination *ol* appears in relatively few words, yet the words are very common (*hold, told, cold*). Thus, *ol* would be introduced relatively early.

The second sequencing consideration is the similarity of letter combinations. If letter combinations make similar (but not identical) sounds, they should be separated by at least three other combinations. Letter combinations to be separated include:

1. *sh* and *ch*: These consonant digraphs are made by forming the lips in a very similar manner. This factor, along with their similar sound and appearance (both contain the letter *h*), can cause confusion.

2. *oa, oi,* oo, and *ou:* In addition to the fact that these letter combinations sound somewhat similar, they are part of a bigger group of letter combinations that begin with o (*oa, oi, ol,* oo, *ou, ow,* and *oy*). The large number of combinations beginning with the same letter and similar sound can confuse students.

3. *r*-controlled vowels: The three sounds produced by *r*-controlled vowels (/ar/ as in arm, /ur/ as in fur, bird, her, and /or/ as in sport) all sound similar. Thus, the letter combinations which represent these sounds should be separated.

Letter combinations representing the same sound (*ee* and *ea, ai* and *ay, ir* and *ur, oi* and *oy, au* and *aw*) need not be separated. Only letter combinations which represent *similar* sounds should be separated.

In Table 16.2 we have constructed a sample order for introducing letter combinations. Keep in mind that the order suggested is *not* meant to represent the only order for introducing letter combinations. It is only an example of how the sequencing guidelines can be applied.

Table 16.2		Sample Order for Introducing Letter Combinations			
1.	th	10.	ea	19.	ir
2.	er	11.	oo	20.	ur
3.	ing	12.	ee	21.	kn
4.	sh	13.	ai	22.	oi
5.	wh	14.	ch	23.	oy
6.	qu	15.	or	24.	ph
7.	ol	16.	ay	25.	wr
8.	oa	17.	igh	26.	au
9.	ar	18.	ou	27.	aw

Here is the rationale for determining the placement of specific letters in Table 16.2.

1. *Th, wh,* and *ol* are introduced early because they appear in very common, high-frequency words (e.g., this, that, when, where, and sold).

2. *Er* and *ing* are introduced early because, in addition to serving as letter combinations, they also function as affixes (e.g., cutter, cutting).

3. *Sh* and *ch* are separated by nine other combinations because, if introduced too near each other, they might be confused by some students.

Rate of Introduction

Learning to decode words containing a new letter combination is more difficult than simply learning the sound of a letter combination in isolation. When reading a word that contains a letter combination, the student can no longer decode by looking at the word letter by letter, but must see the word as being composed of one or more combinations of letters. For example,

to decode the word *sheet,* the student must see that *sh* and *eet* are units within the word. This transition, from decoding letter by letter to decoding words as units, requires extensive practice. The students' performance in decoding words containing previously taught letter combinations determines when to introduce a new letter combination, rather than their ability to identify a letter combination in isolated sound tasks.

As a general rule, students should be able to read a list of words containing letter combinations introduced to that date with no errors on the first trial at a rate no slower than every 2 seconds with 95% accuracy before a new letter combination is introduced. There are exceptions to this rule. If a student has developed a confusion between two letter combinations, the teacher (while working on alleviating the confusion) might introduce another letter combination. The new letter combination should not be similar to the ones with which the student is having difficulty. For example, if a student is having difficulty with the combinations *oo* and *ou* the teacher might introduce combination *ir* which is not similar to either of the pair the student has confused. (Procedures for alleviating confusions are discussed on page 94 of Chapter 8.) If, however, a student is having difficulty with more than one pair of previously introduced combinations, the teacher should work generally on firming up the student's knowledge of these combinations before introducing a new one. In a developmental program being taught to average-ability students, nearly all letter-combinations can be introduced by the end of the primary grades. This translates into a new letter combination being introduced about every second week.

Teaching Procedure

Two basic formats can be used in teaching students to decode words that contain letter combinations: an isolated-sounds format in which students learn to identify letter combinations in isolation and a sight word-list format in which the students identify words that contain a letter combination.

Isolated-sounds Format

The isolated-sounds format (see Table 16.3) is similar to the formats used to teach the most common sounds of individual letters. The teacher writes the new letter combination, along with several previously introduced letter combinations, on the board. The teacher models the sound of the new letter combination and tests the students on saying the sound. Then the teacher alternates between the new letter combination and previously introduced letter combinations. The teacher uses the same signaling procedures and alternating procedure discussed in Chapter 8.

Critical Behaviors for Teaching Isolated Sounds

Signals, Pacing, and Individual Turns. The signaling procedure would be the same as described on pages 90–93 for isolated letter-sound correspondences. The teacher points to a letter combination, pauses to let the student recall the sound, then signals with an out-in motion. The teacher should point to the letter combination for about a second; then quickly move to another letter.

The pacing should be rapid from letter to letter. When the students respond correctly to a signal, the teacher quickly moves to another sound, allows, the students time to recall the sound, and then signals.

Correcting Mistakes

If a student misidentifies a letter combination or responds late, the teacher tells the

---

Table 16.3   Isolated Sounds for Letter Combinations (This format introduces the letter combination *ea*.)

Teacher	Students
Teacher writes on the board: ea, or, ee, ea, th, sh, ea, and ing.	
1. Teacher models by saying the sound of the new letter combination and tests by having the students pronounce it. Teacher points to *ea*. "These letters usually say /ē/. What sound?" (Signal.)	"ē."
2. Teacher alternates between the new combination and other combinations. Teacher points to a letter combination, pauses 2 seconds, says "What sound?" and signals with an out-in motion.	Say the most common sound.
3. Teacher presents the remaining letter combinations using an alternating pattern similar to this: ea, or, ea, ee, th, ea, sh, ing, or, ea.	
4. Teacher calls on several individual students to identify one or more letter combinations.	

student the correct sound, has the student say the sound, and then alternates between the missed letter combination and other letter combinations the student knows. If a student continues to make errors on a previously introduced letter combination, extra practice should be provided on that combination in the next lessons.

Example Selection

The format should include six to eight letter combinations. The following are guidelines for selecting examples:

1. Review the most recently introduced letter combinations daily until students correctly produce the correct sound for the letter combination on the first trial for three consecutive lessons.

2. Exclude previously taught, similar letter combinations the first day a new letter combination appears. On the second day after the new combination appears, include any previously introduced letter combinations similar to the newly introduced combination. For example, on the second day *ch* is introduced, the combination *sh* should be included because it sounds similar. Similarly, on the second day after the letter combination *or* is introduced, the letter combination *ar* should be included. Do not, however, include a similar letter combination unless it has been taught earlier.

Word-list Format

The word-list format (see Table 16.4) gives students practice reading words with letter combinations. Words containing a new letter combination can be introduced when the students correctly produce the sound of the combination for two consecutive days

---

Table 16.4   Format for Words With Letter Combinations

Teacher	Students
Teacher writes on the board: <u>bout</u>, r<u>ou</u>nd, l<u>ou</u>d, b<u>oo</u>t, b<u>ea</u>m, tr<u>ou</u>t, stain, proud, moon, pound.	
1. a. Students identify the sound of the letter combination, then read the word. Teacher points under the underlined letters and asks, "What sound?" (Signal.)	"Ou."
b. Teacher points to left of word. "What word?" (Signal.)	"Bout."
c. Teacher repeats step 1(a–b) with remaining words.	
2. a. Students reread the list without first identifying the sound of the letter combination. Teacher points to *bout*, pauses 2 seconds, and asks, "What word?" (Signal.)	"Bout."
b. Teacher repeats step 2(a) with remaining words.	
3. Teacher calls on individual students to read one or more words.	

---

in the isolated-sounds format. The word-list format should include 10–15 words. In the first half of the words, the letter combination are underlined. The students first read the words with the underlined combination. For each word, the students first say the sound for the letter combination, then they say the entire word. The students then reread those words and the remaining words without first identifying the sound of the letter combination.

Critical Teaching Behavior

When presenting word-list exercises, the teacher uses the same procedures discussed for practicing sight-word reading in the beginning stage. (See page 118.) The teacher points to the left of a word, pauses to let students figure out the word, then signals by using an out-in motion. The teacher monitors the students by watching their eyes and mouths. When giving individual turns, the teacher points to a word, pauses to let students figure out the word, then calls a student's name. This procedure increases the probability of high student attentiveness.

Correction Procedure for Word Reading. If a student misidentifies a word or does not respond, the teacher points to the letter or letter combination pronounced incorrectly, then asks the student to say its sound. For example, if a student says "boot" for *bout*, the teacher points under *ou* and says "What sound do these letters make?" If the student does not respond or responds incorrectly, the teacher tells the sound and has the student repeat it. After the student produces the correct sound for the letter (or letter combination), the teacher asks, "What word?" Then she returns to the beginning of the list or 4 words earlier in the list, whichever is fewer and re-presents the words.

Example Selection Sight Reading Word Lists

- The first 3 words in the list should contain the newly introduced letter combination.

- Of the remaining words in the list, a third to a half should include the newly introduced letter combination.

- Include words that will appear in passages students will read within the next few lessons.

(Appendix A includes words the teacher can use in constructing word-list exercises.)

Multisyllabic Words Containing Letter Combinations

Two-syllable words containing a letter combination (e.g., *loudest*, *leader*, *beetle*) should be introduced several weeks after the first one-syllable words with that letter combination are introduced. A format for introducing multisyllabic words is discussed in Chapter 17.

Words with a VCe Pattern

In a VCe pattern word, a single vowel is followed by a consonant, which, in turn, is followed by a final *e*. Note the VCe patterns in the following words:

VCe   VCe   VCe
lake, stripe, smile.

In approximately two-thirds of the one-syllable words containing VCe patterns, the initial vowel represents the long sound (the letter name.) In the other one-third of the words in which there is a VCe pattern, the vowel sound is sometimes the most common sound of the initial vowel (give) and sometimes a sound that is neither the most common sound nor the long sound (done).[2]

Since the initial vowel represents its long sound in many one-syllable VCe pattern words, we recommend teaching the rule that when a word ends in *e*, the initial vowel says its name. The one-syllable, VCe pattern words in which the initial vowel makes a sound other than its long sound should be treated as irregular words. Although a few irregular VCe pattern words (e.g., have, give, come) will need to be introduced early because of their high frequency, most irregular VCe words should not be introduced until after students learn to decode "regular" VCe words in which the vowel represents the long sound.

Preskills

The strategy to decode VCe pattern words should be introduced after students have been taught to identify 6 to 8 letter combinations and can decode words containing those combinations. Reading words with letter combinations gives students practice in looking at units of letters. This skill will prepare students for VCe words in which the initial vowel sound is determined by a letter at the end of a word (the final *e*).

Students should also be able to discriminate vowel letter names from vowel letter sounds before VCe pattern words are introduced. Many students will already know letter names.

For those students who do not know the name of the vowel letters, the teacher will need to make a mini-program to teach vowel names. On the first day, the teacher writes two vowels on the board, then tells the students the names of each vowel. "You know the sound these letters make. Today you're going to learn their names." (Points to *a*.) "This letter's name is *a*." (Points to *o*.) "This letter's name is *o*" The teacher then tests the students asking, "What's the name of this letter?" for each letter. The next day, the teacher begins by testing the students: (Points to *a*.) "What's the name of this letter?" (Points to *o*.) "What's the name of this letter?" If the students know both letter names, the teacher can introduce another letter name, then test on all three letter names. The procedure is repeated daily until the students can say the letter names for all vowels.

When the students know all vowel letter names, a discrimination format should be introduced. The teacher writes two letters on the board: *o* and *a*. The teacher models, pointing to the *o* and says, "This letter's name is ō. It's sound is /ŏ/." The teacher then tests the students by asking, "What's its name? What's its sound?" The same procedure is followed with the letter *a*.

The next day the teacher begins by testing. She writes *a* and *o* on the board and for each letter asks, "What's its name? What's its sound?" If the students are able to produce the name and the sound correctly for each letter, the teacher introduces the third letter: *i*. The teacher models saying the name and sound for *i*, then tests for that letter. Afterwards, the teacher tests all 3 letters (*a, o, i*) by asking students to say the names and sound for each letter. The teacher provides daily practice on saying the name and sound of the vowels *a, i,* and *o*. When the students can respond without making any errors for two consecutive days, the teacher can introduce VCe pattern words. Note that we did not include the letters *e* and *u* in the discrimination format. There are relatively few VCe pattern words in which these letters are the

---

2. Various researchers report different percentages for the number of words in which the initial vowel in a VCe pattern represents its long sound. Clymer (1963) found the percentage to be 63%; Burmeister (1968), 61%. The differences result from the different words included in the studies.

initial vowel. We recommend delaying the introduction of VCe pattern words with either *e* or *u* as the initial vowel. This delay reduces the initial demands on the students. The letters *e* and *u* can be introduced when students can decode VCe word that have *a, i,* or *o* as initial vowels.

Teaching Procedure

Two formats are used to teach VCe pattern words. First, there is an introductory format in which the teacher presents the rule and leads the students through decoding VCe pattern words.

In the introductory format (see Table 16.5), the teacher tells students about the VCe rule and prompts its usage. The students tell the teacher first the name of the initial vowel, then says the word. Note that the teacher does not use the term "initial vowel," but instead, points to the initial vowel and says, "An *e* at the end tells us to say the name of this letter." This wording is used because at this stage, students have not learned the terms *vowel* or *initial.* The VCe concept can be taught without the extensive preskill teaching necessary to teach the word meanings.

A discrimination format (see Table 16.6) is used when students can answer the questions in the introductory format without error for two consecutive lessons. Included in the discrimination format is a six-word list with three CVCe words: one with *i* as the initial vowel, one with *a* for the initial

---

Table 16.5   Introductory Format for VCe Words

Teacher	*Students*
Teacher writes on the board: game, rope, mine, tape, note.	
1. Teacher states the rule: "An *e* at the end tells us to say the name of this (pointing to *a*) letter."	
2. Teacher guides students in applying the rule.	
a. Teacher points to game. "Is there an *e* at the end of this word?" (Signal.)	"Yes."
b. Teacher points to *a*. "So we say the name of this letter."	
c. "What's the name of this letter?" (Signal.)	"A."
d. "Get ready to tell me the word." Teacher pauses 2 seconds, then says, "What word?" (Signal.)	"Game."
e. Teacher repeats step 2(a–d) with the remaining four words.	
3. Students read all the words without guidance from the teacher.	
a. "You're going to read these words."	
b. Teacher points to *game,* pauses 2 seconds, then signals.	"Game."
c. Teacher repeats step 2(b) with remaining words.	
4. Teacher calls on individual students to read one or more words.	

Table 16.6   Discrimination Format for VCe Words

Teacher	Students
Teacher writes on board: make, sit, hope, like, ram, hop.	
1. Teacher reminds students of the rule: Remember, an *e* at the end of a word tells us to say the *name* (points to initial vowel) of this letter.	
2. Teacher guides students.	
a. Teacher points to *make*. "Is there an *e* at the end of this word?" (Signal.)	"Yes."
b. Teacher points to *a* in make. "Do we say /ā/ or /ă/ for this letter?" (Signal.)	"/ā/."
c. Teacher points to left of *make*, pauses, then says, "What word?" (Signal.)	"Make."
d. Teacher repeats steps 2(a–c) with remaining words.	
3. Students read words without teacher guidance.	
a. "When I signal, tell me the word."	
b. Teacher points to *make*, pauses 2 seconds, then asks, "What word?" (Signal.)	"Make."
c. Teacher repeats steps 3(b) with remaining words.	
4. Teacher calls on several individual students to read one or more words.	

vowel, and one with *o* for the initial vowel. The remaining three words should consist of regular CVC words: one with *i* as the initial vowel, one with *a* as the initial vowel, and one with *o* as the initial vowel. One or two minimally different pairs should be included (e.g., *hope–hop, dime–dim*). The list would be constructed in an unpredictable order (a CVCe word is not always followed by a CVC word). A list might include these words: make, sit, hope, like, ram, hop. Few words beginning with consonant blends (e.g., *globe, crime*) should appear in the introductory or discrimination format for the first two weeks of practice with VCe pattern words.

The students read the list twice. During the first reading, the teacher guides the students, asking about the presence of an *e* at the end of the word, then asking if the initial vowel says its name. In the second reading, the students simply say the word without teacher prompting.

The sight word list is presented daily (not using the identical words from day to day) until the students are able on the first trial to respond correctly to all the words for at least two consecutive days. Thereafter, VCe pattern words are incorporated into passage reading stories and mixed into sight word-list exercises that contain words with letter combinations, as well as irregular words. VCe pattern words with *e* and *u* can be introduced at this time.

Correcting Mistakes

The most common error is the students saying a CVCe word with the short sound of the initial vowel (e.g., saying "pan" for *pane*.) The correction procedure is illustrated below:

1. Teacher asks "Is there an *e* at the end of this word?" and prompts rule "Remember, if there is an *e* at the end, we say its (pointing to vowel) name."

2. Teacher asks the vowel sound. "What's the name (pointing to initial vowel) of this letter?"

3. Teacher has students say the word. "What word?"

4. Teacher returns to the beginning of the list and re-presents the words.

The same correction procedure is used for any type of mistake involving the vowel sound (e.g., student says "some" for *same* or "dime" for *dome*)

Application Exercises

1. Assume you have taught students the following skills:
   - Most common sound of all individual letters;
   - How to decode all regular word types;
   - Strategy to decode VCe words with long vowel sound;
   - The most common sound of the following letter combinations: *ar, ea, ee, oa, th, sh, wh, ck.*

   Circle each of the following words the student would not be able to decode. Next to each of the circled words, write the abbreviated explanation below that tells why the student could not decode the word.
   - Letter (L)—The word contains a letter combination that the student does not know.
   - Irregular (I)—Some letter or letter combination is not representing its most common sound.

_____ground	_____those	_____warn
_____boat	_____which	_____farm
_____speak	_____spoil	_____break
_____wish	_____cheer	_____sack
_____stew	_____stick	_____done
_____went	_____groan	_____build
_____broad	_____spout	

2. Circle the three pairs of letter combinations below students are most likely to confuse:

   ch–sh   ph–wr   ai–ea

   ea–ou   ou–oo   ar–ir

3. Below are sequences in which teachers introduced letter combinations. State the problems with each sequence.

   Sequence 1: *au, ea, ph, oy, th, ar*
   Sequence 2: *ar, er, th, sh, ch, ou, oi*

4. Describe the differences in teachers' presentation of words, such as *like, made,* and *hope,* and words, such as *have, none,* and *live.*

5. Below are the words three teachers included in VCe discrimination format. One teacher's examples are acceptable. Identify that teacher's examples. Tell why the other examples are unacceptable.

Teacher A: *lake, hope, time, bake, rode, made*

Teacher B: *tape, tap, side, Sid, hope, hop*

Teacher C: *rope, time, sad, Tim, made, lot*

6. The following letter combinations have been taught so far in a program: *th, sh, wh, er, ai, oo, ar,* and *ea.* On an individual test, a student identifies all the letter combinations correctly except *oo.* Assume the program introduces the letter combination *ch* on the next lesson.
Should the teacher delay *ch*? If so, why?
What if the program introduced the letter combination *ou* on the next lesson?
Should the teacher delay *ou*? If so, why?

7. In the following situations, specify what the teacher should do and the wording the teacher would use to correct the error. Then describe what the teacher should do next after the students have responded correctly to the missed item.

a. During an isolated-sounds format, the student says "o" for *ou.*

b. During the word-list format: for one-syllable words containing a letter combination, a student says "bat" for *bait.*

c. During the VCe format, a student says "hop" for *hope.*

8. (Review item)
Describe 6 examples (3 positive and 3 negative) that could be used to teach the concept, *plastic.* Specify what the teacher says and does with each example.

Structural analysis refers to an analysis of words formed by adding prefixes, suffixes or other meaningful word units to a base word. Structural analysis is sometimes referred to as morphemic analysis, morphemes being the smallest meaningful units of language.

In this section, we will present strategies for teaching students to decode words formed by adding morphemes (prefixes, suffixes, or inflected endings) to a base word.

The chart in Table 17.1 lists major word types formed by adding morphemes to base words. The word types appear in their approximate order of introduction into a reading program. Each word type is described in the first column, illustrated in the second column, and special difficulties that arise are commented on in the third column.

Words Formed by Adding Common Endings to Base Words That End with a Consonant

Two factors should be taken into consideration when designing a sequence for introducing prefixes and suffixes: (1) the number of primary level words in which each prefix or suffix appears, and (2) the relative similarity of the prefixes or suffixes. As always, any similar word parts should not be introduced too close to each other. For example, the suffix *le* would not be introduced soon after the suffix *ly* because they both contain the letter *l*, but represent significantly different sounds.

Table 17.2 lists prefixes and suffixes in one possible order of introduction. Although it is not the only acceptable sequence, it does serve as a concrete example of how our recommendations are applied. In column 1 is a word that represents the most-common pronunciation of the particular suffix or prefix. Column 2 tells whether

Chapter

17

Structural Analysis

Word Type	Illustration	Comment
Common ending or prefix added to a known base word ending with a consonant	bat + er = batter farm + ing = farming sun + y = sunny re + pack = repack	When suffixes that begin with a vowel are added to words ending with a consonant-vowel-consonant pattern (CVC), the final consonant is doubled
ed added to words ending with a consonant	stop + ed = stopped hum + ed = hummed hand + ed = handed	When *ed* is added to a base word, the final consonant sound may be /d/ (hummed) or /t/ (stopped). Sometimes adding *ed* adds an extra syllable (handed).
Compound words	in + to = into some + times = sometimes	
An ending added to a word that ends with the letter *e*	hope + ing = hoping like + able = likable care + less = careless	When an ending that begins with a vowel is added to a word that ends with *e*, the *e* is dropped. Students must deal with discriminating word pairs such as *hopped* and *hoped*.
An ending added to base word ending with the letter y	cry + ed = cried happy + ness = happiness stay + ed = stayed	When the base word has a consonant before the *y*, the *y* is changed to an *i*. The *i* may represent the /ē/ or /ī/ sound, depending on the sound of the *y* represented in the base word.
Suffixes or prefixes added to multisyllabic word	in + action = inaction	

the word part is a prefix, suffix, or inflected ending.[1]

Words formed by adding a suffix or prefix to a base word can be introduced when students are able to sight read one syllable words at a rate of about 20 words per minute.

---

1. The discrimination between what is a suffix and what is an inflected ending is not critical for teaching decoding. We list them simply because the terms appear in reading literature.

The basic procedure for teaching students to read words formed by adding a common prefix or suffix to a base word ending in a consonant is to (1) introduce a prefix or suffix in the letter-sound correspondence format; (2) practice the prefix or suffix in isolation for several days; (3) introduce words containing that prefix or suffix in a word-list exercise; and, (4) then include words of that type in passage-reading stories.

	Column 1	Column 2
er	batter	inflected ending
ing	jumping	inflected ending
ed	jumped	inflected ending
y	funny	suffix
un	unlock	prefix
est	biggest	inflected ending
le	handle	suffix
a	alive	prefix
be	belong	prefix
re	refill	prefix
de	demand	prefix
ic	heroic	suffix
ful	careful	suffix
ly	sadly	suffix

Table 17.2 Sample Sequence for Introducing Common Prefixes and Suffixes

The presentation procedure begins with the teacher introducing a new ending or prefix in isolation. The teacher writes the new word part on the board along with several other prefixes or endings that have already been introduced. The teacher:

- Models the sounds made by the suffix: (Teacher points to *er*.) At the end of a word, these letters usually say "er."

- Tests the students: (Teacher points to *er*.) What do these letters say? "Er."

- Provides practice: Teacher alternates between the new ending and other letter combinations and endings. What do these letters say?

(Note that the teaching procedure is similar to that described in Chapter 8 for teaching isolated letter-sound correspondences.)

The new word-ending is practiced for several days in the letter-sounds format, then words containing that ending are introduced in the following manner: Four or five words in which the new ending is added to a known base word are written on the board. The base word is underlined. (Note: In many words there will be a double consonant. The base word is underlined through the double consonant.)

<u>jump</u>ing	<u>trick</u>ing
<u>bet</u>ting	<u>hop</u>ping
<u>swim</u>ming	

The teacher has the students read the list twice. On the first reading, the teacher prompts the students. For each word, the teacher first has the students say the underlined part ("Say the underlined part." (Signal.)), then pronounce the entire word ("Say the whole word." (Signal.)). After completing the list, the students reread the list without reading the underlined part.

After several days, a discrimination exercise with 8 to 12 words is presented. In each word, the base word is underlined. The students read the discrimination list twice. The first time they say the underlined part, then the whole word. The second time they only say the whole word.

The newly introduced word ending should appear in about half the words. The other words should have previously introduced endings. Below is a sample list that might be used to present the ending *est* in a discrimination list. Assume that the endings *er*, *ing*, and *y* have previously been introduced.

<u>big</u>gest	<u>small</u>est
<u>funn</u>y	<u>small</u>er
<u>smart</u>est	<u>sunn</u>y
<u>hop</u>ping	<u>tall</u>est
<u>bett</u>er	<u>runn</u>ing

The most important criteria in selecting words for word-list exercises is that base words to which the prefix or suffix is added must be words the student is able to read, i.e., either an irregular word that has been previously taught or a word that contains letter-sound correspondences the student has been taught. (A list of words containing common prefixes can be found in Appendix A.)

A new prefix or suffix can be introduced when students are able to read the discrimination list without error on the first trial for two consecutive days.

Introducing Words Formed by Adding "ed"

The *ed* ending may represent one of three pronunciations. When *ed* is added to a word that ends in *d* or *t*, the *ed* is pronounced as a separate syllable (e.g., *handed, batted*). When *ed* is added to other words, the *ed* sometimes represents the /t/ sound (e.g., *jumped, tricked*), and sometimes, the /d/ sound (e.g., *hummed, begged*). The suffix *ed* can be introduced when stu-

dents are able to read words with the endings *ing* or *er*.

The teaching procedure for words that contain the *ed* suffix consists of 2 steps. The first step involves a verbal format (see Table 17.3) in which the teacher writes *ed* on the board, says a word, then says the word with the *ed* ending. (e.g., "I'll say hop with this ending. Hopped"). The teacher repeats this procedure with two more words, each ending with a different sound. Then the teacher tests the students on a set of six words. In 2 words, the *ed* represents the /d/ sound (e.g., *filled, hummed*), in two other words the /t/ sound (e.g., *jumped, hopped*), and in the remaining two words the /ed/ sound (e.g., *handed, landed*). The base words should be words the students have learned to decode. A sample list might include: *handed, jumped, filled, landed, hopped,* and *hummed*.

The advantage of using this verbal format is that it clearly demonstrates how the base word determines the sound the *ed*

Table 17.3   Format for Verbally Presented "ed" Words

Teacher	Students
1. Teacher writes *ed* on the board. Teacher then models and tests, saying different words with the *ed* suffix.	
a. "Say hop." (Signal.)	"Hop."
"I'll say hop with this ending."	
Teacher points to *ed*. "Hopped."	
b. Teacher points to *ed*. "Say hop with this ending." (Signal.)	"Hopped."
Teacher repeats steps 1(a–b) with *hum* and *lift*.	
2. Teacher tests students.	
a. Teacher points to *ed*. "Say hop with this ending." (Signal.)	"Hopped."
b. Teacher repeats step 2(a) with *hum, jump, lift, hand,* and *rub*.	
3. Teacher calls on individual students.	

ending will make. Because the students do not have to read the base word, they can concentrate on saying the ending appropriately. The *ed* ending is *not* presented in an isolated-sounds task. Presenting *ed* in an isolated-sounds task would be inappropriate since *ed* can represent one of three sounds.

In the second format (see Table 17.4), written words are presented. This format can be introduced when the students can do the verbal *ed* format without errors for two consecutive days.

The first 3 days the format is presented, the teacher writes on the board a set of 6 regular words to which *ed* had been added. (The same example selection procedure as described above for the verbal format is used.) The teacher underlines the base word (e.g., handed, filled, hummed, batted, hopped, jumped). The students read the list twice. On the first reading, the students

---

Table 17.4   Format for Presenting Written "ed" Words

Teacher	Students
Teacher writes on the board:	

hummed   begged
jumped   tripped
lifted   handed

Part I—Introducing "ed" Words (presented for 3 days only)

1. Students read each word by first identifying the root word and then saying the whole word.
    a. Teacher points to *hummed.* "Say the underlined part." (Signal.) — *"Hum."*
    b. "Say the whole word." (Signal.) — *"Hummed."*
    c. Teacher repeats steps 1(a–b) with remaining words.

2. Teacher tests students on reading words.
    a. Teacher points to *hummed.* "What word?" (Pauses 2 seconds, then signals.) — *"Hummed."*
    b. Teacher repeats step 2(a) with remaining words.

3. Teacher gives individual turns.

Part II—Discrimination Practice (begins on 3rd day)

Teacher writes on the board:

lifted   stopped   handed
handing   skipper   running
hummed   picked   lifting
biggest   picking   tagged

1. a. Teacher points to *lifted,* pauses 2 seconds, says "What word?" (Signal.) — *"Lifted."*
    b. Teacher repeats step 1(a) with remaining words.

2. Teacher gives individual turns.

---

say the base word, then the whole word. On the second reading, the students only say the entire word. On the third day, a practice list that contains 8 to 12 words is be presented. The list should include a mix of word endings. Half with the various *ed* sounds and half with previously introduced endings. The practice list is presented daily. Words with new parts are incorporated into the list.

VCe Derivatives

A VCe derivative is created by adding a word ending to a VCe pattern word (e.g., care + less = careless, hope + ing = hoping).

The easiest VCe derivative is that formed by adding the letter *s* to a VCe word (hope + s = hopes). This word type can be introduced when students have demonstrated mastery of the discrimination between VCe words and CVC words (*hate–hat*). The teacher presents an introductory list of four words. Each word is a VCe word to which *s* has been added (e.g., *hates, likes, names*). The VCe base word is underlined (e.g., hates). For each word, the teacher has the students say the underlined part, then the whole word.

A discrimination exercise can be presented when the students can do the introductory exercise without error for two consecutive days. The discrimination word list should include a mix of CVC and VCe words to which the letter *s* has been added (e.g., hates, cops, names, hopes, taps, tapes). The teacher has the students read the list twice. The first time, students say the underlined part, then the entire word. The second time, students only say the whole word. When the students can do the exercise with no errors for two consecutive days, the teacher can write the list without the underlining and have them read the words in a regular, unprompted sight-word-list list exercise. Keep in mind that the list should be written in a non-predictable order; a VCe word should not always follow a CVC word. When the students can read this type of list without error for two consecutive days, VCe words with *s* endings can be integrated into word-list exercises containing a mixture of regular and irregular words to which various endings have been added (e.g., *handed, lifting, hopes, bigger, likes, hats, jumped, sitter, ropes, funny*).

VCe derivatives formed by adding endings other than *s* are introduced when students can read lists formed by adding *s* to CVCe and CVC words without error.

The teaching procedure for these words must take into account the effect of a spelling rule: When an ending that begins with a vowel is added to a VCe word, the *e* is dropped (e.g., hope + ing = hoping, love + able = lovable, use + ed = used). The difficulty caused by this spelling rule arises because of the likelihood that students may see a CVCe-derivative word as a CVC word plus an ending (e.g., hoping is seen as hop + ing rather than hope + ing).

A 3-step teaching procedure is used to teach CVCe derivatives:

1. Introduce VCe derivatives formed by adding any ending except *ing* to a VCe word.

2. Introduce VCe derivatives formed by adding *ing* to a VCe word.

3. Teach a strategy for discriminating CVCe derivatives from CVC derivatives (hoping vs. hopping).

The introduction of words formed by adding common endings (other than *ing*) to CVCe words is similar to the procedure for introducing words formed by adding *s* to CVCe derivatives.

The teacher constructs a list of 6–9 words, a third with *a* as the initial vowel, a third with *o* as the initial vowel, and a third with *i* as the initial vowel. A mix of common endings is incorporated. The CVCe base word is underlined. Here is a sample list:

named	smiled	hoped
smoker	hopeless	baker
likely	tamer	rider

The students read the list twice: the first time identifying the underlined part, then saying the whole word; the second time only saying the whole word. This format is presented daily until students make no errors for two consecutive words.

A mini-format for introducing words formed by adding *ing* is presented on the second or third day after the other endings are introduced. This format (see Table 17.5) demonstrates how the CVCe spelling rule works. The teacher writes several sets which include the base word, the ending, and the word formed by combining (hope + ing = hoping). The teacher explains that the *e* is dropped when combining the base word and the ending. The teacher then has the students identify and spell each part of each word set.

Two formats can be used to teach students to discriminate CVCe derivatives from regular-word derivatives. The first discrimination format can be presented after the students make no errors in the introductory format for two consecutive days. In this format, the teacher constructs a list of about 8 words—half CVC derivatives, half CVCe derivatives. Below is a sample list:

hopping	liked
hopeless	baker
timer	hitter
madder	likely

Table 17.5 Format for Introducing CVCe Derivatives Formed by Adding "ing"

Teacher	Students

Teacher writes on the board:
  hope + ing = hoping
  care + ing = caring
  ride + ing = riding	

1. Teacher tells students about spelling rule: "Here's a rule about spelling words that end with an *e*. When you add the ending *ing*, you drop the final *e*" (Points to *hoping, caring* and *riding*.) "These are words formed by using this rule."	
2. (Points to hope.) "What word?" (Signal.) (Points to hope.) "Spell *hope*." (Signal.) (Points to ing.) "What ending?" (Signal.) (Points to ing.) "Spell *ing*." (Signal.) (Points to hoping.) "What word?" (Signal.) (Points to hoping.) "Spell *hoping*." (Signal.)	"Hope." "H-o-p-e." "Ing." "I-n-g." "Hoping." "H-o-p-i-n-g."
3. Teacher repeats step 2 with remaining sets.	

4. Teacher has students read 2-syllable words.
  a. (Points to hoping.) "What word?" (Signal.)
  b. Repeats step 4(a) with remaining words.
	
	"Hoping."

The base part is underlined. Note that the underlining extends through the double consonant in CVC derivatives and through the *e* in CVCe derivatives. The students read the list twice: the first time saying the underlined part, then the entire word; the second time they only say the whole word.

Also note that CVCe derivatives that end in *ing* cannot be used in the above format. If the base were underlined (i.e., hop<u>ing</u>) the format would induce the students to say the wrong word.

A special format for discriminating CVCe and CVC derivatives ending with *ing* appears in Table 17.6. In this format, the teacher shows the students how to use the number of consonants in the middle of the word as a cue to the pronunciation of the initial vowel. To discriminate between words such as *tapping* and *taping*, students must cue on the number of consonants in the middle of the word. One consonant in the middle of a word indicates that the word was derived from a VCe pattern and that the initial vowel *will probably* represent its long sound. Two consonants in the middle of a word indicates that the word was *not* derived from a VCe-pattern word and that the initial vowel will *not* represent its long sound.

The format is designed to keep language usage simple. The terms *consonant* and *vowel* are not used. The initial vowel is underlined in each word. The rule students learn is: Double letters after the underlined letter tell you to say its sound. A single letter after the underlined letter tells you to say its name.

Steps 1 and 2 teach students to determine if a word contains a single letter or double letters after the underlined letter. Step 3 presents the rules while in Step 4 the teacher leads students through applying the rules. Appendix A lists words that can be used in this format.

Y Derivatives

Y derivatives are formed by adding an ending to a word that ends in *y* (e.g., marry + ed = married, dry + ed = dried, happy + est = happiest). Y derivatives can cause difficulty because of the variety of sounds that may occur. When an ending is added to a base word that ends in *y*, there is usually a spelling change. The *y* is changed to an *i*. Note that in the following examples, the letters *ie* represents a variety of sounds. In the word *married*, the *ie* represents the /ē/ sound. In *dried*, the *ie* represents the /ī/ sound. And in *happiest*, the *ie* represents two sounds—the long e sound followed by the short e sound. A procedure for teaching students to decode y derivatives must deal with this variability.

Y derivatives can be introduced when the students know at least 5 words in which the *y* represents the /ē/ sound (e.g., *happy, funny, silly, carry, sunny*) and 5 words in which the y represents the /ī/ sound (e.g, *cry, fly, try, sky, dry*).

We recommend a 2-step procedure. The first step involves using word sets to illustrate how *y* derivatives are formed. Each set contains a base word, an ending, and the word formed by adding the ending to the base (e.g., funny + er = funnier). The examples should be carefully controlled. All the variations of sounds that *ie* represents should be included. Note that the list below contains an equal number of words in which the *ie* represents different sounds.

> bunny + es = bunnies
> funny + er = funnier
> try + es = tries
> carry + ed = carried
> happy + er = happier
> cry + ed = cried

Teacher	Students
Teacher writes on the board:	

hoping   taping
tapping   batting
filling   robbing
piling   roping

1. Teacher models presence of double consonants.
   "Some of these words have double letters after the underlined letter. Some of these words have single letters after the underlined letter.."
   Teacher points to hoping.
   "There's one *p* after the underlined letter. That's a single letter."
   Teacher points to tapping.
   "There's two *p*'s after the underlined letter. Those are double letters."

2. Teacher tests on presence of double letters.
   a. Teacher points to hoping. "What comes after the underlined letter. A single letter or double letters?" (Signal.)   *"A single letter."*
   b. Repeat step 2(a) with remaining words.
   c. Teacher gives individual turns.
   (Note: Steps 3 through 5 are not introduced until students are firm on step 2.)

3. Teacher presents rules about what to say.
   a. "Here are the rules about what to say for the underlined letter.
   b. If double letters come next, say the sound. If a single letter comes next, say the name.
   c. What do you say if a single letter comes next? (Signal.)   *"The name."*
   d. What do you say if double letters come next?" (Signal.)   *"The sound."*

4. Teacher leads through steps in applying rule.
   a. (Points to hoping.) "Does a single letter or double letters come next? (Signal.)   *"Single letter."*
   b. (Points to o.) Do we say the name or the sound for this letter? (Signal.)   *"The name."*
      What word?" (Signal.)   *"Hoping."*
   c. Teacher repeats steps 4(a) and 4(b) with remaining words.

5. Teacher tests.
   a. "This time you'll just say the whole word when I signal.
   b. (Points to hoping.)
      What word?" (Signal.)   *"Hoping."*
   c. Teacher repeats step 5(b) with remaining words.

The students read the list twice: the first time for each set they say the base word, then the *y* derivative (e.g., bunny, es, bunnies). In the second reading the teacher erases the base word plus the ending, then the students read only the derivatives. This exercise is continued until the students can do it without error for two consecutive days.

In the second step, a discrimination list focusing on *y* derivatives is presented. Half the words are *y* derivatives, including words in which the *ie* represents different sounds. The other half of the words are CVC and VCe derivatives. Below is a sample list:

sillier	drier
hoped	names
tried	funniest
runner	dropped
bunnies	candies

The students read a different list each day. When students can read the lists without error for two consecutive days, stories containing *y* derivatives can be presented.

Multisyllabic Words Formed with Prefixes and Suffixes

A systematic introduction of prefixes, suffixes, and multisyllabic words should occur throughout the primary and intermediate stage of a reading program.

The average number of syllables in the words students read should increase steadily throughout the grades. At the end of the beginning stage, students are reading primarily one- and two-syllable words. A year later, students will be reading more two- and three-syllable words with occassional four- and five-syllable words appearing.

The following word list might be presented to students reading at an early, third grade level:

refilling	unfairly	complaining
unlocked	returning	countless
belonging	respected	returned
repaying	surrounded	refilled

The length of words grows as students progress through the grades. The word list below might be presented to students reading at a fifth grade level:

occasional	professional	investigation
incredible	advantage	discovered
powerful	enjoyable	tremendous
entertainment	carefully	assortment
inspection	detective	poisonous

Note how the first list is composed of 3-syllable words in which the base word is either regular or contains a common letter combination, while the prefixes and suffixes to the base words are common, easy-to-decode affixes.

The second list contains several 4-syllable words, one 5-syllable word, and a greater variety of prefixes and suffixes.

Common prefixes and suffixes should be systematically introduced throughout the primary and intermediate grades. Table 17.7 gives a possible sequence for introducing prefixes and suffixes. Not all the endings listed in Table 17.7 are suffixes. For example, *tion* and *sion* are not actual suffixes. They are formed by adding the suffix *ion* to a word ending in *t* or *s* (inspect + ion = inspection, profess + ion = profession). Similarly, *ation* is formed by combining *ate* + *ion* (e.g. invite + ate + ion = invitation.) From a decoding viewpoint, it makes sense to present *tion* as an ending because it occurs in many words. Similarly, giving special treatment to *ation* is warranted since it appears in quite a few high-frequency words (e.g., *invitation, congratulations*).

The teaching procedure for the longer, multisyllabic words is similar to that used for words formed by adding common pre-

	Sample Word	Type
con	confuse	prefix
ment	payment	suffix
teen	sixteen	suffix
ful	handful	suffix
dis	distant	prefix
able	enjoyable	suffix
less	useless	suffix
ness	darkness	suffix
pro	protect	prefix
tion	invention[a]	suffix
ist	artist	suffix
ad	address	prefix
ible	sensible	suffix
age	package	suffix
sion	mission[a]	suffix
ence	sentence	suffix
ish	selfish	suffix
ation	vacation	suffix
pre	preschool	prefix
ex	expect	prefix
over	overtime	prefix
ion	million	suffix
ship	friendship	suffix
com	compare	prefix
ist	artist	suffix
ure	adventure	suffix
ive	detective	suffix
ac	accuse	prefix
ous	joyous	suffix
inter	interfere	prefix
ward	forward	suffix
ize	realize	suffix

Table 17.7 Sample Sequence for Introducing Common Prefixes and Suffixes

[a]The suffix *tion* is often formed by adding *ion* to a word ending in *t* (interruption). We list *tion* as a high-frequency suffix for convenience. In addition, *sion* is formed by adding *ion* to a word ending with *s* (miss + ion = mission).

fixes or suffixes to one-syllable words. The prefix or suffix is introduced and practiced in isolation. After several days, a group of words containing the new prefix or suffix is presented. After several days, words containing that new affix are mixed in with words containing previously introduced affixes. One or more word parts in each word are underlined.

The students read the list twice: the first time, they identify the underlined word parts ("What do these letters say?"), then they say the word ("What's the word?"); the second reading of the list, students only say the word. Below is a sample list:

professional	tremendous	instinctively
temperature	triangle	refrigerator
occasionally	exposure	incredible

Several sources are available for finding words to include in word-list exercises. Appendix A lists words containing the prefixes and suffixes shown in Tables 17.2 and 17.7. A more thorough listing of words can be found in a computer study by the University of Oregon *Follow Through* project. In this study, 28,000 words were divided into morphemes. The morphemes for each word were entered into a computer which generated word lists categorized by morpheme. A book entitled *Morphographs: An Alphabetical List with Examplars* contains words for each of the morphemes that appeared in the 28,000 words. A third source of multisyllabic words is an instructional program written by Anita Archer entitled "Learning Multisyllabic Words." (Information on these books can be obtained by writing to: D.I. Reading, P.O. Box 10459, Eugene, Oregon, 97440.)

Application Exercises

1. Each word in the list below contains a phonic or structural element. Circle the phonic (letter combination or VCe word) or structural element(s) unique to each word (see Table 17.4). Identify the type of phonic or structural element represented in each word.

batter	celebration	doting
helped	fried	humming
sail	saves	hardest

2. Assume students know the letter combinations *sh, th, ol,* and *wh,* all single letters, and the suffixes *ing* and *er.* Below are discrimination word lists various teachers prepared several days after the suffix *est* was introduced. Tell which teacher constructed an acceptable list. Specify the problem with the other two lists.

Teacher 1
biggest   hottest   hotter   fattest   coldest   colder   hitting
Teacher 2
hottest   biggest   fattest   coldest   maddest   wettest
Teacher 3
cheapest   cheaper   shortest   trainer   smallest   falling

3. Assume the students know the most common sounds of all single letters and can decode all types of regular words. Circle the prefixes and suffixes below which the students would not be able to decode.

ment   ist   un   pro   re   ion

4. Specify what the teacher would say and do to correct the following error made when reading a list of words:

   a. A student says *"hop-ped"* for the word *hopped.*

   b. A student says *"hopping"* for the word *hoping.*

5. Below are word lists a teacher used in the format for presenting written *ed* words. Two lists are unacceptable. Identify those lists and tell why they are not acceptable.

   List A: handed, lifted, rented, sanded, melted
   List B: fainted, hopped, pounced, jumped, steered, called
   List C: hopped, hummed, handed, jumped, lifted, filled

6. Why are students likely to make more decoding errors on the words *taping* and *hoping* than the words *taped* and *hopes?*

7. Construct a 10-word discrimination list. Assume the students know all single letters, and the letter combinations and suffixes *ar, ee, ea,* and the endings *er, ing, ed, y,* and *est.* The teacher is introducing words that end in *le.*
   Construct a 6-word introductory list for presenting y derivatives. Assume the students know all single letters and the letter combinations *ar, ee, ou, er,* and *ai.*

Irregular Words

Contextual analysis involves using the context of a sentence along with phonic and structural-analysis cues to decode irregular words. We define an irregular word as any word that contains a letter-sound correspondence the students do not know. The students' knowledge at a particular moment in time determines if a word is to be considered irregular. For example, if the students know the most common sound of the letter combination *ea,* the word *treat* would not be considered irregular. However, if the students had not learned the most common sound of *ea,* the word *treat* would be considered irregular.

As students learn phonic- and structural-analysis skills, the number of words to be treated as irregulars significantly decreases. There are two types of words that will always be considered irregular; namely:

- words containing an uncommon letter combinations which will not be taught to the students either because of its low frequency of appearance or lack of consistency in representing any particular sound (e.g., *duel, build, ceiling*). (See Table 18.1 for a list of these combinations.)

- words containing common letters or letter combinations not representing their respective, most common sounds. (For example, in the word *break,* the *ea* is not representing its most common sound.)

We recommend a two-part teaching procedure for irregular words. The teaching procedure is the same for both types of irregular words. First, a systematic and carefully controlled introduction and review of irregular words in word-list exer-

Chapter

18

Contextual Analysis

Table 18.1   List of Letter Combinations NOT to be Taught

Letter Combination	Sample Word	Percentage of Words with Sound
ae	algae	83
	aesthetic	17
ei	reign	40
	deceit	26
	foreign	13
	seismic	11
eo	pigeon	67
	leopard	20
	people	13
ie	chief	64
	tie	36
gh	rough	45
	ghost	48
oe	foe	59
	shoe	22
ue	clue	75
ui	build	47
	fruit	29
uy	buy	100

Note: The words in this table either appeared in less than 10 words and/or did not represent the same sound(s) in more than half the words in which they appeared. The source for these figures is Burmeister (1975), who also utilized Hanna and Hanna's (1966) computer analysis of letter-sound correspondences.

cises and passage-reading exercises. Second, a plan to teach students to use the context of a sentence and the known letter-sound relationships in the word to figure out unknown irregular words.

Systematic Introduction of Irregular Words

The systematic introduction of irregular words involves developing a sequence and a systematic teaching procedure for introducing and reviewing irregular words.

The sequencing guidelines for introducing irregular words remain the same as

during the beginning reading stage. More common words should be introduced before lower-frequency words. Also, words very similar to each other should not be introduced too near each other. Teachers using basal-reader textbooks use the words that will appear in upcoming passages.

Rate

During the beginning reading stage, we recommend introducing irregular words at a relatively slow rate. Initially, one word is introduced every several lessons, then one each second or third lesson. The rate gradually increases until several new words are introduced each day. The students' performance is the factor that determines the rate at which new words can be introduced. If students are able to identify previously introduced words with no difficulty, the teacher can introduce new words. If students misidentify previously introduced words, the teacher concentrates on reteaching these words, rather than introducing new words.

Review

Irregular words require systematic review. New words should appear in word-list exercises for several days, then appear in either or both passages and word-list exercises. The more difficult the irregular word, the more review is required. Two factors determine the difficulty of an irregular word. First is the difference between how the word is sounded out and how the word is pronounced. The greater the discrepancy between the sounds and the actual pronunciation, the more difficult the word is. The word *though*, for example, is more difficult to decode than the word *put* because several letters in *though* do not represent their most common sound (*ough*); whereas, in *put* only one letter does not represent its most common sound (*u*). The second factor that determines the relative difficulty of an irregular word is familiarity. The more familiar a word is to students, the easier it will be for them to decode. A word such as *tough* will be easier for students to remember than a word such as *agile*, because *tough* is more likely to be in the students' speaking vocabulary. Therefore, *agile* needs more review.

Teaching Procedure

The format for introducing and reviewing irregular words appears in Table 18.2. The format has two parts. In part 1, the teacher presents the irregular words being introduced in the current lesson, as well as those introduced in the previous lesson. These words appear in a column. For each word, the teacher

- tells the students the word. "This word is *fuel.*"
- has the students say the word. "What word?"
- has the students spell the word. "Spell *fuel.*"
- has the students say the word again. "What word?"

The teacher repeats the above procedure with each word, then has the students read the column again, just saying each word.

In part 2, irregular words introduced over the 3 prior days, as well as any previously introduced words students may have misidentified, are reviewed. The students read each word without any prompting from the teacher. Any error is corrected by telling the students the word, having them repeat it, then returning to an earlier word in the list and re-presenting the list.

Table 18.2 shows words that might be introduced in mid-third grade. Three new words are introduced each day. The first 3 words in the new word column (*ghost, pour,* and *zero*) are being introduced for the first time. The next 3 words (*weight, earth,* and *wrong*) are being reintroduced. They were presented in the previous lesson. The words in the review column were introduced two and three lessons prior to the current lesson.

Minor Sounds

The procedure for introducing irregular words can be modified when introducing

Table 18.2   Format for Introducing and Reviewing Irregular Words

Teacher	Students
Part 1: *(Teacher introduces new words.)*	

Teacher writes on board:

New Words	Review Words
ghost	agile
pour	fuel
zero	anchor
weight	chew
earth	zero
wrong	

1. Teacher models and has students spell words in new word column.

   a. Teacher points to *ghost*. "This word is *ghost*. What word?" (Signal.) — *"Ghost."*

   b. "Spell *ghost*." (Signal.) — *"G-h-o-s-t."*

   c. "What word?" (Signal.) — *"Ghost."*

   d. Teacher repeats steps 1(a–c) with remaining words in the new word column.

Part 2: *(Students sight read words in new word column and review word column.)*

1. a. "When I signal, tell me the word."

   b. Teacher points to *ghost*, pauses 2 seconds. "What word?" (Signal.) — *"Ghost."*

   c. Teacher repeats step 1(b) with all remaining words.

2. Teacher calls on individual students to read several words.

---

sets of related words and multisyllabic words.

Sets of related irregular words are formed by (1) words in which the letter *c* represents the /s/ sound; (2) words in which the letter *g* represents the /j/ sound; (3) one-syllable words which end with *ow, ew, y,* or *e.*

The letter *c* represents the /s/ sound (as in "cent" and "cill") in about 25% of the words in which it appears, while the letter *g* represents the /j/ sound in about 35% of the words in which it appears. Both these sounds are referred to as minor sounds.

The majority of common words in which *c* and *g* represent their minor sounds are words in which those letters appear in the middle of the word (e.g., *badge, page, bridge, mice, race*). Several groups of related words account for the majority of these words, for example:

ace	ice	age	dge
face	mice	page	badge
grace	spice	cage	bridge
lace	dice	wage	ledge
place	nice	rage	wedge
mace	rice		fudge
pace	slice		budge
race	spice		
space			

The teacher should introduce these words in groups. For example, the teacher might write on the board a group of words ending with the letters *ace* (*lace, face, race, place, space*). The teacher says, "The letters a-c-e say *ace*. All these words rhyme with *ace*." Then the teacher has the students read the set of words. This exercise is repeated for several days. After 2 days of practice, these words are randomly integrated into a practice sight-reading word list. Several days later, the same words would be placed into stories.

A similar procedure is used to introduce words ending with *ow* (*grow, blow, show, throw, mow, snow*), one-syllable words ending with *y* (*my, by, shy, cry, dry, fly, sky, spy, pry*), and *e* (*me, he, she, tree*).

Providing Practice

A peer-testing procedure can be used to provide a systematic review and to ensure that students are, in fact, mastering irregular words. In this procedure, the teacher makes a list of 30 to 50 recently introduced irregular words on a sheet of paper and distributes copies of the list to the students. Students practice reading the list in pairs. To ensure students are attentive, the teacher directs the student who is not reading to point to the words being read. If the reader misses a word, the checker says "Stop," and tells the student the word. The reader says the word, moves back 4 words in the list, then continues to read. The teacher should put in a group reward to encourage cooperation and discourage arguing.

After several days of practice periods, the teacher has a testing period. Higher performing students or adults (volunteers or aides) are the testers. The instructions to the tester are kept simple. If a student misidentifies a word, the tester says the correct word and makes a mark next to the missed word. If a student takes longer than 3 seconds to say a word, the tester tells the student the word, then makes a mark next to the word. The students' goal is to read the list without error at a rate of one word per second.

A new set of words can be introduced after 30 to 50 new words have been presented. The teacher keeps old word lists and has students review them periodically. For example, after the students have been given three worksheets, they might be directed to review worksheets one and two. A danger with this procedure is that the students will memorize the order of words in a list. This danger can be avoided by rewriting the words in a different order every few days.

Context as a Cue

A teacher cannot systematically introduce all the irregular words students will encounter. As students progress through the grades, they will do increasingly more reading outside the structured reading lesson. In this reading, they will encounter irregular words, i.e., words that contain letter-sound correspondences the students do not know. The context of the sentence offers important cues that can be used, with phonic and structural-analysis cues, to decode the new irregular words.

The most difficult aspect of most irregular words encountered in the early grades is the vowel sound. In one-syllable words the difficulty often arises due to the presence of a low-frequency letter combination (e.g., the *ue* in *fuel*, the *ei* in *neither*) or the presence of a letter or letter combination representing a vowel sound which is not its major sound (e.g., *ea* in *break*, *ee* in *been*, *ai* in *said*, *u* in *put*). In two-syllable words the difficulty often arises when there is a single consonant between two vowels in the mid-part of the word (e.g., *camel, hotel, topic, bacon, cupid, study, petal, meter*). Note that in some words the initial vowel sound is the long sound of the first vowel and, in some words, the short sound of the initial vowel. There is no apparent structural cue as in CVC and CVCe derivatives (e.g., *hoped* and *hopped*) as to what sound the initial vowel represents.

Teaching Procedure

The procedure we recommend gives students a strategy to use when they come to a word in which there is no phonic or structural cue for the vowel sound. When the students come to such a word, they are first to pronounce the word with the initial vowel representing its long sound. The students then determine if the word pronounced with the long vowel sound makes sense within the sentence context. If the word pronounced with its long vowel sound does not make sense, the students pronounce the word with another vowel sound to create a word that does make sense in the context. This strategy should not be presented until students have mastered the discrimination between CVCe derivatives and CVC derivatives (*hopped* vs. *hoped*). Introducing the strategy too early can cause confusion.

Two formats are presented to teach the above strategy. The first (see Table 18.3) is

Table 18.3	Preskill Format	
	Teacher	*Students*

Teacher writes on board:
  bugle   fuel
  rapid   topic
  neither   silent

Teacher	Students
1. "These are funny words. In some words, the underlined letter says its name. In some words, the underlined letter says its sound."	
2. "For each word, I'll tell you if the underlined letter says its name or sound. You'll tell me what the letter says. Then you'll say the word."	
3. a. Teacher points to the *u* in *bugle*. "This letter says its name."	
b. b."What's the name of this letter?" (Signal.)	"Ū."
c. "Say the word." (Signal.)	"Bugle."
4. a. Teacher points to the *a* in *rapid*. "This letter says its sound."	
b. "What's the sound?" (Signal.)	"Ă."
c. "What word? (Signal.)	"Rapid."
5. Teacher repeats steps 3 or 4 with the remaining words.	
6. Teacher gives several students individual turns on steps 3 (a–c) or steps 4 (a–c) with one or more words.	

a preskill format in which the teacher presents a list of 6 to 8 words. Half the words should have a long vowel sound and half should have a short vowel sound. (See Appendix A for a list of words.) The initial vowel is underlined. For each word, the teacher tells the student whether the initial vowel says its name or sound, then has the student say the word. The purpose of this format is simply to give the students practice in saying words that have been prompted by the teacher. This preskill format is presented daily until the students can answer with no errors on the first trial for two consecutive days.

The second format (see Table 18.4) introduces students to the actual strategy of what to do when they encounter a new word with a difficult-to-determine vowel sound. The teacher first explains that to figure out a new word the students may have to try several sounds for the under-

---

Table 18.4   Strategy for Words That Have Difficult-to-Determine Vowel Sounds

Teacher	Students
Teacher writes on board: camel neither topic bagel	
1. "These are new words. When you try to figure out a new word, you may have to sound out the word with several different sounds for the underlined letter before you can figure out the word."	
2. "Here's a rule: the first time you figure out the word, say the name of the letter."	
3. **a.** Teacher points to camel. "What's the name of the underlined letter?" (Signal.)	"a."
b. Teacher points to a. "Figure out the word to yourself, saying /ā/ for this letter." (Pause.)	
c. "Say the word." (Signal.)	"Cāmel."
d. " I'll say a sentence with that word: A cāmel is an animal that has humps on its back. Does cāmel make sense in that sentence?" (Signal.)	"No."
NOTE: If the answer to step 3(d) is "yes," do not do steps 3(e–g).	
e. "Teacher points to a. "So let's try the sound. What's the sound?" (Signal.)	"ă"
f. "Get ready to pronounce the word saying the sound." (Pause and signal.)	"Camel."
g. "I'll say the sentence with that word. A camel is an animal that has humps on its back. Does camel make sense in that sentence?" (Signal.)	"Yes."
4. Repeat step 3 with remaining words.	

lined letter (the initial vowel). Furthermore, the teacher tells the students that the first time they sound out the word they should say the name of the underlined letter. The teacher then leads the students through decoding a set of 6 to 8 words, half with a long initial vowel sound and half with a short initial vowel sound. For each word, the teacher prompts the students to pronounce the word, saying the long sound for the initial vowel. Then the teacher says a sentence and asks if what the student said makes sense within the sentence's context. If not, the teacher asks the students to say the word with a different sound. The word should make sense within the context of that sentence. All words should either be in the students vocabulary or have been presented earlier in a vocabulary exercise.

This format is presented daily until students make no errors on the first trial for two consecutive days. Then a worksheet exercise similar to that in Figure 18.1 can be presented. In the worksheet exercise, 4 to 8 irregular words that have not been previously introduced are written. Sentences with a missing word are

written below the words. The students are to fill in the blanks in the sentences with one of the listed words.

The range of examples in the context exercise can be expanded to include words which are irregular either because they (1) contain letter combinations not taught because they appear infrequently, or (2) contain letter combinations representing a sound other than its most common sound. For example, the word *steak* contains the letter combination *ea* which usually makes the /ē/ sound as in the word *neat*. The teacher presents *steak* to the students by saying, "In this word, *e–a* does not say /ē/. I'll say the sentence. You figure out what the word must be. He cooked a big blank. What word?" (Signal.) "Yes, *steak*."

Multisyllabic Words

Students should also be taught how to use context as a cue to decode multisyllabic irregular words. Table 18.5 includes a format for teaching students to use context to figure out multisyllabic irregular words. The teacher has the students identify known word parts, then says the sentence in which the word appears as a cue to help the students figure out the word. The instances presented in Table 18.5 are appropriate for the late-intermediate grades.

The unknown word must be a word that is in the students' receptive vocabulary. If the student has never heard the word before, or does not know what it means, context will not be a useful cue. After several days, worksheet exercises such as those described above are presented.

Figure 18.1 Sample Worksheet for Context Usage

Instructions: Fill in the blanks below with one of these words:

salad   camel   bacon   hotel   copy

1. They stayed in a nice _____ .
2. I love _____ and eggs.
3. The teacher said, "Do not _____."
4. They rode on top of a _____ .
5. We put tomatoes in the _____ .

Table 18.5   Format for Introducing Multisyllabic Irregular Words

Teacher	*Students*
A. Teacher writes on board: isolation recognize demonstrate relationship graduation	
B. Teacher introduces word.	
1. Teacher has students say familiar parts of the word.	
a. Teacher points to *isolation*. "Let's say the parts in this word."	
b. Teacher points to *ol*. "What do these letters usually say?" (Signal.)	*"Ol."*
c. Teacher points to *ation.* "What do these letters usually say?" (Signal.)	*"Ation."*
2. Teacher gives context hint. "Listen, I'll say a sentence: The doctors put him in an (points to *isolation*) ward because they didn't want anyone to catch his disease. Raise your hand when you know the word." Teacher calls on an individual. After the student says the word, teacher asks the group to say it. "What's the word?" (Signal.)	*"Isolation."*
3. Teacher repeats Steps 1 and 2 with all remaining words.	
4. Teacher has students reread words giving only context cues.	
a. "I'll say a sentence that has a missing word. You'll say the missing word."	
b. Teacher points to *isolation.* "The doctors put him in a blank ward. What word?" (Signal.)	*"Isolation."*
c. Teacher points to *recognize.* "I could not blank him. What word?" (Signal.)	*"Recognize."*
d. Teacher points to *demonstrate.* "We asked the salesman to blank how the machine worked. What word?" (Signal.)	*"Demonstrate."*
e. Teacher points to *graduation.* "When he finishes school, he will have a blank party. What word?" (Signal.)	*"Graduation."*

Application Exercises

1. Assume the teacher has taught the following skills:

   - Decoding all types of one- and two-syllable regular words and words containing letter combinations;

   - The most common sounds of all single letters;

   - The most common sound of these letter combinations and affixes: *ai, ar, ea, ee, ck, ou, th, sh, wh, ch, er, ing, ed, y, igh, al,* and *oa;*

   - VCe words with long sound for initial vowel.

   Circle each of the following words the student would not be able to decode. Next to each of the *circled* words, write the abbreviation for the explanation below that tells why the student could not decode the word.

   - Letter (L)—The word contains a letter combination the students do not know.

   - Irregular (I)—Some letter or letter combination is not representing its most common sound.

_____ spoil	_____ float	_____ cough
_____ ground	_____ blame	_____ smell
_____ blew	_____ steak	_____ warn
_____ trait	_____ cheer	_____ done
_____ groan	_____ bleach	_____ roam
_____ soup	_____ sigh	_____ shame
_____ broad	_____ rough	_____ build

2. When teaching the strategy for words that have difficult-to-determine vowel sounds, the teacher states the following sentence and question to which the student answers, "No." Tell the likely reason for this error.
   Teacher: "I'll say a sentence with the new word. Listen: He ate a bagel.
   Does *bagel* make sense in that sentence?"

3. Below are the irregular words a teacher presented in word lists on each day. Tell why the lists are not adequate. Tell what the teacher should do to teach the words.
   Monday: fuel, reign, chaffeur
   Tuesday: bias, puny, tour
   Wednesday: sewn, plaque, chef

4. Put a check in front of the irregular words which can be part of a related set.

_____ said	_____ grace	_____ suit
_____ throw	_____ stood	_____ me
_____ fly	_____ cage	_____ soup

5. It is possible for a teacher to predict the relative difficulty students will have decoding new words. Put a check in front of the six words below students are most likely to have difficulty decoding. Assume students have mastered all phonic and structural-analysis skills taught during the primary stage.

_____ predictable	_____ inactive	_____ peril
_____ hilarious	_____ ratio	_____ invention
_____ detective	_____ souvenir	_____ basketball
_____ hopelessly	_____ returning	_____ buttercup
_____ sodium	_____ inspection	_____ malaria

6. Construct a worksheet exercise that provides practice for using context to decode two-syllable words with a single consonant in the middle. (See word list in Appendix A.)

Chapter

19

Passage Reading

A reading lesson has three basic parts: the word-list exercises, the comprehension-skills exercises, and the passage-reading exercises.

Passage reading refers to a structured activity in which students read stories designed to provide practice and application of decoding and comprehension skills. Passage reading provides students with the practice to become accurate and fluent decoders. Fluency refers to the ease with which a student reads. Accuracy refers to the student's ability to read without making errors.

An emphasis on accuracy in early reading instruction will enable students to develop habitual accuracy. They will develop the concentration to read accurately without great effort. The need for accurate reading becomes increasingly observable as students encounter complex materials where misreading one word can change the meaning of a sentence.

The teacher must take the responsibility to develop both accuracy and fluency. Students who do not get the practice to develop adequate fluency may be handicapped in later grades. If a student reads significantly slower than his peers, the student can develop a negative attitude towards himself as he notes that he is not performing at a level equal to his peers. The student may also encounter frustration as the workload grows in the upper grades and the student's slower reading rate results in the student needing more time than his peers to do assignments.

Story Selection

A successful passage-reading component is possible only if the stories presented in the passage-reading exercises are carefully controlled to ensure the student has a strategy to decode every word in the passage. Not every word appearing in the story must have appeared in an earlier word-list exercise. If a word contains a phonic element the student has already mastered in earlier word-list exercises, the word need not be presented in a word-list exercise prior to its appearance in a story. For example, if the letter combination *ar* had been introduced in early April and the students had read about 20 words containing the letter combination *ar* in word-list exercises, the word *spark* could appear in a story presented in late April without prior presentation in a word list. Any word containing a phonic or structural element the student does not know should be presented as an irregular word in word-list exercises prior to its appearance in the passage.

As the students progress through the grades and have learned most phonetic, structural, and contextual cues, slightly irregular new words can appear in passages without prior appearances in a word-list exercise. The word, however, must be one that is in the students' receptive vocabulary. For example, the word *motel* can present a decoding problem to students because there is no structural cue to indicate the vowel is long. After context-usage cues have been taught, the word *motel* would not need to be presented in word-list exercises because it is already in the students' vocabulary and is not difficult to figure out with the use of context and phonetic skills.

Teaching Procedure

The relationship between the teaching of decoding skills and the teaching of comprehension skills in passage-reading exercises changes throughout the grades.

At the conclusion of the beginning reading stage, about two-thirds of the 30–40-minute reading period is devoted to passage-reading exercises. Most of the passage-reading exercises at that time centers on decoding practice. The teacher concentrates on providing students with practice in applying decoding skills learned in word-list exercises.

As the students progress through the grades, the amount of time the teacher spends focusing on decoding skills gradually decreases, while the amount of time spent on comprehension skills increases.

This section first will present in detail procedures for presenting passage reading during the second year of instruction. Modifications in the passage-reading procedures to be made in later grades will be discussed next.

The major focus of second-year reading is still decoding. This is not to say that comprehension is ignored, but, at this level the words students are able to read constitute only a small proportion of the words in the children's vocabulary. The type of written-comprehension exercises that can be presented are limited.

A major part of passage-reading time should be devoted to the students orally reading stories under the teacher's direct supervision. Whenever possible, passage reading should be conducted in relatively small groups. Higher performing students can be placed in groups of up to 12 students. Groups composed of lower performing students should be smaller. During passage-reading time, the students take turns reading orally. Each student reads anywhere from one to four sentences when called upon.

The challenge for the teacher is to (1) motivate the students to be attentive while other students read, (2) provide motivation to foster careful and accurate reading by the students when it is their own turn to read, (3) provide adequate practice for all students to develop fluency, and (4) provide instruction in specific skills, such as reading with expression.

The following teaching and motivation procedures are based on the assumption that the students in the group have received sufficient teaching to decode all the words appearing in the stories. If one or more students in the group are not able to decode the words in the story or read at a significantly slower rate than the other students in the group, the teacher should do something to increase the student's likelihood of having a successful experience during passage-reading exercises. The most practical procedure involves the student reading stories individually to a volunteer or peer *before* reading it as part of a group.

The basic procedure for conducting story reading during the second year of instruction involves the students reading a story at least twice. In the first reading, the teacher concentrates on decoding. If the students perform at an acceptable mastery level on the first reading, the teacher then focuses in the second reading on comprehension and decoding skills.

The teacher conducts the group reading by calling on individual students to read as the others follow along. The student whose turn it is reads one to four sentences. The teacher calls on different students to read several sentences until the passage is completed. The teacher records any errors the students make. If the group reads the passage with an acceptable number of errors (a 97% criterion—no more than 3 errors per 100 words), the teacher has the students reread the story and asks comprehension questions as the students read. If the students make too many errors (more than 3 per 100 words), they reread the story with the teacher solely concentrating on decoding skills, not asking comprehension questions.

Individual checkouts, in which the teacher has each student read a 100-word passage to her, should be done at least every second week. The checkouts serve to test whether students are developing mastery. The teacher designates a 100-word excerpt from a recently read passage. The teacher records the time the student took to read, as well as the number of errors made.

A format for introducing passage reading appears in Table 19.1. The format begins with the teacher telling the students they will be reading individually when called upon. The teacher instructs the students to talk in a mature voice and to pause at each period when they read. When it is no longer their turn, the students are to point to the words being read. At this early stage, we recommend requiring students to point to words as other students read as a means to increase the probability they will stay actively involved throughout the entire lesson, not only when they are called upon to read. When students read for several weeks without losing their places, the teacher can give them the privilege of not pointing.

After explaining the procedure, the teacher reads part of the story, modeling how to pause at the end of sentences, and monitoring the students as they follow along. The teacher reads at a rate quickly enough to model good expression, but slowly enough to allow students to follow along.

Next, the teacher explains to the students the error limit for reading the story. (A description of procedures for setting error limits appears later in this section, along with a discussion of techniques to motivate students to read accurately.)

The students read the story without the teacher asking comprehension questions. If the students read the story making fewer errors than specified, they read the story

Table 19.1   Format for Introducing Passage-reading Decoding

1. Introducing story reading procedure
   a. "You're going to read this story out loud. I'll call on different students to read. When you're reading, talk in a big voice so everyone can hear you. Pause when you come to a period. If I don't call on another student, read the next sentence. If it's not your turn to read, point to the words that are being read."
   b. "I'll show you how I want you to read. You point to the words as I say them." (Teacher reads several sentences. Students touch words as teacher reads.)
   c. Teacher repeats step 1(b) until all students follow along as she reads.
2. Students read story—decoding
   a. "Your turn to read. When I call on you, read in a mature voice. Pause when you come to a period. If I don't call on another student, read the next sentence. If it's not your turn to read, point to the words that are being read."
   b. "Our error limit for today's story is 8. If you read the story with only 8 errors or fewer, we'll read the story again, and I'll ask comprehension questions."
   c. Teacher calls on students to read individually. Teacher calls on a new student each one to three sentences.
3. Students read story—comprehension
   a. Teacher calls on student to read individually. Teacher asks comprehension questions.

again. During this second reading, the teacher asks comprehension questions. If the students make more errors than allowed on the first reading, they read the story for a second time with the teacher concentrating again on decoding. The next day the story can be reread with comprehension questions asked.

Critical Behaviors

- Call on students to read in an unpredictable order. Students will be more attentive when they do not know when it will be their turn. Sometimes have a student read one sentence, sometimes several sentences.

- Watch the students carefully to make certain they are following along when another student is reading.

- Good timing will facilitate the transition from student to student. When the teacher wants a new student to read, the teacher should start the process of calling on the next student as the student who is reading finishes the last word in the sentence. The teacher should keep her talk to a minimum.

Corrections

The correction procedure a teacher uses depends on the group size the teacher is working with.

When a teacher is working with more than three students, she must consider how her actions effect the attentiveness of the group. If the teacher spends too much time with an individual student, she increases the probability of the other students becoming inattentive. The following correction procedure is designed for use with a group of more than three students.

1. When a student makes an error, the teacher lets the student read several more words, then says, "Stop." The teacher should not use an abrupt or loud voice. The reason the teacher waits is to give the student the chance to self correct.

2. The teacher points out to the student what error was made, indicating whether the reader misidentified a word, skipped a line, reread a word, or omitted a word. For misread words, the teachers says the correct word and asks the student to repeat it.

3. The teacher tells the student to read the sentence from the beginning. ("Go back to the beginning of the sentence and read the sentence again.") The purpose of rereading the sentence is to make certain the student gains the proper meaning.

In a one-to-one situation or with a small group, the teacher can use a more sophisticated correction procedure when the student makes an error. The teacher lets the student read a word or two more, then says "Stop," points to the word, and asks the student to identify it. If the student still cannot identify the word, the teacher either tells the student the word or gives him some type of phonic or structural cue. The cue depends on the type of word missed. If a student misidentifies a word with a letter combination, the teacher points out the letter or letter combination missed, asks the student the sound, then asks the student, "What word?" For example, if a student says "beat" for *beach*, the teacher would point to *ch* and ask, "What do these letters say? Figure out the word." If the

word has a VCe pattern, the teacher would remind the student of the VCe rule. If the student misidentifies an irregular word, the teacher simply tells the student the word, because a phonic or structural cue will not help to figure out an irregular word. For all errors the student should go back to the beginning of the sentence and reread it.

As a general rule, the less said by the teacher when making corrections during passage reading, the smoother the lesson probably will progress.

Modifications for Higher Grades

The procedure for presenting passage reading changes as the students progress through the grades. Starting in early third grade, when the students can read accurately and at the specified reading rate for their instructional level, the teacher can ask comprehension questions on the first reading of the passage. Thus, rereading becomes unnecessary.

Starting in late third grade when students demonstrate consistently accurate and fluent reading, the teacher can introduce structured silent reading. The student reads most of the passage orally, then a small part silently. The teacher asks comprehension questions immediately after the students read. The proportion of the story read silently gradually grows until one-third is read orally and two-thirds silently.

Reading with Expression

Training in reading with expression is necessary to demonstrate to students that written passages express meaning in the same way spoken language does. Oral reading behaviors that characterize reading with expression include pausing at periods and punctuation marks, emphasizing the appropriate words in questions, and when reading quotations, using inflections that reflect the mood of the character speaking. Expression training can begin when students are able to read at a rate of 60 words per minute. A 5- to 10-minute training session can be incorporated into the lesson following the reading of the passage.

We recommend a modeling procedure for teaching students to read with expression. The teacher says, "We're going to practice reading this story as if we were telling it to someone. I'll read a sentence. Then you read it the same way I do." The teacher then reads the first sentence or two, using slightly exaggerated expression. Students should be instructed to keep their fingers on the first word in the sentence and simply follow along with their eyes as the teacher reads. (Pointing to the first word enables the students to find the beginning of the sentence when it is their turn to read.) After the teacher reads, an individual is called upon to read with expression. If the student does not read with expression, the teacher repeats the model. Exercises for teaching reading with expression should be done until students read new material with expression without first receiving a teacher model. This can take months and months of practice.

Recordkeeping

The teacher should maintain a recordkeeping system to keep track of student behavior during passage reading. Two student behaviors are recorded: decoding errors and lost places.

A recording system should provide maximum information with minimum disruption of the group. The teacher should be able to record student performance without becoming distracted from teaching the group.

We recommend that the teacher record student performance on a photocopy of the passage the students are reading. The teacher transfers the data to summary sheets used to diagnose student performance and to serve as the basis for implementing a motivational system.

Recording Errors

Any time a student makes an error, the teacher should write the student's initials in capital letters over the missed word. Lower-case letters should be used to describe the decoding error.

The teacher needs a consistent system for describing student errors. Below is one possible system for recording various types of decoding errors:

- Student says word incorrectly: The teacher writes the reader's initials in capital letters over the word. The teacher then writes what the student said over the word, using lower-case letters. The teacher need not write the entire student response. If the student left off an ending (e.g., saying "mark" for *marked*), the teacher might make a slash through the ending (e.g., marke$\cancel{d}$). The teacher's slash indicates that the *ed* ending was not said. If the student says one sound incorrectly, the teacher can write the lower-case letter representing that sound (e.g., p$\overset{a}{o}$rk). The *a* indicates that the student said *park* instead of *pork*. Remember, the teacher uses lower-case letters when writing what the student said and upper-case letters to designate who made the error (e.g., we ate $\overset{EM}{}$p$\overset{a}{o}$rk). The teacher wrote EM for a student named Ellen Manco, and the *a* because the student said *park* instead of *pork*.

- Student is unable to identify a word within a reasonable amount of time: The teacher writes the initials for the student's name in capital letters over the word and circles the word (e.g., (mystery)). As a general rule, the teacher should allow the student no more than 5 seconds to figure out a word. Allowing the student too much time can be punishing for the student unable to figure out the word and can disrupt the flow of the lesson. However, not allowing sufficient time for a student to attempt a word can also be frustrating to the student. The teacher must use his judgment. If the student seems on the verge of figuring out the word, the teacher can allow the student several more seconds.

- Student omits a word: The teacher writes the initials for the student's name in capital letters over the omitted word and writes an "o" with a slash through it above the word (e.g., The man went to the old house).

- Student inserts a word: The teacher writes an ∧ to indicate that the student said a word not appearing in the text and writes student's initials in capital letters next to the inserted word. The teacher writes the word the student inserted (e.g., The student read the sentence, "He went to the game" as "He went to the *big* game." The teacher writes "He went to the big game").

- A student sometimes will pronounce a word incorrectly, but immediately correct himself. This is referred to as a self-correction. The teacher writes the student's initials in capital letters and records the error by writing the letters "sc" over the word.

- When a student is called on to read, the student should say the first word of the sentence to be read within a second or two after being called on. If the student does not start reading within this time, it is probably because the student has not been attending. The teacher writes the student's initials over the period and a circled L for lost place (e.g., went home. They play). Some students may not start reading when called on because their reading rate is slow. If it is obvious a student has been following along, the teacher need not record a circled L. Similarly, if the first word is a difficult word, the teacher should allow more time. The teacher must, however, make it clear to the students that she expects them actively to follow along when other students read.

Group and individual performance during passage reading should be kept on summary sheets. As a rule, any error is counted as a mistake. Omissions and insertions, as well as misread words, count as errors. Self-corrections need not be counted as long as they happen infrequently. Group performance can be recorded on graph paper. Lesson numbers are written across the horizontal axis, while the number of errors is recorded up and down the vertical axis. Table 19.2 displays a sample chart. Numbers 1 through 9 on the vertical axis refer to the number of errors. Note that only one space is provided for more than 9 errors. Numbers 30 through 40 across the horizontal axis refer to lesson numbers.

Individual student performance could be recorded on a simple table as shown in Table 19.3. The students' names are listed vertically. Lesson numbers are written horizontally. Daily performance is recorded on the table.

Motivation System

A motivation system should focus on two behaviors: accurate reading and student attentiveness.

Table 19.2   Group Performance Chart

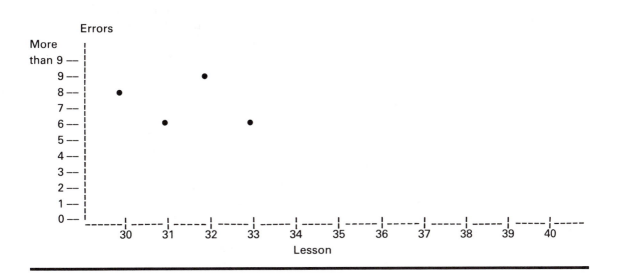

Accurate Reading

A motivation system to foster careful reading begins with the teacher setting up payoffs based on the number of errors a group makes when reading stories. The fewer the number of mistakes, the greater the payoff.

The critieria for accurate reading should be set at a high level. We recommend a 97% accuracy goal (no more than 3 errors per 100 words). This criterion is based on the assumptions that students have received adequate practice to master word-list exercises and that the word-list exercises were adequately designed and implemented to prepare students to read all the words in the assigned stories. One purpose of story reading is to give students practice employing decoding skills they have already mastered. If the students have not had adequate preparation in word-list exercises, the high criterion will be unreasonable and cause frustration. If students

Table 19.3   Individual Student Performance Table

Name	43	44	45	46	47	48	49	50
Billy								
John								
Sally								
Tim								

have had adequate preparation, the 97% criterion will be a realistic goal.

A variety of pay-offs may be used. The pay-offs employed should be based on the type of students involved. Teachers working with higher-performing students, who work more carefully, can rely solely on verbal and written acknowledgements of performance. Teachers working with difficult-to-motivate students may need to utilize more powerful pay-offs, such as extra recesses, and tangibles, as well as acknowledgements of good performance.

Below is a sample system used by a teacher. The students were reading stories of approximately 300 words. The students would be reading at a 97% accuracy rate if they made 9 errors. The teacher set up an economy in which the students' performance earned an extra recess once a week. (Note: The recess was not awarded during reading time, but at another time during the day. Missing 15 minutes of reading a week would deprive students of nearly 10% of their instructional time.) The students earned minutes of recess each day if they read at a 97% accuracy level. They earned more minutes if they read at a higher accuracy level. Table 19.4 shows the schedule the teacher used for a 300-word story.

Attentiveness

A motivation system also should be designed to keep students attentive when it is not their turn to read. The best indicator of attentiveness is the student's knowing his place when called on to read.

A minimal consequence can be used to discourage inattentiveness. A second lost place in a week might mean a 5-minute practice session during recess time in which the teacher reads while the student follows along. For most students, this minimal consequence will be effective. If, however, a student continues to have problems with lost places, the teacher must take further actions to alleviate the problem.

First, the teacher should test the student's reading rate to determine if the problem results from the student's inability to keep up. If the student's rate is not adequate, the teacher should provide extra practice. Ideally, the student should have a chance to read the story to a volunteer the day before the group reads the story. If the student's reading rate is adequate, the teacher then can set up a more powerful motivation system. We recommend setting up a system whereby gradual improvement by the student enables the whole group to earn a reward. For example, if a student loses his place an average of 3 times a lesson, the teacher might set up a system wherein the student's improvement to only 2 lost places per lesson earns a small reward for the group. Once the student improves to only 2 lost places per lesson, the teacher would up the criterion to 1 lost place per lesson, then 2 or 3 per week. It is important to maintain the reward system after the student improves. Paying attention to students when they are performing well and constantly acknowledging their good performance is very important.

Other Behaviors

Two student behaviors very important to a smoothly run passage-reading exercise are: (1) students pausing when they reach a period, and (2) students talking in a loud

Table 19.4	Reward Schedule for Passage Reading

Student Errors	Minutes of Extra Recess
0–1 errors	4
2–4 errors	3
5–7 errors	2
8–9 errors	1

enough voice when called on for an individual turn.

During the story-reading exercise, the teacher should do a lot of specific praising (e.g., "Good stopping at the period," "You talked in a big voice," "Good reading"). This praise will usually be effective with most students in the group. If one or two students have difficulty, the teacher should make individual systems with those students (e.g., "Billy, each time you read loud, I'll give you a point. When you get 10 points, you'll earn a sticker for everyone in the group").

Monitoring

A motivation system is not a fixed thing. A teacher must continually monitor the motivation system to ensure that each student is feeling successful and competent. The teacher must always resist the temptation to nag students having difficulty or implore them to work harder. Both of these teacher behaviors rarely result in student improvement. Instead, the teacher should always test individually to determine if a skill deficit is involved, and if so, set up a remediation program. If no skill deficit is involved, the teacher should set up an individualized reinforcement system. A more in-depth treatment of how to set up a motivation system can be found in a book entitled "The Solution Book" (Sprick, 1981).

Diagnosis and Remediation

Any student whose accuracy rate is below 97% in passage reading should receive remediation. The type of remediation to be provided depends on the basic cause of the errors. Errors can be divided into two broad categories: context-related errors and skill-deficit errors.

Context-related errors are usually indicated by inconsistent student performance. The student reads a word correctly in one sentence and, later in the passage, reads it incorrectly.

Specific-skill deficits are indicated by a consistent error pattern (e.g., the student misses all words with the letter combination *ou*).

A teacher must make a correct diagnosis before planning a remedy for inaccurate reading. The first step in any diagnosis procedure is to present an exercise similar to the one on which the student has been performing poorly and to make available a powerful reinforcer for improved performance. The teacher might give a student who has been reading inaccurately a passage to read and say, "If you read this passage with 2 or fewer errors, you'll earn 5 minutes extra recess for the class." The purpose of the motivator is to see if there is a significant improvement in the student's performance with only the introduction of an increased motivator.

If the student reads significantly more accurately with the increased motivator in force, the teacher should provide a more powerful motivator to the student for reading performance during group reading. As a general rule, we recommend letting a student earn something extra for the entire group. This procedure prevents shrewder students from figuring out that poor performance can eventually lead to greater rewards.

If the increased-motivation procedures do not result in significant improvement, the teacher should give an in-depth test to find specific phonic and structural weaknesses, as well as test the student's knowledge of irregular words. A diagnostic test that focuses on phonic and structural analysis appears in Chapter 20 on pages 245–248. A test of irregular words can be created by going through the text being used and making a list of the irregular words introduced to that point.

Students with deficits in previously taught phonic, structural, or irregular-word skills should receive daily remediation on the specific deficits. Remediation would involve the systematic reintroduction and practicing of the skills the student has not mastered. For example, if the student did not know one or more letter combinations, the teacher would reintroduce the letter combination(s) one at a time using the procedures specified in Chapter 16. While the word-list remediation is being provided, the teacher would prompt the students in passage reading on words containing the unknown elements (e.g., "That word has the letters *o–u*. Remember, those letters say /ou/."

Ideally, remediation should be provided by the teacher in a 5 to 10-minute daily one-on-one setting. The realities of the classroom however, often, make it impossible for the teacher to provide ongoing individualized remediation. Several options are available: The teacher can integrate the remediation into the word-list presentations being made to the group or set up peer tutoring. In peer tutoring, the teacher prepares word-list exercises and trains a higher performing student to work with the student having difficulty.

Context errors may involve either an over- or underreliance on context cues. An overreliance on context cues is indicated by the student misidentifying many words (more than 3 per hundred) which the student is able to identify correctly in isolation. The student says a sentence that is syntactically correct but isn't what is written (e. g., reading "The boy was not happy" as "The boy was happy").

The remediation procedure for a pattern that indicates an overreliance on context involves instituting a motivation system to encourage accurate reading. The criteria depends on the student's current performance. The teacher should set up a system to improve performance in graduated steps. If a student is currently reading at a 90% accuracy level, the system could be set up so that a student is awarded for reading at a 92% or higher criterion. The criterion would gradually be increased as the student's performance improved.

Inaccurate readers often make many self-corrections. Whereas, an occasional self-correct is not important, frequent self-corrects hamper the story flow. A student who makes too many self-corrects should be put on a motivation system like the one described in the previous paragraph. Some students who overrely on context will also have a reading-rate deficit. The teacher should not work on remediating both types of deficits at first. He should work first on developing accuracy. Only after the student has begun reading accurately on a consistent basis should the teacher work on increasing rate. Remember, the key to a successful remediation is ensuring that the passage contains no words that have phonic or structural elements the students do not know.

An underreliance on context would be indicated by students saying words that do not make sense in the context of a passage. For example, when reading, *The man went to the shop*, a student reads, "The man went to the she." If students make many nonsense errors, the teacher should institute oral language training exercises to teach students to identify context errors. In one type of exercise, the teacher says sentences, and students indicate whether the sentence makes sense. Once students learn to identify errors in spoken sentences, they are more likely to identify context errors when they read. In presenting this exercise, a teacher might say, "I'll say some sentences. You tell me whether they make sense."

1. "The ran ate the corn. Does that make sense?"

2. "The rat are corn. Does that make sense?"

3. "The boy played on the pouch. Does that make sense?"

4. "The girls ran to the sore. Does that make sense?"

5. "The boy played on the porch. Does that make sense?"

In addition to exercises such as this one, the teacher should establish a motivation system to encourage more careful reading.

Protecting a Student's Self-Image

In addition to providing remediation exercises, the teacher should take other actions to ensure that the self-image of lower-performing students is not being hurt. If one student makes a disproportionate number of errors during group passage reading, the other students may react negatively towards that student. One way of dealing with this situation is to not count the student's errors when determining how many errors the group makes when reading a story. The teacher might tell the group, "Jerry is working hard now to catch up on some skills. While he is catching up, I won't count any errors he makes when you read the story."

Another action that can protect a lower-performing student's self-image is to arrange for the student to receive a tutoring

session on the story *before* it is presented to the group. The pre-reading increases the probability of the student performing well when the story is presented to the group.

Reading Rate

Reading rate refers to the speed at which students read passages. A student's rate is usually expressed in words per minute. Table 19.5 shows minimal desired reading rates at various levels. (See pages 271–272 for research on reading rate.)

Deficits in reading rate are indicated when students read new material at a rate 10% more slowly than the desired instructional-level reading rate (see Table 19.5). Note that a student's instructional level may be different than her grade level. If a student is reading in a book designated for late-second grade, the student's instructional level is at late-second grade, regardless of whether the child is a first-, second-, or third-grader.

We recommend exercises for students whose reading rate is 10% or more below the desired level for their instructional level. The rate-building exercises involve students rereading passages previously read until they can read them at a higher rate.

Table 19.5	Desired Reading Rates for Various Instructional Levels

Instructional Level	Words per Minute on First Reading
Second third of grade 1 materials	45
Last third of grade 1 materials	60
First third of grade 2 materials	75
Second third of grade 2 materials	90
Last third of grade 2 materials	110
First half of grade 3 materials	120
Second half of grade 3 materials	135
Fourth grade and higher	150

To prepare for rereading exercises, the teacher first sets a target-rereading rate. The target-rereading rate should be 40% higher than the student's current reading rate. The purpose of setting the rereading criterion significantly higher than the student's current rate is to ensure that students receive massed practice on familiar material needed to improve his rate on new material. We found that having lower performers reread a story one time results in minimal improvements in rate. Yet, if students reread a passage until they read it at a rate significantly higher than their rate on the first reading, their rate on new material gradually improves.

If a student were currently reading at a rate of 50 words a minute, the teacher would set the target rate at 70 words per minute (50 + [40% of 50 = 20] = 70). If a student were reading at a rate of 90 words a minute, the target rate would be 126 words a minute (90 + [40% of 90 = 36] = 126).

The teacher prepares the reading material by marking off several 100-word excerpts in a previously read story. A teacher might put a star at the beginning and a bracket at the end of each 100-word excerpt.

The teacher uses Table 19.6 to translate the target-rereading rate into seconds needed to read a 100-word passage. In order to read a 100-word passage at a target rate of 70 words a minute, the student would have to read a passage in about 1:26 seconds.

The teacher begins the rereading exercises by pointing out the excerpt a student is to read and telling the student how long he has to complete it. The teacher would let the student time himself while reading the story. The student practices reading the excerpt to himself until he is able to read it within the specified time. When the student feels he is able to read at the specified time, he raises his hand for the teacher to check him out. The teacher times the student as the student reads the excerpt orally. The student's reading of the excerpt would be deemed acceptable if the student read the passage in the specified time with two or fewer errors. If the student read acceptably, he would begin practicing another excerpt. During one 15-minute session, the student might work on three to five 100-word excerpts. If a teacher is working with a group of students, the teacher should structure the session so that while one student is being tested, the other students are practicing reading to themselves.

A motivational system should be incorporated into rate-building exercises. For example, each excerpt read at a faster rate might earn a point with a 2-point bonus for reaching the target rate. Each 20 points can lead to some type of reward.

Every two weeks, the teacher would have a student read a passage the student has never read before. The passage should be of a similar difficulty level to the passages being read in the rate-building exercises. The student's performance tells the teacher if the rate-training exercises are, in fact, working. If the student's rate has improved, the teacher increases the target rate on rereading exercises to the student's new rate plus 40%. For example, if a student had been reading at a rate of 60 words a minute at the beginning of the year and is now reading at 75 words a minute, the target rate for rereading exercises would increase from 84 words a minute (60 + 24) to 105 words a minute (75 + 30).

The exercise described above may be conducted in a small group setting with one adult and 3 or 4 students. Parent volunteers or paraprofessionals could be used to conduct the training sessions. The length and number of training exercises each day would depend on a student's relative deficit. Students reading at a very

Table 19.6   Translation of Seconds Required to Read 100 Words into Reading Rate

Seconds	Words per Minute	Seconds	Words per Minute
:30	200	1:46	57
:32	187	1:48	56
:34	176	1:50	55
:36	167	1:52	54
:38	158	1:54	53
:40	150	1:56	52
:42	143	1:58	51
:44	136	2:00	50
:46	130	2:02	49
:48	125	2:04	48
:50	120	2:06	48
:52	115	2:08	47
:54	111	2:10	46
:56	107	2:12	45
:58	103	2:14	45
1:00	100	2:16	44
1:02	97	2:18	43
1:04	94	2:20	43
1:06	91	2:22	42
1:08	88	2:24	41
1:10	86	2:26	41
1:12	83	2:28	40
1:14	81	2:30	40
1:16	79	2:32	39
1:18	77	2:34	39
1:20	75	2:36	38
1:22	73	2:38	38
1:24	71	2:40	37
1:26	70	2:42	37
1:28	69	2:44	37
1:30	67	2:46	36
1:32	65	2:48	36
1:34	64	2:50	35
1:36	62	2:52	36
1:38	61	2:54	34
1:40	60	2:56	34
1:42	59	2:58	34
1:44	58	3:00	33

slow rate might participate in two 15- to 20-minute sessions daily.

In addition to the rereading exercises, teachers should try to help the student do more reading, both at home and in school. The extra practice at school could be in the form of paired reading in which two students of equal ability read to each other, switching each paragraph. In these practice exercises, students could sometimes read materials they read one time previously and at other times new materials which are at an appropriate level (i.e., contain virtually no words the student does not have a strategy to decode).

Reading at home can be of significant benefit. Below is a series of steps the teacher can follow to encourage home reading:

- The teacher contacts the parent and explains the importance of extra reading to the student. The teacher asks the parent to arrange, at a minimum, a 15-minute daily period during which the student reads. Usually it is best if the student reads silently rather than to the parent. Without careful structure, parent-child sessions often can be negative experiences for both.

- The student brings home a weekly calendar (see Table 19.7). Each day the parent writes how many minutes the student read. The student brings the calendar to school once a week on a specified day.

- As a motivator, the teacher can put the minutes read by each student on a chart.

- A goal with a special event can be planned. "When our class reads 10,000 minutes at home, the principal will come down and give our class a special award."

- Individual motivation systems might be necessary for some children (e.g., "When you read 100 minutes at home you can be in charge of cleaning the erasers for a week").

Table 19.7		Student's Home Reading				
M	**Tu**	**W**	**Th**	**F**	**Sat**	**Sun**

Dear Parent:

Please record the number of minutes your child reads each day at home.

Your child should bring this form to school each _____ so we can add the minutes to the classroom chart.

Thank you.

Application Exercises

1. The errors in each item below reflect a deficit in a particular passage-reading skill. State the skill and describe the procedure for remedying the deficit.

   a. When reading the sentence, *The girl tripped when running down the stairs,* a third grade student says "stars."

   b. When reading the sentence, *Ann built a large house,* student says "bought" for *built.* The student has missed *built* several times.

   c. When reading two sentences, the student ignores the period. The student has done this several times.

   d. A student reading late second-grade material reads at a rate of one word each 2 seconds.

   e. A student reads "bet" for *beat* and "set" for *seat.*

2. Specify the desired reading rates for the following students (see Table 19.5).

   a. A third grade student reading at a mid-second grade level.

   b. A second grade student reading at a late-first grade level.

   c. A fifth grade student reading at a late first grade level.

   d. A second grade student reading at a beginning third grade level.

3. For each student described below, tell if they should receive training to improve their reading rate. If they need such training, specify what the acceptable criterion would be on rereading exercises.

   a. William—A third grader whose instructional level is at early second level. He is reading at a rate of 75 words per minute.

   b. Jackie—A third grader whose instructional level is at mid-third grade. She is reading at a rate of 75 words per minute.

   c. Andra—A second grader whose instructional level is at a early second grade level. He is reading at a rate of 40 words a minute.

4. Listed below are the errors made by two students when reading the following passage. The word the student said is in quotes next to the missed word from the passage.

   The farmer had a gleam in his eye. He was hoping that all his wheat would be cut by that night. Later he would load it on his truck and take it to the coast.

   For each student, tell if the student's errors indicate a specific skill deficit. If so, state the deficit. Remember skill deficits are indicated by patterns of errors rather than a single incorrect response.

   a. Bill—gleam, "glow," load, "lay"

   b. Wilma—load, "land," coast, "cost"

5. Explain the differences between the correction procedure a teacher would use during the large group passage reading and the correction procedure for a one-to-one reading situation

6. During passage reading, a student is constantly losing his place. To remedy this problem, the teacher has decided to call on students in a predictable order as a way of cueing students to their reading turn. Tell the potential problems the proposed remediation may cause. Describe an alternative remediation to correct the student's losing his place.

7. Below is a passage students will be reading. Pick 3 words from the passage that fourth grade students are likely to have difficulty decoding. Specify what the teacher would do and say in presenting each word. Assume students have mastered all phonic and structural skills.

> Alice had an older friend. It was Ann Lewis, a sophomore, who was the school's star soccer player. Ann gave Alice a great deal of encouragement. Some day Alice would be the team's leader. One day the two young women were talking. Alice said, "I want to be a star. I want to tour the country."

This section includes three parts. The first part deals with testing, grouping and placing procedures for primary- and intermediate-grade students. The second part suggests how to incorporate direct instruction procedures into classroom instruction in the primary and intermediate grades. The third part deals with setting up programs for the remedial reader.

Testing, Grouping, and Placing

This part describes a testing procedure a classroom teacher can use to group students homogeneously and place the groups at an appropriate level of instruction. The procedure described is designed to provide maximum information in a relatively short period of time. (In a day or two a teacher with one parent volunteer could administer tests that would provide a basis for initial grouping and placing.) A teacher with 20 to 30 students simply does not have time for time-consuming testing. After a week or two of instruction, the teacher should assess the performance of students to see which students might function better in another group and if groups are placed at appropriate instructional levels. This point is very important: Many students after a week or two of practice will perform significantly better than they did when the school year started. Retesting after one to two weeks of instruction is critical.

We recommend three testing instruments for initial grouping and placing: a diagnostic test of word attack skills, an informal reading inventory, and a written comprehension test.

Diagnostic Test of Word Attack Skills

The testing procedure would begin with the teacher administering the diagnostic

Chapter

20

Using Commercial Materials: Decoding Instruction

test of work attack skills (see Table 20.1) which is designed to serve (1) as a quick screening test to get an idea at what level a student is reading, and (2) as a preliminary indicator of what word attack skills a student does and does not know.

Note that we use the word "indicator" because no one test is definitive. Correctly identifying a word does not necessarily mean that the student could identify the same phonic elements in another test word. For example, the student may read the word *hawk* correctly but not be able to generalize to another *aw* word such as *claw*.

The test is an individually administered oral test in which students read words in a list. The words are ordered according to the sequences we recommend for introducing phonic and structural skills. Each word is designed to test a specific phonic or structural skill. The element tested is written in parenthesis in front of the word.

Administering the Test

The teacher gives the student a copy of the test, and asks the students to read the words beginning with number 1. The teacher records the student's performance on a copy of the test. The teacher and student should be situated so that the student cannot see the teacher recording on the record sheet.

Table 20.1		**Word Attack Skills Test**								
___	1.	(th)	bath	___	21a.		happier	___	41.	(ness)	darkness
___	2.	(er)	matter	___	21b.	(y)	funniest	___	42.	(tion)	invention
___	3.	(ing	handing	___	21c.		cried	___	43.	(ist)	artist
___	4.	(sh)	shop	___	22.	(ay)	pray	___	44.	(ible)	sensible
___	5a.		handed	___	23.	(ou)	proud	___	45.	(age)	package
___	5b.	(ed)	licked	___	24.	(ir)	thirst	___	46.	(sion)	mission
___	5c.		hopped	___	25.	(ur)	curb	___	47.	(ence)	sentence
___	6.	(wh)	when	___	26a.		taped	___	48.	(ish)	selfish
___	7.	(qu)	quiz	___	26b.	(VCe)	hoping	___	49.	(ation)	vacation
___	8.	(ol)	fold	___	26c.		timer	___	50.	(pre)	preschool
___	9.	(y)	sunny	___	27.	(kn)	knock	___	51.	(ex)	expect
___	10.	(est)	biggest	___	28.	(oi)	boil	___	52.	(over)	overtime
___	11.	(oa)	loan	___	29.	(oy)	enjoy	___	53.	(ion)	million
___	12.	(ar)	cart	___	30.	(ph)	graph	___	54.	(ship)	friendship
___	13a.		fine	___	31.	(wr)	wrap	___	55.	(com)	compare
___	13b.	(VCe)	hope	___	32.	(au)	haunt	___	65.	(ure)	adventure
___	13c.		cane	___	33.	(aw)	hawk	___	57.	(ive)	detective
___	14.	(ea)	neat	___	34.	(con)	confuse	___	58.	(ac)	accuse
___	15.	(oo)	toot	___	35.	(ment)	payment	___	59.	(ous)	joyous
___	16.	(le)	candle	___	36.	(teen)	sixteen	___	60.	(inter)	interfere
___	17.	(ee)	meet	___	37.	(ful)	handful	___	61.	(for)	forward
___	18.	(ai)	pain	___	38.	(dis)	distant	___	62.	(ize)	realize
___	19.	(ch)	lunch	___	39.	(able)	enjoyable				
___	20.	(or)	port	___	40.	(less)	useless				

Table 20.2   Group-record Form

Element	Student											
1. th												
2. er												
3. ing												
4. sh												
5. ed												
6. wh												
7. qu												
8. ol												
9. y												
10. est												
11. oa												
12. ar												
13. VCe												
14. ea												
15. oo												
16. le												
17. ee												
18. ai												
19. ch												
20. or												
21. Yderiv.												
22. ay												
23. ou												
24. ir												
25. ur												
26. VCederiv.												
27. kn												
28. oi												
29. oy												
30. ph												
31. wr												
32. au												
33. aw												
34. con												
35. ment												
36. teen												
37. ful												
38. dis												
39. able												
40. less												
41.ness												
42.tion												
43. ist												
44. ible												
45. age												
46. sion												
47. ence												
48. ish												
49. ation												
50. pre												
51. ex												
52. over												
53. ion												
54.ship												
55. com												
56. ure												
57. ive												
58. ac												
59. ous												
60. inter												
61. for												
62. ize												

If a student correctly identifies a word, the teacher writes a plus sign (+) on the line in front of the word. If a student misidentifies a word, the teacher writes the student's response in the space. If the student does not respond to a word within 5 seconds, the teacher can tell the student the word and count it as an incorrect response by writing N.R. for "No Response." The teacher has the student read until the student misses 4 consecutive words. Class results can be summarized on the group record form (see Table 20.2)

Informal Reading Inventory

An informal reading inventory (IRI) is a criterion-referenced test constructed by selecting representative passages from the reading series being used in the classroom. The purpose of administering an IRI is to determine the appropriate lesson in the reading series at which to begin instruction. This lesson is usually referred to as the student's *instructional level.*

Constructing the IRI

The test is constructed by selecting excerpts from various lessons in the student readers. During the first-, second-, and third-grade levels, the stories get more difficult as you progress through a grade level book. The teacher might select a 100-word passage from each 30th lesson.

Starting at fourth grade, the structure of reading books changes. The difficulty level of stories does not increase as you progress through the book. A story early in the fourth grade book may be more difficult than a story appearing later in the fourth grade book. Since the structure of the fourth-grade and higher level books is different from first- through third-grade level books, the way a teacher selects passages for the IRI is different. The teacher

need select only one passage representative of the stories in the reader for each grade level. We recommend selecting a 200-word passage that does not contain any unusual proper nouns (e.g., difficult-to-decode names or phrases).

The teacher should make a photocopy of each excerpt and prepare a booklet with the excerpts ordered from lower to higher grade. A separate booklet would be prepared for each student. The excerpts the students are to read would have stars placed before the first word and after the last word of the part the student is to read.

Administering the Informal Reading Inventory

The student should be seated at a desk facing away from the rest of the class. The teacher should be seated to the side of the student so that the student cannot see the teacher recording errors.

Where to Begin

The teacher can use the student's performance on the diagnostic word attack skills test as a guide at what level to begin. (See Table 20.3 for a schedule telling at what level to begin testing.)

1. The teacher explains the purpose of the test: "I want to find out at what lesson to start you in reading. I am going to ask you to read from different stories. Start here."
   (The teacher points to where students begin.)
   "If you make a mistake, I want you to read the word again and say it the correct way."

2. The teacher should use a stopwatch to time the student on each excerpt. She starts the watch when the student

Table 20.3	Schedule to Determine Beginning Point for IRI
Words Correct on Diagnostic Word Attack Skills Test	**Where to Begin IRI Testing**
0–10 words	Beginning first-grade level. Also, administer the beginning-level diagnostic test (see Table 13.3).
11–20 words	Late first-grade level.
21–30 words	Mid second-grade level.
31–40 words	Late second-grade level.
41–50 words	Early third-grade level.
51–60 words	Late third-grade level.
61–65 words	Early fourth-grade level.
66 or more words	Fourth-grade level or higher. Test students on material for their grade level.

begins to read, and stops it when the student finishes reading the 100th word (first to third grade) or the 200th word (fourth grade and higher).

3. If a student hesitates more than 5 seconds on a word, the teacher should tell the student the word.

4. If a student misses a word, the teacher says nothing (no correction) unless the student tries to figure out the missed word and hesitates for 5 seconds. After 5 seconds, the teacher says the word.

5. If a student is reading a passage very laboriously and is making many errors, the student does not have to read the entire passage. The teacher can stop the student and present an earlier passage.

Recording

As the student reads, the teacher records any errors the student makes on the photocopied excerpt the student is reading. The following are recorded instructions:

- Student mispronounces a word: The teacher writes the word the student said over the word.

- Student is unable to decode a word within 5 seconds: The teacher writes "N.R." over the word.

- Student omits a word: The teacher writes a little "o" above the omitted word.

- Student inserts a word: The teacher writes a (caret) where the insertion occurred.

- Student mispronounces, but immediately self-corrects: The teacher writes "S.C." over the word.

The teacher summarizes the student's performance after the student has completed the excerpt. The teacher records the total number of errors the student made. (Self-corrections should not be considered errors.) The teacher also records the student's total time for the passage. These numbers can be written on the photocopied excerpt.

What to Do

If a student reads below a 95%-accuracy rate (6 errors or more in a 100-word passage), the teacher has the student read the next lower level passage. The teacher continues testing lower level passages until the student reads the passage with a 95%- (or higher) accuracy rate.

If a student reads a passage at a 95%- (or higher) accuracy rate, the teacher tests the next higher-level passage. The teacher continues testing higher level excerpts until the student goes over the error limit.

Written Comprehension Test

The third test we recommend giving is a written comprehension test. To prepare this test, the teacher would select several pages from the student workbook corresponding to the student's instructional level in the textbook (as determined by the student's performance on the IRI). Students whose instructional level was in the first book of the third grade level would be given several pages from early in the 3–1 workbook. Students whose decoding levels in the 2–1 reading book would be given pages from the 2–1 workbook. The purpose of the test is to give the teacher additional information in deciding how to group a borderline student. The test will also indicate any students who have severe comprehension deficits.

The workbook pages selected should be ones requiring little explanation from the teacher. What the students are expected to do should be obvious. If possible, the teacher should try to select some items that test main idea, inference, and sequencing, as well as literal comprehension. A test might include three or four workbook pages.

Grouping and Placing

Each student's instructional level on the informal reading inventory (IRI) is re-corded on a summary sheet on which each student is listed according to his/her performance. Students at the lowest-instructional lesson are listed first. (The instructional lesson is the lesson corresponding to the most advanced IRI passage the student can read with no more than five errors.) The instructional lesson and the time it takes a student to read the passage are listed across from each student's name.

The teacher works from this summary sheet in forming instructional groups. In second and third grade, student performance on the IRI is the major determinant of group composition. The performance on the written comprehension test is referred to when a teacher has doubts about a student's placement. When making groups, teachers should try to place students so there is not a significant spread between the highest and lowest performing student in the group.

In some second- and third-grade classrooms, a teacher may find that instructional levels vary from nonreader to several years above grade level. To illustrate how students in a classroom might perform on an IRI, we have listed in Table 20.4 the testing results for one second grade class. Note that one student (student 22) is performing significantly above grade level and one student (student 1) is performing significantly below grade level. Appropriately placing these students in instructional groups in the classroom is almost impossible since no other student is functioning near their levels.

As mentioned earlier, the best way to minimize the problems involved with grouping is intergrouping among classrooms. If several teachers from adjacent grade levels or from the same grade level join together in grouping students who are either very low or very high, the problems involved in setting up groups will be greatly reduced. The basic rule concerning groups is that the larger the number of students and teachers involved in setting up groups, the easier it will be to form groups that meet the instructional needs of each individual student.

The teacher starts forming groups with the lowest performers, trying to keep the group of the lowest performing students as the smallest group. On the summary score form in Table 20.4, NF appears next to student 1. This indicates the student was not able to finish reading (NF) the lowest level passage. Student 1 has almost no reading skills and must be handled as a special case. Similarly, student 22 (who is reading a year ahead) must be handled as a special case. Students 2, 3, and 4 scored at the same lesson (grade level 1, lesson 80). Student 5 tested out slightly higher (grade level 1, lesson 100), but had a slow-reading rate. We would place him with students 2, 3, and 4 resulting in a low group of four students. Next, we note that eight other students scored at grade 2, lesson 10. The mid- group might, thus, contain eight students (6 through 13). The high group would include the remaining students. Ideally, the high group should contain the most students. However, as in this class, such grouping is not always possible.

Fourth Grade and Up. In fourth grade and above, more consideration should be given to a student's comprehension performance when determining groups. Some students may decode well, but perform poorly on comprehension tasks. Students whose answers to comprehension questions are written significantly below other students in the same group should be considered for a lower group.

Teachers should expect some regrouping to be necessary after the first week or two of instruction. Students who consistently make more errors on comprehension items and/or passage reading should

	Table 20.4	Mrs. Muntz's Second Grade Class		
	Student's Initials	**Instructional Level**		**Time**
		Grade	Lesson	
1.	F.G.	NF	—	——
2.	M.T.	1	80	2:38
3.	T.L.	1	80	2:18
4.	B.N.	1	80	2:15
5.	T.R.	1	100	3:10
6.	T.M.	2	10	2:30
7.	R.J.	2	10	2:18
8.	D.H.	2	10	2:14
9.	J.B.	2	10	2:12
10.	L.T.	2	10	2:10
11.	M.B.	2	10	2:00
12.	R.A.	2	10	1:50
13.	D.C.	2	10	1:50
14.	L.S.	2	40	2:20
15.	R.L.	2	40	2:15
16.	A.M.	2	40	2:00
17.	S.J.	2	40	1:40
18.	E.K.	2	40	1:38
19.	A.L.	2	40	1:35
20.	B.A.	2	40	1:30
21.	G.B.	2	40	1:30
22.	L.G.	3	80	:48

be considered for a lower group. Regrouping might also be necessary if a student shows marked improvement and demonstrates the ability to learn information at a rate more commensurate with a higher placed group. Student personality characteristics also need to be taken into consideration when regrouping. Some students will function better when slightly pressured to keep up with other students; other students may perform much better as the high members of a lower group.

Again, let us stress the need for re-evaluation after the first two weeks of instruction. We recommend that all students be tested again individually for rate and accuracy on a passage. A great deal of instructional time can be wasted if a student is not placed at an appropriate lesson for instruction.

Specifying a Starting Lesson

Group instruction does not allow for perfect individualization because not all students in a group will perform at the same instructional level. A teacher will have to make some deviations from the ideal placement when dealing with groups. There are several alternatives. A teacher may start at the instructional level of the lowest performing student in the group. The advantage of starting at this lesson will be that all students will be successful in initial instruction. A disadvantage of this starting point is that the instruction may not initially challenge the higher students. A second, and usually more practical, alternative is starting at a lesson midway between the instructional lesson of the highest and lowest students in the group. A problem with this starting point is that the initial lessons might be somewhat difficult for the lower performers in the group. The teacher can deal with this problem by providing the lower students with extra help. For example, if five students in a seven-student group were performing at a level 30 lessons higher than the lower two students in a seven-student group, the teacher might start at a lesson midway between the instructional level. During the early weeks of instruction, the teacher would provide supplemental instruction for the lower performing students. The teacher would also have to work to keep the two lower-performing students from becoming discouraged or feeling incompetent. An effective technique is to have a volunteer or aide preteach the lesson to the lower perform-

ing students before the teacher presents it to the entire group.

Using a Commercial Basal Program

Teachers can incorporate direct instruction procedures into both decoding and comprehension teaching.

Decoding instruction during late-first, second, and third grade should include: (1) systematic introduction of phonic, structural, and contextual-analysis skills; (2) introduction of irregular words which will appear in upcoming stories; and (3) adequate practice to enable students to develop fluency.

Teachers using a code-emphasis program will find it relatively easy to incorporate the teaching of phonic and structural elements because the sequencing of passages in code-emphasis (phonic) programs is designed so that a new element is stressed every several stories.

To incorporate direct instruction principles into lessons, the teacher first should examine the upcoming ten lessons in the program to determine what new skills and irregular words are going to appear. The teacher constructs daily word-list exercises to introduce the upcoming skills and irregular words.

Teachers using a meaning-emphasis approach will have to do a lot more work to incorporate the teaching of phonic and structural elements into the program. Meaning-emphasis basals will include supplementary phonic and structural exercises in a student workbook independent of the passages in the program. Rarely is there a systematic pattern of review provided. A new element might appear in a workbook exercise for several days, then not appear again for weeks.

The teacher needs to set up a supplementary program to teach the critical phonic- and structural-analysis skills. The teacher can use the group record form (Table 20.2) as a guide to setting up a sequence for introducing skills.

The teacher begins the supplementary program with the first phonic or structural element that one or more students missed on the diagnostic test of word attack skills. (A zero or NR in a column indicates a missed word on the test.) Before spending significant time teaching a new skill, the teacher might retest the students who missed the word containing that tested skill. The retest is to certify that the student does not know the skill. The teacher retests by selecting several words containing that element and having the student read those words.

Appendix A includes a list of words the teacher can refer to in selecting words for teaching the various elements. When preparing word-list exercises, the teacher should include adequate discrimination practice, presenting not only the new element, but also reviewing the previously introduced elements. The formats for presenting these skills appear in the phonic- and structural-analysis sections (Chapters 16 and 17).

The teacher focuses on a new skill for several days. When the students are able to read words with these new skills, the teacher looks at the chart and determines the next skill a student did not know and reteaches that skill.

Regardless of whether the teacher is using a code-emphasis or meaning-emphasis approach during late-first through third grade, the basic structure of a daily lesson should include the following tasks:

1. Phonic and structural analysis (5–7 minutes):
   a. Isolated letter combination and affix identification;
   b. Word-list reading (15–20 words).

2. Irregular word practice (3–5 minutes):
   a. Introduction of new words;
   b. Practice on previously introduced words (10 words).

3. Passage reading (15 minutes).

4. Preparation for written comprehension exercises (5–15 minutes):
   a. Vocabulary instruction;
   b. Instruction explanation;
   c. Strategy introduction or review.

In the intermediate grades (fourth and above) there is virtually no difference between those reading programs using a code-emphasis approach (phonic) and those programs using a meaning-emphasis approach (non-phonic) to teach beginning reading. By the intermediate level, all the major phonic- and structural-analysis skills have been presented and decoding instruction will consist of introducing irregular and multisyllabic words that will be appearing in upcoming passages and comprehension exercises. The teacher should carefully examine materials students are to read in upcoming weeks. Basal texts at this level contain literature from a variety of sources. A by-product of the literature component is the significant variance in the difficulty of stories within a grade level. By examining materials to be presented several weeks in the future, the teacher will allow herself adequate time to introduce the words that will be appearing in the more difficult passages. Remember, new difficult words should be presented in word lists 1–3 days prior to students encountering them in passages.

Regardless of what type program is being used, remember that students' performance is always the key to when the teacher should proceed to the next lesson or provide review. If students are not performing successfully at the current lesson, the teacher should provide remediation on the skills the student has not mastered before proceeding.

Workbooks

Teachers should examine the student workbook as well as the textbook. They should note the significance of exercises, the readability, and the clarity of directions.

1. Significance of exercises. Teachers must constantly be on guard for what can be described as non-functional workbook exercises. These are workbook exercises often called "busy work." We define a workbook exercise as a "busy-work" activity if (1) it requires that the students use a skill they must have already mastered and the exercise does not provide meaningful review of the skill, or (2) the workbook page presents or practices a non-functional skill, a skill students will not use.
   Below are descriptions of "busy-work" activities:
   a. An exercise requiring students to classify words that have the letter C according to whether they are hard-C words or soft-C words. This exercise is non-functional because the students must already be able to read the words to tell what sound the C makes. The exercise does not teach the students to read words, rather, students can only be successful if they already know the targeted skill.
   b. A syllabication exercise in which students have to put a line between the letters in a word to indicate where one syllable ends and the next syllable begins. The purpose of this skill is to provide practice on decoding, but, in fact, the students would have to already have learned

the words to do the exercise. There are numerous rules governing syllabication. Presenting all these rules to elementary-grade students is inappropriate. The only time a student would use syllabication is when writing a sentence where the student begins a multisyllabic word on one line and must complete it on another. Syllabication is a writing skill, not a decoding skill.

2. Readability.[1] The readability level in each unit's sections should be at the level designated by the publisher. This point is critical. If a great number of selections differ significantly from the designated grade level, the program will not be suitable for independent use by the students without extensive preteaching of difficult words and concepts. Teachers should carefully examine workbook pages to see if they contain words students are not able to decode.

3. Clarity of directions. When a new skill is being taught, the students should

---

1. *Readability* is a term used to describe the relative ease or difficulty of a passage. The level of difficulty is usually expressed in terms of grade equivalent. A book with a rating of 2.5 would be deemed readable by a student in the fifth month of second grade. Numerous formulas have been developed to determine readability. While each formula is somewhat unique, some or all of the following factors are taken into consideration in most:
   a. The average length of words. Passages with longer words are considered more difficult than passages with shorter words.
   b. The relative frequency of the words. Passages with more-common words are easier than passages with less-common words.
   c. The length of sentences. The longer the average sentence, the more difficult the passage.
   d. The relative complexity of the sentences. The more clauses used and the greater the use of passive voice, the more difficult the passage.

concentrate on that new skill. The directions should be brief and clear and the page layout simple. Simplicity of directions will allow a teacher to concentrate on the more significant skills rather than on explaining where to put answers.

Remedial Reading Instruction

Six guidelines were presented (pages 106–107) for teaching students reading materials below their grade level:

- Extra instruction: The more deficient a student is in reading, the greater the amount of instruction the student should receive.

- Early remediation: Remediation efforts should begin as soon as the student begins to fall behind.

- Careful instruction: The more severe the student's deficit, the more careful the instruction must be. A student with skill deficits must receive instruction from a well-trained person.

- Instructionally sound materials: The greater the student's deficit, the greater the need for well-designed programs.

- Rapid progression: The more deficient in skills a student is, the greater the need for optimal progress.

- Motivation: The more severe the student's deficit, the greater the need for a motivational component.

Students whose reading level is years below where it should be need to progress at an accelerated rate if they are to function at their peers' level in later grades. The amount of practice the students receive must be geared to enable students to make this progress. As a general guideline, teach-

ers might provide an extra ½ hour of adult-supervised instruction for each year a student is performing below grade level. Much of the supervised instruction will consist of oral reading. Trained volunteers or paraprofessionals can be used in providing this extra practice.

Types of Remedial Readers

Students not reading acceptably at their respective grade level fall into one of the following four categories: non-readers, confused decoders, moderately deficient decoders, and adequate decoders with comprehension difficulty. Correctly classifying students in one of these categories is extremely important because the different deficits call for entirely different types of remediation.

Nonreaders

Nonreaders are students who are virtually unable to decode. They may be able to identify 50–100 words by sight; however, they have no generalizable strategy for decoding words.

First- and second-grade nonreaders should be placed in a well-constructed code-emphasis program designed for the beginning reader.

Older students, third-grade level and above, should not be placed in materials that are designed for the beginning student. These students should be placed in a program specially designed to teach decoding skills to the older nonreader. The program would teach the same skills described in Part 2 for the beginning reader; letter-sound correspondence, and auditory preskills would be taught first. Sounding out regular words in lists and passages are introduced next. Irregular words are introduced when students have begun sight-reading regular words. The main difference between instruction for the nonreading older student and the beginning student would involve the packaging of the materials and story content. The materials should not look babyish; similarly, story themes should not be too childish.

Confused Decoders

Confused decoders are students who know most letter-sound correspondences, but demonstrate a confusion regarding how letter groups represent sounds in words. They will say "hat" for *hate* and "load" for *loud*. Confused decoders will demonstrate an overreliance on context usage. They will make such errors as looking at a letter or two, then saying a word that makes sense in that context. They will omit or add words in sentences. They will not attend to endings of words, calling *hopping* "hopped" or *played* "plays." They will seem to vacillate in their approach, reading a word correctly in one sentence and incorrectly in the next sentence.

A program for confused decoders should *not* include sounding out, but should concentrate on teaching phonic and structural units such as letter combinations, common affixes, the VCe rule, and minor sounds. It also should include passage-reading exercises designed to teach students how to read carefully and not to overrely on contextual cues. Examples of such exercises appear later in this section.

Moderately Deficient Decoders

Moderately deficient decoders will have mastered most of the phonic, structural, and contextual-analysis skills taught in the primary stage. However, they will not have developed adequate proficiency in decoding multisyllabic words. The deficiency in decoding multisyllabic words will result in them having a halting, choppy reading rate on intermediate-grade-level material. A

program for these students should include remediation of any phonic and structural-analysis skills, and a lot of oral practice on passage reading to develop fluency.

Adequate Decoders with Poor Comprehension

The fourth type of remedial student, the adequate decoder, has no decoding deficits. The student can decode material at her appropriate grade level with acceptable accuracy and speed. The student's problem is poor performance on comprehension exercises. There are three possible causes of this student's problem: (1) vocabulary deficits (the student does not know the meaning of many words), (2) strategy deficits (the student does not have problem-solving strategies), or (3) a motivational deficit. Quite often the student's poor performance will be caused by a combination of these three deficits. A program for this student type should not include intensive decoding instruction, but should deal with vocabulary, comprehension strategies, and motivation.

Commercial Materials— Remedial Reader

The materials used in a remedial reading program should have these five components:

1. Structured teaching of word-attack skills;
2. Passage-reading exercises that provide practice and application of the skills taught in word-list exercises;
3. A comprehension component coordinated with the decoding component;
4. A management system which incorporates motivational procedures;

5. Materials designed to be appealing to the older student.

A model of a complete remedial program is the SRA *Corrective Reading Series* by Siegfried Engelmann (1988). The series includes separate yet coordinated components for decoding and comprehension skills. The program is unique in its comprehensiveness. Not only are there sequential lesson-by-lesson word-list exercises, but the skills taught in word lists are reinforced by carefully designed stories which provide massed practice on skills. The programs are also coordinated so that words do not appear in written-comprehension exercises until students have been taught a strategy for decoding them.

The decoding component includes three levels. The lowest level is designed for the nonreader. Instruction during this level concentrates on teaching students to decode regular words. During the second level, students are taught to read words containing the most common sounds of common letter combinations and a strategy for decoding VCe words and VCe derivatives. They are also taught to decode two- and three-syllable words containing prefixes and/or suffixes. A unique feature of this level is the construction of the stories. Initially, stories are constructed with unpredictable syntax in order to discourage students from overrelying on context usage. Figure 20.1 includes a page from the student workbook. At the top of the page are word-list exercises. The story is about a girl and her talking dog. The dog cannot speak well and uses lots of nonsense sentences. The students must read carefully to read exactly what the dog said. Stories in the mid and latter part of the program are written using more predictable syntax with themes designed to interest older students. Figure 20.2 includes a story from late in the series. Note its theme about animals and also its more regular story syntax.

The third level of the decoding program provides more emphasis on structural-analysis skills as more and longer multi-syllabic words are introduced. Stories on this level are also quite carefully controlled. Longer and more complex sentences, including passive-voice construction and multiple clauses, are introduced. Nonfiction selections, similar to those students will encounter in content area books, are interspersed among the fiction stories.

A structured point system that rewards attentiveness and careful reading is built into the programs. The students receive points for cooperation and performance. In addition, they receive bonus points for accurately rereading excerpts from parts of stories. Rereading is important for developing accuracy and fluency. The procedure of awarding points for the rereading helps to motivate students who otherwise might be reluctant.

The comprehension component of the *SRA Corrective Reading Series* also includes three levels. In the first level, nearly all the tasks are presented orally. The type of tasks presented includes a mixture of basic facts: months, holidays, seasons, etc., and thinking operations, such as analogies, classifications, deductions, true-false, synonyms-opposites, and inference.

The second level of the program makes the transition from oral to written comprehension activities. The words in the comprehension program are carefully controlled so that the students have the skills to decode any word they encounter in a comprehension exercise.

The third level contains more advanced comprehension items. The focus is on reasoning and critical thinking. The SRA Corrective Reading program is designed for students in fourth grade through high school.

Figure 20.1

1 cold st<u>ore</u> <u>th</u>at r<u>ea</u>d <u>b</u>ack s<u>oo</u>n j<u>o</u>b b<u>ea</u>ns h<u>e</u>lped h<u>a</u>m bett<u>er</u> thi<u>ng</u>s mu<u>ch</u>	**3** <u>Gretta</u> <u>Chee</u> let's day pay played stay someone saying door bigger said I've cook other some don't can't folks didn't another their became one
2 name like came note bone home	

4

CHEE, THE DOG

Gretta got a little dog. She named the dog Chee. Chee got bigger and bigger each day.

On a very cold day, Gretta said, "Chee, I must go to the store. You stay home. I will be back."

Chee said, "Store, lots, of, for, no."

Then Gretta said, "Did I hear that dog say things?"

Chee said, "Say things can I do."

Gretta said, "Dogs don't say things. So I must not hear things well."

But Chee did say things. Gretta left the dog at home. When Gretta came back, Chee was sitting near the door.

[1]

Gretta said, "That dog is bigger than she was."

Then the dog said, "Read, read for me of left."

Gretta said, "Is that dog saying that she can read?" Gretta got a pad and made a note for the dog. The note said, "Dear Chee, if you can read this note I will hand you a bag of bones."

Gretta said, "Let's see if you can read."

Chee said, "Dear Chee, if you can read this note, I will ham you a bag for beans."

[1]

Gretta said, "She can read, but she can't read well. Ho, ho."

Chee became very mad. She said, "For note don't read ho ho."

Gretta said, "Chee gets mad when I say ho, ho."

Chee said, "Yes, no go ho ho."

Then Gretta felt sad. She said, "I didn't mean to make you mad. I don't like you to be sad. I will help you say things well."

Then Chee said, "Yes, well, of say for things."

So every day, Gretta helped Chee say things. She helped Chee read, too.

[1]

Chee got better and better at saying things. And she got better at reading. And she got bigger and bigger. When she was one year old, she was bigger than Gretta.

On a hot day Gretta left Chee at home, but when she got back, Chee met her at the door. "Did you have fun at your job?" Chee asked.

"Yes, I did," Gretta said.

"I don't have much fun at home," Chee said. "I think I will get a job. I don't like to stay at home."

"Dogs can't have jobs," Gretta said.

Chee said, "You have a job. So I will get a job, too."

[1]

Figure 20.2

1	**2**
H<u>ur</u>n m<u>ou</u>th <u>fer</u>ns sharp <u>air</u> al<u>so</u> br<u>ea</u>thing h<u>ur</u>led f<u>ir</u> w<u>ou</u>ld cr<u>ou</u>ched f<u>ai</u>th S<u>ur</u>t p<u>oa</u>ch j<u>er</u>k <u>ou</u>ch sla<u>sh</u>ed	<u>forward</u> <u>beware</u> <u>except</u> <u>dead</u> both stiff two knowing clover against snapped sniffed wolves safe fixed battled happened sister smelled peered neck

3

HURN, THE WOLF

Hurn was sleeping when it happened. Hurn didn't hear the big cat sneak into the cave that Hurn called his home. Suddenly Hurn was awake. Something told him, "Beware!" His eyes turned to the darkness near the mouth of the cave. Hurn felt the fur on the back of his neck stand up. His nose, like noses of all wolves, was very keen. It made him very happy when it smelled something good. But now it smelled something that made him afraid.

Hurn was five months old. He had never seen a big cat. He had seen clover and ferns and grass. He had even eaten rabbits.

[1]

Hurn's mother had come back with them after she had been hunting. She had always come back. And Hurn had always been glad to see her. But now she was not in the cave. Hurn's sister, Surt, was the only happy smell that reached Hurn's nose.

Surt was awake. She was leaning against Hurn, and Hurn could feel how hard Surt was shaking.

"Ooooooowww," howled Surt. At the sound of the howl, Hurn jerked. Then he turned his nose back toward the mouth of the cave. He made his ears stand up as high as they would go. Adult wolves have ears that stand up all the way. But puppy wolves, like Hurn, have ears that stand up part way. Then they flop forward.

[2]

Suddenly Hurn's ears grabbed something from the air. They grabbed the sound of a padded paw taking a slow step across the floor of the cave. Then another padded paw came down slowly on the cave floor.

"Run, run," something told Hurn. But there was nowhere to run. Hurn peered at the mouth of the cave. He crouched down as low as he could get, and looked. Then he saw the outline of the big cat. The cat was bigger than Hurn's mother. It was only about two meters from Hurn and it was walking slowly toward Hurn and his sister.

[1]

Hurn tried to back away. But he felt the hard rock of the cave against his back. He could go back no more. Surt was curled next to Hurn.

Without knowing why he did it, Hurn showed his teeth and began to growl. He snapped at the air as if to scare the cat away. The cat stopped for an instant, but then it started to come toward the puppies again.

Suddenly something dashed into the cave. It growled and it slashed at the cat. It was Hurn's mother. She had come back to her puppies. She hurled herself at the cat. The cat spun across and met with sharp claws. Bits of fur floated in the air as the mother wolf battled the cat. Then the cat ran from the cave.

[2]

The mother wolf walked very slowly to Hurn and Surt. She sniffed them. She licked Hurn on the ear. Then she curled up next to her pups. Hurn got as close to her as he could get. She felt good.

Hurn couldn't see that she had been badly hurt in the fight with the cat. He couldn't see that her eyes were fixed and that she was breathing slower and slower.

Hurn went to sleep, feeling very safe. When he woke in the morning, he could feel that something was wrong. His mother was cold, and she was stiff.

His mother was dead and Hurn was all alone, except for his little sister, Surt.

[2]

Application Exercises

1. Below are the results of the IRI administered by Ms. Adamson to her second-grade class. Book A, B, C, D, and E are first grade books; F and G, second-grade books; and H and I, third-grade books.

   a. Would you place student 3 in a group with students 1 and 2 or students 4, 5, and 6? Why?

   b. Would you place student 7 in a group with the students who scored at level C or level E? Why?

   c. Assuming that interclass grouping is not feasible, set up four instructional groups. Tell what you would do to ensure that all students are successful.

Student	Instructional Level Book	Time
1	NF	—
2	NF	—
3	B	2:20
4	C	2:30
5	C	2:40
6	C	2:30
7	D	2:40
8	E	1:50
9	E	1:45
10	E	1:58
11	E	2:04
12	E	1:42
13	F	1:51
14	F	1:38
15	F	1:50
16	F	1:56
17	F	1:48
18	F	1:52
19	F	1:32
20	F	1:30
21	F	1:24
22	F	1:14
23	F	1:38
24	F	1:42
25	G	:51

NF = did not finish passage

2. Below are descriptions of pages that appeared in a reading workbook. Three of the pages contain activities that would be difficult for lower-performing students and would not warrant the time required to teach the skill. Identify these three pages.
Page A
The student is asked to classify a group of words according to their initial vowel sound.

Page B

The student is asked to designate which of two minimally different words belongs in a blank space in a sentence; e.g., The boy is _____it will not rain. (hopping, hoping).

Page C

The student is asked to indicate where a word would be divided into syllables.

Page D

The student is asked to select the word that corresponds to a picture.

Page E

time
tin
tame

The student is asked to place the accent mark over the proper syllable.

3. Explain the differences between a confused decoder and a moderately deficient decoder, and the difference in the programs appropriate for each student.

Chapter

21

Research on Decoding Instruction

Regular Words

Earlier research related to the instruction of regular words has substantiated the teaching of a sounding-out strategy (Carnine, 1977; Muller, 1973; Richardson & Collier, 1971). In addition, the procedure of initially teaching regular words in isolation (Singer, Samuels, & Spiroff, 1973) and providing letter- and word-discrimination practice (Kameenui, Stein, Carnine, & Maggs, 1981; Rayner & Posnansky, 1978) have also been supported. Finally, research suggests that when students first learn to sound out words, corrections would prompt students to sound out words in contrast to a word-supply correction (Carnine, 1981c).

Results of recent investigations have revealed four areas of inquiry related to the instruction and acquisition of regular words: (a) meaning-based vs. phonics-based instruction; (b) the use of illustrations in instruction; (c) practice and fluency and (d) the use of computer software to increase regular word fluency.

Meaning-based vs. Phonics-based Instruction

Instructional studies have indicated that learning to decode facilitates reading acquisition (Bradley & Bryant, 1983; Williams, 1980). Specifically, the direct instruction of a code-based approach to word reading is supported by an extensive research base. Ehri and Wilce (1987) compared the effects of a code-based approach (cipher-reading) to a less explicit phonics

This chapter was written by Deborah C. Simmons, Peabody College, Vanderbilt University, and Cynthia C. Griffin, University of Florida. Assistant Professor in Educational Psychology and Scientist at the Center for the Study of Reading, University of Illinois, Champaign, Urbana.

approach (cue-reading). In the cue-reading condition, novice kindergarten readers were taught to remember words by selecting a distinctive visual feature of the words. Cue-trained students were taught how to say real words in which one of nine previously taught letter-sound correspondences appeared in the initial position. In cipher-reading instruction, students were taught to attend to all the letter-sound correspondences in the word. In the initial study trials, students were taught to read the word by slowly stretching out the sounds in the word and running their finger beneath each letter as it was overtly pronounced. Results indicated that the cipher-reading condition required substantially more time than the cue-reading condition. Substantial practice was required for kindergartners to acquire explicit decoding skills.

A particular advantage of the cipher-reading condition was evidenced on students' abilities to read words containing consonant blends and nonsense words. On word-learning tasks, cipher readers showed consistent gains on successive trials, whereas, scores of the cue readers were more erratic indicating no cumulative acquisition and application of decoding knowledge. Cipher readers were able to learn to read sets of words with complete accuracy. Conversely, cue readers had much difficulty learning to read words accurately and consistently. Such findings indicate the importance of not only learning letter-sound correspondences, but also how these letter-sound relations are blended to form words.

Vellutino and Scanlon (1986) recently posited that the reliance on either a meaning-based or a phonics-based method of reading instruction impairs the fluency of regular-word identification, while the complementary use of both decoding approaches may facilitate the acquisition of fluency in regular-word identification. Poor and normal achieving readers in second and sixth grades were randomly assigned to treatments that simulated three general methods of teaching word identification: (a) the whole-word/meaning-based method, (b) the phonics method, and (c) the whole-word/meaning and phonics methods combined.

In the combined strategy condition, the phonics-based phonemic-awareness training always preceded whole-word training. The phonics-based method did not teach sounds in isolation, but rather, focused on counting phonemes, vocalizing phonemes, and locating the positions of phonemes. Such procedures differed from a sounding-out method in which students mastered sounds in isolation prior to the reading of regular words. In the whole-word condition, students heard nonsense words and were asked to identify all the nonsense words they could remember. In the second component of the whole-word method, nonsense words were associated with a cartoonish character to provide a concrete meaning to the nonsense syllables.

Results indicated that whole-word training had a positive effect on the initial learning of nonsense words; however, students who received the phonemic-awareness training improved steadily across trials. Subjects in the combined condition performed significantly better across all trials on initial learning tasks than subjects in all other groups. On transfer measures, the phonics group performed considerably better than did subjects who received whole-word training only. In fact, in most instances, subjects in the phonemic-segmentation group performed as well as subjects who received both phonemic segmentation and whole-word training.

Given the role of phonemic segmentation in the combined-training condition, such findings suggest the advantage of a code-based strategy in initial word identification. Vellutino and Scanlon (1986) noted the advantage of whole-word instruction in early learning trials and called for the use of this strategy to facilitate the development of a core of words for use in beginning reading activities. Prior to the acceptance of this strategy, the comparison of the sounding-out strategy and the whole-word familiarization procedures seems warranted.

Illustrations

Studies have indicated that the presence of illustrations in reading materials has a more detrimental effect on the reading of poor readers than on good readers (Koenke & Otto, 1969; Samuels, 1967; Willows, 1978). When illustrations were simultaneously presented during instruction of regular words in isolation, lower reading performance rates were obtained by disabled readers (Rose & Furr, 1984). The added visual cues (i.e., the illustrations) actually distracted the reader's attention from the critical stimuli (i.e., the word) (Samuels, 1970).

Practice and Fluency

Research findings reveal that better readers not only decode words more accurately than less able readers, but that they also decode these words more fluently (Ehri & Wilce, 1983). The effect of fluent word reading is explained in LaBerge and Samuels' (1974) theory of automaticity as well as in Perfetti's (1985) bottleneck theory. According to these theories, lower-performing students expend substantial amounts of cognitive resources on decoding rather than comprehension tasks. To reduce the demands of word- recognition activities, investigations have studied the effects of prac-

tice on word recognition and comprehension. Jenkins and Pany's (1981) review of the effects of word-level practice indicated that gains were evidenced in the area of word recognition, but minimal benefits were demonstrated in reading comprehension. Jenkins and Pany qualified these results, indicating that the majority of studies provided no instruction during the practice components and used a limited number of words. Additional research is necessary to substantiate the transfer effect of word-list practice to comprehension.

Computers

Recent advances in computer technology create the possibility of providing greater amounts of fluency-oriented practice than most traditional programs (Torgesen, 1986). Computers can be effectively utilized to build the decoding skills of low-performing students with the use of carefully designed instructional-software packages (Fletcher & Atkinson, 1972; Robyler & King, 1983; Torgesen & Wolf, 1986). Low-performing students appear to have particular difficulties acquiring fluent word-identification skills (Guthrie & Tyler, 1976). Anderson, Hiebert, Scott, and Wilkinson (1985) have recognized and reported the importance of practice for improving word-recognition fluency.

Irregular Words

With the exception of two notable studies, very little research has been conducted on the instruction and acquisition of irregular words. These two studies of note examined two instructional procedures for teaching irregular words. Bryant, Payne, and Gettinger (1982) taught one group of disabled readers irregular words which incorporated mastery-learning strategies. The mastery-learning strategies included: (a) teaching in five-word units; (b) dropping words temporarily as they are learned; (c) providing distributed practice across days; (d) giving discrimination practice; and (e) training for transfer. The comparison group was taught with methods typically used in teaching irregular words (e.g., tracing or copying words and word-list reading). The advantage of the mastery learning model to teach irregular words to disabled readers was documented in this investigation.

Hendrickson, Roberts, and Shores (1978) compared the effects of antecedent modeling and contingent modeling conditions on the irregular-word acquisition of disabled readers. Results of the study revealed that when the irregular word was modeled before subjects were asked to identify the word (i.e., the antecedent modeling condition), word acquisition was more efficient. Subjects required fewer trials to reach criterion during the antecedent modeling training.

Passage Reading

In the 1970s, research conducted on aspects of passage reading focused primarily on (a) reading rate (LaBerge & Samuels, 1974; Spache & Spache, 1977); (b) corrections (Hansen, 1976; Jenkins & Larson, 1977); and (c) the use of daily performance measures for instructional planning (Jenkins, Mayhall, Peschka, & Townsend, 1974). Currently, research on passage reading continues to focus on corrections, with additional emphasis on the use of context, illustrations, and computers in acquiring information from passage-level text. A summary of research in these areas follows.

Corrections

A number of instructional studies comparing different corrective feedback proce-

dures on word recognition have produced conflicting findings. In some studies, word-supply conditions were found to be superior to phonics analysis and a no-correction condition (Jenkins, Larson, & Fleisher, 1982; Pany, Peters, Mastropieri, & Kulhavy, 1982; Rose, McEntire, & Dowdy, 1982), while phonics analysis and no-correction conditions have provided facilitative effects similar to word supply in other studies (Meyer, 1982; Pany & Mccoy, 1983; Pany, McCoy, & Peters, 1981; Singh & Singh, 1985).

McCoy and Pany (1986) summarized the research on corrective feedback during oral reading according to its effect on word recognition and comprehension. Their analysis revealed that corrective feedback enhances learning disabled students' word recognition accuracy. Additionally, the authors concluded that not all corrective feedback techniques on word recognition are equally effective. Based on their findings, drill on the word in error was superior merely to supplying the correct word which was superior to sentence reread, end-of-page review, or word-meaning instruction. Their summary also revealed a differential effect of corrective feedback for learning disabled and average readers.

While corrective feedback revealed facilitatory effects on learning-disabled students' comprehension, results of preliminary studies indicate either the negative or neutral effect of corrective feedback for average readers. Fleisher, Jenkins, and Pany (1979) found that training fourth- and fifth-grade poor readers to read words presented on flash cards resulted in significant reduction in reading times. However, no differences were observed on comprehension. Pany, McCoy, and Peters (1981) examined the effect of corrective feedback during oral reading on primary and intermediate remedial readers. Few significant differences occurred between four dependent measures at either skill level. The results do not support the position that immediate corrective feedback is detrimental to reading comprehension.

Use of Context

Generally, studies have found that good readers use contextual information to facilitate word recognition (Ehrlich, 1981; Ehrlich & Rayner, 1981; Perfetti & Roth, 1981; Smith, 1982; Stanovich, 1980, 1982). More specifically, a number of recent studies have consistently found that when reading materials are within the difficulty range of readers, less-skilled readers show just as large contextual effects on word recognition as more skilled readers (Becker, 1982; Ehrlich, 1981; Schwantes, 1981; Schwartz & Stanovich, 1981; West, Stanovich, Freeman, & Cunningham, 1983). However, when less-skilled readers fail to use the context appropriately, contextual facilitation is hindered by poor-decoding skills, not by a strategic inability to use the context when reading (Stanovich, Cunningham, & Freeman, 1984).

Illustrations

Few studies exist which have examined the effects of illustrations on early passage reading even though they are commonplace in many beginning reading materials. Earlier studies have indicated that the presence of illustrations has a more detrimental effect on the reading of poor readers than on good readers (Koenke & Otto, 1969; Samuels, 1967; Willows, 1978). A recent investigation has confirmed this earlier finding (Harber, 1983). Two recent studies (Harber, 1980, 1983) suggested that low performing students tend to focus their attention during the reading task on the easier cue (i.e., the picture) and have greater difficulty shifting their attention to the printed word once the picture is identified.

Computers

A few beginning studies suggest that microcomputer technology can increase students' passage-reading fluency (Jones, Torgesen, & Sexton, 1987; Roth & Beck, 1987; Rashotte & Torgesen, 1985). However, further research in this area is needed.

Program Comparisons

In response to the documented decoding deficits of low-performing readers, phonics-based decoding instruction has assumed an important place in the traditional reading curricula. Beck (1985) cautioned against the wholesale acceptance of reading curricula which promote such an emphasis. In her evaluation of phonics programs, she (1985) proposed that even when phonics is taught, it is the "wrong kind of phonics instruction" that results in the perpetuation of word-attack difficulties (p. 243). In summary, she suggested that many phonics programs are too abstract and rely on skills that are too difficult for the learner to extract. She found that not all skills taught in phonics programs contribute to reading. Finally, she noted that students are seldom taught an explicit soundblending technique.

A longitudinal study by Evans and Carr (1983) compared the effects of direct decoding instruction to a language experience approach in 20 first-grade classrooms. The code-based approach supplemented basal texts with phonics drills and applications, while the language experience groups were taught to produce their own books of stories in which the teacher directed instruction comprised approximately 35% of the instructional session. Results at year-end indicated the significant effect of decoding instruction on decoding and comprehension tasks.

The effectiveness of the *Corrective Reading Program (CRP)*, a code-based direct-instruction method for teaching older students who experience difficulties in word recognition and comprehension skills, was assessed by Polloway, Epstein, Polloway, Patton, and Ball (1986). Subjects were 78 learning disabled and 41 educable mentally retarded adolescents who were achieving at least three years below grade level. Results indicated that under the CRP period, academic gains in reading recognition and comprehension were significantly greater than gains evidenced during the implementation of other reading programs. Findings further indicated that, under the CRP program, the LD group improved at a greater rate in reading recognition than the EMR group when taught. Similar advantages of the direct instruction decoding methods prescribed in the *Corrective Reading Program* have been documented in other studies involving intermediate-aged learning disabled students (Lloyd, Cullinan, Heins, & Epstein, 1980; Lloyd, Epstein, & Cullinan, 1981).

In a quasi-experimental investigation of direct-decoding instruction involving 63 primary grade, learning-disabled children, Stein and Goldman (1980) contrasted the effectiveness of two phonics-based programs, DISTAR and *Palo Alto*. In the initial stages, DISTAR used only phonics decoding instruction, while *Palo Alto* combined phonics and contextual cues. *Palo Alto* programs also viewed the teacher as a facilitator of learning. In contrast, the teacher directed the learning process in DISTAR instruction. Results indicated that the DIS-

TAR reading program was significantly more effective than the *Palo Alto* program in terms of both reading recognition and comprehension measures. Although both reading programs enhanced the reading abilities of students, the DISTAR group showed an approximate mean gain of more than 15 months over a 10-month treatment period, while subjects in the *Palo Alto* program evidenced an approximate 7-month gain during a 10.8-month treatment period.

Phonic Analysis

Teaching students letter combinations greatly reduced the irregularity of common words by allowing students to treat them as a special type of regular word (Mason, 1977). Other studies indicate that good readers attend to letter combinations. Glass and Burton (1973) and Spoeky and Smith (1973) studied successful readers to determine how they decode. In the Glass and Burton study, the possibilities included generalizations, syllabication rules, single letter analysis, affixes, and letter clusters. According to self-reports from the readers and experimenter observations, over 80% of the successful identifications were accounted for by a letter-cluster analysis. Our assumption is that, if students learn the most common (and in some cases, minor) sound for letters and letter combinations, the students will automatically learn to combine letters and combinations into larger chunks (letter clusters) so that they can sight read. Decoding individual letters and combinations is too slow a process for fluent sight reading.

For example, Spache (1939) identified several high-frequency letter clusters that exhibit a consistent sound-symbol relationship:

ail	con	ick	ter	it
ain	eep	ight	tion	ite
all	ell	ill	ake	le
and	en	in	ide	re
ate	ent	ing	ile	ble
ay	er	ock	ine	
	est			

It is interesting to note that all these clusters are composed of letters and letter combinations discussed earlier in the text; e.g., *ail* is composed of *ai* and *l; ain* is composed of *ai* and *n*. Research is needed to determine whether teaching letters and combinations results in students automatically mastering letter clusters or whether letter clusters need to be directly taught after single letters and letter combinations have been taught.

A great deal of research has been conducted concerning the utility of phonic generalizations taught to students. Clymer (1963) identified 121 generalizations that appeared in four basal reading programs. By combining overly specific generalizations and deleting overly general ones, Clymer ended up with 45 generalizations. He then prepared a composite list of all the words introduced in the four basic series from which the words were drawn, plus the words for the *Gates Reading Vocabulary for the Primary Grades*. Once this list was prepared, each phonic generalization was checked against the words in the list to determine which words were pronounced as the generalization stated and which were not. A percent of utility was computed for each generalization by dividing the number of words pronounced as the generalization claimed by the total number of words the generalization applied to.

Of the 45 generalizations, 6 were found to be extremely nonfunctional as they had only a 35% utility figure. Another 6 of the generalizations had a utility rate between 36 and 50%. An additional 16 had a utility

rate between 51 and 75%, and 17 had a utility rate of above 75%. Further studies by Emans (1967), Baily (1967), and Burmeister (1968) showed similar but not exact findings due to the variations in the words studied. The results of these studies point out the need for teachers to have a specific knowledge of phonic generalizations so that they may delete or modify ill-founded generalizations appearing in commercial programs.

Unfortunately, little research has been conducted on teaching words that contain letter combinations or VCe patterns. Two studies by Carnine and Stein (1979) dealt with issues relevant to teaching procedures. They compared the efficacy of two common procedures for teaching students to decode words with letter combinations. In one procedure, words containing *oi* were introduced in a passage, which the students read twice. If the students missed the word, the teacher told it to them. In the other procedure, the letter combination *oi* was introduced in isolation followed by *oi* words in introductory and discrimination word lists. Then students read the training passage containing *oi* words one time. Both groups were tested on a transfer passage containing *oi* words the students had never before seen. The results showed that the group introduced to the letter combination in isolation and in word lists identified significantly more *oi* words on the transfer passage than the passage-reading group.

Another important question regarding letter combinations is sequencing. Should one sound value be introduced when a new letter or letter combination is introduced, or should several sound values be introduced? We recommend a constant introduction in which just one sound is presented for a letter or letter combination when it is first introduced. In contrast, Gibson and Levin (1975) recommend a variable introduction, in which multiple sound values are presented for a letter when the letter first appears; i.e., a vowel is introduced in isolation and as a member of letter combinations to demonstrate that it represents various sounds. Stein and Carnine (1978) compared constant and variable introductions by constructing two sequences made up of three-vowel and six-letter combinations; each vowel appeared alone and as part of two letter combinations. In the constant treatment, the sound represented by each single letter was taught before the sounds of any letter combinations; the order of introduction was *a, o, u, aw, or, ur, ow, oa,* and *ou.* In the variable treatment, different sound values represented by a single letter were taught before a second vowel; the order of introduction was *a, aw, oa, o, or, ow, ou, u,* and *ur.* Nonreading preschoolers were pretrained on consonant sounds, on the vowel *a,* and on the sounding-out strategy. After pretraining, the preschoolers were presented a set of introductory words, all of which contained the most recently introduced single-vowel or vowel-letter combination. After the introductory words, the preschoolers were presented a set of discrimination words, including those which contained the recently introduced letter or combination, and others containing previously introduced letters and combinations. Introductory and discrimination-word lists were presented for each letter and letter combination. The results were mixed: preschoolers receiving the constant introduction made more correct responses to words that contained three of the nine letters and combinations (*o, oa, ow*), while preschoolers in the variable treatment made more correct responses to one-letter combination (*ou*). Transfer scores for the two treatments were comparable.

The mixed findings may have resulted from the limited practice received in the fixed-trials design and from the brevity of the constant introduction. In the constant introduction, only three vowels were presented before letter combinations with different values for the vowels were introduced. The limitations that result from a fixed-trials design are illustrated by two experiments on separating similar sounds (Carnine, 1976d) where the post test scores were over three times higher for students involved in the trials-to-criterion experiment than for students who received a fixed number of trials. Further research comparisons of constant and variable introductions with more letters and using a trials-to-criterion design are needed.

Kameenui, Stein, Carnine, and Maggs (1981) also conducted a study concerning varying teaching procedures with VCe pattern words. Three procedures for teaching VCe words to lower performing children were compared to a control group: rule stated, rule applied to introductory and discrimination list, and rule applied to introductory list. The VCe rule was "When there's an *e* at the end of the word, this letter (tester points to the vowel) says its name." The students in the rule-stated group were told the rule, then presented with three introductory words (all VCe words) until they correctly identified all three consecutively or until the list had been presented three times. After the introductory list, the students were asked to identify nine words in a discrimination list (VCe and CVC words) until they correctly identified six consecutive words or until the list had been presented three times. All errors were corrected by the teacher's saying the word and asking the students to repeat it.

The students in the rule applied to introductory list group were also presented the VCe rule. When they were presented the introductory word list, however, the tester prompted each word by asking: "Is there an *e* at the end of the word? So, what does this letter say? What is the word?" Following the introductory list, the tester presented the discrimination list. To correct errors on the discrimination list, the tester used the same VCe-rule prompt that was used with the introductory words.

The third group differed from the second group in that the discrimination words were replaced by five additional VCe words; i.e., the students were presented an introductory list only. In all other ways, the groups were alike.

Following training, all three groups were tested on an 11-word transfer-discrimination list and a paragraph containing 5 new VCe words. Mistakes were not corrected. The students in the control group were given the transfer test without having had any previous training on VCe words. Students in the two-rule application groups made significantly more correct transfer-list responses than students in the rule stated or in the control group. This result suggests that students should be prompted to apply the VCe rule and not simply told it. Also, all students who were presented word lists made significantly more transfer responses than the control group, indicating that practice on word lists improves decoding performance on new words in lists. The absence of significant differences in paragraph reading indicates that the relatively brief intervention (3.19 minutes on the average) did not substantially affect reading performance in context. Mean correct identification of VCe words in passages was about 35%. Longer interventions that include some passages with transfer words are needed to replicate the earlier finding (Carnine & Stein, 1979a) that word and passage training contribute to superior transfer passage performance.

Another study on procedures for teaching VCe words (Kameenui et al., 1981) evaluated the importance of discrimination lists. The results indicated that teaching with discrimination lists results in superior-transfer performance in both lists and passages compared to training with all VCe words and to passage reading with a high density of VCe words. A second finding was that transfer performance for the group with list training on all VCe words was also superior to the transfer performance for the group that received paragraph reading training.

Although research has found that students have difficulty learning minor sounds (Calfee, Venezky, & Chapman, 1969), we could find no research relating to teaching procedures for words with minor sounds. The strategy of trying the most common sound for a letter or combination, then trying the minor sound, needs to be compared with a sight or context procedure for teaching words that contain minor sounds. Additional research is also needed to determine what kind and how much phonic instruction is beneficial for various skill levels. We assume that in the beginning stage, much of the instruction involves word lists; but, in the primary stage, more instruction occurs in passage reading. Research on how best to make this transition would be helpful.

Structural Analysis

The research concerning structural analysis deals with syllabication generalizations and correlations of student performance rather than experimental studies to determine more effective ways of teaching structural-analysis skills.

Waugh and Howell (1975) discussed various problems associated with syllabication rules. They pointed out that syllables are often treated as a group of letters rather than a unit of speech. When syllables are viewed as conventions for where to divide a word, they are not functional decoding units. The syllables for *abrupt* are *ab-rupt*, but people don't say "ab rupt"; they say "a brupt." Thus the most widely accepted syllabication rule—a word is divided between adjacent consonants and before a consonant—is of questionable utility.

Spache and Badgett (1965), McFeely (1974), Aaron (1960), Burmeister (1968), and Canney (1976) suggested that most syllabication rules are not worth teaching. Rather than emphasizing generalizations and rules, various researchers suggest teaching students to identify root words, suffixes, and prefixes (Venezky, 1967, 1970; Chomskey, 1970; and McFeely, 1974). Also, several affixes can be taught as letter combinations: *ing, est, iest, pre, re, de, pro, con, tion, tain, ly,* and *ness* (McFeely, 1974; Venezky, 1970). We agree that teaching syllabication rules is not a good use of time. We would rather see teachers concentrate on demonstrating how to find prefixes, roots, and suffixes in longer words and how to use a strategy of trying various sounds when encountering a syllable one does not know how to pronounce.

Although the correlation research and analyses of syllabication are important, they are no substitute for experimental research. Experimental research is needed to answer several questions. Many of these questions are the same ones raised with regard to teaching letter combinations: Should affixes be introduced in isolation? What is the optimal mix of word-list training and passage reading? How proficient should students be with a set of affixes before a new affix is introduced? When should identification errors be corrected by prompting the missed structural element rather than through a context or whole-word correction, or no correction at all? Other research questions relate more specifically to structural analysis. How should spelling, morphemic analysis (for deriving meaning), and structural analysis (for purposes of decoding) be integrated? Can syl-

labic analysis exercises be designed to help students decode new words? When should y derivative and VCe derivative words be introduced? What formats should be used? As can be seen from this extensive list of questions, many of the suggestions we make in this section have not been investigated experimentally. Although our recommendations are consistent with research in phonic analysis and our own experience, research studies could provide information that would improve the recommendations.

Contextual Analysis

Correlational evidence indicates that proficient readers read in phrases and multiple-word units while less skilled readers focus on individual words or letters within words. Clay and Imlach (1971) found that the best readers read 7 words between pauses while the poorest readers read only 1.3 words between pauses. Taylor reported that twelfth graders made one fixation (eye movement) for approximately every 2 words while first grade readers made about two fixations for each single word. A comprehensive comparison of three methods for instructing students to read in units larger than single words was conducted by Dahl (1979). She compared single-word recognition training, repeated readings, and hypothesis-test training, in which students were trained to use context cues to predict the next word in a sentence. On various reading measures, Dahl found that the repeated readings and hypothesis-test procedures produced significant gains, but isolated-word drill did not. This study points out the need for specific training in passage reading. Teachers cannot assume that training in word list reading will result in students acquiring passage-reading skills. Specific teaching is needed to develop the various passage-reading skills.

Table 21.1   Average Reading Rates of Students Scoring 70% or Better in Comprehension

Grade	1	2	3	4	5	6	7	8	9	12
Words per Minute	80	115	138	158	173	185	195	204	214	250

Note: From *Grade Level Norms for the Components of the Fundamental Reading Skill,* Bulletin #3 by S. E. Taylor et al. New York: Huntington, Educational Development Laboratories, 1960.

Another variable involved in passage reading is student interest. In reviewing the literature on the importance of student interest, Collins, Brown, Morgan and Brewer (1977) reported that interest significantly affects the performance of boys up through third grade, but has no effect after third grade. This finding would suggest that using high-interest material is important for boys in the first three grades. However, more recent research included in the review suggested that students may be more interested in areas in which they are knowledgeable, in which case, an appropriate knowledge base, and not interest, would be the critical variable in student performance. The data are insufficient to resolve this question. (See Table 21.1.)

A major longitudinal study investigated whether students taught over several years with a code emphasis program would also become proficient in reading from context. Using students from three states, Carnine, Carnine, and Gersten (1984) found that students taught with the code-emphasis program *Reading Mastery* achieved high levels of proficiency in using both letter and context cues to read for meaning. Other research on context is often correlational.

Taylor, Frackenpohl and Pettee (1960) studied students who scored 70% or better in comprehension when reading material was of average difficulty for the grade. The average reading rates are shown in Table 18.5.

Unfortunately, experimental studies have not been conducted to establish optimal accuracy and rate criteria for various skill levels. Nor have studies compared differing passage-reading procedures. Studies of this type might determine an optimal mix and sequence for oral and silent reading activities. Questions about how to correct errors during passage reading also need to be researched. The contribution researchers could make in the area of instructional practices for passage reading is substantial.

Comprehension

Comprehension is the label for a myriad of skills that involve getting meaning from the printed page. The teaching of comprehension should be approached in the same manner as the teaching of decoding. Instruction should be carefully planned to facilitate a high degree of student success in the learning process. Specific skills are taught and then integrated into passage-reading exercises. Isolated skills have little value if they are not used in comprehending the text.

The following sections are designed to provide an in-depth view of the instructional variables to be considered when teaching comprehension. Unlike the rather inclusive sections on decoding, the sections on comprehension do not include discussions of how to teach all aspects of comprehension. Rather, we have picked a few areas and provided in-depth discussions of how program-design principles are applied to comprehension.

A comprehension program should have the following components:

1. A systematic introduction of vocabulary and information appearing in passage-reading exercises. A program should teach the meaning of words critical to the understanding of a passage prior to the students encountering the word in a passage. Similarly, information the students will need to comprehend a passage and make inferences should be presented prior to the students' reading the passage. If the students were to be given stories about the life of Jackie Robinson, information about baseball should be presented before students read the stories about Jackie Robinson.

2. A sequence for introducing specific comprehension skills should be carefully designed. Skills should be

Chapter

22

Overview of Comprehension Instruction

taught systematically. Structured presentations of strategies, careful example selection, and cumulative practice and review should be provided.

3. Passage reading should be the vehicle for integrating the various specific skills into a meaningful whole. When conducting passage reading, the teacher integrates specific comprehension skills, asking students to explain why characters act the way they do, to anticipate what characters might do, to determine if a character is thinking critically, etc. The teacher guides the student to see the overall meaning of the story.

There are five chapters after this one in this part of the book. Chapter 23 discusses methods for teaching vocabulary. In addition to demonstrating how the vocabulary-teaching techniques used in the beginning stage can be applied to teaching new words in the primary and intermediate grades, new techniques for teaching vocabulary are presented. Procedures for teaching students to figure out the meaning of words from the context of the sentences surrounding the word are presented. Use of the dictionary and the meanings of word parts are also discussed as methods for teaching vocabulary.

Chapter 24 illustrates procedures for teaching skills that are presented in the early-primary level. Three skill areas are discussed: literal comprehension, summarization, and sequencing.

Chapter 25 illustrates procedures for teaching several skills normally presented during the intermediate grades. These skills include making inferences and critical thinking.

Chapter 26 presents procedures for facilitating the students' understanding of fiction. Chapter 27 focuses on instructional procedures for expository or content-area material.

Teaching Specific Skills

Chapters 24 and 25 illustrate procedures for teaching specific comprehension skills in the early primary and intermediate grades. These chapters do not cover all aspects of comprehension; rather, the discussions are aimed at demonstrating how the principles of program design are applied to teaching comprehension skills.

Six aspects of program design are relevant when designing lesson plans to teach comprehension skills:

1. specifying objectives,
2. devising strategies,
3. sequencing skills,
4. selecting examples,
5. developing teaching procedures,
6. providing practice and review.

Specifying Objectives

Objectives must be stated as specific observable behaviors. The teacher's first step is to examine the skills she wishes to teach then to describe specifically each type of activity she wishes to present.

Table 22.1 contains a sample sequence for introducing items that teach main ideas. Note that the type of passage, as well as the type of response, is specified. For each item, the objective is either to generate or select a main idea. Note the specificity.

The more specific the teacher is in specifying what the students will be expected to do, the better the teacher can construct a program to teach the skill and help the students encounter success in the learning process.

Devising Strategies

Whenever possible, an instructional program should teach students strategies that

Table 22.1   Description of Item Types—Main-idea Sequence

Passage Specifications	Example of Passage	Type of Response
1. 3–4 sentences: subject is single person, predicate actions can be categorized	Bill picked up his dog. Bill put the dog in the tub. Bill turned on the water. Bill scrubbed the dog.	Generate sentence: Bill gave his dog a bath.
2. 3–4 sentences: subject names different persons	Alice climbed the bars in the park. Mary slid down the slide. Jane swung back and forth in the swing.	Generate sentence: The girls played in the park.
3. Same as #2 with multiple choice	Alice climbed the bars in the park. Mary slid down the slide. Jane swung back and forth in the swing.	Select the main idea: 1. The girls went on the swings. 2. Jane played in the park. 3. The girls played in the park.
4. Same as #3 except there is a one-sentence distractor. One choice is an inference.	A dog walked on its back legs. A seal played a horn. The seal wore a dress. A bear rode a bike.	Select the main idea: 1. A seal did a trick. 2. The animals did tricks. 3. The animals were hungry.

will enable them to figure out the answers to problems. The strategies must be carefully designed to help students answer the current problem type, yet not interfere with strategies to be taught in the future.

The area of main idea is one which typically causes students difficulty. The basic rule for finding out the main idea is to determine what the entire passage says. There is a lot of variety in the passage types presented to students. In some, the main idea may be stated in the first or last sentence. This is usually found in expository writing. In narrative writing, however, the main idea is almost never stated in the first or last sentence in the passage.

It would be unwise to begin instruction by teaching students the strategy of examining the first or last sentence to determine the main idea. If the items were multiple-choice items, the students might not read the story, but instead would examine the first and last sentences to find the one that matches one of the multiple-choice answers.

The initial strategy taught to students should be one which clearly shows the students the need to read the entire passage. In the discussion presented in Chapter 25, a strategy which encourages students to read the entire passage is presented.

Strategy Selection

Reading comprehension skills are usually taught with one of three strategies: (1) rule statements, (2) multi-step procedures, or (3) demonstration examples. In other words, when deciding how best to teach a comprehension skill, teachers can use: (a) a rule statement that alerts the reader to a specific relationship (e.g., "If it tells about the whole passage, it's the main idea");

(b) a series of individual steps that make up a multi-step procedure; or (c) a set of demonstration examples.

Rule Statements. Rule statements specify a reliable connection between two events or concepts. By knowing about one event or concept, the reader is able to predict the other event or concept mentioned in the rule. For example, identifying the main idea of a passage could be taught by using the rule statement: "If it tells about the whole passage, it's the main idea." If a student had to choose the main idea statement from among a group of five statements, the rule would alert the student to choose the statement that describes "all" of the events in the passage. The student would then be able to label the statement as "the main idea" of the passage. The rule statement allows the student to determine if a clear connection exists between the main idea statement and the information in the passage.

Multi-step Procedures. Some comprehension skills are best taught through chaining a series of individual steps, some of which might include a rule. For instance, evaluating testimonial statements or propaganda would consist of the following steps: (1) Identifying the point the author wants the reader to believe (e.g., "Madonna, the popular rock singer, says that Bubba Baths makes the best pedestal sinks in the country"); (2) Identifying the argument that is likely to be compelling to the reader (e.g., "If Madonna says something is the best, it must be the best"); (3) Evaluating the argument (e.g., "Madonna is a singer; does she know what's best about pedestal sinks?"); and (4) Deciding whether to believe what the author wants the reader to believe (e.g., "Are pedestal sinks the best because Madonna says so?").

Demonstration Examples. Although many comprehension skills can be taught through rule statements or multi-step procedures, there are some skills that can not be easily reduced to a rule or a multi-step procedure. These skills are taught simply through the presentation of examples and teacher feedback. Unlike the two previous approaches (rule statements and multi-step procedures), this approach does not require students to follow a prescribed sequence of procedures for learning a comprehension skill. Instead, students are presented with an example of the skill (e.g., a passage and a set of comprehension questions specific to the passage) and receive feedback on their response.

Sequencing Skills

Sequencing involves determining an optimum order for introducing the sets of items identified after objectives are stated. Item sets should be sequenced from easier to more difficult. In the process of devising a sequence, the teacher should examine each set and note the preskills assumed in that set. The sequence of skills should be designed so that these skills are taught before the teacher presents items of that particular set.

For example, when teaching the main idea, one of the sets requires students to make class names for the persons or things doing the actions (e.g., boys, girls, vehicles, children), as well as classifying the actions (e.g., played, cleaned, fixed, made). Exercises to teach these class names should be presented before the students are given passages and asked to construct main-idea sentences.

Selecting Examples

Enough examples of a particular type of item must be constructed to enable the students to have adequate practice in order to master that particular type. Constructing examples for comprehension exercises is much more complicated and time consuming than selecting items for decoding exercises. Most comprehension exercises require the students to read a passage that may vary in length from a couple of sentences to many pages.

Many variables must be considered when constructing passages. Among these are:

- Length: the length of items in a particular set of items should be consistent;

- Readability: the passage should contain no important words the student is unable to decode;

- Sentence structure: a consistent use of sentence types in the items is important; sentences with clauses or passive constructions make comprehension more difficult;

- Vocabulary information: a passage should contain words with which the students are familiar.

Developing Teaching Procedures

After objectives are specified and a strategy has been devised (rule, multi-step procedure, or demonstration example), the strategy must be translated into a format that specifies exactly how the teacher is to present the strategy. The teacher must be certain that her explanations are clear and succinct. The words used in the format must be words the students understand.

Many comprehension skills involve a multi-step procedure. Teaching should be sequenced so that the teacher initially provides a lot of structure, leading the students step-by-step through applying a strategy. The teacher should make a gradual transition from highly structured activities to the guided-practice stage in which the teacher gives little or no help.

Providing Practice

Students need adequate practice to help them master skills before the teacher proceeds to more difficult items. Teachers should also provide intermittent review to facilitate student retention of skills they have mastered. Without intermittent review, students are likely to forget what they have learned.

Practice should always be cumulative. Cumulative review means that, after a new skill is introduced, students are given an assignment in which examples of the most recently introduced type are integrated with items of previously introduced types. In these exercises, the students get the practice necessary to learn not only how you apply a strategy but also when you apply a particular strategy. Cumulative review is a critical, but often overlooked, part of instructional design.

Chapter

23

Vocabulary Instruction

Vocabulary used in primary-grade reading books is usually controlled in that nearly all words appearing in stories are in the average student's speaking vocabulary. In the intermediate grades, vocabulary is not as carefully controlled and, consequently, becomes a source of difficulty for many students. Many passages are written at almost adult reading levels, particularly books in the content areas of social studies, English, science, and math. Teachers must be prepared to spend additional time teaching vocabulary. They must work on increasing students' general vocabulary and knowledge of specific words that will appear in upcoming passages students will read either during reading group or in other assignments.

The procedures we discuss in teaching vocabulary during the intermediate grades include those discussed earlier (modeling, synonyms, and definitions), plus several new strategies: morphemic analysis, contextual analysis, and dictionary usage.

Examples, Synonyms, and Definitions

We discussed three methods for teaching vocabulary in Chapter 12 on oral language training: (1) teaching through modeling examples, used when students do not understand words which could explain the meaning of the new word, (2) teaching through synonyms, used when students know a word with a meaning similar to a new word; for example, the word *deceive* can be taught by using the synonym *trick*, and (3) teaching through definition, used when a longer explanation is needed to define a word and students already understand the words that make up the explanation.

Modeling examples are used when there are no words available to define the concept adequately (e.g., How do you explain a color?). Modeling examples are used primarily to teach basic concepts to children.

Synonym teaching begins to supplement modeling examples as the child's vocabulary grows. For example, a parent explains that *below* means the same as *under,* or that *glad* means the same as *happy.* Synonym teaching can be continued throughout all grade levels. Some examples of less common words that can be taught through synonyms are:

- merge—join
- exterior—outside
- amity—friendship
- assault—attack
- secure—safe
- brief—short
- vary—change
- mentor—teacher

An excellent resource for the teacher in finding synonyms is a thesaurus.

Definitions are used more often as students progress through the grades and the meanings of words become increasingly more complex. The major way to define a word involves putting the new word in a class, then specifying the unique characteristics of that word distinguishing it from other words in that same class:

- decathlon—an athletic contest that includes ten track and field events;
- pediatrician—a doctor who works with children;
- slander—a false report that says bad things about someone;
- cutlery—tools used for eating;
- nonentity—a thing that is of no importance.

Teaching Procedure

The teaching procedure for new vocabulary involves three steps. First, the teacher communicates the meaning of the word, either through modeling examples, giving a synonym, or giving a definition. Second, the teacher tests the students on various positive and negative examples. This step ensures that students really understand the meaning of the word and are not simply memorizing a rote definition. Third, the teacher incorporates the new word into review exercises. The teaching procedure is illustrated in Table 23.1. In the format, the teacher presents the word *respite* using a synonym (a short rest), then tests the students on a series of positive and negative examples.

Note that for testing new vocabulary, the teacher asks, "How do you know?" after each question (e.g., The bear slept all winter. Is that a *respite*? How do you know?).

Sequence and Examples

The words that are taught and the sequence in which they are introduced will be dictated by what the students are expected to read. Teacher's guides for basal reading programs, supplementary comprehension programs, and content area programs usually specify words to be introduced before students read selections. Unfortunately, many difficult words naive students may not understand are not included in these lists. Teachers should preview selections students are to read to determine with which words students will have difficulty. New words should be taught two days prior to their appearance in a passage. Fortunately, teachers do not have to preteach every difficult word likely to be unfamiliar. Rather, teachers should concentrate on words that are (1) critical to the meaning of the story or necessary to

Table 23.1   Format for New Vocabulary (*Respite*)

Teacher	Students
1. Teacher models the pronunciation and definition of *respite*.	
a. "Listen, *respite*.	
Say that." (Signal.)	*"Respite."*
b. "A respite is a short rest.	
What is respite?" (Signal.)	*"A short rest."*
2. Teacher tests definition.	
a. "John worked hard all day. Then he went home and worked all night.	
Did he take a respite?" (Signal.)	*"No."*
"How do you know?"	*"He didn't take a rest."*
b. "Ann worked hard all morning. At twelve, she stopped and relaxed for awhile then she went back to work.	
Did she take a respite? (Signal.)	*"Yes"*
"How do you know?"	*"She took a short break."*
c. "Sue did fifty push-ups. Then she splashed cold water on her face and lay down for five minutes. Then she did twenty-five more push-ups.	
Did she take a respite?" (Signal.)	*"Yes."*
"How do you know?" (Signal.)	*"She rested for five minutes."*
d. "Bill did fifty push-ups this morning, then he slept on the bed all night.	
Did he take a respite?" (Signal.)	*"No."*
"How do you know?" (Signal.)	*"He slept too long."*
3. Teacher reviews recently introduced words.	

answer a question and (2) not defined in the context of the story. The question of which words to teach, though, is not as difficult as the question of which words to review. Students will encounter hundreds of new words during a year. There is not enough time adequately to review all the words. Teachers must decide which words to review.

In selecting words to review, teachers should consider student ability as well as the likelihood of students encountering the word in future assignments. Teachers working with higher performing students can focus on less common words, while teachers working with low performing students should review more common words.

The second criterion for selecting review words is usefulness. The more likely students are to encounter a word in the future, the more frequently it should be reviewed. Only by allocating extra time to lower performing students will teachers be able to review less common words with them. All practice need not be in the form of directed instruction or worksheets. Teachers can make up game-like activities.

For example, a "Bingo" game might involve each student's getting "Bingo" cards with several words written on them. The teacher would give a definition or synonym, then the students would find the card with the correct word and put an "x" over it.

A final note on review deals with the expressive versus the receptive use of a word. *Expressive usage* refers to how a person uses words to communicate with other people, while *receptive usage* refers to a person's understanding of the words another person has said. Teachers should keep in mind that expressive language (using a word properly) is much more difficult than receptive language (understanding the word). Thus, exercises in which students are asked to generate sentences using a new word should not be done until at least several days after the word has been introduced. During the introductory period, the teacher should model how the word is used in sentences. The more often the teacher can use the word throughout the school day, the better. Using the word in sentences during the school day provides excellent models of how to apply the word.

Figurative Speech

Intermediate-grade textbooks contain hundreds of figurative or idiomatic expressions such as *down and out, bottom of the heap, in hot water,* and *to be out of line.* Students should be taught the meaning of figurative expressions just as they are taught the meaning of any unknown vocabulary word. Teachers should preview upcoming passages students will read and select figurative or idiomatic expressions they may not understand and are not explained by the passage's context. These expressions should be taught and reviewed before the passage is presented. As extra practice, the teacher can prepare worksheets in which the students must match figurative expressions with their meanings, then have them fill in the blanks in sentences with the appropriate expressions (see Table 23.2).

Contextual Analysis

In contextual analysis, a reader uses the words in a sentence surrounding an un-

---

Table 23.2   Figurative Speech Example Worksheet

Draw a line from each numeral to the correct letter.

Phrases	Meanings
1. down and out	a. in trouble
2. in hot water	b. very happy
3. high as a kite	c. without hope
4. heavy heart	d. sad

Fill in the blanks with the phrases.

1. That kid was _____ after she spilled the ink on her dad's shirt.
2. With a _____ the coach told the team that he was leaving.
3. We were _____ after winning the game.
4. The old tramp was _____ .

---

known word to figure out the unknown word's meaning. Contextual analysis is an essential skill for students in the intermediate grades because it allows them to determine the meaning of many unknown words they will encounter. Writers often define words they feel the reader is unlikely to know. Many times the definition is given through the use of an appositive construction containing a synonym or definition which immediately follows the unknown words in the passage:

1. The *drouge,* a small parachute for slowing down an object, shot out of the rear of the space capsule at 10,000 feet.
2. The *surplus,* that is, the amount left over, was so great that the storage bins were full and grain was lying on the ground.

A definition or synonym can also be stated as a negation, a form more difficult for students to understand:

1. The older brother was quite *affable,* not argumentative, as his younger sibling.
2. Jamie was a *versatile* athlete, while Ann, who was not so versatile, was able to play only one sport.

Contextual analysis is made more difficult not only when negative examples are used, but also when a synonym or definition is separated from the unknown word in a passage. In example 1 below, the definition immediately follows the new word. In example 2, the definition is separated from the new word, which makes example 2 more difficult:

1. The food is *preserved,* or kept from spoiling, by special refrigeration cars.

2. The food is *preserved* by special refrigeration cars. These specially made cars keep the food from spoiling.

Contextual analysis is also more difficult when the meaning of a word is implied by description rather than by direct use of a synonym. Often a paragraph or a series of sentences provides example(s), either positive or negative, that students must use as the basis for inferring the meaning of a new word:

1. Byron's muscles strained as he pulled at the door. He leaned back and pushed as hard as he could. He *exerted* all the force he could.
2. In the sea, bones and shells are not eaten away and harmed by the air. Objects are covered with protective layers of sand so that years from now they will be undamaged. Life from the sea is being *preserved* for the future.

Teaching Procedure

The teaching procedure involves leading students through a series of passages where context is used to define an unknown word. For each passage, the teacher (1) points out the unknown word, (2) has the students find the words that tell what the unknown word means, and (3) has the students restate the sentence substituting a synonym or description for the unknown word. The definition or synonym would be derived through contextual analysis. Table 23.3 shows a format that can be used in the intermediate grades for teaching students to infer meaning from a passage.

Critical aspects of teaching contextual analysis involve the sequencing of examples from easy to difficult and providing

Table 23.3   Format for Teaching Vocabulary through Context

Teacher	Students

An advanced exercise might include four to six passages such as this one:

When the first people came to our country, they saw a dark, living cloud of birds. The cloud was so huge that it almost *eclipsed* the sun. When this happened, the people could hardly see what was happening.

1. Teacher calls on a student to read the passage and identify the unknown word.

   a. "Read the passage."

   b. "A new word is underlined, what word is that?" (Signal.) — *"Eclipsed."*

2. Teacher calls on a student to find the synonym or definition.

   a. "What happened when the birds eclipsed the sun?" (Signal.) — *"The people could hardly see."*

   b. "Because of the eclipse of the sun, the men could hardly see. What do you think an eclipse does to the sun?" (Signal.) — *"Covers it up."*

   c. "Yes, it covers it up."

3. Students say the sentence substituting the meaning of the new word.

   a. "Read the sentence with *eclipse* in it." (Signal.) — *"The cloud was so huge that it almost eclipsed the sun."*

   b. Teacher calls on a student. "Say the sentence using a different word for *eclipse*." (Signal.) — *"The cloud was so huge that it almost covered up the sun."*

4. Teacher repeats steps 1 through 3 with several more passages.

---

adequate practice. Students will learn the skill if they are given enough practice and review on the various types of context construction: synonym or definition (which can be close to or separated from the new word), negation, and inference. Providing sufficient and appropriate examples is as important as the teaching procedure itself.

Dictionary Usage

Using the dictionary to determine a word's meaning is more difficult for the young student than an adult may suppose. First, a definition may include words a student does not understand. For example, a dictionary may define *habituate* as to *accus-*

tom; unfortunately, many students will not know what *accustom* means. Teachers should try to select dictionaries written at an appropriate level for the students. The dictionary itself should use clear definitions composed of words with which students are familiar.

Second, many words have more than one meaning listed for them (e.g., the word *bark* can mean (1) covering of a tree; (2) a noise a dog makes; or (3) a small sailing ship). Teachers cannot take for granted that students will know how to find the appropriate meaning. Exercises should be presented to teach students how to determine which of several meanings listed for a word is appropriate for a given sentence. To teach the skill of finding the appropriate meaning, we recommend an exercise in which the teacher writes on the board (or worksheet) a sentence that contains a word having several meanings. The students look up the word, examine each meaning listed for the word, indicate which meaning seems most appropriate for the sentence, and explain why. The first exercises should be limited to words in which the differences between the meanings are fairly obvious. For example, two possible meanings for the word *cold* are chilly and emotionless. In the sentence *The doctor's eyes were cold as he performed the operation,* the meaning of *cold* is somewhat obvious. To correct mistakes, the teacher would have the student read the sentence substituting the dictionary definition, then ask the student if the sentence makes sense.

As the students become more proficient in finding words in the dictionary, the teacher can use dictionary exercises as a means of introducing new vocabulary words that will appear in future passages. Review can be provided through written worksheets similar to the one in Table 23.4 where the students are to match a word

with its meaning. The meanings should be written using words the teacher is certain the students know. For example, in a dictionary the word *inflate* might be defined as "to swell up with air or gas." Some students are not likely to know what *swell up* means. An alternative definition might be "to make bigger with air."

Using a Dictionary during Independent Reading

Although teachers should encourage students to look up new words encountered during independent reading, teachers should not require students to look up so many words that reading becomes tedious. Looking up every unknown word makes reading too laborious, while never looking up words can result in students' reading without understanding what they read. The decision of whether a word is important depends on the students' purpose for reading the passage. When reading to learn new information, students should look up most unknown words. Yet, students do not need to look up all adjectives or adverbs during pleasure reading. Knowing when to figure out the meaning of a new word is an important skill usually not taught. Students should be taught to rely on context rather than going immediately to the dictionary.

The basic strategy students need to learn when encountering an unknown word, is that they should continue reading the paragraph in which the word appears to see if the context gives the word meaning. If the context does not give the meaning, the students decide if knowing the word's meaning is important to understanding the paragraph. If so, the students look up the word. To demonstrate when looking up a word is necessary, a teacher should conduct exercises where he leads

Table 23.4   Matching Words with Their Meanings

1. Look up the meaning of each word in your dictionary. Make a line from the word to its meaning.

Words	Meanings
inflate •	• able to be bent or changed
picturesque •	• about to happen
flexible •	• leave out
imminent •	• very colorful or attractive
omit •	• to fill up with air

2. Fill in the blanks in the sentences with the words below:

   inflate   picturesque   flexible   imminent   omit

   This postcard shows a _____ fall day in Oregon.

   Don't _____ any words when you copy the sentence.

   Rubber is a _____ material.

   We asked the mechanic to _____ our front tires.

   With only two seconds left and our team ahead by eight points, I think victory is _____ .

students through several passages, helping them to see if the context gives the unknown word's meaning. If the context does not provide the meaning, he asks if knowing the meaning of that particular word is essential to understanding the passage.

Morphemic Analysis

All words are composed of *morphemes,* the smallest linguistic units that have meaning. Morphemes may be free (whole words) or bound (found only as parts of words such as prefixes, suffixes, and non-word bases). Morphemic analysis as a vocabulary aid involves dividing a word into its component morphemes, then using the meanings of the individual morphemes to figure out the meaning of the entire word. Morphemic analysis, as a vocabulary aid, can be illustrated with the word *unworkable,* which includes three morphemes: *un*

meaning *not, work,* and *able* meaning *able to.* Through morphemic analysis, *unworkable* can be translated as *not able to work.* Teaching students the meanings of morphemes will give them a strategy for analyzing some unknown vocabulary words. However, teachers must realize that this strategy works with only a limited set of words. Thus, the time allotted to teaching morphemic analysis should not be too lengthy.

Three factors limit the usefulness of morphemic analysis. The first factor is the difficulty of translating individual morphemes into a functional definition. For example, the word *accurate* is composed of three morphemes: *ac,* which means *toward; cure* which means *care;* and *ate* which means *that which is.* The literal morphemic definition of *accurate* is *that which is toward care.* For a sophisticated reader, this definition might be helpful; however, for the less sophisticated students, such a definition would be difficult to use.

A second reason why morphemes are of limited value in figuring out word meanings is that many morphemes have dual meanings. For example, the morpheme *dia* sometimes means *through* as in *diameter* and sometimes means *day* as in *diary*.

A third reason for the limitations of morphemic analysis is that students often cannot determine the morphemes that have been combined to make up the word. For example, the word *recognition* is composed of the morphemes *re + cogno + ite + ion*.

Table 23.5 includes some morphemes that lend themselves to relatively easy translation. Next to each morpheme is a word that illustrates use of that morpheme and the morpheme's common meaning. Note that the meaning we use is designed to be functional rather than technically correct. We tried to construct definitions to make morphemic analysis easier for students.

Teaching vocabulary through morphemes can begin when the students can read at about mid-third-grade level.

Two rules for sequencing the introduction of morphemes are: (1) to introduce the most functional ones first, and (2) to separate morphemes likely to be confused. Morphemes are functional when they enable students to understand words they could not understand without knowledge of the morpheme. The morpheme *re*, which means *again*, is an example of a morpheme that is quite functional. Morphemes *inter* and *intra* can serve as examples of morphemes likely to be confused. The introduction of these morphemes should be separated by at least five other morphemes.

Teaching Procedure

Our teaching procedure includes a format (see Table 23.6) for presenting the meaning of new morphemes and several types of

Table 23.5		Morpheme Meanings*
Morpheme	**Sample Word**	**Approximate Meaning**
able	portable	able to be
bi	bicycle	two
dis	dishonest	not
	disappear	opposite of
est	biggest	the most
ful	hopeful	full of
il	illegal	not
inter	interstate	between
intra	intrastate	inside
less	fearless	without
pre	preschool	before
re	repay	again
sub	submarine	below
tri	tricycle	three
un	unable	not
	untie	opposite of

*For a more thorough listing of morpheme meanings see *Dictionary of English Word-Roots* (R. Smith, 1966).

independent exercises: one exercise requires students to match morphemes and meanings, one in which students match words and meanings, and finally, one exercise in which students fill in missing words in sentences.

The rate of introducing new morphemes depends on the students' performance. A new morpheme can be introduced when the students can do the verbal and worksheet exercises that review previously introduced morphemes without error.

The format includes several steps. In the first step, the teacher tells the students the meaning of a new morpheme, then tests students on the meaning of several words that contain that morpheme (e.g.,

Table 23.6 Format for Introducing Morphemes

Teacher	Students
1. Teacher introduces a new morpheme.	
a. "Listen. *Less* usually means *without*."	
b. "What does *less* usually mean?" (Signal.)	"Without."
"So *careless* means without a care."	
"What does *careless* mean?" (Signal.)	"Without a care."
c. "What does *less* usually mean?" (Signal.)	"Without."
"So what does the word *winless* mean?" (Signal.)	"Without a win."
d. "What does *less* usually mean?" (Signal.)	"Without."
"So what does *homeless* mean?" (Signal.)	"Without a home."
2. Teacher reviews morphemes.	
a. "What does *pre* mean?" (Signal.)	"Before."
b. "What does *un* mean?" (Signal.)	"Not."
c. "What does *tri* mean?" (Signal.)	"Three."
d. "What does *less* mean?" (Signal.)	"Without."
e. "What does *able* mean?" (Signal.)	"Able to be."
3. Teacher applies morphemes to figuring out meaning.	
a. "Listen. *Careful.* Tell me the first morpheme in *careful*." (Signal.)	"Care."
"What's the next morpheme in *careful*?" (Signal.)	"ful."
b. "What does *ful* mean?" (Signal.)	"Full of."
c. "What does *careful* mean?" (Signal.)	"Full of care."
d. Teacher repeats steps 3(a–c) with these words: *preschooler* (one who is before school), *triangle* (three angles), *winless* (without a win).	

the morpheme *less* added to the word *win* creates the word *winless* which means *without a win*.) In the second step, the teacher provides practice for the meaning of the new morpheme and previously taught morphemes. In the third step, students use their knowledge of those morphemes to determine word meanings.

Corrections

In Part 2, the teacher presents a set of morphemes, asking the meaning of each morpheme. If a student does not respond correctly, the teacher tells the student the meaning of the morpheme, repeats the question, then alternates between that morpheme and other morphemes the students know.

Seatwork Exercises

Practice on morphemic analysis can be provided through independent worksheet activities such as those in Table 23.7. In Part 1 of the worksheet, students write the correct

Table 23.7   Worksheet for Morphemic Analysis

Part 1: Write the correct meaning next to each morpheme.

un_____   less_____   re_____   mis_____

ful_____   able_____   est_____   er_____

Part 2: Fill in the blanks using these words:

hopeful   hopeless   misspell   winless   preschool

a. Tom did not want to _____ any words on the test.

b. My brother is too young for this school; he goes to a _____ .

c. We are _____ our team will win.

d. After trying for two months to get his dog to sit, Tom thought it was _____ to continue.

e. The team was sad because it was _____ .

Table 23.8

Fill in the blanks using these words:

prediction   predicted   predictable   unpredictable

a. Yesterday Tom _____ we would lose the game.

b. Tom's _____ did not come true.

c. The hot weather in Hawaii is usually _____ .

d. Take a jacket because the weather here is _____ .

---

meaning for each morpheme. In Part 2, students select words for sentence completion items. The students are given a worksheet with 5–10 sentences. A list of words appears above the sentences. From the list, the students are to select the words that should be in each sentence and go in the blanks.

Similar exercises can be done with related words formed by adding affixes to the same root word. For example, when *predict* is introduced, the words *predictable, predicted, unpredictable,* and *prediction* can be used in a written exercise similar to the one in Table 23.8.

Application Exercises

1. Circle the five words in which the use of morphemes will enable intermediate-grade students to figure out the meaning of a word. Assume the students know the meaning of the root word.

unusable	emphasis
decisive	discord
misspell	dejected
careless	rewashable
absent	useful

2. Rank the following three passages according to the difficulty students would have determining the meaning of each underlined word through contextual analysis. Write 1 for the easiest, 2 for moderate, and 3 for most difficult. Explain why 2 is more difficult than 1 and why 3 is more difficult than 2.

- Our center fielder, Bill, is <u>ambidextrous</u>. He bats third in the lineup. He can use his right hand and his left hand.
- I wish I were <u>ambidextrous</u>. Then I would be able to use my left hand as well as my right.
- Our center fielder, Bill, is not <u>ambidextrous</u>. He bats third in the lineup. He can use his right but not his left hand.

3. Which three of the following dictionary definitions would be most difficult for fifth graders to understand? Why?

malpractice—dereliction of professional duty
mammoth —a very great size
burnish —to polish using something hard
fossil —trace or impression of the remains of a plant or animal preserved in the earth's crust from past ages
infirm —deficient in vitality
fortunate —coming by good luck

Rewrite the more difficult definitions to make them more understandable.

4. Tell which method (examples only, synonym, definition) you would use to teach the meaning of the following words. If you would use a synonym or a definition, specify the wording you would use.

a. residence   **d.** invalid
b. retrospect   **e.** sanctuary
c. diabolic

5. Specify a set of examples (two positive and two negative) you would use in the teaching of *residence*.

6. Which five of the following vocabulary words should a fourth grade teacher review in later lessons when working with more naive students?

congress   region
impend   myriad
defend   professional
ensconced   suspend
wrest   trough

7. The following words are to appear in passages the students will be reading several days from now. Write V in front of each word that should be included in a vocabulary exercise. Write D in front of each word that should be included in a decoding exercise. (Some words need not be included in either type of exercise.)

_____ pauper	_____ exported	_____ extinction	_____ cleft
_____ surround	_____ finch	_____ gymnasium	_____ footstep
_____ essay	_____ architect	_____ void	_____ dynamite
_____ noun	_____ swear	_____ neutral	_____ brittle

Chapter

Specific Comprehension Skills for the Primary Level

In this chapter we illustrate the aspects of program design with three primary grade comprehension skills: literal comprehension, sequencing and summarization. Literal comprehension involves teaching students to retrieve information stated in a passage. The discussion of literal comprehension is presented to demonstrate how attention to specific details can help lower performing students succeed in the early stages of learning.

Sequencing requires students to order several events from a passage according to when they happened in a passage. The discussion on sequencing also is meant to illustrate how a step-by-step procedure can help the instructionally naive student succeed.

Both the discussions of literal comprehension and sequencing present rather mechanical-type skills that show students how to extract information from a passage.

Teachers working with average and higher performing students will likely not have to utilize the strategies presented in this section because their students will be able to do the tasks without teacher guidance.

Summarization involves teaching students to generate or select a sentence that expresses the main idea. The discussion is designed to show how a teacher can introduce a higher level thinking skill in a manner that can foster success for all students.

Literal Comprehension

Literal comprehension, which is the simplest written comprehension exercise, is the first type of written exercise introduced in reading programs. In a literal comprehension exercise, the answer is directly stated in passage. The difference between literal and nonliteral comprehension is illustrated in the passage and items in Table 24.1. Item 1 is literal because the answer is directly stated in the passage. In contrast, Item 2 is not literal since the answer (afraid) does not appear in the passage. In Item 2, students must infer that, since the cat ran from the dog and hid, the cat was afraid.

Teaching Procedure for Literal, Passage-Related Items

The following procedure is designed to introduce literal comprehension items. The procedure would be used only if students were unable to work literal items on their own. Even with students who initially require the structured teaching procedure, the procedure should be faded as soon as students can accurately work literal items independently.

In presenting passage-related items (see Table 24.2), the teacher (1) has the students decode the passage until they can do so fluently, (2) explains and tests the students' understanding of the instructions, and (3) has the students read the first item, asks if they remember the answer, and, if not, directs them to reread the passage until they come to the sentence that contains the answer.

Developing Student Retention

After a few days of teacher directed instruction, the students should do several passage-related items independently. The teacher watches students carefully while they read the passage and answer the items. She notes the strategy students use: Do students refer to the passage for every item or just for unknown items?

If students refer to the passage to answer most of the items, they should be encouraged to remember what they have read. One way of doing this is to present a passage and items on separate pages or require the students to cover the passage before they begin answering the items. The teacher says, "Today you're going to have to remember what you read. When you remember what you read, you can write your answers without looking back at the story. Let's try it. Read the story over until you remember what happens. Then cover the story like this (demonstrates) and write the answers." The teacher monitors the students to make certain they cover the passage before they begin to work the items. When students make an error or cannot remember an answer, they are allowed to refer to the passage. The teacher calls attention to students who correctly answer all the items without looking at the passage; for example, "Students who didn't have to look at the story are in the good remembering club." The teacher reads the names of students who are members of the club for that day. This procedure for building retention can be used on almost all comprehension exercises. In order to ensure a successful experience for instruc-

---

Table 24.1

Passage:
  A cat was sleeping in the sun. Then a dog walked by. The cat jumped up and hid in a can.

Items: Write the right word in the blank.
     literal 1. The cat hid in a _____ . can   house   box
nonliteral 2. The cat was _____ . happy   afraid   big

Table 24.2   Format for Literal Comprehension

Passage:

A little cat lived in a mud house. It rained. A bug ran in the house. The mud house got wet and fell apart. The cat and the bug sat in the rain and got wet.

Items: Fill in the blanks.

1. What got wet and fell apart? _____
2. A cat lived in a mud _____. house   bug   hut
3. The _____and the bug sat in the rain. bug   dog   cat

Teacher	Students

1. The teacher focuses on decoding fluency. **"Touch the first word."** Teacher checks pointing. The teacher alternates between unison and individual responses until the students read the passage fluently. Students may need to reread the story several times.

   Students read the passage.

2. Teacher tests students' understanding of the instructions. Often the instructions for early comprehension activities are not written because the students do not have the decoding skills necessary to read the words that appear in instructions. Whether the teacher gives the instructions or the students read them, the teacher then asks, **"How are you going to answer the question? Tell me what you're going to do. Show me where you put the answer."**

3. Students read the first item and then mark the answer. If necessary, they find the appropriate sentence in the story that answers the item.

   a. **"Touch the first question."** Teacher calls on a student to read.

      Student reads the question.

   b. **"Raise your hand if you know the answer to that question."** If the question has only one possible correct answer, the teacher calls on the group to respond. If the question has several possible correct answers, she calls on individuals to respond. **"What's the answer?"**

      Students answer.

   c. If any students do not remember the answer, the teacher says, **"Let's find the answer in the story. Find the words *got wet and fell apart.*"** If students cannot find the words, have them read each sentence. After students find the sentence, the teacher repeats the item. **"What got wet and fell apart?" "Right, the mud house. Write the answer."**

      "the mud house"
      Students write the answer.

   d. The procedure in step 3 is repeated until the students have completed all the items.

tionally naive students, initial exercises should include relatively short passages. Passage length should be increased gradually.

Difficulty of Literal Comprehension Items

Several variables affect the difficulty of passage-related items: (1) the degree to which the items are literal, (2) the length of the passage, (3) the order in which questions are asked, (4) the complexity of the instructions, and (5) the use of pronouns.

Literal Items

The easiest type of passage-related item is one that can be answered by matching words in the item with those in the sentence. The following item, written in a nonsense language, illustrates a strictly literal item.

    Sentence: yjr, sm gr;; gpp jod jptdr
    Item: yjr, sm gr;; gpp jod_____

Adults cannot decode the nonsense item; yet, they can answer it correctly by matching the words in the item with those in the sentence and writing *jptdr* in the blank. Similarly, a child can answer a completion item by using a matching strategy rather than decoding each word.

Items become less literal when they are not identical to a corresponding sentence in a passage.

Question word items are also less literal (e.g., *Where did the cat live?*) because the word order is altered and the student must understand particular question words (e.g., *where* calls for a location answer).

Passage Length

Finding the sentence that contains the answer to a completion item is more difficult in longer passages. For example, extracting the answer to the question, "Who sat on a mat?" is easier in the sentence "A mad cat sat on a mat" than in this passage: "A rat sat on a mitt. A mad cat sat on a mat. A sad man sat on a bed."

Question Order

Items ordered so that they parallel the sequence of events in a passage are easier than items that do not. When items follow the sequence of a passage, students can start at the beginning of the passage and work through the items in order. Otherwise, they must skip around in the passage to locate the answers. Below are two sets of items, one that follows the sequence of events in the passage (set a) and one that does not (set b).

> Passage:
> Sam ran in a hut. He sat in a cup. He said, "I am hot." He fell off the cup. He got wet. "I am not hot," he said.
>
> Items: Fill in the correct answer.
> a. Items follow the order of events in the passage:
>   Did Sam run in a hut?_____
>   Where did Sam sit?_____
>   He said, "I am not _____."
> b. Items do not follow the order of events in the passage:
>   He said, "I am not _____."
>   Did Sam run in a hut?_____
>   Where did Sam sit?_____

Instruction Complexity

Instructions indicating how students are to respond range from simple ones in which students circle the word that goes in a blank or fill in a missing word to more complex ones in which students make several different responses, e.g., "Circle the word that tells what the boy did. Underline the word that tells what the girl did."

Pronouns

Pronouns increase the difficulty of items because students must identify a pronoun antecedent before they can answer the item. Note the differences between passage a and passage b.

> Passage a: Tom got a car. It was dirty.
> Passage b: Tom got a car. The car was dirty.
> Item: Was Tom dirty?

A naive student would be more likely to answer incorrectly yes after reading passage a because of the pronoun *it*. Passage b is easier because it directly states that the car was dirty. If students do not understand pronouns, they will have some difficulties with comprehension. To prevent these difficulties, teachers should present oral language exercises to teach pronouns. Students can then apply their understanding of pronouns when reading. Although most students will *not* require instruction in pronouns, teachers should be prepared to work with students who need the instruction.

Teaching Procedure for Pronouns

The first step in teaching proper pronoun usage involves oral exercises to ensure that students know the meaning of key pronouns: *he, she, we, they, it, you, them, her, him.* Pronouns that cause particular difficulty are *it, they,* and *them* because they can refer to inanimate objects. The format in Table 24.3, which assumes students know *he, she,* and *it,* demonstrates how the pronoun *they* might be taught. Note that students are taught that the pronoun *they* refers to objects as well as people. This is

an example of including a full range of positive examples.

The second step in teaching pronoun usage involves leading the students through a series of passages containing pronouns. A sample passage appears below.

> Passage:
> Tom and Lisa got in trouble with their parents. They had to stay in all weekend. He cried. She got mad.
>
> Item:
> a. Did Lisa stay in all weekend?
> b. Did Tom get mad?
> c. Who cried?

The teacher or students read the passage. The teacher asks questions after each sentence:

1. "Tom and Lisa got in trouble. Who got in trouble?" "Tom and Lisa."
2. "They had to stay in all weekend. Did Tom have to stay in?" "yes" "Did Lisa have to stay in? "yes"
3. "He cried. Did Tom cry?" "yes" "Did Lisa cry?" "no"
4. "She got mad. Did Tom get mad?" "no" "Did Lisa get mad?" "yes"

If students make errors, the teacher refers to the pronoun; e.g., "She got mad. She tells about a girl. Is Tom a girl?"

Sequencing

Sequencing requires ordering several events according to when they occur in a passage. For example, a student reads a passage and then writes numbers in front of several phrases that describe events, writing 1 in front of the event that occurred first, 2 in front of the event that occurred next, etc. The difficulty of

Table 24.3   Format for Teaching Pronouns

	Teacher	Students
1.	Teacher demonstrates. "Here's a new pronoun. *They. They* tells about more than one."	
2.	Teacher provides practice on saying the definition. "What does the pronoun *they* tell about?"	*"More than one."*
3.	Teacher provides practice on applying the definition. "Listen: John and Mary. Do we say *they* when we talk about John and Mary?"	*"Yes."*
	"How do you know?"	*"John and Mary are more than one."*
4.	"Listen: John. Do we say *they* when we talk about John?"	*"No."*
	"How do you know?"	*"John is only one."*
	"What pronoun could tell about John?"	*"He."*
5.	"Listen: fork. Do we say *they* when we talk about a fork?"	*"No."*
	"Why not?"	*"Fork is only one."*
	"What pronoun could tell about a fork?"	*"It."*
6.	"Listen: fork and spoon. Do we say *they* when we talk about a fork and spoon?"	*"Yes."*
	"How do you know?"	*"Fork and spoon are more than one."*
7.	"Listen: boys. Do we say *they* when we talk about boys?"	*"Yes."*
	"How do you know?"	*"Boys are more than one."*
8.	"Listen: Mary. Do we say *they* when we talk about Mary?"	*"No."*
	"Why not?"	*"Mary is only one."*
	"What pronoun could tell about Mary?"	*"She."*

sequencing items depends on the length of the passage and the number of items to be sequenced. Obviously, the longer a passage and the more items to be sequenced, the more difficult the exercise will be.

Teaching Procedure

The strategy we recommend works only for very simple passages in which the first action appears in the story first; the second action appears second, and so forth. The strategy involves these steps (see Table 24.4): (1) the students read the passage; (2) for each event, the students underline the words in the passage that coincide with the event; (3) the students number the events underlined in the passage, beginning with one; and (4) the students then write the numbers in front of the appropriate items in the question.

The teacher can fade the structure of the format over a period of days. When the students do the items without teacher help, the teacher need not insist on students using the underlining strategy if they are able to answer the items correctly without underlining.

The length of the passage, and the number of items to be sequenced, should increase gradually. The increases in difficulty occur when the students are able to do the current type without error for two consecutive days.

Summarization

Summarization not only allows the students to identify the key ideas from a

---

Table 24.4   Format for Sequencing

Passage:

Alice went home after school. Later she went to the park. At the park she saw her friend, Bob. Alice and Bob played catch all day. Then they got an ice cream cone.

Directions:

Write 1 in front of what happened first, a 2 in front of what happened next, and a 3 in front of what happened third.

Items:

_____ Alice went home.

_____ Alice got an ice cream cone.

_____ Alice and Bob played catch.

Teacher	*Students*
1. Teacher has students read the story and directions. **a.** Read the story. **b.** Read the directions.	*Students read the story.* *Students read directions.*
2. Touch the item that says *Alice went home.*	*Students find event below directions.*
3. Now find in the story where it says *Alice went home* and underline those words.	*Students locate and underline the sentence.*
4. Teacher repeats steps 2 and 3 for the remaining two events.	
5. Look at the passage, find the first event in the story that is underlined and place a 1 over it. Then place a 2 over the second underlined event, and a 3 over the third underlined event.	*Students locate the first event and write a 1 over it. Students locate the next item and write a 2 over it, etc.*
6. **a.** Look at the items. Touch *Alice went home.*	*Students locate item and touch it.*
b. Now touch where it says *Alice went home* in the passage.	*Students touch sentence in the passage.*
c. What number is written over the words *Alice went home?*	*"One."*
d. Write that number in front of *Alice went home.*	*Students write 1.*
e. Teacher repeats steps a–d with remaining items.	

---

passage, but it also reduces the information in a passage to key ideas that students can remember. Since students cannot remember everything they hear or read, acquiring summarization skills ensures they will remember major events rather than random details. A summary condenses a passage into a few sentences. A one-sentence summary can be considered a main idea.

Teaching Procedure

The teaching procedure we recommend begins with exercises in which the students create main idea sentences for short passages in which the subjects are persons or things, and the predicates include actions that can be easily classified.

The first type of item involves one person doing a series of actions that can be easily classified. Table 24.5 includes a sample set of items. Note that in each item the main idea can be written by naming the person, then telling the main thing the person did in all the sentences. The teaching procedure includes these steps: (1) the teacher tells the students a rule for writing a main idea sentence (e.g. "Name the person and tell the main thing the person did in all the sentences"); (2) the students read the passage; (3) the teacher asks the students to figure out a main idea sentence by naming the person and telling what the person did in all the

sentences; (4) the teacher calls on a student to say the sentence. The teacher corrects the student by telling the correct answer; (5) the teacher repeats the same procedure with the remaining passages; (6) the teacher has the students write the main idea sentence for each paragraph (difficult-to-spell words would be written on the board).

A slightly more complex type item is introduced when the students master writing main idea sentences for the item type described above. This type includes sentences that name different persons or things and tell the actions they did. The students must give the people or things a group name, then say a verb that classifies the action. A typical item appears below:

> Mr. Smith dug holes for the rose bushes. Mr. Jones put rose bushes in the holes. Mr. Adams put dirt back in the holes around the rose bushes.

An acceptable main idea sentence for the item above would be "The men planted rose bushes."

The teaching procedure for this type of item is basically the same as described above, except that the teacher directs the students to make the sentence by naming the group (the men) and telling the main thing the group did (planted rose bushes).

The value of these exercises is that they demonstrate that main idea sentences tell what an entire passage is about.

Table 24.5	Items for Main-Idea Single-Person Class Action
Tom cooked two eggs. He poured orange juice into a glass. He put cereal in a bowl. He poured milk into the bowl.	Ann went to the park. She swung on the swings. She slid down a slide. She climbed on the bars.
Sally took the flat tire off her bike. She put a patch on the hole in the tire. She put the tire back on her bike. She filled the tire with air.	Robert threw a fish to a seal. He poured milk in a bowl for a cat. He put hay in the barn for the cows.

Multiple-choice items, in which students are asked to select the sentence that is the main idea sentence for a passage, could be introduced next. Below is a sample item.

Passage:
A dog walked on its back legs. A bear rode a bicycle. A seal balanced a ball on its nose.

Which sentence is the best main idea sentence?

1. An animal walked on its back legs.
2. The animals wanted food.
3. The animals did tricks.
4. A dog did a trick.

Note the variety of possible main idea sentences used in the item. The correct answer is "The animals did tricks." Two sentences do not express the main idea because they merely describe one of the animals. One incorrect answer names the group (the animals), but makes an inference (the animals *wanted* food).

The teaching format includes these steps: (1) the students read the passage; (2) the teacher tells the students that one of the sentences is a good main idea sentence for the passage; and (3) the teacher has the students read each sentence and asks if it is a good main idea sentence for the passage, asking why or why not after each response.

The next step in the sequence is to introduce passages in which one or more sentences are not related to the main idea. We can call these sentences *distractors*. When distractors appear, the rule for creating a main idea changes from telling what a person or group did in all the sentences to telling the main thing the person or group did in most of the sentences. Look at the following passage.

Passage:
Tom got home and took out his school books. He did three pages of math. He was going to have a math test soon. He studied twenty spelling words. He wrote a report about birds. Tom was very interested in birds.

Note that two sentences in the above passage do not tell what Tom did, The main idea is still clearly "Tom did homework."

The teacher introduces the passage by saying, "Most of the sentences in this passage tell about the main thing a person did. The main idea sentence for the passage tells what the passage is mainly about."

Multiple-choice items in which the sentences the students must select are written as questions can be introduced next. The sentences usually begin with what, how, where, when, or why.

A preskill for these types of items is the sentence-analysis skills which teach students to determine if a sentence tells where, why, when, etc. (see Chapter 12). Below are examples of paragraphs that tell why something occurred and where something occurs. This paragraph tells *why* a boy was sad:

Bill got an F on his test. Bill lost his favorite toy. Bill's team lost the big game. Bill's best friend moved to another school.

Circle the best main idea:

1. Why Bill failed his test.
2. Why Bill was sad.
3. What happened to Bill's friend?
4. What Bill is going to do.

This paragraph tells *where* you can do something:

Football is lots of fun. You can play football in the street. You can play football in the park if there aren't too many trees. You can play football on a soccer field.

Circle the best main idea:

1. What you can do in a street.
2. Why football is fun.
3. Where you can play football.
4. When you can play football.

Where and *why* items can be introduced concurrently because they are relatively easy to distinguish from each other.

The teaching procedure presents the strategy of having the students examine each possible main idea, noting how many sentences tell about that particular main idea. The teacher leads the students through several examples, then has them do several independently.

Passages that tell when something occurs, how something is done, or how something looks may be introduced later.

Application Exercises

1. Specify whether each question below is a literal question or a non-literal question:

The rocket landed on the soft sand. Minutes later Zorn walked out of the rocket. He had never seen such a place. The sky was black. He could see nothing but sand.

   a. Did Zorn land at noon time?

   b. What landed on the soft sand?

   c. What color was the sky?

   d. Did Zorn land in New York City?

2. Assume some teaches are presenting sets of examples to teach the range of the word *it*. Tell which of the three teachers below has constructed the best set of examples. Explain why.

Teacher A—a pen, a fork, a pencil, a knife

Teacher B—a bed, a chair, a table, a dresser, a stool

Teacher C—a lion, a dresser, the moon, a pen, a spider

3. Specify the teacher wording to correct the following errors made by a student on a worksheet assignment. (Assume the student can decode all the words.)

   a. Passage: The beach was crowded. It was Sunday, and it was hot. Babies played in the sand. Children jumped in the waves. Parents sat and talked.

   Item: Circle the best title.

   1. Babies make sand piles.

   2. People had a good time at the beach.

   (3. Children play in the waves.)

   b. Passage: Bill and Sally walked to the park this morning. Sally played baseball and Bill ran around the track. They got a drink of water. Then they went home.

   Item: Write 1, 2, 3 in front of the events in the order they happened.

        3 They got a drink of water.

        1 They went home.

        2 Bill and Sally went to the park.

4. A teacher tested a group of students and found the students did not know the meaning of the following words that will appear in a written-comprehension task within the next few days: daring, contented, rudder, and parallelograms. For each word,

   a. describe the procedure you would use to teach the word (examples, synonyms, or definitions) and, if applicable, write the synonym or definition.

   b. write a set of four examples that could be used in teaching *daring* (specify two positive and two negative examples).

Chapter

25

Specific Comprehension Skills for the Intermediate Level

In this chapter we illustrate the aspects of program design reviewed earlier in Chapter 22. The illustrations involve three intermediate-level comprehension skills: making inferences based on relationships, comprehending sentences with complicated syntactic structures, and critically reading passages (i.e., identifying an author's conclusion and evaluating the adequacy of the evidence and the legitimacy of the arguments). Because we cannot explain how to teach all the important comprehension skills for the intermediate grades, we have limited our discussion to these few examples. However, these topics are very important in their own right. Making inferences based on relationships is a fundamental thinking skill. Similarly, critical reading is necessary if students are to intelligently evaluate material they read.

Inference

Inferential questions require knowledge of relationships between two objects or events. The statement "When people run faster, their hearts beat faster" implies a relationship between changes in running rate and changes in heartbeat. Sometimes the relationship is directly stated in a passage (see example A in Table 25.1). More often, the relationship is not specified; students are expected to know a particular relationship (see example B in Table 25.1) or are expected to infer the relationship using the information stated in a passage (see example C in Table 25.1). In passage A the relationship "When people run faster, their hearts beat faster" is directly stated. Since the relationship is stated, students are more likely to answer the item about Rachel correctly. In passage B, the relationship is not stated, and examples are not provided that allow the reader to figure out or induce the relationship. Obviously, students who do not know the relationship between exertion and heart rate have no basis for answering the item. Although the relationship is not directly stated in passage C either, several examples illustrate the relationship between running rate and heart beat. When Rachel ran a mile in 8 minutes, her rate was 78 beats per minute. When she ran faster (a mile in 6 minutes), her rate was faster (93 beats per minute). Students are given information that enables them to induce the relationship and then figure out the answer. (Using specific information to derive a general relationship, as in example C, is called induction. Applying a stated relationship to come up with a specific answer is called deduction.)

First, we discuss procedures for teaching students to make inferences based on stated relationships. Second, we discuss procedures for teaching students to complete items when a relationship is not stated. This type of item accounts for the majority of inference items in commercial programs. Third, we discuss procedures for teaching students to induce relationships when examples are provided to illustrate the relationship.

When introducing inference items, the teacher can refer to them as "detective" problems. The students must use the information in the passage to figure out the answer to the question.

Table 25.1   Inferential Questions

Relationship Stated	Relationship Not Stated	
	Knowledge of Relationship Is Assumed	Examples for Figuring Out the Relationship Are Provided
A. When people run faster, their hearts beat faster. On Monday, Rachel ran a mile in 5 minutes. On Tuesday, she took 7 minutes. On Wednesday, she took 4 minutes.	B. On Monday, Rachel ran a mile in 5 minutes. On Tuesday, she took 7 minutes. On Wednesday, she took 4 minutes.	C. On Friday, Rachel ran a mile in 8 minutes. Her heart was beating 78 times a minute. On Saturday, Rachel ran a mile in 6 minutes. Her heart was beating 93 times. On Sunday, she ran a mile in 9 minutes. Her heart was beating 68 times. On Monday, Rachel ran a mile in 5 minutes. On Tuesday, she took 6 minutes. On Wednesday, she took 4 minutes.

On which day did Rachel's heart beat fastest?
  Monday
  Tuesday
  Wednesday
	On which day did Rachel's heart beat fastest?
	  Monday
	  Tuesday
	  Wednesday
		On which day did Rachel's heart beat fastest?
		  Monday
		  Tuesday
		  Wednesday

Relationship Stated

Much of the material students read in the intermediate grades is expository. It is designed to convey information. A common characteristic of expository material is the inclusion of key sentences which specify a relationship. Table 25.2 includes examples of sentences which specify relationships with items that can be used to test students' ability to draw inferences.

Table 25.3 includes a sample worksheet exercise that can be used to teach students to work from stated rules. The rule is presented; then a series of questions that contain information relating to the rule are given. Note that after each question, the students are expected to explain why they gave a particular answer.

Teaching Procedure

The teaching procedure always begins with the students reading the rule, then saying it. Some students may have a lot of trouble

---

Table 25.2   Simple Relationships and Items for Teaching Inference

Relationship	Items
1. Students who study *hardest* make the best grades.	1. Jim got a lower mark on the test than Bill. Who studied *harder?*
2. The steeper a stream, the faster the water flows.	2. Bill is fishing in a stream on some flat land. Sarah is fishing in a stream on a hill. Which steam is moving faster?
3. The higher you go up, the less oxygen in the air.	3. There is less oxygen where Ann is walking than where Margie is walking. Who is walking at a higher place?
4. The greater the rainfall, the greener the grass.	4. There were 5 inches of rain in Oregon last month, 2 inches in New York, and 1 inch of rain in Arizona. Where is the grass greener?
5. When you buy a lot of the same thing, the price is cheaper.	5. Ann, Tom, and Jill bought some cans of chicken soup. Ann paid 14 cents for each can. Tom paid 13 cents for each can. Jill paid 11 cents for each can. Who bought more cans of soup?
6. The more weight you lift, the bigger your muscles get.	6. Bob's and Susan's muscles were the same size in November. Now Bob's muscles are smaller than Susan's muscles. Who lifted more weight?
7. The faster you run, the more energy you use.	7. On Monday Agnes ran 3 miles in 15 minutes. On Tuesday she ran 3 miles in 13 minutes. On which day did she use more energy?
8. The less a car weighs, the further it goes on a gallon of gas.	8. Tim's car went 23 miles on a gallon of gas. Bill's car went 17 miles on a gallon of gas. Who's car is heavier?
9. The less you eat, the thinner you get.	9. Bill lost 4 pounds in January, 3 pounds in February, and 5 pounds in March. In which month did he eat the least?

---

saying the rule. See the statement repetition procedures on pages 146 through 147 for suggestions.

The first several days these worksheets are presented, the teacher models by relating the answer to the rule (e.g., "My turn. Item 1: Who used more oxygen?" Bill. "How do you know?" Bill ran faster than John. "The rule says: The faster you run, the more oxygen you use.") After modeling several items, the teacher repeats the items, calling on different students to respond, then presents new items.

When students can do rule worksheets without error for two consecutive days, simple passages containing "rules" should be introduced. A sample passage appears below. Note that the rule sentence is underlined.

John runs the track every day. When he finishes, he counts his breath to see how hard he ran. When he breathes harder, it means that he ran faster. On Monday he took 100 breaths in 1 minute. On Tuesday, he took 90 breaths in 1 minute. On Wednesday, he took 110 breaths in 1 minute. When do you think John ran the hardest? Why?

The teacher tells the students that the underlined sentence gives the rule they should use to find the answer. The teacher (1) has the students read the entire passage; (2) find the rule and say it; (3) points out what the information given tells ("We know how many breaths he took on each day"); (4) reminds students of the rule; and (5) asks students why they gave that answer.

Relationship Not Stated

In many inference items, the student is assumed to have the prerequisite information and knowledge of a less common relationship needed to answer the question. For example, a social studies book might ask, "Is the border between the U.S.A. and Mexico or the border between Oregon and Washington more heavily watched by police?" To answer the question, the students must know that since the U.S.A. and Mexico are separate nations,

---

Table 25.3   Sample Worksheet—Rule-related Inference

Rule: The faster you run, the more oxygen you use.
Item I:
   a. John and Bill had a race. John lost the race.
       Who used more oxygen?_____
   b. How do you know?_____

Item 2:
   a. Ann and Sally ran a race. Ann breathed more oxygen than Sally.
       Who ran faster?_____
   b. How do you know?_____

Item 3:
   a. Jerry ran 3 miles in 15 minutes. Al ran 3 miles in 12 minutes.
       Who used more oxygen?_____
   b. How do you know?_____

---

that border is more closely watched than the border between Oregon and Washington, which are states. Knowledge of the relationship between the type of boundary and how heavily it is guarded is assumed. Teachers, especially those working with lower-performing students, should preview inference items in all types of material—content area, literature, and workbooks. When previewing the material, the teacher notes what information the student needs to comprehend the material and answer questions. The information may be a simple fact (e.g., Oregon is a state) or an unstated relationship (e.g., international boundaries are watched more closely than state boundaries). Teachers should preteach prerequisite information or relationships students are not likely to know and not stated in the passage. The distinction between items which do and do not require preteaching can be seen in the following sets of passages and items. Note that the first set will not require preteaching because it assumes knowledge of a relationship most students will, in fact, know ("When you play in the rain you may get a cold"). The second set assumes knowledge of a less well-known relationship ("If a cactus is watered every day it will die"). This relationship should be taught before students are assigned the item.

Exercise 1—obvious relationship, no preteaching needed

Passage:
Thomas was big for his age and tired quickly; but, today he kept on playing handball even after the rain started. He was so concerned about improving his serve, he didn't care about being tired or notice the cold rain beating down on his head and arms.

Item: Circle the best answer.
Thomas_____

1. is probably a ninth grader.
2. plays handball every day.
3. may get a cold.

Exercise 2—less common relationship, preteaching required

Passage:
Tom brought his mother two plants, a cactus and a fern, for her birthday. He watered the plants every day for three weeks. He wanted the plants to look nice when he gave them to his mother.

Item: Circle the best answer.
Tom_____

1. probably will be very happy when he gives his mother the plants.
2. will be disappointed because one of the plants will be dead.
3. probably took a course in how to care for plants.

Relationship-based inference items, in which students must induce a relationship (i.e., the relationship is unstated), are much more difficult than items in which a relationship is directly stated in a passage. Items of this type can be introduced after students have learned to answer questions based on stated and assumed relationships.

Teaching Procedure

A format for teaching students to induce a relationship based on information in a passage appears in Table 25.4. First the students read a passage about what happens when several beggars make different types of requests of a girl named Alice. If

Table 25.4   Format for Inducing Relationships

Passage:

A beggar asked Alice Jones for some food. Alice said, "No." Another beggar came by and asked to sit on the porch and rest. Alice said, "Yes." The next day a different beggar came to the house. He asked to stand by the fire and warm up. Alice said, "Yes." A week later, a beggar asked for some gas for his car. Alice said, "No."

Items:

1. A beggar asked to lay in Alice's yard and sleep. What do you think Alice said?
2. Another beggar asked for some clothes. What do you think Alice said?

Teacher	*Students*
1. "You're going to read about Alice and some beggars. We're going to figure out why Alice treats them the way she does. Start reading the story."	*Students begin reading the passage. "A beggar asked Alice Jones for some food. Alice said, 'No.' Another beggar came by and asked to sit on the porch and rest. Alice said, 'Yes.' "*
2. "One time Alice said yes; one time she said no. What happened before she said yes?"	*"The beggar asked to sit and rest."*
"What happened before she said no?"	*"The beggar asked for food."*
"Why do you think Alice said no to food and yes to sitting and resting? How is letting someone have food different from letting someone sit down and rest?" If students do not indicate that food costs money but letting someone sit and rest doesn't, the teacher should point out this relationship. "Let's read on and see if Alice says no when beggars ask for things that cost money."	*"The next day a different beggar came to the house. He asked to stand by the fire and warm up."*
3. "Would it cost money to let the beggar stand by the fire?"	*"No."*
"So what do you think Alice will do?"	*"Let him stand by the fire."*
"Read on and see if she does."	*"Alice said, 'Yes.' A week later, a beggar asked for some gas for his car."*
4. "Would it cost money to let the beggar have some gas?"	*"Yes."*
"So what do you think Alice will do?"	*"Not give him any gas."*
"Read on and see what happens."	*"Alice said, 'No.' "*
5. "You were right. Giving the man gas would cost money, so Alice said no. Read and work the items on your own."	

the request will cost Alice money, she says "no." If the request will not cost Alice money, she says "yes."

Difficulty Variables

Three factors contribute to the difficulty of inference items:

1. the degree to which the stated relationship is separated from the relevant information;

2. the ease with which relevant information can be used in drawing an inference;

3. the number of distractors that appear in the passage. (A distractor is irrelevant information that calls attention to a plausible but incorrect answer).

These three difficulty variables are illustrated in the two passages that appear in Table 25.5. Most students find passage A easier because relevant information is directly stated, the sentences containing the stated relationship and the relevant information appear together, and passage A contains no distractors.

1. In passage A, the information about the speed of the planes immediately follows John's statement about wanting to fly on fast planes. In passage B, John's statement about wanting to fly on fast planes is separated from the relevant information about the speed of planes. Students reading passage B must remember the stated relationship that John's major concern is flying on a fast plane.

2. In passage A, relevant information can be easily processed since the flying

time for each plane is stated: 1 hour and 1½ hours. On the other hand, students reading passage B must know to translate departure and arrival times into total flying time: "The Air Worst plane is a small jet which leaves at 10:30 and arrives at 11:30."

3. Finally, passage A contains few distractors. In passage B, many advantages of one plane are listed: it is big, serves a good meal, and shows movies. Students who read passage B must be careful to apply John's criterion for selecting a plane and not be misled by all the benefits listed for the plane.

While no single format can prepare students to handle all inference items, a general teaching procedure can be helpful. The first step is to teach students to find the stated relationship and the information needed to draw an inference based on the stated relationship. Instructionally naive students must be shown that they sometimes have to skim a passage to find both the stated relationship and the information they need to draw an inference based on the stated relationship. For example, if students had just read the item asking about which plane John will take, the teacher would say, "In what kind of plane does John like to fly?" "Fast planes." "Find the part of the story that tells about how long it takes the planes to get to San Francisco." Note that this passage assumes student knowledge of the unstated relationship: vehicles that get to a place the quickest travel the fastest. This relationship may have to be taught to some naive students before presenting the passage.

Next, students must learn to translate any relevant information into a form that directly fits the stated relationship. In the example about John, who likes to fly on

Table 25.5   An Illustration of Passage Related Difficulty Variables

---

Passage A

John was planning a short vacation. He walked into a travel agency and said, "I like to visit big cities. The city I enjoy visiting the most is San Francisco."

"Are you sure you want to go to San Francisco?" asked the agent. "It's raining there and you won't be able to enjoy the parks and beaches."

"Yes, I'm sure," John replied. "It's a beautiful city with many interesting people and lots of fun things to do. I can see friends, go to museums, see new plays, and enjoy good food. The last time I was in San Francisco the weather was stormy. It was a holiday and there was a special show at a theater. I went and saw folk dancers, listened to music, and watched a magic show. There is always something new and exciting to do there."

"Let me tell you about the flights to San Francisco then," said the agent. "There are two planes that travel non-stop to San Francisco."

"Well," said John, "when I travel, all I care about is flying on fast planes."

The agent said, "The Air Worst plane takes one hour. The Untied plane takes one-and-a-half hours."

Which plane do you think John will take?

Passage B

John was planning a short vacation. He walked into a travel agency and said, "I want to fly to San Francisco. When I travel, all I care about is flying on fast planes."

The agent said, "Are you sure you want to go to San Francisco? It's raining there and you won't be able to enjoy the parks and beaches."

"That's all right," said John, "I don't mind rain. I'm sure I want to go to San Francisco. It's my favorite city. There is always something new and exciting going on there. I can visit friends, go to concerts, see new plays, and enjoy good food. I always have a good time in San Francisco. The rain won't matter."

"Let me tell you about the flights to San Francisco," said the agent. "There are two planes that fly non-stop. The Air Worst plane is a small jet which leaves at 10:30 and arrives at 11:30. The Untied plane is a huge jet. It has one of the fastest engines built. It carries 300 passengers, serves a great meal, and shows a movie. If you don't want to see the movie you can listen to music with headphones. Or, you can just rest comfortably. The Untied plane leaves at 9:30 and arrives at 11:00. I think you would enjoy flying on the Untied plane, but it's up to you."

Which plane do you think John will take?

---

fast planes, the student must be able to subtract time notations and determine that 10:30 until 11:30 is 1 hour while 9:30 to 11:00 is 1½ hours. When students do not have the skills needed to translate information into a direct form, they will have trouble with comprehension items. Consequently, teachers must preview comprehension exercises and identify assumed preskills. The teacher must then either

---

teach preskills that students do not have or delete items requiring those preskills.

Finally, students must learn to deal with distractors in a passage. The distractors in the item about John consist of the positive aspects of the Untied plane, which is the slower plane. The Untied plane is bigger, serves a meal, and has music and a movie. Students who do not carefully attend to the statement that John wants to fly in the fastest plane might think that John would take the Untied plane. When introducing items with distractors, teachers must emphasize the statement that determines the answer to the item. For example, after students read, "Which plane do you think John will take?" the teacher says, "In what kind of plane does John want to fly?" "The fastest plane." "Did John say he wanted a plane with a meal or with a movie?" "No." "So what kind of plane are you going to look for when you answer the item?" "The fastest plane." "Figure out what plane John picked." Whenever students make a mistake because of a distractor, the teacher should require the students to locate the part of the passage that specifies the stated relationship. The teacher then points out that the distractor has nothing to do with the stated relationship and does not lead to the correct answer.

Although teachers can and should use formats for teaching students to handle the various difficulty variables, the most critical aspect of teaching involves providing a carefully designed sequence of items in which difficulty variables are introduced one at a time.[1] They should sequence items from simple to complex and provide sufficient practice on easier types before introducing more difficult types. When sequencing items, teachers should begin with relatively simple items which call for commonly known relationships; complexity of passages should be gradually increased, and new difficulty variables should be introduced one at a time. More specifically, teachers should pretest, and, if necessary, teach students to make inferences based on stated relationships. Next, items based on assumed relationships can be introduced. Less common relationships should be pretaught. Items for both stated and unstated relationships should be drawn from the students' reading assignments. Next, the difficulty variables can be introduced, one at a time: separation, ease of using relevant information, and distractors. Finally, induction items should be presented. Again, the items should be taken from literature and content area assignments.

Sentence Structure

During the intermediate grades, sentence syntax becomes increasingly complicated.

---

1. Education has long been enamored with higher order or inference questions. While educators are correct in calling for numerous inferential items, they must realize that large doses of inferential items will not necessarily improve students' inference skills, especially for instructionally naive students. The problem occurs when the inference items assume knowledge and skills the students do not have; and yet, teacher guidance is not provided. For example, consider this inference item: "As the location of a subatomic particle becomes more precise, what would you infer about its momentum?" Or consider this example: "When John walked out onto the street, he nictitated rapidly. Where do you think John had been?" These are inference items, but working many items similar to these would not improve an average adult's skill in drawing inferences. Similarly, exposing students, especially low-performing ones, to inference items is not sufficient. The examples must be carefully selected and sequenced, and careful instruction must be provided. Students must know relevant vocabulary, assumed relationships, and how to draw inferences if practice exercises are to be helpful.

A great variety of sentence constructions are introduced including these:

1. Participles (underlined words):
   The man <u>taking the money</u> looked to his side.
   The mountain <u>towering above the plain</u> was 12,000 feet high.
   <u>Thinking about the upcoming test,</u> Jack decided not to go out last night.
   <u>Wearing her new sneakers to the meet,</u> Ann was confident she would be the next state champion.

2. Clauses: Trig, who comes from the planet Floss, was over 80 feet tall.
   Eugene, which is in west-central Oregon, has a population of 100,000.

3. Sentences containing these connectives:
   consequently, although, therefore, provided that, unless, so that, as, whether, while, yet, whether or not, while, during, some, all, none, either, or, neither, nor.
   Note the difference in the meanings in these sentence pairs:
   a. Neither Jim nor John will win.
      Either Jim or John will win.
   b. They played while it rained.
      They played until it rained.
   c. He gave pencils to some of the students.
      He gave pencils to all of the students.

4. Passive constructions:
   John was carried down the mountain by Liz.
   The man was led into the arena by a black stallion.

5. Numerical and class-inclusive notations:
   The lion and the gladiator walked into the arena, the former snarling and vicious, the latter tense and alert.
   (*Former* and *latter* are numerical terms.)

His dog barked a lot during the night. The animal seemed to be on edge. (Dog is included in the class of animals.)

6. Pronouns referring to an action or series of actions:
   The baseball game went into extra innings. <u>This</u> caused Tom to worry if he would be late getting home.
   The rocket took off. Faster and faster it went until it had climbed 386 feet. <u>It</u> was the beginning of the space age.

The teaching procedure for each type of construction is somewhat different. Since we cannot discuss the procedures for each type of syntactic construction, we will illustrate direct instruction procedures that can be used to show students how passive voice construction functions. Similar procedures can be used for other constructions. (Note: Directly teaching all types of syntactic structures is not necessary since many may not cause difficulty for students. However, syntactic structures that cause students difficulty in comprehension could be taught using the steps similar to those outlined for passive constructions.)

Passive Voice

In the procedure for teaching students to understand passive voice, the teacher asks questions about a pair of minimally different active- and passive-voice sentences. The format involves the teacher's presenting an active-voice sentence and asking (1) who was acted upon; and (2) who did the acting. After each active-voice sentence, the teacher presents a passive-voice sentence and asks the same questions. By answering these questions, students will learn to comprehend both active and passive constructions. For example:

1. "I'll say sentences and then ask a question."
   "John hit Mary." (Active)
   "Who was hit?" ("Mary")
   "Who did the hitting?" ("John")

2. "Listen to a different sentence."
   "John was hit by Mary." (Passive)
   "Who was hit?" ("John")
   "Who did the hitting?" ("Mary")

In the active construction ("John hit Mary"), Mary was hit. In the passive construction ("John was hit by Mary"), the subject, John, was hit. Since the question, "Who was hit?" is identical for both the active and passive constructions, the students must attend carefully to the words *was* and *by*. These words signal a passive construction, in which the subject is the recipient of the action ("John *was* hit *by* Mary. Who was hit? John"). Only by carefully watching for the words that signal a passive construction will students learn to distinguish passive from active constructions and, thereby, be able to answer questions such as, "Who was hit?"

The situation is almost identical for the "Who did the hitting?" question. This question is asked about both the active and passive constructions. Again, only by watching for the words that signal a passive construction (*was* and *by* in this example) will the students learn to distinguish active from passive voice and, thereby, be able to answer the question. More specifically, "John hit Mary" is active so the subject (John) did the hitting. "John was hit by Mary" is passive so the subject (John) didn't do the hitting; Mary did. The verbal exercises should include three to five pairs of sentences. Corrections should involve modeling and testing.

After several days, a worksheet exercise can be presented in which pairs of similar sentences, one in the active voice and one in the passive voice, are followed by literal-comprehension questions (see Table 25.6). Note that in both sentences in each item the names appear in the same order; e.g., in item 1 the order is rabbit—chicken. Maintaining a consistent order prevents students from learning a misinterpretation that the actor in a sentence always comes first.

The items included in these tasks should be low-probability items. That means the answer should not be one that would be expected based on common knowledge. An example of a poor item is "The child was bitten by the dog." Since the answer is highly predictable from common knowledge (dogs bite children), the item is of high probability. It can be answered through common sense without the students carefully attending to the words that signal a passive-voice construction.

Table 25.6	Worksheet Practice on Passive-voice Constructions

Item 1. a. The rabbit helped the chicken.
Who got helped?_____
Who did the helping?_____
b. The rabbit was helped by the chicken.
Who got helped?_____
Who did the helping?_____

Item 2. a. John was found by Mary.
Who was found?_____
Who did the finding?_____
b. John found Mary.
Who was found?_____
Who did the finding?_____

Item 3. a. The dog sold the cat.
Who was sold?_____
Who did the selling?_____
b. The dog was sold by the cat.
Who was sold?_____
Who did the selling?_____

In contrast, the items on our sample worksheet are low-probability items. Common sense does not indicate whether a rabbit or a chicken is more likely to be helpful, whether a dog would sell a cat, or whether John would find Mary rather than Mary find John. Since the answers for items 1, 2, and 3 are not based on common knowledge, students must learn sentence structure to determine who is the actor and who is the recipient of the action.

Critical Reading

Critically evaluating assertions, arguments, and proposals, whether presented orally or in print, is possibly the most important comprehension skill related to preparing students for their various roles in life. Many personal, professional, and social decisions are based on what we are told by other people. Because faulty arguments and propaganda are so common, critical thinking has a role in almost every important decision we make. To simplify instruction in critical reading, we will outline a standard procedure students can apply to increasingly sophisticated arguments. As in all comprehension instruction, sequencing exercises from simple to complex and providing sufficient practice for students to master one level of complexity before introducing the next are indispensable if students are to learn a strategy for critical reading. The steps in teaching critical reading involve teaching students to do the following:

1. Identify the author's conclusion; i.e., what does the author want the reader to believe?

2. Determine what evidence is presented; i.e., what does the author present to convince the reader? Evidence or opinion?

3. Determine the trustworthiness of the author; i.e., can the reader trust what the author says?
   a. Does the evidence come from a qualified person?
   b. Does the person have biases?

4. Identify faulty arguments; i.e., does the conclusion derive from the evidence?
   a. Tradition, either old or new (sometimes called a bandwagon effect);
   b. Improper generalization;
   c. Confusing correlation with causation (or coincidence).

A rather advanced example of the propaganda devices students will encounter and how students should analyze them are illustrated in the following passage and discussion:

> Thomas Edison, the inventor of the light bulb, was seriously concerned about the increasing use of alternating current as a form of electricity. Edison believed that because alternating current involved so much more current than direct current, alternating current was a threat to the nation. Many fires were caused by alternating currents. In fact, alternating current was used in Sing Sing to electrocute criminals. Direct current was used with light bulbs for many years. Edison felt direct current was still the best form of electricity.

First, the students must use details from a passage (seriously concerned, a threat to the nation, direct current is still the best) to form a main idea (or an author's conclusion). Identifying an author's conclusion is a continuation of summarization skills (main idea, best title) discussed earlier.

The second step is for the student to decide whether the author's conclusion is based on opinion or evidence. If a conclusion is based on opinion, students should know that the author's conclusion is really nothing more than a suggestion by the author about what people should think. A conclusion based on opinion does not imply the student should believe or act on it. In the alternating current example, both opinion and evidence are used to support the author's conclusion. The statement that alternating current is a threat to the nation is an opinion. The other details are evidence used to justify the author's interpretation, i.e., the occurrence of fires, electrocution of criminals, and the initial use of direct current as an energy source.

The third step consists of several questions, all relating to the reliability or trustworthiness of the person presenting the argument. Question a is whether the evidence comes from a qualified person. Since Edison was definitely an expert on electricity in the late 1800s, he was qualified. Question b concerns biases the expert might have. In Edison's case, two major biases existed. One was his deep personal and financial involvement in a company that provided direct current. He stood to lose money if alternating current replaced direct current. Also his reputation was at stake. He became famous, in part, because of his discovery of the light bulb and a distribution system for electricity based on the use of direct current. If alternating current replaced direct current, his reputation might be diminished. Since Edison's biases contribute to the passage's conclusion, the evidence may not be trustworthy.

Since there is doubt about the trustworthiness of the author, students must seek information from different experts. The statement that direct current is the best form of electricity is disputed by many experts. Alternating current can be transmitted great distances, but direct current cannot. If remote areas are to receive electricity at a reasonable rate, alternating current is a necessity. Since the expert is biased and alternative interpretations of the evidence are compelling, the evidence is probably not trustworthy.

The final step in the critical reading process is deciding whether a conclusion legitimately derives from the evidence. In many arguments, valid evidence will be presented, but then a conclusion will be drawn that does not derive from the evidence. In the alternating-current example, one possible interpretation is that since direct current has been used with light bulbs for many years, it should continue to be the best form of electricity. This improper argument illustrates the use of tradition; what has been the best must continue to be the best. Conclusions based on tradition are not necessarily true. What has worked well may continue to be the best procedure, or a better procedure may be developed. Students can disregard conclusions based on tradition. (Note that the same attitude can be taken toward newly developing traditions; i.e., "Everybody is starting to use alternating current; therefore, you should, too." A conclusion that a product or procedure is better because it is popular is not reasonable.)

Since the passage about alternating current does not illustrate the other two types of improper arguments (improper generalization and confusing correlation with causation), the following additional passages provide illustrations of these invalid forms of conclusions. The first additional passage illustrates improper generalization. One valid example is presented, but then a conclusion is drawn that applies to all examples:

> Another example of the dangers of
> alternating current has just occurred. A
> house wired with alternating current
> caught fire and burned to the ground. The

fire started when an electrical wire became so hot that a wall caught fire. Alternating current will eventually cause a fire whenever it is used. Direct current rather than alternating current should be used for lighting.

One fire caused by alternating current does not mean that alternating current will cause a fire every place it is used. Improper generalization occurs often: "I saw a rich person who was rude. What makes rich people so rude?" "We sat next to a long-haired man in the movies. He smelled. I'll bet he hadn't bathed in weeks. Long hairs should take better care of their bodies."

The next passage involves a confusion of causation and correlation. An event that is associated with success or some other positive outcome through coincidence is erroneously concluded to be the cause of the positive outcome:

The Daily Post used direct current to light its press room for over a year. Reporters are much happier now. They say that the light from bulbs does not hurt their eyes as much as the gas lights the paper used before. Also the rooms are much cooler in the summer because the light from direct current does not give off heat as gas lights do.

Direct-current lighting is associated with less eye strain and more comfortable temperatures; however, direct current did not necessarily cause reporters to be happier. The electric lighting that produced the positive outcomes could have been achieved with direct or alternating current. Conclusions suggesting causation that are, in fact, based on correlation can be disregarded. Confusion of correlation and causation is often made: "Joe Blow uses Squirt-Squirt deodorant, and girls always chase him." "Sally took You-Bet-Your-Life vitamins every day. She lived to be 106!"

Sequence

Before the complete critical reading strategy can be introduced, the component skills must be taught separately, then combined to form the strategy. The four steps in the critical reading process can be treated as the major component skills: (1) identifying the author's conclusion; (2) distinguishing opinion from evidence; (3) determining the trustworthiness of evidence (qualifications of evidence source, biases, alternative interpretations of evidence); and (4) identifying faulty arguments (tradition, improper generalization, and a confusion of correlation and causation).

Students can be taught relatively early to identify an author's conclusion and details that support the conclusion. Next, procedures for discriminating evidence from opinion can be introduced. After that, instruction in determining the reliability of evidence and then the validity of arguments can occur. Finally, the component skills can be combined to form the complete strategy.

Teaching Procedure

We will discuss separately teaching procedures for the four component skills of the critical reading strategy.

Identifying an Author's Conclusion

This skill is closely related to selecting a main idea. The major difference is that students must generate a conclusion rather than select the best alternative in a multiple-choice format. Since every passage is unique, specifying a detailed format to teach students to generate an author's conclusion is difficult. This skill, however, can be taught through modeling and extensive practice. A teacher models by presenting a passage, identifying the author's conclusion, and listing supporting details from the passage that led to the conclusion. Then the teacher tests by presenting a series of passages, asking students to identify the author's conclusion, and then justify their conclusion by citing supporting details. The teacher and the students should discuss unacceptable answers by pointing out why they are unacceptable. At first, items should be quite simple. Below are examples of items that might be presented initially:

1. I hope Tom comes back to our team. Ever since he left, we have lost every game. (Conclusion: We are losing because Tom isn't on the team.)

2. Those ABC tires are great. I've been getting super gas mileage on my new car with ABC tires. (Conclusion: I'm getting better gas mileage because I'm using ABC tires.)

3. Mary has looked so sad since our team lost the game. She doesn't go out at night. I never see her in the store after school. (Conclusion: Mary doesn't go out any more because she's sad about our team losing the game.)

Verbal exercises are conducted for several days and then replaced with written exercises. The length of the passages should be increased gradually.

Discriminating Evidence from Opinion

Teaching students to discriminate fact from opinion is done in two stages. In the first stage, all opinion statements include phrases that indicate that an opinion is being given (I think, I believe, I feel, in my opinion, in my judgment). The examples include about 10 statements, half of which are opinions and half of which are facts. Below is a set of statements that might be included in such a format.

1. I believe Tom won the race.
2. Tom won the race yesterday.
3. I believe he is faster than his brother.
4. He beat his brother in a race.
5. I think it will rain.
6. It is raining.
7. I think chocolate is the best flavor.
8. More people eat chocolate than any other flavored ice cream.
9. In my opinion she is the best player on the team.
10. She is the oldest girl on our team.

The teacher might introduce the items by explaining the difference between fact and opinion saying, "When somebody tells you something that actually happened they are telling you a *fact*. When somebody tells you how they feel about something they are telling you an *opinion*. Sometimes the way a person tells you something lets you know if it's an opinion. If a person says 'I think,' 'I believe,' or 'I feel,' they are giving an opinion." The teacher would then present the statements asking the students to tell if the statement is one of fact or opinion.

The second stage of the procedure introduces more sophisticated items which do not include phrases such as "I think" or "I believe". Teaching students to distinguish fact from opinion with this type of statement involves consensus. If, on the one hand, a person says something with which almost everybody who is knowledgeable agrees, the statement is one of fact. If, on the other hand, it is a statement with which knowledgeable people disagree, the statement is one of opinion. Consider the following statements:

1. *Traveling by train is not as exciting as traveling by car.* This is a statement of opinion. No special knowledge base is needed. In the general population, there are many people who would not agree with the statement.

2. *Traveling across the country by plane is faster than by car.* This is a statement of fact. Most people knowledgeable about travel agree.

3. *It rains too much in Oregon.* This is a statement of opinion. It reflects how some people feel, but not how all people feel.

4. *Oregon has more rain than New Jersey.* This is a fact.

Distinguishing opinion from fact is not easy. It will require lots of practice with a great variety of statements. For example, when an author uses opinion rather than evidence to sway the reader, he may use emotional words as a tactic. (See Table 25.7 for teaching students how to identify emotionally charged words when evaluating conclusions. Since this format is independent of the other formats, it can be introduced at a teacher's convenience.)

Determining the Trustworthiness of an Author

An important aspect of determining author trustworthiness is examining the qualifications of the person stating the argument. Much advertising is based on nonexpert endorsements. Sometimes a popular figure will endorse products about which he or she has no knowledge.

The first step in determining the trustworthiness of the author is determining his expertise regarding what he is talking about. A second step involves examining the motives of an author to determine if he has anything to gain by convincing the reader of his position. For example, if a student knows that a person invented an object and stands to make a good deal of money if the object is sold, there is good reason to be suspicious of the person's claims. Passages such as the one below could be presented to develop the concept of author motive:

> Edwin Water, an inventor of the Sunglass Water Camera and owner of Water Camera Company of America, made the following remarks at a photographer's convention: "I was a professional photographer for several years. During that time I felt that a PHXTVW-23 Sunglass Water Camera gave me the greatest resolution, both with close work and when using a telephoto lens. Its light weight and small size make it very convenient. I don't need to tell you the importance of quality and convenience when it comes to cameras."

After students have been taught to evaluate an author's trustworthiness, they should work exercises that incorporate the critical-reading skills discussed thus far. A sample exercise appears below. (Assume that the students have previously learned to identify an author's conclusion and to distinguish evidence from opinion.)

> Thomas Edison invented the electric light bulb and a system for distributing direct current to people to light their homes and businesses. He owned part of a company that made light bulbs and one that sold direct current. After direct current had been in use for a few years, alternating current

Table 25.7   Format for Identifying Emotional Words

Teacher	*Students*
1. Teacher explains emotionally charged words. **a.** "Most people like some words and don't like other words. Here are some words that most people like: love, freedom, beauty, democracy, kindness, confidence, creativity. Here are some words that most people do not like: murder, hate, ugliness, loneliness, cruelty, selfishness. Sometimes words people like are used to convince people to accept a conclusion."	

2. Teacher models.
   a. "Listen to this conclusion. The F.U.N. Reading Program is colorful, fun packed, and enlightening. All teachers should use the F.U.N. Reading Program."
   b. "When you read or hear an argument, ignore words that people like or dislike. When we get rid of the words people like or dislike, we see that there is no evidence for using the F.U.N. Reading Program. It's just someone's opinion."	

3. Teacher tests.
   a. "I'll make a claim. You tell me the words people like or dislike. Then you tell me if any evidence is left to support the conclusion."
   b. "Everybody should use Smiley Toothpaste. It makes them pleasant all day and free to do all the things they really want to do."
   c. "What are the words people like or dislike?" Teacher calls on individuals.
   d. "Is there any evidence left to support the conclusion?"
	
	"Pleasant, free."
	
	"No."

4. The teacher presents several more items. After students can correctly respond to verbally presented items, they should be assigned written items. The students cross out emotionally charged words and then indicate what evidence remains to support the conclusion.	

was invented. Many people bought alternating current because it was cheaper and could be distributed long distances. Edison opposed the use of alternating current, though. He felt it was a threat to the nation. Edison argued that people should continue to use direct current.

1. What was the author's conclusion?
2. Was evidence or opinion used to support the conclusion?

3. Was Edison a qualified expert on electricity? Explain your answer.
4. Was Edison biased? Did Edison have any personal reason for opposing alternating current? Explain your answer.
5. Would you be suspicious of Edison's conclusion? Why?

Items 1 and 2 assume that students have been taught to identify an author's conclusion and to distinguish evidence from opinion. To answer items 3 and 4, students use information in the passage about Edison. If students have doubts about the trustworthiness of an author, they must seek additional information about the subject. Item 5 requires the student to synthesize the information from items 1–4.

Identifying Faulty Arguments

Earlier we mentioned three types of fallacious arguments: those based on tradition ("It's been done this way in the past, so it should be done this way in the future"), improper generalization ("X is no good, X is a Y, so Y is no good"), and coincidence or a confusion of causation and correlation ("S and Y happened at the same time, so S must cause Y"). We picked these three fallacies since they occur relatively often. For a discussion of other fallacies, we recommend a book by Alex C. Michalos (1970) entitled *Improving Your Reasoning*.

The formats are similar for each of the three types of invalid arguments (tradition, improper generalization, and a confusion of causation and correlation). The teacher states a rule about an invalid form and presents a series of examples, asking whether the argument in each example is valid. After students have learned the first two forms of invalid conclusions, they receive discrimination practice in determining which form accounts for an invalid conclusion. In this discrimination exercise the teacher presents a series of examples and asks, "Is the argument faulty?" If students answer yes, the teacher asks, "Why?" The students then have to indicate what invalid argument was used to draw the conclusion. This discrimination exercise also appears again after the third form of invalid argument is introduced; students identify which of three forms accounts for an invalid conclusion. Table 25.8 contains a format for identifying invalid conclusions based on *tradition*. Table 25.9 contains a format for identifying invalid conclusions based on *improper generalization*. Note that the format for improper generalization is identical to the format for tradition. Only the rule for explaining why the argument is invalid is different.

After arguments based on improper generalizations are introduced, a discrimination exercise in which students must discriminate between tradition and improper generalization should be given (see Table 25.10). The teacher reviews the definitions of tradition and improper generalization and then presents a series of items.

The final type of faulty argument is a confusion of correlation with causation. When two things happen at the same time, one does not necessarily cause the other.

Table 25.11 presents a format for introducing this type of faulty argument. A discrimination exercise with all three types will be presented later.

An Overall Critical-reading Strategy

Exercises in which students must apply several of the critical-reading-component skills in analyzing the validity of an author's conclusion should be presented after

Table 25.8   Format for Identifying Invalid Conclusions Based on Tradition

Teacher	Students
1. "Sometimes an author makes a conclusion that is based on a faulty argument."	
2. "One type of faulty argument is called tradition. A conclusion based on tradition says that something should be a certain way because it has always been that way. What does a conclusion based on tradition say?"(signal)	"That something should be a certain way because it has always been that way."
3. "Here is an example. Mr. Rotter said our family has always bought Brand-X shoes and should keep on buying Brand-X shoes. The conclusion that we should continue doing something just because we have done it in the past is based on the faulty argument of tradition."	
4. "Listen to this argument: Mr. Jones said the Yankees are a sure bet to win this year since they won last year. Do you agree with Mr. Jones' conclusion? (signal) "Why not?" Teacher calls on individual students and accepts reasonable answers. "Correct, his conclusion was based on tradition. Just because something has been done a certain way in the past doesn't mean that is the way it should be done."	"No."
5. "Listen to this argument. Mrs. Spencer told her daughter, 'When I was a young girl, my mother had me come home at 9 P.M. from a date. So when you go out, you should be home at 9 P.M.' Do you agree with Mrs. Spencer's conclusion?"(signal) "Why not?" Teacher calls on individual students and accepts reasonable answers. "Correct, the conclusion was based on tradition."	"No."

students have been taught the component skills (identifying conclusion, distinguishing evidence from opinion, determining reliability of evidence, and spotting faulty arguments). Exercises should include a mixture of supportable and unsupportable conclusions so that students do not develop a habit of automatically disagreeing with an author's conclusion. There should be variety among the passages that have unsupportable conclusions. In some passages, the cause of the invalid conclusion should be lack of evidence; in others, faulty arguments; and in others, lack of reliable evidence. Below is a sample worksheet exercise:

Table 25.9   Format for Identifying Invalid Conclusions
Based on Improper Generalization

Teacher	Students
1. "Sometimes authors make a conclusion that is based on improper generalization. An improper generalization says that because a part has a certain characteristic, the whole thing must have that characteristic. What does an improper generalization say?" (signal)	*"That because a part has a certain characteristic, the whole thing must have that characteristic."*
2. "Here are some examples. When a store sells a gallon of spoiled milk, that doesn't mean that all the milk they sell is spoiled. The conclusion that the store always sells spoiled milk because it once sold some spoiled milk is based on the faulty argument of improper generalization. When a student does well in sports, that doesn't mean that all the student's brothers and sisters are athletic. The conclusion that everyone in the family is athletic because one person is athletic is based on improper generalization."	
3. "Listen to this argument. The cobra car has super tires. You should buy the cobra car. Do you agree with the conclusion?" (signal) "Why not?" Teacher calls on individual students and accepts reasonable answers. "Correct, that argument is faulty because it is based on improper generalization. Just because one part of something is good doesn't mean the whole thing is good."	*"No."*

Mrs. Asper was talking to her neighbor, Mr. Trump. Mrs. Asper told him she thought it would be terrible if he sold his house to the Parkinson family. Mrs. Asper said that the Parkinsons were from that terrible country Lispania. Her husband had been in the war against Lispania. She had worked with a person from Lispania who always came late to work and did not dress neatly. She said that if the Parkinsons moved into the neighborhood, it would never be the same.

1. What is Mrs. Asper's conclusion?

2. Did Mrs. Asper use evidence? If so, list the evidence used.

3. Would you be suspicious of Mrs. Asper's evidence? If so, explain why.

4. Are faulty arguments used? If so, tell which type.

5. Do you agree with Mrs. Asper's conclusion? Explain your answer.

Table 25.10   Discrimination Format

	Teacher	Students

1. "An argument may be faulty because it is based on tradition or because it is based on an improper generalization."

2. "What does an argument based on tradition say?" (signal)

"Something should be a certain way because it has always been that way."

3. "What does an argument based on improper generalization say?" (signal)

"That because a part has a certain characteristic, the whole thing must have that characteristic."

4. "I'll say some arguments that are faulty. You tell me why the argument is faulty, because of tradition or because of improper generalization."

   a. "Thomas can spell very well. I bet he is the smartest student in the class. Why is that argument faulty?"

"It is based on improper generalization."

   b. "New York had the first good subway system. Its subway system must be the best. Why is that argument faulty?"

"It is based on tradition."

   c. "Mr. Ricardo has lived on this street since 1970. He'll never move. Why is that argument faulty?"

"It is based on tradition."

   d. "That restaurant serves delicious pies. It is the best restaurant in town. Why is that argument faulty?"

"It is based on improper generalization."

When initially presenting exercises of this type, the teacher instructs the students to answer the questions one at a time, occasionally inserting additional instructions. More specifically, before students identify the author's argument, the teacher instructs the students to cross out all emotionally charged words. In the example above, the students cross out the phrase *terrible country*. The teacher also makes certain the students explain why Mrs. Asper's opinions are unreliable. The teacher checks the students' answers to each item before instructing them to answer the next item.

After carefully monitoring student performance on several exercises, teachers should allow students to work independently. After students can successfully work items independently, the teacher can omit the first four items, and only present the question, "Do you agree with the author's conclusion? Explain your answer." In explaining their answers, students should discuss the reliability of the author's opinions, the evidence, and any faulty arguments. Working exercises of this final form is difficult and requires extensive practice.

Table 25.11   Format for Identifying Faulty Arguments Based on Coincidence

	Teacher	Students
1.	"An argument is faulty if it is based on coincidence. An argument is based on coincidence when we say that one event caused another event just because they both happened at the same time. When is an argument based on coincidence?" (signal)	"When we say that one event caused another event just because they both happened at the same time."
2.	"Here are some examples. Joe is shown eating muscle-man hotdogs. Joe is handsome and strong. Eating muscle-man hot dogs and looking handsome and strong happen at the same time. A conclusion that muscle-man hot dogs caused Joe to be handsome would be faulty. Just because two things happen at the same time, you cannot make a conclusion that one caused the other to happen. That argument is based on the faulty argument of coincidence."	
3.	"Listen to this argument. Sam fights a lot, and he has lots of friends. Sam has lots of friends because he fights a lot. Do you agree with the conclusion?" (signal)	"No."
	"Why not?" Teacher calls on individual students; accepts reasonable answers. "Correct, a conclusion that fighting causes people to have friends would not be reasonable; it is based on coincidence. Just because two things happen to the same person, you cannot make a conclusion that one caused the other"	

Application Exercises

1. Label each passage with an *RS* (relationship stated), *PKA* (prior knowledge assumed), and *IIP* (information for induction provided).

    _____ Fresher vegetables contain more vitamins. The two pounds of carrots in the blue bag were picked today. The two pounds of carrots in the red bag were picked three days ago. Which carrots have more vitamin A?

    _____ The two pounds of carrots on the ground have four hundred units of vitamin A. They were picked today. The two pounds of carrots on the table have two hundred units of vitamin A. They were picked a week ago. The two pounds of carrots in the can were picked yesterday. Which carrots have the most vitamin A?

    _____ These carrots are all from the same garden. The two pounds in the sack were picked today. The two pounds in the box were picked a week ago. Which carrots have more vitamins?

2. Specify what the teacher should say to correct a student who answered the question below incorrectly.

"Fresher vegetables contain more vitamins," Mrs. Ampston told her boy, Robbie. "When you go to the store, always try to buy the freshest vegetables." Saturday morning Robbie went shopping for his mother. When he got to the vegetable counter he asked the man about carrots. The man told him they had two types of carrots, Mighty-Fine carrots and Blue Label carrots. Mighty-Fine carrots were delivered to the store Tuesday. They were from the biggest farm in the state. They were also on sale today, one pound for 36¢. Blue Label carrots had been delivered just after the store opened this morning. They were packed in plain wrappers and cost 38¢ a pound. They had been grown on a small farm outside the city. Which carrots should Robbie buy?
(The student answers, "Mighty-Fine carrots.")

3. For each of the following selections:

   a. Identify the author's conclusion;

   b. List the evidence;

   c. Determine the author's trustworthiness by indicating whether she is qualified or has biases;

   d. Identify any faulty arguments.

   • Mr. Ragster had been a top race car driver and mechanic when he was young. Now he was a salesman for the Snazy Truck Company. Mr. Ragster had heard that Kevin McNeer wanted to buy a new truck. Wednesday morning Mr. Ragster called Kevin. He said "Kevin, you should buy a Snazy truck. Your Dad always drove a Snazy truck. I bet I sold him 10 different Snazy trucks. *Automotive News,* a magazine that has reports on trucks, says that the new Snazy truck gets better mileage than any truck that is comparably priced. You'd be making a mistake if you didn't buy a Snazy truck."

   • Tom Jackson was a star baseball player. He worked for the Ace Toothpaste Company during the winter. He said, "I think Ace toothpaste is the best toothpaste there is. I have white shiny teeth and I use Ace toothpaste. If you want bright shiny teeth, you, too, should use Ace toothpaste."

4. For each of the following inference items, state any information students must know to answer the item correctly:

   a. Tim lived in San Francisco. Bill lived in New York. When waking up each morning, one of the boys would look out his window and watch the sun rise over the ocean. Tell which boy. Tell why you chose that boy.

   b. Janice was a star athlete. She hoped to make the Olympic team; however, first she wanted to complete medical school. It is now 1990. Janice has 3 years of medical school left. Do you think Janice will try out for the next Olympics? Why?

   c. Bill and Susan were carpenters who were building a house. They had completed everything, except putting in the floor. Jack, their good friend, told them that he had lots of cedar wood left over and would sell it to them for a cheap price. Do you think they will buy the cedar? Why?

5. Which two of the following four sentences would not be good items for a passive-voice exercise?

    a. The dog was put in the house by Tom. Who was put in the house?

    b. Bill was put in the house by Bob. Who was put in the house?

    c. Ann is getting a scolding from Jill. Who is scolding?

    d. Ann is getting a scolding from her mother. Who is scolding?

6. (Review)

The following words will appear in passages the students will read several days from now. Write *V* in front of each word that should be included in a vocabulary exercise. Write *D* in front of each word that should be included in a decoding exercise:

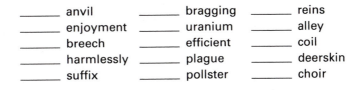

_____ anvil	_____ bragging	_____ reins
_____ enjoyment	_____ uranium	_____ alley
_____ breech	_____ efficient	_____ coil
_____ harmlessly	_____ plague	_____ deerskin
_____ suffix	_____ pollster	_____ choir

Chapter

26

Narrative-Comprehension Strategies

Overview

During the primary grades, basal reading programs consist mainly of narrative or storybook reading passages. In the intermediate grades, expository or textbook reading is introduced; however, a significant part of these programs still includes narrative stories.

This section deals with teaching students to comprehend narrative stories. Stories have their own text structure called *story grammar*. This structure often revolves around the conflicts or problems faced by the characters in the story and the characters' attempts to resolve the problem. The story-grammar components of (1) conflict, (2) goal, (3) resolution of the conflict, (4) plot, and (5) the characters' thoughts and feelings are common to many stories. By keying on the presence of these components in a story, the reader is better able to comprehend the story. The structure of a story can be simple (e.g., the components are few and written in a predictable sequence) or complex (e.g., the components are numerous and their sequence unpredictable).

Students who do not have problems with literal comprehension may still have problems answering questions about the structure of a story. For example, a student may be able to identify the characters in a story, but not the characters' goals and motives and actions for achieving those goals. For these students, the teacher needs to demonstrate a strategy for identifying, understanding, and relating these different components of story grammar to each other in comprehending the story's general message.

This section presents procedures for presenting the components of story grammar during story-reading activities. These procedures are designed for students who decode passages accurately, do not have significant fluency problems, and can accurately answer literal-comprehension questions.

Story Selection

The primary rule for developing a sequence for introducing stories in story-grammar exercises is to progress from simple stories to more complex stories. Factors to consider are (a) the number of characters, plots, goals, and subgoals, (b) the number of attempts by characters to achieve the goals, (c) the explicitness of the story-grammar components (the main characters, goals, conflict), (d) the length of the story, (e) the readability of the story (structure of sentences, multisyllabic words), and (f) the amount of background knowledge required of students.

Stories can differ in the amount of background knowledge required for students to comprehend the story. Some stories may rely heavily on a reader's background knowledge about a topic, while others may provide the reader with the information necessary to comprehend the story. For example, in some stories the information the reader needs to comprehend the characters' goals, conflicts, motives, and actions is given in the story. This type of story is called *textually explicit* because the text gives the reader all the information needed to comprehend fully what's going on in the story. Stories somewhat dependent on the reader's background knowledge are called *textually implicit*. Stories heavily dependent on the reader's background knowledge are called *scriptally implicit*.

Figure 26.1 includes an example of a textually explicit text, the fable of "The Mouse and the Hawk."

In this fable, the actions of the mouse in wanting to help the people of the town get rid of the hawk are explicit. The relationship between the mouse's motivation for ridding the town of the hawk and the goal are stated in the text.

Figure 26.2 contains an example of a textually implicit text, the fable of "Clover and the King."

In the fable, Clover wants the lettuce, knows the King dislikes him, recognizes

---

Figure 26.1   Example of Textually Explicit Text

The Mouse and the Hawk

Long ago in a small western town lived a hawk that attacked almost all the chickens in the whole town. He ate them one by one until finally there were only two chickens left.

Nobody in the town could kill the hawk. They talked about it in the big tent where a little mouse was listening when she heard the bad news. The little mouse was very brave and she also liked to help people. The mouse wanted to help the people in the town, so she worked out a plan.

First, she cut a small hole in the top of the tent. Then she made a very sharp point on one end of a stick. She put that stick through the hole. Next she went outside and sat on top of the tent very close to the sharp stick.

She knew the hawk would see a tiny mouse and come diving down from the sky to get her. Even though she was afraid that the hawk would kill her, she sat there waiting.

Finally, the hawk saw the brave mouse and came flying toward her ready to attack. The mouse waited until the hawk was almost on her. Then she jumped aside and the hawk flew onto the sharp stick and was killed instantly.

The mouse was a hero and everyone in the village came to the big tent to praise and thank her.

Figure 26.2   Example of Textually Implicit Text

Clover and the King

Clover was a very clever rabbit who, along with the other rabbits, loved lettuce. They lived outside the King's castle, and soon they had all the lettuce from nearby gardens except for the King's own garden.

The King loved his garden and grew the best lettuce in all the land. He did not want the rabbits to get any of his lettuce so his garden was well guarded. The rabbits didn't like the King either and just wanted his lettuce.

One day Clover got an idea. A rabbit could not sneak into the King's garden, but a rabbit could sneak into the King's kitchen. Clover sneaked into the King's kitchen every morning for several days. Each day the King's men brought in some lettuce for dinner, and each day Clover poisoned the lettuce. Soon, everyone in the King's palace was sick.

The King was very sad when he learned that his lettuce was making everyone sick. He ordered his soldiers to dig up the lettuce from his garden. Then he ordered the lettuce dumped outside the castle, near where the rabbits lived.

The King was very pleased with himself. He would solve two problems at once.

the King loves his subjects, and poisons the lettuce cut for royal consumption. To appreciate Clover's motivation for poisoning the lettuce, students must take the information about Clover's stated goal (poisoning the lettuce) and the King's response to the poisoned lettuce, then make an inference about the relationship between those events. By making the connection between those events, actions, goals, and intentions of the characters, students will appreciate why Clover, the rabbit, is so clever, and why the King thought he had solved two problems at once. This text is textually implicit because the reader has to use the information in the story to make inferences about the character's actions and goals.

An example of a scriptally implicit text, the fable "The Fox and the Grapes," is given in Figure 26.3.

Figure 26.3   Example of Scriptally Implicit Text

The Fox and the Grapes

One day a sly fox was running along a dry, dusty road and he was very hot and thirsty. After a long period, he saw a large bunch of purple grapes hanging from a tree on a vine in a garden by the side of the road. These grapes were large, ripe, and very juicy looking. They looked especially good to the fox. "How I wish I could eat some of those beautiful grapes," said the fox as he licked his lips. The fox jumped high into the air to get the grapes, but he did not get them the first time he tried. He jumped again and again, but he still could not reach the grapes. He was still very thirsty, but he kept trying. After awhile, he became tired and at last he gave up. He said as he wandered away, "I am sure they are very sour grapes and I don't like sour grapes at all."

In the "Fox and the Grapes," the relationship between the fox's goal of getting the grapes and its final observation that the grapes were sour is not made explicit. To understand the fox's reasons for calling the grapes sour, the reader must identify with the fox's frustrated and unsuccessful efforts in not achieving an important goal. The conclusion that the fox called the grapes sour in order to feel better about not reaching them is drawn exclusively from the reader's own experiences, not from the story.

We recommend beginning story-grammar instruction with stories that are textually explicit (i.e., require little or no background knowledge), short in length, and structurally simple. There should be few characters, and the conflicts, actions, goals, and resolutions should be rather straightforward. As students progress, longer, more complex stories can be gradually introduced. However, the teacher should avoid introducing too much that is new too quickly. For example, it would be inappropriate to introduce scriptally implicit stories that involve multiple characters with many goals, subgoals, plots, and actions after a student has read only textually implicit stories with few characters and a simple story line.

Teaching Procedure

The following teaching procedures are based on the assumption that students can decode the words in the stories and are capable of answering basic literal-comprehension questions. To introduce story-grammar instruction, the teacher relies on a facilitative questioning strategy that consists of four basic story-grammar questions: (1) Who is the story about? (2) What is s/he trying to do? (3) What happens when s/he tries to do it? and (4) What happens in the end? These core questions will be used to direct the students' attention to the critical parts of each story. The questions are aligned with the important components of story grammar, such as identifying the characters in the story; identifying their goals, the actions and obstacles related to achieving those goals; a resolution, and the final circumstances surrounding the characters' goal-related actions; and the story ending. The core questions can also be eventually used as a framework for teaching students to summarize the story in either oral or written form.

Table 26.1 contains a format for introducing story grammar. In this format, students read the story, the teacher stops students at the appropriate points in the story, then asks each story-grammar question. The students then answer the questions. The specific wording used in the format is for such textually explicit texts as "The Mouse and Hawk." The teacher begins the format by telling students the four core questions that they will find answers to when reading the story. The students read the story orally, one student reading several sentences at a time. During the story reading, the teacher asks each story-grammar question at the appropriate place in the story. In addition, the teacher sometimes stops and conducts a cumulative review of the questions previously answered. In the final step of the format, the teacher summarizes by asking the four questions again. Following students' oral answers to the four questions, the teacher requires students to answer written comprehension questions.

In general, the strategy communicates to students that answers to comprehension questions can be retrieved reliably from the story itself. With sufficient practice and guidance, students will eventually learn when to rely on the story to answer questions and when to rely on their own background knowledge and experiences to answer questions.

Teacher	*Students*
The teacher writes on the board: Who is the story about? What is the main character trying to do? What happens when the main character tries to do it? What happens in the end?	

1. The teacher introduces the story-grammar questions: "When we read this story, we are going to ask four questions."
   The teacher reads and points to each question on board.
   a. "What's the first question?" Teacher calls on a student. — *"Who is the story about?"*
   b. "What's the next question we're going to ask about the story?" — *"What is the main character trying to do?"*
   c. "What's the next question?" — *"What happens when the main character tries to do it?"*
   d. "What's the last question?" — *"What happens in the end?"*

2. The teacher calls on individual students to read the title.
   a. "During the reading of the story, I will stop you to ask one of the questions. The answers to the questions can be found in the story. Let's start by reading the title of the story."
   Teacher calls on a student to read the story title. — *"The Mouse and the Hawk."*
   b. "Yes, the title tells us that story will be about a mouse and a hawk. So when we read the story, what main characters will we read about?" Teacher calls on a student. — *"A mouse and a hawk."*

3. Teacher calls on individual students to read the story. Teacher stops students at different points in the story and asks questions.
   a. After reading through the second paragraph, the teacher stops the reader and calls on individual students to answer the following question:
   "What is the hawk trying to do?" — *"Kill all the chickens."*
   "What is the mouse trying to do?" — *"Help the town people."*
   b. After reading the next two paragraphs, the teacher stops the reader and asks:
   "What is the mouse trying to do?" — *"Kill the hawk by getting the hawk to fly down on the sharp stick."*

Table 26.1   Continued

Teacher	Students
c. After reading the last paragraph, the final two questions are asked: "What happens when the hawk tries to get the mouse?" "What happens in the end?"	"It flew onto the sharp stick and was killed." "The mouse is a hero and the people thank the mouse."
4. The teacher summarizes the story using the four questions. "First, who is the story about?" "What are the hawk and mouse trying to do?" "What happens when they try to do these things?" "What happens in the end?"	"The mouse and the hawk." "The hawk is trying to kill chickens and the mouse is trying to help the town people get rid off the hawk." "The mouse gets rid of the hawk and the chickens are saved." "The mouse is a hero."

Corrections

The teacher must demonstrate the relationship between answering the four questions and finding those answers in the story. Sometimes, students' answers will be incomplete or partially correct. For example, when identifying who the story is about, the student may identify a secondary character instead of the main character. In this case, the teacher should respond as follows: "Yes, that tells about one character in the story, but tell me the character the story is mostly about."

In general, the correction procedure should be tailored to the kind of response the student provides. If the response is partially correct, the teacher should acknowledge the specific parts that are correct. When appropriate, the teacher should require the student to locate the correct answer in the story. If an inference is required, the teacher might summarize the relevant information. For example, in the fable "Clover and the King," the student might know that Clover poisoned the lettuce, but not understand the King's motive for dumping the lettuce next to where the rabbits lived. The teacher should summarize the actions of both Clover and the King and discuss with the student the motives of the characters.

Advanced Story-reading Comprehension Strategy

Overview

Story reading in the upper-grade levels typically involves the reading of short stories. Unlike stories in the primary-grade levels that are fairly simple, upper-grade short stories are fairly complex. As a result, the comprehension strategy for identifying and understanding story-grammar components needs to be more thorough than the strategy described previously for beginning story reading.

In intermediate grades, stories become more scriptally implicit and students need to have more background knowledge to comprehend the stories. Similarly, stories are more likely to contain words critical to the meaning of sentences but not known by the student. Before presenting stories to the student, the teacher should preteach any critical information or vocabulary words students need to know.

This section will present teaching procedures for introducing short story comprehension based on the research by Gurney (1987) and Dimino (1988). The procedures will provide a basic understanding of how to teach intermediate- and secondary-level students to identify and interpret the wide range of characters, actions, events, and situations that take place in short stories.

Story Selection

The short stories that students are required to read in intermediate grades, middle school, and high school are typically found in literature textbooks, basal readers, and student magazines. These stories may range from well-known classics, such as Jack London's "To Build a Fire," to contemporary selections concerned with the problems faced by today's adolescents. Many of these stories have been modified or edited by the publisher. We do not recommend any stories be further rewritten or modified. The preteaching of words difficult to decode or unknown to students should be done prior to short story reading. By requiring students to read the original stories instead of modified versions, they acquire the comprehension and decoding skills necessary to meet the demands placed upon them in regular reading and English classes.

Although short stories are quite varied in their structure, story grammar, and story line, the comprehension strategy we propose builds on the four core story-grammar questions taught for comprehending simple stories. We expand these four questions to categories as more complex stories are introduced. These categories, based on Dimino's (1988) analysis, are described below.

Category 1: Character Information

The teacher expands the first question, "Who is the story about?" by asking questions about the character. The teacher tries to have students anticipate what a character might do based on the information given. Questions can be asked about the following characteristics:

a. Actions: What the characters do.

b. Dialogue: What the characters say to themselves and each other.

c. Thoughts: What the characters are thinking.

d. Physical Attributes: How the characters look.

Category 2: Conflict or Problem

The second question, "What are the characters trying to do?" is expanded to asking questions about the conflict or problem that exists. The types of conflicts or problems the teacher asks questions about are:

a. Disagreements: A problem arises between two characters. For example, parents disagree with a son over using the car.

b. Tough Decisions: A character is faced with two difficult choices. For example, a character must choose between keeping quiet or revealing a friend's crime.

c. Struggle for Survival: A character tries to overcome the forces of nature. For example, a character tries to survive in the wilderness during the extreme cold.

Category 3: Attempts/Resolution/Twist

The third question, "What happens when the characters try to do it?" expands to questions about how the characters attempt to solve the conflict or problem. The teacher asks questions about the following:

a. Attempts: What the character does to resolve the conflict or solve the problem.

b. Resolution: The final outcome or attempt that solves or fails to solve the problem.

c. Twist: An unexpected complication that occurs at the end of the story and usually differs from the resolution of the problem.

Category 4: Reactions and Theme

The final question, "What happens in the end?" is expanded in a different way. Instead of focusing on what actually happens at the end of a story, the teacher requires students to focus on the meaning of the author's message. Questions are asked about the following:

a. Reactions: What is the character's response to the events in the story?

b. Theme: What is the underlying meaning of the story? What is the author of the story trying to tell the reader? What is the moral of the story?

Teaching Procedures

The teaching strategy utilizes two unique procedures: (a) a story notesheet designed to help students summarize and clarify the story-grammar components during short story reading (the outline notesheet appears in Table 26.2), and (b) a think-aloud procedure in which the teacher summarizes and points out how to anticipate story-grammar questions to be asked.

Unlike the strategy for simple stories requiring students to ask whom the story is about first, the strategy for comprehending complex stories requires students to identify the problem or conflict first.

The format for teaching short story reading comprehension appears in Table 26.3. Because short stories vary in content and complexity, this format is unlike other formats in the book. Instead of providing detailed teacher wording for each step of the strategy, we provide descriptions of how each of the four categories of story-grammar components can be presented. This format is developed around the short story "To Build a Fire" by Jack London. A summary of this short story follows:

> The story begins on an "exceedingly cold and gray" day. The main character is a newcomer to the Yukon Territory and this is his first winter in the land. The man, as London notes, was "without imagination," "quick and alert in the things of life, but only in the things, and not the significances." It is fifty degrees below zero and the man is bound for an old claim where he is to meet "the boys." The man decided to leave the main Yukon trail and is accompanied by a "big native husky" who knew it was not time to be traveling. The man was making four miles an hour as he made his way up Henderson Creek. Unexpectedly, the man broke through the ice and wet himself "halfway to the knees." The man built a fire. He felt safe and thought the fire was a success. However, the man had built the fire under a big spruce

Table 26.2   Notesheet for Short-story Comprehension Strategy

Student Notesheet

Name_____ Date_____

Story_____

1. Name the problems or conflict._____

_____

_____

_____

2. Identify the main characters and tell about them._____

_____

_____

_____

3. Tell how the characters try to solve the problem._____

_____

_____

_____

4. Tell how the problem is or is not solved._____

_____

_____

_____

5. Is there an added twist or complication at the end of the story?_____

_____

_____

_____

6. What is the theme of the story? What is the author trying to say?_____

_____

_____

_____

tree. The fire had warmed the snow until a load of it had fallen on the fire. The man made several attempts to build another fire, but the attempts failed. Soon the newcomer to the Yukon fell asleep in the snow as the day drew to a close and eventually died.

The teacher begins the lesson by giving each student a notesheet. During-story reading, students are stopped at designated points and asked the appropriate story-grammar question. The teacher records the information on a transparency of the notesheet while students record it on their individual notesheets. Students are allowed to copy from the transparency, but are encouraged to record the information in their own words. Students are advised that after a few stories, they will be responsible for determining and recording the components without the benefit of the transparency or class discussion.

During the first days of story reading, the teacher models asking questions and giving answers. After several lessons, the teacher calls on students to answer questions. For example, after the problem is stated in the story, the teacher asks, "Do we have a problem?"

After weeks of practice, independent exercise is given. In this independent-practice phase, identification and discussion of the story-grammar components does not take place until students have recorded the information on their notesheets. Students' responses on the notesheets are monitored, and time is allotted for students to correct their incorrect answers after each story-grammar component is discussed. Since answers are no longer being recorded on the transparency, the teacher must monitor students' written responses carefully.

Correction Procedures

Although the complexity of short stories and the lengthy application of the strategy could prompt a variety of errors, three different types of errors are likely to occur. Each type of error is addressed separately.

Errors Involving Textually Explicit Information

These errors occur when students incorrectly answer questions that require recalling information stated explicitly in the story (e.g., What was the first thing the main character did to solve the problem?). To correct these errors, students should be directed to the portion of the text that contains the answer, then asked to read the passage to find the answer.

Errors Involving Textually Implicit Information

These errors are likely to be more frequent than errors involving textually explicit information. These errors occur when students incorrectly respond to questions that require them to make inferences and judgments about the characters, events, or situations (e.g., What is the main character like? What is the author's message in the story?). To answer these questions correctly, students must assimilate the information given in the story and render a judgment or opinion. To correct these errors, the teacher should first direct the student to the appropriate information on the notesheet or in the story. Once the correct information is found, the teacher should ask questions to assist the student in making a correct inference. For example, if a student responds incorrectly to the following question "Do you think the character will do well in this environment?" The teacher corrects by modeling the following answer: "When the author says that the man was without imagination and was not alert to significances of life, he is using this information to tell the reader that the man was not in tune with his new environment." This correction procedure demonstrates to students the relationship between information in the story and the process of making judgments or inferences about that information.

Errors Involving Theme Identification

Theme identification is likely to be the most difficult aspect of the instructional

Table 26.3   Format for Introducing Short-Story Reading Comprehension

1. **You're going to learn a strategy that will help you understand short stories. When you read short stories, you're going to be reading about characters, their problems, and how they solve their problems. We'll read a short story and apply the strategy to the story.**

2. **I'll call on different students to read different parts of the story. Read clearly and loudly so that everyone can hear you. If I don't call on another student, continue reading. If you're not reading, be certain to follow along in case I call on you.**

3. [The teacher begins instruction by calling on students to read the title of the short story. Once the title is read, the teacher asks students to make predictions about the story to be read by asking] **"So what do you think the story is going to be about?"**

4. *Identifying the main problem/conflict.*
   [Students begin reading the story and stop at points predetermined by the teacher. At these designated points, the teacher simply asks students to stop. Utilizing a think-aloud strategy, the teacher states] **"I see a problem"** or **"It looks as if we have a problem."**

   [The teacher states the problem/conflict and writes it on Part I of the notesheet that is projected on the transparency for students to see].

   [When stories contain both major and minor problems, the teacher identifies the problems. For example, during the reading of "To Build a Fire," the teacher states] **"I see a problem. The man is a newcomer and this is his first winter traveling in the Yukon. This may not be a major problem, but I will record it on Part I of the notesheet. As we read on, we will be able to see if this is the major problem."**

   [Students are told to watch carefully as the teacher writes on the notesheet. The teacher should choose the main problem by identifying the one which encompasses most of the action or is the most difficult to solve. Once this problem is identified, the teacher circles it on the notesheet and explains the reasons for its selection].

5. *Identifying the main character.*
   [Once the main problem is identified, the teacher points out to students that the problem revolves around the main character. The teacher models the thinking-aloud process by restating the problem, then specifying whose problem it is.] **"Now that I found the problem, we can choose the main character by asking ourselves who the problem revolves around. In "To Build a Fire," the problem is a struggle for survival, which revolves around a man who is a newcomer to the winters in the Yukon territory. The man is on a journey through the woods with his dog and his goal is to join some other men at a camp miles away."** [The teacher writes the main character on Part 2 of the notesheet.]

strategy. Students may have difficulty assimilating the events in the story and formulating a general statement that captures the underlying message. The teacher can model how to state a theme by reviewing themes from previous stories to illustrate how events in a story can be used to develop a theme.

Table 26.3   Continued

6. *Identifying attempts, resolution, and twist.*

   "Now that I have found the problem and main character, we can identify the attempts. The attempts are what the main character does to try to solve the problem." [Students are told to follow along as a group until they are stopped at a designated point. At that point, the teacher models the process by identifying attempts. For example, in "To Build A Fire," the teacher states the following] **"It looks as if the main character tried to solve the problem here. His problem is that he is alone and making his way to a camp that is miles away. It is the middle of winter and it's fifty degrees below zero. He tried to solve his problem by building a fire."** [The students observe as the teacher records the attempt on Part 3 of the notesheet placed on the transparency.]

   The fire kept him warm for a while, but it melted the snow on a tree. The snow fell and put out the fire. The man couldn't get warm again and died of the cold. [The teacher records the events on parts 4 and 5 of the notesheet.]

7. *Summary and retell.*

   Students are told that information recorded on Parts 1 (problem), 2 (main character), 3 (attempts), 4 (resolution), and 5 (twist) of the notesheet are used to retell the story. The teacher models retelling the story while pointing to the pertinent information on the notesheet. An example of a retell for Jack London's "To Build a Fire" follows:]

   "This is a story about a man and his dog (main characters) **who make a journey alone in the middle of winter when the temperature is fifty degrees below zero** (problem). **The man tried to avoid the springs** (attempt) **along the Yukon river, but fell through the ice** (problem) **and was forced to build a fire** (resolution). **He built the fire under a big spruce. The snow on the spruce melted and put out the fire** (twist). **The man ran to keep warm** (attempt) **but fell and eventually died."**

8. *Identifying the theme.*

   "Now we can talk about the theme of this story. The theme is what the author of the story is trying to tell you. It is the advice the author is giving to the reader."

   a. [Teacher calls on students and asks] **"What is the author trying to tell us?"** [The teacher accepts reasonable answers, then reviews the theme:]

      "The author might be telling us we must be sensitive to the environment. The man was a newcomer to the cold winters in the Yukon and he tended to ignore the significance of things, such as the significance of temperature when it was fifty degrees below zero."

   b. [The teacher calls on several students to retell the story.]

Application Exercises

Clover and the King

Clover was a very clever rabbit who, along with other rabbits, loved lettuce. They lived outside the King's castle, and soon they had all the lettuce from nearby gardens except for the King's own garden.

The King loved his garden and grew the best lettuce in all the land. He did not want the rabbits to get any of his lettuce, so his garden was well guarded. The rabbits didn't like the King either and just wanted his lettuce.

One day Clover got an idea. A rabbit could not sneak into the King's garden, but a rabbit could sneak into the King's kitchen. Clover sneaked into the King's kitchen every morning for several days. Each day the King's men brought in some lettuce for dinner, and each day Clover poisoned the lettuce. Soon, everyone in the King's palace was sick.

The King was very sad when he learned that his lettuce was making everyone sick. He ordered his soldiers to dig up the lettuce from his garden. Then he ordered the lettuce dumped outside the castle, near where the rabbits lived.

The King was very pleased with himself. He would solve two problems at once.

1. Assume the role of an elementary student. Fill out the Notesheet (Table 26.2) for the story above.

2. Assume the role of the teacher. Rewrite the format for introducing short story reading comprehension (Table 26.3) so that it could be used with the story above. Indicate where you would ask questions during story reading, what the questions would be, and what are acceptable student responses.

3. Predict two serious mistakes students might make. Describe how you would correct each mistake.

The major emphasis in the intermediate grades should move from learning to read to reading to learn. Intermediate children begin extensive reading in expository materials, such as content area textbooks and reference books designed to convey factual information or to explain what is difficult to understand. These materials differ significantly from the narrative or story material generally found in basal readers. New organizational structures are used, the vocabulary is often more difficult to decode and understand, unique typographic features as well as graphics are introduced, and the density of concepts is higher. Not only are the characteristics of expository materials more difficult for the naive reader to cope with, the demands placed on the reader also increase. The reader is expected to extract, integrate, and retain significant main ideas and details presented in the material and to learn many specialized vocabulary terms, expectations seldom demanded in narrative reading. Due to the unique characteristics of expository materials and the demands placed on the reader, explicit instruction in reading and understanding expository materials must be provided for the intermediate student beginning with classroom content-area textbooks.

This section focuses on content area reading instruction, beginning with an analysis of the differences between expository and narrative materials. Next, procedures for teaching content area reading lessons are outlined, including the following steps: (1) teacher preparation for instruction, (2) prereading activities, (3) reading activities, and (4) postreading activities.

Chapter

27

Direct Instruction in Content Area Reading

This chapter was written by Anita Archer and Mary Gleason. Anita Archer is Associate Professor at San Diego State University. Mary Gleason is Assistant Professor at the University of Oregon.

Characteristics of Expository Materials

Before discussing teaching procedures for content area textbooks, it is helpful to examine the unique characteristics of expository materials and some of the problems these characteristics might pose to naive readers. To illustrate these characteristics, examine Figure 27.1, a selection from a sixth-grade science book.

Vocabulary

One of the major differences between narrative and expository materials is the vocabulary used. The vocabulary of content area materials is often more difficult to decode and pronounce than that found in narrative material. For example, in the selection in Figure 27.1, the student must decode the words *seismograph, identify, geologists, properties,* and *classify.* The density of multisyllabic words and words containing unfamiliar morphemes increases the decoding difficulty of expository materials.

Pronunciation is made more difficult by lack of familiarity with the words and their absence from the student's listening or speaking vocabulary. Though the student may use appropriate decoding strategies, he may make slight errors in pronunciation because of his inability to correct the pronunciation against his known vocabulary.

The challenges posed by expository vocabulary go beyond decoding. Expository materials are more likely to include vocabulary terms difficult to understand or unfamiliar to the student. It is unlikely that the sixth grade student has had an opportunity to use such terms as *geologist, seismograph,* or *minerals* in his own speech or has had much prior exposure to their meanings. Expository materials not only present a large number of new vocabulary terms, but also include technical terms (e.g., *meters*), words used in unusual ways (e.g., "the earth's *mantle*"), symbols and abbreviations to convey concepts or to replace vocabulary terms (e.g., 1290° F, 700° C), and figures of speech.

Not only is the vocabulary difficult to decode and unfamiliar to the reader, but the terms are often presented in rapid succession. For example, in one paragraph the terms *geologists* and *minerals* are presented using definitions or contextual cues but with little elaboration. Students, particularly students new to the content area or naive readers in expository materials, will need careful preparation in order to handle the vocabulary and concept load found in content area selections.

Content

In addition to the vocabulary terms, the general content of expository materials is often beyond the student's experiences. While narrative stories generally focus on situations, events, or concepts that the student has dealt with or been exposed to, expository materials include content that is new and unique to the student. Within the illustrated passage, the reader is introduced to the use of the seismograph, the layers of the earth, the characteristics of each layer, the role of geologists, the term *mineral*, and the use of physical properties in classifying rocks. The content includes many unfamiliar concepts as well as a much higher density of ideas than found in narrative materials.

Style and Organization

Expository material is usually written in a terse, straightforward style with explana-

Figure 27.1   Selection from a Content Area Textbook

Chapter 4

How Rocks Are Formed

Picture Analysis

This rock is made up of different layers. Look closely at the thick layers. Do these layers appear to be about the same size? How does the color of the thin layers differ from the color of the thick ones? Notice the shapes of the two kinds of layers. Are they the same or different?

The rock has been exposed to the weather. What effect do you think heavy rains and strong winds might have had on the rock? What effect do you think they will have in the future?

Preview and Share

Look at the pictures in this chapter. Choose one picture that you want to know more about. Write two questions about it. After you have finished reading the chapter, share your questions with a classmate. Try to answer the questions together.

Science Vocabulary

seismograph	physical property	lava
core	weathering	volcano
mantle	sediment	igneous rock
crust	sedimentary rock	metamorphic rock
rock	pressure	rock cycle
geologist	geyser	
mineral	magma	

From HOLT SCIENCE (Sixth Grade), by Joseph Abruscato and others, pp. 81–85. Copyright 1989 by Holt, Rinehart and Winston, Publishers. Reprinted by permission.

Figure 27.1   Continued

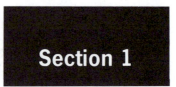

Section 1

THE EARTH'S LAYERS

This is Bryce Canyon in southwest Utah. It was named for Ebenezar Bryce, a pioneer who settled in Utah in 1875. Wind and rain have carved the rocks into these unusual shapes. The rock in this canyon is colored in over sixty shades of red, pink, and beige. Because of the placement of the rock layers, scientists are able to determine the history of their formation. Over one billion years of history are recorded in the layers. When you finish this section, you should be able to:

Figure 27.1   Continued

- **A.** Identify the layers of the earth.
- **B.** Explain how *rocks* and *minerals* are related.
- **C.** Explain how *rocks* are classified.

Bryce Canyon is 300 meters (1,000 feet) deep. That depth is only a scratch in the surface of the earth. Yet we know what the inside of the earth is like. How do we know? Earthquakes tell us. When there is a strong earthquake, vibrations, or waves, are sent through the earth. The waves are recorded on a **seismograph** (size-muh-graf). The *seismograph* measures the strength of the earthquake waves. It also notes how often the waves occur.

Seismograph: An instrument that detects and records earthquake waves.

Two kinds of earthquake waves travel through the earth. One kind travels through liquids and solid materials. A second kind travels only through solid material. The center of the earth is called the **core**. Scientists have been able to identify earthquake waves that pass through liquid and solid materials in the *core*. Thus, scientists believe that the core is partly liquid. They further believe that the inner core is made of the solid metals iron and nickel.

Core: The hot, partly liquid center of the earth.

Around the core is a thick hot layer called the **mantle**. The earth's *mantle* is a little like plastic. It is not liquid, but it does flow. The kind of earthquake wave that moves only through solids moves through the mantle. So it is thought to be a solid layer.

Mantle: The hot, rocky layer that surrounds the core of the earth.

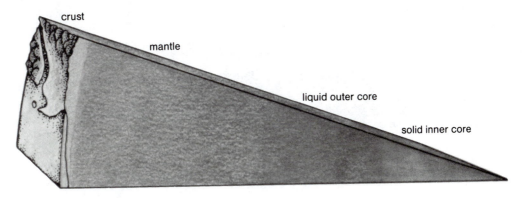

crust

mantle

liquid outer core

solid inner core

Figure 27.1   Continued

Crust: The thin, rocky outer layer of the earth.

Rock: The material of which the earth's crust is built.

Geologist: A scientist who studies rocks and other features of the earth.

Mineral: A solid material that occurs naturally in the earth's crust.

Physical property: A characteristic, such as color, of a material.

The crust of the earth is the part we know most about. The very top part of the *crust* is the surface of the earth, where we live. The crust is only 5 to 70 kilometers (3 to 43 miles) deep. The basic material that makes up the earth's crust is **rock**. *Rock* is what mountains are made of. Stones and pebbles are broken pieces of rock. Sand and soil are very small pieces of broken rock.

Scientists who study rocks and other features of the earth are called **geologists** (jee-**ahl**-uh-jists). *Geologists* have found that all rocks have things in common. All rocks are made of **minerals**. A *mineral* is a solid material that is found in the earth's crust.

The **physical properties** of a mineral are the same no matter where it is found. The *physical properties* of a material make it different from other materials. Color, hardness, and luster are some properties of minerals. About 10 to 15 minerals are commonly found in rocks. The picture on the left shows a rock called granite. To the right of the granite rock are the three minerals of which it is made: quartz (**kworts**), feldspar (**feld**-spahr), and mica (**my**-kuh). Granite may also have a little of some other minerals in it.

Rocks can be classified, or grouped, by their physical properties, such as color. Or they can be classified by their minerals. One way geologists classify rocks is

Figure 27.1 Continued

according to the way in which the rocks were formed.

Rocks are formed in three different ways. Some rocks are formed from pieces of other rocks and from plant and animal remains. The second kind of rock is formed from hot, melted rock deep in the earth's crust. The third kind is formed from heat and pressure on the other two kinds of rocks.

---

tion minimized, a pattern seldom found in narrative materials. The organization of ideas presented in narrative and expository materials often differs. In narrative or story selections, there is generally a gradual building of sequential events or related ideas, climaxing near the end of the selection and tapering to the selection's conclusion. The reader is literally carried by the author from event to event, from situation to situation, from idea to idea. Unlike narrative materials that provide a continuous, uninterrupted stream of information, expository materials usually segment the selection into a number of topics delineated by headings and subheadings. Like a huge puzzle, each paragraph provides an explicit or inferred main idea with supportive details which, when combined with other paragraphs, define a single topic. These topical segments, in turn, are combined with other segments to form a body of knowledge. For example, the selection in Figure 27.1 begins with a title that presents the chapter's theme. Each of the subsequent major headings introduces a different topic concerning the formation of rocks: The Earth's Layers, Sedimentary Rocks, Igneous Rocks, and Metamorphic Rocks. To develop the topic, a series of paragraphs, each containing a main idea and supportive details, follows each heading.

Other characteristics of organizational design also contribute to the complexity of expository materials. For example, cause-and-effect relationships and comparisons are prevalent in expository materials, particularly in science and social studies textbooks. These relationships occur less often in narrative materials. Inverted time sequences are also found in expository materials but seldom in story material. Within narrative materials, the discourse is smooth and seldom disturbed until the selection's conclusion. However, expository reading is interrupted by subheadings and headings; referrals to glossaries and pronunciation keys; and references to graphic aids. These complex organizational patterns and disruptions in the discourse can pose problems for the naive reader who has not been systematically introduced to this type of organizational design.

Special Features

Narrative stories have few special features outside of the title and occasional illustrations. The student, however, must cope with and attend to many special features in content area material. Graphics and illustrations that accompany narrative stories are included to enhance enjoyment and interest and to enrich the story. Graphics

Direct Instruction in Content Area Reading   **345**

and illustrations found in expository materials, however, contribute directly to the information presented either by supplementing or expanding on concepts found in the discourse. In narrative materials, the student need not examine illustrations with any intensity. However, in expository materials, she must scrutinize graphics and illustrations with special attention given to the title, explanatory notes, and labels. Each new type of graphic aid must be carefully introduced so that the student can locate information, make comparisons, formulate inferences, and draw conclusions based on the information presented. In the selection on rocks, a diagram is presented illustrating the various layers of rock found in the earth. Although the written discourse discusses the various layers of rock (e.g., the crust, mantle, and core), their interrelationships are not clear until the student has examined the labeled graphic.

Content Area Lessons

Content area lessons should be designed to promote *mastery of the salient information* presented in the selection and *acquisition of critical-reading study skills* that can be applied to other expository materials and, at the same time, *foster independence in the learners.* This is a difficult but important balance to reach. Often teachers give total responsibility to students for reading the selection and answering questions on the content. Although independence is maximized in this case, the lack of preparation for reading and guidance given during reading may result in lowered comprehension and inadequate use of reading-study skills. Yet teachers may provide extensive prereading activities and extensive direction to students across all selections throughout the year. This introduction to

critical-reading study skills would not foster student responsibility for learning or independent use of previously taught reading study skills. For the majority of elementary students and the majority of selections found in content area textbooks, a compromise between these extremes should be reached. Prereading activities and guidance during reading should be limited to critical passage variables and should be gradually faded as the students become more sophisticated in their reading.

Content area lessons should include the following steps: (1) teacher preparation for instruction, (2) prereading activities, (3) reading activities, and (4) postreading activities. Prior to instruction, the teacher should determine critical content that students should master, design a chapter examination, and divide the chapter into teachable units. During the prereading activities, instruction is presented on significant variables within the material (e.g., unknown vocabulary concepts, difficult-to-decode words, unique graphics, the structure of the passage) that can contribute to passage comprehension. Prereading activities may also include a survey of the passage's content. These activities are followed by reading of the passage under teacher direction (guided reading or reciprocal reading), in cooperation with a peer (partner reading), or independent reading using a specified learning strategy. Following reading of the selection, students engage in postreading activities (e.g., answering chapter questions, writing a summary of the selection) designed to summarize and synthesize the salient chapter information.

Teacher Preparation for Instruction

Selecting Critical Content

Before you can select appropriate prereading, reading, or postreading activities, you must first decide exactly what you would like your students to gain from studying the chapter in the content area textbook. What ideas, vocabulary, concepts, generalizations, events and related details would you like them to retain? What concepts are necessary for future study in the content area? To make these determinations, careful reading of the chapter is necessary. Many teachers find it helpful to take notes on the chapter and to consult the objectives provided in the student or teacher's edition of the textbook. Table 27.1 is a content analysis for the introductory expository material on rock formation. Here, the teacher has listed the vocabulary concepts and general understandings to be stressed for each segment of the chapter. As the teacher prepares prereading, postreading, and reading activities, as well as test items, she can refer to her content analysis. Whether your content analysis takes this form or another form, it is always important to have an instructional map to guide your work with students.

Designing or Adapting a Chapter Test

When students have completed study on a chapter, it is useful to give a chapter test for a number of reasons. First, an examination over critical content benefits *students*. It encourages students to study and rehearse the salient information that has been stressed in lessons and within the chapter. If the test is well designed, it can also reinforce what is important in the body of knowledge and, thus, should be retained. Finally, when feedback is given on the test, students have another opportunity to review the critical content. Of course, examinations also serve the *teacher*. Certainly, tests allow us to measure the information obtained by our students and to hold them accountable for studying. However, as a teacher, you also need feedback on the

quality of your instruction. Were the prereading, reading, and postreading activities adequate? Did students focus on the most important information? Without this feedback, instruction cannot be enhanced in the future. Finally, a test on the critical content allows you to determine which concepts need reteaching.

While most teachers formulate a chapter test after the chapter has been taught, it is more beneficial to develop it before instruction. If this is done, it will reinforce your instructional focus on critical concepts and ideas. The test that you develop or adapt should directly measure the concepts, ideas, and general understandings that you have deemed important and worth retaining. If the test measures irrelevant details, students will come to believe that details should be the focus of their self-study. Whether you utilize a chapter test provided in the program or design your own, your first concern is the importance of the information measured. Next, be certain that the types of items are appropriate to measure the specific concept or general understanding. For example, if you want students to be able to identify the layers of the earth, a labeling task requiring this behavior would be the most appropriate. Examples of objectives and parallel test items are found in Figure 27.2.

Dividing the Chapter into Teachable Units

Finally, in preparation for teaching a content area chapter, divide the chapter into smaller, teachable segments that represent a body of connected discourse on a topic in an amount that can be introduced in one lesson. While many elementary textbook chapters are already broken into teachable segments indicated by lesson numbers and concluding questions, other textbooks have reading seg-

Table 27.1   Determination of Critical Content

CHAPTER 4: How Rocks Are Formed
Section 4.1: The Earth's Layers

Vocabulary: seismograph, core, mantle, crust, rock, geologist, minerals, physical properties
General Understandings:
   The student will be able to
   1. identify the layers of the earth;
   2. describe each layer;
   3. explain how minerals and rocks are related;
   4. tell how rocks are classified.

Section 4.2: Sedimentary Rocks

Vocabulary: weathering, sediment, sedimentary rock, pressure
General Understandings:
   The student will be able to
   1. describe what makes up sediment;
   2. explain how sedimentary rocks are formed;
   3. describe how different sedimentary rocks (shale, sandstone, limestone, gypsum) are formed.

Section 4.3: Igneous Rocks

Vocabulary: geyser, lava, volcano, magma, igneous rock
General Understandings:
   The student will be able to
   1. describe the difference between magma and lava;
   2. describe two ways that igneous rocks are formed and give examples of rocks formed in each manner;
   3. explain how the rate of cooling affects igneous rocks.

Section 4.4: Metamorphic Rocks

Vocabulary: metamorphic rock, rock cycle
General Understanding:
   The student will be able to
   1. describe how metamorphic rocks are formed;
   2. tell what quartz, slate, and marble are made from;
   3. trace the steps in the rock cycle.

Based on HOLT SCIENCE (Sixth Grade), by Joseph Abruscato and others, pp. 81–85. Copyright 1989 by Holt, Rinehart and Winston, Publishers.

ments that are much too long for the naive student. The prereading, reading, and postreading activities will be structured around these lesson-length chapter segments.

Prereading Activities

When critical information that students will be held accountable for has been determined and translated into chapter ob-

For each objective or combination of objectives, select a type of test item that matches the outcome you wish. Use a limited number of types of items, particularly in the early grades.

Examples

Objective: Can identify the layers of the earth.
Type of test item chosen: Labeling
Directions: Label each part of the earth.

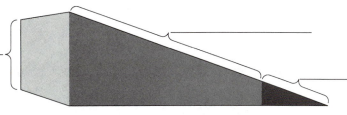

Objective: Describe each layer of the earth.
Type of test item chosen: Multiple choice
Directions: Circle the letter for the best answer.

1. The core of the earth is
   a. at the center of the earth
   b. partly liquid
   c. very hot
   d. all of the above.

2. The mantle of the earth is
   a. a hot liquid
   b. a thick, hot, solid layer
   c. a thick, cool layer of rock
   d. none of the above.

3. The crust of the earth is
   a. a thin, hot liquid
   b. the thick outer layer of the earth
   c. the thin, rocky, outer layer of the earth
   d. all of the above.

Objective: Can define the following vocabulary terms: core, mantle, crust, mineral, sedimentary rock, lava, magma, igneous rock, metamorphic rock.
Type of test item chosen: Matching
Directions: Write the number for the correct definition on the line.

_____ core
_____ mantle
_____ crust
_____ mineral
_____ sedimentary rock
_____ lava
_____ magma
_____ igneous rock
_____ metamorphic rock

1. Rock formed from particles of rock.
2. Hot, melted rock as it comes out of the earth.
3. The thin, rocky, outer layer of the earth.
4. The hot, partly liquid center of the earth.
5. Hot, melted rock under the earth's surface.
6. A solid material that occurs in the earth's crust.
7. The hot, rocky layer that surrounds the core.
8. Rock formed from melted material that has cooled and hardened.
9. Rock formed from sedimentary and igneous rock that has been changed by heat and pressure.

jectives and test items, the other steps in the content area lesson can be initiated. The first step, preparing students for selection reading, is designed to preteach or alert students to significant variables within the material (e.g., new vocabulary, difficult-to-decode words, organizational patterns, new graphics) that will facilitate comprehension and extraction of the desired information.

The amount of preparation needed for a given selection depends on the complexity of the material, the experience of the students with the given textbook, the amount of prior knowledge that students have on the topic, and the reading skills of the students. Certainly, the fourth grade student reading the first selection in her new social studies book will need substantially more preparation than the more advanced student.

Teaching Difficult-to-decode Words

Given the increased difficulty of words found in content area textbooks, the teacher needs to ensure that students can decode and pronounce the words. When selecting words for decoding instruction, focus on words that are difficult "stopper" words, central to the understanding of the passage, and whose pronunciations are not cued within the discourse. When presenting the words, the teacher should not restrict the presentation to whole-word methodology, though this will be necessary when teaching irregular words. Instead, she should capitalize on the phonic and structural decoding skills that have been introduced to students using the formats presented throughout this book. Many of the multisyllabic words in content area textbooks include known prefixes or suffixes. The teacher can ask students to pronounce these known parts and then the

entire word. For example, in presenting *mantle*, the teacher can have students pronounce *le*, then the entire word. In other cases, the teacher can indicate parts of the word, have each part read, and have the entire word pronounced. Generally, the pronunciation of words can be introduced at the same time as important word meanings, since the difficult-to-decode words are often the unfamiliar vocabulary. The important thing is that the accurate pronunciation of the words is not assumed, but taught directly. Decoding, while not sufficient for passage comprehension, is necessary.

A potentially important aspect of decoding instruction in content areas involves directly teaching children to use the phonetic spelling often found in parentheses following foreign words or difficult-to-pronounce words. The teacher should not assume that children will be able to use these prompts without direct instruction, substantial practice, and occasional review of the process. Begin by examining the textbook and determining the pronunciation key used for respelling in the text. The following were extracted from two science texts.

Ginn Science
(Ginn and Company, 1975)

igneous	ig̀ nē es
sedimentary	sed ə meń tə re
metamorphic	met ə môŕ fik

Modern Elementary Science
(Holt, Rinehart and Winston, 1971)

vegetarians	veh-juh-TAIR-ee-unz
algae	AL-jee
aphids	AY-fids
forsythia	for-SITH-ee-uh

As noted in these examples, some authors use pronunciation keys similar to those found in glossaries and dictionaries, while others use phonetic respellings. After discovering the system used by the author, the teacher should present lessons that teach students to use this decoding strategy. The teacher should present the pronunciation system, demonstrate decoding of words using the system, lead children through decoding of unknown words written in the author's style, and, finally, test students on their use of this strategy. If the pronunciation system is very complex and difficult to interpret or will directly interfere with use of the dictionary pronunciation system used in the classroom, you may elect not to introduce the pronunciation key, and, instead, present the words using direct instruction.

Vocabulary Instruction

One of the most critical prereading activities is vocabulary instruction. The number of word meanings and concepts that students know directly relates to their ability to comprehend text. Thus, the teacher should introduce the essential vocabulary within a passage to enhance comprehension. Students do not automatically acquire new concepts, suggesting that direct instruction is essential.

Words for vocabulary instruction should be limited to a small number of words that are crucial for passage understanding and beyond the student's experiential background. Children should not be overwhelmed with a large number of difficult-to-understand words in a single presentation. Critical words should be carefully introduced, practiced, and reviewed in subsequent lessons.

There are many methods that the teacher can use to teach and provide practice in vocabulary concepts. However, our discussion will be limited to four procedures: (1) direct instruction procedures,

(2) concept diagrams, (3) concept maps, and (4) feature analysis procedures.

Direct Instruction Procedures

In this book, we have discussed a number of strategies for vocabulary instruction that apply equally well to content area instruction: (1) teaching through examples, (2) teaching through synonyms, (3) teaching through definitions, (4) locating the meaning in the dictionary or glossary, or (5) using context clues. Though all of these strategies can be used in content area materials, emphasis should be placed on developing contextual analysis. Since authors of elementary textbooks realize that many of the words will not be in the student's experiential background, explicit and inferred context clues are generally given. Contextual analysis is a student's major tool for vocabulary expansion. Because contextual analysis can be used by the reader when no instructor is present, proficiency in its use leads to independent vocabulary growth. Many children (and adults) have developed the habit of reading right past unfamiliar words. Direct instruction on contextual analysis will alert children to the use of these clues and encourage them to hunt for the word's meaning within the discourse.

During the vocabulary lesson, students can be asked to determine a word's meaning using context clues found in the passage, the glossary, or a dictionary. When this is not possible, the teacher can directly present a definition or a synonym for the unfamiliar word. However, reading the definition, even verbally repeating the word and its definition, may not improve comprehension of the selection (Pany & Jenkins, 1977). In all cases, explicit instruction should follow the introduction of the word and its meaning to ensure that students

Table 27.2   Format for Teaching Vocabulary Using a Synonym or Definition

Teacher	Students
1. Teacher states the new word. Students locate the word's definition in the passage (contextual analysis) or in the glossary. If the definition is not clear in either place, the teacher states the definition.	
a. **This word is** *export*. **What word?**	*"export"*
b. **Find** *export* **in your glossary.**	
c. **Read the definition.**	*"Something that is sent out of the country to be sold in another."*
2. Teacher tests understanding of the definition by asking questions and by having the definition repeated.	
a. **Where is an export sent?**	*"to another country"*
b. **Why is an export sent out of the country?**	*"to be sold"*
3. Teacher presents examples or uses the word in sentences to ensure clarity of the definition.	
a. **For example, Japan sends cars to the United States to be sold. Cars are an important Japanese export.**	
b. **The United States sells wheat to the Soviet Union. That wheat is an important U.S. export.**	
4. Teacher presents examples and non-examples in random order. Students identify examples and non-examples and tell why it is an example or a non-example.	
a. **Tell me if this is an** *export*. **Australia sells wool to other countries. Is wool an export of Australia?**	*"yes"*
Why is it an export?	*"Because it is sent out of Australia and sold."*
b. **The United States buys lots of wool from Australia. Is the wool an** *export* **of the United States?**	*"no"*
Correction: If students make an error, lead them to the correct response.	
Listen again. The United States buys lots of wool from Australia. Does the United States send wool to other countries to sell?	*"no"*
So is wool an export from the United States?	*"no"*
c. **South Korea sells lots of radios and stereos to Canada. Are radios and stereos an export of South Korea?**	*"yes"*
Why are they exports?	*"Because South Korea sells them to Canada."*

Table 27.2   Continued

Teacher	Students
d. South Korea buys some of the lumber it needs from Canada. Is the lumber a South Korean export?	*"no"*
Why isn't the lumber a South Korean export?	*"Because South Korea doesn't sell the lumber, it buys it."*
e. The United States raises lots of cattle and sells the beef in many countries. Is the beef a U.S. export?	*"yes"*
Why?	*"Because the U.S. sells the beef to other countries."*
Remember—an export is something that a country sells to another country.	

5. (Optional) Students generate additional examples.

a. Think carefully. What are some U.S. exports?	*(Students suggest U.S. exports.)*
b. Recently we studied about China. What do you think some of China's exports might be?	*(Students suggest Chinese exports.)*

(NOTE: Similar instruction is repeated for other words and definitions. In this lesson, the teacher also taught the following vocabulary terms: import, necessity, and luxury.)

6. Teacher reviews the new words and their definitions. If related words have been taught, she highlights their relationships.

a. Is an *export* something that we buy or sell?	*"sell"*
b. Is an *import* something that we buy or sell?	*"buy"*
c. If Australia sells wool to the United States, is wool an Australian export or import?	*"export"*
Is wool a U.S. export or import?	*"import"*
d. What is a necessity?	*"Something you need."*
e. What is a luxury?	*"Something you want but don't need."*
f. Tell me if this is a necessity or a luxury:	
television	*"luxury"*
food	*"necessity"*
warm clothing	*"necessity"*
a fancy sweater	*"luxury"*

have adequate practice in using the word. A format similar to those presented earlier in this book can be used. First, the teacher should introduce the word and ask students to locate the definition in the glossary or within the chapter (context analysis). If the word is not adequately defined in the context or included in the glossary, the teacher can directly present a definition or synonym for the word. After the definition has been presented, the teacher should check students' understanding of the definition by having it repeated or by asking questions about the definition. Next, the teacher should present a number of examples of the word's use to ensure the definition is clear. After this, the teacher should test students' understanding by presenting examples and non-examples. Finally, the teacher can ask students to generate examples or to use the word in verbal sentences. These teaching procedures are illustrated in Table 27.2.

As children become more familiar with the use of context clues, direct instruction on vocabulary meanings explicitly stated in the material or reliably inferred should be faded. However, prior to passage reading, the teacher may wish to delineate the important vocabulary to alert students to the use of context clues:

> In your chapter today on rocks, these are the most important words: *sedimentary, sediments, sandstone, conglomerates,* and *limestone* (words written on the board). As you read, watch for these words. Read the sentences around these words carefully to determine their meanings. Write down the meanings so we can discuss them after your reading.

After the children have read the selection, elicit their definitions. If their definitions are inadequate or too limited, go back

to the context and lead them to the correct definition. The majority of elementary content-area textbooks indicate important words to the reader through boldface type, alternate type style, underlining, color highlighting, or italics. If this occurs in the textbook, the teacher may simply remind children to attend carefully to the highlighted, key words.

Concept Diagrams

Another effective method for teaching specific vocabulary concepts, *concept diagrams,* also involves presenting an unknown word, its definition, examples, and non-examples (Bulgren, Schumaker, & Deshler, 1988). In preparing for this instruction, the teacher selects a vocabulary concept from the text material. Next, the teacher constructs a concept diagram that includes the word's definition; characteristics of the concept that are always present, sometimes present, or never present; and examples and non-examples of the concept. A concept diagram for *natural resources* is found in Table 27.3.

When presenting the concept, the teacher places a blank Concept Diagram on the board or overhead transparency. The teacher then presents and fills in the diagram following a specially designed routine including the following steps: (1) presenting the word and its definition; (2) discussing the "always," "sometimes," and "never" characteristics; (3) discussing one of the examples and one of the non-examples in relationship to the characteristics; (4) checking other examples and non-examples to determine if they match the characteristics. Throughout the presentation of the concept diagram, students are actively involved in the discussion.

Table 27.3   Example of a Concept Diagram

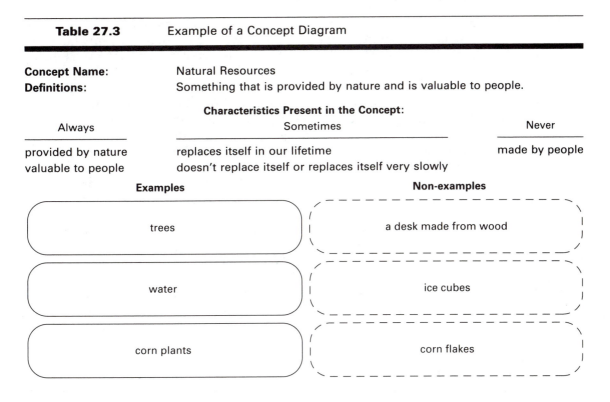

Concept Name: Natural Resources
Definitions: Something that is provided by nature and is valuable to people.

Characteristics Present in the Concept:

Always	Sometimes	Never
provided by nature	replaces itself in our lifetime	made by people
valuable to people	doesn't replace itself or replaces itself very slowly	

Examples	**Non-examples**
trees	a desk made from wood
water	ice cubes
corn plants	corn flakes

Based on research by J. Bulgren, J. Schumaker, and D. Deshler, "Effectiveness of a concept teaching routine in enhancing the performance of LD students in secondary-level mainstream classes." Presented in *Learning Disability Quarterly, 11* (1988): 3–17.

Concept diagrams are a very powerful procedure for presenting new concepts, especially to secondary students. The structure of the presentation, if used over time, will not only assist students in learning concepts, but teachers in designing concept instruction.

Concept Maps

In expository text, unlike narrative text, the difficult or unfamiliar concepts are generally semantically related. For example, in the text material on the formation of rocks, the highly related terms *core*, *mantle*, and *crust* are presented. It would be useful to teach these terms stressing their interrelationships. Concept maps, also referred to as graphic organizers, (Barron & Earle, 1973; Boothby & Alvermann, 1984; Earle, 1976; Tierney, Readence, & Dishner, 1985), graphic representations (Jones, Pierce, & Hunter, 1989; Van Patten et al., 1986), structured overviews (Sanacore, 1983), and visual-spatial displays (Darch, Carnine, & Kameenui, 1986) allow the teacher to preteach concepts stressing their interrelationships. This not only facilitates initial attainment of the concepts, but subsequent retention and retrieval of information.

A concept map visually represents a body of knowledge including the critical concepts, vocabulary, ideas, events, generalizations and/or facts using a diagram or other type of visual display. As a result, students gain a holistic view of the body of knowledge before the chapter is read. Not only do students learn critical content before passage reading, they gain an understanding of the chapter's structure. As the name implies, the concept map can serve as a guide to the chapter's content and structure.

The structure of the concept map is dictated by the different types of structure found in expository materials. In many cases, the text material represents a *hierarchy* in which the relationships between major concepts, subordinate concepts, and related details are stressed. The concept map presented in Figure 27.3 illustrates a hierarchical body of knowledge. In this case, the chapter presented the organization of the federal government, the branches of the government, the functions of each branch and their components. As seen in Figure 27.3, a hierarchy was used to present the major concepts, the subordinate concepts, and the related details.

In some cases, the body of knowledge is best illustrated with a *diagram* that shows the relationship of the *parts* to the *whole*. In Figure 27.4, the concept map illustrates the four layers of the atmosphere using a diagram. This allows the teacher to preteach the four major chapter concepts as well as related ideas (e.g., The density of gas molecules changes in each atmosphere layer. The temperature changes across atmosphere layers). In Figure 27.5, a diagram is used to illustrate the respiratory system. Once again, a diagram is the most appro-

priate representation since the relationship of the parts (e.g., mouth, larynx, lungs) to the whole (respiratory system) is being stressed.

Many chapters or sections of chapters compare and contrast times (e.g., before and after the Industrial Revolution), objects (e.g., the different types of rocks), people (the past and current cultures of Southwest Native Americans) or concepts (e.g., democracy and communism). In these cases, a chart can be constructed to *compare* and *contrast* information presented in the chapter. This type of structure can be seen in the concept map prepared for a science chapter on land biomes (Table 27.4). Using this chart, students can compare the climates, common plants, and animals in the *biomes*.

In social studies, the structure of the discourse often reflects a sequence of events over time. The most appropriate concept map in this case is a *timeline*. The concept map found in Table 27.5 is a timeline listing the major events in the American Revolution. Before reading each section of the chapter, the teacher went through the sequence of events involved in each major event (see sequences listed under Stamp Act and Boston Massacre). As a result of this preview, students brought a lot of prior knowledge to the passage reading. They could focus on the critical information and fit the new-chapter information into their existing scheme concerning each event.

Other expository materials present *processes* (e.g., how cotton cloth is manufactured) or *cycles* (e.g., the food cycle; the rock cycle). Once again, the structure of the concept map should reflect the structure of the body of knowledge. For example, one science chapter introduced the process involved in the formation of coal, petroleum, and natural gas. A concept map was developed to preteach the basic steps

Figure 27.3   Example of a Concept Map: Hierarchy

A New Constitution (1787)

1. What kind of government?

Democracy—a government that is run by the people who live in it

Republic—a nation or state in which citizens elect representatives to manage the government.

2. How can we be sure that no part of the government is too powerful?

ANSWER: Divide the powers of the Federal government.

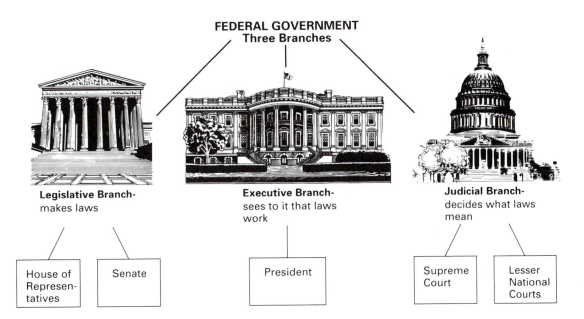

FEDERAL GOVERNMENT
Three Branches

Legislative Branch- makes laws

Executive Branch- sees to it that laws work

Judicial Branch- decides what laws mean

| House of Represen- tatives | Senate | | President | | Supreme Court | Lesser National Courts |

ANSWER: Each branch of government needs help of another branch to do its job.

      Legislative Branch makes laws **but President** must sign.

      President commands army **but Legislative Branch** decides to spend money for army.

(Note: All words printed in bold face type are provided by the teacher on the worksheet. All words printed in light face type would be added by students during the lesson.)

Based on AMERICA PAST AND PRESENT by Joan Schreiber and others. Copyright 1983 by Scott, Foresman and Company.

in the process using arrows to show the relationships between each step (see Figure 27.6).

    To construct a concept map, you use the following steps:

1. Determine the critical content (vocabulary, concepts, ideas, generalizations, events, details, facts, etc.) that you wish to preteach to your students.

Figure 27.4   Example Concept Map: Diagram

The Atmosphere—
The air that surrounds the earth.
Two Main Gases. _____
_____

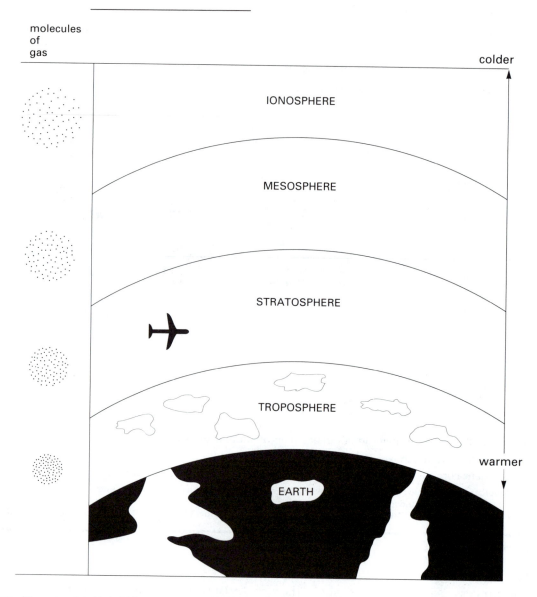

molecules
of
gas

colder

IONOSPHERE

MESOSPHERE

STRATOSPHERE

TROPOSPHERE

warmer

EARTH

(Note: All words printed in bold face type are provided by the teacher on the worksheet. The words in light face type would be
added by the students during the lesson.)
Based on HOLT SCIENCE (Fourth Grade), by Joseph Abruscato and others. Copyright 1989 by Holt, Rinehart and Winston,
Publishers.

Figure 27.5   Example of a Concept Map: Diagram

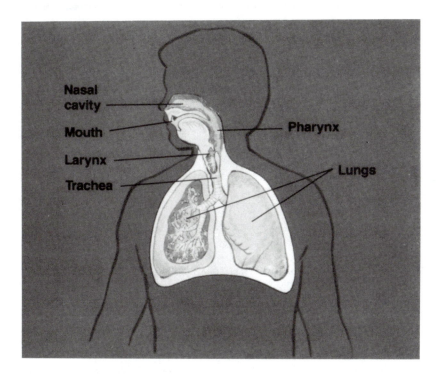

Respiratory System
pharynx—connects nasal cavity and trachea.
trachea—tube that leads to the lungs.
larynx—contains the vocal cords.
lungs—organ where the gas exchange between air and blood takes place.

From ACCENT ON SCIENCE by Robert B. Sund and others, p. 178. Copyright 1985 by Merrill Publishing. Reprinted by permission.

2. **Organize the concepts in a visual representation that reflects the structure of the content: hierarchy, diagram, compare-contrast, timeline, or process/cycle.** In some cases, a combination of these structures might be used. For example, in constructing a concept map on a science chapter on protists, the teacher began with a *hierarchy* showing the relationship of organisms to kingdoms and to the three groups of kingdoms. Next, the teacher used a *compare-contrast* chart to present the various types of protists and their characteristics (see Table 27.6).

3. **Design a completed concept map.** Write in the vocabulary, concepts, definitions, details, events, facts, etc. that you wish to preteach. (See Figure 27.7 for an example of a completed conceptual map.) It is helpful to add minimal graphics to your concept map (e.g., an outline of the White House

Table 27.4   Example of a Concept Map: Compare/Contrast

Biomes A large ecosystem that has similar populations and climate.

	Climate	Land Biomes Common Plants & Protists	Common Animals
Tundra	very cold, little rain	mosses, grasses, shrubs, lichens	reindeer, foxes wolves, owls, hawks, eagles, falcons, flies, lemmings
Taiga			
Grassland			
Tropical Rain Forest			
Temperate Forest			
Desert			

Based on ACCENT ON SCIENCE by Robert B. Sund and others. Copyright 1985 by Merrill Publishing. (Note: All words printed in bold face type are provided by the teacher on the worksheet. All words printed in light face type would be added by students during the lesson. The remainder of the chart would be completed as the chapter was read.)

next to the executive branch, a sketch of a tree next to the word *tree*). These graphics will increase interest in the concept map and will also help your students remember information when a blank concept map is presented.

4. **Create a partially completed concept map.** (See Figure 27.8.) A partially completed conceptual map includes the major terms and the actual diagram. During the instructional lesson, the partially completed conceptual map will be distributed to students. They will add information such as definitions, examples, and events. Since they will be writing on the concept map, active participation, subsequent attention, and learning will be increased.

5. **Create a blank concept map.** Delete all words, leaving only the diagram or structure of the concept map and any added graphics. The blank conceptual map will be used in a number of ways. First, during initial instruction, it will be used to review and firm up concepts that have been presented. Second, the blank map can be used as a postreading activity in which students or a group of students can recreate the concept map by adding missing information. Third, the blank map can be used in review exercises in which students determine missing information.

The teaching procedures for introducing concept maps will vary considerably depending on the structure of the map. However, the following procedures can generally be used. (See Table 27.7 for an example script that parallels the concept map on natural resources.)

Table 27.5   Example of Concept Map: Timeline

The Struggle for Independence

American Revolution 1775-1783

Stamp Act	Boston Massacre	Boston Tea Party	Battles at Lexington and Concord	Declaration of Independence	Peace with Britain
1765	1770	1773	1775	1776	1783

- Parliament passed stamp act.
  ↓
- Colonists had to buy stamp taxes.
  ↓
- Colonists angry.
  ↓
- Colonists sent message to Britain.
  ↓
- Act couldn't be enforced.
  ↓
- Britain did away with Stamp Act.

- Parliament put a tax on tea and said colonists could only buy tea from Britain.
  ↓
- Many stopped drinking tea. Some smuggled in tea.
  ↓
- British soldiers searched for tea.
  ↓
- Colonists upset.
  ↓
- Small fight broke out and 5 colonists killed.

Based on UNITED STATES by G. Vuicich and others. Copyright 1983 by McGraw-Hill, Inc. NOTE: The timeline represents information presented in the entire chapter. The related events are presented before students read each section of the chapter.

1. **Distribute partially completed concept maps to your students.** During the lesson, they will fill in additional information.
2. **Place a transparency of the completed map on an overhead projector.** Place a piece of paper under the transparency so that you will expose only those portions you wish students to attend to.
3. **Introduce the information on the concept map, proceeding in a logical order, stressing the relationships between the vocabulary concepts, events, details,**

facts, etc. When introducing vocabulary concepts, use the direct instruction procedures discussed earlier. Introduce the vocabulary concept and its meaning. Check students on the definition by having students repeat the definition or asking questions about the definition. Have students record the definition on their concept map. Next, check understanding by presenting examples and non-examples and by asking students to generate examples. When presenting other aspects of the concept map (e.g., facts, details, events), present the fact, have students repeat

Figure 27.6   Example of a Concept Map: Process

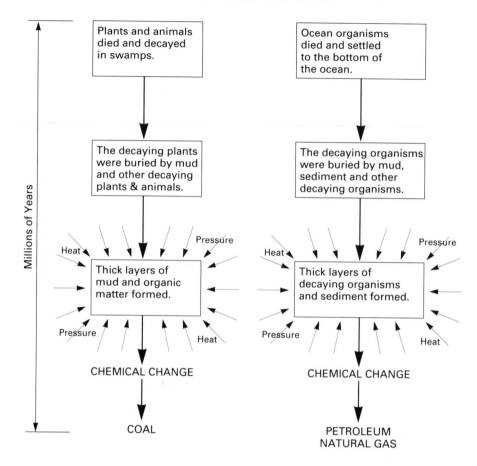

How Fossil Fuels Were Formed

Based on ACCENT ON SCIENCE (Sixth Grade) by Robert B. Sund and others. Copyright 1985 by Merrill Publishing.

the fact or ask questions about it, then have students record the fact on their concept map. Active participation is critical if you wish students to attend during the lesson. Continually ask students questions and have them record information on their concept maps.

4. **At natural junctures, review and firm up concepts you have introduced.** This can be done by placing the blank map on the overhead and asking students questions concerning the content.

5. **At the end of the lesson, review the critical content again using the blank concept map.**

Table 27.6   Concept Map: Multiple Structures

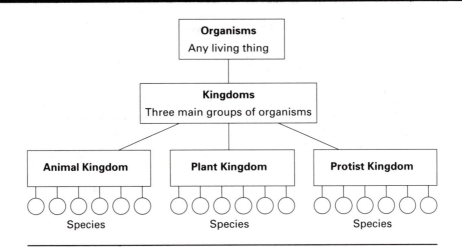

Protists

Description	How it gets food	Where it lives	Examples
Viruses			
Bacteria			
Protozoa			
Fungi			
Algae			
Lichen			

Based on ACCENT ON SCIENCE (Sixth Grade) by Robert B. Sund and others. Copyright 1985 by Merrill Publishing. (Note: The second half of this concept map would be completed in subsequent lessons.)

Figure 27.7   Completed Concept Map on Natural Resources

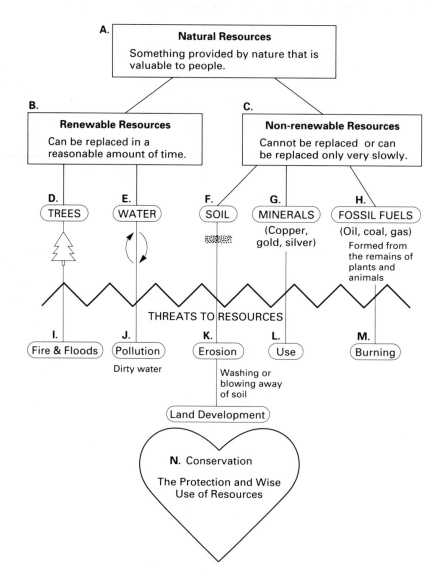

A. **Natural Resources**
Something provided by nature that is valuable to people.

B. **Renewable Resources**
Can be replaced in a reasonable amount of time.

C. **Non-renewable Resources**
Cannot be replaced or can be replaced only very slowly.

D. TREES

E. WATER

F. SOIL

G. MINERALS
(Copper, gold, silver)

H. FOSSIL FUELS
(Oil, coal, gas)
Formed from the remains of plants and animals

THREATS TO RESOURCES

I. Fire & Floods

J. Pollution
Dirty water

K. Erosion
Washing or blowing away of soil

L. Use

M. Burning

Land Development

N. Conservation
The Protection and Wise Use of Resources

Note: During instruction, the teacher displays this map on an overhead projector.

Figure 27.8   Partially Completed Concept Map on Natural Resources

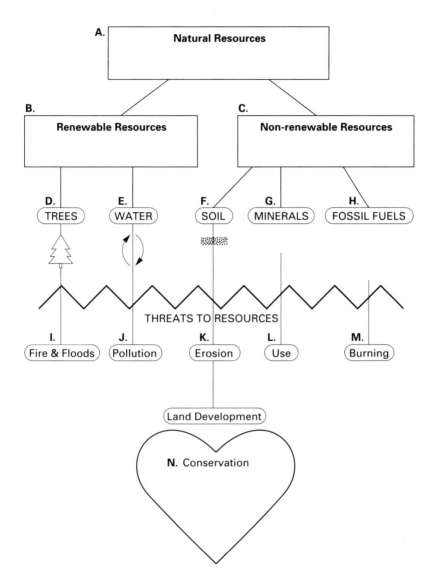

Note: The partially completed concept map would be distributed to students during the lesson. They would add information to the map throughout the lesson.

Table 27.7   Example Lesson for Teaching a Concept Map

Directions: Hand out partially completed concept map (Figure 27.8). Place completed map on overhead (see Figure 27.7).

T: You are going to be reading a chapter on natural resources. Before you read the chapter, let's learn some of the important concepts.
(Point to Box A on the map.) A natural resource is something provided by nature that is valuable to people. What is a natural resource?

S: Something that is provided by nature that is valuable to people.

T: Yes. For example, trees are a natural resource. They are provided by nature and are valuable to people.
Soil is another example of a natural resource. It is provided by nature and is valuable to people. A chair is not a natural resource. Though the chair contains wood and metal, both of which are natural resources, the chair is made by a person.
Tell me if this is a natural resource. Is water a natural resource?

S: Yes.

T: Why? (Call on an individual student.)

S: Because it is provided by nature and is valuable to people.

T: Is gold a natural resource?

S: Yes.

T: Why? (Call on an individual student.)

S: Because it is provided by nature and is valuable to people.

T: Is this gold ring a natural resource?

S: No.

T: Why is this ring not a natural resource? (Call on individual.)

S: Because it was made by a person.

T: You are correct. The ring is made from a natural resource, gold, but the ring itself is not a natural resource.
In Box A, write the definition for natural resource. (Monitor students as they fill in the box.)
There are two kinds of natural resources. (Point to Box B.) The first kind of natural resource is called a renewable resource. What kind of natural resource?

S: Renewable resource.

T: Renewable resources can be replaced in a reasonable amount of time. How quickly can renewable resources be replaced?

S: In a reasonable amount of time.

T: Yes, these are resources that can be replaced in a reasonable amount of time. For example, they might replace themselves in a month, a year, or one hundred years.
Write the definition for renewable resources in Box B. (Monitor students.)
Find D. (Pause.) What word is written next to D?

S: Trees.

T: Yes, trees are examples of renewable resources. The trees produce seeds or cones. From some of these seeds and cones, new trees grow. This may take a few years, or in some cases, a hundred years. Why are the trees in the forest called renewable resources? (Call on an individual.)

Table 27.7   Continued

S: Because they replace themselves in a reasonable amount of time.

T: Why are trees important natural resources?

S: (Accept reasonable answers.)

T: Find E. (Pause.) What word is written next to E?

S: Water.

T: Water is another example of a renewable resource. Water replaces itself in a reasonable amount of time. Look at the arrows. Water on the earth evaporates and goes up into the air. Later, clouds are formed and the water returns as rain or snow. Why is water called a renewable resource? (Call on an individual.)

S: Because water replaces itself in a reasonable amount of time.

T: Why is water an important natural resource?

S: (Accept reasonable answers.)
     (Place blank concept map on the overhead.)

T: Let's review what we have learned to this point. Turn your maps over. (Point to Box A.) What is the topic of this concept map?

S: Natural resources.

T: Who provides natural resources?

S: Nature.

T: To whom are natural resources valuable?

S: People.

T: Get ready to give me an example of a natural resource.

S: (Give examples.)

T: Great! (Point to Box B.) What is one kind of natural resource?

S: Renewable resources.

T: Can renewable resources be replaced?

S: Yes.

T: How quickly can they be replaced?

S: In a reasonable amount of time.

T: (Point to D.) What is one example of a renewable resource? (Call on an individual student.)

S   Trees.

T: Why are trees a renewable resource? (Call on an individual.)

S: Because they replace themselves in a reasonable amount of time. (Accept appropriate explanation.)

T: (Point to E.) What is another example of a renewable resource?

S: Water.

T: Why is water called a renewable resource? (Call on an individual.)

S: Because it replaces itself in a reasonable amount of time. (Accept appropriate explanations.)
     (Place the completed map on the overhead.)

T: Find Box C. (Pause.) Now let's study the other type of natural resource, nonrenewable resource. Listen. Nonrenewable resources CANNOT be replaced or can be replaced only very slowly. Read the definition with me. Nonrenewable resources cannot be replaced or can be replaced only very slowly.

S: Nonrenewable resources cannot be replaced or can be replaced only very slowly.

Table 27.7   Continued

T: When we use some natural resources, we simply use them up. They are not replaced. Other natural resources do replace themselves, but it might take thousands of years. Thus, they are not replaced in our lifetime or in the next generation's lifetime.

T: On your map, write the definition for nonrenewable resources. (Monitor as students write in the definition.)

T: Find F. (Pause.) Read the word written next to F.

S: Soil.

T: Yes, soil is an example of a nonrenewable resource. When soil is blown away, washed away, or carried away, it does replace itself, but it takes thousands of years. Why is soil called a nonrenewable resource?

S: Because it replaces itself very slowly.

T: Why is soil an important natural resource?

S: (Accept reasonable answers.)

T: Find G. (Pause.) Read the word.

S: Minerals.

T: Yes, minerals are another example of a nonrenewable resource. Some examples are copper, gold, and silver. What are some examples of minerals? (Call on individual students.)

S: Copper, gold, or silver.

T: On your map, write *copper, gold,* and *silver* below the word *minerals.* (Monitor.)

T: When we take minerals from rocks or ores to make things, the minerals do not replace themselves. Why are minerals called nonrenewable resources?

S: Because they cannot be replaced.

T: Why are minerals important natural resources?

S: (Accept reasonable answers.)

T: Find H. (Pause.) Read the words next to H.

S: Fossil fuels.

T: Yes, fossil fuels are also nonrenewable resources. Some examples of fossil fuels are oil, coal, and gas. What are some examples of fossil fuels? (Call on individual students.)

S: (Oil, coal, and gas.)

T: Under the words *fossil fuels,* write *oil, coal,* and *gas.* (Monitor.)

T: Fossil fuels were formed from the remains of plants and animals that were buried under the ground millions of years ago.
     What were fossil fuels formed from? (Call on individual.)

S: The remains of plants and animals.

T: Yes, dead animals and plants were buried deep in the ground. Over millions of years, oil, coal, and gas formed from these remains.
     To help you remember how fossil fuels were formed, write "formed from the remains of plants and animals" on your map. (Monitor.)

T: When we burn oil, coal, or gas for energy, they do not replace themselves for millions of years. Why are fossil fuels called nonrenewable resources?

S: Because they can be replaced only very slowly. (Accept appropriate explanation.)

T: Why are fossil fuels important natural resources? (Call on an individual.)

S: (Accept reasonable answers.)

Table 27.7   Continued

T: Now, take some time and study your map. (Monitor.)
     Before we end class today, let's review what we have learned.
     (Place blank concept map on the overhead.)

T: Turn your map over and look here. (Point to Box A.) What are we studying today?

S: Natural resources.

T: What is a natural resource?

S: Something that is provided by nature that is valuable to people.

T: Who uses natural resources?

S: People.

T: (Point to Box B.) What is the first type of natural resource?

S: Renewable resources.

T: Can renewable resources replace themselves?

S: Yes.

T: (Point to D.) What is one example of a renewable resource?

S: Trees.

T: (Point to E.) What is another example of a renewable resource?

S: Water.

T: Excellent. (Box C.) What is the second type of natural resource?

S: Nonrenewable resources.

T: What is a nonrenewable resource? (Call on an individual.)

S: One that cannot be replaced or can be replaced very slowly.

T: (Box F.) What is the first example of a nonrenewable resource?

S: Soil.

T: Can soil be replaced quickly?

S: No.

T: (Box G.) What is the next example of a nonrenewable resource?

S: Minerals.

T: What are some examples of minerals? (Call on an individual.)

S: Copper, gold, silver.

T: Can minerals be replaced quickly?

S: No.

T: What is the last type of nonrenewable resource?

S: Fossil fuels.

T: What are some examples of fossil fuels? (Call on an individual.)

S: Oil, coal, gas.

T: What are fossil fuels formed from? (Call on an individual.)

S: The remains of plants and animals buried in the ground millions of years ago.

T: Can fossil fuels be replaced quickly?

S: No.

T: You have done an excellent job. Tomorrow we are going to talk about some of the things that are
     hurting our natural resources. Please place your map in your notebook.

A concept map may display information from an entire chapter or only a section of a chapter. If it represents information from the entire chapter (as does the concept map on natural resources), introduce the map in sections corresponding to parallel reading assignments. As students proceed through the chapter, the other portions of the concept map can be introduced.

As you can see, concept maps are a powerful tool for preteaching and reviewing bodies of knowledge found in science, social studies, and health textbooks. They not only show students the relationship of the concepts, the structure of the chapter, but visually represent the information for easier acquisition, retention, and retrieval. Concept maps are also very useful when teaching students with very low reading skills. While they may not be able to read the content area textbook, there is no reason why they cannot learn the important ideas. In addition, early experience with teacher-prepared concept maps will prepare students for designing and using their own concept maps in secondary schools.

Feature Analysis Procedures

Another procedure for presenting related concepts found in a content area chapter is feature analysis (Johnson & Pearson, 1984). This procedure can be used when the concepts fall in one category (e.g., types of governments, different rock formations, the nine planets). When using this procedure, the teacher organizes the concepts and the features of those concepts in a matrix. For example, a feature analysis on types of government leadership might stress whether the leader's position is inherited, maintained by force, elected by the people or elected by legislators (see Table 27.8). A feature analysis concerning planets might examine whether the planet has life, is hotter or colder than the Earth, is small or large in comparison to the Earth, has rings or satellites, and has physical characteristics similiar or different from those of Earth (see Table 27.9).

When presenting the feature analysis matrix, the teacher assists students in determining if the concept possesses each of the features. A (+) is recorded if the feature is present and a (−) if the feature is not present. If the students have little prior knowledge of the concepts, the teacher can directly present each of the concepts and their features. The entire feature matrix can be completed prior to reading, or students can complete some aspects of the matrix during or after reading. Once the matrix is completed, the teacher can assist

Table 27.8	Example of Feature Analysis				
	Inherited	Governs by Force	Elected	Elected by People	Elected by Legislators
Monarch (King, Queen)	+	−	−	−	−
Dictator	−	+	−	−	−
President	−	−	+	+	−
Prime Minister	−	−	+	+	+

Based on OUR WORLD, LAND & CULTURE by Joan Schrieber and others. Copyright 1983 by Scott Foresman and Company.

Table 27.9   Example of Feature Analysis

		Life	Hotter than Earth	Colder than Earth	Big in Relation- ship to Earth	Small in Relation- ship to Earth	Rings	Satellites	Physical Character- istics Similar to Earth	Mostly Gaseous
INNER:	Mercury	−	+	−	−	+	−	−	+	−
	Venus	−	+	−	−	−	−	−	+	−
	Earth	+	−	−	−	−	−	+	+	−
	Mars	−	−	−	−	+	−	+	+	−
OUTER:	Jupiter	−	−	+	+	−	+	+	−	+
	Saturn	−	−	+	+	−	+	+	−	+
	Uranus	−	−	+	+	−	+	+	−	+
	Neptune	−	−	+	+	−	−	+	−	+
	Pluto	−	−	+	−	+	−	+	+	−

Based on EARTH SCIENCE by E. Danielson and E. Denecke. Copyright 1986 by Macmillan Publishing Company.

students in noting similarities and differences between the concepts. For example, the teacher might ask the following questions concerning the planet feature analysis: Which planets have satellites? Which planets are hotter than Earth? Which planets are colder than Earth? Which planets have a temperature similiar to Earth? How does Mars differ from Earth? How is Venus similiar to Earth?

Assistance with Graphics

In addition to assistance with vocabulary meanings and decoding, students will often need preparation adequately to read and interpret visual aids found in the chapter. Since content area materials generally provide students with their first exposure to charts, tables, graphs, diagrams, maps, and interpretive illustrations and photographs, direct instruction must be provided. The goals of this preparation are to increase the student's ability to read and interpret the information presented as well as to increase awareness of the importance of these features to expository writing.

At the beginning of the school year, the teacher should determine the types of visual aids to be included in the content area textbook. Generally a few types of visual aids will be repeated throughout a textbook. For example, a social studies textbook might include maps, line graphs, circle graphs, timelines, and tables. Next, the teacher should provide instruction on reading and interpreting each major type of visual aid, preferably before the content area instruction begins. For example, if maps occur throughout a social studies book, the teacher might teach the following map reading skills: determining the topic of the map from the map's title, determining directions, locating various places, understanding symbolic language presented in the map, reading the legend of the map, identifying geographic characteristics presented in the map, and reading the map's scale. In the same manner, the teacher can teach students how to read each type of graph (e.g., line graph, pictograph, bar graph) found in the book, stressing the following skills: (1) determining the topic of the graphic material using the title and caption; (2) understanding the organization of the graph; (3) locating information in the graph; (4) making comparisons using the non-numerical information in the graph (e.g., height of the bars; height of the lines); (5) making comparisons using the numerical information in the graph; and (6) making inferences based on the information. (See Table 27.10 for example teaching script.)

Table 27.10   Format for Introducing Different Types of Graphs

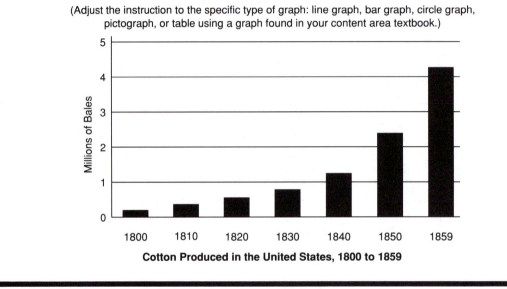

(Adjust the instruction to the specific type of graph: line graph, bar graph, circle graph, pictograph, or table using a graph found in your content area textbook.)

Cotton Produced in the United States, 1800 to 1859

Teacher	Students
1. Introduce the name of the graph (e.g., line graph, bar graph, circle graph, pictograph, table) and the type of information conveyed in the graph.	
a. *Look at the graph on page 221.* This graph is called a bar graph. What do we call this type of graph?	"A bar graph"
b. A bar graph lets us compare things by comparing the height of the bars.	
2. Introduce the importance of reading the title of the graph and determining the type of information presented.	
a. We read the title of the graph to find out what the graph is about. Read the title of the graph.	"Cotton Produced in the United States, 1800 to 1859."

Table 27.10   Continued

Teacher	Students
b. What will the information in the graph be about?	*"Cotton production"*
3. Introduce the organization of the graph.	
a. This bar graph lets us compare the millions of bales of cotton produced from 1800 to 1859. Look at the numbers across the bottom of the graph. These numbers tell the different years that are compared. Above each of these numbers is a bar.	
b. Put your finger on the highest bar. The highest bar tells you the amount that was produced in 1859. Find the shortest bar. The shortest bar tells you the amount of cotton produced in 1800.	*(Students touch the different bars.)*
4. Guide students in making comparisons, using the visual display, not the numerical information.	
a. Look at the first two bars. Was more cotton produced in 1800 or 1810?	*"1810"*
Was more cotton produced in 1850 or 1859?	*"1859"*
b. Did cotton production go up or down from 1800 to 1859?	*"Up"*
When was cotton production greatest?	*"1859"*
5. Guide students in making comparisons using the numerical information.	
a. Now, look at the numbers on the left side of the bar graph. We can figure out the millions of bales of cotton by looking at these numbers.	
b. Find the highest bar. Now, look over at the numbers on the left side. A little more than 4 million bales of cotton were produced in 1859.	
c. Find the bar for 1850. Now, look at the numbers on the left side.	*"2 billion"*
Approximately, how many millions of bales of cotton were produced in 1850?	
Find the bar labeled 1840. Approximately, how many millions of bales were produced in 1840?	*"1 billion"*
6. Guide students in making inferences based on the information reported in the graph.	
a. In the 1800s, did the production of cotton go up or down?	*"Up"*
b. Slaves were used in all aspects of cotton production. In which of these years would the plantation owners need the most slaves?	*"1859"*
Do you think the end of slavery would have threatened the plantation owners? Why?	*"Yes"*

If these skills are taught early in the year, the teacher can focus on interpreting information, forming conclusions, making comparisons, and/or using the information for problem solving when graphics for a specific chapter are introduced. The teacher can ask structured questions about the graph found in the chapter. The following questions were asked about a bar graph on automobile production from 1900 to 1929: What type of graph is this? What is the title of the graph? What will this graph be about? What do the numbers at the bottom of the graph refer to? What do the numbers on the left side of the graph refer to? In which time period were the most cars produced? In which time period were the fewest number of cars produced? Approximately how many cars were produced between 1910 and 1919? Approximately how many cars were produced between 1920 and 1929? How many more cars were produced in the years 1920–1929 than 1910–1909? Do you think that car production would be higher today? Why?

In addition to instruction on reading and interpreting graphic aids, students must be taught *when* to refer to graphic material and how to move from discourse to the graphic aid and back. Authors use different techniques to direct the reader's attention to graphic material: explicit directions to refer to graphic material (e.g., "see diagram," "the scale shown in the margin"), general discussion of the graphic material within the discourse, and symbols that appear in the text to indicate to what graphic material a statement refers.

Naive readers could be taught to read the discourse until the author refers to a graphic aid, place their finger at that place in the discourse, refer to the graphic material, examine the material carefully reading all captions, and then resume reading. The critical concept to convey to students is that in content area material, you don't skip over graphs, maps, diagrams, charts, pictures, and other illustrations. You examine them carefully.

Previewing the Selection

Another prereading activity for expository reading involves previewing information-laden sections of the chapter, such as the chapter title, introduction, headings, subheadings, summaries, and end-of-chapter questions. Through this preview, the reader gains an idea of the content material covered in the chapter and the organization of that information, thus developing a framework for reading the selection.

Previewing the chapter should be teacher guided when the content or organizational structure is complex, the textbook is new to the reader, the readers are less skilled in expository reading, or the information presented in the chapter is beyond students' prior knowledge. Aukerman's (1972) teacher-guided Survey Technique consists of (1) analyzing the chapter title, (2) analyzing the subtitles, (3) analyzing the visual aids, (4) reading the introductory paragraph, (5) reading the concluding paragraph, and (6) deriving the main idea. Similarly, Archer and Gleason (1989) developed a teacher-guided survey procedure called *Warm-up*. When using this strategy, the teacher guides students in examining different parts of the chapter and formulating predictions as to the major points to be learned from the chapter. This teaching procedure is outlined in Figure 27.9.

As children become more familiar with the text organization and general content of the book, the teacher may simply review the sections to be previewed to gain a global understanding of the content. Students can then be given a structured activity, such as the worksheet found in Table 27.11 to complete by themselves or with a partner. When all students have previewed

Figure 27.9   Format for Previewing a Chapter: Warm-up

Warm-up

Before you read a chapter in your science, social studies, or health book, **warm up**. Use these steps to find out what the chapter is about <u>before</u> you begin to read.

Step 1:   Read the TITLE of the chapter and the INTRODUCTION.
Step 2:   Read the HEADINGS and SUBHEADINGS.
Step 3:   Read the CHAPTER SUMMARY.
Step 4:   Read the QUESTIONS at the end of the chapter.
Step 5:   Say to yourself, "This chapter will talk about. . . ."

Example Lesson

(This format can be adapted to any chapter in an expository chapter. Distribute copies of the warm-up strategy to students before the previewing activity.)

1.   Today we will learn how to *warm up* before reading a chapter in a book. People often warm up before doing an activity. If you go to a baseball game, you see players throwing the ball back and forth and swinging the bat. Before a football game, you see players exercising to warm up their muscles before they start playing the game. Can you think of some other times that people warm up before doing an activity?

2.   Before you read a section in a textbook, you need to warm up your mind, just as you warm up your body before an athletic event. When you warm up for reading, you find out what the chapter is about. Let's find out *how* to warm up for reading.

3.   Read Step 1.—*Read the title of the chapter and the introduction.*—We read the chapter title and the introduction to learn what the chapter is about. Read the title of the chapter.—What will this chapter be about?—(Write the title on the chalkboard.)—Next, we read the the introduction. (Do it.) What will this chapter be about?

4.   Read Step 2.—*Read the headings and subheadings.*—Each chapter is divided into parts. These parts have titles called headings and subheadings. We read the headings and subheadings to find out more about what we are going to read. Find the first heading.—What is the first heading?—So, what will this section of the chapter be about?—(Write the heading on the chalkboard. Continue until all headings and subheadings have been read and written on the chalkboard.)

5.   Read Step 3.—*Read the chapter summary.*—Next, we read the summary. Find the summary at the end of the chapter.—Follow along as I read the summary. (Do it.) Tell me some important ideas in this chapter.—As we read the chapter, we will want to learn more about these ideas.

6.   Read Step 4.—*Read the questions at the end of the chapter.*—This is the most important part of **warm-up**. Reading the questions at the end of the chapter tells you what you are supposed to learn by reading the chapter. Find the questions at the end of the chapter.—Let's read the questions. (Call on individual students to read each question.)

7.   Now, think about the information we have read. What will you learn by reading this chapter?—Let's complete Step 5 together. Tell me what this chapter will be about.

From SKILLS FOR SCHOOL SUCCESS by A. Archer and M. Gleason. Copyright 1989 by Curriculum Associates. Reprinted by permission.

Table 27.11 Student Worksheet for Previewing Chapter

Directions: As you warm up with your partner, fill in the blanks.

Step 1. **Read the title of the chapter and the introduction.**

What is the title of this chapter?_____

Does this chapter have an introduction?_____

Based on the title and the introduction, what is this chapter about?

_____

Step 2. **Read the headings and subheadings.**

List the headings and subheadings you found in this chapter.

_____

_____

_____

_____

Step 3. **Read the chapter summary.**

Does this chapter have a summary?_____

Based on the summary, what are two things that you will learn in this chapter?

_____

_____

Step 4. **Read the questions at the end of the chapter.**

Does this chapter have questions at the end?

_____

Based on the questions, what are two things that you will learn in this chapter?

_____

_____

Step 5. **Tell yourself, "This chapter will talk about. . . ."**

Finish this sentence. This chapter will talk about

_____

_____

the chapter, the teacher and the students can discuss the structure of the chapter and the information that is to be gained by reading the chapter.

Reading Activities

Once students have been properly prepared for reading the passage, the teacher must select a format for the actual passage reading. The type of reading activity depends on the students' reading and comprehension skills and their experience with expository reading. For example, if the students were third-grade students reading the initial chapters of a science textbook, the teacher might choose a teacher-directed procedure to maximize the amount of guidance given students. As students progress, the teacher might involve the students in a dialogue procedure (reciprocal teaching) in which the students participate as "teachers," asking other students questions about the content area material. The teacher might also maximize student participation by having students read with a partner, retelling the critical information to their partner. Finally, as students' experience with expository materials increase, the teacher could give the students an independent reading/learning strategy that can be used for any expository reading.

While the options for reading activities are great, four procedures will be stressed in this section: (1) guided reading, (2) reciprocal teaching, (3) partner reading, and (4) learning strategies. All four reading activities will be modeled using an expository passage about fish. Read the passage in Figure 27.10 before continuing with this section.

Guided Reading

When working with young students, such as those having difficulty with comprehension or new to a content area textbook, the teacher can use a teacher-directed strategy, *guided reading*, similar to the reading formats presented earlier in the book for narrative reading. In this procedure, the teacher presents a guided-reading question or directive (e.g., "Read to find out . . .") concerning a paragraph or series of paragraphs in the content area material.

Figure 27.10   Expository Text Material

Fish

Fish are the simplest group of vertebrates. They are also the largest group of vertebrates. All fish have similar characteristics. They all have skeletons. Most of the fish you have seen have skeletons made of bone. A few have skeletons made of cartilage (KART ul ihj).

Cartilage is a firm, flexible substance that forms parts of some skeletons. Sharks and rays have cartilage instead of bone. Your body has both bone and cartilage. Feel the tip of your nose. Wiggle it. Compare the tip of your nose to the upper part of your nose. How does the cartilage feel? Where else on your head can you feel cartilage?

Fish also have scales. **Scales** are thin, smooth pieces of a bonelike material that cover the entire body of the fish. Each scale overlaps another scale. The tough, hard scales help protect fish. How are the scales like a coat of armor?

Doug Martin

Figure 27.10   Continued

Central Ohio School of Diving (Joey Jacques)

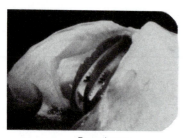

Russ Lappa

Fish live in water. **Gills** are organs through which fish get oxygen from the water. You can see the gills on the side of the fish's head through the openings or slits. As water enters the mouth, it passes over the gills. Oxygen in the water moves into the gills. Carbon dioxide from the body is given off through the gills. The water then passes out of the body through the slits. Find the slits visible on the fish in the pictures. The gills are beneath the slits.

Fish are cold-blooded animals. **Cold-blooded animals** have a body temperature the same as their environment. For example, fish living in warm water have a warm body temperature. Fish living in cold water have a cold body temperature.

Most fish have fins which are bony limbs covered with thin skin. Fish use fins and body movements to move through the water. Count the fins on the fish. How many does it have? Where are the fins located?

This question is meant to direct students' attention to the critical content in the segment of discourse. Next, the students read the segment silently, or with very poor readers, silently and then orally. After the segment has been read, the teacher asks students questions concerning the main idea of the segment and any critical facts or details that the teacher wishes the students to retain.

To optimize this procedure, the teacher should structure the questions to model the type of self-questioning students should engage in when reading independently. For example, the teacher might begin by asking students the topic of the segment. Next, the teacher might ask students to summarize the information reported about the topic, asking them to stress the most important information. Next, the teacher could ask questions to help students clarify any confusing aspects of the passage. Finally, the teacher could ask students to predict what would be reported in the remaining discourse. As you will see when you examine the remaining reading activities, this type of questioning would prepare students for participation in *reciprocal teaching,* for the verbal retell in the *partner reading,* and for the rehearsal steps in *learning strategies.* An example of guided reading is found in Table 27.12.

Reciprocal Teaching

In reciprocal teaching (Palincsar, 1984; Palincsar & Brown, 1984; Palincsar & Brown, 1986; Palincsar, Ogle, Jones, & Carr, 1986), the reading activity proceeds in much the same manner as in guided reading; however, the burden of asking questions on the content is shared by the teacher and the students. The students are directly taught four strategies: questioning, summarizing, clarifying, and predicting. Once these strategies have been taught, students, as well as the teacher, ask questions on the content. In this manner, they engage in a dialogue concerning the chapter content. The four strategies are explained below:

- **Question generating:** Using this strategy, the students identify important information within the content, formulate questions concerning this content, and address the questions to peers. Since students are involved in posing as well as answering, the questions, they are more involved than if only responding to teacher-generated questions.

- **Summarizing:** Here the students are to summarize the information in the segment that has been read, reporting the most important information. As reading proceeds, the students are asked to summarize content across paragraphs and sections of the passage.

- **Clarifying:** Using the clarifying strategy, the students identify elements of the segment that they have read that are unclear (e.g., vocabulary that is unknown) so that they can respond appropriately to facilitate comprehension (ask for help or reread the material).

- **Predicting:** Using this strategy, the students predict what the author will discuss in subsequent paragraphs or sections of the discourse. To do this, students use their prior knowledge of the topic and the information that has already been presented in the discourse.

As Palincsar and Brown (1986) discuss, each of these strategies must be taught before they are used in reciprocal dialogue. Once each of the strategies has been introduced and students have demonstrated some competency with each, the teacher models the use of the strategies within the context of reading an expository passage.

Table 27.12   Format for Teacher-directed, Guided Reading

Teacher	Students
1. Students read the heading or subheading. The teacher asks them to tell what the section will talk about.	
a. Read the heading.	*"fish"*
b. What will this section of the chapter talk about?	*"fish"*
2. The teacher directs students to read a segment of the selection, generally a paragraph or a series of paragraphs on the same topic. The segment may be read silently, or the teacher can have the segment read silently and then orally when working with students having decoding difficulties. Before the segment is read, the teacher presents a guided-reading question or directive.	*(Students read the paragraph silently.)*
a. Read the first paragraph to find out what is the same about all fish.	
b. Look up when you have finished reading.	
3. The teacher asks structured questions about the segment's content. The questions should help students to identify the topic of the paragraph and summarize the critical information. In addition, questions could help students clarify confusing elements of the segment and to predict what might be discussed in subsequent segments.	
a. Tell me in a word or phrase what this whole paragraph talked about.	*"fish"*
b. Yes, it talked about fish. Tell some of the important things that it said about fish.	*"That fish are the largest group of vertebrates."*
c. From our past reading, what are vertebrates?	*"Animals with backbones."*
d. What other important thing did this paragraph tell us about fish?	*"That all fish have skeletons."*
e. Excellent. Yes, this paragraph talked about fish. It said that fish are the largest group of vertebrates and that all fish have skeletons.	
f. What are most fish skeletons made from?	*"bone"*
g. What are some fish skeletons made from?	*"cartilage"*
h. Did the paragraph tell us what cartilage is?	*"No."*
i. What do you think we will learn about in the next paragraph?	*"cartilage"*
j. You all know something about fish. Tell me some of the things that we might learn about fish.	*"Fish have scales. About the fins on fish. About how fish swim."*

Table 27.12 Continued

Teacher	Students

4. Repeat this procedure for the remaining paragraphs or segments in the passage.

5. When the selection has been read, ask students questions over the entire selection that will assist them in summarizing the information and give them practice in rehearsing the critical information.

a. Let's review what we learned in this selection. Fish are the largest group of vertebrates. What do all fish have?

"skeletons"

b. What two materials can the skeletons be made of?

"bone and cartilage"

c. What is cartilage?

"Flexible stuff like the tip of your nose."

d. What covers the body of fish?

"scales"

"They protect the body of fish."

e. How do the scales help fish?

f. What organs help fish get oxygen from the water?

"gills"

g. Are fish warm- or cold-blooded animals?

"cold-blooded"

h. What are cold-blooded animals?

"Animals that have the same temperature as their environment."

i. So if a fish lives in cold water, what would be the temperature of the fish?

"cold"

j. Fish don't have arms or legs, but they do have limbs. What are those limbs called?

"fins"

k. How do fins help fish?

"They help them move through the water."

6. If time permits, have students retell the content of the selection to a partner. When the partner is done, have their partner add any information that was deleted. This will give your students practice in summarizing the information. This skill can be used in reciprocal teaching, partner reading, and in the independent-learning strategies using verbal rehearsal.

a. Partner #1, tell your partner what you learned about fish.

(Student retells content to partner.)

b. Partner #2, tell your partner any information that they left out.

(Student tells additional information to his/her partner.)

Initially, the teacher leads the dialogue, modeling how the strategies can be used during reading. As instruction proceeds, more responsibility for initiating questions and maintaining the dialogue is transferred to the students. Over time, students take more responsibility for the dialogue, but the teacher continues to guide them in using the strategies. Using the passage on fish, the dialogue (shown in Table 27.13) might result when the teacher and students engage in reciprocal teaching.

Partner Reading

As Palincsar and Brown, Larson and Dansereau (1986) were concerned with actively engaging students in the reading process. However, they used paired-student learning rather than teacher-student dialogue to meet this goal. Using their procedure, students silently read a designated portion of the chapter. After reading, one of the partners acts as "recaller" and the other as "listener." The recaller orally retells the content of what was read without looking back at the textbook. The listener can interrupt only to ask for clarification. When the recaller has completed the retell, the listener does two things. First, the listener can correct any misunderstandings that the recaller has reported. Second, the listener can add any information that the recaller deleted. When this elaboration process is completed, the students read the next portion of the chapter.

Table 27.13   Example Dialogue Resulting from the Use of Reciprocal Teaching

(Following silent reading of paragraph #1.)

Teacher:	Who will be our teacher?
Student 1:	My question is, how are fish all the same?
Student 2:	They all have skeletons.
Student 1:	What are the skeletons made out of?
Student 3:	They are made out of bone.
Student 4:	They are also made out of cartilage.
Student 1:	For my summary now: This paragraph was about fish. All fish have skeletons. Some of the skeletons are made out of bone. Other fish skeletons are made out of cartilage.
Teacher:	Are there any things that need to be clarified?
Student 1:	I think we need to clarify cartilage.
Teacher:	Is cartilage defined in the paragraph?
Student 1:	No.
Teacher:	What do you predict the authors will talk about in the next paragraph?
Student 5:	Cartilage.
Student 1:	Yes, I predict the authors will tell us what cartilage is.
Teacher:	Can you predict any other things that the authors might tell us about fish?
Student 6:	They might tell us about how fish move.
Student 7:	Maybe they will tell us about parts of fish, like the fins.
Student 8:	I bet they will tell us about different kinds of fish.
Teacher:	Those are excellent predictions. Let's read the next paragraph and see if any of your predictions are true.

Then, the partners exchange roles and repeat the retell and elaboration procedures.

When using this procedure with naive learners, the teacher would need to model structured retell. The teacher should first read a paragraph; then, she should retell the content by stating the topic of the paragraph, then giving the important details using his/her own words. For example, using the first paragraph in the article about fish, the teacher might retell the content in this manner, "This paragraph talked about fish. It said that all fish are vertebrates and have skeletons. Their skeletons can be made from bone or cartilage." This modeling should be repeated with many paragraphs to ensure that students understand the retelling procedure. Once retelling has been modeled, guided practice should be provided where students retell paragraph content to the class and the teacher provides feedback on the adequacy of the paraphrasing. When students demonstrate facility with retelling, they can work with a partner. However, the teacher must carefully monitor students to ensure on-task behavior and the appropriate use of procedures.

Use of Independent Learning Strategies

Our ultimate goal in content area reading, as in all areas of instruction, is to develop independent students who can analyze a task, devise a plan for attacking that task, carry out the plan, and evaluate their own performance. One way to accomplish this goal is to teach our students task-specific *learning strategies*. While learning strategies are defined in many ways throughout the literature, we are referring to systematic, student-directed procedures for responding to a specific type of task (e.g., reading expository materials). Learning strategies generally involve a series of steps that the student performs. These steps are meant to enhance students' cognition and attention to critical variables (e.g., important concepts in the expository material) and to increase metacognition, thinking about your thinking, through self-monitoring, self-evaluation, and self-correction.

Many learning strategies for reading expository materials have been developed and studied with elementary and secondary students (e.g., Adams, Carnine, & Gersten, 1982; Schumaker, Denton, & Deshler, 1984; Schumaker, Deshler, Alley, Warner, & Denton; Manzo, 1969). However, there are some similarities between these strategies. First, all of the strategies attempt to make students more actively involved in the reading process. Instead of passively reading and rereading the chapter, students are asked to formulate questions, take notes on the content, or verbally paraphrase the critical information. Second, all strategies attempt to direct the student's attention to the most important concepts, ideas, and details. Finally, the learning strategies for content area reading engage the student in some type of information rehearsal and practice involving either reciting or writing down critical information. We will explore two types of expository learning strategies: those that involve verbal rehearsal and those that involve written rehearsal.

Verbal Rehearsal Strategies

Since Robinson's development of SQ3R (Survey, Question, Read, Recite, Review) in 1941, many similar strategies involving verbal rehearsal or recitation have been developed for use with elementary and secondary students (Archer & Gleason, 1989; Adams, Carnine, & Gersten, 1982; Burmeister, 1974; Laurita, 1972; Manzo, 1969; Schumaker, Deshler, Alley, Warner, & Denton, 1982). One of these strategies, *active reading*, is particularly appropriate for elementary students and low-performing secondary students because of its simplicity. The steps in active reading are outlined in Figure 27.11.

Using active reading, the student reads a single paragraph, cover the paragraph, recite the important information, then check his/her statement of the critical information by examining the paragraph again. This process continues for the entire selection. The student is actively involved in the reading process through a number of overt behaviors: reading the material, placing his/her hand over the material, and verbally reciting the content. Cognition (thinking about the information) is enhanced through verbal rehearsal; metacognition (thinking about your thinking) is activated in the check step, where students evaluate their recitation.

As Archer and Gleason (1989) outline in their instructional materials, it is important to teach students verbally to retell content before the strategy is introduced. First, they teach students to identify the topics for paragraphs. Once students can say a word or phrase topic for a paragraph, then they are taught to identify critical details in the paragraph and to retell the topic and details in their own words. When students can retell paragraph content, the entire strategy is modeled; guided practice is provided until proficiency is reached, then students practice the strategy independently.

Written Rehearsal Strategies

Another way actively to involve students in the reading of expository material is to have them take notes on the critical content. When students take notes, they have to attend closely to the author's message and evaluate what information is important and should be recorded. They emerge from notetaking with a short summary of

---

Figure 27.11　　Active Reading Procedure

Active Reading

R = Read

Read a paragraph.
Think about the topic.
Think about the important details.

C = Cover

Cover the material with your hand.

R = Recite

Tell yourself what you have read.
Say the topic.
Say the important details.
Say it in your own words.

C = Check

Lift your hand and check.
If you forget something important, begin again.

From SKILLS FOR SCHOOL SUCCESS by A. Archer and M. Gleason. Copyright 1989 by Curriculum Associates. Reprinted by permission.

---

the content that can be used in subsequent study, writing a paragraph summary of the content, answering chapter questions, or writing a report.

When selecting a notetaking style to teach students, it is important that the form does not take attention from the content. Often teachers introduce formal outlining in which the relationship of ideas in the passage are shown through indentation, numbers (Roman and Arabic), and letters (upper- and lower-case). While outlining might help students organize their *own* ideas in preparation for a speech or writing a paper, it is not an appropriate form when taking notes on written material since many students will be concerned about the appropriate designation (e.g., Should this be a Roman numeral I, a capital A, or a lower-case a?) rather than the author's information. Instead, a simple form of notetaking in which the subordination of ideas is illustrated through systematic indentation of topics and supporting details should be taught. This system is far less complex than parallel systems using number and letter designations, allowing the student to focus on the relationships between ideas rather than the formality of the outlining system.

One simple system of notetaking developed by Archer and Gleason (1989) is particularly appropriate for elementary students and lower-performing students because the notes follow the structure of the text material and again use the paragraph as the unit of analysis. In this system, students record the heading or subheading in the center of the paper followed by the corresponding page number. Next, students take notes on each paragraph in the section. First, they record a topic for the paragraph. Then, they indent and record the important details in the paragraph. When the notes have been completed and checked for clarity, students go back and record questions in the left-hand margin for each of the paragraphs. Later, when studying their notes, students are taught to cover their notes, ask themselves the question, recite the answer, then check their verbal answer with their notes (see example notes in Table 27.14).

As with all complex skills, careful instruction on notetaking should be given. First, students will need training in identifying paragraph topics and critical details. Next, the notetaking procedure should be modeled. The teacher should read a paragraph, determine the topic of the paragraph and record it on the board or overhead, then indent and record critical details. As you model, "think out loud," telling students why the topic and details were chosen. Stress that the notes should be brief and written in their own words. Students can then be asked to copy your example notes to reinforce the organization of ideas through indentation.

After modeling notetaking, lead your students in taking notes. Have them read a paragraph and determine a paragraph topic. Ask students to suggest possible topics and select one topic. Write the topic on the board or overhead transparency and have students record it on their papers. Next, have students suggest important passage details and provide feedback on their selections. Have students indent and record the important details under the topic. Again, stress brevity and paraphrasing rather than copying as they record their details. This type of guided practice should be provided for many days until students show proficiency in this skill. At this point, independent practice should be provided and students should be expected to take notes on information-laden portions of their chapters. These same instructional procedures can be used to teach *mapping*, an alternative notetaking system that illustrates the subordination of ideas through a visual display (see Figure 27.12 for an example of mapping).

Table 27.14   Example of Indentation Notes

These notes follow the structure of the text material. Notes are taken on each paragraph with a topic and the important details recorded.

Fish

Fish Group
  —simplest group of vertebrates
  —largest group
  —have skeletons
      —bone
    —cartilage

Cartilage
  —firm, flexible
  —some fish skeletons
  —sharks & rays

Scales
  —thin, smooth, bonelike material
  —cover fish
      —scales overlap
      —protect fish

Gills
  —organs that get oxygen from water
      —water comes into mouth
      —oxygen goes into gills
      —water goes out through slits

Cold-blooded
  —temperature same as environment
  —warm water = warm body

Fins
  —limb covered with skin
  —use to move through water

Notetaking will only benefit students if they are required to take notes and actually study the notes. While collection and grading of students' notes is not necessary, completion and non-completion of required notes should be recorded in the gradebook to increase accountability. Students should also be taught how to study their notes. They can use a verbal-rehearsal strategy (e.g., Read, Cover, Recite, Check) or a self-questioning strategy (e.g., Read your question. Answer the question. Check your answer with your notes). Class activities can also be structured for use of the notes. The teacher can ask questions on the content and have students locate the answers in their notes. Similarly, students can ask questions and have their peers locate the answers in their notes. Both of these procedures provide students practice in using their notes and feedback on the adequacy of those notes.

Postreading Activities

The goal of postreading activities is to integrate, synthesize, and consolidate the information that has been read in the selection. Of many postreading activities (e.g., filling in a blank concept map, discussing content using class notes, developing a visual representation of the information), two postreading activities have particular merit: (1) answering written questions and (2) writing a summary of the content. In both cases, the students have an opportunity to study and practice the important information once again and to for-

Figure 27.12   Example of Mapping

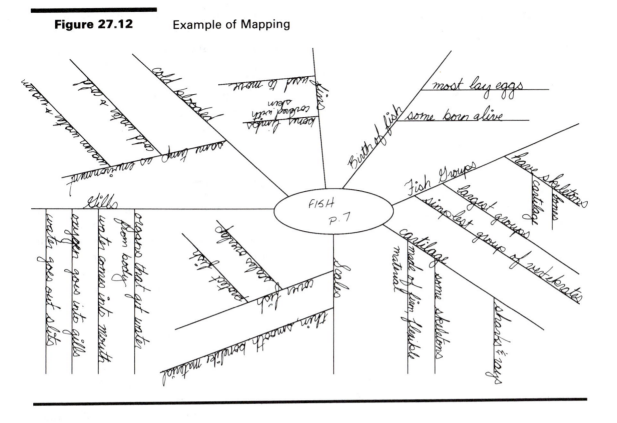

Written Questions

After reading a passage, students can be assigned written questions on the passage content. To make this activity valuable to students, the teacher should write or select questions that match the following criteria. The questions should (1) stress major concepts presented in the material, not insignificant facts, (2) include both literal- and inferential-comprehension responses, (3) go beyond yes and no responses, and (4) be well worded to promote ease of interpretation. Since one of the purposes of the questions is to ascertain passage understanding, the ma-jority of questions should be "passage dependent," that is, the answers should be based on passage information rather than solely on experiential background. The answers should also involve significant concepts and relationships. Often teach-ers and authors write questions that focus on insignificant facts rather than main ideas. As a result, students become detail seekers who cannot separate the impor-tant from the unimportant. Teachers can change this pattern through the prudent selection of questions. Ask yourself, "What do I *really* want the students to remember from this selection?"

Many students lack a strategy for an-swering chapter questions. For example, they may not read the questions carefully or have a procedure for locating the answer

mulate a written product that can be used in subsequent study.

within the chapter. In addition, many students write incomplete sentence answers that do not incorporate wording from the question. To alleviate these problems, students should be taught a specific learning strategy for answering written questions. Using the strategy developed by Archer and Gleason (1989), students are taught to read the question carefully and to change the question into part of the answer and write it down. This step has many benefits. First, it gives the students a way to get the task started. Second, the resulting answer will be a complete sentence and will reflect the question's wording. Finally, changing the question into part of the answer encourages the student to contemplate the question before referring to the chapter. This reduces the possibility of an answer that appears to have no relationship to the question. Next, students locate the section of the chapter that talks about the topic by examining the headings and subheadings. Finally, students locate and complete the answer (see Table 27.15).

As with other learning strategies, the teacher should present the steps in the strategy, model the strategy, guide students in practicing the strategy, and provide independent practice. If this strategy is carefully taught and practiced, the accuracy and quality of students' answers will increase significantly. Once this strategy has been taught, most teachers no longer require that students copy the question since the question wording is incorporated into the answer.

Written Summaries

Writing a summary on a passage is an excellent postreading activity for a number of reasons. First, summarizing can better help the students understand the organization of the text material. Second, it provides students with practice in determining main ideas and critical concepts in the selection. Third, it provides students needed practice in expressive writing. Finally, the effort to identify critical content during the summarizing process can help students remember those ideas (Murrell & Surber, 1987).

Despite its many benefits, summarizing is a difficult skill that even high-school students may not be able to do proficiently (Brown & Day, 1983; Hare & Borchardt, 1984). Summarizing places great demands

---

Table 27.15   Strategy for Answering Chapter Questions

Answering Chapter Questions

Use this strategy when you need to answer questions in your science, social studies, or health book. Remember, words from the question can be used in your answer.

Step 1:   Read the question carefully.

Step 2:   Change the question into part of the answer and write it down.

Step 3:   Locate the section of the chapter that talks about the topic. Use the headings and subheadings to help you find the section of the chapter that talks about the topic.

Step 4:   Read the section of the chapter until you find the answer.

Step 5:   Complete the answer.

From SKILLS FOR SCHOOL SUCCESS by A. Archer and M. Gleason. Copyright 1989 by Curriculum Associates. Reprinted by permission.

on the student. The student must decide what information should be included in the summary, what information should be deleted, and how the information should be organized and reworded. Young and low-performing students are likely to have difficulty deciding what to include and how to condense the information into a concise summary.

Sheinker and Sheinker (1989) have developed a powerful learning strategy to guide students in summarizing content area material. Their strategy involves the following steps: (1) skim a passage; (2) list key points; (3) combine related points into single statements; (4) cross out least important points; (5) reread list; (6) combine and cross out to condense points; (7) number remaining points in logical order; and (8) write points into paragraph in numbered order (Sheinker & Sheinker, 1989, p. 135). The steps in this process are illustrated in Figures 27.13, 27.14, and 27.15. This step-by-step strategy will benefit all students in learning this important, but difficult skill.

Figure 27.13   Initial Steps in Writing a Summary

Following the strategy developed by Sheinker and Sheinker (1989), students skim the chapter and list key points. Next, they combine related points that could be written as single statements. Then, they eliminate least important points by crossing them out. The first four steps in the strategy are illustrated in this example.

Figure 27.14   Additional Steps in Writing a Summary

Fish

① Fish are vertebrates.

② (All fish have skeletons.)
~~The skeletons are~~ made of bone
  or cartilage.
~~Cartilage is like the tip of my nose.~~

③ Fish have scales.
  (Scales (that) cover ~~the body of the fish~~ and
   Scales protect the body of the fish.

   ~~(Gills are organs.)~~
⑥ Gills: special (organs) of fish
   ~~remove~~ oxygen from the water.

④ Fish are cold-~~blooded~~ animals.

⑤ Fish use fins to move through water.

In completing their written summary, students next reread their list and combine and cross out additional points to condense further their list. Next, they renumber the points in a logical order. These steps are illustrated in this example.

In the instructional procedures outlined by Sheinker and Sheinker, the teacher introduces the purpose of summarizing, situations in which summarizing would be helpful, and a model summary. In a series of carefully structured lessons, the teacher introduces the steps in the strategy, a rationale for each step, and provides drill on the strategy steps. Next, the students write a written summary on a selection following the prescribed steps. Then, all class members brainstorm through the steps, creating a group summary. Students compare their written summary to that generated by the group. This type of instruction is repeated until the students can write summaries both accurately and fluently.

Review Procedures

Feedback on written assignments should be provided through answer keys, whole class or small group corrections, or through either written or verbal teacher feedback. Students should be required to complete incorrect or incomplete responses using their textbook. Performance

Figure 27.15   Paragraph Summary of Key Points

Fish

Fish are vertebrates. All fish have skeletons made of bone or cartilage. They have scales that cover and protect their bodies. Fish are cold-blooded animals that use fins to move through the water. Gills, special organs of fish, remove oxygen from the water.

Finally, the student composes a paragraph summary by writing the listed points into a paragraph in the numbered order.

on written exercises should be recorded on some type of chart, grade sheet, or assignment sheet. All students should be performing at about a 90% accuracy level. If students are not performing at this level, teachers should increase the preparatory activities and the amount of practice. Typically, lower performing students function at a low accuracy level because the assignments presented are too difficult and/or the students do not receive adequate preparation. When students constantly encounter failure, they are likely to develop faulty study habits (random answering just to finish an assignment) and negative attitudes.

Whole class or small group discussion designed to firm up difficult concepts can follow individual corrections. The teacher may pose additional literal and inferential questions on the content, elicit verbal answers, and engage the children in discussion. Questions recorded during the chapter preview can be used. To clarify concepts, the teacher may visually summarize information using a table, chart, graph, time line, or flow chart.

In addition to firming up difficult concepts immediately after completion of passage reading and written assignments, critical concepts and relationships should be reviewed in subsequent lessons through teacher-posed verbal questions, written items on later written assignments, or on daily quizzes. End-of-chapter or unit tests can also be used to insure review of critical concepts. Only through cumulative review will students learn that information presented in the content area textbook is important and should be retained beyond completion of daily assignments.

Summary

Reading in content area textbooks presents new challenges to intermediate students due to the divergence of expository material from more familiar narrative or story material. Students need explicit instruction on the use of content area textbooks that not only promotes mastery of information presented in the text, but also assists students in the acquisition of critical-reading study skills that can be used independently. Preparation for content area lessons begins with the teacher's determination of the information in the selection that should be mastered by the students. This information is translated into a chapter examination and into written assignments that will be completed during or after reading of the selection. The assignments may consist of written questions, directions for completing a written summary, or a visual representation of the information, such as a chart, graph, time line, outline, or concept diagram. The chapter should also be divided into teachable units.

When the critical information has been determined and the written assignment either designed by the teacher or selected from the materials accompanying the content area textbook, the teacher can prepare students for reading of the selection. Preparatory activities may include preteaching of vocabulary (decoding and meanings), introduction of critical graphics, previewing the selection, instruction on the structure of the passage, and preteaching of concepts through concept diagrams or maps and feature analysis procedures. The amount and type of preparation for passage reading should be adjusted to accomodate the individual differences among students with more preparation given to low-performing students. As the students become more competent content area readers, the amount of preparation should be gradually faded, leading to independent reading of the selections.

Following preparation for passage reading, students should read the selection through guided, reciprocal, partner, or independent silent reading and use of learning strategies, then complete written exercises on the material. Students should be taught how to take notes, answer questions, and write summaries. When the written assignments are complete, corrections, either group or individual, should be given followed by students correcting any incorrect or inadequate answers. Additional follow-up activities to extend or review critical concepts should also be included.

Application Exercises

Select a chapter in a science, social studies, or health textbook. Complete the following exercises.

Teacher Preparation for Instruction

1. Read the chapter carefully. Determine the critical concepts, vocabulary, general understandings, facts, etc. that you want students to gain from reading the chapter. Write a content analysis similar to that found in Table 27.1.

2. Write or adapt a test for the chapter. Be certain that your test focuses on critical content and uses appropriate items to measure the content.

3. Divide the chapter into teachable segments. Be certain that each segment represents connected discourse on a specific topic and can be taught in one class session.

Prereading Activities

Complete the remaining activities for one segment of the chapter.

1. Reread the segment of the chapter and list words that would be difficult to decode. For each of the words, tell how you would introduce the pronunciation of the word (e.g., as a whole word; by precorrecting affixes; by indicating parts of the word).

2. Select one critical vocabulary concept from the segment. Write an instructional script similar to that found in Table 27.2 for teaching the vocabulary concept.

3. Select another vocabulary concept from the segment. Design a concept diagram (see Table 27.3) that could be used in teaching the concept.

4. Design a concept map that could be used visually to present the critical content within the segment or within the entire chapter. Be certain that the structure of your concept map matches the structure of the discourse (e.g., hierarchy, diagram, compare-contrast, timeline, or process/cycle).

5. For each paragraph or series of related paragraphs in your text selection, write questions that could be used in the guided reading procedure. See Step 3 of Table 27.12 for example questions.

6. Write example notes for your text selection using the indented notetaking and the mapping styles.

Postreading Activities

1. Write a set of questions that students can complete after passage reading. Be certain that your questions focus on the critical concepts delineated in your content analysis.

2. Create a series of examples that can be used in teaching summary writing. List the key points from your selection. Next, combine related points into single statements and cross out the least important points. Then, condense points further by combining and deleting statements. Number the remaining points in a logical order. Finally, write a summary of the selection.

Chapter

Using Commercial Materials in Comprehension Instruction

The main source of materials used in classrooms are the comprehension components of basal reading programs. The versions of the basal programs published in the late 1980s showed significant improvement in the teaching of comprehension. Specifically, many workbook activities of questionable value were deleted and more systematic introduction of new skills was provided. Despite the improvements, nearly all basal programs will require significant modifications to make them effective tools for teaching the instructionally naive learner.

Problems with Basal Programs

Most basal reading programs have what can be referred to as "too little of too much." In an effort to keep their products competitive on the marketplace, publishers include a wide range of activities. It is not unusual to see a 150-page student workbook include 100 types of activities. The problem this structure creates for the instructionally naive student and many average students is that they do not receive adequate practice to develop mastery and do not receive enough review to facilitate retention.

A second major problem found in basal workbooks is that too much is introduced at one time. For example, a program might introduce singular and plural possessives (a boy's hat, a boy's hats, the boys' hats) in a short span. The fast introduction results in student and teacher frustration.

A third problem is the lack of guidance provided for the teacher regarding how to teach particular skills. Teaching suggestions will often be vague. Clear, concise explanations and a provision for a transition from structured to independent will not be provided in the teacher's guides.

This chapter will provide suggestions for using commercial materials to provide efficient and humane comprehension teaching.

Components of a Comprehension Lesson

A basal program has two main components: the basal text stories, used as a base for applying comprehension skills, and the worksheets, used to teach specific comprehension skills.

The teacher can structure story-related comprehension by preteaching critical vocabulary and information, carefully controlling the type of questions asked during story reading, and preparing worksheet exercises to test the students' comprehension of the story.

Most basal reading programs now have provisions for teaching vocabulary that is to appear in an upcoming story. Teachers working with instructionally naive students should examine stories at least several days prior to having students read the passage. The teacher should note the words that students are not likely to know the meaning of. The teacher should then compare these words with the words the program presents. If there is a discrepancy, the teacher should thereafter be prepared to supplement the vocabulary teaching in the basal program using the procedures specified in Chapter 23.

The new basal programs also provide for teaching information relevant to stories before the stories are presented. Instructionally naive students encounter difficulty because exercises students are given assume knowledge the students do not have. Again the teacher should examine stories, determine the information the student needs to comprehend the story, and compare it to the information presented by the basal program. Teaching essential information is critical for providing students with a successful learning experience.

Basal programs will list questions the teachers can ask as the students read a story. Most basals though do not include worksheets that test students on the passages they read. Such worksheets are necessary to assess if all students are in fact comprehending the passages. We recommend that teachers prepare worksheets relating to the story.

A motivation and follow-up system should be established. A motivation system includes recordkeeping provisions and a reward schedule. The recordkeeping involves recording the number of items a student answered correctly and incorrectly when doing assignments. The reward schedule involves setting up criteria for rewarding student performance. With higher performing, intrinsically motivated students, the reward can be minimal. Sending a "good-work" letter home for meeting a specified criteria (e.g., 90% or better) for specified periods (e.g., 10 lessons) will usually be sufficient. With less motivated students, a more powerful reinforcement system will be needed. In addition to letters home for good work, rewards such as stickers and extra recesses can be powerful motivators.

A follow-up system is established to ensure that students are retaught any items they miss and that provisions are made to reduce student errors in the future. A follow-up system should have the following components:

1. Papers should be marked daily.
2. Students should have to redo any items missed. Note: If students are unable to figure out an answer, they circle the item or write a question mark.
3. The teacher should inspect the items the student redid to see if they are correct.
4. The teacher helps students on items they are unable to answer correctly.

Diagnosis and Remediation

If students are not functioning at about a 90% accuracy level, teachers should determine what is causing students difficulty. There are five main reasons why students may miss items:

1. Lack of effort;
2. Decoding deficits;
3. Lack of knowledge of critical vocabulary;
4. Inability to understand directions;
5. Lack of appropriate strategy.

The first step in the diagnosis process involves setting aside a time when the students redo any items they missed on daily worksheet assignments. The students' performance on redoing the items may tell if the errors were caused by lack of effort; e.g., a student who usually is able to answer all the missed items correctly when redoing a worksheet is likely to have a motivation problem. A special procedure to increase the student's motivation should be instituted. The teacher sets up a goal of increased accuracy. The goal should involve a small improvement from the student's current level. Reaching the goal results in a reward for the entire group. "Amy worked hard. She earned a sticker for everyone." The teacher gradually increases the goal (e.g., from 75% to 80%, then to 85%, and so on). Teachers should be quite cautious in diagnosing errors as being caused by lack of effort. Sometimes students seem not to be trying when, in fact, they do not know what to do.

A second step in the diagnosis procedure involves individual testing of students who are functioning below the 90% level and who do not respond to increased motivation. Teachers have students reread missed passages and items aloud to determine whether errors were caused by decoding deficits. If the students can decode the words with minimal errors and at a rate which does not interfere with compre-

hension, the teacher will have to continue the diagnostic process. The remaining three steps can be done in any order. The teacher should start with the step that deals with the probable cause of the students' errors. One step would be to determine if a vocabulary deficit caused the problem. The teacher does this by testing the students on key words. If the problem is not vocabulary, the teacher has the students redo the item, watching them carefully to see the strategy they use and noting whether they follow the directions. Once the cause is determined, whether it involves motivation, decoding, vocabulary, directions, or strategy, remediation on the particular skill deficit should be provided.

Practice and Review

Teaching isolated comprehension skills is done to prepare students for comprehending text. As mentioned earlier, basal programs do not usually provide adequate practice and review of specific skills. Providing massed practice when a skill is introduced is critical if students are to master it. In most commercial reading programs, a new skill appears in a workbook one day and then does not appear again for several weeks. For example, in one program the initial exercise on choosing the best title appears on page 59 of the student's first workbook. Only one more exercise on selecting the best title is included in the rest of the 140-page workbook. That exercise in on page 127. This pattern of limited practice, scattered throughout a program, characterizes most basal programs. They seldom provide adequate massed practice when new skills are introduced.

Problems resulting from inadequate practice and review on a skill are difficult to remedy. One possible solution is to assign all written tasks of one type from a workbook at the same time. For example, if a program has sequencing tasks on workbook pages 18, 47, and 73, the teacher might make copies of the activities on pages 47 and 73 and present them on the same day as the task on page 18, or wait until lesson 73 and present them all. The problem with introducing worksheets from later lessons earlier is that they may contain words the students will not know. The teacher either must identify these words as the students encounter them or preteach the words as irregular words before students are assigned the worksheets.

An alternative to presenting all the items of one type at the same item is for the teacher to prepare written exercises or use exercises from supplementary comprehension programs.

In addition to providing massed practice when a skill is introduced, teachers also need to provide review after a skill is introduced. For example, when main idea is introduced, the teacher might present three main idea items every day for about two weeks. Thereafter, the teacher should include a main idea exercise each several lessons. Similarly, when any new skill appears, it should be reviewed heavily at first, then systematically reviewed.

Other Programs for Comprehension

Constructing comprehension exercises is very time consuming, especially at the intermediate level where exercises become more complex. A more practical alternative to providing adequate practice is to use supplementary comprehension materials. Many publishers produce materials designed to teach comprehension. The materials can vary from a workbook that presents a particular skill to a coordinated set of materials that present a wide range of skills at different levels.

Teachers should be very selective in choosing supplementary materials. Below are some factors to consider:

1. Significance of exercises. Does the program teach worthwhile skills? Avoid programs that present busy-work activities.

2. A progression from simple to more complex skills.

3. Readability. The readability level of the selections in each unit should be at the level designated by the publisher. If a great number of selections differ significantly from the designated grade level, the program will not be suitable for independent use by the students without extensive preteaching of difficult words and concepts.

4. Clarity of directions. When a new skill is being taught, the students should be able to concentrate on that new skill. The directions should be brief, clear, and the layout of the page simple. Simplicity of directions will allow a teacher to concentrate on the more significant skills rather than on explaining where to put answers.

Few commercial programs provide the teacher with specific in-depth guidance on how to teach skills or correct student errors. Teachers should examine teachers' guides days before they are to teach a specific skill and determine the adequacy of teaching procedures suggested in the teacher's guide. Teachers should be prepared to provide extra structure. Often it will not be possible to devise a multi-step procedure. In such cases, we recommend a modeling procedure in which the teacher tells students the correct answer for several items, then explains why the particular answer is correct but other similar answers are incorrect.

Using parts of various commercial programs to construct a comprehension sequence will be time consuming and will result in some degree of fragmentation. An ideal solution obviously is for the teacher to obtain a basal program which has incorporated the principles of effective instructional design. The SRA Reading Mastery Series (copyright 1988) is a basal reading series with materials for grades 1 through 6.

The program can serve as a model to demonstrate the careful introduction of vocabulary, specific story-related information, and specific comprehension-skill teaching into a general comprehension strategy.

In summary, keep in mind that the higher the degree of structure provided in teaching comprehension, the higher the degree of success a teacher can bring to her students. Comprehension skills, as well as decoding skills, should be taught in a manner that fosters a successful learning experience.

This research brief presents findings from experimental studies investigating the effectiveness of various direct instruction approaches for teaching reading comprehension skills, strategies, and processes. The studies included in this selective review are grouped according to the types of comprehension skills or strategies (e.g., main idea, metacomprehension, etc.) that have been investigated.

Teaching Main Idea and Summarization Skills[1]

A popular line of direct instruction research has involved teaching students to comprehend main ideas and to summarize informational text. Williams (1986; Williams, Taylor, Jarin, & Milligan, 1983) designed a program of main idea instruction for learning disabled middle-school students based on a categorization model of importance in text. The learning disabled students who received systematic, focused, main idea instruction outperformed matched non-learning disabled controls in ability to generate main-idea sentences for paragraphs and identify anomalous details. Kameenui (1986) developed an instruction-analysis program of main idea instruction for learning disabled and low-performing students, although its efficacy is yet to be tested empirically.

Baumann (1984) used a five-step direct instruction paradigm (Baumann, 1983, 1986) to teach sixth-grade students a variety of main idea skills. Students who received intensive, direct instruction demonstrated superior performance on multiple-dependent measures of main idea comprehension when compared to students who were taught main idea skills according to a basal reading program and to controls who received vocabulary-development instruction. Reutzel, Hollingsworth, and Daines (1988) con-

Chapter

Research on Comprehension and Vocabulary Instruction

1. This section was written by James F. Bauman and Nancy Seifert-Kessell. James F. Baumann is Professor of Elementary Education at Purdue University. Nancy Seifert-Kessell is a doctoral candidate in Elementary Education at Purdue University.

ducted a modified replication of Baumann's study with first-grade children and found an equally powerful treatment effect for directly instructed students.

It has also been established that students can be directly taught various summarization skills. Bean and Steenwyk (1984) reported that sixth-grade students who were directly taught to summarize text through either a rule-governed approach or an intuitive approach outperformed controls, who were simply given advice about how to summarize, on a summary writing task and on a standardized paragraph-comprehension test. Additional support for the success of direct instruction approaches in summary training is found in studies by Cunningham (1982, fourth graders), McNeil and Donant (1982, fifth graders), Rinehart, Stahl, and Erickson (1986, sixth graders), Taylor (1986, sixth graders), and Taylor and Beach (1984, seventh graders).

Teaching Metacognition and Metacomprehension Abilities

Metacognition refers to theory and research on learners' knowledge of and use of their own cognitive resources (Garner, 1987). *Metacomprehension* involves the metacognitive abilities required for understanding oral and written text. Specifically, metacomprehension refers to readers' ability to reflect on, monitor, and evaluate their understanding as they read, and to apply correction strategies when comprehension is impaired (Palincsar & Brown, 1987; Wong & Jones, 1982). Behaviors such as summarizing, paraphrasing, retelling, self-questioning, predicting and verifying, thinking aloud, and rereading or reading on to clarify meaning are typically referred to as metacomprehension strategies.

Recent research has demonstrated that direct instruction methods are effective in

teaching normally achieving and low-performing elementary and middle-grade students a variety of metacomprehension and comprehension monitoring abilities. For example, several studies have examined the effects of training students to monitor comprehension by detecting semantic inconsistencies. Miller reported that fourth-grade average readers (1985) and fifth-grade above-average readers (1987) were more skilled in detecting semantic errors after training in a self-verbalization comprehension monitoring procedure than students not receiving such training. Similarly, Reis and Spekman (1983) were successful in teaching middle-school poor comprehenders to detect semantic inconsistencies.

Basal reader instruction has served as the comparison group for several studies. Schmitt (1987) infused direct metacomprehension strategy instruction within the basal directed reading activity and reported that third-grade students were more metacognitively aware and demonstrated greater comprehension than controls who engaged in a traditional directed reading of basal stories. Baumann, Seifert-Kessell, and Jones (1987) used the Baumann and Schmitt (1986) direct instruction paradigm to teach fourth-grade students a series of comprehension monitoring strategies through the use of a think-aloud procedure. Their experimental group outperformed control students who engaged in guided reading of the same basal stories; it was also superior on several measures to students who engaged in a directed reading-thinking activity. Duffy, Roehler, Sivan, Rackliffe, Book, Meloth, Vavrus, Wesselman, Putnam, and Bassiri (1987) trained third-grade teachers to explain explicitly to students in their low basal reading groups the mental acts associated with strategic reading. Results indicated that experimental group students were more metacognitively aware and demonstrated superior comprehension than treated controls. Similarly, Paris, Cross, and Lipson (1984) reported that third- and fifth-grade students trained to employ various meta-comprehension strategies were more highly skilled than controls who did not receive such instruction.

Jenkins, Heliotis, Stein, and Haynes (1987) trained third- through sixth-grade learning disabled students in a paragraph restatement procedure and reported that experimental subjects were more highly skilled than learning disabled controls in applying the strategy and generalizing it to other comprehension conditions. Chan and Cole (1986) reported that 10- to 12-year-old learning disabled students taught to use a self-questioning procedure demonstrated higher levels of comprehension than subjects taught a read-and-reread procedure. Schunk and Rice (1987) demonstrated that fourth- and fifth-grade remedial readers who received general- and specific-strategy value information about finding main ideas (i.e., conditional knowledge about the importance of main idea comprehension) were more skilled in finding main ideas and demonstrated higher levels of self-efficacy (confidence in ability to complete specific academic tasks) than students who received only general, only specific, or no strategy-value information.

Raphael and her colleagues (Raphael & McKinney, 1983; Raphael & Pearson, 1985; Raphael & Wonnacott, 1985) demonstrated that elementary- and middle-school students could be trained to achieve sensitivity to different sources of information when answering questions, that is, to be metacognitively aware of not only the kinds of questions that might be asked, but also the sources of information readers must use to answer those questions. Raphael taught students three categories of question-answer relations: (a) questions and answers which deal with information stated explicitly in the text ("Right There"); (b) questions and answers that involve inferences made from text-based information ("Think and Search"); and (c) questions and answers that require inferences to be made on the basis of students' extra-textual (prior knowledge) information ("On My Own"). Results of several experiments (Raphael & McKinney, 1983; Raphael & Pearson, 1985; Raphael & Wonnacott, 1985) indicated that students could be taught directly to recognize these multiple sources of information which, in turn, enhanced their understanding of text. Poindexter (1985) reported success in using a modified version of Raphael's question-answer relationship procedure for teaching inferential comprehension to students in grades four through six.

Narrative Text-structure Instruction

Several experiments have evaluated the effects of narrative text-structure instruction with normally achieving students. Fitzgerald and Spiegel (1983) instructed fourth-grade students who lacked a keen sense of story in narrative text structure. Instructed students improved their story structure knowledge and also evidenced improved general comprehension when compared to students who were assigned to a word-study/dictionary-usage group. Spiegel and Fitzgerald (1986) replicated and extended these findings with another group of fourth-grade students who were similarly deficient in story-structure knowledge. Working with middle-school students and using the existing English curriculum (American short stories), Ballard (1988) contrasted the performance of students who received direct instruction in a story-mapping procedure (Baumann & Ballard, 1987) to students who experienced a directed reading-thinking procedure and instructed controls who engaged in a guided-reading procedure. The direct instruction group outperformed both DRTA and controls in ability to answer story plot questions and write well-formed original stories.

Other studies have evaluated the effectiveness of narrative text-structure instruction with low-performing students. Carnine and Kinder (1985) instructed low-performing intermediate-grade students who had difficulty comprehending narrative text to use story-grammar questions to improve their comprehension. Results indicated that through demonstration, guided practice, and repeated use of the strategy, students were able to use the procedure effectively and improve their understanding of stories. Similarly, Short and Ryan (1984) taught students who achieved low scores on a comprehension screening test to answer questions based on common story elements. Specifically, fourth-grade students who were taught to use the strategy were as skillful at answering comprehension questions after instruction as non-instructed controls who had been identified as highly skilled comprehenders (92nd percentile and above) according to the same comprehension screening test.

Direct Instruction in Making Inferences

Direct instruction procedures have also been shown to be effective in teaching students to infer unstated information. In addition to the previously cited work by Raphael (Raphael & McKinney, 1983; Raphael & Pearson, 1985; Raphael & Wonnacott, 1985) and Poindexter (1985) on metacognitive inference training, several other researchers have also reported effective inference-training techniques. Hansen (1981, second graders) and Hansen and

Pearson (1983, fourth graders) demonstrated the effectiveness of intensive instruction in how to make inferences by integrating textual information with a reader's prior knowledge. Somewhat similarly, Carnine, Kameenui, and Woolfson (1982) used direct instruction procedures to train fifth grade students to make text-based inferences. Holmes (1985) also reported that a direct instruction approach was effective in improving fourth- and fifth-grade students' inferential comprehension abilities. Finally, Dewitz, Carr, and Patberg (1987) demonstrated that training fifth-grade students to make inferences not only improved their overall comprehension of text, but it also enhanced students' ability to monitor comprehension.

Specific Skill Training

Several studies have evaluated the effectiveness of direct instruction procedures in facilitating children's comprehension of specific skills. Patching, Kameenui, Carnine, Gersten, and Colvin (1983) compared three strategies for teaching three critical reading skills: a direct instruction strategy, a workbook with feedback strategy, and a no-intervention condition. The results of this study suggest that fifth-grade students who were taught utilizing a direct instruction rule-based strategy performed at a higher level on a series of critical-reading tests than students in the other two conditions. Darch and Kameenui (1987) replicated the Patching et al. (1983) study with elementary-age learning disabled students and found the same results. This line of research has recently been extended to constructing and critiquing arguments (Collins, Carnine, & Gersten, 1987).

In another study on critical thinking and reasoning skills, Fielding, Kameenui, and Gersten (1983) taught secondary students a strategy for evaluating legal cases. Direct instruction students were explicitly taught the meaning of legal concepts such as a fact, an issue, a holding, and a legal test or principle. They were also taught how to use these concepts to relate new cases with cases studied earlier. Direct instruction students scored higher than students taught an inquiry method on both multiple-choice and essay tests designed to assess knowledge of and ability to apply legal concepts and principles. These effects were also maintained over a two-week period.

In a study concerned with the teaching of complex syntactical construction, Kameenui, Carnine, and Maggs (1980) taught three mildly handicapped children to simplify passive-voice and clause constructions. Each syntactical construction was taught through a series of component skills that included (1) identifying the construction in isolated sentences, (2) transforming the constructions into simpler forms at the sentence level, (3) answering comprehension questions specific to the construction at the sentence level, and (4) answering comprehension questions specific to constructions embedded in passages. Utilizing a within-subjects, multiple baseline design, the direct instruction component skill training appeared to be more effective than systematic practice only.

Other direct instruction studies have looked specifically at variables that influence the effectiveness of rules used in teaching skills: example selection, subjects' age, syntactic complexity, rule repetition, and concept training. These studies have been conducted with handicapped (Carnine, Gersten, Darch, & Eaves, 1985) and non-handicapped students (Ross & Carnine, 1982; Carnine, Kameenui, & Maggs, 1982).

In many cases the explicit modeling of an overt, step-by-step comprehension strategy may not be necessary. Sometimes, the careful selection and sequencing of examples coupled with systematic practice and with corrective feedback is just as effective as an explicit modeling strategy. For example, in a study on learning vocabulary from context, Carnine, Kameenui, and Coyle (1984) found that fourth-, fifth-, and sixth-grade students who received extensive practice and corrective feedback performed at the same high level as students who were taught an explicit, overt strategy for selecting the meaning of unfamiliar vocabulary words embedded in short and long passages. Similar results were also found in the teaching of other specific comprehension skills. For example, Carnine, Stevens, Clements, and Kameenui (1982) found the same results in teaching fourth-, fifth-, and sixth-grade students to identify a character's true motive. Dommes, Gersten, and Carnine (1983) also found the same results in teaching elementary-age students to simplify pronoun constructions.

Research on Vocabulary Instruction[2]

Two seemingly contradictory facts constrain the direct instruction of word meanings. First, direct instruction of vocabulary cannot possibly teach more than a fraction of the words that the average (or even below-average) student will learn during twelve years of schooling. Second, direct instruction of vocabulary can have significant effects on comprehension of both passages containing taught words and comprehension in general.

---

[2] This section was written by Steve Stahl, Associate Professor in the Department of Elementary Education and Reading at Western Illinois University.

Direct Instruction and Learning from Context

The Importance of Incidental Learning

Regarding the first fact, Nagy and Anderson (1984) estimate that an average child will encounter approximately 88,500 words in school material in grades 1–12. Given that about half of these will occur in very low frequencies and will not necessarily be learned and given that students enter school with a fairly sizable vocabulary, they estimate that children will learn about 3000 words per school year (see also Graves & Slater, 1987). Since the best vocabulary teaching programs can teach 350–400 words per year, this suggests that the vast majority of words children learn must have been learned through exposure to words in context, not through direct instruction. Other estimates of children's ability to learn words from a single exposure in context (e.g., Nagy, Herman & Anderson, 1986) suggest that, even though the probability of learning a given word from a single exposure is low, a moderate amount of reading over the course of a year could account for a 3000-words-per-year growth. These, of course, are averages. Ranges may vary from 1000 to 5000 words growth per year (Graves & Slater, 1987).

Even though direct instruction of individual words cannot account for a large portion of vocabulary growth, it may play a significant role. Stahl and Fairbanks (1986) suggest that teaching 350 words per year may augment learning from context by 10 to 30%, a significant amount.

Improving Learning from Context by Direct Instruction

It is possible that direct instruction can be used to teach children to gain meaning out of context, although the research in this area is still inconclusive. Sternberg (1987) reports two evaluations of programs designed to teach how to use context to get the meanings of unknown words. The first, conducted with high school sophomores and juniors, directly taught six different cue types how to paraphrase sentences to figure out unknown words and were given practice in how to use these skills to ascertain the meanings of neologisms. While there was a significant gain from pretest to posttest for the training group, the posttest scores were not significantly different from those of a control group. The second study, using adult non-college students, was more successful. Of three of the training groups—one teaching a set of contextual cues as in the first study, one teaching and giving practice in the mental processes involved in learning from context (selective encoding, selective combination, and selective comparison), and one training students in using moderating variables that affect learning from context, (e.g., the location of a cue relative to the unknown word)—all produced better learning from context than two control conditions with one providing the same practice the other groups received without the training and one asking subjects to memorize the definitions of extremely rare words.

Carnine, Kameenui, and Coyle (1984) were also able to train intermediate-grade students to improve their learning from context, but, in contrast to Sternberg, they found that rule-based instruction and extensive practice in getting word meanings from context were equally effective. Beck, Perfetti, and McKeown (1982) found that students given direct instruction in word meanings were better able to discern meanings of words not taught than control subjects. They suggest that their vocabulary training made students more aware of word meanings, leading to better learning from context.

Jenkins, Matlock, and Slocum (1988) compared the effects of training in learning from context and specific instruction in vocabulary. They found that training in specific words was more effective for the learning of those specific words, while training in learning from context was more effective for learning of words not taught (see also McDaniel & Pressley, 1984).

Contexts Are Not Always Clear

One reason that direct instruction in learning from context may not be consistently effective is that contexts vary in their helpfulness (Beck, McKeown, & McCaslin, 1983). Some contexts may give a lot of information about a word's meaning, such as providing a synonym, but these are relatively rare, except in contrived texts written for some content area textbooks. Often context can be misleading so that readers get the incorrect impression from a single exposure (Schatz & Baldwin, 1986). There are some indications, however, that good readers will modify these misimpressions by further exposure, while less proficient readers may cling to these misimpressions which interfere with acquisition of meanings from context (Elshout-Mohr & van Daalen-Kapteijns, 1986; McKeown, 1985; Werner & Kaplan, 1952). It may be possible that learning from context training might be improved by specific training in modifying predictions with additional information, thus teaching poorer readers to act as if better readers.

Direct Teaching of Word Meanings

As for the second fact that vocabulary instruction can improve reading-comprehension abilities, Stahl and Fairbanks (1986) in their meta-analysis of vocabulary-instruction studies found an effect size for vocabulary instruction on passage comprehension using taught words of 0.97, indicating that the average child in the taught group scored as well as a child in the 83rd percentile of an untaught group. This is considered to be a large effect. On passages in standardized tests not necessarily containing taught words, vocabulary instruction produced an average effect size of 0.30, indicating that the average child in a taught group scored as well as a child in the 62nd percentile of an untaught group—a moderate effect. This also may be considered an estimate of the long-term effects of vocabulary instruction because this group contained the studies with the longest duration.

Definitional and Context Information

Not all different types of vocabulary instruction had this effect, however. Stahl and Fairbanks (1986) found that methods which involved only definitional knowledge and required only that children memorize an association between a word and information about that word (e.g., a synonym drill or dictionary look-up activities) did not improve comprehension. Examples of such studies include Pany and Jenkins (1977) and Jenkins, Pany, and Schreck (1978), who studied the effects of associative drill (e.g., "Debris means trash. What does *debris* mean?", etc.) on vocabulary learning and comprehension. They found that such drill improved students' ability to recognize definitions and to detect anomalous sentences, but not to comprehend passages containing taught words.

However, methods which mixed definitional and contextual information, or information about how the context changes in different contexts, were generally successful in improving comprehension. Kameenui, Carnine, and Freschi (1982) found that adding practice in integrating word meanings into sentence contexts to a synonym drill similar to that used by Pany and Jenkins (1977) was successful in improving comprehension. Such specific practice in integrating the definitional information into sentence contexts seemed necessary for students to improve their comprehension of the words in passages. Stahl (1983) also found a "mixed" method to produce significantly higher comprehension of passages containing taught words than a purely "definitional" treatment.

Involving Students in a More Active, Deeper Processing

There is also some evidence that methods of instruction which involve students in a deeper, more meaningful, or more active processing of a word's meaning may also lead to better learning of vocabulary. What Stahl and Fairbanks (1986) termed "depth-of-knowledge" approaches involving students in the active processing of words in different types of context produced strong effects on measures of passage comprehension.

Multi-dimensional Approaches

Examples of multi-dimensional approaches found to be successful include Wixson's (1986) adaptation of the Frayer method for teaching concepts, Beck and McKeown's "rich" vocabulary instruction, and semantic mapping and semantic feature analysis (Johnson, Pittelman, & Heimlich, 1986).

Wixson (1986) found that a concept method using systematic exposure to examples and non-examples generally produced higher vocabulary learning and comprehension than a definition method. However, these effects were not found on all measures and there were significant interactions suggesting these effects were not consistent with all sets of words tested.

She found that children who were instructed on words relating to noncentral ideas in the text recalled those ideas better than children who were not instructed; however, vocabulary instruction did not improve the recall of central ideas. A similar concept development program (Eeds & Cockrum, 1985) has been found to improve recall of taught words.

Beck and McKeown (Beck, Perfetti, & McKeown, 1982; McKeown, Beck, Omanson, & Perfetti, 1983; McKeown, Beck, Omanson, & Pople, 1985) examined the effects of a "rich" program of vocabulary instruction involving multiple meaningful encounters, elaboration and discussion of word meanings, and incentives for using the words outside the classroom. Such a program was found significantly to improve comprehension of texts containing instructed words and to have effects on general measures of comprehension (Beck et al., 1982; McKeown et al., 1983). McKeown et al. (1985) examined the effects of "rich" instruction, using a variety of activities to provide an elaborate knowledge of word meanings; "extended/rich" instruction, including the same activities as in rich instruction but adding incentives for using the words outside of class; and "traditional" synonym-association activities, using words encountered either 6 or 12 times in a seven-day cycle. They found that all three treatments had similar effects on a multiple-choice vocabulary test, but that the two "rich" approaches produced significantly greater effects on story comprehension and interpretation of the meanings of the words in context. The extended/rich instruction method produced significantly greater recall than the rich approach, although the two had similar effects on the contextual interpretation measure. More encounters also produced greater learning than fewer encounters, except that with the "traditional" approach to the story comprehension task, neither the high-encounter nor the low-encounter conditions yielded performance significantly different from the control.

A number of studies have found that semantic mapping and semantic feature analysis produce significant effects on both vocabulary measures and comprehension of passages containing taught words (e.g., Johnson, Pittelman, Toms-Bronowski, & Levin, 1984; Johnson, Toms-Bronowski, & Pittelman, 1982), when compared to either "traditional" instruction (providing both contextual and definitional information) and a no-exposure control. Pittelman, Levin, and Johnson (1985) found that semantic mapping was equally effective for poor readers in small groups or large class settings.

Stahl and Vancil (1986) "decomposed" semantic mapping into discussion and mapping components; they found students who discussed the target words and their relation to other known words but did not develop a map performed as well as those who received a full semantic mapping treatment. Both of these groups outperformed a third group who only studied the map. Thus, they concluded that discussion seemed to be the key factor in the success of semantic mapping (similar to the discussion component in the Beck et al. "rich" instruction).

Stahl and Vancil (1986), as did Pittelman et al. (1985), also found a nonsignificant correlation between the number of responses children made in class and their scores on the vocabulary posttests. Stahl and Clark (1987) hypothesized that children in a classroom discussion anticipate being called upon and covertly generate possible answers. They suggest that the generation of these covert answers, rather than actual participation, leads to the ef-fects found for discussion. To test this, they compared the vocabulary recall of fifth graders taught semantic mapping in a repeated-measure design under three conditions: a "listening" condition where children were told they would not be called upon and, thus, would neither participate nor anticipate; a "participation" condition where children were called upon; and an "anticipation" condition where they anticipated being called upon, but were in fact ignored. As hypothesized, children who anticipated being called upon (the "participation" and "anticipation" conditions) performed better than when they did not anticipate being called on (the "listening" condition) on a delayed posttest measure. (There were no differences among the three groups in an immediate posttest.) Also all three groups outperformed comparison groups who received no training.

Computers

One approach to the trade-off between the need for direct instruction and the time such instruction takes away from the opportunity to read widely and thus learn words incidentally is through the use of computer-based instruction. Johnson, Gersten, and Carnine (1987) taught learning disabled high school students new word meanings through computer-assisted direct instruction. The computer-based direct instruction procedure pretested students so that instruction would be targeted to their needs; they also systematically reviewed words over time so that mastery would be reinforced. They found this program produced significantly better retention of taught word meanings than a CAI program which did not incorporate such direct-instruction principles. They did not measure the effects on comprehension. Their program, and that of Beck,

McKeown, and Roth (1987), are promising approaches to using computer-based technology to aid in vocabulary growth.

Vocabulary Instruction in the Content Areas

In addition to semantic mapping and semantic feature analysis, approaches such as structured overviews (Herber, 1978) and graphic displays (Moore & Readence, 1980; Simmons, Griffin, & Kameenui, 1986) have been found effective not only for teaching the meanings of particular words, but also for teaching relationships among the concepts, thus facilitating understanding of the content material.

Mnemonic Keyword Methods

Another well-researched vocabulary training method is the keyword method in which children learn to associate a word with a short definition through interactive imagery (see Pressley, Levin, & McDaniel, 1987, for review). Although this study has produced consistent and powerful effects on measures of vocabulary recall, there is no research to prove that this learning transfers to comprehension. Since the effects of this associative learning might be similar to the "synonym drill" studied by Pany and Jenkins (1979) which led to better performance on vocabulary recall measures but not on comprehension measures, the effects of the keyword method on measures of comprehension need to be examined specifically.

Morphology

The effects of specific training in morphology, or word parts, have not been well researched. Both Otterman (1955) and O'Rourke (1974) report that specific training in prefixes and roots does increase children's knowledge of word meanings. Wysocki and Jenkins (1987) found that fourth-, sixth-, and eighth-grade students were able to generalize from taught words to morphologically related words; but, this effect was found only when a lenient standard of word meaning was used, not when a strict standard was employed.

A Total Vocabulary Program

Full vs. Partial Knowledge

Kameenui, Dixon, and Carnine (1987) argue that full-concept knowledge, such as that produced by depth of knowledge approaches that mix definitional and contextual information, might not be necessary for students to comprehend words in particular contexts. Instead, only partial information may be needed. For example, to know that gold is a heavy, yellow metal may not constitute full knowledge of gold, but may involve enough information to comprehend it in most contexts. Partial knowledge, through less intensive instruction, may involve enough information to improve children's comprehension in certain situations. Full knowledge about concepts may then evolve over time, through repeated exposure in context. Providing partial knowledge, however, may be more efficient in a long-term program, and may allow for the direct teaching of many more words than approaches which produce full-concept knowledge.

Balancing Direct Instruction and Incidental Learning

An effective vocabulary program, then, should contain both direct instruction of specific words as well as procedures for developing additional word meanings from context. The principles of providing both definitional and contextual information about each word's meaning, engaging the student in active and "deep" processing about each word's meaning, and providing as many exposures as practical seem to be valid for the direct instruction component if full knowledge is required. For developing word meanings from context, it is necessary for the student to read as much connected text as practical in order to be exposed to as many new words as possible. Specific training in the use of context may or may not improve word learning; it may be enough to encourage children to look for new word meanings. Effective vocabulary instruction involves trade-offs between full and partial instruction as well as incidental learning and direct instruction. These trade-offs need to be made deliberately by matching children's needs to instructional approach. Attention to vocabulary development will result in children's improved ability to comprehend texts and should be an important component of any reading program.

Other reviews of direct instruction of vocabulary can be found in Graves (1986), Jenkins and Dixon (1983), McKeown and Curtis (1987), and the *Journal of Reading* (April 1986).

References

Aaron, I. A. (1960). What teachers and prospective teachers know about phonics generalization. *Journal of Educational Research, 53,* 323–330.

Abramson, T., & Kagan, E. (1975). Familiarization of content and differential response modes in programmed instruction. *Journal of Educational Psychology, 67,* 83–88.

Abt Associates (1977). *Education as experimentation: A planned variation model.* Volume IV–B, Effects of Follow Through Models. Cambridge, MA: Abt Books.

Action Books (1971). New York: Scholastic Book Services.

Adams, A., Carnine, D., & Gersten, R. (1982). Instructional strategies for studying content area texts in the intermediate grades. *Reading Research Quarterly, 18*(2), 27–55.

Anderson, R. C. (1977). The notion of schemata and the educational enterprise. In R. C. Anderson, R. J. Spiro, & W. E. Montague (Eds.), *Schooling and the acquisition of knowledge.* Hillsdale, NJ: Erlbaum.

Anderson, R. C., & Freebody, P. (1983). Reading comprehension and the assessment and acquisition of word knowledge. In B. Hutson (Ed.), *Advances in reading/language research: A research annual* (pp. 231–256). Greenwich, CT: JAI Press.

Anderson, R. C., Heibert, E. H., Scott, J. A., & Wilkinson, I. A. G. (1985). *Becoming a nation of readers: The Report of the Commission on Reading.* Champaign-Urbana, IL: National Academy of Education, National Institute of Education, Center for the Study of Reading.

Anderson, R., Reynolds, R., Schallert, D., & Goetz, E. (1977). Frameworks for comprehending discourse. *American Educational Research Journal, 14,* 367–382.

Anderson, R., Reynolds, Schallert, & Goetz, (1977).

Anderson, Spiro, & Anderson, (1977).

Anderson, R., Spiro, R., & Montague, W. (1977). *Schooling and the acquisition of knowledge.* Hillsdale, NJ: Erlbaum.

Archer, A., & Gleason, M. (1989). *Skills for school success* (Book 4). North Billerica, MA: Curriculum Associates.

Armbruster, B. B., Echols, C. H., & Brown, A. L. (1983). *The role of metacognition in reading to learn: A developmental perspective* (Reading Education Report No. 40). Champaign-Urbana, IL: University of Illinois, Center for the Study of Reading.

Armbruster, B. B., & Gudbransen, B. (1986). Reading comprehension instruction in social studies programs. *Reading Research Quarterly, 21,* 36–48.

Arter, J. A. & Jenkins, J. R. (1978). *Differential diagnosis-prescriptive teaching: A critical appraisal* (Technical Report No. 80). Champaign-Urbana: University of Illinois, Center for the Study of Reading.

Aukerman, R. C. (1972). *Reading in the secondary school.* New York: McGraw-Hill.

Ausubel, D. P. (1967). A cognitive-structure theory of school learning. In L. Seigel (Ed.), *Instruction.* San Francisco: Chandler.

Baily, M. H. (1967). The utility of phonic generalization in grades one through six. *Reading Teacher, 20,* 413–418.

Baker, L., & Brown, A. L. (1982). Cognitive monitoring in reading. In J. Flood (Ed.), *Understanding reading comprehension.* Newark, DE: International Reading Association.

Baker, L., & Brown, A. L. (1984). Metacognitive skills and reading. In P. D. Pearson, R. Barr, M. Kamil, & P. Mosenthal (Eds.), *Handbook of reading research.* New York: Longman.

Ballard, P. Q. (1988). *Effects of instruction on story mapping on eighth-grade students' comprehension and composition of short stories.* Unpublished doctoral dissertation. Purdue University, West Lafayette, IN.

Balow, B. (1965). The long-term effect of remedial reading instruction. *The Reading Teacher, 18,* 581–586.

Baron, J. & Strawson, C. (1976). Use of orthographic and word-specific knowledge in reading words aloud. *Journal of Experimental Psychology: Human Perception and Performance, 2,* 386–393.

Barron, R. F., & Earle, R. A. (1973). An approach for vocabulary instruction. In H. L. Herber & R. F. Barron (Eds.), *Research in reading in the content areas: Second year report* (pp. 84–100). Syracuse, NY: Syracuse University Reading and Language Arts Center.

Bateman, B. D. (1971). *The essentials of teaching.* San Rafael, CA: Dimensions Publishing Co.

Baumann, J. F. (1983). A generic comprehension instructional strategy. *Reading World, 22,* 284–294.

Baumann, J. F. (1984). The effectiveness of a direct instruction paradigm for teaching main idea comprehension. *Reading Research Quarterly, 20,* 95–115.

Baumann, J. F. (1986). The direct instruction of main idea comprehension ability. In J. F. Baumann (Ed.), *Teaching main idea comprehension* (pp. 133–178). Newark, DE: International Reading Association.

Baumann, J. F., & Ballard, P. Q. (1987). A two-step model for promoting independence in comprehension. *Journal of Reading, 30,* 608–612.

Baumann, J. F., & Schmitt, M. B. (1986). The what, why, how, and when of comprehension instruction. *The Reading Teacher, 39,* 640–646.

Baumann, J. F., Seifert-Kessell, N., & Jones, L. A. (1987). *Effect of think aloud instruction on elementary students' ability to monitor their comprehension.* Paper presented at the 37th Annual Meeting of the National Reading Conference, St. Petersburg, FL.

Bean, T. W., & Steenwyk, F. L. (1984). The effect of three forms of summarization instruction on sixth graders' summary writing and comprehension. *Journal of Reading Behavior, 16,* 297–306.

Beck, I. L. (1985). Five problems with children's comprehension in the primary grades. In J. Osborn, P. Wilson, & R. Anderson (Eds.), *Reading education: Foundation for a literate America* (pp. 239–254), Lexington, MA: D.C. Heath.

Beck, I. L., McKeown, M. G., McCaslin, E., & Burkes, A. (1979). *Instructional dimensions that may affect reading comprehension: Examples from two commercial reading programs* (LRDC Publication 1979/20). Pittsburgh: Pennsylvania Learning Research and Development Center.

Beck, I. L., McKeown, M. G., & Roth, S. (1987). *Word Wise I, II, III, IV.* Austin, TX: Developmental Learning Materials.

Beck, I. L., Perfetti, C., & McKeown, M. G. (1982). The effects of long-term vocabulary instruction on lexical access and reading comprehension. *Journal of Educational Psychology, 74,* 506–521.

Becker, C. A. (1982). The development of semantic context effects: Two processes or two strategies? *Reading Research Quarterly, 17,* 482–502.

Becker, W. C. (1973). Applications of behavior principles in typical classrooms. In *Behavior modification in education: The seventy-second yearbook of the National Society for the Study of Education.* Chicago, IL: NSSE.

Becker, W. C., & Carnine, D.W. (1980). Direct instruction as a direct approach to educational intervention with disadvantaged and low performers. In B. Lakey & A. Kazdin (Eds.), *Advantages in clinical child psychology* (Vol. 3). New York: Plenum Press.

Becker, W. C., & Englemann, S. (1976a). *Teaching 3: Evaluation of instruction.* Chicago, IL: Science Research Associates.

Becker, W. C., & Englemann, S. (1981). The direct instruction model. In R. Rhine (Ed.), *Encouraging change in America's schools: A decade of experimentation.* New York: Academic Press.

Berger, N. (1975). *An investigation of linguistic competence and organizational processes in good and poor readers.* Unpublished doctoral dissertation, University of Pittsburgh.

Biedorf, J.R., & Pear, J. J. (1977). Two-to-one versus one-to-one student-teacher ratios in the operant verbal training of retarded children. *Journal of Applied Behavioral Analysis, 10,* 506.

Biggins, C., & Uhler, S. (1979). Is there a workable decoding system? *Reading Improvement, 16,* 47–55.

Bishop, C. H. (1964). Transfer effects of word and letter training in reading. *Journal of Verbal Learning and Verbal Behavior, 3,* 214–221.

Blank, M., & Frank, S. M. (1971). Story recall in kindergarten children: Effect of method of presentation on psycholinguistic performance. *Child Development, 42,* 229–312.

Bleismer, E. P., & Yarborough, B. H. (1965). A comparison of ten different reading programs in first grade. *Phi Delta Kappan,* pp. 500-504.

Bond, G. L., & Dykstra, R. (1967). The cooperative research program in first-grade reading instruction. *Reading Research Quarterly, 2,* 5–142.

Boothby, P. R., & Alvermann, D. E. (1984). A classroom training study: The effects of graphic organizer instruction on fourth graders' comprehension. *Reading World, 23,* 325–339.

Bourne, L. E., Jr., & Pendleton, R. B. (1958). Concept identification as a function of completeness and probability of information feedback. *Journal of Experimental Psychology, 56,* 413–420.

Bradley, L., & Bryant, P. E. (1983). Categorizing sounds and learning to read: A casual connection. *Nature, 301,* 419–421.

Bradley, L., & Bryant, P. (1985). *Rhyme and reason in reading and spelling.* Ann Arbor: University of Michigan Press.

Britton, B. K., & Westbrook, R. D., & Holdredge, T. (1978). *Reading and cognitive capacity usage: Effects of test difficulty.* Paper presented at the annual meeting of the American Education Research Association, Toronto.

Brophy, J. E., & Evertson, C. M. (1976). *Learning from teaching: A developmental perspective.* Boston: Allyn and Bacon.

Brophy, J. E., & Good, T. L. (1986). Teacher behavior and student achievement. In M. Wittrock (Ed.), *Third handbook of research on teaching* (pp. 328–375). Chicago: Rand McNally.

Brown, A. L. (1976). Semantic integration in children's reconstruction of narrative sentences. *Cognitive Psychology, 8,* 247–262.

Brown, A. L. (1978). Knowing when, where, and how to remember: A problem of metacognition. In R. Glasser (Ed.), *Advances in instructional psychology.* Hillsdale NJ: Erlbaum.

Brown, A. L. (1980). Metacognitive development and reading. In R. J. Spiro, B. C. Bruce, & W. F. Brewer (Eds.), *Theoretical issues in reading comprehension.* Hillsdale, NJ: Erlbaum.

Brown, A. L., Capione, J. C., & Day, J. D. (1981). Learning to learn: On training students to learn from texts. *Educational Researcher, 10,* 14–21.

Brown, A. L., & Day, J. D. (1983). Macrorules for summarizing texts: The development of expertise. *Journal of Verbal Learning and Verbal Behavior, 22,* 1–14.

Brown, R. M. (1977). An examination of visual and verbal coding processes in preschool children. *Child Development, 48,* 38–45.

Bryant, N. D., Payne, H. R., & Gettinger, M. (1982). Applying the mastery learning model to sight word instruction for disabled readers. *Journal of Experimental Education, 50,* 116–121.

Bulgren, J. A., Schumaker, J. B., & Deshler, D. D. (1988). Effectiveness of a concept teaching routine in enhancing the performance of LD students in secondary-level mainstream classes. *Learning Disability Quarterly, 11,* 3–17.

Burmeister, L. E. (1968). Usefulness of phonic generalizations. *Reading Teacher, 21,* 349–356.

Burmeister, L. (1974). *Reading strategies for secondary school teachers.* Reading, MA: Addison-Wesley.

Burmeister, L. E. (1975). Final-vowel consonant-e. The* ing. Reading, MA: Addison-Wesley.

Calfee, R. C., Venezky, R. L., & Chapman, R. S. (1969). *Pronunciation of synthetic words with predictable and unpredictable letter-sound correspondences.* (Tech. Rep. No. 71). Madison WI: University of Wisconsin, Wisconsin Research and Development Center for Cognitive Learning.

Canney, G. F. (1976). A study of the relationship between pupil's aural vocabulary and their ability to apply syllabication rules or to recognize phonogram patterns to decode multiple syllable words. *Journal of Reading Behavior, 8,* 273–288.

Carnine, D. W. (1976a). *Conditions under which children learn the relevant attribute of negative instances rather than the essential characteristics of positive instances.* Unpublished manuscript, Follow Through Project, University of Oregon.

Carnine, D. W. (1976b). *Establishing a discriminative sequence by distributing attributes of compound stimuli between instances and not-instances.* In W. C. Becker & S. E. Englemann (Eds.), Technical Report 1976–1 Appendix B. Eugene, OR: University of Oregon, Follow Through Project.

Carnine, D. W. (1976c). Effects of two teacher presentation rates on off-task behavior, answering correctly, and participation. *Journal of Applied Behavioral Analysis,* 199–206.

Carnine, D. W. (1976d). Similar sound separation and cumulative introduction in learning letter-sound correspondence. *Journal of Educational Research, 69,* 368–372.

Carnine, D. W. (1977). Phonics versus look-say: Transfer to new words. *Reading Teacher, 30,* 636–640.

Carnine, D. W. (1978a). *Three procedures for presenting minimally different positive and negative instances.* In Technical Report 1978–2, Formative Research on Direct Instruction. Eugene, OR: Follow Through Project, University of Oregon.

Carnine, D. W. (1978b). *Two procedures for sequencing instances in discrimination learning tasks: Simultaneously presenting minimally different instance pairs and changing a single stimulus to generate successive instance.* In Technical Report 1978–2, Formative Research on Direct Instruction. Eugene, OR: Follow Through Project, University of Oregon.

Carnine, D. W. (1978c). *The effects of progressive increase in the number and/or magnitude of differences between positive and negative concept instances.* In Technical Report 1978–2, Formative Research on Direct Instruction. Eugene, OR: Follow Through Project, University of Oregon.

Carnine, D. W. (1978d). *The effects of two correction procedures on word acquisition by pre-school children.* In Technical Report 1978–2, Formative Re-

search on Direct Instruction. Eugene, OR: Follow Through Project, University of Oregon.

Carnine, D. W. (1978e). *High and low implementation of direct instruction teaching techniques.* In Technical Report 1978–2, Formative Research on Direct Instruction. Eugene, OR: Follow Through Project, University of Oregon.

Carnine, D. W. (1980a). Three procedures for presenting minimally different positive and negative instances. *Journal of Educational Psychology, 72,* 452–456.

Carnine, D. W. (1980b). Two letter discrimination sequences: High-confusion alternatives first versus low-confusion alternatives first. *Journal of Reading Behavior, 12,* 41–47.

Carnine, D. W. (1980c). Phonic versus whole-word correction procedures following phonic instruction. *Education and Treatment of Children, 3,* 323–330.

Carnine, D. W. (1980d). Relationships between stimulus variation and the formation of misconceptions. *Journal of Educational Research, 74,* 106–110.

Carnine, D. W. (1981a). Reducing training problems associated with visually and auditorily similar correspondences. *Journal of Learning Disabilities, 14,* 276–279.

Carnine, D. W. (1981b). High and low implementation of direct instruction teaching techniques. *Education and Treatment of Children, 4,* 42–51.

Carnine, D. W., & Fink, W. T. (1974). *Effects of eye contact on attending and correct responding during small group instruction.* Unpublished manuscript, University of Oregon.

Carnine, D., & Fink, W. T. (1978). *A comparative study of the effects of individual versus unison responding on the word reading performance of preschool children.* (Technical Report 1978–2,

Formative Research on Direct Instruction.) Eugene, OR: Follow Through Project, University of Oregon.

Carnine, D., Gersten, R., Darch, C., & Eaves, R. (1985). Attention and cognitive deficits in learning disabled students. *Journal of Special Education, 19,* 319–331.

Carnine, D. W., Kameenui, E., & Coyle, G. (1984). Utilization of contextual information in determining the meaning of unfamiliar words. *Reading Research Quarterly, 19,* 188–204.

Carnine, D. W., Kameenui, E. J., & Maggs, A. (1982). Components of analytic assistance: Statement saying, concept training, and strategy training. *Journal of Educational Research, 75,* 374–377.

Carnine, D. W., Kameenui, E. J., & Woolfson, N. (1982). Training of textual dimensions related to text based inferences. *Journal of Reading Behavior, 14,* 182–187.

Carnine, D. W., & Kinder, D. (1985). Teaching low-performing students to apply generative and schema strategies to narrative and expository material. *Remedial and Special Education, 6,* 20–30.

Carnine, D. W., & Stein, M. (1979a). *Two methods for teaching words with an unfamiliar letter combination.* Unpublished manuscript, Follow Through Project, University of Oregon.

Carnine, D. W., & Stein, M. (1979b). *Use of a deductive rule in teaching students to decode VCe pattern words.* Unpublished manuscript, Follow Through Project, University of Oregon.

Carnine, D. W., Stevens, C., Clements, J., & Kameenui, E. J. (1982). Effects of facilitative questions and practice on intermediate students' understanding of character motives. *Journal of Reading Behavior, 14,* 179–190.

Carnine, L., & Carnine, D. W. (1978). Determining the relative decoding difficulty of three types of simple regular words. *Journal of Reading Behavior, 10* (4), 440–441.

Carnine, L., & Carnine, D. W. (1980). Determining the relative decoding difficulty of three types of simple regular words. *Journal of Reading Behavior, 10,* 440–441.

Carnine, L. M., Carnine, D. W., & Gersten, R. M. (1984). Analysis of oral reading errors made by economically disadvantaged students taught with a synthetic-phonics approach. *Reading Research Quarterly, 19,* 343–356.

Carrol, J. B. (1977). Developmental parameters of reading comprehension. In J. Guthries (Ed.), *Cognition, curriculum, and comprehension.* Newark, DE: International Reading Association.

Chall, J. (1967). *Learning to read: The great debate.* New York: McGraw-Hill.

Chall, J. (1978a). Clues on research on programs for poor readers. In S. Samuels (Ed.), *What research has to say about reading instruction.* Newark, DE: International Reading Association.

Chall, J. S. (1983). *Learning to read: The great debate* (updated edition). New York: McGraw-Hill.

Chall, J. S. (1987). Two vocabularies for reading: Recognition and meaning. In M. G. McKeown & M. E. Curtis (Eds.), *The nature of vocabulary acquisition* (pp. 7–17). Hillsdale, NJ: Erlbaum.

Chall, J. S. (1988). *Stages of reading development.* New York: Academic Press.

Chan, K. S., & Cole, P. G. (1986). The effects of comprehension monitoring training on the reading competence of learning disabled and regular class students. *Remedial and Special Education, 7,* 33–40.

Chapman, R. S., & Kamm, M. R. (1974). *An evaluation of methods for teaching initial sound isolation.* Washington, DC (ERIC Document ED 066–231).

Chomsky, C. (1970). Reading, writing, and phonology. *Harvard Educational Review, 40,* 287–309.

Clay, M. M., & Imlach, R. H. (1971). Juncture, pitch, and stress as reading behavior variables. *Journal of Verbal Learning and Verbal Behavior, 10,* 133–139.

Clymer, T. (1963). The utility of phonic generalizations in the primary grades. *Reading Teacher, 16,* 252–258.

Coleman, E. B. (1970). Collecting a data base for a reading technology. *Journal of Educational Psychology Monograph, 61* (4, Part 2).

Collins, M., & Carnine, D. (1988). Evaluating the field test revision process by comparing two versions of a reasoning skills CAI program. *Journal of Learning Disabilities, 21* (6), 375–379

Collins, M., Carnine, D., & Gersten, R. (1987). Elaborated corrective feedback and the acquisition of reasoning skills: A study of computer-assisted instruction. *Exceptional Children, 54,* 254–262.

Collins, R., Brown, A. L., Morgan, J. L., & Brewer, W. F. (1977). *The analysis of reading tasks and texts.* (Technical report 43). Champaign-Urbana, IL: Center for the Study of Reading, University of Illinois.

Corder, R. (1971). *An information base for reading: A critical review of the information base for current assumptions regarding the status of instruction and achievement in reading in the United States.* Washington, DC: USOE, Project No. 0–9031. (ERIC Document ED 054–922)

Cossairt, A., Hall, V., & Hopkins, B. L. (1973). The effects of experimenter's instructions, feedback, and praise on teacher praise and student attending behavior. *Journal of Applied Behavior Analysis, 6,* 89–100.

Cowart, J., Carnine, D. W., & Becker, W. C. (1976). The effects of signals on attending, responding, and following in direct instruction. In W. C. Becker & S. E. Englemann (Eds.), *Technical Report 1976–1 Appendix B.* Eugene, OR: University of Oregon.

Cronbach, L. J., & Snow, R. E. (1977). *Aptitudes and instructional methods: A handbook for research interactions.* New York: Irvington Publishers.

Cunningham, J. (1982). Generating interactions between schema and text. In J. A. Niles & L. A. Harris (Eds.), *New inquiries in reading research and instruction, Thirty-first yearbook of the National Reading Conference* (pp. 42–47). Rochester, NY: National Reading Conference.

Cunningham, P. M. (1975–76). Investigating a synthesized theory of mediated word identification. *Reading Research Quarterly, 11,* 128.

Dahl, P. (1979). An experimental program for teaching high speed word recognition and comprehension skills. In T. Lovitt (Ed.), *Communications research in learning disabilities and mental retardation.* Baltimore, MD: University Park Press.

Darch, C., & Carnine, D. (1986). Teaching content area material to learning disabled students. *Exceptional Children, 53,* 240–246.

Darch, C., Carnine, D., & Gersten, R. (1984). Explicit instruction in mathematics problem solving. *Journal of Educational Research, 77,* 350–359.

Darch, C., Carnine, D., & Kameenui, E. (1986). The role of visual displays and social structure in content-area instruction. *Journal of Reading Behavior, 18,* 275–295.

Darch, C., & Gersten, R. (1985). The effects of teacher presentation rate and praise on LD students' oral reading performance. *British Journal of Educational Psychology, 55,* 295–303.

Darch, C., & Kameenui, E. J. (1987). Teaching critical reading skills to learning disabled children. *Learning Disabilities Quarterly, 10*(2), 82–92.

Darch, C., Carnine, D., & Gersten, R. (1984). Explicit instruction in mathematics problem solving. *Journal of Educational Research, 77,* 350–359.

Darch, C., Gersten, R., & Taylor, R. (1987). Evaluation of the Williamsburg County Direct Instruction program: Factors leading to success in rural elementary programs. *Research in Rural Education, 4,* 111–118.

Davis, F. B. (1968). Research in comprehension in reading. *Reading Research Quarterly, 3,* 449–545.

Davis, F. B. (1972). Psychometric research on comprehension in reading. *Reading Research Quarterly, 7,* 628–678.

Denburg, S. E. (1976). The interaction of picture and print in reading instruction. *Reading Research Quarterly, 12,* 176–189.

Dewitz, P., Carr, E. M., & Patberg, J. P. (1987). Effects of inference training on comprehension and comprehension monitoring. *Reading Research Quarterly, 22,* 542–546.

Dieterich, P. B., II. (1973). *Research 1960–1970 on methods and materials in reading.* Princeton, NJ: Educational Testing Service, (TM Report 22), ERIC Clearinghouse on Tests, Measurement and Evaluation.

Dimino, J. (1988). *The effects of a story grammar comprehension strategy on low-performing students' ability to comprehend short stories.* Unpublished doctoral dissertation, University of Oregon.

Dommes, P., Gersten, R., & Carnine, D. (1983). Instructional procedures for increasing skill deficient fourth graders' comprehension of syntactic structures. *Educational Psychologist, 42,* 155–166.

Duffy, G. G., Roehler, L. R., Sivan, E., Rackliffe, G., Book, C., Meloth, M.S., Vavrus, L. G., Wessleman, R., Putnam, J., & Bassiri, D. (1987). Effects of explaining the reasoning associated with using reading strategies. *Reading Research Quarterly, 22,* 347–368.

Duncan, C. P. (1959). Transfer after training with single versus multiple tasks. *Journal of Experimental Psychology, 55,* 63–72.

Durkin, D. (1981). Reading comprehension instruction in five basal reader series. *Reading Research Quarterly, 26,* 515–544.

Durkin, D. (1987). Influences on basal reader programs. *The Elementary School Journal, 87,* 331–341.

Durling, R. & Schick, C. (1976). Concept attainment by pairs and individuals as a function of vocalization. *Journal of Educational Psychology, 68,* 83–91.

Dykstra, R. (1968a). Summary of the second grade phase of the cooperative research program in primary reading instruction. *Reading Research Quarterly, 4,* 49–70.

Dykstra, R. (1974). Phonics and beginning reading instruction. In C. C. Walcutt, J. Lamport, & G. McCracken (Eds.), *Teaching reading: A phonic/linguistic approach to developmental reading.* New York: Macmillan.

Earle, R. A. (1976). *Teaching reading and mathematics.* Newark, DE: International Reading Association.

Edelman, G. (1963). The use of cues in word recognition in a basic research program on reading. (Final Report, Project No. 639). Ithaca NY: Cornell University and the U.S. Office of Education.

Eeds, M., & Cockrum, W. (1985). Teaching word meanings by expanding schemata vs. dictionary work vs. reading in context. *Journal of Reading, 28,* 492–497.

Ehri, L. C. (1983). A critique of five studies related to letter-name knowledge and learning to read. In L. M. Gentile, M. L. Kamil, & S. S. Blanchard (Eds.). *Reading research revisited* (pp. 143–151). Columbus, OH: Merrill.

Ehri, L. C. (1984). How orthography alters spoken language. In J. Downing & R. Valtin (Eds.), *Language awareness and learning to read* (pp. 119–147). New York: Springer-Verlag.

Ehri, L. C. & Wilce, L. S. (1983). Development of word identification speed in skilled and less skilled beginning readers. *Journal of Educational Psychology, 75,* 3–18.

Ehri, L. C. & Wilce, L. S. (1987). Cipher versus cue reading. *Journal of Educational Psychology, 79,* 3–13.

Ehrlich, S. F. (1981). Children's word recognition in prose context. *Visible Language, 15,* 219–244.

Ehrlich, S. F., & Rayner, K. (1981). Contextual effects on word recognition and eye movements during reading. *Journal of Verbal Learning and Verbal Behavior, 20,* 641–655.

Elkonin, D. B. (1973). In J. Downing (Ed.), *Comparative reading.* New York: Macmillan.

Elshout-Mohr, M., & Van Daalen-Kapteijns, M. M. (1987). Cognitive processes in learning word meanings. In M. G. McKeown & M. E. Curtis (Eds.), *The nature of vocabulary acquisition* (pp. 53–71). Hillsdale, NJ: Erlbaum.

Emans, R. (1967). The usefulness of phonic generalization above the primary grades. *Reading Teacher, 20,* 419–425.

Enfield, M. L. (1976). *An alternative classroom approach to meeting special learning needs of children with reading problems.* Unpublished doctoral dissertation, University of Minnesota.

Englemann, S., & Bruner, E. (1974). *DISTAR reading I.* Chicago IL: Science Research Associates.

Englemann, S., & Carnine, D. (1976). A structural program's effect on the attitudes and achievement if average and above average second graders. In W. C. Becker, & S. Englemann (Eds.), *Technical Report 76–1. Appendix B: Formative Research.* Eugene, OR: University of Oregon.

Englert, C. S. (1984). Examining effective direct instruction practices in special education settings. *Remedial and Special Education, 5,* 38–74.

Evans, M. A., & Carr, T. H. (1983). *Curricular emphasis and reading development: Focus on language or focus on script.* Symposium conducted at the biennial meeting of the Society for Research on Child Development. Detroit, MI.

Farmer, A. R., Nixon, M., & White, R. T. (1976). Sound blending and learning to read: An experimental investigation. *British Journal of Educational Psychology, 46,* 155–163.

Fielding, G. D., Kameenui, E. J., & Gersten, R. (1983). A comparison of an inquiry and a direct instruction approach to teaching legal concepts and applications to secondary school students. *Journal of Educational Research, 76* (5), 387–293.

Fink, W. T. (1976). *Effects of a pre-correction procedure on the decoding errors of two low performing fourth grade girls.* In W. C. Becker & S. E. Englemann (Eds.), *Technical Report 1976–1 Appendix B.* Eugene, OR: University of Oregon.

Fink, W. T., & Carnine, D. W. (1975). Control of arithmetic errors using informational feedback and graphing. *Journal of Applied Behavioral Analysis, 8,* 461.

Fink, W. T., & Sandall, S. R. (1977). *A comparison of one-to-one and small group instructional strategies on a word identification task by developmentally disabled pre-schoolers.* Unpublished manuscript, Center on Human Development, University of Oregon.

Fitzgerald, J., & Speigal, D. L. (1983). Enhancing children's reading comprehension through instruction in narrative structure. *Journal of Reading Behavior, 15* (2), 1–17.

Flanders, D. (1978). *Teaching receptive and expressive usage of plurals to a language delayed mentally retarded child.* Unpublished master's thesis, University of Oregon.

Flavall, J. H. (1976). Metacognitive aspects of problem solving. In L. B. Resnick (Ed.), *The nature of intelligence.* Hillsdale, NJ: Erlbaum.

Flavall, J. H., & Wellman, H. M. (1977). Metamemory. In R. V. Kail, Jr., & J. W. Hagen (Eds.), *Perspectives on the developmental memory and cognition.* Hillsdale, NJ: Erlbaum.

Fleisher, L. S., Jenkins, J. R., & Pany, D. (1979). Effects of poor readers' comprehension of training in rapid decoding. *Reading Research Quarterly, 15,* 30–48.

Fletcher, J. D., & Atkinson, R. C. (1972). Evaluation of the standard CAI program in initial reading. *Journal of Educational Psychology, 63,* 597–602.

Foss, D. J., & Swinney, D. A. (1973). On the psychological reality of the phoneme: Perception, identification, and consciousness. *Journal of Verbal Learning and Verbal Behavior, 12,* 246–257.

Fox, B., & Routh, D. K. (1976). Phonemic analysis and synthesis as word attack skills. *Journal of Educational Psychology, 68,* 70–74.

Frase, L. T. (1967). Learning from prose material: Length of passage, knowledge of results and position of question. *Journal of Educational Psychology, 58,* 266–272.

Frase, L. T. (1968). Questions as aids to reading: Some research and theory. *American Educational Research Journal, 5,* 319–332.

Frase, L. T., Patrick, E., & Schumer, H. (1970). Effect of question position and frequency upon learning from text under different levels of incentive. *Journal of Educational Psychology, 71,* 52–56.

Frase, L. T., & Schwartz, B. J. (1975). Effect of question production and answering on prose recall. *Journal of Educational Psychology, 67,* 628–635.

Garner, R. (1987). *Metacognition and reading comprehension.* Norwood, NJ: Ablex.

Gersten, R., Becker, W. C., Heiry, T. J., & White, W. A. T. (1984). Entry IQ and yearly academic growth of children in Direct Instruction programs: A longitudinal study of low SES children. *Education Evaluation and Policy Analysis, 6,* 109–121.

Gersten, R., Carnine, D., & Williams, P. (1982). Measuring implementation of a structured educational model in an urban setting: An observational approach. *Education Evaluation and Policy Analysis, 4,* 67–79.

Gersten, R., Carnine, D., Zoref, L., & Cronin, D. (1986). A multifaceted study of change in inner city schools. *Elementary School Journal, 86,* 257–276.

Gersten, R., White, W., Falco, R., & Carnine, D. W. (1982). Teaching basic discrimination to handicapped and nonhandicapped individuals through a dynamic presentation of instructional stimuli. *Analysis and Intervention in Developmental Disabilities, 2,* 305–317.

Gibson, E. D., & Levin, H. (1975). *The psychology of reading.* Cambridge: MIT Press.

Gibson, E. J. (1965). Learning to read. *Science, 148,* 1066–1072.

Gibson, E. J. (1976). Trends in perceptual development: Implications for the reading process. In H. Singer and R. B. Ruddell (Eds.), *Theoretical models and processes of reading*. Newark, DE: International Reading Association.

Ginn 720. (1976). Lexington, MA: Ginn and Company.

Gipe, J. P. (1978). *Investigating techniques for teaching word meanings*. Paper presented at the annual meeting of the American Educational Research Association, Toronto.

Glass, G. G., & Burton, E. H. (1973). How do they decode? Verbalizations and observed behavior of successful decoders. *Education, 94*, 58–64.

Golinkoff, R. A. (1975–76). Comparison of reading comprehension processes on good and poor comprehenders. *Reading Research Quarterly, 4*, 623–659.

Goodman, K. S. (1965). A linguistic study of cues and miscues in reading. *Elementary English, 42*, 639–643.

Gough, P. B. (1976). One second of reading. In H. Singer & R. B. Ruddell (Eds.), *Theoretical models and processes of reading*. Newark, DE: International Reading Association.

Gough, P. B. & Tunmer, W. E. (1986). Decoding, reading, and reading disability. *Remedial and Special Education, 7*, 6–10.

Grant, E. M. (1973). *A study of comparison of two reading programs (Ginn 360 and DISTAR) upon primary inner city students*. Unpublished doctoral dissertation, University of Wisconsin.

Granzin, A. C. & Carnine, D. W. (1977). Child performance on discrimination tasks: Effects of amount of stimulus variation. *Journal of Experimental Child Psychology, 24*, 332–342.

Graves, M. F. (1986). Vocabulary learning and instruction. *Review of Research in Education, 13*, 49–90.

Graves, M. F. (1987). The roles of instruction in vocabulary development. In M. G. McKeown & M. E. Curtis (Eds.), *The nature of vocabulary acquisition* (pp. 165–184). Hillsdale, NJ: Erlbaum.

Graves, M. F. & Slater, W. H. (1987). *The development of reading vocabularies in children from three social, economic, and linguistic settings: A preliminary report*. Paper presented at the annual meeting, American Educational Research Association, Washington, DC.

Groff, P. (1976). Limitations of context cues for beginning readers. *Reading World, 16*, 97–103.

Gurney, D., Gersten, R., Dimino, J. & Carnine, D. W. (in press). Story grammar: Effective literature instruction for learning disabled high schools. *Journal of Learning Disabilities*.

Guthrie, J. T. (1977). Follow Through: A compensatory education experiment. *The Reading Teacher*, 240–244.

Guthrie, J. T., & Seifert, M. (in press). Education for children with reading disabilities. In H. R. Myklebust (Ed.), *Progress in learning disabilities* (Vol. IV). Orlando: Grune.

Guthrie, J. T., & Tyler, S. (1976). Psycholinguistic processing in reading and listening among good readers. *Journal of Reading Behavior, 8*, 415–426.

Guthrie, J. T., & Tyler, S. J. (1978). Cognition and instruction of poor readers. *Journal of Reading Behavior, 10*, 57–78.

Haddock, M. (1976). Effects of an auditory and an auditory-visual method of blending instruction on the ability of prereaders to decode synthetic words. *Journal of Educational Psychology, 68*, 825–831.

Haddock, M. (1978). Teaching blending in beginning reading instruction is important. *The Reading Teacher, 31*, 654–658.

Hall, V., Lund, D., Jackson, D. (1968). Effects of teacher attention on study behavior. *Journal of Applied Behavior Analysis, 1,* 1–12.

Hammill, D. D., & Larsen, S. C. (1974). The effectiveness of psycholinguistics training. *Exceptional Children, 41,* 5–14.

Hanna, G. S. (1976). Effects of total and partial feedback in multiple-choice testing upon learning. *Journal of Educational Research, 69,* 202–205.

Hanna, P. R., Hanna, J. S., Hodges, R. E., & Rudlof, E. H. (1966). *Phoneme-grapheme correspondences as cues to spelling improvement.* Washington, DC: U.S. Government Printing Office.

Hansen, C. (1976). *The generalization of skills and drills versus corrective feedback instruction to the independent reading performance of intermediate aged learning disabled boys.* Unpublished doctoral dissertation, University of Washington.

Hansen, J. (1981). The effects of inference training and practice on young children's reading comprehension. *Reading Research Quarterly, 16,* 391–417.

Hansen, J. & Pearson, P. D. (1983). An instructional study: Improving the inferential comprehension of fourth grade good and poor readers. *Journal of Educational Psychology, 75,* 821–829.

Harber, J. R. (1980). Effects of illustrations on reading performance: Implications for further LD research. *Learning Disability Quarterly, 3,* 60–70.

Harber, J. R. (1983). The effects of illustrations on the reading performance of learning disabled and normal children. *Learning Disability Quarterly, 6,* 55–60.

Hare, V. C., & Borchardt, K. M. (1984). Direct instruction of summarization skills. *Reading Research Quarterly, 21,* 62–78.

Hargis, C., Terhar-Yonkers, M., Williams, P., & Reed, M. (1988). Repetition requirements for word recognition. *Journal of Reading, 88* (1), 320–327.

Haring, N. G., & Bateman, B. (1977). *Teaching the learning disabled child.* Englewood Cliffs, NJ: Prentice- Hall.

Harris, A. J., & Sipay, E. R. (1975). *How to increase reading ability* (6th ed.). New York: David McKay.

Harris, A. J., & Sipay, E. R. (1980). *How to increase reading ability.* (7th ed.). New York: David McKay.

Harzem, P., Lee, I., & Miles, T. R. (1976). The effect of pictures on learning to read. *The British Journal of Educational Psychology, 46,* 318–332.

Hayes, R. B., & Wuerst, R. C. (1967). ITA and three other approaches to reading in the first grade-extended into the second grade. *The Reading Teacher, 20,* 694–698.

Hayes, R. B. & Wuerst, R. C. (1969). *Four instructional approaches to beginning reading—three years later.* Paper presented at convention of the International Reading Association, Boston. (ERIC document Reproduction Service No. ED 020098)

Helfgott, J. A. (1976). Phonemic segmentation and blending skills of kindergarten children: Implications for beginning reading acquisition. *Contemporary Educational Psychology, 1,* 157–169.

Hendrickson, J., Roberts, M., & Shores, R. E. (1978). Antecedent and contingent modeling to teach basic sight vocabulary to learning disabled children. *Journal of Learning Disabilities, 11,* 524–528.

Herber, H. L. (1978). *Teaching reading in the context areas.* (2nd ed.). Englewood Cliffs, NJ: Prentice Hall.

Hochberg, J. (1970). Components of literacy: Speculations and exploratory research. In H. Levin & J. P. Williams

(Eds.), *Basic studies on reading*. New York: Basic Books.

Hoffman, J. V. & Roser, N. (1987). The basal reader in American reading instruction. Elementary School Journal, Vol. 87, No. 3 Special Issue.

Hohn, W. E., & Ehri, L. C. (1983). Do alphabet letters help prereaders acquire phonemic segmentation skill? *Journal of Educational Psychology, 75*, 752–762.

Holmes, B. C. (1985). The effects of a strategy and sequenced materials on the inferential comprehension of disabled readers. *Journal of Learning Disabilities, 18*, 542–546.

House, E., Glass, G. V., McLean, L., & Walker, D. F. (1978). No simple answer: Critique of the Follow Through education. *Harvard Educational Review, 48*, 128–160.

Hunres, (1976). *Instructional procedures and effects on measures of reading comprehension with learning disabled students*. (ERIC No. Ed 136237).

Jarvella, R. J. (1971). Syntactic processing of connected speech. *Journal of Verbal Learning and Verbal Behavior, 10*, 409–416.

Jeffrey, W., & Samuels, S. J. (1976). Effect of method of reading training on initial training and transfer. *Journal of Verbal Learning and Verbal Behavior, 6*, 354–358.

Jenkins, J. R., Bausell, R. B., & Jenkins, L. M. (1972). Comparison of letter name and letter sound training as transfer variables. *American Educational Research Journal, 9*, 75–86.

Jenkins, J. R., & Dixon, R. (1983). Vocabulary learning. *Contemporary Educational Psychology, 8*, 237–260.

Jenkins, J. R., Heliotis, J. D., Stein, M. L., & Haynes, M. C. (1987). Improving reading comprehension by using paragraph restatements. *Exceptional Children, 54*, 54–59.

Jenkins, J. R., & Larson, K. (1977a). *Differential effects of error correction procedures for oral reading* (Technical Report No. 55). Champaign, IL: Center for the Study of Reading, University of Illinois.

Jenkins, J. R., & Larson, K. (1978). *Evaluating error correction procedures for oral reading* (Technical Report No. 55). Champaign, IL: Center for the Study of Reading, University of Illinois.

Jenkins, J., Larson, K., & Fleisher, L. (1982). Effects of error correction on word recognition and reading comprehension. *Learning Disabilities Quarterly, 6*, 139–154.

Jenkins, J. R., Matlock, B., & Slocum, T. A. (1988) *Effects of specific vocabulary instruction in deriving word meaning from context*. Paper presented at annual meeting, American Educational Research Association, New Orleans, LA.

Jenkins, J. R., Mayhall, W. F., Peschka, C. M., & Jenkins, L. M. (1974). Comparing small group and tutorial instruction in resource rooms. *Exceptional Children, 40*, 245–250.

Jenkins, J. R., Mayhall, W. F., Peschka, C. M., & Townsend, V. (1974). Using direct and daily measures to influence learning. *Journal of Learning Disabilities, 7*, 14–17.

Jenkins, J. R., & Pany, D. (1976). *Curriculum biases in reading achievement tests* (Technical Report No. 16). Champaign, IL: Center for the Study of Reading, University of Illinois.

Jenkins, J. R., & Pany, D. (1977). *Reading comprehension in the middle grades: Instruction and research*. NIE Deliverable. Champaign, IL: Center for the Study of Reading, University of Illinois.

Jenkins, J. R., & Pany, D. (1978). Learning word meanings: A comparison of instructional procedures and effects on measures of reading comprehension with learning disabled students. *Learning Disability Quarterly, 1,* 21–32.

Jenkins, J., & Pany, D. (1980). Research on teaching reading comprehension: Instructional variables. In J. Guthrie (Ed.), *Reading comprehension and education.* Newark, DE: International Reading Association.

Jenkins, J. R., Pany, D., & Schreck, J. (1978). *Vocabulary and reading comprehension: Instructional effects* (Technical, Report No. 100). Champaign, IL: Center for the Study of Reading, University of Illinois. (ERIC Document Reproduction Service No. Ed 160 99)

Jenkins, J., Stein, M., & Osborne, (1981). What next after decoding? Instruction and research in reading comprehension. *Exceptional Education Quarterly,* Vol. 2, No. 1, pp. 27–39.

Jitendra, A., & Kameenui, E. J. (1988). A design of instruction analysis of concept teaching in five basal language programs: Violations from the bottom up. *The Journal of Special Education, 22,* 199–219.

Johnson, D. D. (1973). Suggested sequences for presenting four categories of letter-sound correspondences. *Elementary English, 50,* 888–896.

Johnson, D. E., & Baumann, J. F. (1984). Word identification. In D. Pearson, R. Barr, M. Kamil, & P. Mosenthal (Eds.), *Handbook of reading research.* New York: Longman.

Johnson, D. D., & Pearson, P. D. (1984). *Teaching reading vocabulary* (2nd ed.). New York: Holt, Rinehart & Winston.

Johnson, D. D., Pittelman, S. D. & Heimlich, J. E. (1986). Semantic mapping. *The Reading Teacher, 39,* 778–783.

Johnson, D. D., Pittelman, S. D., Toms-Bronowski, S., & Levin, K. M. (1984). *An investigation of the effects of prior knowledge and vocabulary acquisition on passage comprehension* (Program Report 84–85). Madison, WI: Wisconsin Center for Educational Research, University of Wisconsin.

Johnson, D. D., Toms-Bronowski, S., & Pittelman, S. D. (1982). *An investigation of the effectiveness of semantic mapping feature analysis with intermediate grade level children* (Program Report No. 83–3). Madison, WI: Wisconsin Center for Education Research, University of Wisconsin.

Johnson, G., Gersten, R., & Carnine, D. (1987). Effects of instructional design variables on vocabulary acquisition of LD students: A study of computer-assisted instruction. *Journal of Learning Disabilities, 20,* 206–213.

Johnson, R. E. (1970). Recall of prose as a function of the linguistic units. *Journal of Verbal Learning and Verbal Behavior, 9,* 12–20.

Johnson, R. J. (1970). *The effect of training in letter names on success in beginning reading for children of different abilities.* Paper presented at American Educational Research Association, Minneapolis, Minnesota.

Jones, B. F., Pierce, J., & Hunter, B. (1989). Teaching students to construct graphic representations. *Educational Leadership, 46*(4), 20–25.

Jones, K., Torgeson, J. K., & Sexton, M. A. (1987). Using computer guided practice to increase decoding fluency in learning disabled children: A study using the Hint and Hunt I program. *Journal of Learning Disabilities, 20,* 122–128.

Jorm, A. F. (1977). Children's reading processes revealed by pronunciation latentcies and errors. *Journal of Educational Psychology, 69,* 166–171.

Kameenui, E. J. (1985). Direct instruction of reading comprehension: Beyond teacher performance variables to the design of instruction. In J. Niles & R. Lalik (Eds.), *Thirty-fourth yearbook of the National Reading Conference. Issues in Literacy: A research perspective* (pp. 257–262). Rochester, NY: National Reading Conference.

Kameenui, E. J. (1986). Main idea instruction for low performers: A direct instruction analysis. In J. F. Baumann (Ed.), *Teaching main idea comprehension* (pp. 239–276). Newark, DE: International Reading Association.

Kameenui, E. J., Carnine, D. W., & Freschi, R. (1982). Effects of text construction and instructional procedures for teaching word meanings on comprehension and recall. *Reading Research Quarterly, 17,* 367–388.

Kameenui, E. J., Carnine, D. W., & Maggs, A. (1980). Instructional procedures for teaching reversible passive-voice and clause constructions to three mildly handicapped children. *The Exceptional Child, 27,* 27–40.

Kameenui, E. J., Dixon, R. C., & Carnine, D. W. (1987). Issues in the design of vocabulary instruction. In M. G. McKeown & M. E. Curtis (Eds.), *The nature of vocabulary acquisition* (pp. 129–146). Hillsdale, NJ: Erlbaum.

Kameenui, E. J., & Simmons, D. C. (1990). Designing instructional strategies: The prevention of academic learning problems. Columbus, OH: Merrill.

Kameenui, E., Stein, M., Carnine, D., & Maggs, A. (1981). Primary level word attack skills based on isolated word discrimination list and rule application training. *Reading Education, 6,* 46–55.

Kavale, K. A., & Forness, S. R. (1987). Substance over error: Assessing the efficacy of modality testing and teaching. *Exceptional Children, 54,* 228–239.

Keeney, T. J., Canizzo, S. R., & Flavell, J. H. (1967). Spontaneous and induced verbal rehearsal in a recall task. *Child Development, 38,* 953–966.

Keisler, E. R., & McNeil, J. D. (1968). Oral and non-oral methods of teaching reading. *Educational Leadership, 25,* 761–764.

Keith, C., & Carnine, D. W. (1978). *Recognition of syntax violation in oral and written sentences by good and poor readers.* Unpublished manuscript, Follow Through Project, University of Oregon.

Kennedy, M. M. (1978). Findings from the follow through planned variation study. *Educational Researcher, 7,* 3–11.

Kinder, D. & Carnine, D. (1985). Teaching low-performing students to apply generative and schema strategies to narrative and expository material. *Remedial and Special Education, 6*(1), 20–30.

King, E. M. (1978). Prereading programs: Direct versus incidental teaching. *The Reading Teacher, 31,* 504–510.

Klausmeier, H., & Allen, P. (1978). *Cognitive development of children and youth: A longitudinal study.* New York: Academic Press.

Klausmeier, H., & Feldman, K. (1975). Effects of a definition and a varying number of examples and nonexamples on concept attainment. *Journal of Educational Psychology, 67,* 174–178.

Kleinfeld, J. (1975). Effective teachers of Eskimo and Indian students. *School Review, 83,* 301–344.

Koenke, K., & Otto, W. (1969). Contribution of pictures to children's comprehension of the main idea in reading. *Psychology in the Schools, 6,* 298–302.

Kryzanowski, J., & Carnine, D. W. (1980). Effects of massed versus spaced formats in teaching sound/symbol correspondences to young children. *Journal of Reading Behavior, 12,* 225–230.

Kryzanowski, J. A. (1976). *Praise effects on on-task behavior during small group instruction.* In W. C. Becker and S. En-glemann (Eds.), *Technical Report 76–1, Appendix B, Formative Research Studies.* Eugene, OR: Follow Through Project, University of Oregon.

Kryzanowski, J. A., Carnine, D. W. (1978). *The effects of massed versus distributed practise schedules in teaching sound-symbol correspondences to young children.* In Technical Report 1878–2, Formative Research on Direct Instruction. Eugene, OR: University of Oregon.

LaBarge, D., & Samuels, S. J. (1974). Toward a theory of automatic information processing in reading. *Cognitive Psychology, 6,* 293–322.

Larson, C., & Dansereau, D. (1986). Cooperative learning in dyads. *Journal of Reading, 29,* 516–520.

Laurita, R. E. (1972). Rehearsal: A technique for improving reading comprehension. *Academic Therapy, 8,* 103–111.

Leiberman, J. (1967). *The effect of direct instruction in vocabulary concepts on reading achievement.* Bloomington, IN: ERIC Clearinghouse on Reading. (ERIC Document ED 010985)

Leinhardt, G., Zigmond, N., & Cooley, W. (1981). Reading instruction and its effects. *American Educational Research Journal, 18,* 343–361.

Levin, J. R. (1971–72). Comprehending what we mean: An outsider looks in. *Journal of Reading Behavior, 4,* 18–19.

Lewkowicz, N. K. (1980). Phonemic awareness training: What to teach and how to do it. *Journal of Educational Psychology, 72,* 686–700.

Lewkowski, N., & Low, L. (1979). Effects of visual aids and word structure on phonemic segmentation. *Contemporary Educational Psychology, 4,* 238–252.

Lloyd, J. W. (1984). How shall we individualize instruction or should we? *Remedial and Special Education, 5,* 7–15.

Lloyd, J., Cullian, D., Heins, E. D., & Epstein, M. H. (1980). Direct instruction: Effects on oral and written language comprehension. *Learning Disabilities Quarterly, 3,* 70–76.

Lloyd, J., Epstein, M. H., & Cullian, D. (1981). Direct teaching for learning disabilities. In J. Gottleibs & S. Strichart (Eds.), *Perspective on handicapping conditions: Current research and application in learning disabilities.* Baltimore, MD: University Park Press.

Lynn, L. (1973). *Basal reading program: Keys to reading* (Research Report No. 73–144). Dallas, TX: Department of Research and Evaluation, Dallas Independent School District.

Madsen, C., Becker, W. C., & Thomas, D. R. (1968). Rules, praise, and ignoring: Elements of elementary classroom control. *Journal of Applied Behavioral Analysis, 1,* 139–150.

Manzo, A. V. (1969). The ReQuest procedure. *Journal of Reading, 13,* 123–126.

Marchbanks, G., & Levin, H. (1965). Cues by which children recognize words. *Journal of Educational Psychology, 56,* 57–61.

Mason, J., Osborn, J., & Rosenshine, B. (1977). *A consideration of skill hierarchy approaches to the teaching of meaning.* Champaign, IL: Center for the Study of Reading, University of Illinois at Champaign-Urbana.

Mason, J. M. (1977a). Questioning the notion of independent processing stages in reading. *Journal of Educational Psychology, 69,* 288–179.

Mason, J. M., & Au, K. H. (1987). *Reading instruction for today.* Glenview, IL: Scott, Foresman.

Massad, V. I., & Etzel, B. C. (1972). Acquisition of phonetic sounds by preschool children. In G. Semb (Ed.), *Behavior analysis and education.* Lawrence, KS: University of Kansas.

McClelland, J. (1977). Letter configuration information in word identification. *Journal of Verbal Learning and Verbal Behavior, 16,* 137–150.

McCoy, K., & Pany, D. (1986). Summary and analysis of oral reading corrective feedback research. *The Reading Teacher, 39,* 548–555.

McCullough, C. (1969). What does research in reading reveal about practices in teaching reading? *English Journal, 58,* 688–706.

McCutcheon, B. A., & McDowell, E. E. (1969). Intralist similarity and acquisition and generalization of word recognition. *The Reading Teacher, 23,* 103–107.

McDaniel, M. A., & Pressley, M. (1984). Putting the keyword method in context. *Journal of Educational Psychology, 76,* 598–609.

McDonald, F. J. (1976). *Beginning teacher evaluation study, phase II:* Executive summary. Princeton, NJ: Educational Testing Service.

McFeely, D. C. (1974). Syllabication usefulness in a basal and social studies vocabulary. *The Reading Teacher, 27,* 809–814.

McKeown, M. G. (1985). The acquisition of word meaning from context by children of high and low ability. *Reading Research Quarterly, 20,* 482–496.

McKeown, M. G., Beck, I. L., Omanson, R. C., & Perfetti, C. A. (1983). The effects of long-term vocabulary instruction on reading comprehension: A replication. *Journal of Reading Behavior, 15,* 3–18.

McKeown, M. G., Beck, I. L., Omanson, R. C., & Pople, M. T. (1985). Some effects of the nature and frequency of vocabulary instruction on the knowledge and use of words. *Reading Research Quarterly, 1,* 522–535.

McKeown, M. G., & Curtis, M. E. (1987). *The nature of vocabulary acquisition.* Hillsdale, NJ: Lawrence Erlbaum.

McNeil, J. D., & Donant, L. (1982). Summarization strategy for improving reading comprehension. In J. A. Niles & L. A. Harris (Eds.), *New inquiries in reading research and instruction, Thirty-first Yearbook of the National Reading Conference* (pp. 215–219). Rochester, NY: National Reading Conference.

Meyer, L. A. (1982). The relative effects of word-supply correction procedures with poor readers during word-attack training. *Reading Research Quarterly, 17,* 544–555.

Meyer, L. A. (1983). Increased student achievement in reading: One district's strategies. *Research in Rural Education, 20,* 47–51.

Meyer, L. A. (1984). Long-term academic effects of the direct instruction Project Follow Through. *Elementary School Journal, 84,* 389–394.

Meyer, L. A., Gersten, R., & Gutkin, J. (1983). One came through: Supervisory and administrative factors that led to a Follow Through success story. *Elementary School Journal, 84,* 241–252.

Meyer, L. A., Hastings, C. N., Wardrop, J. L., & Linn, R. L. (1988). *How entering ability and instructional settings, not the length of the school day, mediates kindergartners' reading performance.* Final report submitted to the OREI.

Michalos, A. C. (1970). *Improving your reasoning.* Englewood Cliffs, NJ: Prentice-Hall.

Miller, G. E. (1985). The effects of general and specific self-instruction training on children's comprehension monitoring performances during reading. *Reading Research Quarterly, 20,* 616–628.

Miller, G. E. (1987). The influence of self-instruction on the comprehension monitoring performance of average and above average readers. *Journal of Reading Behavior, 19,* 303–317.

Moore, D. W., & Readence, J. E. (1980). A meta-analysis of the effect of graphic organizers on learning from text. In M. L. Kamil & A. J. Moe (Eds.), *Perspectives on reading research and instruction. Twenty-ninth Yearbook of the National Reading Conference.* Washington, DC: National Reading Conference.

Morrisett, L., & Hovland, C. I. (1959). A comparison of three varieties of training in human problem solving. *Journal of Experimental Psychology, 58,* 52–55.

Muller, D. (1973). Phonic blending and transfer of letter training to word reading in children. *Journal of Reading Behavior, 5,* 13–15.

Murphy, J., Weil, M., & McGreal, T. L. (1986). The basic practice model of instruction. *The Elementary School Journal, 87,* 83–95.

Murrell, P. C., Jr., & Surber, J. R. (1987). *The effect of generative summarization on the comprehension of main ideas from lengthy expository text.* Paper presented at the annual meeting of the American Educational Research Association, Washington, DC.

Nagy, W. E. (1988). *Teaching vocabulary to improve reading comprehension.* Newark, DE: International Reading Association.

Nagy, W. E., & Anderson, R. C. (1984). How many words are there in printed school English? *Reading Research Quarterly, 19,* 304–330.

Nagy, W. E., Anderson, R., & Herman, P. (1987). Learning word meanings from context during normal reading. *American Educational Research Journal, 24,* 237–270.

Nagy, W. E., Herman, P., & Anderson, R. C. (1985). Learning words from context. *Reading Research Quarterly, 20,* 233–253.

Neef, N. A., Iwata, B. A., & Page, T. J. (1977). The effects of known-item interspersal on acquisition and retention of spelling and sight reading words. *Journal of Applied Behavior Analysis, 10,* 738.

Neville, M. (1968). Effects of oral and echoic responses in beginning reading programs. *Journal of Educational Psychology, 59,* 362–369.

New starts for America's third century. (1976, April). *Time* (p. 29).

O'Malley, J. M. (1973). Stimulus dimension pretraining and set size in learning multiple discrimination with letters of the alphabet. *Journal of Educational Psychology, 67,* 41–45.

O'Rourke, J. P. (1974). *Toward a science of vocabulary development.* The Hague: Moulton.

Oaken, R., Wiener, M., & Cromer, W. (1971). Identification, organization, and reading comprehension for good and poor readers. *Journal of Educational Psychology, 62,* 71–78.

Ohnmacht, D. D. (1969). *The effects of letter knowledge on achievement in reading in the first grade.* Paper presented at the American Educational Research Association meeting, Los Angeles.

Osborn, J. H., Jones, B. F., & Stein, M. (1985). The case for improving textbooks. *Educational Leadership, 42,* 9–16.

Otterman, L. M. (1955). The value of teaching prefixes and word roots. *Journal of Educational Research, 48,* 611–616.

Otto, W., & Pizillo, C. (1970–1971). Effect of intralist similarity on kindergarten pupils' rate of word acquisition and transfer. *Journal of Reading Behavior, 3,* 14–19.

Pace, A. J., & Golinkoff, R. M. (1976). Relationship between word difficulty and access of single word meaning by skilled and less skilled readers. *Journal of Educational Psychology, 68,* 760–767.

Palincsar, A. (1984). The quest for meaning from expository text: A teacher guided journey. In G. Duffy, L. Roehler, & J. Mason (Eds.), *Comprehension instruction: Perspectives and suggestions.* New York: Longman.

Palincsar, A., & Brown, A. (1984). Reciprocal teaching of comprehension- fostering and comprehension-monitoring activities. *Cognition and Instruction, 2,* 117–175.

Palincsar, A., & Brown, A. (1986). Interactive teaching to promote independent learning from text. *The Reading Teacher, 39,* 771–777.

Palincsar, A. M. S., Ogle, D. S., Jones, B. F., & Carr, E. M. (1986). *Teaching reading as thinking: Trainer's manual.* Arlington, VA: Association for Supervision and Curriculum Development.

Palincsar, A. S., & Brown, A. L. (1987). Enhancing instructional time through attention to metacognition. *Journal of Learning Disabilities, 20,* 66–75.

Pany, D., & Jenkins, J. R. (1977). *Learning word meanings: A comparison of instructional procedures and effects on measures of reading comprehension with learning disabled students* (Technical Report No. 25). Champaign, IL: Center for the Study of Reading, University of Illinois. (ERIC Document Reproduction Service Ed 134 979)

Pany, D., McCoy, K. M., & Peters, E. (1981). Effects of corrective feedback on comprehension skills of remedial students. *Journal of Reading Behavior, 13,* 131–143.

Pany, D., Peters, E., Mastropieri, M., & Kulhavy, R. (1982). *Effects of corrective feedback on comprehension of adolescents at two skill levels: Acquisition and fluency.* Paper presented at the Council for Exceptional Children's International Convention, Houston, TX.

Pany, D., & McCoy, K. M. (1983). *Effects of corrective feedback on word accuracy and reading comprehension of learning disabled and average readers.* Paper presented at the American Education Research Association International Convention, Montreal, Canada.

Paris, S. G., Cross, D. R., & Lipson, M. Y. (1984). Informed strategies for learning: A program to improve children's reading awareness and comprehension. *Journal of Educational Psychology, 76,* 1239–1252.

Paris, S. G., & Jacobs, J. E. (1984). The benefits of informed instruction for children's reading awareness and comprehension skills. *Child Development, 55,* 2083–2093.

Paris, S., Wasik, B., & Van der Westhuizen, G. (1988). *Meta-metacognition: A review of research on metacognition and reading.* Paper presented at the National Reading Conference, St. Petersburg, FL.

Patching, W., Kameenui, E. J., Carnine, D. W., Gersten, R., & Colvin, G. (1983). Direct instruction in critical reading skills. *Reading Research Quarterly, 18,* 406–418.

Pearson, D. (1984). *The explicit teaching of reading comprehension.* Paper presented at 34th Annual National Reading Conference, St. Petersburg, FL.

Pehrsson, R. S. V. (1974). The effects of teacher interference during the process of reading or how much of a helper is Mr. Gelper? *Journal of Reading, 17,* 617–621.

Perfetti, C. A. (1977). Language comprehension and fast decoding: Some psycholinguistics prerequisites for skilled reading comprehension. In J. T. Guthrie (Ed.), *Cognition, curriculum, and comprehension.* Newark, DE: International Reading Association.

Perfetti, C. A. (1985). *Reading ability.* New York: Oxford Press.

Perfetti, C. A. (1986). Continuities in reading acquisition, reading skill, and reading disability. *Remedial and Special Education, 7*, 11–21.

Perfetti, C. A., Beck, I., & Hughes, C. (1981, March). *Phonemic knowledge and learning to read.* Paper presented at the meeting of the Society for Research in Child Development, Boston.

Perfetti, C. A., & Curtis, M. E. (1986). Reading. In R. F. Dillon & R. J. Sternberg (Eds.), *Cognition and instruction.* Orlando, FL.: Academic Press, Inc.

Perfetti, C., & Hogalboam, T. (1975). Relationship between single word decoding and reading comprehension skill. *Journal of Educational Psychology, 67*, 641–649.

Perfetti, C. A., & Roth, S. (1981). Some of the interactive processes in reading and their role in the reading skill. In A. Lesgold & C. Perfetti (Eds.), *Interactive processes in reading* (pp. 269–297). Hillside, NJ: Erlbaum.

Petty, O., & Jansson, L. (1987). Sequencing examples and nonexamples to facilitate concept attainment. *Journal for Research in Mathematics Education, 18* (2), 112–125.

Petty, W., Herold, C., & Stoll, E. (1968). *The state of knowledge about the teaching of vocabulary.* Champaign, IL: National Council of Teachers of English.

Pflaum, S., Walberg, H. J., Karigianes, M. L. & Rasher, S. P. (1980). Reading instruction: A quantitative analysis. *Educational Researcher,* 12–18.

Pittelman, S. D., Levin, K. M., & Johnson, D. D. (1985). *An investigation of two instructional settings in the use of semantic mapping with poor readers* (Program Report 85–4). Madison, WI: Wisconsin Center for Education Research, University of Wisconsin.

Pittsburg Learning Research and Development Center. *Report of the first year implementation of the new primary grades reading system (NRS) in Kelly School* (1974–1975 school year). Mimeo, updated.

Poindexter, C. (1985). *The effects of a metacognition question-answering strategy on the inferential comprehension abilities of fourth, fifth, and sixth grade students.* Unpublished doctoral dissertation, University of California at Los Angeles.

Polloway, E., Epstein, M., Polloway, C., Patton, J., & Ball, D. (1986). Corrective reading program: An analysis of effectiveness with learning disabled and mentally retarded students. *Remedial and Special Education, 7*, 41–47.

Pressley, M., Levin, J. R., & McDaniel, M. A. (1987). Remembering versus inferring what a word means: Mnemonic and contextual approaches. In M. G. McKeown & M. E. Curtis (Eds.), *The nature of vocabulary acquisition* (pp. 107–127). Hillsdale, NJ: Lawrence Erlbaum.

Putnam, L. R., & Youtz, A. C. (1972). Is a structured reading program effective for disadvantaged children? *Reading World, 12*, 123–135.

Ramsey, W. Z. (1972). *Evaluation of assumptions related to the testing of phonics skills* (Final Report). St. Louis: National Center for Educational Research and Development (ERIC Document ED 068–893).

Raphael, T. E., & McKinney, J. (1983). An examination of fifth- and eighth-grade children's question-answering behavior: An instructional study in metacognition. *Journal of Reading Behavior, 15*, 67–86.

Raphael, T. E., & Pearson, P. D. (1985). Increasing students' awareness of sources of information for answering questions. *American Educational Research Journal, 22*, 217–236.

Raphael, T. E., & Wonnacott, C. A. (1985). Heightening fourth-grade students' sensitivity to sources of information for answering comprehension questions. *Reading Research Quarterly, 20,* 282–296.

Rashotte, C. A., & Torgesen, J. K. (1985). Repeated reading and reading fluency in learning disabled children. *Reading Research Quarterly, 20,* 180–188.

Rayner, K., & Posnansky, C. (1978). Learning to read: Visual cues to word recognition. In A. M. Lesgold, J. W. Pellegrino, S. D. Fokkena, & R. Glaser (Eds.), *Cognitive psychology and instruction.* New York: Plenum Publishing.

Reis, R., & Spekman, N. (1983). The detection of reader-based versus text-based inconsistencies and the effects of direct training of comprehension monitoring among upper-grade poor comprehenders. *Journal of Reading Behaviors, 15,* 49–60.

Reith, H., & Frick, T. (1982). *An analysis of academic learning time of mildly handicapped students in special education service delivery systems. Initial report on classroom process variables.* Bloomington: Center for Innovation in Teaching the Handicapped, Indiana University.

Reutzel, D. R., Hollingsworth, P. M., & Daines, D. (1988). *Teaching beginning readers main idea comprehension using dictated texts: A modified replication of Baumann's direct instruction paradigm.* Manuscript submitted for publication.

Reynolds, G. S. (1961). Attention in the pigeon. *Journal of Experimental Analysis of Behavior, 4,* 203–208.

Rhine, R. (Ed.) (1981). *Encouraging change in America's schools: A decade of experimentation.* New York: Academic Press.

Richards, J. P. (1975–76). Processing effects of advance organizers interspersed in text. *Reading Research Quarterly, 11,* 599–622.

Richardson, E., & Collier, L. (1971). Programmed tutoring of decoding skills with third and fifth grade non-readers. *Journal of Experimental Education, 39,* 57–64.

Richardson, E., Winsberg, B. G., & Binler, I. (1973). Assessment of two methods of teaching phonics skills to neuropsychiatrically impaired children. *Journal of Learning Disabilities, 10,* 628–635.

Rinehart, S. D., Stahl, S. A., & Erickson, L. A. (1986). Some effects of summarization training on reading and studying. *Reading Research Quarterly, 21,* 422–438.

Rist, R. (1970). Student social class and teacher expectations: The self-fulfilling prophecy in ghetto education. *Harvard Educational Review, 40,* 411–451.

Robinson, R. P. (1941). *Effective study.* New York: Harper & Row.

Robyler, M. D., & King, F. J. (1983). *Reasonable expectations for computer-based instruction in basic reading skills.* Paper presented at the meeting of the Association for Educational Communications and Technology, Cincinnati, OH.

Rose, T. L., & Furr, P. M. (1984). Negative effects of illustrations as word cues. *Journal of Learning Disabilities, 7,* 334–337.

Rose, T. L., McEntire, E., & Dowdy, C. (1982). Effects of two error-correction procedures on oral reading. *Learning Disability Quarterly, 5,* 100–105.

Rosenshine, B. (1976). Classroom instruction. In N. L. Gage (Ed.), *The psychology of teaching methods, Seventy-seventh yearbook of the National Society for the Study of Education.* Chicago, IL: University of Chicago Press.

Rosenshine, B. (1979). Content, time, and direct instruction. In J. Peterson and H. Walberg (Eds.), *Research on teaching: Concepts, findings and implications.* Berkeley, CA: McCutchan.

Rosenshine, B. V. (1986). Synthesis of research on explicit teaching. *Educational Leadership, 43,* 60–69.

Rosenshine, B. V., & Berliner, D. C. (1978). Academic engaged time. *British Journal of Teacher Education, 4,* 3–16.

Rosenshine, B., & Stevens, R. (1984). Classroom instruction in reading. In D. Pearson (Ed.), *Handbook of research on reading.* New York: Longman.

Rosenshine, B., & Stevens, R. (1985).

Rosenshine, B., & Stevens, R. (1986). Teaching functions. In M. C. Wittrock (Ed.), *Handbook of research on teaching* (3rd ed.), pp. 376–391. New York: Macmillan.

Ross, D., & Carnine, D. W. (1982). Analytic assistance: Effect of example selection, subject's age, and syntactic complexity. *Journal of Educational Research, 75,* 294–298.

Roth, S. F., & Beck, K. L. (1987). Theoretical and instructional implications of the assessment of two microcomputer word recognition programs. *Reading Research Quarterly, 22,* 197–218.

Rowe, M. (1987). Wait time: Slowing down may be a way of speeding up. *American Educator,* Spring, 38–43.

Rozin, P., & Gleitman, L. (in press). The reading process and the acquisition of the alphabetic principle. In A. S. Reber & D. Scarborough (Eds.), *Reading: The CUNY Conference.* New York: Erlbaum.

Ruddell, R. B. (1976a). Language acquisition and the reading process. In H. Singer & R. B. Ruddell (Eds.), *Theoretical models and processes of reading.* Newark, DE: International Reading Association.

Sabatino, D. A., & Dorfman, N. (1974). Matching learner aptitude to two commercial reading programs. *Exceptional Children, 41,* 85–90.

Samuels, S. J. (1967). Attentional process in reading: The effect of pictures on the acquisition of reading responses. *Journal of Educational Psychology, 58,* 337–342.

Samuels, S. J. (1970). Effects of pictures on learning to read, comprehension, and attitudes. *Review of Educational Research, 40,* 397–408.

Samuels, S. J. (1971). Letter-name versus letter-sound knowledge in learning to read. *Reading Teacher, 24,* 604–608.

Samuels, S. J. (1976a). Automatic decoding and reading comprehension. *Language Arts, 53,* 323–325.

Samuels, S. J. (1976b). Modes of word recognition. In H. Singer & R. B. Ruddell (Eds.), *Theoretical models and processes of reading.* Newark, DE: International Reading Association.

Samuels, S. J., Biesbock, E., & Terry, P. R. (1974). The effect of pictures on children's attitudes toward presented stories. *The Journal of Educational Research, 67,* 243–246.

Samuels, S. J., & Jeffrey, W. E. (1966). Discriminability of words and letter cues in learning to read. *Journal of Educational Psychology, 57,* 337–340.

Sanacore, J. (1983). Improving reading through prior knowledge and writing. *Journal of Reading, 26,* 714–720.

Santa, C. M. (1976–77). Spelling patterns and the development of flexible word recognition strategies. *Reading Research Quarterly, 12,* 125–144.

Saving, H. B., & Bever, T. G. (1970). The nonperceptual reality of the phoneme. *Journal of Verbal Learning and Verbal Behavior, 9,* 295–302.

Schatz, E. K., & Baldwin, R. S. (1986). Context clues are unreliable predictors of word meanings. *Reading Research Quarterly, 21,* 408–421.

Schmitt, M. C. (1986). *The effects of an elaborated reading activity on the meta-comprehension skills of third graders.* Unpublished doctoral dissertation, Purdue University, West Layafette, IN.

Schumaker, J. B., Denton, P. H., & Deshler, D. D. (1984). *The paraphrasing strategy.* Lawrence, KS: The University of Kansas.

Schumaker, J. B., Deshler, D. D., Alley, G. R., Warner, M. M., & Denton, P. H. (1982). Multipass: A learning strategy for improving reading comprehension. *Learning Disabilities Quarterly, 5,* 295–304.

Schunk, D. H., & Rice, J. M. (1987). Enhancing comprehension skill and self-efficacy with strategy value information. *Journal of Reading Behavior, 19,* 285–301.

Schwantes, F. M. (1981). Effect of story context on children's ongoing word recognition. *Journal of Reading Behavior, 13,* 305–311.

Schwartz, R. M., & Stanovich, K. E. (1981). Flexibility in the use of graphic and contextual information by good and poor readers. *Journal of Reading Behavior, 13,* 263–269.

Scribner, S. & Cole, M. (1972). Effects of constrained recall training of children's performance in a verbal memory task. *Child Development, 43,* 845–857.

Shankweiler, D. & Liberman, I. Y. (1972). Misreading: A search for causes. In J. F. Kavanagh & I. G. Mattingly (Eds.), *Language by ear and by eye.* Cambridge, MA: MIT Press.

Shannon, P. (1987). Commercial reading materials, a technological ideology, and the deskilling of teachers. *The Elementary School Journal, 87,* 307–329.

Sheinker, J., & Sheinker, A. (1989). *Metacognitive approach to study strategies.* Rockville, MD: Aspen.

Short, E. J., & Ryan, E. B. (1984). Metacognitive differences between skilled and less skilled readers: Remediating deficits through story grammar and attribution training. *Journal of Educational Psychology, 76,* 225–235.

Siegel, M. A. (1977). Teacher behavior and curriculum packages: Implications for research and teacher education. In L. J. Rubin (Ed.), *Handbook of curriculum.* New York: Allyn & Bacon.

Siegel, M. A., & Rosenshine, B. (1973). *Teacher behavior and achievement in the Engelmann-Becker Follow Through Program.* Paper presented at the meeting of the American Educational Research Association, New Orleans. (ERIC Document Reproduction Service No. ED 076–564.)

Siegler, R. S., & Liebert, R. M. (1973). Effects of presenting relevant rules and complete feedback on the conservation of liquid quantity task. *Developmental Psychology, 7,* 133–138.

Silberman, H. F. (1964). *Exploratory research on a beginning reading program.* Santa Monica, CA: System Development Corporation.

Siler, E. R. (1973–74). The effects of syntactic and semantic constraints on the oral reading performance of second and fourth graders. *Reading Research Quarterly, 9,* 583–602.

Simmons D. C., Kameenui, E. J., & Darch, C. (1988). Learning disabled children's metacognition of selected textual features. *Learning Disabilities Quarterly, 11,* 380–395.

Simmons, D. C., Griffin, C. C., & Kameenui, E. J. (1986). *Effects of pre and post graphic display instruction on sixth-grade students' comprehension and recall of science content area text.*

Paper presented at annual meeting, National Reading Conference, Austin, TX.

Singer, H., Samuels, S. J., & Spiroff, J. (1973). The effect of pictures and contextual conditions on learning responses to printed words. *Reading Research Quarterly, 9,* 555–567.

Singh, S., & Singh, N. N. (1985). Comparison of word-supply and word-analysis error-correction procedures on oral reading by mentally retarded children. *American Journal of Mental Deficiency, 90,* 64–70.

Skailand, D. B. (1971). *A comparison of four language units in teaching beginning reading.* Paper presented to the American Educational Research Association, New York.

Smith, F. (1969). Familiarity of configuration vs. discriminability of features in the visual identification of words. *Psychonomic Science, 14,* 261–262.

Smith, F. (1982). *Understanding reading.* New York: Holt, Rinehart and Winston.

Smith, H. D. (1967). The responses of good and poor readers when asked to read for different purposes. *Reading Research Quarterly, 3,* 53–83.

Smith, R. W. L. (1966). *Dictionary of English word-roots.* Totowa, NJ: Littlefield, Adams & Co.

Spache, G. D. (1939). A phonics manual for primary and remedial teachers. *Elementary English Review, 16,* 147–150 and 191–198.

Spache, G. D., & Baggett, A. (1965). What do teachers know about phonics and syllabication? *The Reading Teacher, 19,* 96–99.

Spache, G. D., & Spache, E. B. (1977). *Reading in the elementary school* (4th ed.). Boston: Allyn & Bacon.

Spear, L. C., & Sternberg, R. J. (1986). An information processing framework for understanding reading disability. In S. Ceci (Ed.), *Handbook of cognitive, social, and neuropsychological aspects of learning disabilities* (Vol. 2). Hillsdale, NJ: Erlbaum.

Speer, O. B., & Lamb, G. S. (1976). First grade reading ability and fluency in naming verbal symbols. *Reading Teacher, 29,* 572–576.

Spiegel, D. L., & Fitzgerald, J. (1986). Improving reading comprehension through instruction about the story parts. *Reading Teacher, 39,* 676–682.

Spoeky, K. T., & Smith, E. E. (1973). The role of syllables in perceptual processing. *Cognitive Psychology, 5,* 71–89.

Stahl, S. A. (1983). Differential word knowledge and reading comprehension. *Journal of Reading Behavior, 15,* 33–50.

Stahl, S. A., & Clark, C. H. (1987). The effects of participatory expectations in classroom discussion on the learning of science vocabulary. *American Research Journal, 24,* 541–555.

Stahl, S. A., & Fairbanks, M. M. (1986). The effects of vocabulary instruction: A model-based meta-analysis. *Review of Educational Research, 5,* 72–110.

Stahl, S. A., & Vancil, S. J. (1986). Discussion is what makes semantic maps work in vocabulary instruction. *The Reading Teacher, 40,* 62–69.

Stallings, J. A. (1975). Implementation and child effects of teaching practices in Follow Through classrooms. *Monographs of the Society for Research in Child Development, 40* 7–8, (Serial No. 163).

Stallings, J. (1980). Allocated academic learning time revisited, or beyond time on task. *Educational Researcher, 8,* 11–16.

Stanford Program on Teaching Effectiveness. (1975). *A factorially designed experiment on teacher structuring, solicit-*

ing, and reacting. Stanford, CA: Stanford Center for Research and Development in Teaching.

Stanovich, K. E. (1980). Toward an interactive compensatory model of individual differences in the development of reading fluency. *Reading Research Quarterly, 16,* 32–71.

Stanovich, K. E. (1982). Individual differences in the cognitive processes of reading I: Word decoding. *Journal of Learning Disabilities, 15,* 485–493.

Stanovich, K. E. (1986). Matthew effects in reading: Some consequences of individual differences in the acquisition of literacy. *Reading Research Quarterly, 21* (4), 360–406.

Stanovich, K. E., Cunningham, A. E., & Freeman, D. J. (1984). Relation between early reading acquisition and word decoding with and without context: A longitudinal study of first grade children. *Journal of Educational Psychology, 76,* 668–677.

Stein, C., & Goldman, J. (1980). Beginning reading instruction for children with minimal brain dysfunction. *Journal of Learning Disabilities, 13,* 52–55.

Stein, M., & Carnine, D. W. (1978). Constant and variable introduction of letter-sound correspondences. In *Technical Report 1978–2, Formative Research on Direct Instruction.* Eugene, OR: Follow Through Project, University of Oregon.

Sternberg, R. J. (1987). Most vocabulary is learned from context. In M. G. McKeown & M. E. Curtis (Eds.), *The nature of vocabulary acquisition* (pp. 89–105). Hillsdale, NJ: Erlbaum.

Stolurow, K. A. C. (1975). Objective rules of sequencing applied to instructional material. *Journal of Educational Psychology, 67,* 909–912.

Stromer, R. (1975). Modifying letter and number reversals in elementary school children. *Journal of Applied Behavioral Analysis, 8,* 211.

Suppes, P., & Ginsberg, R. (1962). Application of a stimulus sampling model to children's concept formation with and without an overt correction response. *Journal of Experimental Psychology, 63,* 330–336.

Taylor, A. M., & Whitely, S. E. (1972). *Overt verbalization and the continued production of effective elaborations by EMR children.* Research Report No. 38, Project No. 332189, Grant No. OE–09–332189–4533(032), University of Minnesota.

Taylor, B. M. (1986). Teaching middle-grade students to read for main ideas. In J. A. Niles & L. A. Harris (Eds.), *Solving problems in literacy, Thirty-Fifth Yearbook of the National Reading Conference* (pp. 99–104). Rochester, NY: National Reading Conference.

Taylor, B. M., & Beach, R. W. (1984). The effects of text structure on middle-grade students' comprehension and production of expository text. *Reading Research Quarterly, 19,* 134–146.

Taylor, S. E., Frackenpohl, H., & Pattee, J. L. (1960). *Grade level norms for the components of the fundamental reading skill.* Bulletin #3. New York: Huntington Educational Development Laboratories.

Tennyson, R. D. (1973). Effect of negative instances in concept acquisition using a verbal learning task. *Journal of Educational Psychology, 64,* 247–260.

Tennyson, R., & Cocchiarella, M. (1986). An empirically based instructional design theory for teaching concepts. *Review of Educational Research, 56* (1), 40–71.

Tennyson, R., & Park, O. (1980). The teaching of concepts: A review of the instructional design literature. *Review of Educational Research, 50,* 55–70.

Tennyson, R. D., Steve, M. W., & Boutwell, R. C. (1975). Instance sequence and analysis of instance attribute representation in concept attainment. *Journal of Educational Psychology, 67,* 852–859.

Terry, P., Samuels, S. J., & LaBarge, D. (1976). The effects of letter degradation and letter spacing on word recognition. *Journal of Verbal Learning and Verbal Behavior, 15,* 577–586.

Thomas, D. R., Becker, W. C., & Armstrong, M. (1968). Production and elimination of disruptive classroom behavior by systematically varying teacher's behavior. *Journal of Applied Behavior Analysis, 1,* 35–45.

Tierney, R. J., Readence, J. E., & Dishner, E. K. (1985). *Reading strategies and practices: A compendium* (2nd ed.). Boston: Allyn & Bacon.

Tobias, S., & Ingber, T. (1976). Achievement-treatment interactions in programmed instructions. *Journal of Educational Psychology, 68,* 43–47.

Torgesen, J. K. (1986). Computers and cognition in reading: A focus on decoding fluency. *Exceptional Children, 53,* 157–162.

Torgesen, J. K., & Wolf, H. (1986). Computers and reading instruction: Lessons from the past, promise for the future. In G. T. Pavlidis & D. Fisher (Eds.), *Dyslexia: Neurophysiology and treatment* (pp. 239–252). Sussex, England: John Wiley and Sons.

Trabasso, T. R. (1963). Stimulus emphasis and all or none learning in concept identification. *Journal of Educational Psychology, 65,* 398–406.

Vandever, T. R., & Neville, D. D. (1976). Transfer as a result of synthetic and analytic reading instruction. *American Journal of Mental Deficiency, 30,* 498–503.

Van Patten, J. R., Chao, C. I., & Reigeluth, C. M. (1986). A review of strategies for sequencing and synthesizing information. *Review of Educational Research, 56,* 437–472.

Vellutino, F. R., & Scanlon, D. M. (1986). Experimental evidence for the effects of instructional bias on word identification. *Exceptional Children, 53,* 145–155.

Venezky, R. L. (1967). English orthography: Its graphical structure and its relation to sound. *Reading Research Quarterly, 2,* 75–106.

Venezky, R. L. (1970). *The structure of English orthography.* The Hague: Mouton.

Venezky, R. L. (1975). Pre-reading skills: Theoretical foundations and practical applications (Theoretical Paper No. 54). Madison, WI: Wisconsin Research and Development Center for Cognition Learning, University of Wisconsin.

Venezky, R. L., & Calfee, R. C. (1970). The reading competency model. In H. Singer & R. B. Ruddell (Eds.), *Theoretical models and processes of reading.* Newark, DE: International Reading Association.

Venezky, R. L., & Shiloah, Y. (1972). *The learning of picture-sound associations by Israeli kindergartners* (Technical Report No. 227). Madison, WI: Wisconsin Research and Development Center for Cognitive Learning, University of Wisconsin.

Venezky, R. L., Shiloah, Y., & Calfee, R. C. (1972). *Studies of prereading skills in Israel* (Technical Report No. 227). Madison, WI: Wisconsin Research and Development Center for Cognitive Learning, University of Wisconsin.

Waechter, M. (1972). *A methodology for a functional analysis of the relationship between oral reading and comprehension in beginning readers.* Unpublished doctoral dissertation, University of Oregon.

Waugh, R. P., & Howell, K. W. (1975). Teaching modern syllabication. *The Reading Teacher*, 20–25.

Werner, H., & Kaplan, E. (1952). The acquisition of word meanings: A developmental study. *Monographs for the Society for Research in Child Development, 15*, Serial No. 1 (Entire).

West, R., Stanovich, K., Freeman, D., & Cunningham, A. (1983). The effect of sentence context on word recognition in second- and sixth-grade children. *Reading Research Quarterly, 19*, 6–15.

Williams, J. P. (1979). The ABD's of reading: A program for the learning disabled. In L. B. Resnick & P. A. Weaver (Eds.), *Theory and practice of early reading* (Vol. 3). Hillsdale, NJ: Erlbaum.

Williams, J. P. (1980). Teaching decoding with an emphasis on Phoneme analysis and phoneme blending. *Journal of Educational Psychology, 72*, 1–5.

Williams, J. P. (1984). Phonemic analysis and how it relates to reading. *Journal of Reading Disabilities, 17*, 240–245.

Williams, J. P. (1985). The case for explicit decoding instruction. In J. Osborn, P. Wilson, & R. Anderson (Eds.), *Reading education: Foundation for a literate America* (pp. 205–214). D.C. Health.

Williams, J. P. (1986). Research and instructional development on main idea skills. In J. F. Baumann (Ed.), *Teaching main idea comprehension* (pp. 73–95). Newark, DE: International Reading Association.

Williams, J. P., Taylor, M. B., Jarin, D. C., & Milligan, E. S. (1983). *Determining the main idea for expository paragraphs: An instructional program for the learning-disabled and its evaluation* (Technical Report No. 25). New York: Research Institute for the Study of Learning Disabilities, Teachers College, Columbia University.

Williams, P., & Carnine, D. W. (1978). *Introducing words in lists and in isolation*. Unpublished manuscript, Follow Through Project, University of Oregon.

Williams, P., & Carnine, D. (1981). Relationships between range of examples and attention in concept attainment. *Journal of Educational Research, 74*, 144–148.

Willows, D. M. (1978). A picture is not always worth a thousand words: Pictures as distractors in reading. *Journal of Educational Psychology, 70*, 255–262.

Wisler, C. E., Burns, G. P., Jr., & Iwamoto, D. (1978). Follow Through readers: A response to the critique by House, Glass, McLean, and Walker. *Harvard Educational Review, 48*, 171–185.

Wittrock, M., Marks, C., & Doctorow, M. (1975). Reading as a generative process. *Journal of Educational Psychology, 67*, 484–489.

Wixson, K. K. (1986). Vocabulary instruction and children's comprehension of basal stories. *Reading Research Quarterly, 21*, 317–329.

Wolf, C. G., & Robinson, D. O. (1976). Use of spelling-to-sound rules in reading. *Perceptual and Motor Skills, 43*, 1135–1146.

Wong, B. Y. L., & Jones, W. (1982). Increasing metacomprehension in learning disabled and normally achieving students through self-questioning training. *Learning Disabilities Quarterly, 5*, 228–239.

Wong, B. Y. L., & Wong, R. (1986). Study behavior as a function of metacognitive knowledge about critical task variables: An investigation of above average, average, and learning disabled readers. *Learning Disabilities Research, 1*, 101–111.

Wyatt, N. M. (1976). *Reading achievement of first grade boys versus approach with boys and girls separately* (Cooperative Research Project No. 2735). Lawrence: University of Kansas.

Wysocki, K., & Jenkins, J. R. (1987). Deriving word meanings through morphological generalization. *Reading Research Quarterly, 22*, 66–81.

Yawkey, T. (1973). Attitudes toward black Americans held by rural urban white early childhood subjects based upon multi-ethnic social studies materials. *The Journal of Negro Education, 42*, 164–169.

Zimmer, J. W. (1978). *A processing activities approach to memory for prose.* Paper presented at the annual meeting of The American Educational Research Association, Toronto.

Appendix A
Word Lists*

Contents

- CVC Words Beginning with a Continuous Sound
- CVC Words Beginning with a Stop Sound
- CVCC Words Ending with a Consonant Blend or Double Consonants
- CCVC Words Beginning with a Consonant Blend
- CCVCC, CCCVC, and CCCVCC Words
- VCe Pattern Words in Which the Vowel Is Long
- Letter Combinations
- Suffixes (Listed Alphabetically)
- Prefixes (Listed Alphabetically)
- CVCe Derivative Words
- Y-derivative Words
- Two-syllable Words with a Single Consonant in the Middle

---

*Parentheses in Appendix A indicate a minimally different word that can be used in discrimination exercises.

CVC Words Beginning with a Continuous Sound (Chapter 9)

a	i	o	u	e
fad				fed
fan	fin		fun	
fat	fit			
lad	lid			led
lag		log		leg
lap	lip			
	lit	lot		let
mad	mid		mud	
		mom	mum	
man				men
map		mop		
mat	mit			met
		nod		Ned
Nat	nit	not	nut	net
nap	nip			
	rid	rod		red
rag	rig		rug	
ram	rim		rum	
ran		Ron	run	
rap	rip			
rat		rot	rut	
sad	Sid	sod		
Sam			sum	
	sin		sun	
sat	sit			set
sap	sip			

CVC Words Beginning with a Stop Sound (Chapter 9)

a	i	o	u	e
bag	big		bug	beg
bad	bid		bud	bed
bam			bum	
bat	bit		but	bet
cap		cop	cup	
cab			cub	
can		con		
cat			cut	
dad	did		dud	
Dan		Don		den

	a		i		o		u		e
		dig		dog		dug		
		dip						
	gas					Gus		
	gag							
						gun		
	had	hid						
	ham	him				hum		
	has	his						
	hat	hit		hot		hut		
		hip		hop				
				hog		hug		
								hen
	jab			job				
	jam	Jim						
								jet
		jig		jog		jug		
		kin						Ken
		kid						
	pan	pin						pen
	pat	pit		pot				pet
		pig						peg
				pop		pup		pep
	tab					tub		
	tag					tug		
	tan	tin						ten
	tap	tip		top				
		Tim		Tom				

CVCC Words Ending with a Consonant Blend or Double Consonants (Chapter 9)

a		i		u		e		o
act	(at)	fill		bump	(bum)	bend	(Ben)	golf
and	(add)	film		bunt	(bun)	bent	(Ben)	honk
ant	(an)	fist	(fit)	bust	(but)	best	(Bess)	lock
band	(bad)	hint	(hit)	dump		belt	(bell)	pond
bank		ink		dust		bent	(Ben)	pomp
camp	(cap)	lick		gulp		dent	(den)	rock
can't	(can)	lift		gust	(gut)	end	(Ed)	romp
cast	(cat)	limp	(lip)	hunt	(hut)	felt	(fell)	sock
damp	(dam)	milk		hung	(hug)	held	(help)	soft
fact	(fat)	mint	(mit)	jump		left	(let)	

a		i		u		e		o
fast	(fat)	mist	(miss)	junk		kept		
gasp	(gas)	sick		luck		melt	(mell)	
hand	(had)	tilt	(till)	lump		mend	(men)	
lamp	(lap)			must		neck		
land	(lad)			punk		nest	(net)	
last				runt	(run)	pest	(pet)	
mask				rust	(Russ)	self	(sell)	
mast	(mass)			suck		send		
pant	(pan)			sung		sent		
past	(pass)					test		
raft	(rat)					tent	(ten)	
sack						weld	(well)	
sand	(sad)					went	(wet)	
sank								
		wind	(win)					

CCVC Words Beginning with a Consonant Blend (Chapter 9)

bl—bled (bed), blot
br—brag (bag), brat (bat), bred (bed), brig (big), brim
cl—clad, clam, clan (can), clap, clip, clot, club (cub)
cr—crab (cab), cram, crib, crop (cop)
dr—drag, drip (dip), drop, drug (dug), drum
fl—flag, flap, flat (fat), fled (fed), flip, flop
fr—frog (fog), from
gl—glad, glum (gum)
gr—grab, gram, grim, grin, grip
pl—plan (pan), plop (pop), plot (pot), plug, plum, plus
pr—prop (pop)
sc—scan, scat (sat), scab
sk—skid, skim, skin, skip, skit
sl—slam (Sam), slap (sap), slat, sled, slim, slip (sip), slob (sob), slot, slug, slum (sum)
sm—smog, smug
sn—snag, snap (sap), snip, snub, snug
sp—span, spat (sat), sped, spin, spit, (sit), spot, spun (sun)
st—stab, stem, step, stop, stun (sun)
sw—swam (Sam), swim
tr—trap (tap), trim (Tim), trip (tip), trot (tot)
tw—twig, twin (tin)

CCVCC, CCCVC, and CCCVCC Words (Chapter 9)

bl—blast, blimp, blunt (bunt), blond, blend (bend), blink, bliss, black, (back), block, bluff

br—bring, brunt, brand (band), brass (bass)

cl—clamp (camp), clasp, cling, clump, clung, clink, class, cliff

cr—cramp, crust, craft, crisp

dr—drink, drank, drift, draft, dress, drill

fl—fling, flung, flunk

fr—frost, frank, frisk, frill (fill)

gl—gland, glint, glass (gas)

gr—gramp, grand, grump, grant, grasp, grunt, grass (gas), grill

pl—plant (pant), plump (pump), plank

pr—print, prank, press

sc—scalp

sk—skunk, skill

sl—slang, slant, slump, slept, sling

sm—smack (sack), smell (sell)

sn—snack (sack), sniff

sp—spend (send), spent (sent), spank (sank), spunk (sunk), spell (sell), spill

st—stand (sand), stamp, stump, sting (sing), stink (sink), stomp, still, stiff, stack (sack), stuck (suck)

sw—swift, swang (sang), swung (sung), swing (sing), swell (sell)

tr—tramp, trunk, trust, trend, trick (tick)

tw—twang, twist

spl—split (spit), splint, splat

str—strip, strap, strung, strand, struck

scr—scrap, scram, script

VCe Pattern Words in Which the Vowel Is Long (Chapter 16)

1. Words Beginning with a Single Consonant (CVCe)

a		i		o		u		e	
vane	(van)	time	(Tim)	hope	(hop)	cute	(cut)	Pete	(pet)
fade	(fad)	like	(lick)	note	(not)	use	(us)	eve	
made	(mad)	site	(sit)	robe	(rob)	mule			
bake	(back)	Mike	(Mick)	home		cure			
cane	(can)	mile	(mill)	joke		pure	(purr)		
tape	(tap)	ripe	(rip)	hole		fume			
mate	(mat)	file	(fill)	nose		mute			
hate	(hat)	tile	(till)	rope					
sake	(sack)	pile	(pill)	mope	(mop)				
Jane	(Jan)	ride	(rid)	pope	(pop)				
pane	(pan)	mite	(mit)	bone					
same	(Sam)	fine	(fin)	cone	(con)				
cape	(cap)	wine	(win)	dope					
wave		pike	(pick)	hose					
tame	(tam)	bite	(bit)	note					
take	(tack)	kite	(kit)	yoke					
save		dime	(dim)	poke					
make	(Mack)	hide	(hid)	pole					
gaze		pine	(pin)	rose					
		tide		rode	(rod)				
		side	(Sid)						
		hire							
		fire							
		wire							
		dine							
		dire							
		line							
		like							
		dive							
		five							
		lime							
		bike							
		nine							
		size							

2. Words Beginning with a Consonant Blend (CCVCe)

a		i		o	u
skate		slide	(slid)	spoke	brute
state		snipe	(snip)	broke	
trade		gripe	(grip)	close	
stale	(stall)	prime	(prim)	drove	
scale		spine	(spin)	globe	
snake	(snack)	spite	(spit)	froze	
slave		bride		scope	
slate	(slat)	crime		smoke	
scare		pride		stone	
plate		prize		stove	
plane	(plan)	smile		slope	(slop)
grape		stripe	(strip)		
grade					
frame					

3. Multisyllabic Words with a VCe Syllable

a	i	o	u	e
careless	perspire	hopeless	excuse	complete
escape	dislike	explode	confuse	stampede
inhale	likely	backbone	reuse	
take-off	umpire	pinhole	costume	
handmade	entire			
grateful	lifetime			
pancake	ninety			
	timeless			

Letter Combinations (Chapter 16)

<u>ai</u> aid, aim, bail, bait, claim, fail, fair, laid, maid, mail, main, pail, paid, pain, paint, plain, rain, tail, plain, stair, trait, afraid, complain, remain, explain, tailor, daily, ailment, maintain, obtain, aimed, failing, mailing, painter, raining, aid (add), aim (am), bait (bat), fair (far), maid (mad)

<u>al</u> fall, call, tall, ball, small, wall, mall, salt, false, bald, waltz, also, always, almost, salty, all right, walnut, hallway, walrus, alter

<u>ar</u> arm, bark, barn, card, cart, farm, far, star, hard, harm, mark, park, part, art, car, dark, mars, smart, start, yard, starve, shark, artist, darling, barber, target, party, carpet, partner, harvest, barking, starring, parked, smarter, started, bark (back), hard (hand), art (at), car (care), star (stare), bar (bare)

<u>au</u> fault, vault, sauce, cause, taught, haunt, laundry, author, autumn, August, daughter, applaud, because, auto

<u>aw</u> bawl, brawn, claw, dawn, hawk, jaw, law, lawn, paw, pawn, raw, saw, straw, crawl, shawl, yawn, awful, drawing, lawful, sawmill, lawyer, seesaw, outlaw, strawberry, awkward, awning

<u>ay</u> day, gay, may, ray, say, clay, gray, play, pray, spray, tray, payment, today, played, saying, player, playing, prayed, praying, away, Sunday

<u>ch</u> chap, chat, chip, chop, cheek, chug, charm, chimp, chain, cheap, chest, chill, chair, champ, catch, match, patch, pitch, switch, ditch, much, march, starch, crunch, arch, pinch, teach, touch, rich, hunch, chip (ship), chop (shop), chap (clap), ditch (dish), catch (cash), catcher, pitcher, pitching, chopped, teacher, touched, rancher, chuckle, chilly, marching

<u>ea</u> bead, bean, beat, beast, dean, deal, fear, hear, heal, heat, Jean, lead, meal, least, mean, meat, neat, read, sea, seal, seat, speak, steam, east, eat, freak, leave, please, sneak, wheat, treat, bean (ben), beat (bet), beast (best), meat (met), speak (speck), reason, season, peanut, teacher, eastern, dealing, speaker, sneaker, treated, eating, leaving, hearing, healed, heated, steaming

<u>ee</u> bee, bleed, creep, see, weed, deer, flee, free, green, keep, wheel, three, jeep, creep, beet, peep, creek, fleet, bleed (bled), beet (bet), peep (pep), weed (wed), beetle, between, canteen, fifteen, sixteen, indeed, needle, freedom, coffee, bleeding, creeped, wheeled, peeping

<u>ue</u> cue, due, sue, rescue, argue, tissue, value, statue

<u>ew</u> new, few, flew, chew, slew, stew, drew, grew, curfew, nephew

<u>ey</u> hockey, money, donkey, turkey, whiskey, valley, alley, monkey, honey

<u>igh</u> fight, light, right, tight, might, high, sigh

<u>ir</u> bird, birth, dirt, first, shirt, sir, skirt, stir, third, whirl, bird (bid), first (fist), shirt (short), stir (star), dirty, birthday, stirring, whirled, thirsty, thirty

<u>kn</u> knock, know, knee, knife, knight, knit, knob, knot, known

<u>oa</u> boat, boast, coal, coat, cloak, float, load, road, roast, oak, oar, soap, throat, toast, boat (boot), coal (cool), load (loud), oar (our), oatmeal, toaster, unload, approach, railroad, seacoast, soapy, charcoal, coaster

oi boil, coin, coil, foil, join, noise, point, spoil, soil, moist, oil, voice, coil (cool), foil (fool), coin (con), boiler, appoint, adjoin, disappoint, poison, avoid, joined, noisy, boiling

ol bold, bolt, cold, colt, roll, fold, gold, hold, hole, scold, sold, told, toll, volt, control, enroll, folder, golden, holder, holster, roller, swollen, unfold, roller, folding, holding

oo boot, cool, food, fool, hoop, mood, moon, moose, room, soon, tool, pool, stoop, shoot, smooth, tooth, too, spoon, shoot (shot), stoop (stop), soon (son), hoop (hop), cartoon, bedroom, noodle, poodle, shampoo, igloo, bamboo, fooling, moody, shooting, raccoon, teaspoon, harpoon

or born, corn, for, lord, pork, port, porch, torn, short, stork, shore, fort, sport, torch, storm, north, corn (con), for (far), pork (park), port (part), short (shot), normal, order, organ, ordeal, border, conform, escort, forty, hornet, perform, inform, popcorn, story, morning

ou bout, cloud, clout, loud, mouse, noun, pout, pouch, scout, mouth, blouse, count, ground, found, out, our, round, sound, about, aloud, amount, around, counter, thousand, trousers, outside, cloudy, counting, grounder, bout (boot), mouse (moose), noun (noon), mouth (moth), our (or)

ow blow, crow, glow, grow, know, low, owe, row, slow, show, throw, shown, thrown, grown, elbow, fellow, below, follow, hollow, pillow, shadow, yellow, window

oy boy, toy, joy, Troy, annoy, employ, enjoy, cowboy, oyster, royal

ph phone, graph, photo, phrase, photograph, physics, typhoon, alphabet, elephant, dolphin, orphan, pamphlet, trophy, nephew, paragraph

sh ship, shot, shop, shed, shin, shut, shack, shell, shun, cash, dish, fish, wish, rush, lash, flash, fresh, crash, brush, trash, shine, chime, shame, shape, share, ship (slip), shot (slot), shop (stop), shell (sell), shack (sack), cash (cast), fish (fist)

th that, them, this, than, with, tenth, eleventh, twelfth, thirteenth, fourteenth, fifteenth, sixteenth, seventeenth, eighteenth, then (ten), than (tan)

ur burn, church, curb, curl, cur, hurt, purr, spurt, surf, turn, burst, curse, curve, purse, nurse, purple, turkey, Thursday, disturb, further, return, turtle, injure, burn (born), fur (far), curl (Carl)

wh when, whip, which, what, white, while

wr wrap, wreck, wrench, wring, wrist, write, wrong, wrapper, wreckage, wrestle, wrinkle, writer, wrongful

Suffixes (Chapter 17)

a panda, comma, Anna, soda, drama, china, zebra, mamma, papa

able likeable, teachable, touchable, expendable, drinkable, enable, unable, portable, reasonable, returnable

age luggage, package, village, image, voyage, storage, passage, hostage, cottage, manage, language, wreckage, usage

al sandal, formal, postal, local, vocal, final, journal, metal, total, legal, criminal

ance clearance, entrance, performance, distance, instance, annoyance

ed hugged, killed, missed, ripped, tipped, bumped, helped, jumped, picked, rocked, clapped, dripped, dropped, flipped, grabbed, grinned, gripped, pressed, smelled, spelled, tricked, flipped, dotted, patted, petted, dusted, handed, landed, tested, lasted, hunted, ended, blasted, planted, slanted, trusted, twisted

ence absence, sentence, audience, patience, silence, influence, evidence, confidence

er batter, bigger, butter, fatter, hotter, letter, madder, sadder, bumper, faster, helper, hunter, blacker, dresser, slipper, speller, sticker, swinger, swimmer

es glasses, misses, passes, messes, foxes, mixes, taxes, boxes, wishes, dishes, fishes, mashes

est biggest, fattest, hottest, maddest, saddest, dampest, fastest, blackest, flattest, stiffest

ful handful, careful, useful, helpful, cheerful, mouthful, watchful, faithful, fearful

ible horrible, sensible, possible, flexible, admissible, responsible, permissible, convertible, terrible, invisible

ic traffic, picnic, arctic, antic, frantic, plastic, magic, tragic, comic, panic, basic, music, critic

ing batting, betting, cutting, digging, filling, getting, killing, letting, petting, bending, dusting, ending, helping, jumping, picking, testing, clapping, dripping, grabbing, grinning, planning, smelling, spending, swimming

ion fashion, champion, region, union, companion, opinion, religion, million, billion

ish snobbish, selfish, sluggish, publish, foolish, furnish, establish, accomplish, astonish, punish, finish, radish

ive active, captive, attentive, expensive, impressive, attractive, constructive, corrective, defective, destructive, positive

le battle, cattle, juggle, middle, paddle, riddle, saddle, wiggle, apple, bottle, giggle, little, puddle, handle, ankle, bundle, candle, jungle, uncle, grumble, twinkle, trample

ment agreement, argument, basement, attachment, development, employment, movement, payment, appointment, shipment

less endless, groundless, matchless, toothless, speechless, sleepless, helpless, careless, restless, lifeless, nameless, useless

ness madness, badness, freshness, dullness, witness, dryness, likeness

tion action, mention, fraction, question, invention, inspection, section, suction, portion, construction, celebration, circulation, congratulation, combination, decoration, education, formation

ture feature, creature, fracture, lecture, picture, puncture, structure, culture, venture, capture, torture, mixture, adventure, furniture, nature, future

ward northward, inward, forward, backward, coward, skyward, onward, awkward

y funny, muddy, penny, bunny, happy, jelly, silly, rocky, jumpy, handy, lucky, rusty, sandy, windy, candy, empty, fifty, sixty, smelly, snappy, sticky, clumsy, drafty, grumpy, plenty, sloppy, twenty

Prefixes (Chapter 17)

a about, alive, alarm, around, along, amount, among, apart, asleep, atop

ab absent, absentee, absorb, absurd

ad address, adjust, admire, admit, adverb, advertise

ap appear, appeal, appendix, applaud, appoint, approach

at attack, attempt, attend, attic, attach

be because, become, before, begin, behave, behind, behold, belong, beneath, besides, between, beware

com combine, command, commit, compete, complain, complex, compute

con concrete, conduct, confess, confine, confirm, conflict, conform,confuse, connect, conserve, consist, control, consult, convict, conserve, contract

de decay, declare, decoy, defeat, define, defrost, delay, delight, demand, depart, depend, describe, design, desire, destruct, detail, devote

dis disappear, disappoint, discount, disconnect, discuss, dismiss, dismount, display, displease, disagree, disbelieve, discharge, dishonest, discolor, distance

ex explain, expect, expense, expert, explode, expand, expire, export, explosive, extoll, exclaim, excuse, exact, exam, except, exit, examine, example

for
fore forbid, forearm, forecast, forgive, forehead, forest, forget, forty, foremost, foreman, foreclosure, forefront

im imperfect, impact, impeach, impress

in inclose, income, index, infect, inflate, inform, inspect, intend

mis miscount, misdeal, misfit, misjudge, mislead, misplace, mistake, mistreat, misspell, misprint, mistrust, mismatch

non nonsense, nonstop, nonprofit, nonconform, nonsupport

over overall, overboard, overcast, overcome, overdue, overhead, overload, overlook, overrun, oversight, overtake, overtime, overturn, overstep, overshoes, overshadow

per percent, perfect, perfume, perhaps, permanent, persist, person, perplex, perspire, perturb

post postage, postcard, postman, postpone, postmark, postal

pre predict, pretend, preheat, prepay, prepare, precook, preside, precede

pro profile, protest, propose, produce, protest, provoke

re return, rebake, recall, recount, refill, reflex, reform, refresh, refuse, regain, regard, relay, release, remark, repair, repay, report, replay, reprint, respect, retreat, reverse

sub subdue, subject, submerge, submit, subnormal, subside, subsist, subtract, suburb, subway

super superman, supervise, supertanker, supersonic, supermarket, supersede, supernatural

trans transfer, transform, transit, translate, transmit, transparent, transplant, transport un unable, unarm, uncage, unchain, unclean, unhappy, uneven, unlock, unreal, untie, unfair, unseen, unsafe, unlucky, unsure

under undercharge, underdog, undergo, underline, understand, underground, undertake, understood, underworld, underwear

up uphill, upkeep, uplift, upright, upsidedown, uptown, upward, uphold, upon, uproar, upstream

CVCe Derivative Words (Chapter 17)

(Not all the words in parentheses are minimally different.)

1. Words with *s* Endings

a		i		o		e-u	
canes	(cans)	bites	(bits)	cones	(cons)	Petes	(pets)
cares	(cars)	files	(fills)	globes	(globs)	cubes	(cubs)
hates	(hats)	fines	(fins)	hopes	(hops)	uses	
mates	(mats)	miles	(mills)	mopes	(mops)		
planes	(plans)	shines	(shins)	robes	(robs)		
shakes	(shacks)	times					
stares	(stars)	wines	(wins)				

2. Words with *er* Endings

a		i		o		e-u	
later	(latter)	filer	(filler)	closer	(hotter)	cuter	(cutter)
shaver	(slammer)	diner	(dinner)	smoker	(robber)	ruder	(rudder)
crater	(batter)	finer	(winner)	homer	(logger)	user	
braver	(hammer)	riper	(hitter)				
saver	(madder)	timer	(ripper)				
		biter	(bigger)				

3. Words with *ed* Endings

a		i		o		e-u
hated	(tapped)	filed	(filled)	hoped	(hopped)	used
named	(jammed)	smiled	(ripped)	closed	(robbed)	
waved	(fanned)	timed	(kidded)	smoked	(nodded)	
skated	(rammed)	piled	(fitted)	stoned	(rotted)	
blamed	(batted)	glided	(fibbed)	roped	(logged)	
faded	(matted)					

450   Appendix A

4. Words with *ing* Endings

a		i		o		e-u
naming	(batting)	filing	(filling)	hoping	(hopping)	using
skating	(tapping)	riding	(hitting)	roping	(robbing)	
waving	(slamming)	timing	(ripping)	closing	(logging)	
hating	(napping)	piling	(kidding)	smoking	(stopping)	
shading	(snapping)	biting	(winning)	roving	(mopping)	

5. Words with *y* Endings

a		i		o		e-u	
gravy	(Tammy)	spicy	(Timmy)	bony	(Tommy)	cuty	(nutty)
shady	(batty)	shiny		smoky	(Dotty)		tummy
wavy	(fanny)	tiny		stony	(foggy)		
shaky	(Sammy)	wiry					

6. Words with *est* Endings

a	i	u
bravest	ripest	cutest
latest	wisest	rudest
safest	widest	surest
tamest		

Y-derivative Words (Chapter 17)

	ier	*iest*	*ied*	*ies*
army				armies
buddy				buddies
bumpy	bumpier	bumpiest		
clumsy	clumsier	clumsiest		
foggy	foggier	foggiest		
funny	funnier	funniest		
greedy	greedier	greediest		
greasy	greasier	greasiest		
grumpy	grumpier	grumpiest		
handy	handier	handiest		
happy	happier	happiest		
holy	holier	holiest		
hungry	hungier	hungriest		
kitty				kitties

	ier	*iest*	*ied*	*ies*
lucky	luckier	luckiest		
muddy	muddier	muddiest		
party				parties
penny				pennies
rusty	rustier	rustiest		
silly	sillier	silliest		
skinny	skinnier	skinniest		
smelly	smellier	smelliest		
ugly	uglier	ugliest		
windy	windier	windiest		
baby			babied	babies
berry				berries
body				bodies
bury			buried	buries
busy	busier	busiest	busied	
carry	carrier		carried	carries
copy	copier		copied	copies
country				countries
hurry			hurried	hurries
lady				ladies
marry			married	marries
sorry	sorrier	sorriest		
study			studied	studies
worry			worried	worries

Two-syllable Words with a Single Consonant in the Middle (Chapter 18)

a	e	i	o	u
paper	legal	Bible	frozen	music
satin	fever	visit	holy	bugle
travel	pedal	china	local	punish
cable	meter	prison	profit	human
label	clever	final	moment	super
planet	zebra	limit	copy	pupil
table	seven	finish	motor	humid
chapel	metal	minus	topic	study
rapid	defend	silent	robin	rumor
magic	second	tiger	poker	
crazy	seven	pilot	soda	
favor	devil	spinach	total	
vacant	petal	spider	solid	
taxi	evil	river	robot	
crater		tiny	modern	
panic			proper	
maple			pony	
			comic	
			motel	
			motor	
			promise	
			model	
			robin	
			total	

Appendix B
List of 400 Common Words

a	ball	box	colds	eight	fox
about	balloon	boy	come	end	friend
after	bark	bring	could	enough	from
again	barn	brought	cow	even	full
airplane	bear	brown	cry	ever	fun
all	because	build	cut	every	funny
almost	bed	bus	daddy	fall	game
along	be	but	dark	family	gave
also	bee	buy	day	far	get
always	been	by	did	farm	girl
am	before	cage	didn't	fast	give
an	began	cake	different	fat	go
and	behind	call	do	father	goat
animals	below	called	does	feet	goes
another	best	came	dog	few	going
anything	better	can	done	fight	gone
are	between	can't	don't	find	good
around	big	car	door	fire	good-bye
as	bike	carry	down	first	got
ask	bird	cat	draw	fish	grass
at	birthday	catch	dress	five	great
ate	black	children	drink	fly	green
away	blue	city	drop	food	grow
baby	boat	clean	duck	for	guess
back	book	coat	each	found	had
bag	both	cold	eat	four	hair

half	land	nothing	red	sun	upon
hand	large	now	ride	sure	us
happy	last	number	right	surprise	use
hard	laugh	of	road	table	used
has	left	off	rocket	take	very
hat	leg	often	room	talk	wagon
have	let	oh	round	tell	walk
he	letter	old	run	ten	want
head	life	on	said	than	warm
hear	light	once	same	thank	was
heard	like	one	sang	that	wash
hello	line	only	sat	the	water
help	little	open	saw	their	way
hen	live	or	say	them	we
her	long	other	school	then	well
here	look	our	see	there	went
hill	looked	out	seen	these	were
him	lost	over	set	they	what
his	made	own	seven	thing	when
hold	make	paint	shall	things	where
home	man	pan	she	think	which
hop	many	part	shoe	this	while
horse	may	party	should	those	white
hot	maybe	peanut	show	thought	who
house	me	penny	side	three	why
how	men	people	sing	through	will
hurry	met	pet	sister	time	window
hurt	might	pick	sit	to	wish
I	miss	pig	six	today	with
ice	money	picnic	sleep	together	won't
if	more	picture	so	told	word
I'll	morning	place	soon	tomorrow	words
I'm	most	play	some	too	work
in	mother	please	something	took	world
into	much	pocket	sound	town	would
is	must	pony	small	toy	write
it	my	pretty	start	train	year
its	myself	prize	stay	tree	yellow
it's	name	pull	step	truck	you
jump	need	put	still	try	your
just	never	rabbit	stop	turtle	yes
keep	new	race	stopped	TV	zoo
kind	next	rain	store	two	
kitten	night	ran	story	under	
knew	no	read	street	until	
know	not	ready	such	up	

Appendix C
Outline of Lessons for Beginning Phonics Program

Formats listed in this outline can be found on the following pages:

letter intro.—88
letter disc.—89
telescoping—77
segmenting—79

sounding out—102, 104
sight reading—116, 117
irregular word—134
passage reading—111

Lesson One
letter intro.—a
telescoping—sad, if, at
letter intro.—a

Lesson Two
letter intro.—m
letter disc.—m, a
telescoping—it, mad, am
letter intro.—a
letter disc.—m, a

Lesson Three
letter disc.—m, a
segmenting—am, it
letter disc.—m, a
segmenting—Sam, at

Lesson Four
letter intro.—t
letter disc.—t, a, m
segmenting—at, it, Sam
letter intro.—t
letter disc.—t, a, m
segmenting—am, sit

Lesson Five
letter intro.—t
letter disc.—m, a, t
segmenting—am, sad, sit
letter disc.—m, a, t
segmenting—mad, if

Lesson Six
letter intro.—s

letter disc.—m, a, s, t
segmenting—am, sit, Sid
letter intro.—s
letter disc.—m, a, t, s
segmenting—Sam, it

Lesson Seven
letter intro.—s
letter disc.—m, a, s, t
sounding out—am
letter disc.—m, a, s, t
segmenting—at, sit, if
sounding out—am

Lesson Eight
letter intro.—i
letter disc.—m, a, s, t, i
sounding out—am, at
segmenting—sat, it, am
letter intro.—i
letter disc.—m, a, s, t, i
sounding out—am, at

Lesson Nine
letter intro.—i
letter disc.—m, a, s, t, i
sounding out—sat, am
segmenting—if, fat, miss, fig
letter disc.—m, a, s, t, i
sounding out—mat, Sam

Lesson Ten
letter intro.—i
letter disc.—m, a, s, t, f, i
sounding out—am, sat
segmenting—mad, Sid, fit, rat
letter intro.—f
letter disc.—m, a, s, t, f, i
sounding out—at, sat

Lesson Eleven
letter intro.—f
letter disc.—m, a, s, t, f, i
sounding out—Sam, sit
segmenting—rag, fit, sad, add
letter disc.—m, a, s, t, f, i
sounding out—am, it, sat

Lesson Twelve
letter intro.—d

letter disc.—m, a, s, d, f, i
sounding out—mat, sit, sat
letter intro.—d
letter disc.—a, d, i
segmenting—lot, rag, luck

Lesson Thirteen
letter intro.—d
letter disc.—m, a, s, d, f, i
segmenting—not, nut, in, on
letter disc.—a, d, i
sounding out—if, fit, am, fat, Sam
passage reading—am
(sounding out)

Lesson Fourteen
letter disc.—a, m, s, t, i, f, d
segmenting—lot, rat, sick, rip
letter disc.—t, d, i
irregular—is
sounding out—Sid, mad, fat, sad, sit, if
passage reading—Sam
(sounding out)

Lesson Fifteen
letter intro.—r
letter disc.—m, a, s, i, t, r, d
irregular—is
sounding out—mad, sat, it, if, at, sad
letter disc.—r, a, i
segmenting—on, in, ran, rag
passage reading—am, Sam
(sounding out)

Lesson Sixteen
letter intro.—r
letter disc.—m, a, i, t, f, d, s, r
irregular word—is
sounding out—sad, sat, am, fit, mit, mad
letter disc.—r, i, s
segmenting—sick, sock, lot, on, in
passage reading—Sam is sad
(sounding out)

Lesson Seventeen
letter intro.—o
letter disc.—o, a, i, r, d, f, s, t
segmenting—lock, fig, cat, rag
sounding out—at, it, am, fit, mad, Sam

sight reading—at, it, am
passage reading—it, is, Sam
(sounding out)

Lesson Eighteen
letter intro.—o
letter disc.—o, a, i, r, d, f, s, t
segmenting—top, got, dad, Tag
sounding out—ram, rid, fit, am, rat, Sam,
  sit
sight reading—it, at, Sam, sit
passage reading—Sam is sad. Sid is mad.
(sounding out)

Lesson Nineteen
letter intro.—g
letter disc.—o, a, i, r, d, f, t, g

segmenting—rug, cut, cat, did, hot
sounding out—Sam, it, am, sat, rim, fit,
  mad
sight reading—Sam, it, am, sat
passage reading—Sid is mad at Sam.
(sounding out)

Lesson Twenty
letter intro.—g
letter disc.—o, a, i, r, d, f, t, g
segmenting—dad, got, can, dig, him
sounding out—mom, rod, rat, sit, at, Sid,
  fit, ram
sight reading—sit, am, at, sad
passage reading—Sam is fat. Mom is fit.
(sounding out)

Appendix D
Basic Vocabulary for Beginning Readers and Suggestions for Assessing Student Knowledge

1. **Colors** blue, red, black, orange, green, yellow, pink, brown, white, gray, gold, purple, olive

   Testing Suggestion Use crayons to make marks of each color. Point to each mark and ask, "What color?".

2. **Prepositions** (Synonyms are in parentheses.) in, on, under (below), over (above), next to (beside), between (in the middle of), in front of (ahead), in back of (behind)

   Testing Suggestion Use a pencil and two cups. Place the pencil in various positions and ask, "Where is the pencil?"

3. **Common Objects and Locations**
   Classroom:
   board, window, reading corner, teacher's desk, bookcase, bulletin board, light switch, doorway, chalk, clothing area, globe, map, stapler, clip, folder, calendar, lunch card holder
   Foods:
   fruits: apricot, apple, cherry, pear, plum, grape, orange, grapefruit, pineapple, blueberry, strawberry
   vegetables: beet, broccoli, cabbage, carrot, celery, onion, pepper, radish, squash
   meats: chicken, ham, liver, steak, turkey
   dairy products: cottage cheese, yogurt, Swiss cheese, American cheese
   miscellaneous: mustard, catsup, salt, pepper, sugar, honey, puddings, bread, cereal

Locations:
park, zoo, restaurant, grocery store, drug store, shoe shore, department store, school, garage, church, library, post office, hotel, hospital, forest

Testing Suggestion Obtain pictures or real objects. Ask, "What is this?"

4. **Pronouns**
subject—he, she, they, it, you, we
object—him, her, them, you
possessive—his, her, their, your, its

Testing Suggestion Get several pictures that are identical except for gender of people (e.g., a picture of girl running and a picture of boy running). Point to appropriate picture and ask questions such as: "Touch *her* hair. Touch *his* hair. Touch the picture that shows *he* is running. Touch *them*."

5. **Parts of Objects**
match—stick, head
pencil—eraser, point, shaft
hammer—handle, head, claw
purse—bag, clasp, handle
wagon—wheels, handle, body
shoe—sole, heel, laces, top, tongue
egg—yolk, white, shell
jacket—hood, zipper, front, back, sleeve
clock—case, hands, face
cabinet—handle, doors, shelves
refrigerator—door, handle, body, freezer door, shelves
tree—roots, branches, trunk, leaves
chair—seat, back, legs, rungs
door—doorknob, key hole, hinges, lock, rod
cup—bowl, handle
pot—body, lid, handle
table—top, legs
umbrella—frame, handle, covering
fish—body, tail, fins
nail—head, shaft, point
flower—roots, stem, leaves, petal
glasses—frame, earpieces, lenses
shirt—collar, pocket, sleeves, cuffs, buttons
window—frame, lock, handle, panes
coat—sleeves, collar, buttons, button holes, front, back
pants—zipper, legs, cuffs, pockets
broom—handle, bristles
toothbrush—handle, bristles
glove—thumb, fingers, cuff, palm
car—wheels, fenders, windows, doors, bumpers, hood, windshield, headlights, seats, seat belts, steering wheel
rake—handle, prongs

fork—handle, prongs
knife—blade, point, handle
dashboard—speedometer, glove compartment, radio, clock, gas gauge
shovel—handle, scoop
jar—lid, mouth, neck, body, label
belt—strap, buckle, prong, loop, holes
lamp—shade, stand, cord, switch, bulb
garbage can—handles, lid, body
spoon—handle, bowl
staircase—railing, post, stairs
person
  face: hair, eyebrow, eyelash, forehead, nostrils, chin
  upper body: waist, shoulder, upper arm, lower arm, index finger, ribs, backbone, hips, wrist, elbow, palm, knuckles
  lower body: ankle, knee, arch, hips, thigh

Testing Suggestion Obtain pictures or actual objects. Ask, "What part is this?"

6. Characteristics (adjectives)

long—short	few—many	dark—light
big—little	same—different	deep—shallow
hot—cold	old—new	raw—cooked
full—empty	skinny—fat	stale—fresh
wet—dry	clean—dirty	ripe—spoiled
straight—crooked	fast—slow	early—late
rough—smooth	young—old	happy—sad
wide—narrow	tiny—huge	sick—well
quiet—noisy	mild—stormy	easy—difficult
safe—dangerous	ugly—beautiful	careful—careless
sharp—dull	open—closed	tight—loose
whole—part	shiny—dull	
wild—tame	cool—warm	

Testing Suggestion Obtain pictures of objects or actual objects that contain a characteristic. Ask either, "Is this _____?" or "Which one is _____?"

7. Occupations

baker	doctor	hair dresser
barber	dressmaker	jeweler
brick layer	druggist	librarian
bus driver	electrician	lifeguard
carpenter	elevator operator	logger
cashier	farmer	maid or butler
clerk	firefighter	mail carrier
cook	fisherman	mechanic
custodian	forest ranger	milkman
dentist	garbage collector	minister
dishwasher	grocer	nurse

painter	priest	taxi driver
paper carrier	printer	teacher
photographer	rabbi	telephone-repair person
pilot	roofer	truck driver
plasterer	secretary	TV-repair person
playground supervisor	shoe repairperson	veterinarian
plumber	stewardess or steward	waiter or waitress
police officer		

Testing Suggestion Obtain pictures. Ask, "What do we call this person?"

8. **Quantity Words** all, some, none, most, a few, a lot

   Testing Suggestion Put five pencils on a table. Ask, "Give me _____ (all, some, none, most, a few, a lot) of the pencils."

9. **Materials** cardboard, cloth, fur, glass, leather, metal, plastic, rubber, wood, brick

   Testing Suggestion Obtain a piece of material or a picture. Ask, "What is this made of?"

10. **Figures** circle, square, rectangle, oval, triangle

    Testing Suggestion Draw each figure. Ask, "What is this?"

11. **Patterns** plaid, striped, plain, spotted, flowered, checkered

    Testing Suggestion Fill in squares with different patterns. Ask, "What pattern is this?"